RECORDS OF EARLY ENGLISH DRAMA

Records of Early English Drama

DORSET

EDITED BY ROSALIND CONKLIN HAYS and C.E. McGEE

CORNWALL

EDITED BY SALLY L. JOYCE and EVELYN S. NEWLYN

BREPOLS ❧ PUBLISHERS

and

UNIVERSITY OF TORONTO PRESS

© University of Toronto Press Incorporated 1999
Toronto Buffalo
Printed in Canada

First published in North America in 1999 by University of Toronto Press Incorporated
ISBN 0-8020-4379-8
and in the European Union in 1999 by Brepols Publishers
ISBN 2-503-50813-8

Printed on acid-free paper

Canadian Cataloguing in Publication Data

Main entry under title:

Dorset. Cornwall

(Records of early English drama)
Includes bibliographical references and index.
ISBN 0-8020-4379-8

1. Performing arts – England – Dorset – History – Sources. 2. Performing
arts – England – Cornwall – History – Sources. 3. Theater – England –
Dorset – History – Sources. 4. Theater – England – Cornwall – History –
Sources. i. Hays, Rosalind C. ii. McGee, C. Edward, 1949–   .
iii. Joyce, Sally. iv. Newlyn, Evelyn. v. Title: Cornwall. vi. Series.

PN2595.5.D67D67 1999   790.2'094233   C98-932491-5

The research and typesetting costs of
Records of Early English Drama
have been underwritten by the
National Endowment for the Humanities and the
Social Sciences and Humanities Research Council of Canada

1002445509

Contents

CORNWALL

Records of Early English Drama

The aim of Records of Early English Drama (REED) is to find, transcribe, and publish external evidence of dramatic, ceremonial, and minstrel activity in Great Britain before 1642. The executive editor would be grateful for comments on and corrections to the present volume and for having any relevant additional material drawn to her attention at REED, 150 Charles St West, Toronto, Ontario, Canada M5S 1K9 or reed@chass.utoronto.ca.

ALEXANDRA F. JOHNSTON University of Toronto DIRECTOR
SALLY-BETH MACLEAN University of Toronto EXECUTIVE EDITOR

EXECUTIVE BOARD

PETER CLARK University of Leicester
C.E. MCGEE University of St Jerome's College
PETER MEREDITH University of Leeds
DAVID MILLS University of Liverpool
A.H. NELSON University of California, Berkeley
BARBARA PALMER Mary Washington College
J.A.B. SOMERSET University of Western Ontario
ROBERT TITTLER Concordia University

DEVELOPMENT BOARD

JENNIFER CLARK
EDWARD JACKMAN op
PATRICIA KENNEDY
J. ALEX LANGFORD
MOIRA PHILLIPS
ROSEANN RUNTE

EDITORIAL ADVISORY BOARD

J.J. ANDERSON University of Manchester
HERBERT BERRY
DAVID BEVINGTON University of Chicago
L.M. CLOPPER Indiana University
JOANNA DUTKA University of Toronto
IAN LANCASHIRE University of Toronto
RICHARD PROUDFOOT King's College, London
JOHN M. WASSON
GLYNNE WICKHAM
LAETITIA YEANDLE Folger Shakespeare Library

EDITORIAL STAFF

ARLEANE RALPH Associate Editor
WILLIAM ROWCLIFFE Graphic Artist / Typesetter
MIRIAM SKEY Bibliographer / Copy Editor
ABIGAIL ANN YOUNG Associate Editor

Symbols

BL	British Library	PRO	Public Record Office
Bodl.	Bodleian Library	RIC	Royal Institute of Cornwall
CRO	Cornwall Record Office	SRO	Somerset Record Office
CUL	Cambridge University Library	SSL	Sherborne School Library
DRO	Dorset Record Office	WM	Weymouth Museum
JRL	John Rylands Library	WRO	Wiltshire and Swindon Record Office

A	Antiquarian Compilation
AC	Antiquarian Collection
DNB	*Dictionary of National Biography*
DNHAS	Dorset Natural History and Archaeological Society
JRIC	*Journal of the Royal Institution of Cornwall*
PDNHAFC	*Proceedings of the Dorset Natural History and Antiquarian Field Club*
PDNHAS	*Proceedings of the Dorset Natural History and Archaeological Society*
REED	Records of Early English Drama
SDNS	*Somerset and Dorset Notes and Queries*
STC	A.W. Pollard and G.R. Redgrave (comps), *Short-Title Catalogue ... 1475–1640*
VCH	*The Victoria County History of the Counties of England*
Wing	D.G. Wing (comp), *Short-Title Catalogue ... 1641–1700*
*	(after folio, page, membrane, or sheet number) see endnote
⟨...⟩	lost or illegible letters in the original
[ ]	cancellation in the original
(blank)	a blank in the original where writing would be expected
° °	matter in the original added in another hand
⌈ ⌉	interlineation above the line
⌊ ⌋	interlineation below the line
^	caret mark in the original
...	ellipsis of original matter
|	change of folio, membrane, sheet, or page in passages of continuous prose
®	right-hand marginale
†	marginale too long for the left-hand margin

DORSET

Acknowledgments

Any REED collection represents the collaboration of many generous scholars. Our work on the Dorset records owes a great deal to the interchange between REED editors and other students of the drama, interchange fostered by REED and nurtured by the project's founder and director, Alexandra F. Johnston, and the indefatigable efforts of executive editor, Sally-Beth MacLean. Their wisdom, expertise, breadth of vision, and sheer energy teach and inspire and also serve as catalysts for a remarkable generation of ideas. We are enormously grateful to them and to other REED editors from whom we have learned a great deal.

We would like, in particular, to thank Sally-Beth MacLean for her unfailing encouragement, her skilful coordination of REED's work on the Dorset records, her insightful assessment of each section of the collection, and her work on first proofs. Associate editor Abigail Ann Young's editorial suggestions have been invaluable, as have her meticulous paleographical corrections, translations of Latin documents, and creation of the Latin Glossary; we greatly admire the breadth and precision of her knowledge. The patience and skill Miriam Skey brought to the sometimes frustrating process of copy-editing and proof-reading the text have been enormously helpful as has been her relentless bibliographical work. We are most grateful for Arleane Ralph's many hours of work on the lists of patrons and travelling companies, for her scrupulous but genial attention to detail in proofing the entire collection, and for her willingness to tackle the thankless task of a two-collection index. REED: Dorset owes a great deal also to Sheena Levitt's expertise in financial administration; to Theodore DeWelles' bibliographic work; to William Cooke for the English Glossary; to Richard Gyug, Philip Collington, and William Cooke for paleographical checking; to Catherine Emerson for checking the Latin Glossary and Translations; and to William Rowcliffe for typesetting the collection. Subash Shanbhag of the Department of Geology at the University of Toronto furnished us with a modern map of Dorset.

British archivists, librarians, and holders of manuscript collections have welcomed two North American scholars and given us a great deal of much-needed assistance in locating, identifying, and interpreting the records. Most important has been the help given by the several archivists at the Dorset Record Office and their staffs: Hugh Jaques, Dorset County Archivist, and his predecessor, Margaret Holmes; principal archivist, Sarah Bridges; assistant and junior archivists, Caroline Ferris, Jennifer Hofmann, M. Prescott, David C. Reeves, and Mary Rose; and reading room assistant Felicity Cohen. I.K.D. Andrews, Town Clerk of Poole, and G.M. Smith, then Curator of Museums at Poole, were extraordinarily helpful, permitting us to see some damaged records in early stages of repair and to examine manuscripts on display in the Poole

Museum as well as those then held in the Poole Borough Archives. John Warmington, Librarian of Sherborne School, made available some of the parish's earliest manuscripts, then kept in the subterranean reaches of the school. We also thank Tom Mayberry of the Somerset Record Office, S.D. Hobbs, County Archivist, and J. d'Arcy, Principal Archivist, at the Wiltshire Record Office and his staff. Mark Nicholls, Deputy Keeper of Manuscripts, Cambridge University Library, and Peter McNiven, head of Special Collections at the John Rylands Library in Manchester, kindly checked documents for us. Others who checked documents included Michael Heaney, who verified entries at the Bodleian and other Oxford libraries and also transcribed quotations from the manuscript of Leland's Itinerary; Alasdair Hawkyard, who worked on the voluminous and scarcely legible membranes of Condytt v. Chubbe at the Public Record Office; Eileen White, who confirmed readings of manuscripts at the Wiltshire Record Office and who also located and did preliminary transcriptions of ecclesiastical court records; and Julia Merritt and Monica Ory, who checked PRO records. Claire Breay checked records at the British Library and helped us secure reproductions of the earliest map of Dorset, Alan Fletcher checked records at Marsh's Library, Dublin, and Adrian Moon did some early checking of records at the Dorset Record Office. We are especially appreciative of the efficient and expert work of Richard Samways who did extensive checking of records at the Dorset Record Office, the Poole Borough Archives, and the Weymouth Museum as well as locating and transcribing records at the PRO.

Among the many scholars with whom we have discussed this collection we particularly thank James Stokes, REED editor for neighbouring Somerset, for his generous sharing of records relevant to both counties and for the assistance his findings gave us in interpreting the Dorset records. John Elliott, Jr alerted us to relevant material in Robert Ashley's autobiography and Father Owen Lee clarified crucial aspects of the Dorchester show for Bishop Thornborough. Early discussions of Dorset material with John Fowles, David Underdown, Adrian Moon, and the late Maureen Weinstock were also helpful. Each of us has benefitted from the enthusiasm and informed interest of colleagues as well, particularly Sister Mary Clemente Davlin, O.P., of Dominican University (formerly Rosary College), Lynne Magnusson of the University of Waterloo, and Paul Stevens of Queen's University, Kingston, Ontario.

Financial support for the work on the Dorset records has included grants to REED from the Social Sciences and Humanities Research Council of Canada (SSHRCC) and the National Endowment for the Humanities, a substantial individual SSHRCC research grant, and generous grants from Father Edward Jackman, O.P., and the Jackman Foundation. A sabbatical leave from Dominican University supported work with the records. St Jerome's University offered both moral and financial support for the research and both universities supported the presentation of preliminary results at several scholarly conferences.

We are most grateful to the following libraries and owners for permission to quote extracts from documents in their possession: the Bodleian Library, University of Oxford; the British Library; the Dorset Record Office; the Public Record Office; the Somerset Record Office; the Wiltshire and Swindon Record Office; and the Weymouth and Portland Borough Council. Crown copyright material in the Public Record Office appears by permission of the Controller of Her Majesty's Stationery Office and excerpts from the Gillingham Manorial Court Orders

(Nicholas MS 69) are reproduced by courtesy of the Director and University Librarian, the John Rylands University Library of Manchester. Extracts from manuscripts and early printed books in the Cambridge University Library collection appear with the kind permission of the Syndics of Cambridge University Library. The excerpt from William Kethe's *Sermon made at Blanford Forum* (*STC*: 14943) appears by permission of the Bodleian Library, University of Oxford, the owner of a copy (Mason CC 73) of the printed book, and the excerpt from John Stow's *Chronicle of England* (*STC*: 23333) by permission of the Folger Shakespeare Library. We thank also the owners of copies of episcopal visitation articles from which we print extracts: the Rector and Fellows of Exeter College, Oxford; the Master and Fellows, Magdalene College, Cambridge; Manchester College Library, Oxford; the Governors and Guardians of Archbishop Marsh's Library, Dublin; and the Master and Fellows of St John's College, Cambridge.

Finally, we thank our families. Rebecca and David Hays' enjoyment of enforced Dorset vacations taught their mother about parts of Dorset she might otherwise have missed and they tolerated many more 'bo-o-oring' conversations about Dorset records than any child or teenager should have to endure. Haley McGee, first as a baby and then as a toddler, made research trips to Dorset more complex – and enormously more fun – for her father, and Rory McGee has graciously put up with stories of times and travels before his time. Donna Penrose has been a constant source of perspective, support, and love throughout all the years of work on this project. Jo Hays provided a willing ear, a thoughtful editorial eye for drafts of the historical introduction, and love that is beyond price.

Historical Background

Modern Dorset – apart from her eastern urban complex – has remained a pre-eminently rural county, still displaying much of the rustic and sometimes wild country and parochial culture described by Thomas Hardy and the Dorset poet William Barnes. The shire attracts fewer tourists than more spectacular Devon and Cornwall, Hampshire's Southampton overshadows Dorset's ports, and the main routes westward from London or Salisbury to Exeter or Bristol now cross through only the narrow northern part of the county. There seems a striking continuity between the modern shire and the sixteenth- and seventeenth-century county: it, too, was prosperous, overwhelmingly rural, and of little importance in national affairs, and early modern travellers to the west country tended to bypass most of the county.[1]

Dorset's terrain is extraordinarily varied. The centre of the county is dominated by the broad crescent of the chalk downs that sweeps north and west from the rocky coast east of Portland, turning east to join eventually with the range that continues through Wiltshire to the Marlborough and Berkshire downs. This high and broad range of hills has encouraged continuous patterns of settlement and farming since at least Roman times. The hilltops are most useful as pastureland, land that supports the animals so important for the fertilizing value of their manure on the rich arable in the well-watered river valleys between the hills.[2] The downs were first settled in neolithic times and more thoroughly cultivated during the four centuries of Roman dominance in Dorset; the pattern of settlement continued and expanded after the belated Saxon conquest of the county. Thus, cultivation of the chalk down country after Domesday was an extension and development of long-standing patterns of land use. Both the pastures on the hilltops and the use of valley ploughland favoured collective agriculture, and medieval and early modern downland Dorset was typified by nucleated villages and important manors.

The heath country between the rocky Isle of Purbeck in southeastern Dorset and the arc of the chalk downs has relatively acidic and, hence, poor soil; it was perhaps settled and cultivated most fully by the Saxons. Early Purbeck farmers could eke out a living but the area was most valuable in the medieval period for the limestone and marble quarried for building. And although there were isolated farmsteads throughout the county from prehistoric times, the heavier clays in Blackmoor Vale and in northern and western Dorset, regions also more heavily wooded than the down country, were more profitably cultivated only after the development of medieval agricultural technology.

Seventy-five miles of coast and easy access to important shipping routes have meant that much of Dorset's history and several of her more important towns have been linked to the sea. Both small river mouths and natural harbours could admit the vessels bringing Roman, Saxon, or Danish invaders or the small ships carrying medieval and later coastal commerce. Much of that coast is dominated, however, by magnificent but unmanageable cliffs; havens useful in the medieval centuries were less accessible to the larger sixteenth-century ships. Only the natural harbours at Weymouth-Melcombe Regis and Poole and the artificial harbour at Lyme Regis were to be of more than local importance after 1500. Nonetheless, much of Dorset's interchange with the world outside the county was by sea, so much so that sometimes the coastal towns seem to have had more to do with their trading partners outside the shire than with inland regions of the county itself.

Dorset was relatively well-developed at the time of the Conquest. Its country was 'heartland' that boasted nearly 300 mills, and the moderate development and expansion of the arable in the twelfth and thirteenth centuries was accompanied by population growth but not radical social change.[3] The county borders are ancient and have changed but little from the borders implicit in the process of the Saxon conquest (modern county reorganizations have exchanged a few parishes between Dorset and Devon; more importantly, territory including Bournemouth and Christchurch was added to the eastern end of the county). In the medieval period the county had close connections with the king: nearly forty Dorset manors made William I the most important landlord in the shire, and several medieval kings spent fair periods of time in Dorset, with Dorchester an important point on the itineraries of Edward I and Edward II. The west country had, of course, been the core of Alfred's territory in the ninth century; it witnessed civil war both immediately after the Conquest and during the conflict between Stephen and Matilda when Dorset castles at Sherborne, Powerstock, Wareham, and Corfe were besieged. Sharing a sheriff with Somerset during much of the medieval period, Dorset was a frequent source of supply for royal ventures.[4]

Dorset's religious life was shaped by institutions initially founded in the Saxon period. The county was originally in the diocese of Sherborne: that see was united to that of Ramsbury, Wiltshire, in 1058 and the bishop moved to Old Sarum after 1075. Under the bishop of Salisbury's jurisdiction until 1542 (when the county was joined to the new diocese of Bristol), several sections of the county were in one or another peculiar jurisdiction that provided some ecclesiastical independence, most notably the very large parish and royal peculiar centred on the royal free chapel of Wimborne Minster, and the peculiar of the dean of Salisbury that preserved both the property rights and influence of the dean and prebends of Salisbury Cathedral within Dorset even after the shire was joined to Bristol diocese. Much of the pattern of parish and monastic life was firmly rooted, however, in the Saxon church. Saxon Dorset was dominated by the huge parishes of the minster churches, some of which still served large parishes in the nineteenth and twentieth centuries, although many former dependencies had acquired parochial independence in the intervening years. Sizeable monasteries at Abbotsbury, Cerne Abbas, Shaftesbury, and Milton Abbas were beginning to serve as centres for towns by the time of the Conquest. These houses and three others – Sherborne Abbey (the Benedictine monastery which became the focus of Sherborne life after Sherborne's bishop moved to Sarum), the college of secular canons at Wimborne Minster (founded after an earlier monastery was destroyed in the late tenth-century Danish invasion), and the twelfth-century Cistercian house at Bindon – dominated monastic life in Dorset until the Dissolution; although the friars were active in the county, their houses were never so influential as the large pre-Conquest monasteries.[5]

Expanded land use, such technological developments as the horizontal loom and the fulling mill, and the emigration of skilled craftsmen from guild-dominated towns to the countryside were among the factors that stimulated the growth of west country cloth production in the twelfth and thirteenth centuries, particularly in the cheese country of Somerset and Wiltshire. The Dorset sheep herds also grew during this period and contributed to the growth of local wool cloth production. As prosperous agricultural communities developed markets, the Dorset markets and small market towns also grew. J.H. Bettey tells us that four Domesday Dorset boroughs (Bridport, Dorchester, Shaftesbury, Wareham; Wimborne Minster also had burgesses) were joined by ten other boroughs by the end of the fourteenth century, including the successful ports of Lyme Regis, Melcombe Regis, Poole, and Weymouth.[6]

The Black Death entered England through Melcombe Regis and it is probable that Dorset lost a higher percentage of its people than other rural counties to the initial epidemic and frequent recurrence of disease in the next three centuries. Some villages were deserted, particularly in wilder, more heavily wooded west Dorset and in the Blackmoor Vale. In the chalk country and in most towns, population loss resulted in the contraction of economic activity in the fourteenth and fifteenth centuries, although it is possible growing sheep flocks may be linked to shrinking population and arable acreage in the downlands. Fifteenth- and sixteenth-century growth of such coastal towns as Poole and Lyme Regis, on the other hand, was important to the general economic recovery of Tudor Dorset.[7]

An early seventeenth-century description of the county may serve to emphasize the continued rural character of the shire in the early modern period:

Though the Aire of this Territorie bee good and healthfull, yet is not the Soyle barren, but rich and fruitfull … The more Northerne Part, divided from the South almost by a continuall Ridge of high Hills, is somewhat flat, and was in foregoeing Ages wholely Forrests; neither is it yet in this decaying Age of ours altogether destitute of Timber Trees, and Woods; abounding also with verie good Pastures, and Feedeings for Cattell; watered with fine Streames, which take their Courses through rich Meadowes … the South Parte … consisteth altogether of Hills, (Downes we call them …) all overspread with innumerable Flockes of Sheepe, for which it yeelds very good and sound Feedeing, and from which the Countrie hath reaped an unknowen Gaine. Valleys it hath diverse, but not large, in the which, for the most parte, the Townes and Gentlemens Houses are seated, for avoideing those sharpe Blasts which this Southerne Parte is subject to; for it is somethinge wilde, and verie destitute of Woods; Cornefeilds they have plentie, which seldome deceive the Husbandmans Expectation; and adjoyneing to the Rivers good Meadowes, though not in soe great Plentie as the North Parte of the Shire…

It is generallie well watered with Rills, and swift runneing Brookes; which, passeing through the Plaines and Valleys, doe at the last in a most loveing manner unite themselves, and of their manie Branches make two bigge bodied Streames, Frome and Stower, both passeing full of good Fish, which neverthelesse is not soe much respected there, because the adjoyneing Sea doeth furnish the Countrie with all Kindes of Fish.[8]

Most striking about Thomas Gerard's description of Dorset is the extraordinarily rural tone of his account, perhaps to be expected in the voice of a member of the gentry most interested in the fortunes of his own kind. But some circumstances conspired to preserve Dorset's relative isolation. There were in the county few large landholders of national prominence: Henry VII's mother, Margaret Beaufort, had close connections with Wimborne and was eventually buried in the minster; Sir Christopher Hatton was for a time at Corfe Castle, later purchased by Sir John Bankes, attorney-general to Charles I; and Sir Walter Ralegh spent much time at his seat at Sherborne Castle and exercised both patronage and authority in Sherborne. For the most part, however, such figures from national politics had little to do with the county and Dorset politics remained in the hands of prosperous local gentry families, headed by the Strangways of Abbotsbury and Melbury Sampford. Gerard's impression in the 1620s was that the Dorset gentlemen were 'for the most parte ... of antient Descent' although freeholders, profiting from 'rakt Rent ... doe now beginne much to encroch upon the Gentrie,' producing occasionally new 'Families of note.'[9] It is notable that he found Dorset gentlemen essentially local worthies, although they sometimes bought lands or intermarried with families from neighbouring counties. The considerable social upheaval in Dorset in the sixteenth and seventeenth centuries – almost 50 per cent of the leading families in the 1630s first appeared among the Dorset gentry after 1529 – was fed by immigration, notably of Devonshire gentry families, the purchase of confiscated monastic properties by lesser Crown servants and local gentry, the social rise of local farmers, the economic success of Dorset merchants, and the occasional movement of local town patricians into the ranks of country gentlemen. As David Underdown has argued eloquently in *Fire from Heaven*, prominent Dorset men could be very much aware of national and international events. But Dorset's own affairs were generally her own; the county was largely free from the domination of aristocrats or of political figures of national influence.[10]

Dorset apparently adapted successfully and reasonably peacefully to the changing agricultural markets of the sixteenth and seventeenth centuries. The flocks pastured on the downs increased greatly and there were frequent enclosures of downland commons for both sheep pasture and arable, often by common agreement of the tenants or between the tenants and a great landlord. By the seventeenth century the county boasted twenty-one important markets and forty-six annual fairs; by far the most important fair was the centrally-located September fair at Woodbury Hill near Bere Regis, which attracted many visitors from outside the shire.[11] From the early seventeenth century there were also experiments with water meadows, and some increased specialization and some expansion of pasturage and arable into cleared and enclosed waste and forest also occurred in the claylands of Blackmoor Vale and the west country. Apparently such developments occasioned little social upheaval in most cases, although in the 1620s and early 1640s riots followed the disafforesting of Gillingham, riots Joan Thirsk associates with general, multifaceted economic depression and David Underdown with attacks on the 'clique of courtiers and Londoners' whom local villagers saw as responsible for the disaf-forestation.[12]

Expanded exploitation of the land contributed to Dorset's general prosperity. Indeed, in general, the pattern of Dorset's early modern development was one of growth and successful adaptation of an economy that nonetheless remained second rank. Dorset's growing herds supplied a sizeable Dorset broadcloth manufacture in the fifteenth century, for example; weavers were turning to both the newer dyed cloths and narrower and cheaper kersies and 'Dorset dozens' by the early seventeenth, and Dorset ports exported cloth made in Somerset as well as Dorset. But the centre of marketing for the expanding cloth trade lay to the north in Wiltshire and Somerset, and Dorset cloth was considered inferior to that of neighbouring counties. Similarly, enterprising Dorset coast towns took advantage of new opportunities for growth. Poole and Weymouth early joined the new trade with the fisheries of Newfoundland, import-ing and re-exporting Newfoundland fish with great profit, and Bridport and Lyme Regis may have helped redistribute the fish in southwest England. The manufacture of sailcloth and rope, particularly for shipping and the navy, were important industries in west Dorset, especially at Bridport, and Dorset was also one of the chief sixteenth-century woad-producing shires. But despite considerable growth, Dorset's coastal commerce was adversely affected by the shift of commercial shipping to London: the harbours at Lyme Regis, Weymouth-Melcombe Regis, and Poole were also too small or shallow to allow for the increasingly large ships that became the commercial carriers and more important naval vessels of the sixteenth century.[13]

Tudor governments – like their medieval predecessors – brought sometimes reluctant Dorset coast towns into the structure of coordinated English maritime defence, building additional coastal forts, such as Sandsfoot Castle, near Weymouth. Dorset coast towns were all involved to some extent in furnishing ships to fight the Armada but their participation was mainly through money or the provision of small, armed merchant ships, a fact reflecting the strong but secondary prosperity of these small, vital ports, important for supporting the larger ships against the Armada, as they were important for supporting coastal shipping increasingly dominated by London. Perhaps symbolic of the enterprising, flexible, and very localized character of county commerce is the county's involvement in privateering, smuggling, and piracy in the late sixteenth century. At least thirty-six ships from Weymouth, Lyme Regis, and Poole captured foreign prizes as part of the privately financed maritime activities against Spain after 1585. Pirates based first in West Lulworth, and later in Purbeck, were linked to members of the Dorset gentry, to the deputy of the vice admiral for the Isle of Purbeck, and to the deputy searcher for Weymouth-Melcombe Regis, as was discovered during Crown in-quiries of the 1570s and 1580s, and both pirates and smugglers operated with the cooperation of villagers in the hinterlands, town officials from several towns, and profit-taking merchants and gentry. The piracy was suppressed and the pirates hanged from gallows stretched out over the sea. But smuggling continued as a cooperative local enterprise adding to the profits of enterprising agriculture and successful town adaptation to the Tudor market economy.[14]

The prosperity of the county is reflected in the growth of Dorset's towns in the sixteenth century (records of performance activity survive largely from towns that were successful), in the increased amount of land brought under cultivation and the innovative techniques used in agriculture, and in the apparent complacency and increasingly visible affluence of Dorset gentry. Prosperity is also reflected in the relative placidity of the shire's relationship to national signs of conflict. Dorset was divided, for example, about religion in the sixteenth and seventeenth centuries. But signs of Lollardy had been less frequent in Dorset than elsewhere in the west country – there was a great deal of church rebuilding in fifteenth-century Dorset – and Dorset monasteries surrendered to Henry VIII's commissioners peacefully.[15] Conflict about religion seems generally confined to town or parish in the succeeding generations, perhaps in part because Dorset's 1542 assignment to the often headless diocese of Bristol and the consequent lack of effective episcopal supervision during Elizabeth's reign made difficult enforcement of any policy against local sentiment. When Devon and Cornwall rose in the conservative 'prayerbook rising' of 1549, Dorset remained calm. The county's quiescence probably did not, however, mean enthusiastic support for reformed religion, for the county militia fought only reluctantly against their more passionate neighbours.[16] In the Elizabethan period Puritanism gradually gained a hold in many towns, particularly in Dorchester and Poole, but several prominent Dorset families preserved Catholic traditions. Attempts to stamp out undesirable religious opinion tended to be inconsistent and probably limited in their effect. For example, Elizabethan efforts against Catholicism resulted in the execution of priests at Dorchester in the 1580s and 1590s, but in 1592 a member of one of Dorset's more prominent Catholic families was appointed to the commission supposed to uncover Jesuits in the county; seventeenth-century presentments from the Wimborne peculiar show the church pursuing both recusants and sabbath breakers. Religious factionalism was a prominent factor in the quarrels that divided several Dorset towns early in James I's reign, and by the 1630s Archbishop Laud's visitors found many Dorset Puritans, particularly in Poole, Dorchester, and Lyme Regis, but the Dorset countryside still harboured considerable anti-Puritan sentiment.[17]

Any interpretation of the records of performance activity in Dorset must consider Underdown's recent challenging interpretation of early seventeenth-century popular politics and culture, particularly in the west country. In *Revel, Riot, and Rebellion*, Underdown argues for a model of understanding popular culture in the region, based on contrasts between '"traditional" areas of open-field, sheep-corn husbandry in the nucleated villages of the chalk downlands, and the more individualistic economies and settlement patterns of the north Somerset and Wiltshire cheese and cloth-making country; with the less industrially developed pasture region in south-east Somerset and Blackmore Vale representing an intermediate type in respect of both economic and settlement patterns.'[18] He describes a Tudor and Stuart England in which there was a natural survival of popular traditions of various sorts. Communities often maintained such traditions because of civic pride as well as local sentiment and sometimes abandoned them for practical reasons, when other fund-raisers or fund-raising techniques seemed more efficient or profitable than traditional merry-makings. Moreover, campaigns against traditional feasts – against traditional popular culture – were fuelled by a 'preoccupation with social discipline ... visible at all levels of English life'[19] that ranged 'the Protestant country gentry and middling sort ... against what they perceived as the corrupt and popish extravagance of the Court and its hangers-on' and also 'ranged many of the gentry, the Puritan clergy and their allies among the respectable parish notables against the bulk of their social inferiors and the poor.'[20] The campaign for moral reform was generally more successful, he believes, in wood-pasture regions. 'Traditional festivals and other plebeian amusements survived longer, and continued to reflect an older notion of community' in the arable downlands, while a few pasture regions – including Dorset's Blackmoor Vale – remained 'as culturally conservative as the downlands.'[21]

Underdown's work has been the object of much cogent criticism, summarized succinctly by Ronald Hutton.[22] As Hutton indicates, Underdown's topographical analysis has borne the brunt of criticism, notably by Martin Ingram, who found similar patterns of declining festivity in Wiltshire regions of all types. Finding revels and Robin Hood games throughout all regions of Somerset and staunch defence of 'traditional entertainment' in the 'heart of wood-pasture areas,' James Stokes similarly concludes that 'reform-minded justices' had more to do with efforts at controlling traditional entertainment than Somerset's topography and that 'support for traditional culture' had 'less to do with class and income level than with whether one was native to the area or a recent immigrant.'[23] Nor does our examination of Dorset evidence yield more support for Underdown's model, although our conclusions must be even more tentative than Stokes' or Ingram's. A major difficulty in fitting Dorset into Underdown's framework is the peculiarities of the Dorset evidence. For much of the period with which we are concerned ecclesiastical records are fragmentary; no sixteenth-century Bristol bishops' registers or ecclesiastical court books survive, for example. Although there are extant quarter session records for other counties – the Somerset evidence is particularly rich – for Dorset there is only a single order book (1625–37). Most of the Dorset evidence for performance activity comes from towns, generally outside the framework of Underdown's regional analysis (although he suggests that most of the towns shared political views with the rural areas around them). In general, we find it difficult in Dorset to distinguish clear geographical patterns for survival or disappearance of popular custom. Indeed, Underdown's model implies a general cultural conservatism in the Dorset countryside, where there was little that could rival the 'individualistic' enterprise of the north Somerset and Wiltshire cheese country. Much of the Dorset evidence does suggest, however, that the decline or continued support for revelry or traditional custom was partly associated with 'religious beliefs and the fear of disorder.' Like Hutton, we think that Underdown's 'stress upon the power of ideology may well be correct.'[24]

Second, a detailed examination of the Dorset evidence suggests that individual pieces do not always fit Underdown's use of them. For example, Underdown talks of James 1's reign as a 'transitional period,' during which festivals survived in many places; he states that at 'Cerne Abbas the maypole survived the earlier Puritan attack, only to be cut down to make a town ladder in 1635, just when maypoles were reappearing in other places after the second Book of Sports.'[25] Since the only surviving reference to the Cerne Abbas maypole relates to its destruction, the Cerne maypole may have languished unused for several years before the parishioners used it for timber, or it may first have been built in 1634. Surely the reference cannot support Underdown's indication on a map showing Dorset popular festivals that 1635 was the 'latest recorded date' for a public revel in Cerne Abbas.[26] Other points where we think Underdown or others have used Dorset evidence incorrectly will be indicated in endnotes to the records.

In brief, we find Underdown's discussion of patterns of social and economic change stimulating, as is much of his discussion of the geographical distribution of Dorset political sentiment during the 1640s and 1650s; we can, however, only regard his framework for understanding regional patterns of cultural conflict as unproved in the case of the county whose records we have examined. Sixteenth- and seventeenth-century Dorset, like the rest of England, was experiencing far-reaching changes in economic and social structure. Generally Dorset's reflection of the national pattern is seen both in the county's moderately successful response to economic setbacks and opportunity and in the increasing gulf between the expanded ranks of the gentry and successful middling sort and the expanding ranks of the poor. Various communities succeeded in different ways in adapting to change, just as individuals succeeded in different ways; some of the differences in success or failure are almost certainly reflected in the continuance or abandonment of traditional culture, including both revelry and performance. A comprehensive and convincing model for understanding those differences, however, has yet to be written; promising elements of that model may be the ideology stressed by Hutton and his suggestion that 'the principal development of the early Stuart period in the history of [the old festive] culture [was] to turn it into a national political issue.'[27]

Boroughs and Major Market Towns

BLANDFORD FORUM

'A faire Markett Towne' in the 1620s, 'pleasantlie seated upon the River, and neare unto the Downes,'[28] Blandford Forum had begun to develop as a trading centre by the mid-twelfth century. The town had several advantages over its immediate neighbours: it straddled a major crossing of the Stour, one of Dorset's two largest rivers, and several roads converged there, including both the road connecting Poole to the hinterland of northwest Dorset and Somerset, and the main route from Dorchester to Salisbury, described by a writer of 1588 as part of a major secondary route between Exeter and London.[29] Although medieval Blandford only twice sent members to parliament, there were markets in the town by the early thirteenth century and Edward 1 granted fairs on the feast of the apostles Peter and Paul (29 June) and on the vigil of saints Simon and Jude (28 October) and the fifteen days following, and James 1 would confirm a one-day fair on St Mathias' Day (24 February).[30] By the Elizabethan period Blandford Forum was a thriving country town with well-known markets and fairs. A council of ten capital burgesses, headed by a bailiff, ran the town with advice from a steward appointed by the duchy of Lancaster.[31] The burgesses appointed chamberlains to carry out the main executive responsibilities of the town's government. In 1605 the community, then numbering perhaps 500–800 people, received a charter confirming its customs and giving the town lordship of the manor for which it would pay fee farm to the duchy. By that time Blandford was exempt from manorial control and could appoint stewards for its own court leet.[32]

Several signs suggest that in the sixteenth century Blandford was profiting from its position as a county market town. A fire in 1570 had destroyed the town hall, and the community undertook to build a new one, drawing on loans and gifts from individual burgesses as well as on funds from various Blandford charities. The new hall was built by 1593 and in 1610

Camden, commenting on the town's phoenix-like recovery, would claim the town was 'built more elegantly, and is better peopled with inhabitants.'[33] The town's sense of community appeared not only in its successful building campaign but also in the variety of ways the town raised funds, ranging from the several different ales featured in the Elizabethan chamberlains' accounts and the renting of space to players to the sponsorship of annual races after 1600.[34] The Puritan preacher William Kethe, rector of tiny Child Okeford, denounced a Dorset parish in his sermon to the justices at Blandford sessions in 1571 and it is tempting to guess that the parish that profaned its sabbath with 'bulbeatynges, boulynges, drunkennes, dauncynges, and such lyke' (see p 118) was Blandford itself. If so, the parish, according to Kethe, staunchly resisted the reforming minister. We know little of Blandford's internal affairs, however; repeated and devastating town fires, most notably that in 1731, destroyed most Blandford records.

BRIDPORT

The Brit river flows into the sea through an impressive gap between East and West Cliffs; the cliffs thus provide a sheltered river anchorage for small ships. Some distance north of the anchorage, in the angle formed by the Asker and Woth rivers as they join the Brit, was the settlement that became Bridport, perhaps originally developed in connection with Anglo-Saxon defence. By the time of the Conquest the town numbered about 120 houses. In the thirteenth century the draining and cultivation of the Marshwood Vale fostered the growing of hemp on land ideally suited to it; King John, who had visited the town a few years earlier, ordered Bridport sailcloth and hemp thread for ships' cables in 1211. The development of flax and hemp growing between Bridport and Beaminster contributed in turn to Bridport's growth; the harbour and the manufacture of rope and sailcloth – particularly for naval stores – were to prove the focus of Bridport's economy. By the fifteenth century the growing urbanity of a town increasingly shaped by its relationship to trade and manufacturing may be seen in the numerous confraternities founded in each of the two local churches.[35]

Although until the late fourteenth century Bridport's river was still too underdeveloped to provide more than a mooring for ships perhaps a mile and a half from the town itself, by the reign of Edward III Bridport sea captains participated in the Gascon wine trade and Bridport rope and sail manufacture was recognized by the Crown. Late fourteenth-century efforts to dredge the Brit and build a well-developed harbour set what was to be the pattern for the remainder of our period: time and again Bridport tried to gain permission and raise funds to build a well-equipped harbour but never managed to construct and maintain anything but a safe landing site for small ships.[36]

In the meantime, Bridport activity in an increasingly complex rope manufacture had grown. Even by 1315 many of the townsmen's assets included flax, hemp, and rope, and by 1530 Bridport successfully petitioned for a local monopoly of hemp selling and rope making. The town's prominence in the industry came 'mainly as a result of the very high quality of the local hemp and flax.'[37] So well known was the Bridport hemp that a sixteenth-century morality play could use 'taw halters of Burporte' as an image for a hangman's noose.[38] By the 1590s, however, the town's rope production had begun to decline as did seventeenth-century Bridport's domination of the industry. Contributing to the decline were Bridport's cumbersome organization of the trade, high transportation costs related to relatively poor overland transport as well as the silted-up harbour, and competition, both from rope-walks near to the naval yards and from Dutch and Russian hemp, of somewhat higher quality than the Dorset product.[39]

Bridport sent members to parliament regularly after 1295; her government was a self-perpetuating council of capital burgesses. In his Itinerary Leland called her a 'fair larg town' in the 1530s[40] but it was not until 1593 that Elizabeth granted the town a market and fairs, including a one-day fair on the feast of the Annunciation (25 March), a three-day fair on the feast of the Ascension (the Thursday following Rogation Sunday), and a one-day fair at Michaelmas. In her grant the queen stated that Bridport was 'an ancient Borough and mercantile town and formerly was a port of great celebrity and resort until the entrance and ascent of the same port were lately choked by the sand of the sea and almost blocked up, by reason of which the same Borough in commerce and merchandise is diminished and deteriorated and the buildings and edifices of the same Borough are in great decay ruin and dissolation.'[41] The queen was probably responding to requests from Bridport burgesses, whose determination to revive the town's economic health Robert Tittler sees in the celebrations surrounding the opening of a new market house in 1593.[42] The influence of an active local group of Puritans may also be visible in Bridport's quick support for parliament in 1642.[43] Consensus like that of 1642 was not easily obtained earlier in the century, when Puritanism set Bridport citizens at odds with one another. In 1614 allegedly libellous verses attacked 'The puritans of Bridporte Towne' as smug, self-righteous hypocrites whose supposedly religious gatherings masked sexual self-indulgence and adultery (see p 158). Named in the verses were many members of the town's leading families, men who had held or would go on to hold Bridport's highest civic offices.

DORCHESTER

The Romans probably chose to build a fort and administrative centre at Durnovaria (Dorchester) because of its proximity to British hill forts at nearby Poundbury and Maiden Castle: the site had been 'pre-eminent in the area' since the Bronze Age. Although there is no clear evidence of continuous occupation, the wealth of Roman remains at Dorchester and the prosperity of the town during the medieval period suggest that the city on the Frome River maintained its importance. In the time of Edward the Confessor the town boasted over 170 houses, of which perhaps 100 were destroyed by 1086. Bettey estimates the population of the town as about 700 at the time of the Conquest.[44]

Its location, economic role, and continuing political role in the neighbourhood all contributed to Dorchester's growth in the Middle Ages. The town was on one of two major sixteenth-century routes between Exeter and Salisbury or London, although the main road between Bristol and Weymouth bypassed the town. Growing agricultural prosperity in the region seems to have contributed to Dorchester's revival and growth as a market town. By the thirteenth century Dorchester had borough status and routinely sent members to parliament after 1295.[45]

K.J. Penn sees a sizeable local Jewish community as evidence of Dorchester's thirteenth-century participation in more than local commerce.[46] In the first half of the fourteenth century the town was granted several market days a week and several days of fairs a year. The town also had the right to maintain a prison. It was 'the main commercial and political centre for south Dorset during the medieval period,'[47] important both as a centre of exchange for the wool from the surrounding sheep farming areas and as a textile manufacturing town. As the king's justice became more influential in the shires, Dorchester also grew in importance as the 'county town' and the town where the king's justices came when they sat the assizes.

In the sixteenth and seventeenth centuries Dorchester remained important primarily as a market town, selling a wide range of commodities at her weekly markets in addition to the cattle, sheep, and corn that were the markets' mainstays. The town held fairs on the day after Trinity Sunday, St John's Day (24 June), St James Day (25 July), and received an early Elizabethan grant for a fair at Candlemas (2 February).[48] Camden found Dorchester 'neither great nor beautifull, being long since despoiled of the walls by the Danes,'[49] but perhaps he visited the town when sixteenth-century depression and inflation had had their worst impact on Dorchester's population and economy.[50] His opinion was not shared by Gerard a generation later. Although in 1613 a devastating fire had consumed 300 houses and Dorchester suffered more fire damage in 1622, Gerard could comment, nonetheless, that Dorchester 'hath encreased and flourished exceedeinglie, soe that nowe it maye justlie challenge the Superioritie of all this Shire, as well for quick Marketts and neate Buildings, as for the Number of the Inhabitants; manie of which are Men of great Wealth.'[51] At least some of Dorchester's élite were drawn from an influx of substantial immigrants to the town in the late sixteenth and early seventeenth centuries; besides such newcomers to Dorchester, Underdown tells us the élite included Dorset men who parlayed land investments into wealth, some even moving to the ranks of the gentry. The importance of the town's men of substance may be seen influencing the reshaping of Dorchester's cultural milieu in the seventeenth century, in their contributions to local charities and support for the Free Grammar School founded after the 1613 fire, in their leadership in the Dorchester Company, and in their successful campaign for a new Dorchester charter, one that was to give Dorchester a unique form of municipal government after 1629.[52]

By Gerard's time many Dorchester men were Puritans, many of them relative newcomers, and all of them greatly influenced by the preacher John White, rector of Holy Trinity and of St Peter's, 1605–48. White's dominance in the town had met some initial resistance. As early as 1607 well-to-do burgesses of Dorchester were engaged in factional wrangling, perhaps best seen as resulting from schisms among members of a ruling élite. The reciprocal accusations employed the rhetoric of religion: White was reported to preach extreme Puritan doctrine and, in turn, he and his friends accused opponents of sabbath breaking as well as recusancy. A dispute of this type, one which incidentally associated opposition to drama with hypocrisy and foolishness, eventually reached the Star Chamber (see pp 173–98 and 340–5). In this nest of quarrelling the fire of 1613 seemed to provide heavenly support for the Puritan interpretation of Dorchester's condition as well as for the town faction allied to its godly rector. In his recent study of Dorchester, Underdown shows how events after the fire brought White and his allies to dominance by the 1620s, placing them in a position to engage in a ferocious and partly successful campaign to suppress frivolity and enforce godliness in Dorchester. Underdown also suggests ways in which there may have been substantial resentment against the Puritan reformers, particularly from among the young and the poor.[53] The 1631 catalogue of the Dorchester library describes a collection which seems to mirror Dorchester's religious interests and the continuing religious controversy in the town. Although there are many Puritan tracts and several 'answeres' to Catholic treatises, the catalogue also lists tracts defending English Catholics or relating the lives of English Catholic martyrs.[54]

White was also deeply engaged in the organization of companies and the recruitment of investors interested in the promotion of trade and colonization in New England. In 1623 fifty Dorset gentry as well as humbler men and some men from other counties were subscribers to the New England Planters Parliament that was to become the Dorchester Company of Adventurers. White was influential in both the Dorchester Company and its successor, the Massachusetts Bay Company, in which west country investors cooperated with those from East Anglia to send expeditions to New England.[55] Such endeavours, initially stimulated by the commercial enterprise of Dorset gentry and Dorchester townspeople, probably also owed much to the desire to provide a haven for those dissatisfied with the increasingly less puritan Anglican church.

The era of White's predominance in Dorchester saw the drastic curtailment of freedom of behaviour and thought within the community, but it also encouraged a strongly independent spirit with respect to outsiders, a spirit visible in the town's reaction to an incident in the parliament of 1629. Denzil Holles, one of the Dorchester MPs, held the speaker in his seat while opposition resolutions were read in the Commons; hearing of their representative's subsequent imprisonment, the Dorchester townsmen voted him a silver cup.[56]

LYME REGIS

Sixteenth-century Lyme Regis was a 'praty market toun set in the rootes of an high rokky hille down to the hard shore' and close to the Devon border.[57] A settlement noted for its processing of salt in pre-Conquest England, by the second half of the thirteenth century Lyme had also developed as a port. The town was in competition with Dartmouth for overseas trade by the 1260s; in 1284 Edward I chartered Lyme as a free borough with a merchant guild and with institutions like those of nearby Melcombe Regis. By the 1280s Lyme seems to have been an active participant in the French wine trade. In the thirteenth century the townsmen 'with much Industrie and Charge'[58] built the Cobb, a massive breakwater curving into the sea to create Lyme's artificial harbour. Lyme Regis began to send members to parliament in the 1290s and the town was asked to provide ships for the Crown. By the early fourteenth century Lyme Regis was apparently a very prosperous port.[59]

A series of fourteenth-century misfortunes, including partial destruction of the Cobb by heavy November gales in 1377 and devastating French raids, left the town too impoverished to pay its fee-farm; the patent rolls picture the town in 1401 as so devastated by disease, war, and natural disaster that 'scarcely a twentieth part of it is now inhabited.'[60] Lyme's port continued to develop in the fifteenth century, however, exporting locally-produced cloth and importing

various goods destined for the Dorset hinterland.[61] By the sixteenth century the town's fortunes were again improving; Leland said Lyme 'hath good shippes and usith fisshing and
marchauntice,' commenting also on the wine trade with Brittany.[62] There are many signs of
Lyme's continued revival and growth in the sixteenth century, largely connected with her
continued development as a port. Public building included extension of the church, repair of
the guildhall and almshouse, and maintenance of the Cobb.[63] Elizabeth's reign witnessed Lyme's
seamen's involvement in profitable smuggling and in the semi-legal piracy that accompanied
late sixteenth-century diplomacy: according to Kenneth R. Andrews, eleven of the twenty-six
Dorset privateers operating between 1589 and 1591 were from Lyme Regis, second only to
Weymouth-Melcombe Regis among the Dorset privateering ports; in 1598 four of ten Dorset
privateers came from Lyme.[64]

On the basis of evidence from Dorset port books, W.B. Stephens believes Lyme Regis to
be the most prosperous Dorset port in the early seventeenth century.[65] His analysis does not
take into account the thriving Newfoundland trade of Poole and Weymouth – from which
Lyme also profited after 1608[66] – but it is nonetheless suggestive of Lyme's continued growth
and relative prosperity, even during the depression years of the 1620s. A 1618/19 royal assessment of the ports to fund an expedition against Moorish pirates demanded that Lyme Regis
and Weymouth pay four times as much as Poole.[67] Stephens suggests that Lyme had better
physical facilities than Poole and Weymouth because of the depth and protected waters of its
harbour, which a visitor of 1635 said was 'so strongly encompass'd, as they feare no wracke …
although they have incroach'd so farre into Neptunes bosome.'[68] Stephens' figures show Lyme
exporting almost as much cloth as Weymouth in 1622 and considerably more than both Poole
and Weymouth by the late 1630s, importing almost as much wine as Weymouth and much
more than Poole before 1640, and rapidly expanding both imports in general and her share
of Dorset imports before 1640. During this period Lyme served as an export centre for cloth
merchants from Bristol, Bridgwater, Chard, Taunton, Tiverton, and Exeter, as well as exporting
cloth produced in the Dorset-Wiltshire-Berkshire area; she also 'was unique in being the only
provincial cloth port continuing to deal chiefly with [the French] market on a large scale' during
the 1630s.[69] Evidence of the town's growing sense of civic pride may be seen in the construction
of a new town hall in 1612, partly financed – as had been earlier repairs to the Cobb – by
drawing on funds intended for the poor.[70]

Factionalism about religion, social conduct, and economic activity was expressed in acrimonious and reciprocal attacks in both religious and secular courts in the next several years. All
these causes of social discord came together in the Star Chamber libel suit of Robert Salter v.
Benjamin Cowper, Richard Harvey, and Edward Rotheram. The conflict had an economic
basis since Salter was one of the farmers of the king's customs and Cowper, Harvey, and
Rotheram were officers of the borough engaged in the same work. However, their allegedly
libellous attack focused on Salter's conduct, which they represented as relentless, adulterous
sexual hunting. Given the inclusion of Robert Hassard and John Viney among the confederates of this libellous action, this case may well have had a religious aspect as well; Hassard
and Viney were deprived of their magistracy by an order of the town council in October 1608
in part because they were supporters and special favourites of John Geare 'an vnbeneficed

Preacher who hath bin a cause of great factions & deuisions amongst vs.'[71] The interactions among Lyme's citizens at this time were very complex, far more complex than a simple binary opposition between moderate and radical Protestant factions. John Viney, for instance, who lost his civic office because of his loyalty to Geare, fought the vicar in the borough court for several years in the second decade of the seventeenth century.[72] And John Geare, whose activism probably helped put an end to the Cobb ale, did not dominate the corporation; indeed, in 1616 Lyme parishioners reported their vicar for over-zealous Puritanism, but Bettey describes the town as strongly Puritan by the 1630s.[73]

POOLE

Although its entrance tends to silt up and only frequent dredging permits the passage of very large vessels, Poole Harbour is one of the world's largest natural harbours. The medieval town of Poole was situated on a rounded and very visible promontory extending into the protected harbour; Leland said the peninsula 'standith almost as an isle in the hauen.'[74] It is in some ways surprising that the first port to develop in the harbour was not at Poole but at the Saxon settlement of Wareham to the north and west.

In the thirteenth century Poole, then merely a settlement 'at the edge of the great heath and commons belonging to the parish of Canford,'[75] began to develop as a settlement of fishermen and traders; the town acquired the right to hold markets and fairs by 1239 and in 1248 the community purchased its first charter from William Longespee, lord of Canford Manor. These were the first of many steps in Poole's gradual achievement of commercial success and greater political independence.[76]

Medieval Poole continued to thrive as a port serving the Dorset hinterland and as a haven for ships plying the coastal and Channel trades. Asked to supply ships to Edward I, it also sent occasional burgesses to fourteenth-century parliaments. Early fourteenth-century feuds with the Cinque Ports presaged Poole's recognition as their equal in 1364, shortly before William Montacute, earl of Salisbury, sanctioned its mayoral government and jurisdiction over breaches of market assizes. Poole's prosperity as a port made it not only the home base for the pirate, Henry Paye, but also the target of French raids during the fourteenth century. By the fifteenth century Poole had become the richest port on the Dorset coast. The wool staple was moved to Poole from Melcombe Regis in 1433 in letters patent recognizing Poole's larger population and more secure harbour. The town also profited from a lively trade with the Channel Islands. In 1453 Poole's mayor and bailiffs received jurisdiction over weekly Thursday markets and two week-long annual fairs beginning on the feast of the apostles Philip and James (1 May) and the feast of All Souls (2 November); after 1453 the town always sent two members to parliament.[77]

With the fifteenth-century decline of the wool trade, Poole may also have declined. Leland insists that 'Ther be men alyue yat saw almost al ye town of Pole kyuerid with segge and risshis,' but by the 1540s, he asserts, the town has recently been 'much encreasid with fair building and use of marchaundise.'[78] By then the town may also have benefited from the enterprise of several immigrant families from the Channel Islands who were, for example, to provide the town with five sixteenth-century mayors named Havilland. Poole's early sixteenth-century record books reveal the town's developing civic pride, reflected in the development of civic ceremony and the quest for civic autonomy by the emerging town élite. A charter from Henry VIII exempted the town from admiralty jurisdiction (the records of Poole's court of admiralty date from the 1550s). Finally, in 1568, after a great deal of expense and effort, Poole won the Great Charter that made the town a separate county corporate.[79]

The 1568 charter added to Poole's autonomy, probably both confirming and stimulating the further development of the town's civic pride and spirit of enterprise. The records reveal the continuous sixteenth-century development of a community with great adaptability and little deference to outsiders. With the Great Charter, Poole acquired legal recognition of the relative freedom from external authority that in some senses it already enjoyed. Earlier sixteenth-century records show Poole's mayor or bailiffs exercising many of the powers confirmed by the charter and assigned to the mayor or to the new sheriff. County status, however, provided an unusually strong basis for preserving town autonomy and for ensuring the role of prominent Poole men in influencing the exercise of royal authority in Poole as well as wielding power of their own.[80]

Although many south coast towns suffered reverses in the second half of the sixteenth century, Poole 'maintained distinct prosperity right up to the 1580s.'[81] The town's population (1,200–1,400 in the early Elizabethan period) grew by about 1.5 per cent per year for at least part of the period, growth paralleled by substantial public and private building and by growing overseas trade, which partly compensated for a decline in Poole's share of coastal shipping. Periods of lively building and commercial activity occurred from 1520 to 1545 and in the 1560s and 1570s. Before the 1580s the brewing, shipbuilding, and butchery industries were important to the town but Poole's main business was commerce and, according to Tittler, it proved relatively immune to the competition and dominance of Elizabethan London, perhaps partly because of the diversity of Poole's trade, perhaps partly because of the town's healthy relationship with the Channel Islands.[82] Only in the 1580s did Poole's commercial vigour decrease; Tittler suggests that by then the decline of Poole's coastal trading partners hindered the resale of its imports. Poole was also troubled by epidemics in the early 1580s. An atmosphere of crisis may also have been generated by incompetent government, reflected by the enormous debts contracted by townsmen who had financed 'over-expansion and ... bad management.'[83] But although the slump was to last until the end of Elizabeth's reign, Poole retained commercial viability and was also developing new areas of activity during the late sixteenth century.

Poole's interest in the Newfoundland fisheries began in the 1550s and developed steadily in the late sixteenth century. In 1583 the town bailiff, Christopher Farwell, thought the Newfoundland trade so important and potentially profitable that he left for Newfoundland despite his office and without the town's consent; he was heavily fined, probably as a part of the party quarrels of Poole's leading political figures of the period. By the early seventeenth century, Poole was regularly sending ships to Newfoundland and re-exporting several hundred pounds' worth of Newfoundland fish to European ports; in 1619 the mayor claimed that the 'Newfoundland fishery and one other trade together occupied all the port's shipping.'[84]

The mayor's comment, however, may suggest more about the decline of Poole's other commercial activities than about prosperity based on Newfoundland fish: by 1622 Poole was a distant third to Weymouth and Lyme Regis in the export of cloth and the town was similarly placed with respect to the import of wine and other trade by the 1630s.[85] Despite the flexibility that led her merchants to change their cargoes with changing markets – Poole was, for example, shipping considerable tonnage of Purbeck clay for tobacco pipes to London by the 1630s[86] – Poole's fortunes ebbed in the seventeenth century. In the 1620s the town suffered from the general depression experienced by cloth exporters after the failure of the Cokayne experiment. One of several ports reporting 'shrinking markets, unfavourable trading conditions, credit tightness and widening poverty' in 1621, Poole pleaded her poverty to avoid taxation in 1622;[87] in 1625 Gerard said Poole was 'much fallen from the pristine Glorie, yea, and soe much, that nowe the Houses beginne to decaye for want of Dwellers.'[88] In the 1630s the town was again ravaged by plague and seems not to have recovered its prosperity until some time after the Restoration.

During Edward vi's reign, Thomas Hancock, one of the more avid Puritan preachers, served as curate to Poole's church of St James. Hancock himself was initially distressed because, he said, Poole's citizens 'lacke the favor and frendship of the godly rewlars and governors to defend them,' and some of his parish walked out while he was preaching. The town remained generally Puritan in its religious preferences, however, although in Poole's late sixteenth-century internal political turmoil it is unlikely that any controversial opinion could have gone unchallenged. Like Dorchester and Weymouth, Poole supported parliament in the 1640s.[89]

SHAFTESBURY

Shaftesbury was one of King Alfred's three Dorset burhs; it was built on the flat-topped spur of a high down in the northern part of the county. Alfred also founded a Benedictine abbey for nuns under the protection of the fortress walls and, perhaps partly because Edward the Martyr's grave was there, the house grew to be England's largest and richest nunnery. A secular settlement sprang up in the shadow of both the protective fortress and the prosperous monastery, probably profiting from the patronage of both at various times, but the town was almost certainly less able to develop as an independent community than the coastal ports or Blandford Forum.[90]

Thus, Shaftesbury's prominence and role in the countryside were very ancient. The town had perhaps 1,000 inhabitants at the time of the Domesday survey and was the largest of Dorset's five Domesday boroughs; its prosperity depended on both the prominence of its abbey and its developing economic role in the neighbourhood.[91] As early as 1252 Shaftesbury's charter gave assurance that the king's justices would regularly visit the borough. Despite confusing jurisdictions (the town lay within two manors) and some conflict with the abbey, the town remained generally prosperous. By the fourteenth century Shaftesbury had a mayor and constables, although both king and abbess continued to profit from the town market and tolls. Friction between abbey and the town may have had several sources: the abbey's church was large and beautiful and, as at Sherborne, the townspeople had to make do with a much smaller church and were generally barred from the abbey precincts. After the abbey's dissolution in 1539, the monastic property was granted to Sir Thomas Arundell; Sir Thomas' heir let the buildings fall into ruins and they came eventually to serve as quarry for building stone.[92]

By the sixteenth century, however, Shaftesbury's location along the main London-Exeter road and position as an entrepôt between the Blackmoor Vale and the downlands of Wiltshire and Dorset had made the town largely independent of the nunnery. Although it is a steep climb from any direction except the northeast and the town had to be supplied with water from communities down the slopes, Shaftesbury served as the major distributor of much of the grain grown in the countryside. Town markets also sold fish and salt and other goods as well: ironware, candles, gloves, leather, and cloth are among the wares listed by Bettey; Shaftesbury's fairs were held the Saturday before Palm Sunday, 22 November, and for the four days before and four days after Midsummer Day (24 June).[93] By the seventeenth century its role as a town with 'one of the most frequented of all the markets in the region'[94] enabled Shaftesbury to support twenty-four licensed inns and alehouses, although the numbers of the poor grew as well.[95] An active Puritan faction in the early seventeenth century seems not to have prevailed; Shaftesbury was the home of a disproportionate number of royalist pensioners after the Civil War.[96] A charter of James I (1604) incorporated the ancient borough; the borough's pride is evident in its public building (a new hall in 1568 and possibly another in the 1620s, according to Tittler[97]) and in the town's faithful adherence to its traditional ceremonial.

SHERBORNE

Sherborne nestles between the hills that surround the Yeo River valley of northwest Dorset, near enough to the Somerset border so that the town has sometimes had more developed relationships with Somerset than with other Dorset communities. Made the episcopal see of the Saxon diocese in the early eighth century, the town continued to grow both as a service centre for its ecclesiastical core and as a market town, even after the bishop transferred to Salisbury in 1075, for by then a large abbey for Benedictine monks had grown up in Sherborne. In the early twelfth century Salisbury's bishop built a castle outside the town; the castle was designed primarily as a domestic residence and was near an extensive deer park.[98] Taken over by the Crown in the 1140s, the castle remained a potential local customer for trade and services, and the town could also profit from its position on the main London-Exeter road.

The town grew as a market centre, always dominated by the great abbey at its core and its relationship to its manorial landlord, the bishop of Salisbury. The bishop's men also controlled the hundred courts that had jurisdiction over Sherborne and Sherborne's abbot had a voice in the bishop's chapter in Salisbury. The thirteenth-century markets and fairs of the community proved profitable; in the sixteenth and early seventeenth centuries the town 'for Largenesse, Frequencie of Inhabitants, and quicke Marketts, giveth place to none in these Partes.'[99]

Like Shaftesbury, the community of Sherborne was sometimes restive under the domination of a large and wealthy monastery. Originally the townspeople worshipped in the nave of St Mary's, the abbey church; later the townspeople met in All Hallows', Sherborne, a small chapel of ease built close to the west end of the abbey church in the fourteenth century.[100] The

All Hallows' priest was subordinated to the abbot as rector of Sherborne and incumbent of the prebend belonging to the abbot and monastic congregation. Tithes and other parish revenue had been appropriated to the prebend in 1091.[101] By the fifteenth century there seems to have been a number of long-standing disputes between the parish congregation and the monastic community, notably a suit in the bishop's court in which the monks opposed a new parish baptismal font. The lay congregation claimed their font was needed because the monks had narrowed the processional door connecting All Hallows' ambulatory to the west end of St Mary's. The quarrels remained intense even after an episcopal attempt to reconcile the disputants and in 1436 the townsmen reportedly set fire to the roof of the abbey church with a flaming arrow. Although they were forced to contribute to rebuilding St Mary's, it was at this time that All Hallows' became an independent, parochial church.[102] A further contemporary sign of the growing autonomy of the town community may be seen in the fifteenth-century development of the community almshouse. In granting letters patent empowering the masters of the almshouse as a corporation, Henry VI was both recognizing the recent efforts of local philanthropists and providing a structure for community action. A building drive was shortly underway and new almshouses were soon built with funds raised by a house-to-house collection; the institution remained a focus for civic charity and civic spirit throughout the period before the English Civil War.[103]

The Reformation made possible the development of still more autonomous town institutions. After the Dissolution the abbey passed to Sir John Horsey, a privy councillor and former steward of the monastery. He in turn sold St Mary's Church to the vicar and parish of Sherborne at 100 marks for the abbey church; the roof leads and bells brought the total to nearly £250.[104] The parish promptly tore down tiny All Hallows' and parochial life henceforth was centred in the same church that still effectively dominates Sherborne's landscape. Although the parish was annexed – with the rest of Dorset – to the newly-formed diocese of Bristol in 1542, the manor and castle of Sherborne continued to belong to the estates of the bishop of Salisbury, and Sherborne was one of the parishes in the peculiars that continued in the jurisdiction of the diocese of Salisbury. The see of Bristol was also vacant for much of Elizabeth's reign and the parish perhaps gained autonomy because of the unenforceable and conflicting claims of powerful and absent ecclesiastics. Moreover, Sir John Horsey obtained the farm of the prebend of Sherborne, which, before the Dissolution, had supplied revenue to Sherborne's vicar as well as to Sherborne Abbey's abbot and sacrist; Sir John and his heirs enjoyed the revenues from the leased lands of the prebend until the early seventeenth century; thus, after about 1540 the income Sherborne's vicar received was inadequate to attract powerful clergy.[105] A single vicar held sway from 1538 to 1566; interestingly enough he and the parish apparently cooperated in adapting to the prevailing religious winds during that period.[106] Some later clerics accepted the Sherborne living only on condition that their income be supplemented from other sources and this may sometimes have made them dependent on the continued goodwill of neighbouring lords like the Horseys or on the townspeople themselves; other vicars did not live in Sherborne.[107] For a time Sherborne's churchwardens may have been more independent of the incumbent than were those in other parishes. Although after 1632 the Sherborne vicar was a Puritan preacher and the town's autonomy may have dwindled, Underdown can still refer to mid-century Sherborne as the 'least puritan town in the entire west country.'[108]

Fragmentary evidence shows the existence of a medieval grammar school in Sherborne, closely associated with the abbey, although the schoolmaster seems to have been a layman by the 1530s. Lands of five suppressed Dorset chantries were used by Edward VI to endow a new grammar school in 1550. Men who became governors of the school might also have held office as masters or brethren of the almshouse corporation or as churchwardens of the parish; all three institutions thus became foci for growing community feeling and civic pride, particularly among Sherborne's multi-occupational élite citizens.[109] Members of the corporations of the almshouse and the school took the reversion of the lease of the bishop of Salisbury's fairs and markets in Sherborne in 1582, in Fowler's opinion a distinct stage in the 'evolution of the town's freedom from manorial control.'[110] After that date community records increasingly use the word 'town' to refer to an autonomous entity, according to Joseph Fowler; he suggests that by the end of the century community affairs were beginning to pass from the hands of the lay churchwardens to some body made up of the townspeople.

Almshouse, parish, and eventually school were also active in the economic life of a town that was enjoying at least modest growth as a market centre. Each of the three institutions derived revenue from shops and the like, and each might build so as deliberately to take advantage of greater opportunities for commercial rentals. A good example of the phenomenon may be seen in the history of the parish church house, also of interest because its upper storey was used for both church ales and later dramatic productions. A series of false starts was finally concluded in the 1520s by the decision to build a church house with a large upper-storey room and a well-equipped kitchen, enabling it to function as a parish hall, and with several ground-floor shops that could be let to tenants for income that would help to support the main building.[111]

But if the parish was growing in independence and civic pride, and the economy of market-minded Sherborne seems generally prosperous during the sixteenth and seventeenth centuries, the town was still less independent than other large Dorset towns, perhaps because of the continued presence in the town of important landlords and its close proximity to the seat of a prominent family. Sherborne Old Castle, still standing until it was destroyed in the Civil War, was joined in the 1590s by Sherborne Castle, built to replace an early Tudor hunting lodge by Sir Walter Ralegh, who had first admired Sherborne on a journey from London to Plymouth, and who found Sherborne a congenial place to live after his amorous adventures lost him favour with Elizabeth. While there he was fêted by the town, served as MP for Dorset, and organized a salon society of intellectuals who may have dabbled in magic and certainly aroused suspicions of heterodoxy among their more orthodox neighbours.[112] Ralegh was based at Sherborne when he sailed for Guiana, Cadiz, the Azores, and Jersey. After Ralegh's attainder and imprisonment, Sherborne Castle passed through several hands; by 1620 the lease had been sold to Sir John Digby, later first earl of Bristol.

WEYMOUTH AND MELCOMBE REGIS

The shelter of the remarkable limestone formations of Portland Bill and of the peculiar deposit of sea-swept stones that forms the eighteen miles of Chesil Beach make the mouth of the Wey a natural and pleasant harbour. Although there is some evidence of earlier settlement, both the medieval towns that attempted to use and profit from the harbour date from the thirteenth century. Weymouth was founded before 1244 on a narrow strip of land on the south side of the river where it leads from the placid waters of Radipole Lake to Weymouth Bay itself. Weymouth's church was a dependent chapel of Wyke Regis, a rural village on top of the steep hill rising sharply behind the town. A bailiff and a royal steward headed the sixteenth-century town government. Facing Weymouth from less than a sixty-yard ferry ride across the Wey River, Melcombe Regis was established by 1268 on a peninsula perhaps 3/8 mile wide, between Radipole Lake on the west and Weymouth Bay on the east. Melcombe became a borough in 1280 and Edward III granted the town an eight-day fair on the eve, day, morrow and five days following the feast of St Botolph (17 June). Medieval Weymouth and Melcombe Regis seem to have had similar populations; in each the more well-to-do townsmen made their livings from trade. Both were summoned to send members to parliament from the early fourteenth century. Vulnerable like other Dorset coast towns to the depredations of pirates and of the French during the late fourteenth-century wars, and the site of the first devastating inroads of the Black Death in 1349, Melcombe Regis was decayed enough in the early fifteenth century for the king to transfer the wool staple to Poole.[113]

Both towns grew in the early sixteenth century, both apparently profiting from the rise of overseas trade in the reign of Henry VIII. But by the 1560s the towns were continually embroiled in competition for control of the harbour and its shipping, vying for rights to collect customs, maintain wharves, and so on. Disputes between them were supposedly formally resolved in 1564 but neither that agreement nor the forced union of the two boroughs in 1571 'saving their ancient liberties and privileges,' ended the controversy between them.[114] The corporation created by the union was to be governed by a mayor, two bailiffs (whom Weymouth saw as continuations of her pre-union government), six aldermen, and twenty-four capital burgesses, with the aldermen and burgesses forming a council. But until 1597, when a bridge across the Wey physically united the two towns, the governments and citizens of the boroughs continued to be at odds; lengthy and acrimonious disputes were accompanied by reciprocal arrests and lawsuits. The bridge induced rich Weymouth men to settle in expanding Melcombe Regis and by 1616, when letters patent of James I cleared up remaining ambiguities about the form of the union, the town was more peaceful. The late sixteenth-century records, however, are dominated by internecine fights between the formerly independent towns.

They are also dominated by Weymouth-Melcombe Regis' adaptations to the opportunities of Tudor economic growth. Perhaps not so forward in the Newfoundland trade as Poole, by the early decades of the seventeenth century Weymouth would be as active as her Dorset rival in the trade and transshipment of Newfoundland fish to continental ports. Together with Lyme Regis, Weymouth was active in privateering attacks on Spanish shipping, activities that brought considerable wealth to prominent families of both boroughs. There also seems to have been a great deal of piracy in the town, although the distinction between privateering and piracy was not always clear. Judging from the expansion of the town settlement on the Melcombe Regis peninsula in the Elizabethan and early Stuart periods, the town seems to have grown rapidly, dominated, as one might expect, by merchant families. Community experience was also coloured by more than ordinarily bitter local politics and more than ordinarily complex relations (for such a relatively small town) with the national courts and central government.

In the seventeenth century, although hampered by the low draught of her harbour, Weymouth-Melcombe Regis came to outstrip Poole as a port, particularly in the export of cloth before the slump of the 1620s; by the 1630s Weymouth's cloth exports were clearly declining but the port continued to be an important importer of wine and her general trade continued to exceed Poole's, although lagging behind that of Lyme Regis.[115]

Since both Weymouth and Melcombe Regis were served by dependent chapels during most of the period (a newly built church in Melcombe Regis was finally made parochial in 1606), in neither town did the parish church serve as a focus for community activity. Puritan influence may be seen in the early seventeenth-century municipal court's stern attitude to tippling or games on the sabbath or during evening service and Bettey describes the town as 'strongly Puritan' by the 1630s.[116]

WIMBORNE MINSTER

Jude James subtitles his 1982 history of Wimborne Minster 'A Country Town,' a title connoting Wimborne's past and present central function as market place for the surrounding countryside.[117] The town is still dominated visually by the imposing minster church and its dual centrality in the religious and commercial affairs of a large area was the community's distinctive trait for the whole of its early history. Indeed, when sources mention 'Wimborne Minster' it is often not clear whether what is meant is the town itself or the much larger rural parish, including the several villages within the parish. The site of the town, where the Allen River flows into the Stour, is 'so low you have to cross water from almost every approach,'[118] and much of the surrounding country was heathland and did not encourage such dense settlement as the valleys of western Dorset, for example. A settlement at Wimborne may have preceded the eighth-century founding of a Benedictine nunnery there by Cuthburga, the sister of King Ine of Wessex; the town, however, flourished after the monastery was founded and the church was, by the time of Alfred the Great, a minster at the centre of a huge rural parish with several dependent chapels. In the late tenth century the monastery was probably destroyed by Danish raids; it was converted, perhaps by Edward the Confessor, into a house for a dean and college of secular canons. By the time of the Conquest the town had developed into a 'small and flourishing township with the monastic church at its centre,' a township with close connections to several manors at least partly within the parish, and a town whose inhabitants generally depended, directly or indirectly, on agriculture for their livings.[119]

The college of canons came to include chaplains for the dependent chapels of St Peter in the Wimborne town square, St Catherine at Leigh, and St Stephen at Kingston Lacy, and Wimborne was also a royal free chapel with considerable independence from the diocesan bishop. This freedom was reflected in the status of the parish as a royal peculiar with its own ecclesiastical court. By 1218 the town had a market under the minster's dean and was growing both to the south on minster property and in the present East and West Boroughs, perhaps creations of the lords of Kingston Lacy, who ran markets in competition with the dean's market. Similarly both the manorial courts of Kingston Lacy and those of the dean held jurisdiction over some Wimborne parishioners.[120]

The Black Death must have greatly reduced the parish population (estimated by James at slightly over 1,400 in about 1330; the town itself had a population then of about 325). Demographic loss probably occasioned the desertion of the Leaze, that part of the expanded town on land controlled by Wimborne's dean,[121] and probably resulted in the beginnings of the gradual conversion of much of the land in the parish to copyhold tenure, a process that began in the early fifteenth century. Both markets and two annual fairs at nearby Pamphill – on the feast of St Luke (18 October) and the feast of St Thomas the Martyr (29 December) – contributed to the parish revenues after 1496; the parish fair of St Cuthburga was on 31 August.[122] At least from the early fifteenth century the parish churchwardens had considerable responsibility for maintaining the minster building and managing the properties and functions that provided the church revenues. These included several church houses during the fifteenth and sixteenth centuries and the proceeds of church ales and church 'cakes,' as well as rent from several properties in the parish. For most purposes the town as a secular community and the parish are indistinguishable before the reign of Elizabeth. Leland tells us that the early sixteenth-century town was 'meatly good and reasonably welle inhabitid.'[123]

Some conflict – notably in 1539 – preceded the dissolution of the college of canons and the minster chantries in 1547. The Wimborne community was particularly upset by the threat to their college-run school, founded by Henry VII's mother, Margaret Beaufort, and determinedly continued by the parish in the years following the Dissolution, despite royal interference and inadequate resources. In 1563 Elizabeth yielded to petitions from the parish and granted Wimborne a charter, establishing a corporation to run both town and grammar school, the latter endowed with many of the former properties of the Wimborne canons.[124] The twelve Elizabethan governors of church and school also appointed an official to preside over the ecclesiastical peculiar court.[125]

Although Wimborne undoubtedly experienced some social dislocation during the sixteenth and seventeenth centuries, the general impression left by the Wimborne records is that of a sleepy country town, dominated by what continued to be overwhelmingly local concerns. Many of the same individuals served as both churchwardens and governors of the grammar school; they could also, through the peculiar court, supervise much of the life of the town. As late as the 1590s the parish of Wimborne seems to have had an unusual number of Catholic recusants; Thomas Norman, the Wimborne minister after 1597, also offended many of the church-wardens and sidesmen with his Puritan views and preaching. Town dissension arising from such diversity of religious views is reflected in the records of the peculiar court, quoted extensively below for their references to local festival and games. Devastation by plague in 1638 seems, however, to have been of more importance to the community than economic change or religious controversy. The spirit of the age was also shown in the endowment of a number of late sixteenth- and early seventeenth-century charities.[126]

Miscellaneous Parishes

Three of the scattered parishes represented in the records were of some importance in the sixteenth and seventeenth centuries. Beaminster and Bere Regis were commercial centres, Corfe Castle a focus of military and judicial authority.

Today Beaminster is a charming village in a lovely west Dorset vale at the head of the Brit River valley, north of Bridport and west of Sherborne. In the sixteenth century, Leland described it: 'Bemistre is a praty market town ⌈in Dorsetshire⌉ and usith much housbandry and lyith in one streat from north to south: and in a nother from west to est.' Leland also stressed the subordination of Beaminster's chapel of ease to Netherbury's parish church, as well as its closeness to Salisbury.[127] A local historian estimates that the population grew from less than 500 in the first quarter of the sixteenth century to about 1,350 in 1642, growth supported by Beaminster's participation in cloth manufacture and hemp growing as well as by its market.[128] Leland comments that the land from Bridport to Netherbury and on to Beaminster 'is in an exceding good and almost the best uain of ground for corne and pasture and wood yat is in al Dorsetshire.'[129]

From the time of the Conquest when the manor at Beaminster had been part of the endowments of the episcopal see relocated at Salisbury, Beaminster had ordinarily boasted little self-government. The town market was granted in the thirteenth century and the town may have become a 'minor trading centre' with some craftsmen as citizens by the first half of the fourteenth century. Some sense of community may be seen in the extension of the church in the fifteenth century and the building of a market house in 1626. During Elizabeth's reign quarter sessions were held in Beaminster, probably because it was the most convenient central town in the relatively underpopulated western reaches of Dorset.[130]

The village of Bere Regis was the centre of a manor at the intersection of chalk downlands east of Dorchester and of forest country extending east to Poole Harbour. King John frequently visited the manor. By the end of the thirteenth century it was held jointly by the nuns of Tarrant Keynston (southeast of Blandford) and the Turberville family; after the Dissolution the whole was held by the Turbervilles, who lived in a manor house within sight of the parish church.[131] The latter dates from at least the twelfth century and Bere was a market town by the end of the thirteenth century. The wealth of the village was almost certainly increased by the annual celebrations at the September fair on Woodbury Hill, a nearby Iron Age hill fort; the fair was important enough for seventeenth-century communities several miles away to date their records by. Fires in 1633 and 1634 consumed much of the town; damage was estimated at about £7000, which small grants from the county and neighbouring towns can have done little to alleviate.[132]

Corfe Castle originated in a Saxon village and a Norman keep commanding a break in the long chain of chalk downs running across the Isle of Purbeck, a 'natural gate ... in to the most fertile part of the peninsula.'[133] Nestled in the shadow of the castle hill, the medieval town profited greatly from its role in the quarrying and shipping of Purbeck marble for which there was something of a national market. Corfe markets and fairs date from the early thirteenth century, although the town was not incorporated until the sixteenth century, a period when the influence of the relatively important holders of the castle tended to dwarf any independent stirrings on the part of the village.[134] Elizabeth made Sir Christopher Hatton constable of the castle and vice admiral of the Isle of Purbeck c 1571, creating an enclave of independent jurisdiction for Hatton. The mayor of Corfe Castle was to hold petty sessions twice annually, and Purbeck was exempted from Dorset jurisdiction. Something of the castle's influence may be seen in the requirement that a Purbeck father obtain the constable's permission to marry his daughter to a Dorsetman. Hatton ordinarily ruled Corfe itself through his deputy, Francis Hawley. Another prominent castle constable was Sir John Bankes, attorney-general to Charles I, appointed to Corfe in 1635.[135]

Local Customs, Music, and Drama

Much of the performance activity in Dorset was local in origin. Church ales and drinkings under civic sponsorship, musters and maypoles, Dorset-born fiddlers and fortune-tellers, bonfires and bell-ringing, parish plays and Corpus Christi processions and, of course, all the games people played (legally and illegally) when they were not playing plays[136] combined to produce a rich, varied cultural scene. Assessing how widespread and long-standing such activities were is difficult because the records often document only those events at which something occurred to attract the attention of ecclesiastical or civic authorities. Had Benjamin Goodwin not shot 'a piece into the church at Puddleton' during the Whitson ale in 1617, no trace of that seasonal custom there would survive.[137] Had the city fathers of Cerne Abbas not turned their maypole into a ladder (see p 169), had some of the citizens of Wimborne Minster not fornicated 'at the setting vpp of a may pole in Spettisbury' (see p 275), had the mayor of Poole not interfered with the use of a maypole with 'a parret vppon the topp therof' (see p 245), had a 'good man Paul' not died, 'smitten by the stroke of God,' because of his determination to see the summer pole set up at Symondsbury (see p 276), we would have scant evidence of the survival of this popular custom in Dorset. Similarly some bullbaitings, some drumming, some singing and dancing by individuals, and one performance by a disguised morris dancer were noticed because they occurred at the time of divine service or in the middle of the night.

Such evidence, however, is misleading to the extent that it suggests that there was a solid, steadily increasing block of opposition to such forms of celebration. In Dorset there was on-going debate about such practices.[138] William Whiteway, writing in 1633 about the reissuing of *The kings majesties declaration ... concerning lawful sports*, suggested what tensions existed when he noted that ministers were required to publish the book in church but 'diuerse in conscience refused to do, & many after they had read it shewd that it was against the word of God.'[139] In spite of such clerical opposition some civic authorities supported such festivities. As late as 1641, for example, the city fathers of Weymouth (where a maypole had been so important a landmark that, even after it had been taken down, it was used to locate other things and places) spent 3s on a maypole at Wyke Regis (see p 283). Although Shaftesbury's early records are fragmentary they also include evidence in 1655–6, 1662, and thereafter until 1830 that the borough continued to observe its annual custom.[140] In Lyme Regis John Geare, the zealous vicar whom several historians credit with the demise of the Cobb ale,[141] failed to extirpate all such activities. Even after thirty years in Lyme he had to accept local citizens making bonfires on Sundays and holy days 'for the Christninge of Apples' (see p 224). Indeed he some-times had to contend with them, as on Ascension Day 1635 when one William Alford, 'callinge himself a Captaine,' disturbed the morning prayer and Geare's sermon by organizing a muster of men who marked the occasion with 'Gunninge and drumminge and shootinge' (see p 224). Perhaps the best indication that opposition to civic festivities and entertainments did not build steadily toward 1642 and Cromwell's regime is to be found in the visitation articles for the diocese. From 1569 to 1640 episcopal visitation articles register the abiding anxiety about pro-fane uses of the church by lords of misrule, dancers, minstrels, and participants in may games or by those enjoying plays, feasts, or ales (see pp 113–116).

Several Dorset communities had their 'olde custums,' traditional, ritualized celebrations peculiar to specific boroughs or parishes and employing basic elements of drama: procession, spectacle, costume, role-playing, music, dance. Annually on Whitsunday morning citizens of Lyme Regis marched forth with a flag, drummer, and other musicians to gather boughs and returned for breakfast at the Cobb house (see pp 222–3). At Wimborne Minster 'the great cacke was browght thorowe the churche' and in Bridport there was a riding of the jack-o-lent (see p 138).[142] Hocktide was the season for fund-raising by the women of Charlton Marshall probably in 1600 and certainly in 1603–4, Poole in 1573–4, and Blandford Forum from 1567 until 1617. Bridport, Netherbury, and Poole also had collections or ales associated with Robin Hood. The records of Netherbury suggest that acting was involved since in 1568, according to an undated commonplace book probably of the seventeenth century, the people kept their Whitsunday ales and 'had their Robert hoode and Littell Iohn & the gentle men of the said parish the cheef acters in it.' Although this entry provides the last explicit reference to a Dorset Robin Hood the character may have persisted for several years. Almost all of the basic dramatic elements listed at the beginning of this paragraph come together in the annual 'Coostom' of Shaftesbury, an annual procession with a bejewelled bezant to Enmore Greene in nearby Motcombe where there was music, dancing, and 'play⌈ei⌉ng in the greene' (see p 250).[143] The custom of Shaftesbury has further significance for, in addition to the performance elements, the festivity had a political and economic purpose. The mayor of Shaftesbury presented the bailiff of Gillingham Manor two penny loaves of bread, a calf's head, a gallon of the best ale, and a pair of gloves as a symbolic way of securing access to the water from the spring-fed wells of Motcombe. Shaftesbury's use of civic entertainment to reaffirm its right to an invaluable resource is not unusual.

Ales, the dominant form of festivity, were regularly used to raise the funds needed to finance local projects such as paving the streets in Sherborne, building the market house and the school house in Bridport, caring for the sick in Blandford Forum, and maintaining the Cobb in Lyme Regis. Unfortunately the records are often frustratingly vague about what kinds of performance enlivened the ales. The only aspect of the Cobb ale of Lyme Regis that adverts to the possibility of musical entertainment is a silver whistle to be passed on each year to the new Cobb wardens and to be worn at the ale (see p 299). Though they may have played the whistle, it seems more likely that the whistle was a device for commanding the attention of a tippling crowd. The accounts of the stewards of the special ale organized in 1592–3 by Brid-port for the building of their new market house and school are unusually detailed in registering payments not only for the wages, liveries, and lodging for musicians, but also for wine for 'the kinge of loders.' This ale had both music and role-playing, the latter being a feature of the Robin Hood ale of Bridport and the Sherborne church ale, over which the 'king of Sherborne' presided. These celebrations frequently achieved their principal purpose – fund-raising. In the early 1590s the annual street ale of Sherborne, for example, never gathered less than £20 and in 1592 the take exceeded £30.[144] The Cobb ale of Lyme Regis had earned more than enough to cover the annual cost of repairing the Cobb so that in 1591–2 the city appropriated over £58 from the profits of the ale to cover the costs of purchasing the charter for the fee farm (see p 303). In Elizabeth's reign Blandford Forum held annual ales (the St Katherine's ale, the Maiden ale, the Bailiff's ale) and organized special purpose ales, such as those in 1592 and 1593 in support of the new guildhall. Robert Harden learned how important such fund-raising endeavours were when in 1582 he gave the town of Blandford 57s 10d 'for that hee did not keep the bailifes Ale this yeare.'[145] The Blandford bailiff might organize as many as ten festive meals at the race meetings the town sponsored in the early seventeenth century, on one occasion hiring Sir Ralph Horsey's cook to help prepare the feasts; the town cleared more than £30 from the races of 1605. Apart from the economic utility of ales and ancient customs, such celebrations had an important social role to play for, in the words of Underdown, they not only provided 'welcome relief from toil' but 'also brought neighbours together and affirmed the links that bound them to each other and to the world of nature.'[146]

As church and civic ales occurred at regular intervals and on special occasions, so various forms of music marked the cultural scene of many Dorset towns annually and occasionally. For some of the townsfolk of early sixteenth-century Poole, music seems to have been a daily experience, given the minstrel or piper who played 'the hole yer goyng mornyges & yeuenyng' (see p 239). Poole, however, is the exception, Dorchester closer to the rule. There each year the bells of Holy Trinity were rung on Accession Day and on Guy Fawkes Day; but bell-ringing also heralded special occasions in a way that connected this small town in the southwest of England with newsworthy events for the nation: a successful treaty with France in 1624, the birth of Prince Charles, a victory by the king of Sweden, the arrival of the vicar general, the success of the parliament in 1640.[147] In Bridport the bells rang out to welcome local gentry to the town and to celebrate (normally along with bread and beer laid on at the expense of the bailiffs) the monarch's coronation day. Lyme Regis rewarded two drummers, musicians regularly associated with musters in Dorset, at the time of the proclamation of King Charles I, and a trumpeter accompanied the city fathers of Poole when they 'went to Broonesey to see the shippe of london.'[148] The frequency with which Poole and Weymouth had to repair their town drums may be an indication of how often this basic form of music was used to enhance the dignity of such formal occasions.[149] Less dignified but no less purposeful were the libellous verses allegedly sung by defendants in cases heard in Star Chamber. Motivated by intense religious beliefs or by economic rivalries citizens of Bere Regis, Bridport, Dorchester, Lyme Regis, Melbury Osmond, and Over Compton satirized their enemies in poems which they nailed to the pillory or church door, reproduced and distributed, recited in public places, or sang in inns, taverns, and alehouses (or so, at least, plaintiffs alleged).

Royal visits to Dorset were marked by such ceremony as well as by the discharge of local ordnance. Henry VII had rewarded players from Wimborne Minster on New Year's Day, 1494, and made offerings at the minster in 1496. The parish of Wimborne Minster spent 6d 'for Redyng and makyng clene of the chyrche yard' for the king's visit in 1505–6. Far more costly was the visit of the queen in 1511, when Wimborne paid to one of the king's footmen what was, in effect, a fine of 2s 'for defawte of ryngyng at ye quene ys departyng.'[150] Poole cleaned up the town gates and relocated ordnance there in order to welcome with some ceremony King Edward VI when he visited the southwest in 1552.[151] Bere Regis laid on beer for the men who rang the bells when King James I came through the town in 1615.[152] These scraps of information suggest how seldom members of the royal family travelled through Dorset in the late medieval and early modern periods and how simple (compared with the pageantry laid on by boroughs such as York, Bristol, Coventry, Chester, or Worcester) was the ceremony with which they were received. Sometimes the problems for the Dorset towns were compounded by uncertainty about the royal itinerary. This happened in 1623 when Prince Charles and the duke of Buckingham returned from Spain. The first report of their landing, in September of that year, prompted some Londoners to write ballads but when the reports proved to be unfounded the ballad singers were imprisoned (see p 199). When the prince did arrive in October, landing at Portsmouth, there was great joy in Dorchester, where the bells were rung and the great ordnance of the town shot off.[153]

In addition to evidence of singers of ballads and other allegedly libellous songs, Dorset records provide information about several musicians, professional and amateur. An apprenticeship agreement identifies one, William Keele of Bridport (see p 154),[154] and a deposition to the peculiar court of Wimborne Minster extends what is known about the organist of that village, Robert Durham, by noting his skill on the harp, lute, and rebeck.[155] Like these apparently well-established, respectable members of their local communities, a 'W. C.' and his son 'H. C.' had the authority of a licence from Queen Elizabeth 'to wander & goe abrode with there instrumentes vsinge there trade of Minstrelcye, pleyinge or singynge throwghe & in all places within ye seyd countye onlye.' Two conditions obtained however: that they behave themselves 'orderlye' and that they use their licence 'accordinge to ye seyd statut' (see p 118). Unfortunately no record of any of the performances of these musicians is extant. When performances of minstrels or fiddlers are recorded their names are never specified unless the performance was in some way illegal. The churchwardens of Wimborne Minster, for example, presented John Pyke, minstrel, for playing at the time of evening prayer on 20 September 1601 and for playing on Midsummer Day, a Sunday, ten years later (see pp 284 and 286). In 1624 Thomas Angell, fiddler of Wyke Regis, was twice fined (and once stocked) by the constables of the mayor's court for playing in at least one alehouse in nearby Weymouth (see p 282). William Scot, a fiddler of Hinton Martell, was required in 1629 to answer unspecified charges against him at the next assizes. William Lucas, alias Bright, minstrel of Holt, four times ran afoul of the ecclesiastical officials of Wimborne Minster, in 1591–2, 1606, 1610–11, and 1620. In every case his offence was playing at the time of divine service. The performance in 1620 (at Cowgrove), however, was associated with drinking and a dancing match. Moreover, in 1620 'old bright' was presented 'with his boy and his daughter,' all of whom played their fiddles. Despite his conflicts with legal authorities old William Lucas (Bright), illustrates how acceptable and how popular was minstrelsy in Dorset, for he used his trade for almost thirty years and trained his young companions to follow in his footsteps.[156] The accounts of Sir Giles Strangways, the most influential of local magnates, confirm this impression in registering his New Year's gift to fiddlers who visited his estate to enliven the Christmas celebrations of 1638 and 1639. He also rewarded fiddlers when he was on his travels, as he did at Knebworth and Oxford in 1638 and at London in 1640, where he also paid 5s for a place to see the king ride to parliament (see pp 290 and 291).

The records of Dorset men connected to shows of various kinds are fraught with uncertainty. The one Dorset patron, Sir Richard Rogers of Bryanston, never appears in the records of his home county but he does turn up in those of Plymouth in 1569–70, Bath in 1577–8, and Exeter in 1582–3. How many entertainers he sponsored and what kind of entertainment they provided remain uncertain, for his performer(s) are associated with possible bearbaiting in Plymouth, bullbaiting in Exeter, and some undefined form of 'playing' in Bath.[157] The same is true for Trustrum and company, who rented the guildhall of Blandford Forum in 1594–5, and for the young men of Sherborne, who rented its churchhouse in 1599–1600; in both cases the income is entered as proceeds from 'playing.' Other individuals associated with the production of plays, such as John Merywether in Wimborne Minster (see p 283) or Andrew Pope and John Gawler of Blandford Forum (see pp 127 and 128), were collectors of the rent for the playing place rather than performers. Since Pope and Gawler (and perhaps Merywether too) acted as local agents for a production mounted outside the town, their involvement cannot be taken as a sure sign of local dramatic activity. What solid evidence we have of drama that originated in the county is to be found in the records of Sherborne or in those of Dorset schools.

The plays by schoolboys had a dual function. Schoolmasters used performances as pedagogical devices which helped students master the content of a work, strengthened their grasp of languages, and developed their oratorical skills. When Paul Rawlins, schoolmaster of Bloxworth, confessed to the court of the dean and chapter of Salisbury that he had arranged for the performance of a dialogue in the parish church on Shrove Tuesday, 1589, he gave as his rationale 'the better exercyse of his scholers.' The educational value of performing was surely a factor, though on the face of it not the crucial factor, in the production of plays at Corfe Castle in 1575/6 and at the Free School in Dorchester in 1623. In these two cases the plays were part of the festivities for the entertainment of a powerful visitor. Robert Ashley, who later represented Dorchester in parliament, mentions in his autobiography his involvement in the performance at Corfe Castle, where comedies and solemn spectacles were presented for the entertainment of Henry Herbert, earl of Pembroke. According to the Dorchester merchant, William Whiteway, comedies also provided the entertainment there in 1623 when Bishop Wright visited (see p 199). Judging from Whiteway's entry in his diary both the schoolboys and their master, Robert Cheeke, performed: 'Mr cheeke acted two comedies at the sheerehall for his comming, by his schollers.' For this use of drama Cheeke had a precedent since he had produced a theatrical presentation on the occasion of a visit by Bishop Thornborough (see pp 171–2). The plays at Dorchester have important political implications given the allegations that Robert Cheeke was of the Puritan faction led by John White. At a time when other boroughs were paying travelling companies 'for sendinge them out of towne' (see p 224), Dorchester's use of plays to entertain and to edify the ecclesiastical authorities suggests that some local Puritans were not opposed to plays or playing per se. More subtle issues were at stake, so that a schoolmaster, like Robert Cheeke, satirized in a poem for sharing the anti-theatrical prejudice of other Puritans, could use plays both to educate his pupils and to enhance the festivities in honour of a powerful guest (see pp 171–2).

Of local Dorset drama the Corpus Christi plays of Sherborne are the most fully developed instance. These plays, like the procession they replaced, were 'an expression of different versions of community at different stages in the town's history.'[158] Although Sherborne Abbey dominated the skyline of the town, the parish of All Hallows' remained fiercely independent of the Benedictine monks who owned the abbey. Each year the parish confirmed its communal life through two special celebrations: a Whitsun ale and a Corpus Christi procession. The latter appears to have been a modest affair in which four men, later in the company of others with banners, carried a shrine. Records of the procession, which begin in the first decade of the sixteenth century, break off abruptly in 1538, the last year (1537–8) in which the churchman who collected at the church ale was referred to as 'king.' Perhaps this is an indication that the parish had given up its customary procession in favour of a different form of celebration but it is difficult to know for certain because there is an unfortunate gap in the records after the account of 1538–9.

A turning point in the dramatic life of Sherborne can certainly be seen in 1540, however. Following the dissolution of the monastery in 1539 Sir John Horsey obtained Sherborne Abbey; he then sold the abbey church to the townspeople, who tore down the little church of All Hallows' and celebrated the acquisition of the abbey with a play on the feast of Corpus Christi. Although the churchwardens' records from 1540 to 1548 never mention the subject matter of the play, they do indicate clearly that Sherborne's Corpus Christi festivities had taken a dramatic form: 'pynnes for the pleyeres' were purchased; costumes were made, painted, and repaired; boards were set up for the performers; money was collected from the 'Stondynge of peopell vppon the Churche at the pley'; and 'the bokes off corpus christi' were registered in the inventories of the parish. In this dramatic activity Sherborne resembles Tewkesbury in Gloucestershire, Chelmsford in Essex, and Bishop's Stortford in Hertfordshire.[159] All these substantial southern communities, where the parish and the town coincided, developed an elaborate production of their own and facilitated dramatic activity elsewhere by renting their players' gear to other towns. But when through the 1550s Sherborne began to rent its costumes, it was apparently no longer producing its Corpus Christi play. The playbook disappears from the inventories after 1548–9, boy bishop's garments acquired from the abbey were sold in 1550–1, and in 1561–2 the churchwardens sold the 'olde Corpuschristi Garmentes' to Richard of Yeovil and the sepulchre cloth and two 'Bannerclothes' to his fellow townsman, Richard Damper.

Not until 1571 did Sherborne revive the practice of producing plays for the feast of Corpus Christi. The churchwardens hired John Dier to oversee the designing and the making of costumes 'Towardes Corpus Christi playes.' Dier may well be Dorset's only theatrical entrepreneur. His involvement in drama in Sherborne goes beyond the Corpus Christi play. In 1567 he rented the church house for the performance of interludes and he may have been associated with the only Dorset touring company, the 'sherborn players,' who performed in the church in Lyme Regis in December 1567. Dier's experience in theatre would have helped him meet the challenges presented by Sherborne's Corpus Christi play in the 1570s. The fairly detailed accounts for 1572–3 and 1573–4 suggest the scale and the difficulty of the project as they register the costs of numerous costumes as well as of tents, boards for stages, stands for the audience, properties, banners, visages for the players, a gilded face for one of them, a canvas giant, a 'vyse coote,' gunpowder, carriage, storage, security, and a trumpeter among other aspects of the production. These accounts, along with the brief one for 1575–6, also provide hints about the content of the play or plays, for they note expenditures for 'staynynge of Sodom clothes' and for 'the new dressyng of Lottes wyffe,' whose transformation into a salt stone was represented by a figure made of wheat meal. The revival of dramatic activity in Sherborne in the 1570s was short-lived. After the production of the play(s) of the destruction of Sodom and the punishment of Lot's wife in 1575–6, the evidence in the churchwardens' accounts of the performance of the play ceases. Thus, Sherborne's celebration of the feast of Corpus Christi with procession or plays comes to an end at about the same time as the great cycles of mystery plays did.

Were there connections between local festivities, customs, and performances and the various kinds of touring players travelling through Dorset? John Dier is one performer who worked both on plays that he mounted independently and on a play sponsored by a community but his case suggests a separation of the non-local, secular drama from the parochial, sacred drama. Whereas his interludes were mounted in the church house, a space later regularly rented to touring players such as the queen's men, the Corpus Christi play remained in the church and the churchyard. The church house served only as a place from which some members of the audience could view the play. Perhaps, however, a tradition of dramatic activity within a community fostered a taste for the same and led to a more receptive attitude toward travelling players. That seems to be the case, judging from the many times that players performed in Sherborne compared with the few occasions when they visited Wimborne Minster, both of which parishes provided the actors with a playing place.[160] Two minstrels were licensed to tour within Dorset but no evidence survives to connect their putative tour with occasions of local festivity (see p 118). Only one travelling performer, Thomas Nehellyng, who 'kepeth three fyghting bulls,' securely links travels through the county with local customs (see p 274). Arrested in Somerset in 1608, he confessed that since the preceding Easter he had been on a profitable tour of church ales and watches from Ilton in Somerset, through Mere in Wiltshire, to Sturminster and Sherborne in Dorset.

Playing Places

Many of the local festivities of the type Underdown would link to the 'traditional culture' in Dorset predictably occurred in public spaces. Bullbaiting and maypoles, of course, were outdoor affairs. Weymouth's maypole was in a central place on the Melcombe Regis peninsula (see p 363), for example, and according to local tradition Dorchester's bullring was between the river and High East Street. Church ales or town ales might be held in community buildings like the church house that hosted the King revel at Sherborne (see pp 250–8 and 356–8) or they might be outdoors like the later Sherborne street ale or the Bere Regis church ale where a fiddler ran afoul of the vicar's musical preferences in 1590. Some of the dancing and revelry censured by Wimborne's early Stuart sidesmen seems to have been outdoors, perhaps in the greens of the parish's subordinate villages, although fiddlers or minstrels might play in inns, and private houses might also host dancing (see pp 284–7). Shaftesbury's ceremonial procession down the wide, steep road linking Shaftesbury to Motcombe certainly symbolized the debt owed by the larger town to the supplier of its water; perhaps the festival was also a symbolic suspension of hierarchy, a liminality encouraging Motcombe and Shaftesbury to experience a temporary community of the type described in David Harris Sacks' discussion of Bristol's ceremonials.[161]

Playing places at Sherborne may stimulate further speculation on the political import of parish celebration and its association with place. The pre-Reformation Corpus Christi procession was outside All Hallows', the small parish chapel of ease sheltering under the west doors of the abbey church. Men carried a shrine in procession into the churchyard where tents were erected; from 1530 the tents were raised at the church door (see pp 255–8). The dramatic innovations of the 1540s, coming shortly after the parish acquisition of the abbatial church – the first reference to 'players' is in 1542–3 – may represent the townsmen's triumph over the monks and pride of ownership of the monastic church.[162] The evidence suggests that events were staged both inside and outside St Mary's: players 'plaid vppon' boards 'in the churche' in 1543–4 and may have acted on 'bordes before the ij lowe alteres' in 1547–8 when the parish also collected money for the 'Stondynge of peopell vppon the Churche at the pley,' and although the procession was apparently discontinued, the wardens continued to have tents set up outdoors for the Corpus Christi festivities (1543–4, 1546–7, and 1547–8).

When Sherborne again mounted a Corpus Christi play in the 1570s – after a more than twenty-year hiatus – it seems to have been an outdoor production in the parish churchyard. The parish collected substantial sums of money from spectators standing on the leads of the church roof (1572–3, 1573–4, and 1575–6), or using the 'roume a gaynste the churche' (1572–3) or the ground in the churchyard (1573–4). Expenses for the play include many payments for tents, including a 'heygh te[ay]nte' (1572–3) and 'backer' tents used as dressing rooms (1573–4). Parish memories of indignities suffered at the hands of the monks had faded and the parish now took for granted its splendid place of worship. The 1570s production was probably an outgrowth of community spirit in the decades Sherborne's historian finds decisive in the transition from parish to civic institutions; public presentations in the churchyard seem to mirror this transition, preserving the distinction between the Tudor citizen 'drama of worship' to which Ian Lancashire refers and the secular drama staged by John Dier in the church house, but also shifting celebration from clearly sacred space to a more ambiguous church exterior.[163]

Most of what we would now call drama in Dorset was performed by travelling players, individuals or companies, who visited the county more and more frequently during the course of the sixteenth century. Where did they play? The evidence is frustrating, for the sites of most performances are unknown. The boroughs record many payments telling us as little of playing places as they tell us of scripts or the size of companies. If the references we have are at all representative, however, some patterns emerge.

Before and early in Elizabeth's reign performers might play in the homes of leading burgesses of boroughs: Richard Allyn of Poole (see p 240); Richard Leonard (see p 211), Richard Buckford (see p 212), and Robert Davey (see p 213), all of Lyme Regis. In the first decades of the seventeenth century playing places might still be private: fiddlers performed in private homes of wealthy magnates such as Sir Giles Strangways of Melbury Sampford (see pp 290–1) and of commoners such as Julian Facy of Fordington (see p 209). Morris dancers, perhaps making their rounds of households in Wimborne Minster in 1611–12, were reported to have performed at Robert Fulford's home there. But increasingly public meeting places were the normal venue for performances by travelling companies from outside Dorset and sometimes for local players as well. Such meeting places included the churches of Poole (1551–2), Lyme Regis (1558–9, 1567–8, 1568–9), Beaminster (1591–3), Bloxworth (1589), and Bere Regis (1599); the shire hall in Dorchester and by default rooms in the George Inn there (see pp 177 and 191); and the schoolhouse in the Lyme Regis churchyard (1606–7). The churches of St Michael the Archangel in Lyme Regis, St Mary in Beaminster, and St John the Baptist in Bere Regis survive relatively unchanged. They must have been attractive places in which to perform. St Michael, for example, provided a spacious playing space, with the nave measuring 61' x 16.5', the chancel 32' x 16.5', and aisles 85' x 16.5'. St Andrew, Bloxworth, was substantially rebuilt in the seventeenth century and unfortunately St James, Poole, was torn down in 1819. The schoolhouses of Lyme Regis and Dorchester and the George Inn and guildhall of Dorchester are no longer still standing.[164]

Perhaps most interesting is the theatrical use of certain Dorset parish or town halls ordinarily available to players for a fee. Such halls included the guildhall at Blandford Forum (see pp 14–15, 41), a church house at Wimborne Minster (see pp 40–1), and the church house at Sherborne (described below, p 40).[165] Tittler has shown us that in the Elizabethan and early Stuart period many Dorset towns experienced a rise of self-conscious civic pride and sense of themselves as autonomous communities, a civic-mindedness associated with the construction of secular buildings.[166] We may also associate such community building with other material civic improvement (the rebuilding of the Cobb at Lyme Regis, for example), the deliberate acquisition of broader rights to self-government (Dorchester, Poole, and Weymouth-Melcombe Regis), or the founding of charities designed to succour the poor by teaching them self-sufficiency. Innovative civic fund-raising and changing civic ceremony could reflect the needs or aspirations of a new town spirit. In few communities were changes in civic consciousness as drastic as in Dorchester where Pastor White's Puritan regime greeted the 'fire from heaven' of 1613 with a systematic attempt to build a 'city on a hill.' But there were changes in many places, nonetheless, and their relationship to the performance climate for players is intriguing. We can certainly link growing civic consciousness, for example, to the prideful spirit in which some communities – Lyme Regis, Poole, and Weymouth – made sure that companies associated with prominent patrons were amply rewarded.[167] The decision to charge players for playing space may represent a different manifestation of a similar growth of community.

In the early Tudor period the Sherborne churchwardens had paid about 4s per year for the use of a building with a furnace and at least some dinnerware for large parties. During that period the major parish fund-raiser was a relatively elaborate and quite profitable ale at Whitsuntide, at which the 'King of Sherborne' presided and collected the parish profits. In about 1530 the churchwardens rented a site in Half Moon Street from the master of Sherborne's almshouse at 26s 8d per annum; hiring temporary quarters for the ale in 1534–5, they built a long two-storey building on the almshouse property. The ground floor was divided into four shops and a kitchen and would be rented out by the Elizabethan churchwardens for total receipts of more than 20s a year. The upper storey seems to have been a single long room, 116' x 19', although one end may have been partitioned off as a storeroom. Curved oak rafters and beams supported a ceiling that rose from a height of 7' above the floor where it met the walls to 18' 2" at the peak. The room was lit along the long south wall by fourteen windows, each with four vertical panes, 41" high x 12" wide. A large fireplace in the east wall and an elaborate staircase with nine stone steps, probably at the west end, completed the room.[168]

Sherborne's churchwardens paid for numerous repairs to the building during the 162 years it was used as a church house. Elizabethan inventories for the house, complete for most years after 1567, tell us that its equipment included trestles and table boards, cooking and brewing gear, platters and pottingers, and, for a time, the parish armour. Other parish necessities – ladders, buckets, racks for weighing – appear in the lists after the 1580s.[169]

The Sherborne community might use the large room that was 'our part' of the church house for community functions like the church ale, but the room and its inventory were also frequently rented out after 1567. When the building was first built in 1533 the rate for using the room on 'hallemasse fayre daye' was set at 16d. Elizabethan parishioners seem to have been able to hire the hall for as little as 4d, paying as much as 2s 9d for the use of both church house and the church house vessels. Rented out more than sixty times, the room was used for several late Elizabethan weddings as well as for the mayor to entertain Sir Walter Ralegh (1595–6).[170] Elizabethan players paid the churchwardens for the use of the room on twelve separate occasions. In addition to John Dier and his interludes in 1567–8, players hired the room five times between 1588 and 1591, paying the churchwardens between 6d and 4s. Between 1597 and 1603 companies hired the hall six times. The queen's players and two anonymous companies paid 2s, 'Certayne' players paid 4s 6d, but the young men of the town paid 16s, four times the ordinary fee. It is possible that local youths contributed all their net receipts to the parish or that they could expect a more profitable run than visiting companies.

Wimborne Minster also maintained one or another church house throughout the sixteenth and early seventeenth centuries. A thatched house at the west end of the church was used in the late fifteenth century (and stocked with dishes probably used for church ales or other parish functions). This building was supplanted in the 1540s when the parish repaired the former St Peter's Church in the town centre and converted it to use as a church house. The building had glass windows, a chimney with a hearth furnished with an iron bar, and plastered walls. Repairs and other parish expenses for the church house for the rest of the century suggest it served the same community purposes as Sherborne's church house. In 1636 when the church house was leased to a town clothier, the school governors (who by then controlled the property) reserved the use of 'all that vpper roome towards the East end of the said house now and heretofore vsed by the inhabitants of Wimborne Minster aforesaid for publike meetings.'[171] Although Wimborne churchwardens' accounts record many fewer rentals of the church house facilities than Sherborne records, 'a rome' in the church house might be hired for a 'bruyng' or other purposes.[172] Twice in 1573–4 and once in 1589–90 the churchwardens recorded receipts of rentals for 'a playe' or from 'players that played' in the church house. The building decayed in stages: the last remaining wall of St Peter's was levelled in about 1800 and the whole of the ground on which St Peter's and the later town hall stood is now buried under the pavement of the Wimborne Minster town square.[173]

Between 1587 and 1599 companies of players hired the Blandford guildhall on at least six occasions; if, as seems likely, the customary fee in the 1590s was 2s 6d, the records probably represent as many as fifteen different visits of groups of players.[174] Further players' rentals occur in 1608–9, 1615–16, and 1620–1. Although the records do not demonstrate private rentals like those common in Sherborne and Wimborne Minster, town-sponsored ales, including the Bailiff's ale, may also have met in the guildhall (the last ale was in 1594–5). The building was destroyed in the great Blandford fire of 1731.[175]

Evidence that towns charged players to play is generally much rarer than records of rewards to players. Elsewhere in Dorset, even when economic restraint, fear of sickness, or religious scruples led seventeenth-century town fathers to forbid a performance, they often paid players not to play. In more welcoming times some Dorset towns made up the difference between what players collected from the audience and what the town thought a reasonable reward. Nothing tells us with any certainty why these three northern Dorset towns chose to charge players rent during the period when companies were most likely to visit the county and most likely to receive rewards from other communities.

If we presume that each of these towns was experiencing a growing sense of autonomy and that each also was experimenting with new sources of revenue, the choice made by these three communities seems more explicable, although other towns made other choices. Late Elizabethan Blandford's sense of greater civic pride was, says Tittler, reflected in the construction of a guildhall costing many times the town's ordinary annual revenue.[176] Although the town ales or collections were profitable, the community was seeking new sources of funds. Fees from players never raised more than £1 a year but we may still see the rental charged players as part of a complex of experiments with new sources of revenue; after all, players played in the building that represented the town's greatest expenditure. As Sherborne groped toward a clearer identification as a secular community, the old church ale gave way to a newer street ale, a more clearly secular affair. The Sherborne church house had been designed partly to pay for itself: the hard-headed spirit animating the Sherborne churchwardens would incline them to see visiting players in the same terms as other tenants. Wimborne, too, was moving toward a rational, planned government, the traditional ale yielding less and less revenue, the parish looking for more consistent sources of funds that would eventually be available in the pew rents and funeral fees of the seventeenth-century parish. As at Sherborne the ordinary uses for the building the players rented influenced the town's reception of visiting companies more than did the town's desire to please performers' influential patrons.

Travelling Players

Evidence of travelling performers in Dorset extends from 1511 to 1636. The picture produced by performances by troupes and individuals from outside the county might be seen as a triptych, the first panel dominated by minstrels and the last one by miscellaneous entertainers, such as William Sands and his puppeteers (see pp 121–2 and 200), William Gosling with his representation of the city of Jerusalem (see p 207), and Mrs Provoe, 'a french woman that had no hands, but could write, sow, wash, & do many other things with her feet' (see p 206).[177] In the central panel, covering the years from about 1565 until 1625, acting companies, rising then declining, occupy the foreground.

The very first record of travelling performers in Dorset epitomizes the cryptic, uncertain quality of so many of these documents. Although this entry undoubtedly served the accountant's purposes perfectly, the lump sum payment 'for Mynstrelles' who visited Poole in the 1511–12 accounting year fails to answer the questions posed by historians of early English drama. Were the minstrels from Dorset or from outside the county? Whose minstrels played there? When did they give their performance? What did they play? How were they received by the audience? Such travelling troupes were an important part of the cultural scene for Poole, which one year later formalized (perhaps not for the first time) the financial arrangements for rewarding minstrels. Costs were to be shared by the mayor and the town, the former being responsible for expenses associated with a performance, the latter covering the cost of the reward to the troupe. The amount of a stipend, which other towns often pro-rated according to the rank of the patron, was not specified but left to the judgment of the city fathers 'as they thynnge conuenyentt' (see p 239). In singling out 'the kyng mynstrellys' among the troupes that might visit Poole, the memorandum of 1512/13 reveals the city's awareness that these travelling players were playing a role in an elaborate patronage system. By providing the reward to the players the town was not simply generously easing the mayor's financial burdens but also garnering what goodwill might come from a report of a gracious reception made by some nobleman's players; in short, the city fathers of Poole were seizing the opportunity 'to show respect for a patron whose influence might be useful.'[178]

The queen's men visited Dorset more often than any other troupe. They visited at least fourteen times during Elizabeth's reign ('at least' because they are presumably sometimes the group identified merely as 'players' in the records; see, for instance, p 217) and they visited regularly from 1588 until 1602. Only the players under the patronage of James Blount, Lord Mountjoy, returned to Dorset with the same consistency. Leicester's men are six times named in the records (once as the lord high steward's players) but their appearances are scattered between 1570 and the year of his death, 1588. The Dorset records identify no other group of players more than three times. Such fragmentary data do not encourage confident generalizations but one factor emerges as important, the strong ties that patrons of the companies which visited Dorset have to the west and/or the south of England either because of substantial estates in those regions or by virtue of their position on the Council in the Marches of Wales. Lord Mountjoy (c 1533–81) is the best example of such ties for he had been a justice of the peace of Dorset and Wiltshire, lord lieutenant of Dorset, and commissioner of oyer and terminer for the southwest, and he held Canford Manor (of which Poole was a part) during Elizabeth's reign. In 1559–60 Lord and Lady Mountjoy visited Poole, which laid on a banquet in their honour and laid out rewards to various people, including players. Perhaps these were Mountjoy's own players, a troupe which performed in Dorset at least five other times: in Lyme Regis in 1568–9, 1572–3, 1573–4, 1577–8, and in Poole in 1569–70. Other patrons with land holdings in Dorset or administrative responsibilities in the region included Thomas Fitz Alan, earl of Arundel, and his son and heir, William; Edward Russell, earl of Bedford; Henry Grey, marquess of Dorset; Arthur Plantagenet, Viscount Lisle, and vice admiral; Charles Howard, lord admiral and captain-general in the south of England; Thomas Seymour, lord admiral, and his brother, Edward, duke of Somerset; John Dudley, duke of Northumberland and lord admiral; and John de Vere, earl of Oxford, and his son and heir, Edward. However, the players of the patron with the strongest Dorset ties, Sir Richard Rogers of Bryanston, are not known to have performed in Dorset. Compared to the regular visits of Queen Elizabeth's players to Dorset during the period from 1588 to 1602, the identifiable appearances by the players of King James in Bridport in 1620–1, 1623–4, and 1624–5 constitute but a brief flurry of dramatic activity. By then Dorset towns were not nearly as hospitable to players as they had been during Elizabeth's reign. During the reign of King James I, the king's men, the queen's men, the prince's men, and the children of the revels were all rewarded but at reduced rates and usually not to play.

Evidence from Dorset confirms many features of the emerging picture of dramatic activity in early modern England: the normal playing places, the arrangements governing payment for playing (and not playing), the players themselves. Neither plays nor playwrights were worthy of note, though occasionally an actor's name was recorded. For some reason John Hayes, mayor of Lyme Regis, registered the town's gift to 'the queenes plaiers the duttons' when they played there in 1592–3. Gilbert Reason, one of the prince's men, gave the authorities of Dorchester reason to record his name in 1615 by being insolent both to Sir Francis Ashley and to John Gould, bailiff. The rewards to players who did perform were, it seems, pro-rated according to the rank of the patron[179] and consisted of money collected plus a grant from the city. In 1560–1, for example, Lyme Regis gave the players of the duchess of Suffolk 2s 'over & aboue that was gatherid.' In 1590–1 the mayor of Poole noted in his account book his calculation of the players' reward: 'ther was gatherell xj s. and I made it xx s. of the townes mony.' In 1592–3 Lyme Regis paid the difference between the 4s 8d given and the 10s reward to Worcester's men and shortly after, it gave the queen's men twice that amount thanks to a subvention of 12s 6d. Twenty shillings for the queen's men was half what the company usually received from large towns such as Bristol and Norwich and two-thirds of Gloucester's reward but it was certainly not an inappropriate sum for a borough the size of Lyme Regis. Occasionally the hospitality offered the players was extended to include wine. In 1616–17 Bere Regis even went so far as to make a 'visard' for the players – special treatment, perhaps for a local troupe.

Why travelling companies returned to perform at some towns and not others is a matter for some speculation, particularly since three Dorset communities – Blandford Forum, Sherborne, and Wimborne Minster – had playing places that the players could rent. Players visited

Sherborne at least a dozen times, Blandford perhaps even more frequently. But Wimborne's church house attracted such visitors only three times. Is the difference explicable?[180] In this we may perhaps look for a combination of reasons. Blandford was a centrally located market town with a population of between five and eight hundred.[181] Sherborne and Wimborne were probably smaller. The Blandford guildhall and Sherborne church house were likely larger than the Wimborne church house and provided better playing spaces, although at higher fees than those charged by Wimborne. We know nothing of earlier dramatic traditions at Blandford – there is really only one set of relevant records from Blandford – but a comparison of activity in Sherborne and Wimborne suggests that Sherborne was also much more likely to provide an audience for visiting players in the 1580s and '90s. Hundreds of years of churchwardens' accounts, decades of school records, and many ecclesiastical judicial records yield precisely three instances when Wimborne may have shown interest in any non-local performers – the three times the church house was let to players. Perhaps the players, learning the hard way that although they could get a good venue in Wimborne they could not attract a substantial and receptive audience, decided to forego a trip to that village. Apart from purely ecclesiastical rituals, the only parish ceremony was a procession bearing the fund-raising parish 'cake.' Late Elizabethan Sherborne, on the other hand, had a rich and varied history of performance activity: the town had kept a boy bishop's costume for a time; a 'king' of Sherborne reigned over the parish ale in the 1530s; the townsmen's Corpus Christi procession was elaborated as religious drama shortly after the parish took control of the former abbey church; Sherborne's play costumes were important in the neighbourhood in the 1550s; and in the 1570s the town and parish presented an elaborate play on Corpus Christi. Perhaps the tradition of performance activity within Sherborne fostered a taste for the drama and led to a more receptive attitude toward travelling players, an attitude that, in turn, influenced the players' choice of public playing places.

Tracking the movements of travelling companies within Dorset is next to impossible. Though the picture of dramatic and musical entertainment there is more complete than ever before, there are still only threee years when we know for sure that the same troupe performed at two different Dorset towns: Leicester's men played Poole and Lyme Regis in 1570; the queen's men performed in Poole and Weymouth-Melcombe Regis in 1590–1; and William Sands' puppeteers turned up in Dorchester in July and then at Beaminster in October 1630. Because only the last of these records dates both performances, it is not clear if the queen's men or Leicester's men were travelling from east to west or from west to east through the county. Nor can we glean much about the travels of players in general from the trip of Sands and his company: that they took about ten weeks to cover the twenty miles from Dorchester to Beaminster suggests that their route was not a direct one.

Dorset's place on a larger map of tours by travelling players is a little clearer. Currently available evidence for the travels of players suggests that Dorset may have been part of a western circuit, one looping down into the southwest and extending as far north as Yorkshire. Worcester's men, for example, visited Poole, Plymouth, Barnstaple, Bristol, Gloucester, and Beverley in 1570–1.[182] Mountjoy's men were rewarded in 1577–8 by Bath, Lyme Regis, and Gloucester.[183] Coordinating information about performances in Dorset with those elsewhere in England suggests the possibility at least that some 'national' companies chose to concentrate their efforts, at least in some years, in the western regions of the country, in those areas where their patrons had power.

More important for Dorset was its place on a southern line running between Kent and Devon. The tour of Leicester's men in 1569–70 illustrates one likely way of proceeding: a spring season in Kent with performances in Canterbury, Faversham, Lydd, and Rye, followed by a summer in the provinces (Poole dates its reward 11 July, Dartmouth its 30 July).[184] Evidence from other years complicates this impression however. In November 1598, for instance, Dartmouth, Devon, rewarded the queen's men and the company went on to receive payments from Winchester in March and Dover in April. They were also rewarded in 1598–9 by Plymouth in Devon, Sherborne in Dorset, Reading in Berkshire, and Faversham and Lydd in Kent. At Sherborne the company rented the church house, perhaps while on route from Dartmouth to Winchester, for the churchwardens rendered their accounts on 21 January 1598/9.[185] In any case, the movement from Dartmouth late in the autumn, through Winchester, to Dover in spring suggests that the so-called southern line was not a straight line, but it was a two-way route and one for all seasons.

The trip through the south of England may also have been part of a much larger, longer tour, such as that of Worcester's men from the autumn of 1567 until that of 1569. The troupe received rewards, some of them dated, from the following towns: Bristol (November 1567), Plymouth (11 June 1568), Lyme Regis (4 August 1568), Winchester, Dover, Canterbury, Folkestone, Fordwich, Ipswich, and Nottingham (August 1569), Gloucester, Bath, and Bristol (September 1569).[186] If we can assume that the dated rewards correspond loosely to the date of performance and if we can assume that Worcester's men toured as a whole those years, then we have the possibility of a large circular route involving many communities in the south and the centre of England. Such a circuit, if it be one, calls into question other long-standing assumptions: that the tours of travelling companies were annual projects and that London was the normal home base for national companies. London may well have been avoided by players who expected to make their living in the provinces and Coventry, or Bristol, or Gloucester may have been the terminus ad quem of a troupe working its way through Dorset.

The heyday for travelling players in Dorset was the last decade of Elizabeth's reign. From that time on various developments – economic decline, measures taken to protect boroughs from the plague, Puritan antagonism to players in general, sabbatarianism in particular, and a concern with social order, which was threatened, some authorities argued, by travelling performers and the kinds of gatherings they occasioned – combined to jeopardize the activity of travelling players.[187] The first payment to a troupe not to play occurred in 1615–16 (see p 279) but opposition, civic and ecclesiastical, had been growing for many years in Dorset. The major forces antagonistic to players came together in 1608 in the events that led to the Star Chamber case of Condytt v. Chubbe.[188] John Condytt, a Dorchester tailor, alleged that he and his wife had been libelled in three poems that Matthew Chubbe, a Dorchester goldsmith and at that time bailiff, had helped to contrive, publicly read, and otherwise distribute. One of the verses attached to the bill of complaint attributes to Puritans a generalized opposition to plays and players and ends with a threatening postscript that they should not put down 'stage plaiers nor Yet trew melody/ ffor yf thou doest thou shalt be calld knave and foole/ and so shall thy sonne in lawe chicke ye maister of the schoole' (p 180). No doubt there were Puritans in Dorset towns who judged plays and players to be anathema but this poem's construction of the attitudes of Puritan reformers oversimplifies the situation: the Mr Cheeke who is alluded to in the last line was the same schoolmaster who entertained ecclesiastical authorities with comedies in 1623. Furthermore, this allegedly libellous poem is the only Dorset document that conjoins Puritans with players in an antagonistic relationship and its self-confessed author was Robert Adyn, a Catholic recusant. Religious opposition to public performances almost certainly existed in Dorset in the early seventeenth century but it came out indirectly. Judging from the bill of complaint in the case of Condytt v. Chubbe the more volatile issue in Dorchester in 1608 was respect for the sabbath. Lord Berkeley's men wanted to play in the shire hall on Sunday, which performance the burgesses would not permit. As a result, through the media-tion of Matthew Chubbe (so it was alleged), whose frustrations led to threats of revenge against his fellow burgesses, the players put on their play before Sir Adrian Scrope and others at one of the local inns. Besides the role of sabbatarianism in this case, the problems produced by the players' refusal quietly to accept the will of the city fathers – the conflict between them and some of the bailiffs, the quarrelling between Chubbe and his peers, ultimately the Star Chamber cases between Chubbe and Condytt – intensified the opposition to the players.

Insolent actors, such as Lord Berkeley's men on this occasion, or Gilbert Reason in Dorchester in 1615, or William Sands the puppeteer in Beaminster in 1630, produced more problems than pleasure for the borough and betrayed the trust placed in them by their patron. The patronage system on which the regional and national tours of minstrels and actors was based lacked the imperative force it once had. The diary of William Whiteway, one of the most influ-ential merchants of Dorchester, confirms this impression. Whiteway seems to have been fascinated by the power of the king, particularly by the king's taste in drama. At three points in his diary Whiteway, whose sympathies were with the Protestant reformers, comes back to the case of William Prynne and notes how brutally he was tortured 'for writing a booke against Stag plaies & dancing' (see pp 202–5). Whiteway also reported the suicide of Dr Butts, vice-chancellor of Cambridge, who hanged himself 'because the king shewed much dislike at a play, which he had caused lately to be acted before him in Cambridge' (see p 202). In an exceptionally long entry in his diary Whiteway also gives an account of the occasion of the second performance of James Shirley's masque, *The Triumph of Peace*. King Charles invited himself to the home of London's lord mayor, Ralph Freeman, for dinner and to Merchant Tailors' Hall for the masque as a way of resolving the dispute between the monarch and the mayor over the new Westminster soap monopoly. This dispute, according to Whiteway, so troubled the mayor 'that he kept his bed a whole moneth after it, & was like to dy, had not the *King*s message reuiued him' (see p 204). Fatal for Butts, restorative (albeit only temporarily) for Freeman: such was the power of Charles as theatre patron – close to the court. Down in Dorset however, Whiteway and Sir Francis Ashley tell a different story: players travelling as the prince's men (see p 198), puppeteers who 'had a warrant vnder the Kings hand' (see p 200), and Mrs Provoe who 'had a commission vnder the seale of the *Master* of the Reuelles' (see p 206) were all summarily dismissed or, in Whiteway's words, 'not allowed here.' Indeed, Gilbert Reason was outraged with Dorchester's recorder, Sir Francis Ashley, and one of its bailiffs, John Gould, because the latter refused 'to look on his Commission.' Reason may have glimpsed the implications of Gould's refusal for the entire patronage system, for the actor accused the bailiff of being 'little better then a traitour' (see p 198).

The true eventual story of the decline not only of travelling performers but also of local customs, sports, and recreation will have to be a complex one. Opposition to players was not monolithic; Lyme Regis in 1607 saw town and church authorities at loggerheads when the churchwardens presented the mayor for permitting players of interludes to perform in the schoolhouse. Sometimes economic factors were crucial, as they were in Weymouth in 1600 and in Poole a year later, when the auditors disallowed gifts to players, a decision suggesting that the boroughs were not opposed to drama but to spending public funds on it – and perhaps only temporarily. Similarly in Lyme Regis in 1622 economic factors and moral duty combined to cause the city fathers to alter a long-standing custom by cancelling the feast upon St Stephen's Day so that the poor might be entertained at each man's private house.[189] Ten years earlier the same group had used borough funds to fight a case initiated by the reformist vicar, John Geare, who had procured an act against the mayor, aldermen, and Cobb wardens for 'the vsing of profane and irreligious abuses.'[190] Sometimes the danger of infection was crucial. Only once was the plague used explicitly as the reason for refusing to permit a performer to play, by Dorchester when William Gosling in October 1636 asked 'to shew the portraiture of the city of Ierusalem.' The 'dangerous tyme of sicknes' need not be taken as a mystification, a cover-up for opposition that was actually sectarian, since Gosling had received a reward from Norwich, one of England's sturdiest Protestant cities.[191] Like many other items registered in account books, the last payments to travelling entertainers fail to disclose the attitude of the boroughs to the players because the entries record merely the reward and the recipient. In the records of Dorset, incomplete as they are in the early seventeenth century, a pattern is clear however: Dorchester arrested Gilbert Reason in 1615; Weymouth-Melcombe Regis paid the queen's men not to play in 1616, as did Lyme Regis an unidentified troupe in 1621–2, and Bridport the king's men in 1623; even Blandford Forum, a town that profited from performances in its town hall as late as 1620, paid the children of the revels, that 'should have acted a stage playe in the Hall,' 10s to depart.

The Documents

The descriptions of the documents from which records are drawn are given in chronological order under four headings: Dioceses, County of Dorset, Boroughs and Parishes (arranged alphabetically), and Households. William Whiteway's records of performance activity in Dorset and elsewhere have been kept together among the records of Dorchester. Whiteway was one of the capital burgesses of the town and frequently one of its officers and Dorchester was the base from which he observed both local performances and dramatic activity in more distant centres such as Cambridge and London. Visitation injunctions and articles appear in the section on Dioceses. With the exception of the records from the peculiar jurisdiction of Wimborne Minster, relatively few ecclesiastical court records for Dorset survive and even fewer refer to public entertainment; descriptions of records from visitations and court records from the diocese of Salisbury are therefore arranged by the borough or parish to which they refer. Within larger boroughs, civic records are listed first, followed by legal records and miscellaneous documents. Shelfmarks and titles given are according to the preference of the individual record offices and libraries where the documents are preserved.

The description of a document yielding entries for more than one place is presented under the first relevant borough or parish; included in the description is a list of other boroughs or parishes from which records have been printed. Brief cross-references direct the reader to the main description from those other locations.

Dioceses

For the diocesan areas of jurisdiction see p 8.

DIOCESE OF BRISTOL

Bishop John Thornborough's Visitation Articles

ARTICLES | TO BE MINISTRED | AND TO BE ENQVIRED | OF, AND ANSWERED IN | the first generall visitation of | the reverend father in God, John, | by Gods permission, Bishop | of Bristoll. | [University device] | OXFORD, | Printed by *Ioseph Barnes* Printer to | the Vniversitie, 1603. *STC*: 10143.

Bishop Robert Skinner's Visitation Articles

ARTICLES | TO BE MINISTRED, | ENQVIRED OF, AND | ANSWERED: | In the first Visitation of the Right Reverend | Father in GOD, ROBERT by Gods | Divine providence, LORD Bishop of | BRISTOL. | [device - motto: ANCHORA. SPEI.] | *LONDON*, | Printed by *George Miller*. 1637. *STC*: 10145.

ARTICLES | TO BE MINISTRED, | ENQVIRED OF, AND | ANSWERED: | In the *(blank)* Visitation of the Right | Reverend Father in GOD, *(blank)* | by Gods Divine providence, Lord | Bishop of BRISTOL. | [rule] | [device] | [rule] | *LONDON*, | Printed by *George Miller* | 1640,. *STC*: 10145.3. In the Exeter College, Oxford, copy the second blank has been filled in with Bishop Skinner's name in a contemporary hand.

DIOCESE OF SALISBURY

Bishop John Jewel's Visitation Injunctions

Iniunctions | giuen by the reuerend father in christ | **Iohn by Gods prouidence, Bishop of** | *Sarisburie, aswel to the Cleargie, as to the* | **Churchewardens and enquirers of euerye seueral** | Parish, aswel of his peculiar as general iurisdiction within | **and of the Diocesse of Sarum to be obserued and kept of euery** | *of them in their offices and callings, as to them shal appertaine, for the* | **aduauncement of gods honor, thincrease of vertue, and good or-** | der to be continued within his sayd Diocesse, and the same to be enqui- | red of and put in vse by all the Archdeacons, Commissaries, and | other officers excercising Ecclesiastical iurisdiction vnder the | sayde Bishop, according to the limittes of their se- | ueral offices and iurisdictions, in their | Synodes, visitations, | inquiries, and | Courts.** | [device] | Imprinted at London, by Henry | *Denham for Richard Iackson,* | **and are to be sold in Gutter Lane** | **at the signe of the red Lion.** | *Anno.* 1569. | February. 22. *STC*: 10326.5.

Bishop Henry Cotton's Visitation Articles

ARTICLES | to bee enquired of, by the | Churchwardens and sworne men, within | the Diocesse of Sarum, in the visitati- | on of the Reuerend Father in God | Henry, Lord Bishop of Sarum, | in his first generall vi- | sitation. | Holden in the 41. yeare of the | raigne of our most gracious soueraigne | Lady Elizabeth, by the grace of | God, Queene of Englande, | France and Ireland, defendor | of the faith, &c. | [device - motto: THOV SHALT LABOR FOR PEACE ⟨&⟩ PLENTIE] | LONDON | Imprinted by Iohn Windet, dwelling at | Paules Wharfe, at the signe of the | Crosse Keyes. 1599. *STC*: 10327.5.

[device] | ARTICLES | OF INQVIRIE, GI- | VEN IN CHARGE BY THE RIGHT | REVEREND FATHER IN GOD, HENRIE BY | the prouidence of Almightie God Bishop of *Sarum*, to be | *answered vnto by way of presentment vpon oath, by the Church-* | wardens and Sidemen of each parish and chapell through- | out the Diocesse of *Sarum*, in his ordinary and trien- | nall Visitation intended to be holden in *(blank)* | next comming, in *Anno Dom.* 1614. | as followeth. | [device] | Imprinted at London by Felix | Kyngston. 1614. *STC*: 10328. In the copy examined at the British Library the blank space for the month has been filled in as 'Iune'; another later hand has added the bishop's surname in the right margin.

Bishop Robert Abbot's Visitation Articles

ARTICLES | TO BE ENQVIRED | OF, VVITHIN THE DIO- | ces of Sarisburie, in the first visitation | of the Right Reuerend Father, ROBERT by the | Prouidence of GOD, Lord Bishop of | SARUM. | [rule] | *HOLDEN* | In the yeare of our Lord God | 1616. | [device] | [rule] | LONDON | Printed by IOHN LEGATT. | 1616. *STC*: 10329.

Bishop Martin Fotherby's Visitation Articles

ARTICLES | to be enquired of, with- | in the Diocese of *Sarisbury*, in the first visi- | *tation of the Right Reuerend Father in* | God, MARTIN by the prouidence of | GOD, Lord Bishoppe | of *Sarum*. | [rule] | *HOLDEN* | Jn the yere of our Lord God, | 1619. | [device] | [rule] | AT LONDON | Printed by *Iohn Beale*, 1619. *STC*: 10329.3.

County of Dorset

A few, very miscellaneous documents yield entries for the whole of Dorset, rather than particular boroughs or villages. These include a sermon given at a court sessions, included here since the speaker, William Kethe, seems to respond to sinful behaviour in the whole of the county, not merely at Blandford Forum where the justices were meeting when the sermon was delivered.

William Kethe's A Sermon made at Blanford Forum

William Kethe was a Protestant divine, forced into exile in Frankfurt during the persecutions of Queen Mary, at which time he wrote metrical versions of the psalms and several anti-Catholic works. When he returned to England in 1561, he became rector of Okeford Superior in the parish of Child Okeford in Dorset. As a result of this appointment presumably, he gathered the evidence of the abuse of the sabbath in Dorset that he describes in the sermon. In 1563 Kethe accompanied the earl of Warwick, Ambrose Dudley, to Le Havre, where he served as minister and preacher to the earl and to the troops resisting Catholic insurgents. When Kethe published the sermon he gave at Blandford Forum, he dedicated the work to Warwick.

A SERMON | made at Blanford Fo- | ru*m*, in the Countie of | Dorset on Wensday the | 17. of Ianuarij last past at | the Session holden there, | before the honorable and | the worshyppefull of that | Shyre, by *William Kethe* | Minister and Preacher | of Gods word. | 1571. | *AT LONDON* | *Printed by Iohn Daye,* | *dwellyng ouer Aldersgate.* | ⸿ Cum gratia & Priuilegio | Regiæ Maiestatis. *STC*: 14943.

Licence for Minstrels

Taunton, Somerset Record Office, DD/HI 469, vol 2; late 16th century; English; paper; 193 leaves + booklet of 4 leaves; 310mm x 210mm; unnumbered; sewn booklets; parchment cover made from a Dorset deed. No date, title, or identification, except the name 'Raphe Barrtt,' which appears on the cover. The book contains precedents from the reign of Elizabeth I or earlier, a court baron description, and orders from a sessions court in Dorset.

Petition of Somerset Clergy to Sir John Denham

An abstract of the relevant item has been printed in John Bruce (ed), *Calendar of State Papers, Domestic Series, of the Reign of Charles I. 1628–1629* (London, 1859), 20.

Kew, Public Record Office, SP 16/96; 15 March 1627/8; English; paper; single sheet; 262mm x 170mm (175mm x 135mm); folio number (15) in pencil in the centre at the bottom; verso blank except for modern dating in pencil, obsolete page or folio numbers ('13' in the upper left corner and, just to the right of that number, '78'), and the dating '1627' in ink and in a hand contemporary with the document; marks and wear from the horizontal folds hamper legibility. Bound as f 15 (of 155 leaves) in modern binding: grey paper over boards, blue cloth corners and spine, bearing the title: 'Domestic Charles I 1627 Mar. 15–21.'

Assize Order for Western Circuit

This volume begins with the Lent circuit 1631 and ends with material from the same circuit of 1640/1. It appears to be a fair copy of the orders for most of the volume is in one hand; however, some relevant documents transcribed by others have been inserted. It is the first of a nine-volume series of Western Circuit Assizes Order Books, which volumes cover the period from the summer assizes of 1629 to the winter assizes of 1648. For a description of the series, see J.S. Cockburn (ed), *Western Circuit Assize Orders: 1629–1648: A Calendar* (London, 1976), who includes on p 33 an abstract of the relevant item.

Kew, Public Record Office, Assi 24/20/140; 1631–40/1; English; paper; 310mm x 200mm (210mm x 150mm); modern foliation; good condition: leaves restored and mounted on guards; modern binding: white cloth over boards, title on spine: 'Assizes 24/20 Part I.'

Boroughs and Parishes

BEAMINSTER

Beaminster was one of the Dorset parishes which remained in the jurisdiction of the peculiar of the deanery of Salisbury when Dorset was incorporated in the new diocese of Bristol in 1542; hence a few visitation documents survive for the parish. Unfortunately Beaminster churchwardens' accounts do not survive.

Churchwardens' Presentments for Salisbury Deanery

Trowbridge, Wiltshire and Swindon Record Office, D5/28/6, item 34; 1591–3; English; paper; single sheet; 203mm x 155mm; written on recto only; condition good but torn at top left corner. One of

176 loose sheets, numbered in modern pencil, tied with a cloth ribbon between two cardboard sheets. A typescript list of the parishes for which presentments are found in this bundle has been inserted at the beginning.

Quarter Sessions Orders

Dorchester, Dorset Record Office, QSM: 1/1; 1625–38; English and Latin; parchment; ii + 642 + iv; 305mm x 200mm; modern pencil and ink foliation; headings in bold, some catchwords; excellent condition; modern brown leather binding with a blue panel on the front and on the spine displaying: 'Dorset Quarter Sessions Orders 1625–37' in gold letters.
   This book also yielded an entry for Hinton Martell.

BERE REGIS

Bere Regis remained in the jurisdiction of the peculiar of the deanery of Salisbury after 1542.

Deposition Book for Salisbury Deanery

Trowbridge, Wiltshire and Swindon Record Office, D5/22/2; 1588–97; Latin and English; paper; 55 leaves; 310mm x 210mm; modern foliation; rebound with modern covers and flyleaves (no original flyleaves survive).

Churchwardens' Presentments for Salisbury Deanery

Trowbridge, Wiltshire and Swindon Record Office, D5/28/7, item 4; 1597–9; English; paper; single sheet; 225mm x 197mm; written on recto only; condition fair, some text obscured by fold at top and tear and hole at centre bottom. One of 128 loose sheets (paper and parchment), numbered in modern pencil, tied with a cloth ribbon in a green cardboard folder.

St John the Baptist's Churchwardens' Accounts

The Bere Regis churchwardens' accounts are detailed to about 1620; several years are missing after that date. The accounting year ran from the Sunday after Easter to the Sunday after Easter.

Dorchester, Dorset Record Office, PE/BER: CW1; 1607–16; English; paper; 27 leaves; 350mm x 200mm; modern pencil foliation; paper booklet; some pages badly damaged; inscription on front cover: 'Bere Regis | A Book belonging to the | Churche of Bere Reges off the church⟨.⟩ ⟨.⟩ardens | a counte | Beere Regis 1607 and 1608 | Bere Reges./ 1616. | Leonard Church | Robert ffrench.'

Dorchester, Dorset Record Office, PE/BER: CW2; 1616–19; English; paper; 4 leaves; 317mm x 200mm; modern pencil foliation; paper booklet; headings in bold; tops of pages stained and some damaged sections.

BLANDFORD FORUM

A disastrous fire in 1731 destroyed most of the civic records of Blandford Forum as well as many of the records of the archdeaconry of Salisbury. Surviving records, on deposit in the Dorset Record Office, relate principally to various Blandford charities; a single, beautifully preserved volume of chamberlains' accounts contains references to public entertainment. The town's accounting year seems to have run from Michaelmas to Michaelmas and the chamberlains usually rendered accounts in November or December.

Chamberlains' Accounts

The front section of the manuscript begins 6 November 1595 and refers to loose town papers in a locked chest; accounts in the series are summary until 1627 and detailed after that date. The series of accounts beginning at the back of the manuscript are mid-seventeenth-century copies of the loose papers then in the town's possession. There is on f B38v the following statement:

All these accomptes att this ende of the Chamberlens booke of accomptes backwarde: from the yeare of our Lorde 1564 beeinge founde in the Councell howse in loose papers vnto the date of our Lorde 1627 (except som of them which are Lost as those from the yeare 1603 vnto the yeare 1608) ware in this yeare of our Lord Christ 1658 entred into the saied Chamberlens booke by Augustine Drake and the loose papers are still remayninge in the Councell howse: and in the 5th yeare of the gouerment of Olliuer Cromwell Lord protector of the 3 nations of England Scottland and Ireland who had that power Conferd on him the 16th daye of december 1653:

> By mee Augustine drake
> transcribed in anno domino 1658

All the accomptes suckseedinge: from the yeare of our Lorde 1627 are constantly entred euery yeare att the other end of this great booke: in particuler: where there is an entry of diuers things worth the readinge & takinge notice of.

Similarly, there is on f F18v the following: 'All the fformer accomptes from 1564 vnto this yeare 1628 ware entred att the other end of this booke taken out of loose papers founde & remayninge in the Councell howse by Augustine drake in the yeare of our Lord Christ 1658.'

Dorchester, Dorset Record Office, DC/BFB: Finance: Chamberlains' Accounts; 1564–1750; English; paper; i + 261; 420mm x 290mm (text area varies); modern ink foliation, 1–159 (front section, here designated F) and 38–1 (back section, here designated B), 63 blank leaves between f F159 and f B38; some folios ruled, some with headings for pounds, shillings, and pence; parchment binding with spine reinforced with 3 pieces of leather sewn with thongs of twisted leather, taped to spine is a piece of paper with typescript: '*Town A/CS etc.* 1564 to 1627.'

BLOXWORTH

Dean and Chapter Act Book for Salisbury Deanery

Trowbridge, Wiltshire and Swindon Record Office, D5/19/12; 1589–91; English and Latin; paper; ii + 275 + ii; 290mm x 200mm; foliated; bottom 60–70mm of all leaves damaged by damp, many pages torn, text faded; bound in grey cloth over boards with olive green cloth spine.

BRIDPORT

Many of the Bridport records were numbered in ink and catalogued by Thomas Wainwright. References to the old classification scheme are included in the present catalogue and documents may be identified within bundles according to their old numbers; 'document numbers' used here to refer to law court records are those of Wainwright's classification scheme.

Civic Records

Bailiffs' Accounts

A letter patent of 37 Henry III (1252–3) established that Bridport was to be governed by a council of fifteen burgesses who elected from their membership two bailiffs each year. Their accounts are extant in thirty-seven separate, unbound booklets, the earliest of which is for 1307, the latest for 1645. Almost half of these account books date from the first half of the seventeenth century. The accounting year extended from Michaelmas of one year to Michaelmas of the next, and the official 'counting day' fell during the last week of October. Normally an account book included a section registering revenue followed by one listing expenses, expenses for the poor, the sick, and other activities of the borough. The account books are tied together with ribbon into two bundles: twelve from the years 1307 to 1464 in one bundle, twenty-five from 1558 to 1645 in the other. The last page of almost every booklet is blank except for an imprint of the Bridport seal and various catalogue reference numbers assigned by Thomas Wainwright in the late nineteenth century. The numbers preceded by the letter K refer to his published catalogue, *The Bridport Records and Ancient Manuscripts*. The more complete and precise reference numbers are those he assigned in 1903 when compiling his manuscript 'Calendar of the Ancient Records of the Borough of Bridport,' now DC/BTB: PQ/28 at the Dorset Record Office. He assigned a number to indicate the class of document (for example, 9 for bailiffs' accounts and 10 for cofferers' accounts), followed by a three- or four-digit number to identify each document. Bailiffs' accounts and cofferers' accounts are hard to distinguish in practice and sometimes the class numbers are inaccurate; however, the reference system currently in use by the Dorset Record Office normally incorporates Wainwright's document class numbers but not the individual document numbers. These individual numbers are given in the document descriptions below, whenever available.

Dorchester, Dorset Record Office, DC/BTB: M2/11; 1614–15; English; paper; original half-sheet folded lengthwise to make a bifolium; 395mm x 155mm (383mm x 134mm); unnumbered; good condition. Assigned reference numbers K21 and 2191 by Wainwright. Contains the account of Robert Miller.

Dorchester, Dorset Record Office, DC/BTB: M2/9; 1616–17; English; paper; 3 bifolia sewn together to make a booklet of 6 leaves; 310mm x 197mm (276mm x 182mm); unnumbered (ff [1v], [2v], and [3v] blank); frayed along the outside edges. Assigned reference number 199 by Wainwright. Contains the account of Stephen Colfox.

Dorchester, Dorset Record Office, DC/BTB: M2/11; 1623–4; English; paper; 1 half-sheet plus 2 bifolia, making a booklet of 5 leaves; 203mm x 154mm (f [1]), 385mm x 154mm (ff [2–5]); un-numbered (f [1v] blank); badly torn (57mm at the widest point) across the bottom so that the last 3 or 4 entries have been lost. Assigned reference number 1669 by Wainwright. Contains the account of Richard Payne.

Dorchester, Dorset Record Office, DC/BTB: M2/9; 1624–5; English; paper; bifolium; 395mm x 154mm; unnumbered; poor condition: wrinkled, stained, torn at the top and the bottom left. Assigned reference number 200 by Wainwright. Contains the account of Robert Miller, dated 3 November.

Dorchester, Dorset Record Office, DC/BTB: M2/9; 1633–4; English; paper; 2 bifolia making a booklet of 4 leaves; 304mm x 197mm (274mm x 172mm); unnumbered. Assigned reference number 1941 by Wainwright. Contains the account of William Wey and Walter Baylie.

Dorchester, Dorset Record Office, DC/BTB: M2/9; 1638–9; English; paper; bifolium; 320mm x 195mm (315mm x 180mm); unnumbered; fair condition. Assigned reference number 904 by Wainwright. Contains the account of William Wey.

Cofferers' Accounts

The incomplete series of Cofferers' Account Books begins in 1400. Bundled and tied with ribbons, there are ten fifteenth-century booklets (DC/BTB: M6), eleven sixteenth-century ones (DC/BTB: M7), and forty-five from the seventeenth and early eighteenth centuries. The accounting year ran from Michaelmas to Michaelmas. A complete account book usually had a section listing revenues (chiefly from rental of properties) followed by a section of payments made on behalf of the borough.

Dorchester, Dorset Record Office, DC/BTB: M7; 1555–6; English; paper; bifolium; 287mm x 198mm (text area varies); unnumbered; good condition (tears along the top and in the centre at the fold line do not damage the text). Assigned reference numbers K98 and 10.2271 by Wainwright. Contains the account of Richard Tygens and John Moyne.

Dorchester, Dorset Record Office, DC/BTB: M7/10; 1574–5; English; paper; bifolium; 310mm x 208mm (290mm x 175mm); unnumbered; fair condition. Assigned reference number 2170 by Wain-wright. Contains the account of Stephen Shower and Peter Cooper.

Dorchester, Dorset Record Office, DC/BTB: M7/10; 1578–9; English; paper; single sheet; 305mm x 204mm; unnumbered; good condition (except for verso, stains on the right corners of which make the text illegible). Assigned reference numbers K102 and 2275 by Wainwright. Contains the account of William Hassard and Thomas Daffege.

Dorchester, Dorset Record Office, DC/BTB: M8/10; 1614–15; English; paper; bifolium; 325mm x 204mm (325mm x 196mm); unnumbered; good condition. Assigned reference numbers K20 and 2190 by Wainwright. Contains the account of Richard Payne and William Wey.

Dorchester, Dorset Record Office, DC/BTB: M8/203; 1620–1; English; paper; 2 bifolia making a booklet of 4 leaves; 314mm x 197mm (303mm x 162mm); unnumbered (ff [5v] and [6] blank, f [6v] blank except for the Bridport seal and the number 203, likely one in Wainwright's K series of reference numbers); fair condition, now held together by paper clips. Contains the account of William Whettam, dated 25 October 1621.

Other Accounts

Bundles of miscellaneous financial records are to be found in DRO: DC/BTB: M13 and DC/BTB: M18. The former contains ten bundles and a total of fifty-three documents from the years 1419 to 1835, but only two of these bundles have material from before 1642. Bills, receipts, summary accounts, payments for the poor, and costs of banquets are the kinds of documents found in DC/BTB: M13. The latter class (DC/BTB: M18) contains thirty-six separate accounts from the years 1555 to 1757, along with other kinds of financial records.

Robin Hood Ale Account
Dorchester, Dorset Record Office, DC/BTB: M18/11; 1555; English; paper; bifolium; 304mm x 210mm (270mm x 160mm); unnumbered; fair condition. Assigned reference numbers K18 and 2188 by Wainwright. Contains the account of Henry Wey and Stephen Shower, collectors.

Ale Account for Town Buildings
Dorchester, Dorset Record Office, DC/BTB: M15/11; 1592–3; English; paper; 5 bifolia sewn with black thread to make a booklet of 10 leaves; 305mm x 204mm (text area varies); unnumbered (ff [1], [1v], and [10] blank); fair condition. Assigned reference number 1947 by Wainwright. Contains the account of Henry Browne and George Francke, collectors.

Town Accounts
Dorchester, Dorset Record Office, DC/BTB: M18/10; 1602–3?; English; paper; 2 bifolia sewn to make a booklet of 4 leaves; 305mm x 205mm (text area varies); unnumbered (ff [1v] and [2v] blank); fair condition except for the faded ink on the upper half of f [1] which makes some entries illegible. Assigned reference numbers K105 and 2278 by Wainwright. The accountant is not named.

Dorchester, Dorset Record Office, DC/BTB: M18/9; undated; English; paper; 1 half sheet; 300mm x 195mm (292mm x 180mm); fair condition. The accountant is not named. Besides the Bridport seal and the document number noted above, the verso has in black ink the number 21B, likely the number in Thomas Wainwright's K series of reference numbers.

See Appendix 1 for this undated document.

Account of Thomas Merefeild

Dorchester, Dorset Record Office, DC/BTB: M13; 1625–6; English; paper; 1 half sheet, formerly folded 3 times (twice horizontally, once vertically) to make a small square; 270mm x 146mm (248mm x 131mm); unnumbered; fair condition. One of twenty items in a bundle of documents from 1567 to 1630.

The account is unusual in that it begins, not on Michaelmas, but on 18 April 1625 and includes a note, dated 19 April 1626 and signed by Merefeild, that he had received from the town all money due to him. It is not clear what office Merefeild held during the period covered by the account, but the current catalogue of Bridport manuscripts asks if he was serving as a constable of the borough during the period covered by the account.

Legal Records

Bridport's voluminous records for the three-weekly and leet courts include many references to citizens amerced for playing unlawful games. The games that are identified include dice, bowls, ball games, and the like; those records that refer to unspecified unlawful games probably refer to gambling or unlawful sports. Miscellaneous sheets recording memoranda from or presentments to the borough court also survive.

Court Leet Proceedings

Dorchester, Dorset Record Office, DC/BTB: C87, item 2; 6 October 1606; Latin and English; vellum; single membrane; 630mm x 285mm; right half of bottom third of document (220mm along right side eating into the document about 150mm) torn away; headings in bold and note to the text in the left margin. Part of a bundle of three court leet records 1606–8.

Dorchester, Dorset Record Office, DC/BTB: C88; 1608–10; Latin and English; parchment; 29 sheets; 305mm x 205mm (280mm x 155mm); modern pencil foliation (followed here) as well as an older pencil pagination beginning on f 1v and numbering odd page numbers through 13; bound in a vellum sheet, right side of the front cover damaged, title on the front: 'Liber Curiarum Burga de Brideport | A tribus septimanis in tres ⟨…⟩ feste sancti | Michaelis Archangeli Anno Domini 1608: vsque idem | festum Anno 1609: tempore Ioha⟨.⟩nis Alforde et Georgii | ffranke ad tunc Ba⟨…⟩ Burgi predicte. Morgano | Moo⟨ne⟩ existente communi Clerici et Georgii Trencharde | Militis ⟨…⟩ senescalli eiusdem Burga'; to the left, opposite the second line of this title, is 'Bridport.' The records are not all in order however. The earliest entry seems to be for Monday 1 August 1608 and the last for September 1610.

Court Leet Presentments

Dorchester, Dorset Record Office, DC/BTB: E2/unnumbered; c 1641; English; paper; single sheet;

205mm x 160mm. Although originally undated a later, pencilled '1641' and the names of the presenters suggest the date *c* 1641. Part of a bundle of forty-two documents of presentments to court leet.

Miller et al v. Maries et al

Four documents comprise the composite manuscript of this case: the bill of complaint (mb 4), which includes a transcription of the allegedly libellous verses, and the answers of several of the defendants: John Abbot (mb 3); Hugh Syms, Anthony Mathew, and William Marshall (mb 2); and William Maries and John Lack (mb 1). The last of these, providing a generalized denial of any guilt and a call for a dismissal of the charges, sheds no light on the reproduction and distribution of the libels; as a result it has not been included here. Naming many of Bridport's leading citizens, this case reveals the divisive force of religious debates among the town's ruling élite.

Kew, Public Record Office, STAC 8/214/2; 1614–15; English and some Latin; parchment; modern pencil numbering; 4 membranes sewn with thread. Individual items include:

mb 4: 1 June 1614; English; 587mm x 680mm (524mm x 617mm); fair condition with some tearing; endorsed with date and style of cause. Contains the plaintiffs' bill of complaint.

mb 2: 11 July 1614; English and some Latin; 200mm x 408mm (125mm x 408mm); fair condition; no endorsements. Contains sworn answer of three defendants.

mb 3: 28 November 1615; English and some Latin; 387mm x 654mm (371mm x 633mm); fair condition; no endorsements. Contains sworn answer of another defendant.

Account of a Sabbath Breaking

This document is one of several (including notes of examinations, presentments, and fines) in connection with the administration for the poor.

Dorchester, Dorset Record Office, DC/BTB: DE10/3; 1637; English; paper; bifolium; 319mm x 204mm; unnumbered; poor condition (worm holes through the top half of the document and dirt hamper legibility). Assigned reference number 809 by Wainwright.

CERNE ABBAS

Cerne Abbas, best known today for the giant carved into the rocky hill that overlooks the village, was prosperous when the abbey of Cerne Abbas dominated the village and provided its principal market, but it declined after the Dissolution.[192] The earliest surviving Cerne Abbas churchwardens' accounts are from 1628; the accounting term for the period represented in the Records ran from Easter to Easter.

St Mary's Churchwardens' Accounts

Dorchester, Dorset Record Office, PE/CEA: CW 1/1; 1628–85; English; paper; 143 leaves; 305mm x 195mm (text area variable); later ink foliation; some parts of text with ruled margins and amounts of payments or receipts in columns; bound in vellum.

CHARLTON MARSHALL

No longer a separate parish, this community is now part of the parish of Spettisbury cum Charlton Marshall. The accounting term during the period relevant for the Records ran from one Easter to the next.

St Mary the Virgin's Churchwardens' Accounts

Dorchester, Dorset Record Office, PE/CHM: CW 1/1; 1582–1642, 1651–6; English; paper; v + 115 + iii; 305mm x 205mm; modern pencil foliation; originally a paper volume of accounts, some now in scraps, restored in 1907.

CORFE CASTLE

John Stow's Chronicles of England (AC)

The Chronicles | of England, from Brute | vnto this present yeare | of Christ 1580 | *Collected by* Iohn Stow | *Citizen of London* | [device] | Printed at London by Ralphe | Newberie, at the assignement | of Henrie Bynneman.| *Cum Priuilegio Regiæ Maiestatis. STC*: 23333.

Autobiography of Robert Ashley

Robert Ashley (1565–1641), elder brother of Sir Francis Ashley (see p 62), studied first at Magdalen College, Oxford, where he performed as a lord of misrule at Christmas 1587. He went on to study at the Middle Temple, where he was called to the bar *c* 1596. Although he practised law and sat as MP for Dorchester in 1597, he made his mark through his avocation as a translator of works in French, Spanish, and Italian.

London, British Library, Sloane MS. 2131; 17th century; Latin and French; paper; i + 24 + xiii; 305mm x 190mm (295mm x 150mm); modern pencil foliation; original pages repaired and mounted on guards; modern leather and cloth binding. Ashley's autobiography, dated *c* 1622 on spine, is on ff 16–20; other works include an 'apologia' dedicated to Edward Sackville, earl of Dorset, by John Bastwick and a section of French poetry.

DORCHESTER

For the early seventeenth century various kinds of records for Dorchester survive: corporation minute books and other administrative documents; the Offenders' Book (otherwise known as the Borough Court Book), a detailed register of legal proceedings of the borough tribunal; ecclesiastical and civil court papers; private journals, such as Dennis Bond's Chronology and William Whiteway's Diary; and churchwardens' accounts of Holy Trinity as well as records of the town's two other parishes. While these records provide a sense of the social life within Dorchester, the lack of financial records like those of Bridport, Lyme Regis, or Poole deprives us of the main source of information about the borough's reception of travelling players and its investment in its own theatrical, musical, ceremonial, or customary activities. Many excerpts from the records of Dorchester have been published by C.H. Mayo (ed), *The Municipal Records of the Borough of Dorchester, Dorset* (Exeter, 1908).

Civic Records

Borough Court Book

Dorchester, Dorset Record Office, DC/DOB: 8/1; 1629–37; English and some Latin; paper; vii + 361; 305mm x 193mm; modern pencil foliation (blank folios: 130–30v, 131, 167, 255–5v, 284v, 285, 296v, 301v, 303, 344, and 361v); 31 quires, each leaf of which has been reinforced with new paper because of worn and torn outside corners, top and bottom (a presentment has been inserted at f 269v); some personal names, titles, and marginalia written in display script; bound into 1 volume with modern flyleaves, covered in red and white modern leather and bearing on the spine in gold: 'Dorchester Borough Court Book 1629–1637.'

Borough Court Minute Book

Dorchester, Dorset Record Office, DC/DOB: 16/4; 1637–56; English; paper; 128 leaves; 303mm x 194mm; unnumbered (last 2 folios blank); some personal names, titles, and marginalia written in display script; vellum cover torn and badly worn.

Legal Records

Condytt et al v. Chubbe et al

Matthew Chubbe was one of the wealthiest and most powerful men in Dorchester. John Condytt was a local tailor, a Puritan, and a follower of Reverend John White, otherwise known as the 'Patriarch of Dorchester.' The conflict between Condytt and Chubbe, which manifested itself on the occasion of a visit by Berkeley's men to Dorchester, exemplifies the antagonistic forces shaping the social history of the borough in the early seventeenth century. While the case as a whole provides a fascinating glimpse of Dorchester life at the time, we have excerpted those parts of the document that deal with the three allegedly libellous verses in which plays are attacked or with the visit of Berkeley's troupe.

Kew, Public Record Office, STAC 8/94/17; 1608–9; English and some Latin; vellum; 22 membranes of various sizes stitched at the top left corner; modern numbering at foot of membranes; written on one side only, with some administrative endorsements; generally good condition except for damage that increases from mb 17 through mb 20 (damage at folds or at outside edges results in loss of text, most but not all recoverable under ultra-violet light). Relevant items include:

mb 19: 21 April 1608; English; 620mm x 784mm; ink rubbed and in some parts illegible except under ultra-violet light; endorsed with date. Contains plaintiffs' bill of complaint.

mb 20: nd; English; 300mm x 220mm; good condition; no endorsements. Contains text of a libellous poem as exhibit accompanying the bill of complaint.

mb 21: nd; English; 428mm x 233mm; good condition; no endorsements. Contains text of a libellous poem as exhibit accompanying the bill of complaint.

mb 22: nd; English; 320mm x 222mm; good condition; no endorsements. Contains text of a libellous poem as exhibit accompanying the bill of complaint.

mb 17: 21 April–7 May 1608 (based on dates of bill (mb 19) and writ to examine defendants (mb 11)); English; single membrane with small attachment (containing final interrogatory); 718mm x 452mm (attachment at foot 105mm x 435mm); condition poor in parts with much fading at edges; no endorsement. Contains plaintiffs' interrogatories for examination of defendants.

mb 18: 2 June 1608; English and some Latin; 628mm x 693mm; good condition; no endorsements. Contains sworn answer of two defendants, Matthew and Margaret Chubbe.

mbs 14–16: 2 June 1608; English and some Latin; 3 membranes (present order is opposite to order of writing: text begins at top of mb 16 and runs to mb 14); 660mm x 283mm, 713mm x 326mm, 717mm x 328mm; good condition; mb 14 endorsed with style of cause and delivery date, 8 June 1608, mb 15 endorsed: 'Conditt et al versus Chubbe et al. Dedimus potestatem.' Contains examinations of the same two defendants.

mb 2: before 13 February 1608/9 (based on date of writ (mb 1) naming commissioners to examine witnesses); English; 642mm x 362mm; condition generally good with some fading at lower right edge; endorsed: 'Condytt versus Chubbe et al. Interrogatoria pro defendentibus.' Contains interrogatories for examination of witnesses drawn up by the defendants.

mbs 7–8: before 13 February 1608/9 (based on date of mb 1); English; 747mm x 311mm, 748mm x 314mm; good condition; mb 8 endorsed with style of cause. Contains interrogatories for examination of witnesses drawn up by the plaintiffs.

mbs 3–6: 26 April 1609; English and some Latin; 640mm x 368mm, 732mm x 298mm, 308mm x 318mm, 348mm x 370mm; good condition; mb 6 endorsed with delivery date, 8 May 1609. Contains examinations of witnesses on behalf of both the plaintiffs and the defendants.

mb 9: 29 June 1609; English and some Latin; single membrane; 386mm x 455mm; good condition; no endorsements. Contains sworn answer of another defendant, Robert Adyn.

Casebook of Sir Francis Ashley

Apart from his practice at the Middle Temple and his work for the Crown as a king's serjeant at law, Sir Francis Ashley held several important offices in Dorset. He became recorder of Dorchester following the resignation of Sir George Trenchard in 1610, sat in the House of Commons for the borough in 1614, 1621, and 1625–6, and served as Dorset justice of the peace from 1614 until his death in 1635. His casebook comes from Ashley's work in the last of these offices; it is a fair copy of notes, some made by Ashley himself (see p 198) and others made by various clerks, of cases in which he was involved. A calendar of the manuscript has been edited by J.H. Bettey, *The Case Book of Sir Francis Ashley, jp, Recorder of Dorchester, 1614–1635*, Dorset Record Society, vol 7 (Dorchester, 1981). A member of a prominent Dorset family, he was the younger brother of Robert Ashley (see p 59) and a cousin of Sir Henry Ashley (see pp 74).

London, British Library, Harley ms. 6715; 1614–35; English and Latin; paper; iii + 106 + iii; 297mm x 197mm; modern foliation (first 2 leaves blank); 2 notebooks, the first ending in 1621, have been bound together in 1 volume, each quire separately mounted on a strip of strong paper sewn in the binding; modern cloth binding with leather spine and corners, stamped in gold. All entries except those for the last two years, occupying ff 93v–106, have been crossed through with large Xs.

    This book also yielded entries for Fordington, Puddletown, Stour Provost, and Winterborne Monkton.

Miscellaneous Records

Prologue for a School Play

The 'Prologue' is one of many items in a miscellany in prose and verse collected by, and partly written by, 'Lew. F.,' probably Leweston Fitzjames, a Dorset MP. Apart from a substantial collection of John Davison's works and a playlet entitled 'Jokey Jenkins,' the volume includes songs, epigrams, poems, legal notes, epitaphs, translations, prayers, notes on primogeniture, and letters on preaching.

Oxford, Bodleian Library, ms. Add. B. 97; *c* 1603–10; English and Latin; paper; 64 leaves; 189mm x 141mm; pencil foliation; 13 quires of 4 leaves each, except for 1 with 10 leaves (ff 39–48v); vellum cover.

William Whiteway's Diary

William Whiteway (1599–1635) was a wealthy merchant of Dorchester and a strong Puritan. Like his father, William Whiteway, Sr (who was mayor of Dorchester in 1631), he traded principally with France, as a result of which connection he had information about Europe, especially about the persecution of Puritans there, that he recorded in his diary. He became one of the fifteen capital burgesses of Dorchester in 1624, sat as one of its MPs in 1626, and served as bailiff of the town in 1628 and 1632. Whiteway's Diary, which covers the years 1618 to 1635 and occupies ff 3–113v of the manuscript, records local, county, national, and international events. The last of these were of particular interest to the first editor of the Whiteway's Diary, W. Miles Barnes, who published selections from the manuscript as 'The Diary of William Whiteway, of Dorchester, Co. Dorset, from November, 1618, to March, 1634,' but his principles of selection concealed Whiteway's interest in drama with political significance.[193] As Thomas Murphy argued in his unpublished edition of the diary ('The Diary of William Whiteway of Dorchester, County Dorset, From the Year 1618 to the Year 1635,' pp lix–lxii), Whiteway drew little of his information from printed sources of news; instead, he relied upon the reports of family, friends, and business associates for the entries in his diary. Although most of the diary appears to have been written as the events occurred, some parts were entered or elaborated upon after the fact. An edition of the entire diary has been published by the Dorset Record Society, *William Whiteway of Dorchester: His Diary 1618 to 1635.*

London, British Library, Egerton MS. 784; 1618–34; English; paper; ii + 127 + ii; 135mm x 75mm; modern foliation 1–121 (+ 5 blank leaves of a lighter (modern?) paper, 1 blank leaf between ff 113–14); 19th-century leather binding, 'Whiteway's Diary. 1618–1634.' stamped in gold on the top of the spine.

William Whiteway's Commonplace Book

William Whiteway's Commonplace Book, compiled between 1625 and 1635, includes in addition to anecdotes about Dorset life a wide range of extracts from, for example, psalms and passages from Greek and Latin authors, verses in French and Latin, Holinshed's *Chronicles* and other historical works, and instructions on painting and limning, as well as a Latin-Polish word list (ff 71–95). Within the commonplace book is Whiteway's private chronology, spanning the period from 1518 to 1635 and consisting chiefly of brief notices of births, marriages, and deaths of his family. In the last year covered, Whiteway's own death is registered by his brother, Samuel. That this younger brother of William came into possession of the commonplace book may help to explain how the volume ended up in the collections of Cambridge University Library, for Samuel Whiteway studied at St Catharine's Hall, Cambridge. In April 1631 he matriculated as pensioner of the college and he went on to earn a BA in 1635.[194]

Cambridge, Cambridge University Library, Dd.11.73; early 17th century; English, Latin, French, Greek, Polish; paper; vii + 187 + vii (flyleaves modern); 193mm x 143mm; modern pencil foliation 1–144, 187–145 (ff 140–4v blank, final 43 leaves written upside-down and from back to front); hard paper cover, leather spine, and gilt lettering, binding badly damaged (front board detached).

Chronology of Dennis Bond

Born on 30 August 1588 and baptized two days later in the parish church of Melcombe Regis, Dennis Bond was the son of John Bond of Lutton and Margaret Pitt of Weymouth and cousin of William Whiteway. Dennis Bond was a woollen draper by trade, who served as constable of Dorchester in 1619, bailiff in 1630, and mayor in 1635. He is listed among the borough's capital burgesses in the charter of 1629. Bond was Puritan in his religious orientation: he supported John White's New England project; he was nominated to try the king for high treason in 1648 (although he seems not to have served in that capacity); and his son, John, became an influential Puritan divine. Having sat for Dorchester in parliament from 1640–53 and for Weymouth-Melcombe Regis in 1654 and 1656, Dennis Bond died in 1658.

Dorchester, Dorset Record Office, D/BOC: Box 22; 1634–46; English; paper and vellum; ii (modern) + ii (original) + 44 + ii (original) + ii (modern); 40 vellum leaves, 390mm x 200mm (gathered in 4s, sewn with 6 stitches), and 4 paper leaves, 340mm x 197mm; pages ruled in 4 columns of unequal width; foliated 1–5 with Latin title on f 1 and table of contents on f 2 (ff 1v, 2v, 3–5 blank), then paginated 7–80 beginning from f 5v (pp [9], 21–5, 27–8, 55, 76, [82–5] blank); good condition; vellum cover marked 'Vol. 1' on the spine, which is badly torn. Contains, in addition to a private chronology of personal and public events from 1100 to 1646, descriptions of property, pedigrees, and a list of Bond's books, dated 1635. The start is dated 1634 on the spine but 1635 is on the title page.

FORDINGTON

The larger centre of Dorchester overshadowed Fordington, which grew up next to the walls of what had been Roman Durnovaria (Dorchester). The fair at Fordington was on the eve, day, and morrow of the feast of St George (22–4 April).[195]

Churchwardens' Presentments for Salisbury Deanery

Trowbridge, Wiltshire and Swindon Record Office, D5/28/35, item 57; 24 September 1635; English; paper; single sheet; 205mm x 166mm; written on recto only; good condition. Now one of 104 items, numbered in modern pencil, kept in a modern folder.

Casebook of Sir Francis Ashley

See Dorchester (p 62) for BL: Harley MS. 6715.

HALSTOCK

Churchwardens' Presentments for Salisbury Deanery

Trowbridge, Wiltshire and Swindon Record Office, D5/28/34, item 41; 16 July 1634; English; paper; booklet made up of 2 bifolia; unnumbered; 300mm x 198mm; good condition. Now one of ninety-seven items, numbered in modern pencil, kept in a modern folder.

HAYDON

Churchwardens' Presentments for Salisbury Deanery

Trowbridge, Wiltshire and Swindon Record Office, D5/28/10, item 62; 2 December 1607; English;

paper; single sheet; 204mm x 123mm; condition generally good. One of 103 loose sheets and bifolia, 1605–10, numbered in modern pencil. A typescript list of the parishes for which presentments are found in this bundle has been inserted at the beginning.

HINTON MARTELL

Quarter Sessions Orders

See Beaminster (p 52) for DRO: QSM: 1/1.

LYME REGIS

In 1943 Cyril Wanklyn began the task of identifying, sorting, and cataloguing the thousands of records of Lyme Regis, a project that led to a series of articles first published in various local magazines and later compiled as *Lyme Leaflets* and published by Spottiswoode, Ballantyne & Co in 1944. Wanklyn's task was a daunting one given the richness and variety of Lyme's muniments, including detailed legal, financial, administrative, property, and parish documents. The financial records of Lyme in the second half of the sixteenth century are especially rich because not only does a fair copy of the town accounts survive but so too do copies of many draft accounts of the mayors. Unfortunately, seventeenth-century records of Lyme reveal less about the community, partly because of big gaps in the records of the town's Hustings Court, partly because draft mayors' accounts are not extant, and partly because changes in accounting practices eliminate the detail necessary to identify performance activity.

Civic Records

Mayors' Accounts

Dorchester, Dorset Record Office, DC/LR: N23/2; 14th–18th centuries; English; paper; miscellaneous documents set into 1 volume with 1 document to each modern guardsheet; modern pencil numbering of guardsheets but no system of foliation or pagination on individual documents; set between boards covered in black buckram with skiver (very thin leather) on the spine and the corners of the fore-edges, and fastened with 2 leather straps with buckles attached to the fore-edges of the covers. Calendared and fully transcribed in DRO: DC/LR: N24/2. The documents include the following:

item 17: 1548–9; bifolium (ff [2–2v] blank); 311mm x 206mm; unnumbered except for '17' in pencil in upper corner of f [1], but this does not provide the basis for a system of foliation; excellent condition. The account of Mayor John Dey.

item 51: 1583–4; 2 bifolia making a booklet of 4 leaves (ff [4–4v] blank), once sewn and formerly folded in 4; 414mm x 152mm; outside left edges ruled to set off 'It' (Item), columns for figures on the right side of each page. The account of Mayor Robert Davey.

item 58: 1589–90; 2 bifolia making a booklet of 4 leaves, once sewn, now loose, the first recto shows evidence of being folded again in half horizontally (ff [2v] and [4v] blank); 412mm x 153mm. The account of Mayor John Davey.

item 75: 1601; bifolium and 1 half-sheet folded to make a booklet; 305mm x 205mm; unnumbered; last page marked by fold lines and dirt on the bottom half but otherwise very clean. Contains the account of Cobb warden John Roze.
    Used in Appendix 3.

Dorchester, Dorset Record Office, DC/LR: G1/2; 1544–73; English; paper; ii + 31 + ii; 31 numbered guardsheets, each bearing a separate booklet with a mayor's account; continuous modern pagination (followed here) in pencil in the bottom right corner of each page, although some blank pages not counted; modern blue leather binding with 'Finance. Vol. II' in gold on spine. Entries transcribed in the calendar (DRO: DC/LR: G1/4a) are marked by a blue pencil line in left margin. The booklets include the following:

no 8: c 1544–5; 3 leaves made up of 1 half-sheet and a sewn bifolium; 308mm x 309mm; modern pagination 81–6; untitled. Pp 81–2 appear to belong to a different account than the rest: the stains on the paper, the lines from folding, and the handwriting differ from those of pp 83–6, which belong to the account of John Tanner, internally dated 1553 and continued on pp 87–92. The date of c 1544–5 has been assigned because the watermark on pp 81–2 resembles that in the paper used by John Tudbold, whose account in DC/LR: G1/2, f 1 is dated 36 Henry VIII, and because the labourers paid by Tudbold for repairing the Cobb house include many of the same workers also named in this account.

no 2: 1547–8; 15 leaves folded and sewn into a quarto-size booklet (leaf following p 40 has been cut out; pp 16, 35ff blank); 217 mm x 160mm; modern pagination includes p 16 but does not count the final blank leaves. Contains the account of Mayor Thomas Ellesdon.

no 9: c 1552–3; 4 leaves made up of 2 half-sheets (second half-sheet has stub of other half remaining) and a bifolium; 313mm x 210mm; modern pagination 87–94 (pp 93–4 blank); untitled. Apparently a continuation of pp 83–6 judging by the similar watermark, stains, and traces of earlier folding. Part of an account, mayor not named.

no 10: 1553; sewn bifolium; 310mm x 210mm; modern pagination 95–8. Contains Mayor John Morris' rough account for Michaelmas quarter.
    Used in Appendix 3.

no 12: 1553–4; 5 sheets folded and sewn into a booklet of 10 leaves; 314mm x 109mm; modern pagination 107–26 (pp 108–10 blank); pp 107–12 stained but not enough to make the text illegible. Account of Mayor John Morris, divided into the quarters Michaelmas, Christmas, Our Lady, and Midsummer; Michaelmas section (pp 111–13) is a fair copy of account in no 10.
    Midsummer section used in Appendix 3.

no 17: 1559; bifolium; 311mm x 108mm; modern pagination 151–4; tattered along the bottom, one blot of ink hampers legibility on p 151; p 154 bears only a title for the entire booklet of which this is a part, a title in a different hand and different ink. The third-quarter account of Richard Hunt (mayor 1558–9), beginning 'at howr lady daye In lente.'

no 19: 1560; 4 half-sheets folded vertically and sewn to make a booklet of 8 leaves; 392mm x 107mm; modern pagination 163–78 (pp 164 and 171–8 blank); stained throughout by water across the top and about three-fifths of the way down the left side of each recto, but legibility excellent. The third-quarter account of John Holcombe (mayor 1559–60).

no 23: 1560; 2 bifolia sewn to make a booklet of 4 leaves; 295mm x 101mm; modern pagination 211–18 (pp 214–18 blank); text from p 212 shows through on p 211 making the reading difficult. The first-quarter account of Richard Buckford (mayor 1560–1).

no 15: 1567–8; bifolium formerly sewn and folded again in half vertically so that the text covers only half the page; 308mm x 214 mm; modern pagination 139–42 (p 142 blank but for 'Iohn Hassard Mayor 1567' in pencil at the top). Accounts cover the first two quarters of John Hassard's mayoralty (1567–8).

no 28: 1568; half-sheet folded to make a bifolium; 316mm x 105mm; modern pagination 262b–d; clean but for show-through on pp 262b and 262d; title on p 262b: 'Iohn hasardes last quarter booke in his mayrallty 1568.' Hassard's fourth-quarter account (mayor 1567–8).

no 24: 1569–70; 5 sheets folded and sewn to make a booklet of 10 leaves; 215mm x 100–107mm; modern pagination 219–38 (pp 231–7 blank); almost the entire booklet is stained but only the stain in the top left corners of rectos makes reading difficult; tightly bound, causing the loss of some figures. The account of Mayor John Garland for the four quarters.

no 31: 1573; half-sheet folded in half vertically to define the writing area; 315mm x 205mm; modern pagination 271–2; text on right vertical half of p 271 and on the left side of p 272; no visible sewing marks. Mayor Hassard's fourth-quarter account for 1572–3.

Dorchester, Dorset Record Office, DC/LR: G1/1; 1549–1665; English; paper (watermark: crowned pot); ii + 197 + ii; 300mm x 195mm (written area variable); original foliation in ink in upper right corner of each leaf to f 78, modern pagination in pencil in lower right corner throughout (pp 2, 8–14, 67, 69, 83, 153, 370–83, 385–7, and 392 blank); opening 'The accompte' and totals in the early accounts larger and lightly decorated; f 26 and the leaf preceding f 46 cut out without any loss of accounts; modern, blue leather binding with 'Finance. Vol. 1' in gold on spine. Preceded and followed by several miscellaneous documents; lacks accounts for 1572, 1576, 1636/7–43/4. Includes accounts for Mayors John Perot (1555–6), John Holcombe (1559–60), Roger Garland (1561–2), Robert Davey (1562–3), and John Bellamy (1591–2); as well as those for Mayors William Kirridge (1621–2), William Davey (1623–4), John Hassard, Jr (1624–5), and Richard Roze (1633–4).
    Sixteenth-century accounts used in Appendix 3.

Dorchester, Dorset Record Office, DC/LR: G2/1; 1550–65; English; paper; 40 leaves sewn into 1 quire (ff [1v], [2v], [4v], [10v–11v], [18v], [19], [21v], [25], [33v], and [35] blank), with a half-page summarizing rents for 1558/9 pinned to f [9]; 312mm x 410mm (written area variable; f [10] different in paper and size (288mm x 202mm)); unnumbered; unbound, first page bears the title: 'Anno *regni regis* E*dwardi* vj^t quarto.' Almost all the material reappears in DRO: DC/LR: G1/1.

Used in Appendix 3.

Dorchester, Dorset Record Office, DC/LR: N23/3, item 2; 1568–9; English; paper; 403mm x 140mm (booklet 1) and 410mm x 153mm (booklet 2); unnumbered; 2 booklets stitched together: the first booklet, bearing the title, is made of 2 bifolia tied by 3 vellum stitches or ties, once folded again in half horizontally (4 notes about payments stitched to the top left corner of f [1v]; a similar note attached to f [3]; ff [3v] and [4–4v] are blank); the second booklet is made up of 2 bifolia bound by vellum ties at the top and bottom (f [4v] blank). Contains the account of Mayor Robert Davey; now bound as no 2 in 'Fugitive Pieces III,' a collection of miscellaneous documents bound up on numbered guard sheets.

Dorchester, Dorset Record Office, DC/LR: G2/2; 1573–1685; English; paper; incomplete collection of mayors' quarter books, each booklet mounted on a separate, unnumbered guardsheet; a system of numeration (followed here) appears on tabs bearing red numbers which correspond to the pagination of the calendar and transcription of the documents made by the Public Record Office (DRO: DC/LR: G2/3g), some pages have more than one tab and number; modern blue leather binding. The year of the account appears in pencil in the upper right corner of each folio and the accounts are arranged in chronological order. Individual booklets include:

1573: single sheet folded to define 3 writing areas; 310mm x 312mm; numbered 5–7 in red ink on tabs glued to the pages. The first-quarter account of Richard Baret (mayor 1573–4).

1573–4: bifolium (marks where it was sewn remain); 310mm x 212mm; numbered 8–12 in red ink on white tabs glued to the pages. The remainder of Baret's account for his mayoralty.

1577–8: 3 bifolia making a booklet of 6 leaves, formerly folded again twice horizontally; 418mm x 150mm; modern numbering on tabs 13–17 omits blank pages. The account of Mayor John Jourdain.

1584–5: 2 bifolia making a booklet of 4 leaves, once sewn; 306–309mm x 206mm; modern numbering on tabs 22–30 (several numbers on tabs appear on individual pages). Mayor Jourdain's account.

1586–7: half-sheet folded to make bifolium, traces of sewing remain; 415mm x 152mm; modern numbering on tabs 31–5. The account of Mayor Walter Harvey.

1587–8: 2 bifolia making a booklet of 4 leaves (outer bifolium now decayed to 2 loose sheets, sewing marks remain); 408mm x 152mm; modern numbering on tabs 36–44 (the entire fourth leaf is blank, as are the versos of the first and third leaves); the top half is stained by water but quite legible. Mayor not named but probably the account of John Jones.

1588–9: 2 half-sheets folded to make a booklet of 4 leaves, once sewn; 305mm x 104mm; modern numbering on tabs 45–51 (the verso of the first leaf is blank; the verso of the fourth has only '1589' and some calculations). The account of Mayor John Hassard.

Used in Appendix 3.

1592–3: 2 bifolia making a booklet of 4 leaves, once sewn, formerly also folded in half horizontally; 402mm x 145mm; modern numbering on tabs 53–60; clean and legible but for the show-through on the last 3 leaves; top of the booklet now folded down to fit the portfolio, the inside edges of leaves in this top part separated and frayed at the cost of some of the figures. The account of Mayor John Hayes.
    Used in Appendix 3.

1593–4: 2 bifolia making a booklet of 4 leaves, once sewn, formerly folded again in half vertically; 305mm x 208mm; modern numbering on tabs 61–6. Mayor Harvey's account.

1594–5: 3 half-sheets folded to make a booklet of 6 leaves; 305mm x 103mm; modern numbering on tabs 70–7. The second of two booklets comprising John Hassard's account; the first payment is dated 12 May (the last in the first booklet is dated 14 April).

1595–6: 7 bifolia making a booklet of 14 leaves (the first half of the fifth bifolium has been cut or torn out, some figuring remains on the stub which is 296mm x 28mm), once sewn and also folded again in half vertically; 308mm x 210mm (but the bifolia making up the fifth and tenth leaves and the sixth and ninth leaves are of different sizes and kinds of paper from the rest); modern numbering on tabs 78–98; repairs to the bottom of the first leaf do not affect the text. The account of Mayor William Ellesdon.
    Used in Appendix 3.

Cobb Records

The Cobb, a breakwater of heavy timber and stone, extended out into the sea to create the harbour of Lyme Regis. The Cobb wardens collected fees from ships that tied up at the Cobb, un-loaded cargo, and had it transported to the town. Because the Cobb did not adjoin the shore the Cobb wardens could control imports tightly for goods would be transferred by smaller vessels from the Cobb to the shore only after the appropriate dues had been paid.

Cobb Wardens' Accounts

Dorchester, Dorset Record Office, DC/LR: G7/3; c 1552–3; English; paper; 4 bifolia making a booklet of 8 leaves (ff [4–4v] blank); 314mm x 215mm; unnumbered; the last page is dirtiest, showing evidence of once being folded again in half vertically and bearing the name, slightly smudged, 'Ion battyn.' F [3v] of the booklet bears a total of the receipts of the Cobb for both this account and that of Richard Leonard. Bound as ff [72–9] of a collection of miscellaneous accounts of the receivers of the Cobb (1546–64 but not in chronological order). Contains the account of John Battyn.

Dorchester, Dorset Record Office, DC/LR: N23/1, item 63; English; paper; 12 June 1601; 1 half-sheet; 303mm x 201mm; show-through hampers legibility somewhat. Now bound as no 63 among a collection of miscellaneous documents 1496–1696; each document is assigned to a numbered modern guardsheet so that these numbers are, in effect, article numbers (individual articles not systematically foliated or paginated). Transcribed by Cyril Wanklyn in DC/LR: N24/1. Contains an account of Cobb warden John Roze.
    Used in Appendix 3.

Grant of Cobb Kitchen to Borough Corporation
Dorchester, Dorset Record Office, DC/LR: N23/4, item 3; 12 October 1579; English; parchment; single membrane; 404mm x 175mm; witnesses' names on the dorse, fragment of a seal attached. Now bound up as no 3 in 'Fugitive Pieces IV,' a miscellany of documents, 1288–1859, in which each document is attached to a numbered modern guardsheet.
　　Used in Appendix 3.

Legal Records

Churchwardens' Presentments for Salisbury Deanery

Trowbridge, Wiltshire and Swindon Record Office, D5/28/9; 1606–8; Latin and English; loose documents in a blue folder tied with cotton, including the following:

item 59: 11 September 1606; English; paper; bifolium; 305mm x 48mm; unnumbered; fair condition: torn along the gutter, water-stained across the top, top right corner torn away.
　　Used in Appendix 3.

item 24: 20 April 1607; English; paper; single sheet; 300mm x 196mm; fair condition: badly stained by water at the top, hole bottom centre.

Trowbridge, Wiltshire and Swindon Record Office, D5/28/11, item 24; 1609; English; paper; bifolium; 204mm x 303mm; condition generally good. One of thirty-nine loose sheets and bifolia, numbered in modern pencil. A typescript list of the parishes for which presentments are found in this bundle has been inserted at the beginning.

Trowbridge, Wiltshire and Swindon Record Office, D5/28/35, item 73; 22 September 1635; English; paper; stitched booklet of 3 bifolia; unnumbered; 298mm x 195mm; good condition. Now one of 104 items, numbered in pencil, kept in a modern folder.

Bill of Complaint in Salter v. Cowper et al

Kew, Public Record Office, STAC 8/258/15; 17 November 1608; English; parchment; single membrane; 710mm x 385mm (667mm x 335mm); stained, faded, and wrinkled along the right edge so that legibility is hampered; inscribed on the dorse: 'Iovis decimo septimo Novembris Anno Sexto Iacobi Regis. Edward Iones.'

MELBURY OSMOND

Gordon et al v. Auncell et al

Kew, Public Record Office, STAC 8/153/29; 1622; English and some Latin; vellum; 3 membranes stitched together at the top left corner; modern numbering on left side. Relevant items include:

mb 3: before 29 November 1622 (based on dates of sworn answers); English; 535mm x 420mm (505mm x 395mm); generally good condition but stained in the bottom right corner and torn down into the text in the top right, wrinkled so as to hamper legibility in the top right corner; endorsed: 'Gordo⟨.⟩ versu⟨.⟩ Auncel⟨…⟩ Mich. *vicesimo* I*acobi* Reg*is.*' Contains the plaintiffs' bill of complaint.

mb 1: 29 November 1622; English; 544mm x 210mm (490mm x 190mm); generally good condition; no endorsements. Contains sworn answer of one defendant, Christopher Auncell.

NETHERBURY

Notes from St Mary's Churchwardens' Accounts (AC)

The compilers of this manuscript (and the scripts are apparently seventeenth century) seem to have had antiquarian interests. Folios [24v] and [25] are notes which the scribe says are based on presentments from the manor of Yondover from 34 Henry VI to 2 Charles I; f [10] is a chronology of events, 1618–40; other sections are more miscellaneous.

Dorchester, Dorset Record Office, D/KAT: 7623; 1455–1640; Latin and English; paper; 24 leaves; 303mm x 190mm (text area variable); unnumbered; paper booklet.

Churchwardens' Presentments for Salisbury Deanery

Trowbridge, Wiltshire and Swindon Record Office, D5/28/11, item 31; 1609; English; paper; single sheet; 200mm x 304mm; condition generally good. One of thirty-nine loose sheets and bifolia, numbered in modern pencil. A typescript list of the parishes for which presentments are found in this bundle has been inserted at the beginning.

OVER COMPTON

Churchwardens' Presentments for Salisbury Deanery

Trowbridge, Wiltshire and Swindon Record Office, D5/28/12, item 20; 1609; English; paper; single sheet; 198mm x 304mm; condition generally good. One of thirty-nine loose sheets and bifolia, numbered in modern pencil. A typescript list of the parishes for which presentments are found in this bundle has been inserted at the beginning.

Bill of Complaint in Abington v. Beaton et al

Kew, Public Record Office, STAC 8/42/14; 1618–19; English and some Latin; parchment; 9 membranes stitched together at the top left corner; modern numbering; folio numbers stamped in the top right corner, written in pencil in the bottom left; good condition. Includes:

mb 9: 19 February 1617/18; English; 688mm x 559mm. Exhibits several styles of handwriting, probably by two different clerks.

POOLE

Most of the Poole documents containing REED material are financial records, although the privately-produced catalogue of Poole records kept both in the Poole Town Clerk's Office and in the Dorset County Library lists many other kinds of records. For the catalogue see Borough and County of the Town of Poole, *Calendar of Local Archives*, vol 1 (compiled by H.P. Smith and Bernard C. Short, 1958). Poole's records have recently been moved to the Dorset Record Office in Dorchester from the Poole Borough Archives and the reference numbers given below, which reflect the classifications used in the *Calendar*, are likely to change after the collection has been fully catalogued.

Poole's year began in January in the early sixteenth century; the Great Charter of 1568 stated that mayoral elections were to be held on the Friday next before the feast of St Matthew the Apostle (21 September) and the accounting year after 1568 ran from September or October to the same date in the following year. Accounts kept by both mayors and bailiffs (who expected to become mayors) may refer to any sort of town expenditure. The purview of the mayors and bailiffs was large. As the sixteenth-century ruling group grew narrower, it also acquired more exclusive powers in town affairs. Choosing churchwardens and auditing church accounts from early in the century, the town government acquired admiralty jurisdiction and independence from manorial authority. Thus great authority was wielded by the small group of families who filled the co-optive group of burgesses and aldermen making up the town council and from whom were drawn the mayors and bailiffs. The records reflect many sixteenth- and seventeenth-century quarrels between Poole burgesses; in particular, controversy between members of the ruling group may have influenced the disallowing of expenditures made by mayors or bailiffs that is sometimes our only evidence of the town's support of performance activity.

The first series of Poole manuscripts to be catalogued carry designations such as P23 or P191. In the past fifteen years the borough has restored a number of damaged manuscripts; these constitute the PA series.

Civic Accounts

Town Accounts

The first part of P26(4), intended as a 'greate boke' for the town, collects material from preliminary accounts by subject, beginning in 1568; some entries made in the 1570s excerpt earlier records. The accounts often contain cross-referenced double-entries. The first twenty-four leaves constitute an incomplete alphabetical index to the accounts.

Dorchester, Dorset Record Office, DC/PL: CLA P23(1); 1490–1553; English; paper; 95 leaves; 203mm x 144mm (190mm x 140mm); modern ink pagination; good condition; contemporary vellum binding reinforced with 2 pieces of dark leather piercing the spine.

Dorchester, Dorset Record Office, DC/PL: CLA P26(4); 1554–78; English; paper; xxiv + 134;

300mm x 205mm (opening index leaves 85mm wide with 10mm tabs); contemporary ink numbering by 'openings,' that is, facing pages assigned the same number (here designated as 'left' and 'right'); headings, particularly in the elaborate first part of the volume, are often in bold; good condition; contemporary vellum binding with 'B 1554' on the cover.

Mayors' Accounts

Dorchester, Dorset Record Office, DC/PL: CLA P51(6); 1551–2; English; paper; 8 leaves; 215mm x 155mm (190mm x 135mm); modern incomplete ink pagination; sewn paper booklet. There are some notes in later hand, including marginal summaries of payments.

Dorchester, Dorset Record Office, DC/PL: CLA PA10; 1552–3; English; paper; 18 leaves; 315mm x 220mm (270mm x 120mm); modern pencil foliation; paper booklet, top badly damaged and whole skilfully repaired on all sides.

Dorchester, Dorset Record Office, DC/PL: CLA P103(60); 1569–70; English; paper; 7 leaves; 220mm x 158mm; unnumbered; sewn paper booklet, stained and with frayed edges.

Dorchester, Dorset Record Office, DC/PL: CLA P106(63); 1577–8; English; paper; 8 leaves; 420mm x 155mm; unnumbered; paper booklet, some holes and frayed edges.

Dorchester, Dorset Record Office, DC/PL: CLA P119(76); 1590–2; English; paper; 4 leaves; 203mm x 145mm (185mm x 90mm); unnumbered; paper booklet, good condition.

Dorchester, Dorset Record Office, DC/PL: CLA P191(A32); 1601–2; English; 6 leaves; 200mm x 153mm (185mm x 105mm); contemporary foliation with facing pages assigned the same number; paper booklet, good condition.

Bailiffs' Accounts

Dorchester, Dorset Record Office, DC/PL: CLA P46(1); 1524–5; English; paper; 8 leaves; 280mm x 204mm (220mm x 155mm); unnumbered; paper booklet, edges frayed.

Dorchester, Dorset Record Office, DC/PL: CLA P49(4); 1546–8; English; paper; 8 leaves; 220mm x 160mm (180mm x 130mm); unnumbered; sewn paper booklet, good condition.

Dorchester, Dorset Record Office, DC/PL: CLA PA20(ii); 1562–3; English; paper; 6 leaves; 208mm x 155mm; modern pencil foliation 7–12 in the bottom centre of each leaf (followed here), incomplete original ink pagination 1–8, starting at f 7v and continuing to f 11; badly torn along left edge with tear extending 70mm into the page just below the centre, repaired by mounting on modern paper. Formerly bound in a Latin vellum book, now an unstitched paper booklet, part of a group of loose papers and unstitched booklets foliated 1–21 by conservators and stored in a modern blue manila folder.

Dorchester, Dorset Record Office, DC/PL: CLA PA12; 1570–1; English; paper; 18 leaves; 300mm x

205mm; modern pencil foliation; paper booklet, top half badly damaged, whole mended on all sides; headings in bold. On the front cover are a number of statements identifying the mayor and bailiff to whose year the account belongs and indicating the booklet was used as evidence in an eighteenth-century lawsuit.

Auditors' Accounts

Dorchester, Dorset Record Office, DC/PL: CLA PA15; 1579 87; English; paper; 27 leaves (ff 1–25 form a stitched booklet in chronological sequence; ff 26–7 comprise an original bifolium account for 1584–5 now out of sequence); 210mm x 150mm; modern pencil foliation throughout (followed here) with contemporary ink pagination beginning on f 1v; recently repaired and placed in modern blue manila repair cover; original paper cover bears title: 'No. 26 1584 | 5 | 6 | 7.'

Miscellaneous Records

Letter of Sir Henry Ashley

Sir Henry Ashley of Wimborne St Giles (1519–88) was one of three deputy lieutenants of Dorset responsible from the early 1580s for organizing the defences of Dorset against the expected Spanish attack. In 1584 he was one of five captains who were to train men from the county; when he and the other deputy lieutenants divided the supervision of Dorset's supply of powder and match in 1586, Poole lay in his district. In July 1588, when the Armada came, Ashley's son, Henry (later Sir Henry Ashley), served as a vice admiral of eight ships, carrying men mostly pressed at Poole. Robert and Sir Francis Ashley (see pp 59 and 62 above) were the first Sir Henry Ashley's nephews; they were also the younger brothers of the Sir Anthony Ashley who inherited Wimborne St Giles when the younger Sir Henry Ashley died leaving only daughters.[196]

Dorchester, Dorset Record Office, DC/PL: CLA P124(81); 21 May 1587; English; bifolium; unnumbered; 290mm x 198mm (240mm x 147mm); some small holes result in brief gaps in the text; addressed on f [2v]: 'To my friende the Mayo⟨.⟩ of the towne of Poole yeue theis' and endorsed: 'xxxviii Henry Ashley to the Mayor adviseinge of 2 Comm*issioners* being appointed to inspect the Caste Fortifications &c on the Sea Coast 2 May 1587.'

PUDDLETOWN

Casebook of Sir Francis Ashley

See Dorchester (p 62) for BL: Harley MS. 6715.

SHAFTESBURY

The rich collection of Shaftesbury records deposited in the Dorset Record Office was arranged by Charles Herbert Mayo, who listed the documents in his catalogue, *The Municipal Records of the Borough of Shaftesbury.* The collection includes documents granting or confirming borough privileges; court rolls from Shaftesbury Abbey; 100 charters of feoffment and other similar instruments; nearly fifty rolls, books, and bundles of accounts and records of payments; 162 documents relating to sixteenth- and seventeenth-century lawsuits; and a dozen miscellaneous documents.

Bishop Simon of Ghent's Register

Trowbridge, Wiltshire, and Swindon Record Office, D1/2/1; 1297–1315; Latin; parchment; i + 410 + i; 270mm x 175mm; original foliation in 2 series superseded by modern foliation 1–174, 175A, 175B (insert), 176–339, 340A, 340B, 341–9, 350A, 350B, 351–88, 389A, 389B, 390–409; modern binding (original limp parchment covers preserved as flyleaves and foliated as 1 and 409).

Depositions in Gower v. Hascoll

Together with DC/SYB: E100–1 and E103–4, these are surviving documents from a lawsuit against Mayor Hascoll for contempt, a suit dismissed February 1625/6.

Dorchester, Dorset Record Office, DC/SYB: E102; 1626; English; paper; 106 sheets; 400mm x 310mm; ink numbering; written on one side only; sheets sewn together at the top and the whole rolled and tied.

Borough Financial Papers

Dorchester, Dorset Record Office, DC/SYB: C11, item 17; 1629; English; paper; single sheet; 175mm x 200mm (156mm x 185mm). Originally one of a number of small slips of paper of varying sizes tied in a roll with a leather thong. This item is now in a folder containing twenty miscellaneous financial documents.

Antiquarian Records

We have not succeeded in tracing the original documents relating to Gillingham Manor which contained references to Shaftesbury's annual procession (Gillingham Manor had jurisdiction over the village of Motcombe; see p 248). By 6 April 1661, Gillingham had been conveyed to Sir Edward Nicholas, secretary of state to Charles I and Charles II, and a member of the Nicholas family of Winterbourne Earls, Wiltshire; a copied reference to Shaftesbury's custom survives in the Nicholas MSS. The antiquarian John Hutchins (1698–1773), who copied other references from sources still extant in the eighteenth century, was the son of a curate of Bradford Peverell who would later serve as rector of All Saints', Dorchester. Educated at Balliol and with a Cambridge MA, Hutchins was ordained in the early 1720s and served as curate and usher to the vicar of Milton Abbas, rector of Swyre (after 1729), rector of Melcombe Horsey (after 1733), and rector of Holy Trinity, Wareham (1734–73). He compiled the history of Dorset between 1736 and 1773; with the aid of generous subscriptions he included material from major libraries and from records in the Tower of London as well as local records.

Gillingham Manorial Court Orders (AC)

Manchester, University of Manchester, John Rylands Library, Nicholas MS 69; 1574–1637; English; paper; 12 leaves; modern pencil foliation; 320mm x 210mm (290mm x 155mm); paper booklet; title on the cover: 'The Orders of the Courte of the Mannor of Gillingham with the Boundarye of the said Mannor Sent upp by Mr Breenker ⌜to yor …⌝ with his letteres in Ianuary 1638.' The orders are apparently all excerpts from court books of the manor.

Gillingham Manor Court Roll (A)

John Hutchins, *The History and Antiquities of the County of Dorset*, 3rd ed, corrected, augmented, and improved by William Shipp and James Whitworth Hodson, vol 3 (Westminster, 1868).
    This work also furnished an entry for Appendix 2.

SHERBORNE

The pre-Reformation parish church in Sherborne was All Hallows'. After the Dissolution the parish took over the former monastic church, St Mary's, and All Hallows' was demolished. The churchwardens' accounts for the two thus represent a single series and are so treated by the Dorset Record Office.
    There are surviving churchwardens' accounts for All Hallows' or for St Mary's for 112 years between the early sixteenth century and 1642. The accounting year varies. The early undated accounts (CW 1/1–1/3) do not indicate when the accounts were made, but they probably date from about 1505–11 (see p 356, endnote to DRO: PE/SH: CW 1/1 f [1]). CW 1/5–1/11 (scattered accounts between 1513–14 and 1525–6) were usually rendered at Christmas, and CW 1/4, dated 5 Henry VIII, was probably also a Christmas account. Accounts for the rest of the sixteenth century (CW 1/12–1/72) were usually rendered in January or February, although on two occasions the accounting year ran to March (1554–5 and 1585–6). After 1602–3 the accounting year ended in late March, April, May, or early June. All Hallows' records were kept by a single warden who ordinarily had served as 'king' of the church ale two or three years before. After 1542–3 there were usually two wardens; the man who ran the parish ale or served as collector for the parish became junior warden the next year and senior warden in the year following.
    The pre-Reformation accounts of All Hallows' are printed with some omissions by Fowler in *SDNQ*, vols 23–4. The accounts for the four years after 1537–8 are missing. Fowler discusses and prints the post-Reformation accounts of St Mary the Virgin, Sherborne, in *SDNQ*, vols 24–6. The last account printed was rendered on 29 January 1558/9.

All Hallows' Churchwardens' Accounts

Dorchester, Dorset Record Office, PE/SH: CW 1/1; undated, probably *c* 1505–8; English; paper; sheet folded to form bifolium (formerly part of booklet); 290mm x 180mm; unnumbered; now repaired.

Dorchester, Dorset Record Office, PE/SH: CW 1/2; undated, probably *c* 1508–10; English; parchment; 2 bifolia sewn as a 4-folio booklet; 285mm x 190mm; unnumbered; now repaired.

Dorchester, Dorset Record Office, PE/SH: CW 1/3; 1510–11; English; parchment; 3 membranes, sewn at top; 385mm x 295mm; unnumbered; mb [2] torn in 2 places.

Dorchester, Dorset Record Office, PE/SH: CW 1/4; 1512–13; English; paper; 4 sheets, sewn at bottom; 315mm x 225mm (largest) and 250mm x 220mm (smallest); unnumbered; top edges frayed.

Dorchester, Dorset Record Office, PE/SH: CW 1/5; 1513–14; Latin; parchment; single membrane with tiny paper list of expenses attached at the bottom; 720mm x 300mm; top torn; heading decorated.

Dorchester, Dorset Record Office, PE/SH: CW 1/6; 1514–15; Latin; paper; single sheet; 750mm x 300mm; badly torn at top and bottom.

Dorchester, Dorset Record Office, PE/SH: CW 1/7; 1515–16; Latin with English inventory on dorse; paper; single sheet; 720mm x 305mm.

Dorchester, Dorset Record Office, PE/SH: CW 1/8; 1517–18; Latin with English inventory; parchment; single membrane; 720mm x 300mm; torn at the top; decorated heading.

Dorchester, Dorset Record Office, PE/SH: CW 1/9; 1523–4; English with Latin headings; parchment; single membrane; 510mm x 320mm.

Dorchester, Dorset Record Office, PE/SH: CW 1/10; 1524–5; English with Latin headings; parchment; single membrane; 550mm x 380mm; top half torn.

Dorchester, Dorset Record Office, PE/SH: CW 1/11; 1525–6; English with Latin headings; paper; single sheet; 450mm x 340mm; ragged top edge.

Dorchester, Dorset Record Office, PE/SH: CW 1/12; 1526/7–27/8; English with Latin headings; paper; single sheet; 570mm x 380mm; badly frayed and torn.

Dorchester, Dorset Record Office, PE/SH: CW 1/13; 1527/8–28/9; English with Latin headings; parchment; single membrane; 560mm x 420mm; stained on the left side.

Dorchester, Dorset Record Office, PE/SH: CW 1/14; 1530–1; English; parchment; single membrane; 570mm x 510mm; decayed, particularly at the top, first heading partially destroyed.

Dorchester, Dorset Record Office, PE/SH: CW 1/15; 1534–6; English; paper; 16 leaves; 217mm x 160mm (200mm x 140mm); modern pencil foliation; paper booklet bound in a vellum leaf with writing on the inside back cover (here designated f [17]).

Dorchester, Dorset Record Office, PE/SH: CW 1/16; 1536–7; English; paper; 6 leaves; 205mm x 150mm (185mm x 130mm); modern pencil foliation; paper booklet, good condition.

Dorchester, Dorset Record Office, PE/SH: CW 1/17; 1537–8; English with Latin headings; parchment; single membrane; 555mm x 355mm; heading decorated.

Dorchester, Dorset Record Office, PE/SH: CW 1/18; 1538–9; English; paper; 10 leaves; 215mm x 160mm (200mm x 135mm); modern pencil foliation; paper booklet, good condition.

St Mary the Virgin's Churchwardens' Accounts

Dorchester, Dorset Record Office, PE/SH: CW 1/19; 1542–3; English; paper; 4 leaves; 465mm x 205mm (380mm x 170mm); modern pencil foliation; headings in bold; generally good condition.

Dorchester, Dorset Record Office, PE/SH: CW 1/20; 1543–4; English; parchment; 5 membranes sewn serially; 530mm x 330mm; unnumbered; headings in bold; top badly torn.

Dorchester, Dorset Record Office, PE/SH: CW 1/21; 1544–5; English; parchment; 5 membranes sewn serially; 555mm x 370mm; unnumbered; top of the first membrane badly torn.

Dorchester, Dorset Record Office, PE/SH: CW 1/22; 1546–7; English; parchment; 6 membranes sewn serially; 380mm x 310mm; unnumbered; headings in bold; top of first membrane stained and frayed.

Dorchester, Dorset Record Office, PE/SH: CW 1/23; 1547–8; English; parchment; 6 membranes sewn serially; 380mm x 305mm; unnumbered; headings centred and in bold; top of first membrane torn and displaying the remains of an old inexpert repair.

Dorchester, Dorset Record Office, PE/SH: CW 1/24; 1548–9; English; parchment; 5 membranes sewn serially; 370mm x 310mm; unnumbered; headings centred and in bold; good condition.

Dorchester, Dorset Record Office, PE/SH: CW 1/25; 1549–50; English; parchment; 5 membranes sewn serially; 385mm x 310mm; unnumbered; headings centred and in bold; top of first membrane damaged.

Dorchester, Dorset Record Office, PE/SH: CW 1/26; 1550–1; English; paper; 7 sheets sewn serially; 380mm x 310mm; unnumbered; headings in bold; top of first sheet fragmented and repaired.

Dorchester, Dorset Record Office, PE/SH: CW 1/28; 1552–3; English; paper; 4 sheets sewn serially; 350mm x 270mm; unnumbered; good condition.

Dorchester, Dorset Record Office, PE/SH: CW 1/30; 1554–5; English; paper; 4 sheets sewn serially; 385mm x 310mm; unnumbered; top sheet frayed at the edges with an old repair at the top of the sheet.

Dorchester, Dorset Record Office, PE/SH: CW 1/31; 1555–6; English; paper; 3 sheets sewn serially; 395mm x 330mm; unnumbered; top of first sheet damaged; headings and some initial words in bold.

Dorchester, Dorset Record Office, PE/SH: CW 1/32; 1556–7; English; parchment; 5 membranes sewn serially; 370mm x 310mm; unnumbered; top of first membrane damaged, making heading illegible; some words, including 'Item,' in bold.

Dorchester, Dorset Record Office, PE/SH: CW 1/33; 1557–8; English; parchment; 4 membranes sewn serially; 595mm x 375mm (largest) and 185mm x 385mm (smallest); unnumbered; top of first membrane cut to form binding for roll and somewhat damaged.

Dorchester, Dorset Record Office, PE/SH: CW 1/34; 1558–9; English; paper; 3 sheets sewn serially; 360mm x 300mm; unnumbered; good condition; 'Item' consistently in bold.

Dorchester, Dorset Record Office, PE/SH: CW 1/35; 1561–2; English; paper; 3 sheets sewn serially; 385mm x 310mm; unnumbered; first sheet very tattered at the top; 'Item' in bold.

Dorchester, Dorset Record Office, PE/SH: CW 1/36; 1565–6; English; paper; 5 sheets sewn serially; 380mm x 310mm; unnumbered; top of first sheet ripped and an old repair has proved inadequate; many words in bold. The heading is missing but churchwardens' names indicate this is the account for 1565–6 made early in 1566.

Dorchester, Dorset Record Office, PE/SH: CW 1/37; 1566–7; English; paper; 3 sheets; 400mm x 270mm; modern pencil foliation; right edges tattered and crumpled; paper booklet bound in vellum, title on the cover: 'The booke off Iohn Elyot Accounte Churche Warden of Sherborne 1566. Et anno *Regni Regine* Elizabeth Nono.'

Dorchester, Dorset Record Office, PE/SH: CW 1/38; 1567–8; English; parchment; 5 membranes sewn serially; unnumbered; 700mm x 210mm (largest) and 240mm x 205mm (smallest); headings in bold; good condition.

Dorchester, Dorset Record Office, PE/SH: CW 1/39; 1568–9; English; vellum; 4 membranes sewn serially; 340mm x 310mm; unnumbered; headings and some initial words in bold; second membrane badly torn.

Dorchester, Dorset Record Office, PE/SH: CW 1/40; 1569–70; English; parchment; 3 membranes sewn serially; unnumbered; 630mm x 300mm; headings and some initial words in bold.

Dorchester, Dorset Record Office, PE/SH: CW 1/41; 1570–1; English; parchment; 3 membranes sewn serially; 685mm x 300mm; unnumbered; decorated heading on first membrane and other headings bold.

Dorchester, Dorset Record Office, PE/SH: CW 1/42; 1571–2; English; parchment; 4 membranes sewn serially; 560mm x 310mm; unnumbered; decorated heading at top of first membrane and other headings bold; good condition.

Dorchester, Dorset Record Office, PE/SH: CW 1/43; 1572–3; English; parchment; 6 membranes sewn serially; 510mm x 300mm; unnumbered; headings in bold.

Dorchester, Dorset Record Office, PE/SH: CW 1/44; 1573–4; English; parchment; 5 membranes sewn serially; 600mm x 270mm; unnumbered; decorated heading at top of first membrane, first 2 marginal headings decorated and other headings in bold.

Dorchester, Dorset Record Office, PE/SH: CW 1/45; 1574–5; English; parchment; 5 membranes sewn serially; 600mm x 210mm; unnumbered; decorated heading at the top of the first membrane and other headings in bold.

Dorchester, Dorset Record Office, PE/SH: CW 1/46; 1575–6; English; parchment; 4 membranes sewn serially; 640mm x 195mm; unnumbered; first heading decorated and other headings in bold; top of first membrane slightly torn.

Dorchester, Dorset Record Office, PE/SH: CW 1/47; 1576–7; English; parchment; 3 membranes sewn serially; 525mm x 250mm; unnumbered; headings, some initial words, and money amounts in bold; good condition.

Dorchester, Dorset Record Office, PE/SH: CW 1/49; 1577–8; English; parchment; 3 membranes sewn serially; 610mm x 193mm; unnumbered; headings, some initial words, and some money amounts in bold; good condition.

Dorchester, Dorset Record Office, PE/SH: CW 1/60; 1588–9; English; parchment; 4 membranes sewn serially; 890mm x 243mm; unnumbered; headings in bold; good condition.

Dorchester, Dorset Record Office, PE/SH: CW 1/61; 1589–90; English; parchment; 3 membranes sewn serially; 795mm x 197mm; unnumbered; headings in bold; good condition.

Dorchester, Dorset Record Office, PE/SH: CW 1/62; 1590–1; English; parchment; 3 membranes sewn serially; 775mm x 210mm; unnumbered; headings in bold; good condition.

Dorchester, Dorset Record Office, PE/SH: CW 1/69; 1597–8; English; parchment; 5 membranes sewn serially; 770mm x 190mm (largest) and 290mm x 193mm (smallest); unnumbered; headings in bold.

Dorchester, Dorset Record Office, PE/SH: CW 1/70; 1598–9; English; parchment; 2 membranes sewn serially; 775mm x 245mm; unnumbered; headings in bold.

Dorchester, Dorset Record Office, PE/SH: CW 1/71; 1599–1600; English; parchment; 3 membranes sewn serially; 815mm x 265mm; unnumbered; headings in bold.

Dorchester, Dorset Record Office, PE/SH: CW 1/72; 1600–1; English; parchment; 5 membranes sewn serially; 740mm x 228mm; unnumbered; headings in bold; good condition.

Dorchester, Dorset Record Office, PE/SH: CW 1/73; 1601–2; English; parchment; 5 membranes sewn serially; 730mm x 238mm (largest) and 150mm x 240mm (smallest); unnumbered; headings in bold; good condition.

Dorchester, Dorset Record Office, PE/SH: CW 1/74; 1602–3; English; parchment; 3 membranes sewn serially; 740mm x 230mm; unnumbered; headings in bold; good condition.

Depositions for the Defendant in Scarlett v. Stocker

Francis Scarlett, vicar of Sherborne, brought suit in 1603 against John Stocker, the purchaser of Sir Ralph Horsey's remaining term 'in the parsonage of Sherborne' and thus also impropriator of the Sherborne prebend. This manuscript is one of those surviving from that lawsuit. Depositions were taken by two commissions in Dorset; three witnesses who appeared before the commission which took evidence in the Hilary term, 1603–4, spoke briefly of incidents related to preparations for a performance of the Sherborne Corpus Christi play, probably in 1572–3.

Kew, Public Record Office, E134/1 James I/ Hil 3; 1603/4; English; parchment; 7 membranes sewn serially; 4200mm x 300mm; modern pencil numbering; good condition.

Somerset Quarter Sessions Roll

An entry from this roll (previously printed in Stokes with Alexander (eds), *Somerset Including Bath*, pp 145–6), refers to a bullbaiter bringing his animals to Sherborne and Sturminster Newton in Dorset.

Taunton, Somerset Record Office, Q/SR 37, pt 2; 1607–8; English and some Latin; paper; 94 leaves; 315mm x 200mm; modern foliation; individual booklets and other documents repaired and bound together as one of a series of volumes following a 1905 order of the county council, all having identical caramel-coloured covers tied with laces. The excerpted presentment originally formed part of Q/SR 2 and was transferred to this volume at some time after the original items were numbered; it is now numbered 101A.

SPETTISBURY

Examination of Anne Barter

Dorchester, Dorset Record Office, PE/WM: CP2/8, item 90; 23 February 1635/6; Latin and English; paper; single sheet; 325mm x 202mm. Filed in a bundle of depositions taken before the peculiar court of Wimborne Minster in cases of fornication.

STOUR PROVOST

Casebook of Sir Francis Ashley

See Dorchester (p 62) for BL: Harley MS. 6715.

STURMINSTER NEWTON

Sturminster Newton was eight miles from Shaftesbury, ten miles from Blandford Forum, and twelve from Sherborne; probably because of this relative isolation, the village developed as a small market centre with thirteenth-century fairs at both Sturminster and Newton.[197]

Somerset Quarter Sessions Roll

See Sherborne (p 81) for SRO: Q/SR 37, pt 2.

SYMONDSBURY

Henry Burton's A Divine Tragedie

Henry Burton's *Divine Tragedie* is a sabbatarian work written to protest against Charles I's reissuing of *The kings majesties declaration ... concerning lawful sports* in 1633. Limiting himself to cases that occurred within two years of the reissuing of this declaration, Burton cites dozens of examples of people who perverted the sabbath and were punished therefore.

A DIVINE TRAGEDIE | LATELY ACTED, | OR, | A Collection of sundrie memorable ex- | amples of Gods judgements upon Sabbath-breakers, | and other like Libertines, in their unlawfull Sports, hap- | ning within the Realme of *England,* in the compasse one- | ly of few yeers last past, since the Book was published, worthy | to be known and considered of all men, especially such, | who are guilty of the sin or Arch- | patrons thereof. | By that worthy Divine Mr. *Henry Burton.* | [woodcut of author entitled: *Ætatis suæ 63*] | Printed in the yeer 1641. Wing: B6161 (also Thomason Tract E176.1).

WEYMOUTH-MELCOMBE REGIS

In the Weymouth Museum is a large metal chest containing the Sherren Manuscripts, a collection purchased at auction in the late nineteenth century, catalogued by the Dorset historian H.J. Moule in 1883, and kept for some time in the town vault. The documents in the collection are kept in manila file folders, most often singly, but sometimes two or three to a folder. Current Weymouth Museum plans to recatalogue the manuscripts collection may result in new shelf marks for the Weymouth manuscripts. Most of the REED material is in the mayors' accounts. The mayor's accounting year ran from Michaelmas to Michaelmas. The accounts were sometimes audited immediately, sometimes only after a two or three-year delay. The auditors often disallowed some expenses although they did not always give their grounds for doing so.

Civic Accounts

Mayors' Accounts

Weymouth, Weymouth Museum, Sherren MS 177; 1590–6; English; paper; 4-leaf booklet; 310mm x

200mm; ink pagination beginning on the verso of the first leaf; slightly stained in centre. Contains the account of Mayor John Bond for 1590–1, with comments from auditors in 1596.

Weymouth, Weymouth Museum, Sherren MS 184; 1596–1600; English; paper; 4-leaf booklet; 308mm x 205mm (295mm x 175mm); unnumbered; good condition. Contains mayor's account for 1596–7 and auditors' remarks dated 23 September 1602; some entries were crossed out by the auditors and their comments are in the left margin.

Weymouth, Weymouth Museum, Sherren MS 185; 1597–1602; English; paper; 2-leaf booklet; 305mm x 201mm; unnumbered; good condition; among various notations on the cover is the inscription: 'Iohn Moket his Acompt In . 1597 . & 1598 / & p[ar]te of 1599.' Includes some marginal notations made by the auditors of 1601.

Weymouth, Weymouth Museum, Sherren MS 186; 1599–1600; English; paper; 4-leaf booklet; 318mm x 218mm; unnumbered; good condition. Includes auditors' comments from 1601 and 1605.

Weymouth, Weymouth Museum, Sherren MS 190; 1603–4; English; paper; 2-leaf booklet; 310mm x 203mm; unnumbered; good condition. Includes auditors' comments from 1606.

Weymouth, Weymouth Museum, Sherren MS 191; 1605–6; English; paper; 2-leaf booklet; 304mm x 196mm; unnumbered; first leaf torn. Includes undated auditors' comments.

Weymouth, Weymouth Museum, Sherren MS 206; 1615–16; English; paper; 4-leaf booklet, sewn; 311mm x 199mm (290mm x 175mm); unnumbered; good condition. Includes auditors' comments and records of repayments from 1617.

Borough Financial Records

Weymouth, Weymouth Museum, Sherren MS 243.1; 1640–1; English; paper; single sheet; 355mm x 159mm (345mm x 130mm); good condition; endorsed with remarks by the mayor about payment of the bill to 'goodman minor,' headed: 'A Noote for the Towne.'

Borough Court Records

Borough Court Minutes

Weymouth, Weymouth Museum, Sherren MS 204; 1612–17; paper; English and Latin; 46 leaves; 310mm x 205mm (300mm x 190mm); modern pencil foliation; good condition; sewn booklet with a glued brown paper cover.

Borough and Borough Court Minute Book

Weymouth, Weymouth Museum, MB.O-B; 1616–83; English and Latin; paper; xxix + 410 + iv; 435mm x 295mm (420mm x 275mm); partly contemporary, partly modern ink pagination to p 378, pencil pagination to p 636, and a separate pencil foliation of miscellaneous leaves bound at the end of the volume; ruled for consistent indentation; generally good condition with some frayed and repaired leaves; 19th-century green leather binding with scalloped metal corners, a shield-shaped escutcheon on the front cover with the legend: 'The Records of the Charters and Matters of Justice for the Town of Weymouth and Melcombe Regis,' a circular escutcheon on the back cover engraved '1646,' and a large, black letter 'B' on the spine.

WIMBORNE MINSTER

St Cuthburga's Churchwardens' Accounts

Wimborne Minster's surviving churchwardens' accounts date from the early fifteenth century, as do references to the parish ale. Many accounts for the 1550s and early 1560s are missing; those that survive were rendered on 14 December and, despite an agreement (p 160) to render accounts on the feast of St Luke the Evangelist (18 October), the accounts resume with ending dates in December in the 1560s. The accounting year ran from December to December until 1605; a blank page in CW 1/42 is followed by an account running from December 1605 until 22 April 1607 and the accounting year ended in April or May from 1607 to 1635.

Dorchester, Dorset Record Office, PE/WM: CW 1/40; 1475–1581; Latin and English; paper; iv + 249 + iv; 425mm x 295mm; modern ink pagination; headings of individual accounts often in bold and sometimes decorated; leaves repaired; modern tooled leather binding with gold decoration on the covers and the ridged spine.

Dorchester, Dorset Record Office, PE/WM: CW 1/41; 1581–1636; English; paper; ii + 267 + v; 435mm x 290mm; modern pagination; generally good condition with some pages repaired; headings in bold with elaborately decorated initials; cardboard binding with a leather spine.

Churchwardens' Presentments to the Peculiar Court

The consistory court of the peculiar and exempt jurisdiction of Wimborne Minster met under the presidency of an official appointed by the twelve governors of the parish and dealt with a great variety of legal and ecclesiastical business.[198] Most REED material occurs in the preliminary itemization of 'presentments' of miscellaneous offenders by the churchwardens and sidesmen, apparently written down hastily by someone present in court and often signed by either or both churchwardens and sidesmen. Later, usually less detailed material concerning some of the incidents presented to the court by the parish officials appears in the Act Book of the peculiar court (PE/WM: CP1/1).

Dorchester, Dorset Record Office, PE/WM: CP2/10; 1589–1714; English; paper; a bundle of documents of varying sizes, 142 of them before 1642, wrapped between sheets of cardboard. Although some documents are folded leaves or several leaves, most are single; the documents are calendared in PE/WM: CP3, where the dating is not always accurate. The present volume includes transcriptions from the following documents:

item 8: 1591–2; single sheet; 200mm x 155mm.

item 16: 12 June 1595; single sheet; 300mm x 195mm.

item 51: 23 September 1601; single sheet; 301mm x 198mm.

item 55: 1602; single sheet; 303mm x 203mm.

item 74: 28 April 1606; single sheet; 198mm x 148mm.

item 75: 26 February 1606/7; single sheet; 300mm x 196mm.

item 82: 1607–8; single sheet; 300mm x 198mm.

item 92: 1609–10; single sheet; 305mm x 198mm.

item 94: 1609–10; single sheet; 306mm x 95mm.

item 95: 1610–11; single sheet; 155mm x 150mm.

item 99: 1610–11; single sheet; 305mm x 205mm; edges torn and some of the ink has run.

item 100: 1610–11; single sheet; 165mm x 190mm.

item 93: 1611–12; bifolium; 278mm x 202mm.

Dorchester, Dorset Record Office, PE/WM: CP2/12, item 60; 1620; English; paper; single sheet; 150mm x 195mm; torn and stained on the left side. Now part of a bundle of seventy-one paper documents, 1619–40, sewn together with a cord, varying considerably in size; the documents at the back of the bundle are in poor condition.

WINTERBORNE KINGSTON

Winterborne Kingston was served by a chapel of ease belonging to the larger market centre of Bere Regis, two miles to the southwest.[199]

Churchwardens' Presentments for Salisbury Deanery

Trowbridge, Wiltshire and Swindon Record Office, D5/28/28, item 92; 3 July 1628; English; paper; bifolium; unnumbered; 305mm x 195mm; written on f [1] only; slight tear at fold. Now one of ninety-eight items, numbered in modern pencil, kept in a modern folder.

WINTERBORNE MONKTON

Casebook of Sir Francis Ashley

See Dorchester (p 62) for BL: Harley MS. 6715.

Households

STRANGWAYS OF MELBURY SAMPFORD

Giles Strangways' Account Book

Giles Strangways (1615–75) was a member of one of the most powerful families of the Dorset gentry. He served as MP for Melcombe Regis in 1640 and for Bridport in 1641, a position from which he was disabled in 1645 because of his fierce loyalty to the royalist cause. Like his father, Sir John, Giles Strangways, colonel of the horse in the army of King Charles I, suffered arrest, imprisonment in the Tower, and severe fines for his loyalty to the monarch. His personal account books indicate that, although the dominant concerns of this country gentleman were hawks, hounds, horses, and haberdashery, he also built up a library to which he added approximately 100 books and pamphlets between 1638 and 1640.

Dorchester, Dorset Record Office, D/FSI: Box 220; English; paper; iv + 82; 265mm x 180mm; foliated, original folio numbers to f 73 in top left corners, ff [74] and [75] lack folio numbers (ff 5v–11, 12v, 76–82 blank); the second flyleaf torn in half vertically; pages ruled for columns of figures along each right side; vellum binding, title on the cover: 'My Booke of Accounts for 1638: 1639 1640 1641.'

Editorial Procedures

Principles of Selection

The records of Dorset, like other collections in the REED series, gather together contemporary evidence of public performance before 1642. Neither 'public' nor 'performance' is interpreted narrowly. The public might be a crowd such as that which assembled on specially built standings for the Sherborne Corpus Christi plays or, no less significant for our purposes, a small group like that entertained by a fiddler in the Dorchester jail. Although most entries refer to performances that occurred, both records of players who were paid not to play or who were arrested for performing and records of antagonism to local customs shed light on the activities of entertainers and on the social scene in which they plied their trade, and they are included for that reason. The range of kinds of performance is also broad, including not only plays, puppet shows, pageants, music, singing, dancing, juggling, fooling, singular exhibitions such as that of 'the portraiture of the city of Ierusalem' (see p 207) and undefined 'feates of actiuity' (see p 223), but also the observance of folk customs and civic ceremonies with maypoles, summer poles, a jack-a-lent, a boy bishop's gear, bullbaiting, racing, a Robin Hood, or a local 'king.'

The category of civic ceremonies also includes civic ales, processions, and local rituals if, on at least one occasion, they included mimetic or musical elements; in such cases all references, even those that do not make explicit the role-playing or music, have been transcribed. Historians have made the Cobb ale of Lyme Regis central to the cultural life of the town but none of the records of that civic ale establishes that performances by dancers, musicians, amateur actors, or professional ones contributed to the festivities. Given the special status of the Cobb ale, records of it have been included as Appendix 3.

In accordance with REED's normal principles of selection, we have excluded performative aspects of liturgies (repairs to musical instruments for use in church and provisions or stipends for singing boys or men there) and ritualistic practices of boroughs: musters, feasts, perambulations of civic boundaries, and bell-ringing. Since the Sherborne Corpus Christi play of the 1540s seems a direct replacement of the pre-Reformation All Hallows' Corpus Christi procession, and it is possible that features of the procession anticipated the more elaborate play in St Mary's, Sherborne, we have, however, printed the references to the Sherborne All Hallows' Corpus Christi procession, last recorded in 1538–9. The pre-Reformation Sherborne parish sometimes also paid for tents on Corpus Christi, probably for use in non-liturgical celebration, additional evidence that Sherborne's earlier practice may have prefigured customs surrounding the parish-sponsored drama of the 1540s.

The materials produced by civil and ecclesiastical courts complicate the meaning of 'play' and 'players' by using these words to refer respectively to illicit games and those engaged in them. The documents sometimes make explicit what such players were playing: handball, tennis, bowls, kayles, fives, cards, and, most often, dice. Unlike performances involving animals (such as the Blandford Forum horse race), such games of athletic skill and such games of chance have not been included.

Normally only the item relevant to performance or performers has been transcribed. For the Dorset records this is the norm because financial records have proven to be the richest source of relevant information and the accountants rarely made explicit connections among the items in their lists of debits and credits. Although, for example, one mayor of Lyme Regis registered the expenditure for reglazing windows immediately after the reward given to a troupe of travelling players, we cannot conclude simply on the basis of the juxtaposition of items in an account that the performers or the audience broke the windows. Similarly, private diaries, official memoranda, and casebooks present material in discrete bits, which we have transcribed as such. For other legal documents we have transcribed the reference(s) to performers or performance in the context of the case. Faced with lengthy Star Chamber cases, for instance, we have transcribed in extenso all passages referring to plays, players, singers, and allegedly libellous songs. Beyond that we have included the bill of complaint, the defendant's answer, exhibits, and excerpts from interrogatories and examinations corresponding thereto so as to put the performance in historical context.

The character of any REED volume is determined in part by the survival of certain kinds of records and the loss of other ones. Unlike Somerset, Dorset lacks extensive quarter sessions records to establish the activity of certain kinds of performers and their circuits within the county. The records of ecclesiastical visitations are limited to the peculiar jurisdictions of Wimborne Minster and that of the dean of Salisbury. For some boroughs for which one would hope to have early records – most notably Wareham, a thriving town in the early modern period – none is extant. It should also be noted that two classes of records have not been searched exhaustively: records of the court of Star Chamber and seventeenth-century diocesan records. Of the former, what appears in this volume is the result of a carefully delimited exploration of the records of the court for their potential relevance to the interests of REED. Only the most accessible cases (those of the reign of King James I), and of those only the ones judged likeliest to include relevant material (cases of defamation, riot, unlawful assembly, and offences against religion), were read. Of the latter, the ecclesiastical court records, churchwardens' presentments were searched entirely but act books, deposition books, and citations were only sampled because preliminary work on them turned up no relevant material beyond that known from the presentments. Otherwise we have tried to live up to the REED ideal to search exhaustively all the manuscripts and printed sources of information about Dorset before 1642. While, like others doing this kind of work, we look forward to the discovery of new materials, we hope, having done this work, that we have not missed too many.

Dating

Documents are dated as precisely as possible, preferably on the basis of evidence in the documents themselves. Dates deduced from information external to a particular document are discussed in the endnotes and undated records are collected in Appendix 1 and cross-referenced by endnotes and the index. When the date is given by regnal year or by reference to the term of a civic official, it has been translated in the heading into a calendar date. However, one aspect of the early modern calendar – the beginning of a new year on Lady Day (25 March) – is acknowledged, indirectly at least: a 'split' year date, 1588/9 for example, is used for an event that occurred between 1 January to 24 March of a year. Most financial records cover an accounting year that went from Michaelmas in one year to Michaelmas in the next.

Entries taken from such accounts are identified in the heading by a double-year, such as 1558–9. Subheadings supply the limits of an accounting year which does not extend from Michaelmas to Michaelmas. Occasionally documents include even more precise information about the date of an entry; when this occurs that date has been transcribed as part of the Records text. Often, however, that more precise information specifies when a payment was made rather than when a performance took place. We have followed a similar procedure in dealing with court records, which are put under the date of the session. Subheadings to these records supply dates of hearings and the Records themselves include specific information about the date of performance if that information appears in the document. See 'The Documents' (pp 48–86) for more specific descriptions of the character of the records, the accounting year of particular boroughs, and gaps in the extant materials.

Although the terminus ad quem of REED volumes is 1642, a few later documents which are especially illuminating in their additional detail and/or establish the survival of a form of entertainment have been included in Appendix 2.

Edited Text

The layout of the edited text approximates as far as practicable the format of the original documents. The paragraphing of the manuscripts has been retained but the lineation has not been kept in prose passages. Left marginalia appear as such. Right marginalia, identified by the symbol ®, have been moved to the left margin. Interlineations above the line are set off with upper half brackets (⌈ ⌉), and the caret that normally signals such additions is retained in the printed text. Square brackets ([ ]) enclose cancelled matter. Diamond brackets (⟨ ⟩) mark places where a manuscript is damaged. Where the damage makes the text altogether illegible, dots are used to suggest the extent of the textual loss; a single dot within the diamond brackets indicates the likely loss of one letter; two dots, two letters; three dots, three or more letters. With one exception all forms of scribal errors appear in the text, with proposed corrections in footnotes. The exception is the use of too few or too many minims in a word; in these cases the printed text has been corrected and the scribal error noted. A change in the hand within a manuscript has been indicated by two raised circles (° °). Where a scribe has left space for words to be added later this is indicated by *(blank)*. When the work of more than two scribes is evident in a manuscript, a note discusses the character and extent of their shares. Manuscript braces, line fillers, and otiose flourishes have as a rule not been reproduced; however, manuscript braces are preserved where it seems advisable for sense both in accounts and in other sorts of texts. When a brace was used to mark a list of receipts or expenditures for which a sum total is given, the sum total appears flush right following the last item in the list. Except in abbreviations for numerals, superior letters have been silently lowered.

The printed text of the long Star Chamber case (see pp 173–98) follows these guidelines concerning format for the individual membranes relevant to the case. However, the order in which the membranes have been sewn together is not reproduced. Instead, the material is set forth in accordance with the sequence of steps by which the court conducted its business: the charge brought by the plaintiff, the defendant's answer, the interrogatories, the several answers to the interrogatories. The decision of the court in this case, were it available, would complete the business. The headings and the endnotes indicate the original arrangement of the documents.

In transcribing the documents, the original spelling, capitalization, word division, and punctuation have been retained. In transcribing original manuscript sources, capital 'I' and 'J' are not distinguished; only 'I' is used, as 'ff' is for 'F.' A thorn has been set as such in documents in which the scribe distinguishes between it and 'y'; otherwise this alternative spelling of 'th' appears as 'y.' Sometimes it is not clear whether an initial letter was intended to be upper-case or lower-case; when such ambiguity exists, the letter has been rendered as lower-case. In instances of ambiguous word division, we have followed the precedents within the document. In documents that are inconsistent in their usage, words that are not clearly conjoined or divided are transcribed as two words. Manuscript virgules have been printed as / and //. The abbreviations 'Xpi' and 'xpi' have been expanded as 'Chr*isti*' or 'chr*isti*.'

Normally scribal abbreviations have been expanded and set in italics, which are used for this purpose only. Hence, the transcriptions do not reproduce the use of italics in manuscripts written in secretary hand or those used for proper nouns or key words in early printed sources. A few types of abbreviations – those for measures and sums of money (such as 'li.,' 'l.,' 'd.,' 'ob.,' and 'di.') and those still current (such as 'Mr,' 'viz.,' '&c.') – have not been expanded. Likewise, in the case of words which have been abbreviated in ways that leave the number or the case of the word ambiguous, the abbreviation has not been expanded; instead, it is indicated by an apostrophe.

A note on the Dorchester Borough Court Book (DRO: DC/DOB: 8/1) is in order because of the difficulty in transcribing the court hand. Words are often abbreviated but not systematically so that it is often impossible to decipher a word letter by letter. To set forth a readable text we have decided not to set every illegible letter in diamond brackets but to transcribe the documents as if every letter were visible and discrete. Footnotes or diamond brackets mark substantive gaps.

Notes

1 For the relationship of Dorset to medieval road systems see the maps in Brian Paul Hindle, 'Roads and Tracks,' *The English Medieval Landscape*, Leonard Cantor (ed) (London and Philadelphia, 1982), 193–217, and in John Ogilby, *Britannia, Volume the First: or, An Illustration of the Kingdom of England and Dominion of Wales: By a Geographical and Historical Description of the Principal Roads Thereof* (London, 1675). For details of the physical description of Dorset see Taylor, *Dorset*, particularly pp 21–4. Any description of Dorset must rely on Hutchins, *History and Antiquities*, and on numerous articles in the *Proceedings of the Dorset Natural History and Antiquarian Field Club* (*PDNHAFC*; continued as the *Proceedings of the Dorset Natural History and Archaeological Society* (*PDNHAS*)). Underdown, *Revel*, is particularly helpful in relating the county's physical characteristics to patterns of agriculture in the sixteenth and seventeenth centuries. See also *VCH: Dorset*, vol 2.

2 Barbara Kerr, *Bound to the Soil: A Social History of Dorset, 1750–1918* (London, 1968), 8–9.

3 Michael Williams, 'Marshland and Waste,' *The English Medieval Landscape*, Leonard Cantor (ed), p 93; Bettey, *Dorset*, pp 39, 41–3; Taylor, *Dorset*, pp 84–101.

4 Hindle, 'Roads and Tracks,' pp 200–1; Bettey, *Dorset*, pp 33–8; Bettey, *Wessex*, pp 29–30, 32–3.

5 *VCH: Dorset*, vol 2, pp 5, 29; David M. Smith, *Guide to Bishops' Registers of England and Wales* (London, 1981), 40, 188. For an introduction to the history of the larger religious houses see *VCH: Dorset*, vol 2, pp 47–90 and 107–13. There are lengthier histories of such houses as Milton Abbas and the college of secular canons at Wimborne Minster; see Clegg, *History of Dorchester*; J.P. Traskey, *Milton Abbey: A Dorset Monastery in the Middle Ages* (Tisbury, 1978); and Patricia H. Coulstock, *The Collegiate Church of Wimborne Minster* (Woodbridge, 1993).

6 Bettey avoids the always vexing question of when a town did or did not have borough status. See *Dorset*, p 63 and *Wessex*, pp 23, 49. Borough status and other technical questions are dealt with in Penn, *Historic Towns*.

7 Taylor, *Dorset*, pp 110–18; Bettey, *Wessex*, p 111; Leonard Cantor, 'Introduction: The English Medieval Landscape,' *The English Medieval Landscape*, Leonard Cantor (ed), pp 21–3.

8 Gerard, *Survey of Dorsetshire*, pp 3–4.

9 Gerard, *Survey of Dorsetshire*, pp 6–7.

10   On local gentry see J.P. Ferris, 'The Gentry of Dorset on the Eve of the Civil War,' *Genealogists' Magazine* 15 (1965), 104–16, particularly p 4; cited in Underdown, *Revel,* p 122; Taylor, *Dorset,* pp 135–40; for examples of immigration to a Dorset town in the late sixteenth century see Underdown, *Fire from Heaven,* pp 41–4. For Dorset's lack of provincialism see Underdown, *Fire from Heaven,* pp 168–75.

11   J.H. Bettey, 'The Marketing of Agricultural Produce in Dorset during the Seventeenth Century,' *PDNHAS* 99 (1977), 1; J.H. Bettey, 'Markets and Fairs in Seventeenth Century Dorset,' *SDNQ* 30 (1974–9), 203–4; for the importance of the fair at Woodbury Hill see also Bettey, *Wessex,* pp 148–9.

12   Bettey, *Dorset,* pp 45–52; Taylor, *Dorset,* pp 126–35; Joan Thirsk, *The Rural Economy of England* (London, 1984), 206; Underdown, *Revel,* pp 107–12. There were some deserted villages: see J.H. Bettey, 'Economic Pressures and Village Desertions in South Dorset,' *SDNQ* 33 (1991–5), 3–6.

13   B.E. Supple, *Commercial Crisis and Change in England, 1600–1642: A Study in the Instability of a Mercantile Economy* (Cambridge, 1964), 5; Joan Thirsk, *Economic Policy and Projects: The Development of a Consumer Society in Early Modern England* (Oxford, 1978), 28, 74; J.H. Bettey, 'Cloth Production in Dorset 1570–1670,' *SDNQ* 31 (1980–5), 209–11; J.H. Bettey, 'The Dorset Wool and Cloth Industry,' *SDNQ* 29 (1968–73), 240–2; Bettey, *Dorset,* pp 74–5; Thirsk, *Rural Economy,* p 210; Bettey, *Wessex,* pp 137–8 and 146; Gillian T. Cell, *English Enterprise in Newfoundland 1577–1660* (Toronto, 1969), 136–44.

14   For a general overview of Dorset's maritime history see M. Oppenheim, 'Maritime History' in *VCH: Dorset,* vol 2, pp 175–228; for Dorset pirates see C. L'Estrange Ewen, 'The Pirates of Purbeck,' *PDNHAS* 7 (1949), 88–109, and Lloyd, *Dorset Elizabethans,* chapter 1; for more sophisticated accounts of Dorset's participation in maritime enterprise and privateering see Kenneth R. Andrews, *Elizabethan Privateering: English Privateering during the Spanish War 1585–1603* (Cambridge, 1964), 252–4, 269–70, and *Trade Plunder and Settlement: Maritime Enterprise and the Genesis of the British Empire, 1480–1630* (Cambridge, 1984), 21, 251.

15   Bettey, *Wessex,* pp 104–7; Taylor, *Dorset,* pp 121–2; Bettey, *Dorset,* pp 98–102.

16   Julian Cornwall, *Revolt of the Peasantry 1549* (London, 1977), 99–103, 115, 121, 178.

17   Lloyd (*Dorset Elizabethans,* chapter 2) discusses the careers of many Dorset Catholics, particularly the Arundells of Chideock and of Wardour Castle; Underdown, *Revel,* p 89; *VCH: Dorset,* vol 2, pp 23–37; J.H. Bettey points out that several Dorset parishes reported unfavourably on the Puritan sentiments of parish clergy. See Bettey, 'Dorset Churchwardens' Presentments: Early 17th Century,' *SDNQ* 29 (1968–73), 263–5 and 'Varieties of Men.'

18   Underdown, *Revel,* p 8. Underdown's analysis draws on national as well as west country evidence and much of his discussion necessarily lies outside the concerns of this volume. His analysis of cultural conflicts, however, relies partly on interpretations of records (from Wiltshire and Somerset as well as Dorset) like those transcribed in this volume.

19   Underdown, *Revel,* p 48.

20   Underdown, *Revel,* p 72.

21   Underdown, *Revel,* pp 103–4.

22   Hutton, *Rise and Fall,* pp 161–4.

23   Stokes with Alexander (eds), *Somerset Including Bath,* vol 2, pp 614–15 n 4.

24   Hutton, *Rise and Fall,* p 163. See Martin Ingram, *Church Courts, Sex and Marriage in England* (Cambridge, 1987), cited by Hutton, *Rise and Fall,* p 162.

25   Underdown, *Revel,* pp 91–2.

26   Underdown, *Revel,* p 92, map iv.

27   Hutton, *Rise and Fall,* pp 163, 198. Hutton vividly depicts the presence or relative absence of national patterns for the rise and decline of customs related to the ritual year from the fifteenth through the seventeenth century. For the rise of church ales, hocktide celebrations, Robin Hood plays, and morris dancing in the fifteenth century, for example, see pp 59– 67; in a tightly reasoned argument, pp 121–52, Hutton concludes that for an Elizabethan decline in festivities, of 'paramount importance' was evangelical Protestantism, not royal or ecclesiastical policy. Hutton's model is, it must be stressed, a national one, in contrast to Underdown's west country model. Hutton's suggestion that late Elizabethan quarrels about revels may depend predominantly on local developments is consistent with the Dorset evidence. But Dorset performance records are too thin or too ambiguous in the early Stuart period to allow us direct comment on Hutton's conclusions.

28   Gerard, *Survey of Dorsetshire,* p 105.

29   William Smith, *The Particular Description of England. 1588. With Views of Some of the Chief Towns and Armorial Bearings of Nobles and Bishops,* Henry B. Wheatley and Edmund W. Ashbee (eds) (London, 1879), 69.

30   Hutchins, *History and Antiquities,* vol 1, pp 216–18; Cox, *Book of Blandford Forum,* p 19.

31   vch: *Dorset,* vol 2, p 139; Cox, *Book of Blandford Forum,* p 21.

32   Weinstock, 'Blandford,' pp 118–22; Cox, *Book of Blandford Forum,* p 39; Hutchins, *History and Antiquities,* vol 1, pp 242–3.

33   dro: DC/BFB: Finance: Chamberlains' Accounts f B11v; Tittler, 'Building of Civic Halls,' pp 38, 42; William Camden, *Britain, or a Chorographicall Description of the Most Flourishing Kingdomes, England, Scotland, and Ireland, and the Ilands Adioyning, out of the Depth of Antiquitie,* trans by Philemon Holland and ed by William Camden (London, 1610; stc: 4509), 215.

34   Hutchins, *History and Antiquities,* vol 1, p 215; Weinstock, 'Blandford,' pp 121–2.

35   Janice Pahl, 'The Rope and Net Industry of Bridport: Some Aspects of Its History and Geography,' pdnhas 82 (1961 for 1960), 143–54, especially pp 144–6; Basil Short and John Sales, *The Book of Bridport* (Buckingham, 1980), 74; Bettey, *Wessex,* p 140.

36   G.W. Hannah, 'The Evolution of Bridport Harbour,' pdnhas 108 (1987 for 1986), 27–31.

37   Pahl, 'Rope and Net,' p 144.

38   *Hycke Scorner,* cited in vch: *Dorset,* vol 2, p 347. See also Ian Lancashire (ed), *Two Tudor Interludes: Youth and Hick Scorner* (Manchester, 1980), 178, l. 243.

39   Pahl, 'Rope and Net,' p 146.

40   Bodl.: ms. Top. gen. e. 10 f 44v.

41   Quoted in Short, *A Respectable Society*, p 1; in 1610, Camden, after praising Bridport's hemp and rope making skill, stated 'Neither is this place able to maintaine the name of an haven, albeit in the mouth of the river being on both sides enclosed within little hilles, nature seemes as it were of purpose to have begun an haven, and requireth in some sort art and mans helpe to accomplish the same' (*Britain*, p 210).

42   Tittler, 'Building of Civic Halls,' pp 38, 44–5.

43   Underdown, *Revel*, pp 54, 166.

44   Bettey, *Wessex*, p 24; Bettey, *Dorset*, p 38.

45   J.S. Roskell, *The House of Commons 1386–1421*, The History of Parliament, vol 1 (Stroud, 1992), 369; Smith, *Particular Description*, p 69; Ogilby, *Britannia*, plate 60; *VCH: Dorset*, vol 2, p 139.

46   Penn, *Historic Towns*, p 61.

47   Taylor, *Dorset*, p 199.

48   Hutchins, *History and Antiquities*, vol 2, p 339.

49   Camden, *Britain*, p 212.

50   Our account of late sixteenth- and seventeenth-century Dorchester relies heavily on Underdown, *Fire from Heaven*. Underdown's brief survey of Dorchester's sixteenth-century economy and Dorchester's response to the problems of poverty is on pp 10–12.

51   Gerard, *Survey of Dorsetshire*, p 69.

52   Underdown, *Fire from Heaven*, pp 8–10 and 22–4; Penn, *Historic Towns*, pp 62–3.

53   Underdown, *Fire from Heaven*, chapters 2–5.

54   'A Catalogue of ye Bookes in ye Library of Dorchester with ye Giuers, taken in ye yeare, 1631' (DRO: DC/DOB: 28/1).

55   Ann Natalie Hansen, *The Dorchester Group: Puritanism and Revolution* (Columbus, Ohio, 1987), 15–34.

56   Cecil N. Cullingford, *A History of Dorset* (London, 1980), 61; Underdown, *Revel*, p 128; for Dorchester's reaction to national policies in general and as they specifically affected the town, see Underdown, *Fire from Heaven*, chapter 6.

57   Bodl.: MS Top. gen. e. 10 f 43v. For the history of Lyme Regis see Fowles, *Short History of Lyme Regis*, and Wanklyn, *Lyme Regis: A Retrospect*. A great deal of the information in Roberts, *Social History*, derives from Lyme Regis records.

58   Gerard, *Survey of Dorsetshire*, p 11.

59   Penn, *Historic Towns*, p 72.

60   Quoted in Bettey, *Wessex*, p 113; See also Hannah, 'Evolution of Bridport Harbour,' p 28; Thomas Cox, 'Dorsetshire,' from *Magna Britannia et Hibernia*, vol 1 (London, 1720–31), 548–604.

61   Bettey, *Wessex*, pp 119–20.

62   Bodl.: MS. Top. gen. e. 10 f 43v.

63   Penn, *Historic Towns*, p 73.

64   Andrews, *Elizabethan Privateering*, pp 32–3 and p 33, Table 2, n 2; Lloyd, *Dorset Elizabethans*, pp 57–9.

65   Stephens, 'Trade Fortunes,' pp 71–3.

66 Fowles, *Short History of Lyme Regis*, p 15.

67 *VCH: Dorset*, vol 2, p 211.

68 The visitor was probably named Hammond. See 'A Relation of a Short Survey of the Western Counties: Made by a Lieutenant of the Military Company in Norwich in 1635,' L.G. Wickham Legg (ed), *Camden Miscellany* 16, Camden Society, 3rd series, vol 52 (1936), iii, 73, quoted in Stephens, 'Trade Fortunes,' p 71.

69 Stephens, 'Trade Fortunes,' p 73; Fowles says Lyme's economic fortunes were at their height in the sixteenth and seventeenth centuries (*Short History of Lyme Regis*, pp 15–19).

70 Tittler, 'Building of Civic Halls,' pp 38, 42.

71 DRO: DC/LR: D1/1 (Order Book) p 29.

72 DRO: DC/LR: B1/8 (Court Book 1613–17) pp 51–4.

73 Roberts, *Social History*, pp 240 and 343–4; Fowles, *Short History of Lyme Regis*, pp 19–20; Bettey, *Dorset*, p 102, and 'Varieties of Men,' p 847.

74 Bodl.: MS. Top. gen. e. 10 f 52v.

75 Bettey, *Dorset*, p 67.

76 Cullingford, *Poole*, pp 35–6. For Poole's history see also Smith, *History of Poole*; Sydenham, *History of the Town and County of Poole*; Bernard C. Short, *Poole: The Romance of Its Early History*, 2nd ed (Poole, 1945). According to the DNB Longespee has often been called the earl of Salisbury although he never actually held the title.

77 *VCH: Dorset*, vol 2, p 139; Cullingford, *Poole*, pp 46–7; W.R. Childs, 'Channel Island Shipping as Recorded in the English Customs Accounts, 1300–1500,' *A People of the Sea: The Maritime History of the Channel Islands*, A.G. Jamieson (ed) (London and New York, 1986), 44–58. Childs points out that Channel Islands trade represented 17 to 34 per cent of late fifteenth-century Poole's shipping, carrying 34 to 63 per cent of Poole's imports and over 40 per cent of the town's cloth exports, 1465–8 (p 47). See also Hutchins, *History and Antiquities*, vol 1, p 20.

78 Bodl.: MS. Top. gen. e. 10 ff 53v, 52v. The early sixteenth-century town records suggest an active and growing municipality; Leland's informants may have been very old.

79 Smith, *History of Poole*, vol 2, p 94.

80 Smith, *History of Poole*, vol 2, pp 87–92.

81 Tittler, 'Vitality,' p 95.

82 Tittler, 'Vitality,' pp 96–107. Southampton had granted trading concessions to the Channel Islands in 1515 and Island trade was to shift from Poole to Southampton during the course of the sixteenth century; J.C. Appleby, 'Neutrality, Trade and Privateering, 1500–1689,' *A People of the Sea*, pp 59–105, particularly pp 79–84.

83 Tittler,' Vitality,' p 107. Some of the town's financial chaos can be seen in the attempt by Mayor John Hancoke to clean up town records and town finance recorded in Hancoke's difficult script in DRO: DC/PL: CLA P26; there are many instances in late Elizabethan records of auditors disallowing expenses incurred by earlier town officials.

84 DRO: DC/PL: CLA P25 f 28; Cell, *English Enterprise in Newfoundland*, p 102.

85 Stephens, 'Trade Fortunes,' p 71.

86 T.S. Willan, *The English Coasting Trade: 1600–1750* (Manchester, 1938), 155–6.

87   Supple, *Commercial Crisis and Change*, pp 55–7.

88   Gerard, *Survey of Dorsetshire*, p 85.

89   Hancock's autobiography, quoted by Hutchins, *History and Antiquities*, vol 1, p 53; Underdown, *Revel*, p 147.

90   Histories of Shaftesbury include Laura Sydenham, *Shaftesbury and Its Abbey*; John Rutter, *An Historical and Descriptive Account of the Town of Shaftesbury* (np, 1827); Bowles, *Shaftesbury Corporation*; and Mayo, *Municipal Records of the Borough of Shaftesbury*.

91   Bettey, *Wessex*, pp 23–5; Bettey, *Dorset*, p 38.

92   Penn, *Historic Towns*, p 88.

93   Bettey, 'Marketing,' p 2; Hutchins, *History and Antiquities*, vol 3, pp 7–8; Mayo, *Municipal Records of the Borough of Shaftesbury*, pp 57–8.

94   Bettey, *Wessex*, p 147; see Bettey's fuller description of Shaftesbury's market in 'Markets and Fairs in Seventeenth Century Dorset,' *SDNQ* 30 (1974–9), 203–6.

95   Underdown, *Revel*, p 37, cites J.H. Bettey, 'Agriculture and Rural Society in Dorset, 1570–1670,' PhD thesis (University of Bristol, 1977), 348–50; for Shaftesbury's inns and alehouses see Bettey, *Wessex*, p 147. See also Bettey, 'Markets and Fairs,' p 206.

96   F. J. Pope, 'Puritans at Shaftesbury in the Early Stuart Period,' *SDNQ* 13 (1912–13), 160–2; Underdown, *Revel*, pp 89, 196.

97   Tittler, 'Building of Civic Halls,' p 38.

98   For a detailed history of Sherborne, including detailed summaries of many Sherborne sources see Fowler, *Mediaeval Sherborne*.

99   Gerard, *Survey of Dorsetshire*, p 122.

100 Fowler (*Mediaeval Sherborne*, pp 164–7) argues from documentary evidence that All Hallows' dates from about 1300; it is assigned to about 1400 by Newman and Pevsner in *Dorset*, p 370.

101 Fowler, *Mediaeval Sherborne*, p 88.

102 *VCH: Dorset*, vol 2, p 67; Fowler, *Mediaeval Sherborne*, pp 264–6. Fowler mistakenly gives the date of the abbey fire as 1437 but see P.N. Dawe, 'Sherborne Almshouse Building Accounts, 1440–1444,' *SDNQ* 29 (1968–73), 74–8; Richard Rochell, the accountant who managed the building of the almshouse and served as its first master, had also served as All Hallows' churchwarden (Fowler, *Mediaeval Sherborne*, p 235).

103 Fowler, *Mediaeval Sherborne*, pp 231–58; the subservice of Sherborne to its ecclesiastical lords in comparison to the relative autonomy of other Dorset towns is stressed by Madeleine C. Fripp and Phyllis Wragge in *VCH: Dorset*, vol 2, p 245.

104 Fowler (ed), 'Post-Reformation Churchwardens' Accounts,' *SDNQ* 24, pp 285–8.

105 Fowler, *Mediaeval Sherborne*, pp 319–21.

106 J.J. Scarisbrick, *The Reformation and the English People* (Oxford, 1984), 103–4.

107 Fowler, *Mediaeval Sherborne*, pp 321–5.

108 Bettey, *Dorset*, p 101; Underdown, *Fire from Heaven*, p 229.

109 Fowler, *Mediaeval Sherborne*, pp 342–7; for the early history of the school see Nicholas Orme, *Education in the West of England: 1066–1548* (Exeter, 1976), 15, 103–4; some indication of the links between pre-Reformation parish and school may be seen in the

fact that Pancras Grout seems to have served as both schoolmaster and parish organist in the 1520s, according to N. Orme, 'Two Tudor Schoolmaster-Musicians,' *SDNQ* 31 (1980–5), 19–26.

110 Fowler, *Mediaeval Sherborne*, p 404. The fair of St Thomas Becket was probably held on 7 July; Sherborne's most profitable fair was held at Michaelmas; see Fowler, *Mediaeval Sherborne*, pp 403–5. In the absence of the rights which would have belonged to an incorporated town, the roles taken by officials of Sherborne's institutions – the parish, the school, and the almshouses – are sometimes confusing. Thus, records for the street ale which succeeded the churchwardens' collection, itself the successor to the earlier church ale, were still held in Sherborne Grammar School in the 1980s, although other records relating to the street ale are in parish vestry accounts. See DRO: S.235: B1/24; S.235: C51/1; S.235: C5/2/1; and S.235: C5/2/7–9 (formerly SSL: MS A26a; MS S1; MS S3; and MSS S10–12), and vestry account DRO: PE/SH: VE1.

111 Fowler, *Mediaeval Sherborne*, pp 286–93; building accounts for the church house and later records of repairs to the building, nearly continuous records of rents paid the parish for the shops on the ground floor of the building, and inventories of the contents of the upper room used as a parish hall are preserved in the numerous sixteenth-century Sherborne churchwardens' accounts.

112 Lloyd, *Dorset Elizabethans*, pp 233–92.

113 Weinstock, 'Weymouth and Melcombe Regis in Tudor and Early Stuart Times,' *More Dorset Studies*, pp 1–46, particularly pp 4–5; Taylor, *Dorset*, pp 190, 192; *VCH: Dorset*, vol 2, pp 139, 242; Hutchins, *History and Antiquities*, vol 2, p 449.

114 Weinstock, 'Weymouth and Melcombe Regis'; R.R. Sellman summarizes the history of the dispute in an essay incorporated within Weinstock's essay, pp 5–17. For seventeenth-century Weymouth government see Maureen Weinstock, 'The Government of Weymouth and Melcombe Regis during the Reign of Charles I,' *Studies in Dorset History*, pp 11–25. The salutary effects of the bridge may be seen in the changes Camden made to his brief references to Weymouth in *Britannia*: in the 1586 Latin edition he merely noted that the two towns had been joined by act of parliament but in the 1610 translation he said they had been 'conjoined of late by a bridge, and growen very much greater and goodlier in buildings by sea-aduentures than heeretofore' (p 211).

115 Cell, *English Enterprise in Newfoundland*, pp 139, 141, and 144; Andrews, *Elizabethan Privateering*, pp 32–3, 241, 252–4, and 269–70; Stephens, 'Trade Fortunes,' p 71; Weinstock, 'Weymouth Trade in the Early Seventeenth Century,' *Studies in Dorset History*, pp 26–51; for the expansion of settlement in Melcombe Regis see the excellent maps in Weinstock, 'Weymouth and Melcombe Regis.'

116 Penn, *Historic Towns*, pp 114 and 118; WM: MB.O-B pp 107, 331, for example; Bettey, *Dorset*, p 102.

117 James, *Wimborne Minster*. Other histories include Clegg, *History of Wimborne Minster*; Mayo, *History of Wimborne Minster*; for a recent history of the medieval church see Patricia H. Coulstock, *The Collegiate Church of Wimborne Minster* (Woodbridge, 1993).

118 Garry Hogg, *History, People and Places in Dorset* (Bourne End, 1976), 88.

119 James, *Wimborne Minster*, p 19.

120 For aspects of the history of the royal peculiar, particularly in the sixteenth century, see A.W. Stote-Blandy, 'The Royal Peculiar Court of Wimborne Minster,' *PDNHAS* 64 (1943 for 1942), 43–57; J.M.J. Fletcher, 'A Century of Dorset Documents,' *PDNHAS* 47 (1926), 25–50; Kaye Le Fleming, 'Notes on the Royal Peculiar of Wimborne Minster,' *PDNHAS* 62 (1941 for 1940), 50 3. The jurisdictional confusion in the parish is exemplified in the systems described by C.C. Taylor in 'Wimborne Minster,' *PDNHAS* 89 (1968 for 1967), 168–70.

121 James, *Wimborne Minster*, pp 24, 27.

122 Clegg, *History of Wimborne Minster*, pp 184–5, citing Henry VII's patent; James says St Cuthburga's fair was on 3 September but the saint's feast day was 31 August (*Wimborne Minster*, p 32).

123 Bodl.: MS. Top. gen. e. 10 f 54v.

124 For the history of the grammar school see Orme, *Education in the West of England*, pp 184–6; Clegg, *History of Wimborne Minster*, pp 75–7; James, *Wimborne Minster*, pp 38–40.

125 Coulstock, *Collegiate Church*, p 191.

126 Clegg, *History of Wimborne Minster*, pp 135–7; James, *Wimborne Minster*, pp 44–52.

127 Bodl.: MS. Top. gen. e. 10 f 45.

128 Eedle, *History of Beaminster*, pp 35–6; Bettey, 'Marketing,' p 1; Bettey, *Wessex*, pp 137, 140.

129 Bodl.: MS. Top. gen. e. 10 f 45v.

130 Penn, *Historic Towns*, p 15.

131 Lloyd, *Dorset Elizabethans*, p 87.

132 Newman and Pevsner, *Dorset*, pp 90–1; Bettey, 'Markets and Fairs,' pp 203–6; Pitfield, *Book of Bere Regis* and 'The Churchwardens' Accounts'; Hutchins, *History and Antiquities*, vol 1, p 158.

133 Hutchins, *History and Antiquities*, vol 1, p 469.

134 Newman and Pevsner, *Dorset*, p 167.

135 See P.W. Hasler, *The House of Commons 1558–1603*, vol 2 (London, 1981), 276 for Hatton's date of appointment; see also Lloyd, *Dorset Elizabethans*, p 30; Bettey, *Wessex*, p 184.

136 John C. Coldewey, 'Plays and "Play" in Early English Drama,' *Research Opportunities in Renaissance Drama* 28 (1985), 181–8.

137 Bettey (ed), *Casebook of Sir Francis Ashley*, p 31.

138 Hutton, *Rise and Fall*, pp 190–1, discusses both the support in the 1620s for the 'yearly cycle of religious ceremonial and ritualized social entertainments' and the conflict between civil and ecclesiastical authorities arising from the effort initiated in 1632 to ban church ales in Somerset and Dorset.

139 BL: Egerton MS. 784 f 96; for a published edition of this manuscript see Whiteway, *William Whiteway of Dorchester: His Diary*.

140 See Appendix 2, pp 293–6.

141 Roberts, *Social History*, pp 343–4; Wanklyn, *Lyme Regis: A Retrospect*, pp 8–9; Fowles, *Short History of Lyme Regis*, pp 19–20.

142 DRO: PE/WM: CP2/10, item 39 single sheet. In 1599–1600 two Wimborne parishioners brought the great cake into the church during a baptism. On a similar occasion in 1600–1 one Robert Allen caused 'many cakes' to be brought into the church (DRO: PE/WM: CP2/10, item 28 single sheet). See Fletcher, 'Church Cakes.'

143 The 'playing' that occurred as part of the Shaftesbury custom may have been a kind of dramatic activity; if it were, then the green can be added to the Sherborne churchyard as outdoor playing places used in Dorset. However, the 'playing' may have involved displays of athletic skills rather than the production of a play.

144 See DRO: S.235: C5/2/7 (the account of Robert Asheborne) for the account of 1592, S.235: C5/2/8 (the account of Steven Exoll) for 1593, and S.235: C5/2/9 (the account of John Lambarte) for 1594. The ale probably raised a comparable sum in 1588, when Edward Knoyle had receipts of £39 19s 10d for the ale, fairs, and markets combined (MS S3).

145 DRO: DC/BFB: Finance: Chamberlains' Accounts f B6v; other ale entries appear on ff B2–7, B10v–11v, B13–14.

146 Underdown, *Revel*, p 45.

147 William Whiteway's diary, BL: Egerton MS. 784 f 45v, notes the king's order that the conclusion of the French match be celebrated with bonfires, discharging of ordnance, and bell-ringing. For payments for ringing the bells to mark the other special occasions, see the Holy Trinity Churchwardens' Accounts, Dorchester (DRO: MS PE/DO(HT) CW 1 ff 45v, 48, 53a, 66v). Payments for ringing on Guy Fawkes Day also appear in the Churchwardens' Accounts on ff 33 (1625), 39 (1627), 42 (1628), 45v (1630), 48 (1631), 50 (1632), 52 (1633), 53a (1634), 54v (1635), 57 (1636), 59 (1637), 61 (1638), and 63 (1639); those for ringing in celebration of the proclamation, coronation, or accession of King Charles I appear on ff 31 (1624), 34 (1625), 50 (1632), 52 (1633), 53a (1634), and 66v (1640). David Underdown and David Cressy suggest that bell-ringing in Dorchester had political significance in that many of the events that were celebrated in this way were seen either as successes for Protestantism in England or in Europe or as Protestant holy days; see, respectively, *Fire from Heaven*, pp 171, 194, and *Bonfires and Bells*, pp 61, 138.

148 Presumably the representatives of Poole attended with some ceremony on this occasion because the borough bore part of the responsibility for the maintenance of Brownsea Castle, which required repairs, munitions, and guards.

149 Weymouth made six payments for drum repair, 1596–1600 (WM: Sherren MS 184 f [2v]; Sherren MS 185 ff [1v] and [2v]; and Sherren MS 186 f [2v]); Poole collected from a citizen 'for spoylinge of the drvm' in 1584–5 (see p 244).

150 DRO: PE/WM: CW 1/41 pp 35 and 43; for the Wimborne Minster players at court in 1494 see BL: Additional MS. 7099 f 13, and W.R. Streitberger, *Court Revels, 1485–1559* (Toronto, 1991), 27, 240, 428; PRO: E101/414/6 f 41.

151 DRO: DC/PL: CLA PA10 ff 13v and 14v.

152 Cressy, *Bonfires and Bells*, p 72.

153 Dennis Bond notes in his Chronology (DRO: D/BOC: Box 22 f 44) that he authorized

the firing of ordnance. The churchwardens of Holy Trinity paid for the ringing; see DRO: PE/DO(HT)/CW1 f 29.

154 One of Dorchester's registers includes in 1624–5 'George Burford barber surgeon borne in Towne and serving Mr. Iohn Burford vj yeares in Town in musick and v yeares in London with a barber surieon is generally admitted to the trade of barber surieon' (DRO: DC/DOB: 13/1 f [18v]), but it seems likely that music is here an error for physic.

155 DRO: PE/WM: CP2/8, item 32 f 1, reporting a conversation dated about the end of September 1590.

156 For provincial evidence of a similar family of players, see John C. Coldewey, 'Some Nottinghamshire Waits: Their History and Habits,' REED Newsletter 7.1 (1982), 40–9.

157 The Devon records include a reward from Plymouth to Mr Rogers' bearward 1569–70 and one from Exeter in 1582–3 to Sir Richard Rogers' man for baiting a bull. In the second of these entries, the phrase following the patron's name, the phrase 'men beinge players,' has been cancelled by the scribe. See John M. Wasson (ed), Devon, REED (Toronto, 1986), 159, 239. Bath posted a payment to 'Sir Richarde Rogers players' in the accounts of 1577–8; Stokes with Alexander (eds), Somerset Including Bath, vol 1, p 12.

158 Hays, '"Lot's Wife",' p 115

159 We are indebted here to Peter H. Greenfield, 'Tewkesbury's Parish Plays and the Southern Dramatic Tradition,' a paper presented at the Twenty-Second International Congress on Medieval Studies, Western Michigan University, Kalamazoo, May 1987.

160 An argument to this effect is developed by Hays, 'Dorset Church Houses,' pp 17–18.

161 David Harris Sacks, The Widening Gate: Bristol and the Atlantic Economy, 1450–1700, The New Historicism: Studies in Cultural Poetics 15 (Berkeley and Los Angeles, 1991), chapters 4 and 5.

162 For an extended discussion of the sixteenth-century Sherborne play, see Hays, '"Lot's Wife",' pp 99–125.

163 Ian Lancashire, 'History of a Transition: Review Article,' in Medieval and Renaissance Drama in England: An Annual Gathering of Research, Criticism, and Reviews 3 (1986), 278–9.

164 Newman and Pevsner, Dorset, pp 84–6, 89–91, 102–3, and 259; Derek Beamish, John Hillier, and H.F.V. Johnstone, Mansions and Merchants of Poole and Dorset, Poole Historical Trust, vol 1 (Poole, 1976), 161.

165 Hutchins, History and Antiquities, vol 1, p 215, and vol 3, p 228.

166 Tittler, 'Building of Civic Halls,' pp 37–45.

167 Apart from many lavish gifts to players by each of these towns, there are more explicit traces of their purposes. In 1512–13, for example, the mayor and his brethren in Poole agreed to procedures for determining town rewards to the king's 'mynstrellys or ffott men.' In 1590–1 the mayor paid the queen's players, who played with the children of the chapel, enough to bring the 11s gathered up to the respectable sum of 20s. In Weymouth, on the other hand, there seems to have been a factional dispute over whether

or not the town should sponsor frivolity; payments to players are sometimes disallowed by later town administrations; see p 277 and the endnote thereto.

168 Much of the information regarding the Sherborne and Wimborne Minster church houses appeared first in Hays, 'Dorset Church Houses.' For references to rents and repair of the early Tudor church house and the dinner vessels of the house see DRO: PE/SH: CW 1/3 mb [2] and CW 1/4 mb [3]. Many of the earliest building accounts of the 1534–5 church house are in DRO: PE/SH: CW 1/15 ff 9–16v. The parish collected 21s 4d in rent for shops, church house cellar, and kitchen in 1570–1 and 25s 4d in the 1590s, according to DRO: PE/SH: CW 1/41 mbs [1]–[2] and CW 1/65 mb [2]. C. Edward McGee explored and described the upper-storey room of the former church house in 1986; his description, repeated here, was first printed in Hays, 'Dorset Church Houses,' p 14. The room is now divided to accommodate the separate shops of the ground-floor tenants and a modern low ceiling in the upper storey creates a third-storey attic. According to Fowler (*Mediaeval Sherborne*, p 293), the conversion of the building dates to about 1700. For a photograph of the exterior of the Sherborne church house see Scott McMillin and Sally-Beth MacLean, *The Queen's Men and their Plays* (Cambridge, 1998), 76.

169 For a slightly more detailed description of the Sherborne church house inventory see Hays, 'Dorset Church Houses,' pp 14–15 and notes 12–14.

170 The rentals are recorded in the Elizabethan churchwardens' accounts. For the weddings and Ralegh's entertainment see DRO: PE/SH: CW 1/46 mb [2], CW 1/52 mb [1], CW 1/67 mb [2], and CW 1/75 mb [1].

171 See DRO: PE/WM: GN8/1/3 single sheet.

172 Almost all information about the Wimborne church house is in DRO: PE/WM: CW 1/41 and CW 1/42. Repairs to the building are also mentioned in the Wimborne school governor's accounts.

173 Hutchins, *History and Antiquities*, vol 3, p 228.

174 As is explained in the description of Blandford's documents and in the notes to Blandford records, the major manuscript reflecting the town's finances includes a 1658 copy of many earlier records, some of them duplicating entries. Thus the records for 1594–5 include copies of three separate accounts: a list of rents received by one of the stewards, specifying that three named companies paid 2s 6d; a list of moneys laid out by the same steward (that is, paid by him to the town); and a stewards' account. Each of these refers to payments from players totalling 7s 6d. If we assume that the standard fee for players hiring the hall was 2s 6d in 1594–5 and that the three accounts do not overlap, we would conclude that players hired the Blandford guildhall on nine separate occasions that year; we can be sure they did so three times. Assuming a 1590s fee of 2s 6d gives us three players' visits in 1594–5, three in 1595–6, and eight in 1598–9, in addition to the visit of 1587–8.

175 DRO: DC/BFB: Finance: Chamberlains' Accounts f B14; Hutchins, *History and Antiquities*, vol 1, pp 215–16.

176 Tittler, 'Building of Civic Halls,' p 42.

177   The identification of this woman is based on the records of her performance in Norwich in July of 1633; see David Galloway (ed), *Norwich 1540–1642*, REED (Toronto, 1984), 211.

178   Mary A. Blackstone, 'Patrons and Elizabethan Dramatic Companies,' *Elizabethan Theatre* 10 (1988), 118.

179   Unfortunately no Dorset civic ordinances prescribing the conditions of performance survive as they do for Gloucester; see Peter H. Greenfield, 'Professional Players at Gloucester: Conditions of Provincial Performing,' *Elizabethan Theatre* 10 (1988), 77–80.

180   See Hays, 'Dorset Church Houses,' pp 16–18 and notes 31–7.

181   Weinstock, 'Blandford in Elizabethan and Stuart Times,' pp 118–19.

182   For Poole see p 243; for Barnstaple and Plymouth, Wasson (ed), *Devon*, pp 44 and 241; for Gloucester, Greenfield and Douglas (eds), *Cumberland/Westmorland/Gloucestershire*, p 301; for Bristol, Pilkinton (ed), *Bristol*, p 79; and for Beverley, Beverley Guild Hall: Governors' Minute Book 3 f 36. We are grateful to Diana Wyatt, editor of the Beverley collection in the REED series, for information about the original records of that borough.

183   For Bath, see Stokes with Alexander (eds), *Somerset Including Bath*, vol 1, p 12; for Lyme Regis, p 214; for Gloucester, Greenfield and Douglas (eds), *Cumberland/Westmorland/Gloucestershire*, p 305.

184   For Canterbury, see Canterbury Cathedral Archives (CCA): CA/FA 17 f 70v; for Faversham, Centre for Kentish Studies, Maidstone (CKSM): FA/FAc 1/2 mb 13; for Lydd, Lydd Town Archives: Ly/FAc3 p 183; for Rye, East Sussex Record Office (ESRO): Rye 60/8 (Chamberlains' Accounts) f 164; for Poole, p 243; for Dartmouth, Wasson (ed), *Devon*, p 67. None of the Kent records assigns performances by Leicester's men to the spring or early summer; however, they likely played there at that time, given the evidence of the troupe's westward movement from Poole to Dartmouth and given the hasty retreat that would have been necessary to return from Devon for a series of performances in Kent prior to Michaelmas, the end of the accounting year for Canterbury, Faversham, Lydd, and Rye. For references to travelling players in Kent and Sussex we are indebted to James Gibson, editor of the Kent: Diocese of Canterbury collection and to Cameron Louis, editor of the Sussex collection, both in the REED series. We are grateful for their permission to use the materials they have deposited at the REED office and to cite the sources of information about players in Kent and Sussex as they have established them.

185   For Dartmouth, see Wasson (ed), *Devon*, p 68; for Winchester, Murray, *English Dramatic Companies*, vol 2, p 406; for Dover, CKSM: Dover Chamberlains' Accounts 1581–1603, f 402; for Plymouth, Wasson (ed), *Devon*, p 257; for Sherborne, p 272; for Reading, BRO: R/FCa 2/81 f 4; for Faversham, CKSM: FA/Fac 28 mb 3; and for Lydd, Lydd Town Archives: Ly/FAc 7 p 217. We are grateful to Alexandra F. Johnston, editor of the Berkshire collection in the REED series, for permission to use her work on the Berkshire records both to track the routes of travelling players and to identify the original manuscript sources of the documents.

186   For Bristol, see Pilkinton (ed), *Bristol*, pp 75 (for 1567) and 76 (for 1569); for Plymouth, Wasson (ed), *Devon*, p 238; for Lyme Regis, p 213; for Winchester, Murray, *English Dramatic Companies*, vol 2, p 404; for Dover, CKSM: Dover Chamberlains' Accounts

1558–81, f 305; for Canterbury, CCA: CA/FA 17 f 27v; for Folkestone, J.O. Halliwell-Phillipps, Literary Scrapbook Fol. W.b. 174, p 10; for Fordwich, CCA: Fordwich, Bundle 8, no. 37 (Chamberlains' Accounts) f 2v; for Ipswich, E.K. Chambers (ed), 'Players at Ipswich,' *Collections*, vol 2, part 3, Malone Society (Oxford, 1931), 266; for Nottingham, Nottingham Chamberlains' Accounts, Nottinghamshire Record Office: CA 1611 f 3v; for Gloucester, Greenfield and Douglas (eds), *Cumberland/Westmorland/Gloucestershire*, p 301; and for Bath, Stokes with Alexander (eds), *Somerset Including Bath*, vol 1, p 10. We are grateful to John Coldewey, editor of the Nottinghamshire collection in the REED series, for permission to cite his research findings for Nottingham.

187 Hutton, *Rise and Fall*, p 163, notes the widespread anxiety about disorder and the ease with which other concerns, such as those about traditional forms of civic celebration, attached themselves to that anxiety.

188 For the disputes between Chubbe and Condytt, see PRO: STAC 8/94/17 and STAC 8/104/10. Excerpts from the former are printed among the records of Dorchester 1608. The latter case alludes to the former one, as John Condytt accuses Matthew Chubbe of prosecuting him in order to get even with Condytt and his wife for their earlier libel suit.

189 DRO: DC/LR: D1/1 (The Old Book of Orders 1594–1671) p 63.

190 DRO: DC/LR: D1/1 (The Old Book of Orders 1594–1671) p 42.

191 Galloway (ed), *Norwich*, p 219.

192 For Cerne Abbas after the Dissolution see Penn, *Historic Towns*, p 30; VCH: *Dorset*, vol 2, pp 54–5; Bettey, 'Dissolution and After,' pp 43–53; G.D. Squibb, 'Cerne Abbas in 1617,' *SDNQ* 28 (1961–7), 4–5; Bettey, *Dorset*, 128; Bettey, *Wessex*, p 133; Gibbons, *Cerne Abbas: Notes and Speculations*.

193 See C. Edward McGee, 'Stuart Kings and Cambridge University Drama: Two Stories by William Whiteway,' *Notes and Queries* 233 (1988), 494–6 and '"Strangest consequence",' pp 311–44.

194 See Murphy, 'Diary,' Appendix 2, and pp xxv, xxx, xliii, and xlv.

195 Hutchins, *History and Antiquities*, vol 2, p 791.

196 Lloyd, *Dorset Elizabethans*, chapter 4; Hutchins, *History and Antiquities*, vol 3, pp 594–5.

197 Hutchins, *History and Antiquities*, vol 4, p 336.

198 See A.W. Stote-Blandy, 'The Royal Peculiar Court of Wimborne Minster,' *PDNHAS* 64 (1943), 43–57.

199 Hutchins, *History and Antiquities*, vol 1, p 146.

Select Bibliography

The Select Bibliography includes books and articles that contain transcriptions of primary documents relevant to this collection as well as reference works that are essential for a study of the county. No attempt has been made to list all works in the Introduction and Endnotes.

Adams, Victor J. 'When "The Players" Came to Blandford,' *The Dorset Year Book* (1975–6), 25–30.
– 'When the Players Came to Bridport,' *The Dorset Year Book* (1977), 61–6.
– 'When the Players Came to Poole,' *The Dorset Year Book* (1978), 129–35.
Barnes, Miles W. 'The Diary of William Whiteway, of Dorchester, Co. Dorset, from November, 1618, to March, 1634,' *PDNHAS* 13 (1892), 57–81.
Bates, E.H. (ed). *Quarter Sessions Records for the County of Somerset*. Vol 1, *James I, 1607–1625*. Somerset Record Society, vol 23 (1907).
Bettey, J.H. *Dorset* (Newton Abbot, Devon, 1974).
– 'Puppet-Players at Beaminster in 1630,' *SDNQ* 30 (1974–9), 19–21.
– 'Varieties of Men: Contrasts among the Dorset Clergy during the Seventeenth Century,' *SDNQ* 32 (1986-9), 846–50.
– *Wessex from AD 1000* (London, 1986).
– (ed). *The Casebook of Sir Francis Ashley, JP, Recorder of Dorchester, 1614–35*. Dorset Record Society, vol 7 (Dorchester, 1981).
[Bowles, Charles]. *Shaftesbury Corporation and Charities*. Copy in Dorset County Library attributed to Charles Bowles of Shaftesbury (Shaftesbury, 1831–2).
Bruce, John (ed). *Calendar of State Papers, Domestic Series, of the Reign of Charles I. 1628–1629* (London, 1859).
Clegg, A. Lindsay. *A History of Dorchester, Dorset* (London, 1972).
– *A History of Wimborne Minster and District* (Bournemouth, 1960).
Clinton-Baddeley, V.C. 'Elizabethan Players in Sherborne,' *Theatre Notebook* 7 (1952–3), 83.
Cockburn, J.S. (ed). *Western Circuit Assize Orders, 1629–1648: A Calendar*. Camden Society, 4th ser, 17 (London, 1976).
Cox, Benjamin G. *The Book of Blandford Forum* (Buckingham, 1983).
Cressy, David. *Bonfires and Bells: National Memory and the Protestant Calendar in Elizabethan and Stuart England* (London, 1989).

Cullingford, Cecil N. *A History of Poole and Neighbourhood* (Chichester, 1988).

Douch, Robert. *A Handbook of Local History: Dorset* (Bristol, 1962).

Eedle, Marie de G. *A History of Beaminster* (Chichester, 1984).

Ferris, J.P. 'The Gentry of Dorset on the Eve of the Civil War,' *The Genealogists' Magazine* 15.3 (1965), 104–16.

Fletcher, J.M.J. 'Church Cakes,' *SDNQ* 18 (1934), 134.

Fowler, Joseph. *Mediaeval Sherborne* (Dorchester, 1951).

– (ed). 'Post-Reformation Churchwardens' Accounts of S. Mary's, Sherborne,' *SDNQ* 24 (1943–6), 285–8, 300–4; 25 (1947–50), 7–11, 23–30, 55–9, 64–8, 83–7, 105–9, 122–6, 169–74, 187–9, 206–10, 226–9, 257–62, 268–9, 287–93; 26 (1951–4), 6–10, 21–3, 24, 28–9, 49–54.

– (ed). 'Sherborne All Hallows Church Wardens' Accounts,' *SDNQ* 23 (1939–42), 179–80, 189–94, 209–12, 229–35, 249–52, 269–72, 289–92, 311–14, 331–4; 24 (1943–6), 6–8, 25–8, 40–3, 66–8, 80–5, 101–6, 121–5, 140–4, 161–6.

Fowles, John. *A Short History of Lyme Regis* (Stanbridge, Wimborne, Boston and Toronto, 1982).

George, David. 'Anti-Catholic Plays, Puppet Shows, and Horse-Racing in Reformation Lancashire,' *REED Newsletter* 19.1 (1994), 15–22.

Gerard, Thomas. *Coker's Survey of Dorsetshire* (written by Thomas Gerard in the 1620s and first published under the name of John Coker in 1732). 2nd ed (Sherborne, 1980).

Gibbons, A.O. *Cerne Abbas: Notes and Speculations on a Dorset Village* (Dorchester, [1962]).

Gourlay, A.B. *A History of Sherborne School* (Sherborne, 1971).

Hays, Rosalind Conklin. 'Dorset Church Houses and the Drama,' *Research Opportunities in Renaissance Drama* 31 (1992), 13–23.

– '"Lot's Wife" or "The Burning of Sodom": The Tudor Corpus Christi Play at Sherborne, Dorset,' *Research Opportunities in Renaissance Drama* 33 (1994), 99–125.

Hutchins, John. *The History and Antiquities of the County of Dorset.* 3rd ed. W. Shipp and J.W. Hodson (eds) (1861–74; rpt East Ardsley, Wakefield, 1973).

Hutton, Ronald. *The Rise and Fall of Merry England: The Ritual Year 1400–1700* (Oxford, 1994).

James, Jude. *Wimborne Minster: The History of a Country Town* (Wimborne, Dorset, 1982).

Lancashire, Ian. *Dramatic Texts and Records of Britain: A Chronological Topography to 1558.* Studies in Early English Drama 1 (Toronto, 1984).

Le Fleming, Kaye. 'Wimborne Minster Archives,' *PDNHAS* 66 (1945 for 1944), 46–64.

Lloyd, Rachel. *Dorset Elizabethans At Home and Abroad* (London, 1967).

March, Henry Colley. *The Giant and the Maypole of Cerne* (Dorchester, 1902).

Mayo, Charles Herbert. *Bibliotheca Dorsetiensis: being a carefully compiled account of Printed Books and Pamphlets relating to the History and Topography of the County of Dorset* (London, 1885).

– *A History of Wimborne Minster: The Collegiate Church of Saint Cuthberga and King's Free Chapel at Wimborne* (London, 1860).

– *The Municipal Records of the Borough of Shaftesbury: A Contribution to Shastonian History* (Sherborne, 1889).

– 'The Shaftesbury Bezant,' *SDNQ* 3 (1892–3), 297–8.

– (ed). *The Municipal Records of the Borough of Dorchester, Dorset* (Exeter, 1908).

McGee, C. Edward. 'Music for Marriage: The Education of Susanna Edwards,' *The Early Drama, Art, and Music Review* 13 (1990), 7–12.

– 'A Performance at a Dorset Inn,' *REED Newsletter* 20.2 (1995), 13–15.

– '"strangest consequence from remotest cause": The Second Performance of *The Triumph of Peace*,' *Medieval and Renaissance Drama in England* 5 (1991), 309–42.

– 'Stuart Kings and Cambridge University Drama: Two Stories by William Whiteway,' *Notes and Queries* 233, no 4 (December 1988), 494–6.

Mills, A.D. (ed). 'A Corpus Christi Play and Other Dramatic Activities in Sixteenth-century Sherborne, Dorset,' *Collections* 9. Malone Society (Oxford, 1977), 1–15.

Moule, H.J. 'Notes on a Minute Book Belonging to the Corporation of Dorchester,' *PDNHAFC* 10 (1889), 71–80.

Murphy, Thomas D. (ed). 'The Diary of William Whiteway of Dorchester, County Dorset, From the Year 1618 to the Year 1635.' PhD thesis (Yale University, 1939).

Murray, John Tucker. *English Dramatic Companies 1558–1642*. 2 vols (1910; reissued New York, 1963).

Nelson, Alan H. (ed). *Cambridge*. 2 vols. REED (Toronto, 1989).

Newman, John, and Nikolaus Pevsner. *The Buildings of England: Dorset* (1972; rpt London, 1975).

Pafford, J.H.P. 'Blandford Forum: Early Records of the Drama,' *SDNQ* 30 (1974–9), 283–7.

Parker, Kenneth L. *The English Sabbath: A Study of Doctrine and Discipline from the Reformation to the Civil War* (Cambridge, 1988).

Penn, K.J. *Historic Towns in Dorset*. Dorset Natural History and Archaeological Society Monograph Series 1 (Dorchester, 1980).

Pitfield, F.P. *The Book of Bere Regis* (Sherborne, 1978).

– 'The Churchwardens' Accounts 1607–1740,' *Bere Regis Parish Magazine* (July 1961–November 1966).

Popham, David. *The Book of Wimborne* (Buckingham, 1983).

Roberts, George. *The History and Antiquities of the Borough of Lyme Regis and Charmouth* (London, 1834).

– *The Social History of the People of the Southern Counties of England in Past Centuries* (London, 1856).

Rose-Troup, Frances. *John White: The Patriarch of Dorchester* (New York, 1930).

Short, Basil. *A Respectable Society: Bridport 1593–1835* (Bradford-on-Avon, 1976).

Smith, Harry Percy. 'A First Glossary of Tudor Words and Phrases Abstracted from the Poole Corporation Records,' *PDNHAS* 63 (1942 for 1941), 41–69.

– *The History of the Borough and County of the Town of Poole*. 2 vols (Poole, 1947–51).

Speed, Peter. *Dorset: A County History* (Newbury, 1994).

Stephens, W.B. 'The Trade Fortunes of Poole, Weymouth and Lyme Regis, 1600–1640,' *PDNHAS* 95 (1974), 71–3.

Stokes, James with Robert Alexander (eds). *Somerset Including Bath*. 2 vols. REED (Toronto, 1996).

Sydenham, John. *The History of the Town and County of Poole* (Poole and London, 1839).

Sydenham, Laura. *Shaftesbury and Its Abbey* (Lingfield, Surrey, 1959).

Taylor, Christopher. *The Making of the English Landscape: Dorset* (London, 1970).

Tittler, Robert. 'The Building of Civic Halls in Dorset, *c.* 1560–1640,' *Bulletin of the Institute of Historical Research* 58 (1985), 37–45.

– 'The Vitality of an Elizabethan Port: The Economy of Poole, c. 1550–1600,' *Southern History* 7 (1989), 95–118.

Trotman, E.E. 'The Church Ale and the Robin Hood Legend,' *SDNQ* 28 (1961–7), 37–8.

Udal, John Symonds. *Dorsetshire Folk-Lore* (Hertford, 1922).

Underdown, David. *Fire from Heaven: The Life of an English Town in the Seventeenth Century* (London, 1992).

– *Revel, Riot and Rebellion: Popular Politics and Culture in England 1603–1660* (Oxford, 1985).

The Victoria History of the Counties of England. *A History of the County of Dorset.* Vol 2. William Page (ed). (London, 1908).

Wainwright, Thomas. *The Bridport Records and Ancient Manuscripts* ([Bridport, 1899]).

Wanklyn, Cyril. *Lyme Leaflets* (Colchester, London, and Eton, 1944).

– *Lyme Regis: A Retrospect* (London, 1927).

Weinstock, M.B. 'Blandford in Elizabethan and Stuart Times,' *SDNQ* 30 (1974–9), 118–22.

– *More Dorset Studies* (Dorchester, [1960]).

– *Studies in Dorset History* (Dorchester, 1953).

– (ed). *Weymouth and Melcombe-Regis Minute Book 1625–1660.* Dorset Record Society, vol 1 (Dorchester, 1964).

Whiteway, William. *William Whiteway of Dorchester: His Diary 1618 to 1635.* Dorset Record Society, vol 12 (London, 1992).

Wildman, W.B. *A Short History of Sherborne.* 2nd ed (Sherborne, 1902).

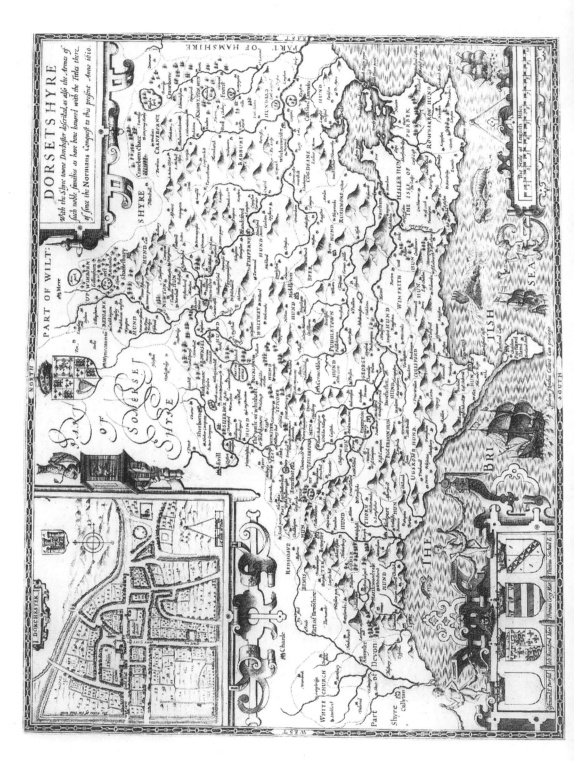

Dorset with Dorchester inset from John Speed, *Theatre of the Empire of Great Britaine* (1611). This item is reproduced by permission of The Huntington Library, San Marino, California.

Dorset coast showing Lyme Regis and the Cobb, from BL: Cotton Augustus I.i.31–3,
by permission of the British Library

Dorset coast showing Weymouth and Melcombe-Regis, from BL: Cotton Augustus I.i.31–3, by permission of the British Library

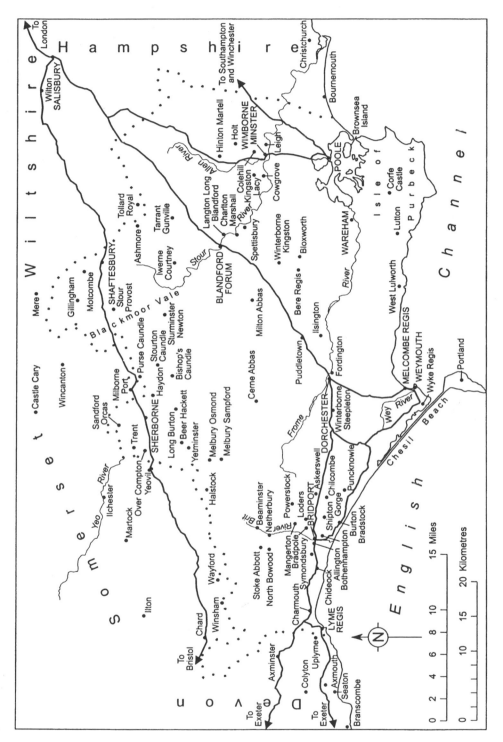

Dorset with principal Renaissance routes

Dioceses

DIOCESE OF BRISTOL

1603
Bishop John Thornborough's Visitation Articles   STC: 10143
pp 10–11 *(Articles concerning the laity)*   5

...

Abuses in
Churches

10. Item, Whether the Ministers and Church-wardens, have suffered any
Lords of mis-rule, or *Summer-Lords*, or Ladies, or any disguised persons,
with may-games morishdances, or the like, to come vnreverently into the
church, or church-yard, & there to dance, or play any vnseemely parts, *with*   10
scofes, iestes, wa*n*ton gestures or ribauld talke, especially in the time of
co*m*mon prayer? And what they be that co*m*mit such disorder, | or keepe
the*m* co*m*pany, or maintaine them? And whether there be any which fight,
braule, or chide in church, or church-yard, or any which strive for seates or
pews, & what be their names.   15

...

1637
Bishop Robert Skinner's Visitation Articles   STC: 10145
sig B1   20

...

® Prophaning of
the Church.

62 Item, whether is your Church or Chappell prophaned by any Playes,
Feasts, Banquets, Church-Ales, drinkings, which are forbidden in the 88.
Canon.

...   25

1640
Bishop Robert Skinner's Visitation Articles   STC: 10145.3
sig B1v *(Articles concerning the church)*

...

Prophaning of
the Church

62. Item, whether is your Church or Chappell prophaned by any Plaies,

Feasts, Banquets, Church-Ales, drinkings, which are forbidden in the 88. Canon.

...

DIOCESE OF SALISBURY

1569
Bishop John Jewel's Visitation Injunctions   STC: 10326.5
sigs Biiij–Biiij verso

...

24. Item, to present likewise, whether there haue | bene any Lordes of misrule, or disguised persons in Christmas, or dauncers, minstrels, or May gamers, at any other time, that haue vnreuerently come into your Church, and there played vnseemely parts, with scoffes, iestes, and ribauldrie talke, or daunsing, and namely in time of Common prayer, and what their names be, and the names also of such others as came with them to maintaine such disorder.

...

1599

Bishop Henry Cotton's Visitation Articles   STC: 10327.5
sigs A6v–B1 *(Articles concerning the clergy)*

...

11. Whether your Preachers or Ministers be peace makers, and exhort their Parishioners to obedience towardes their prince and all that bee in authority to the Ecclesiasticall gouernment now established, and to mutuall loue among themselues: whether they be diligent in visiting the sicke, in comforting them, and in exhorting them in their last wils to relieue the poore, whether they be suspected to be fauourers of the Romish or forrain power, maintainers of sectaries, corrupt in Religion, incontinent persons themselues, reported or suspected to keepe any suspected man or woman in their houses or els where, giuen to riote, idlenesse, drunkennesse, haunters of tauerns, alehouses, or suspected places, giuen to any notorious crymes, light ordered behauiour, or swearers, fighters, quarrellers, gamesters, carders, common table players, dycers, dauncers, hawkers, hunters, stage players, vsing any lay-|call craft disordered in apparell, eyther in colours, guardes, light fashion, great ruffes, or any other waies giuing any iust occasion of offence, whereby their Ministerie should be slaundered or contemned.

...

sig B1v *(Articles concerning the laity)*

...

2. Whether the people of your parish, especially householders, doe faithfully

endeuour themselues to resort with their children & seruants to their parish
church or chappell on the Sundayes and holydaies to morning & euening
prayer, & then and there abide orderly and soberly during the time of
common prayers, sermons, homilies and other seruice of God, there to be
vsed, giuing themselues to the hearing thereof reuerently and deuoutly, who   5
they be that negligentlie absent themselues, or come very late vnto the church,
or that walke, talke slumber, or otherwise vnreuerentlie behaue themselues
in the Church, who doe vse any gaming or pastime abroade, or in any house,
who doe sit in the streetes, churchyeard, or in any tauern, Inne or Alehouse,
vpon the Sundayes, or other holydayes, in the time of common prayer,   10
sermon, reading of homilies, eyther before or after noone, you shall deliuer
the names aswell of such persons that so offend, as of the persons in whose
house the offence is committed.

sig B2   15
...

5. Whether there be any that keepe any shop, or any part of their shop open
vpon the Sabboth daies, or vpon any holydayes: or doe vse any worke or
labour on those dayes, whether in anie fayres or common markets falling
vpon the Sundayes, there bee any shewing of any wares before morning   20
prayer be done, and whether any markets or selling of wares be vsed in the
churchyeards, whether any Lords of misrule, Sommer Lords or Ladyes, or
any disguised persons or Maygames, or any Morris dancers are suffered in
your parish, and being so suffered do come vnreuerentlie into your church
or churchyeard, or there to dance or play at any time: whether there be any   25
that fight or braul within your church or churchyeard, or any that for pues
or seates doe striue or contend, especially in the time of common prayer or
sermon.
...

                                                                               30

1614
Bishop Henry Cotton's Visitation Articles   STC: 10328
f [4v]
...

    57 Item, whether you or your predecessors Church-wardens there, haue   35
suffered any plaies, Feasts, Banquets, Church-ales, Drinking, Temporall
Courts or Leets, Iuries, Musters, or any other prophane vsages to bee kept in
your Church, Chapell, or Church-yard, or bels to bee rung superstitiously
vpon holidaies or eeues abrogated by the booke of Common Prayer, or at
any other time, without good cause to be allowed by your Minister and your   40
selues?
...

1616
Bishop Robert Abbot's Visitation Articles   STC: 10329
f [7] *(Articles concerning parishioners, etc)*

…

17 Whether haue you or your Predecessors, Church-wardens suffered any   5
playes, feasts, banquets, church-ales, drinkings or any other prophane vsages,
to be kept in your church, chappels, or churchyard, or bels to be rung
superstitiouslie vpon holidaies or Eues abrogated by the booke of common-
prayer, contrary to the 88. cannon?

…   10

1619
Bishop Martin Fotherby's Visitation Articles   STC: 10329.3
sig B3 *(Articles concerning parishioners)*

…   15

17. Whether haue you or your Predecessors, Church-wardens suffered any
playes, feasts, banquets, church-ales, drinkings or any other profane vsages,
to be kept in your church, chappels, or churchyard, or bels to be rung
superstitiouslie vpon holidaies or Eues abrogated by the booke of common
prayer, contrary to the 88. canon?   20

…

County of Dorset

1571

William Kethe's A Sermon made at Blanford Forum STC: 14943
sigs Biiij–Biiij verso

…

® The abuse of
the Saboth day.

The Sabboth
day turned into
a Reuelyng day.

    The Lord God hath commaunded, and so do the lawes of this Realme   5
that the Sabboth day should be kept holy, that the people, should cease from
labour, to the end they should heare ye word of God, and geue them selues
to godly exercises, but custome and sufferaunce hath brought it to passe that
the multitude do most I shamefully prophane the Sabboth day, & haue altered
the very name therof, so as where god calleth it his holy sabaoth, the multitude   10
call it there reuelying day, whiche day is spent in bulbeatings, bearebeatings,
bowlings, dicyng, cardyng, daunsynges, drunkennes, and whoredome.

…

sigs Ciij–Ciiij   15

…

    There was within my remembraunce a Minister of this shyre, who
vnderstandyng what great disorders there were commonly at these Church
Ales vpon ye Saboth day, required his flock committed to his charge (as hee
was preachyng vnto them) both in Gods name, ye Queenes Maiesties name,   20
and the Lord Lieutenauntes name of the countrey, that they should not
assemble the people together, to offende God by theyr vngodly behauiours,
but rather geue them selues vppon the Sabboth day to serue God, accordyng
to their duties. The people could in no wise alway with this exhortation, but
certaine of them, went to the Iustices to desire licence for the commyng   25
together of the people. Sondry of the Iustices both godly and wisely denyed
them. At lenght one Iustice they founde who for good considerations (as he
thought) gaue them a licence for certaine dayes I may not say to commit
disorders, for we may well thinke no Iustice would be so vndiscret, but they
abused hys authoritie. The Minister seying ye great disorders in hys Parish,   30
the next Sabboth day after they had obtained licence, wrote to the Iustice of

ye same, and wrote nothyng but that he will yet stand to. The Iustice called
those that had abused hys authoritie and reproued them, but now ye shall
see the multitude. |

   There were (by the Iustices report) 36. whiche offred vp vnto hym theyr
names (which was as much as to saye, as that they would haue periured them   5
celues, if the Iustice would haue put them to their othes) to testifie agaynst
the Minister, that where he complayned of disorder, they to ye contrarie
affirmed, that there was no disorder at all. And yet it was manifest that the
same Sabboth day was shamefully prophaned, with bulbeatynges, boulynges,
drunkennes, dauncynges, and such lyke, in so much as men could not keepe   10
theyr seruauntes frome lyinge out of theyr owne houses the same Sabboth
day at night, but yet in the Iudgementes of .36. (or there aboute) there was
no hurt, nor disorder at al committed.

Late 16th century   15
Licence for Minstrels   SRO: DD/HI 469, vol 2
f [124]

A licence for Mynstrelles

Dorset   H. V. armiger T. H. armiger iustices of ye Quenes Maiesties peace within ye   20
countye of .Dorset. To all & singuler Iustices of peace. Sheriffes, Mayers,
constables, bayliffes, tythyngmen & other ye Quenes Maiestyes officers &
ministers within ye seyd countye to euerye of them, gretinge./. fforasmutch
as itt is not lawfull for anye person or persons to wander or goe abrode from
towne to towne, or from place to place & vse ye trade of Mynstrelles, but   25
onlie for sutche person & persons, as shalbe therevnto licensed bye too Iustices
of peace, whereof one of them to be of the quorum, or belonginge to anye
baron of this realme, or towardes anye other honorable personage of greter
degre. As bye ye statut made in ye .14. yere of ye Quenes reigne amongest
other thinges more att large apperethe. Knowe ye therefore we ye Iustices   30
aforeseyd att ye requeste & sute of .W. C. ye father, & .H. C. his sonne
dwellinge within ye parishe of .G. in ye countye aforeseyd Minstrell, & for
ye good & honeste behauior we our selues doe knowe, & ye lyke reporte yat
we haue hard of ye partyes aforeseyd, We haue licensed ye seyd .W. G. ye
father & .H. C. ye sonne to wander & goe abrode with there instrumentes   35
vsinge there trade of Minstrelcye, pleyinge or singynge throwghe & in all
places within ye seyd countye onlye, behavinge themselues orderlye & vsinge
there seyd lycence accordinge to ye seyd statut, which licence ys to endwer

34/ .W. G.: *for* .W. C.

ye space of one whole yere *after* ye date hereof. In wytnes whereof we ye seyd
Iustic*es* haue to this *our* licence put *our* hand*es* & seales ye .xx. daye etc

...

1627/8   5

Petition of Somerset Clergy to Sir John Denham   PRO: SP 16/96
single sheet* *(15 March)*

To the Hon*orable* S*i*r Iohn Denham Knight one of
the Barrons of his M*aiesties* Excheq*ue*r and Iustice of   10
Assize for the County of Somersett./

The humble Petic*i*on of the ministers whose names are subscribed./
Sheweth
That whereas at the last Summer Assises held for the County of Dorsett;   15
there was an Order made for the suppressing of all Reuells, Church Ales, and
other publique Ales [amongst other things] as by the Copie of the sayd Order
hereunto annexed appeareth.
Yo*u*r Pet*itioners* therfore humbly desier that yo*u*r Lordship would be pleased
to grant the like Order at this Assises for the suppressing of the like Ales   20
and disorders in this County of Som*er*sett.
Soe they shall alwayes pray for yo*u*r L*ordshi*ps long
health and prosperity.

Adam Abraham   Iohn fforde
William Gyllet   Iohn ffathers   25
Ralfe Turner   George Drake./

15° Marcij 1627
Let the Clerke of the Assizes draw vp the like Order for this County
(signed) Iohn Denham./ 30

1631

Assize Order for Western Circuit   PRO: Assi 24/20/140
f 35v* *(21 July) (Summer assizes)*

35

Held at Dorchester before Sir John Denham, baron of the exchequer
...

Whereas vpon Informac*i*on given of soundry misdemeanors and
disorders yeerely happeninge by occasion of the keepinge of publique

---

9/ S*i*r Iohn Denham: *in display script and underlined in* MS   29/ for: *written as correction over other letters*
17/ [amongst other things]: *square bracket in* MS; *no deletion*

Revells Churchales clerkes ales and other ales of like nature It hath ben
heretofore ordered att the Assizes holden att Sherborne in this County of
Dorset the thirteenth day of July .1628. that all suche Revells and publique
ales should be henceforth vtterly suppressed which said order not with standinge
hath not in all thinges taken suche effect as was expected and desired It is   5
nowe therefore farther ordered by this Court that not only the said former
order be henceforth carefully and strictly observed in all things (exceptinge
the dirreccions formerly given for the publishing of the same in euery parishe
Churche in this County) But besides for the better observacion thereof that
the gentlemen of the grand Iury and the Constables of euery hundred &   10
libertie shall make diligent inquiry of the keepinge of all suche revells and
Ales as are formerly mencioned att any tyme hereafter ^⌈And⌉ [neither shall]
the said Grand Inquest receive any presentment from the handes of the high
Constables vnles they particulerly expresse whether any suche Revells or Ales
as aforesaid have ben kept within their hundred yea or nay and the keepers   15
of the said Ales and Revells tiplers and mynstrells resortinge vnto and keepinge
tiplinge & mynstrelsey there with all other misdemeanors and disorders
vsed & committed therein ^⌈&⌉ the same Grand Inquest shall carefully and
faithfully present ^⌈it⌉ to this Court att euery Assizes to be holden hereafter
within this County that suche course may be taken therein as to Iustice shall   20
apperteyne And the Constables of euery hundred & libertie are to publishe
this order throughout their seuerall hundredes and liberties.

12/ [neither shall]: *cancelled in MS but needed for sense*

Boroughs and Parishes

BEAMINSTER

1591–3
Churchwardens' Presentments for Salisbury Deanery   wro: D5/28/6, item 34
single sheet*

...

Item we present that there were stage players played in our parshe Churche.
°dominus monuit quod imposterum non permittant tragediones ludere in
ecclesia &c°

...

1630
Quarter Sessions Orders   dro: QSM: 1/1
ff 272v–3* (5–8 October)

Order made before Thomas Freke and John Strode, knights; John Whetcombe, DD;
John Browne, Leweston FitzJames, Henry Drake, and Roger Gollop, esquires

...

Ordo versus
poppett Players

fforasmuch as complaint was made vnto this Court that William Sands the
elder Iohn Sands and William Sands the yonger doe wander vp and downe
the Countrey and about nine others of their Company with certaine
blasphemous shewes and sights which they exercise by way of poppett
playinge contrary to the Statute. made against such vnlawfull wanderers. And
whereas the Constable of Beamister in this County and other inhabitants
there haue now alsoe informed this Court that the said William Sands thelder
and his Company are come to Beamister aforesaid and there haue sett vp
their shewes of poppett playinge, and there doe exercise their feats not only
in the day tyme but alsoe late in the night to the great disturbance of the
Townsmen there, and the greivance of diuers of the Inhabitants who cannot
keepe their Children and servants in their houses by reason that they frequent

7/ *parshe: for* parshe

the said shewes and sights late in the night in a disorderly manner. And
likewise that the said Iohn Sands and two other of their company on Sunday
last pursued the *pre*cher that *pre*ched at Beamister aforesaid, from the Church
to his house and entred the said house, and there challenged him for his
sermon and gaue him threatninge speeches: and likewise that on Tuesday   5
night last there was an vproare in the said Towne of Beamister by reason of a
brawle between the said Iohn Sands and a disorderly inhabitant of the same
Towne, the said Iohn runninge in a forceible manner into a Townsmans house
there to the afrightinge of the people of the same house: Wherevpon this
Court takinge the said complaint and Informac*i*on into considerac*i*on and   10
findinge the same to be true. And farther consideringe the great dearth of
Corne and other victualls at this time and the extremity that is like to come
on the poore of this Countrey by reason of the said dearth, and alsoe by two
seue*r*all Proclamacons his Ma*ie*stie hath commaunded the puttinge in
execuc*i*on the Law and Statutes ag*ain*st such wanderers, doe hold it very vnfitt   15
and inconvenient to suffer the *said* Sands and his company to exercise their
said feats in this Countrey. It is therefore by this Court ordered that the said
Will*ia*m Sands thelder Iohn. Sands and William Sands the yonger shall
remove themselues and their shewes on Munday next and shall then forthw*i*th
departe out of this County and that neither they nor any of them or any of   20
their Company shall henceforth vse or exercise their said feats or shew | their
said sights in this County but shall forthwith depart out of the County
toward the place of their dwellinge. And if they or any of them shall againe
vse or exercise their said ffeats or make shew of their sightes within this
County That then the Constables Tythingmen or other officers of the place   25
where they shall soe exercise their said feates or shew their said sightes shall
convey all the said parties soe offendinge contrary to this order before some
one of his Ma*ie*st*ies* Iustic*es* of the peace neare or next adioyninge to the place
where they shall soe offend to be by him bound over to the then next Assizes
to be held in and for this County and in the meane tyme to be of the good   30
behavior towards the kings Ma*ie*stie and all his Leige people./

...

BERE REGIS

35

1590
Deposition Book for Salisbury Deanery   WRO: D5/22/2
ff 47v–8* *(17 December) (Examination of Thomas Howlett, husbandman, aged 30)*

Taken before William Wilkinson, LLD, *the dean's official*   40

...

14/ Proclamacons: *for* Proclamac*i*ons; *abbreviation mark missing*   21/ shew: *catchwords* [or shewe] their *follow*

Ad 2^m et 3^m articulos libelli deponit That in the thursdaie in the whitson
weeke was xij moneth in a streete within the parishe of Bere Regis ∧⌈the place⌉
called newe in corner in the eveninge of the same daie this deponent beinge
then and there presente [together] hard harry Gerrard articulated speake to
Thomas whiffen in this article mencyoned these wordes or the like in effect,   5
Thow arte a knave and an arrant knave, thow mightest haue turned att home
and make splites to bottome a seeve like a cuckold knave, and not to troble
vs here, which wordes were so spoken by the said Gerrard in the hearinge of
this examinate Thomas ffawkner, Thomas ffrye, Thomas Coffyn William
Dunstee, and his contestes Ieffry Phipper and ffraunces Blundon, with [may]   10
many more of the parishe, Et plura nescit deponere ad hos articulos vt dicit
…

(Howlett's replies to further interrogatories)

15

Ad 2^m interrogatorium respondet that the articulate whiffen being a minstrell
and playing on his Instrument att the church ale mr woodnutt vicar of Bere
came and [forbid] disliked (as itt should seeme) of his playing then Thomas
ffaw[⟨.⟩]kner one of the church wardens willed him the said whiffen (having
putt upp his instrument | to playe and he would aunswere itt, wherevppon   20
mr woodnutt desired the articulate Gerrard to beare witnes, and presentlie
therevppon the said Gerrard vttered the wordes by this respondent deposed
to the [thirde] second and third articles of the libell Et aliter nescit respondere
isto interrogatorio quam superius per ipsum responsum est dictis 2º et 3º
Articulis libelli predicti   25
…
Ad 4^m respondet That he neuer hard the said Gerrard speke the wordes
libellated but once Et aliter satisfactus est in deposicionibus
Ad 5^m ∧⌈& vltimum⌉ interrogatoria respondet that the articulate Whiffen was
goinge awaye from the company, and as this respondent belevith the said   30
whiffen did not heare the wordes libellated
X

(Examination of Geoffrey Phipper, husbandman, aged 31)
…
35
Ad 2^m et 3^m articulos deponit that in the thursdaie in the Whitson weeke
last was xij moneth Thomas whiffen [libellated] Articulated [playinge] abowt
supper tyme in the eveninge of the same daie [vppon] att the church ale
playinge on his Instrument in the streete within the parishe of Bere Regis the
name of the ⌈place⌉ being called newe Inn Corner, mr David woodnutt   40

1–2/ thursdaie … xij moneth: *22 May 1589*   19–20/ (having putt … instrument: *closing parenthesis omitted*
18/ disliked: *corrected from* disliking   32/ X: *Howlett has signed with his personal mark*

vicer there came and disliked of his playing there, So that *present*lie the said
Whiffen putt vpp his instrument and was goinge awaye, and then certayne
word*es* being passed betwene the said vicer and Thomas ffawcon*er*
Churchwarden there the said vicer called the ar*ticu*lated Henry Gerrard to
be a witnes to the word*es* spoken by the said ffawckner (but what those word*es*   5
w*er*e this depon*ent* cannot tell) And therevppon the said Gerrard vttered
and spake these word*es* ∧⌈viz⌉ he might haue byd away and not haue come
there a fidlinge like an arrant knave he might better haue byd att home a
making of spleet*es* and bottoming of seeves like a cuckolde knave then to come
here a troblinge of the *pa*rishe being then and there *presen*te willi*am* Hick*es*,   10
willi*am* dunster, Richard dunster, [and] Thomas ffawckner, [Thomas] and
his contestes Thomas Howlett & ffraunc*es* Blundon wi*th* dyvers other but
whether they hard the said word*es* these depon*ent* knoweth not w*hi*ch word*es*
were spoken (as this depon*ent* verelie belevith) of the said whiffen by the said
Gerrard Et plura nescit depon*ere* ad hos ar*ticu*los vt dicit   15

...

f 48v *(Phipper's replies to further interrogatories)*

...

Ad 4^m 5^m et vl*timum* inter*ro*gato*r*ia *re*sp*ond*et that he hard the said Gerrard   20
speake the word*es* by this *re*sp*ond*ent in the second & third ar*ti*cles of the
libell deposed) but once/ And as this *re*sp*ond*ent verelye belevith the ar*ticu*late
whiffen [was] did not ⌈then⌉ here the same word*es* so spoken Et plura nescit
*re*sp*ond*ere al*i*t*er* qu*a*m *pre*deposuit.

25

(Examination of Francis Blundon, shoemaker, aged 21)

...

Ad 2^m et 3^m ar*ticu*los depon*it* That on Thursdaie in the whitson weeke last
was xij moneth the church ale being then kept, ∧⌈&⌉ in a streete the place
thereof vsually called newe in corner wi*th*in the *pa*rishe of Bere Reg*is* in ye   30
afternoone toward*es* night of the same daye mr woodnutt co*m*ming to the
place and findinge the ar*ticu*late Thomas whiffen playinge on an Instrum*ent*.
disliked thereof and asked what he was, and who gave him leave to play,
therevpon the said whiffen putt vp his instrum*ent* and was going awaye, then
Thomas ffawckner being one of the churchwardens there willed the said   35
whiffen to come back and play againe and he would beare him owt therein,
wherevppon mr woodnutt called Henrie Gerrard ar*ticu*lated [b] to beare
witness to the word*es* spoken by ffawckner, then the said Gerrard vttered
these word*es* viz [he was] ⌈thow arte⌉ a knave, and an arrant knave and were
more fitter to be att home making of spleet*es* to bottome seeves like a Cuckold   40

10–13/ being then ... knoweth not: *added at foot of sheet and marked for insertion here* knave, which wordes were spoken of and ment by the said whiffen (as this deponent in his conscyence verelie belevith) beinge then and there present and harde the same his *prœcontestes* Thomas Howlett, & ffraunces Blundon and others namelie Thomas ffrye ⌞&⌟ the said Thomas ffawkner with dyvers others whom this deponent cannott nowe well remember/ Et plura nescit ad   5 hos articulos deponere vt dicit/

...

f 49 *(Blundon's replies to further interrogatories)*

...   10

Ad 2ᵐ 3ᵐ 4ᵐ 5ᵐ et ultimùm interrogatoria respondet that he hard the said Gerrard speake the wordes (by this respondent in the second and the third articles of the libell deposed) but once & in that one place, and that as this respondent beleveth) the said whiffen did not then here the said wordes so spoken Et aliter nescit respondere quam in deposicionibus suis per ipsum   15 depositum est.

...

1599

Churchwardens' Presentments for Salisbury Deanery   WRO: D5/28/7, item 4   20
single sheet *(Before 2 April)*

...

Thomas frye the servante of Iohn Spere George Dracke the Sonne of anne Dracke for playing in the Churche and spoyling of the pewe dores./

...   25

1607–8

St John the Baptist's Churchwardens' Accounts   DRO: PE/BER: CW1
f 2* *(12 April–3 April) (Receipts)*

...   30

Item made of the Church Ale   xiij li.

...

f 3* *(Payments)*

...   35

Inprimis paide for mendinge of the drum   vj s.

...

Item paide to the Minstrells in earnest   iiij d.

...

5/ nowe: *written as correction over another word, possibly* doe   23/ Sonne: *3 minims in* MS
13–14/ as this respondent beleveth): *opening parenthesis omitted*

1616–17
St John the Baptist's Churchwardens' Accounts   DRO: PE/BER: CW2
f 2 *(7 April 1616–27 April 1617) (Receipts)*

Money made at our Church ayle at witsvntyde last/ 1616: comes to 13 li. 7 s.   5
9 d./
...

(Payments)

                                                                              10

                                                                    li.   s.   d.

...
Itt*em* for mending the weathercocke, & making a visard
for the pleayers   0   1   2.
...   15
Itt*em* for a meeting for the players   0   9   0
...

BLANDFORD FORUM

                                                                              20

1567–8

A   *Chamberlains' Accounts*   DRO: DC/BFB: Finance: Chamberlains' Accounts
f B2v *(Rendered in December) (Receipts)*
...
Item more of the weamen geathred on hoppe Monday   00   06   0   25
...

1577–8

A   *Chamberlains' Accounts*   DRO: DC/BFB: Finance: Chamberlains' Accounts
f B5   30
...

                                                                    li.   s.   d.

...
geathred att hocktide this yeare   02   00   0
...   35

5/ witsvntyde ... 1616: *19–25 May 1616*
25/ hoppe Monday: *Hock Monday, 26 April 1568*
34/ hocktide: *7–8 April 1578*

1587–8

A   *Chamberlains' Accounts*   DRO: DC/BFB: Finance: Chamberlains' Accounts
f B9* *(Rendered 22 November) (Receipts)*

...

more of players that played in the yeld hall   iij s.   5

...

1594–5

A   *Chamberlains' Accounts*   DRO: DC/BFB: Finance: Chamberlains' Accounts
f B14* *(Rendered 5 November) (John Cleeves' receipts)*   10

...

Rec*eiued* of Trustrum & his company for the hall   00   02   6
Rec*eiued* of my lord Staffor*des* man 2 s. 6 d.: of my
lord Mounteagles man 2 s. 6 d.   00   05   0

...   15

(Additional receipts)

thay Rec*eiued* of will*iam* Bryne for his fyne of adowble
Shamble w*hich* Ioseph Walter had 40 s.: & for players   20
in the yeld hall 7 s. 6 d. all w*hich* is   24   07   2

...

1595–6

Chamberlains' Accounts   DRO: DC/BFB: Finance: Chamberlains' Accounts   25
f F2* *(Rendered 2 December) (Receipts)*

...

...more there was R*eceived* of plaiers that had plaied in the yeld hall this yere
vij s. vj d....

                                                                                     30

1596–7

A   *Chamberlains' Accounts*   DRO: DC/BFB: Finance: Chamberlains' Accounts
f B15v* *(Rendered 2 December) (Receipts)*

...

Rec*eiued* of Gawler for the playes in the gyld hall   00   07   6   35

...

1598–9

Chamberlains' Accounts   DRO: DC/BFB: Finance: Chamberlains' Accounts
f F5* *(Rendered 5 November)*   40

...

There is also dewe to the towne by Androe pope for plaies made in ˄⌈the⌉

yelde hall this yere the some of xx s. dewe to be paied at the next accompte
to the town stewardes

...

This Daye there is Chosen to be stewardes for the borowe for one yere folowing
Iohn Cleves and Iehonadab Sherley and there is dewe oweinge by the towne   5
popes xx s. for plaies abuesaied the some aboue *(blank)* laied out by Ionodab
Shereley the some of *(blank)*

A   ***Chamberlains' Accounts***   DRO: DC/BFB: Finance: Chamberlains' Accounts
f B16v* *(Rendered 5 November) (Receipts)*   10

...

It*em* mr Bailife Rawlingston of hock monye	01	01	0
rec*eiued* of Mr Iohn Gundrye 2 s. of Iohn Sherlye 4 d.	00	02	4
Rec*eiued* of Richard Bishoppe of Ock Monye	00	04	3

...   15

1599–1600

Chamberlains' Accounts   DRO: DC/BFB: Finance: Chamberlains' Accounts
f F6* *(Rendered 3 November)*

...   20

...Receivell Also of Andrewe Pope the som of xx s....

...

1601–2

A   ***Chamberlains' Accounts***   DRO: DC/BFB: Finance: Chamberlains' Accounts   25
f B18v* *(Rents due)*

...

Rec*eiued* of Thomas ffrye & George Harben beeinge soe much restinge by them on the accompt of the benifitt made of the race 1601	01	10	2

30

Rec*eiued* the Monye gathred by the weamen att hocktyde beeinge 1602	01	00	0

...

4/ yere folowing: *words obscured by smeared ink*
6/ abuesaied: *for* abouesaied
12/ hock monye: *Hocktide was 16–17 April 1599*
21/ Receivell: *for* Received
32/ hocktyde: *12–13 April 1602*

1602–3
Chamberlains' Accounts   DRO: DC/BFB: Finance: Chamberlains' Accounts
f F8v

                    The Eight daie of November 1603   5

Richard Keynell bailiff and one of the Towne Stwerd*es* with Rober*t*t Keynell
the other Stwerde hath not as yett made or yelded [⟨...⟩] vpp their Accomptes
for the Towne rent*es* and also of the benefitt of the Race w*hic*h they are
accomptable for to the Towne   10
°This Richard Keynell died in prison for debt°

1603–4

A   ***Chamberlains' Accounts***   DRO: DC/BFB: Finance: Chamberlains' Accounts
f B19* *(Receipts)*   15
…
Rec*eiued* the Monye geathred hock Mondaye   01   00   2
…
Rec*eiued* that was made of the Race   26   02   1
…   20

ff B19v–20*
…
            Monyes Receiued att the Race by Iohn Cleeues 1603
Rec*eiued* on sonday supper   00   17   6 25
Rec*eiued* on monday dynner   02   14   6
Rec*eiued* on Monday att supper   09   06   6
Rec*eiued* att dynner on Tewsday   07   15   6
Rec*eiued* att Supper Tewsday   10   07   6
Rec*eiued* att dynner wensday   10   06 11 30
Rec*eiued* at Supper wensday   09   06   5
Rec*eiued* att dynner Thardsday & supper   16   09   3
                                                         67   04   1
Rec*eiued* ffryday dynner & supper   11   10   6
Rec*eiued* on Satterdaye dynner exc'   04   01   8 35
                                     Sume is   82   16   3

17/ hock Mondaye: *2 May 1603*   33/ 67 04 1: *6, 04, and 1 corrected over other figures*
30/ 06: *6 corrected over another figure*   34/ 6: *corrected over another figure*
31/ 06 5: *0 and 5 corrected over other figures*   36/ 16: *1 corrected over another figure*
32/ 16 09 3: *1, 9, and 3 corrected over other figures*

Rec*eiued* by playe Monday 11 s. 4 d.: Rec*eiued* by				
play Tewsdaye 26 s.	01	17	4	
Rec*eiued* wensday by playe 53 s. 4 d.: rec*eiued*				
Thurdsday by playe 64 s.	05	17	4	
Rec*eiued* ffryday by playe 69 s. 11 d., Rec*eiued* on				5
Satterdaye 2 s. 6d.	03	12	5	
Sume is	11	07	1	

Sume totall   95 li.   09 s.   4 d.†

Rec*eiued* that was made of brand 2 s. 6 d.: rec*eiued*				
made of beeffe that was left 9 s.	00	11	6	10
rec*eiued* for candles left 3 s. 6 d.: rec*eiued* for fish left 12 d.	00	04	6	
rec*eiued* for sewett & dreppinge 4 doz. lack*ing* 2 li. att				
2 s. 8 d. doz. is 10 s.	00	10	0	
Sume is	01	06	0	
				15

payment*es* att the Race 1603 as followeth

p*aie*d to my selfe as by my bill appeareth	08	02	06	
p*aie*d for the hyer of a horse for ij dayes to S*ir* Ralfe Horssyes	00	02	0	
p*aie*d for a messenger sent to S*ir* Care Rawleigh 20 d.:				20
p*aie*d to Arnold 4 d.	00	02	0	
p*aie*d Io*h*n Hawker for 53 li. of Beeffe	00	08	10	
p*aie*d for j load of ffaggott*es* 5 s. 6 d.: p*aie*d for iij sacks				
of Cole to one of ffroome 8 s.	00	13	6	
p*aie*d for fetchinge the broches 6 d.: p*aie*d y*at* S*ir* Georg				25
Morten had *(blank)* 7 s.	00	07	6	
p*aie*d for Carrige of a hogshead of wyne 20 d.: p*aie*d				
Nick*olas* Sole for fishing att brensley 16 d.:	00	03	0	
p*aie*d widdow Boyte for 4 daye*s* fyndinge herselfe 2 s.:				
p*aie*d for 4 sacks of Coles 18 d.	00	03	6	30
p*aie*d for a loade of wood 6 s.: p*aie*d for ij doz. Cotton				
Candles 8 s.	00	14	0	
p*aie*d for 2 doz. of cutt Match Candles 7 s.: p*aie*d for				
ij Sammons 26 s. 8 d.	01	13	8	
p*aie*d him that brought them 12 d.: p*aie*d longs daughter 18 d.	00	02	6	35
p*aie*d for oatmeale 3 d.: p*aie*d for apples 2 s.: p*aie*d for				
pares 12 d.	00	03	3	
p*aie*d for a pecke of cutt salt 6 d. p*aie*d for j doz. of				
(blank) 3 s. 9 d.	00	04	3	
Sume is	13	00	6	40

28/ brensley: *probably Brownsea Island in Poole Harbour*

paied for a bottle for strong watter 2 d.: paied Thomas
Hellier for goinge to gunnell for a nett 6 d.   00   00   08
paied for a shoulder & brest of Mutton 22 d.: paied for
a ribb of beefe 22 d.   00   03   8
paied for a horse to shroton 8 d.: paied for Tapps & Riben 5 d.:   5
paied for salt & lambe 3 s.   00   04   1
paied for eggs 3 s. 8 d.: paied for read herringe 12 d. paied
for Cockells 6 d.:   00   05   2
paied for 301 of oysters 10 s. 8 d. for 3 quarters of Cushinge
Cloth 9 d.   00   11   5   10
paied for 6 sacks of Coles 2 s. 9 d.: paied for a cupple of lings 2 s. 00   04   9
paied for a pynt of white wyne 3 d.: paied for candles 4 d.:   00   00   7
paied for fresh ffish att iij tymes 14 s. 4 d.: paied Thomas
hellyer & his company for fishinge 9 s.: paied for rodds
20 d.: paied for a quarter of bread 3 d.: paied for apples   15
4 s. 9 d.   01   10   0
paied Goodwiffe Gardner for a henn & a capen 2 s. 6 d.:
paied hugh Macham for cuttinge of sayes 8 d.: paied
Thomas Rawlingston for a rostinge pugg 18 d.   0   04   8
paied for a capen 12 d.: paied for a Capen to Mrs Barens   20
16 d.: for a capen to mrs Roove 2 s.:   0   04   4
paied to Byles for 14 quartes of white wyne & 3 pyntes of sack   0   08   6
paied to mr Macham for ij Capons 3 s.: paied George
payne for 2 hennes 18 d.   0   04   6
paied to higgons for 2 quarters & 4 leggs of Mutton   00   10   0   25
paied to Sander for 4 quarters of Mutton 8 s. paied
Thomas Morie for a lambe 5 s. 6 d.   00   13   6
paied to pyne for foynge ye Cloth in ye hall 6 d.: paied for
spriggs 3 d.   00   00   9
paied for 3 neats tongs 2 s. 6 d.: paied for Musterd 6 d.:   30
paied for a ferken of beare 12 d.   00   04   00
paied to davis for naylinge ye railes 16 d.: paied for orenges
& lemons 8 d.   00   02   0
paied to Roberte davis man for carrige a lettere to warham
& poole   00   01   0   35
paied for 5 pyntes of rose watter & d. a pynte of sweete watter   00   04   8
paied for a quarte of head att spennyes 6 d.: paied Mary
Rawlingston for 5 henns 4 s. 2 d.:   00   04   8

2/ gunnell: *5 minims in MS; Tarrant Gunville, about 5 miles northeast of Blandford Forum*
5/ shroton: *Iwerne Courtney, also known as Iwerne Shroton, about 5 miles northwest of Blandford Forum*

paied mrs Keynell for 6 henns 5 s. 6 d.: paied to Shepeard for worke 5 s.	00	10	6
paied Goodwiffe Gardner for ij hogsheads of ye best beare & ij barrells of other	01	05	0
paied william Bremble for j hogshead of Clarrett wyne	04	00	0
paied pellye for Candles 5 s. 10 d.: paied Iohn Munns that hee spent att sherburne 2 s.	00	07	10
paied for vennigeare 3 s. 4 d.: paied william Higgons 10 s. 8 d.	00	14	0
paied william ffreeman 13 s.: paied Thomas pitt 13 s. 4 d.	01	06	4
paied Iohn Roper 5 s.: paied Robert Hamond 5 s.	00	10	0
paied to George Harben 64 s. 6 d.: paied Richard Hardinge 10 s. 6 d.	03	15	0
paied to Iehonadab Sherlye	08	12	6
paied Ione Bryce 22 s. 16 d.: paied Hugh Macham 5 s. 6 d.: paied Ione Iellett 56 s.	04	04	02
paied Iohn Hawker 89 s.: paied to Robert Swayne 14 li. 15 s. 8 d.	19	04	8
Sume is	50	13	0⎮

5

10

15

Monyes paied for waiges as followeth

20

paied Sir Ralfe Horssies Cooke 20 s.: paied Nicholas Cooke & his boy 13 s. 4 d.	01	13	4
paied to the widdow Gawler 2 s: paied to the widdowe harrice 2 s.	00	04	0
paied to old Turnebroch 2 s. 4 d.: paied to the Clarkes wiffe 12 d.: paied Thomas pellyes mayde 12 d.	00	04	4
paied Thomas Sherman 2 s.: paied Henry Mellidge for 7 dayes 7 s.	00	09	0
paied Bishope 2 s. 6 d.: paied the widdowe Baylie 4 s. 6 d.: paied the lame wench 18 d.	00	08	6
paied to Anne Grims 4 s.: paied Ione knight for washinge 2 s. 6 d.	00	06	6
paied Iames Cooke 16 s. 8 d.: paied for makinge Cleane the broches 8 d.	00	17	4
paied that I gaue vnto Ione Hawker 12 d.: paied mr pitt for bricks vsed in ye kitchen 12 d.	00	02	0

25

30

35

6/ 10: *corrected over 6*

15/ 04 02: *4 and 2 corrected over other figures*

18/ 50 13: *corrected over other figures*

23/ 01: 1 *corrected over another figure*

p*ai*ed to muston for ij dayes worke about Robert Swaynes
Kitchen 2 s.   00   02   0
                                        Sume is   04   07   0

more paied for such thinges as ware lost att the Race   5

p*ai*ed for ij stone Iuggs 2 s. j table napken of fine canvas 12 d.   00   03   0
p*ai*ed for ij wyne quart*es* 2 s. 6 d.: p*ai*ed for a great carued
stone Iugg 18 d.   00   04   0
p*ai*ed for a lanterne 12 d.: p*ai*ed for a dieper Napken 12 d.   00   02   0   10
p*ai*ed Iohn Roper for a carpett 8 s.: p*ai*ed for a payer of
snoffers 6 d.   00   08   6
p*ai*ed for a malt seeve 6 d.: p*ai*ed for the mendinge of
a Ioyne stoole of mr pitt*es* 4 d.   00   00   10
p*ai*ed for 2 table Napkens 20 d.: there was lost by apce   15
of gold taken at one of ye tables 3 s.   00   04   8
p*ai*ed for ij halland Napkens that ware lost   00   02   6
                                        Sume is   01   05   6
The total Su*m*me of all the disbursment*es* was   69 li.   06 s.   0 d.
Soe resteth to accompt for the su*m*me of   26 li.   02 s.   1 d.   20

p*ai*ed to George *(blank)*   00   06   6
p*ai*ed for j doz. & d. of *(blank)*   00   09   6
p*ai*ed to Goodwiffe *(blank)*   00   03   6
p*ai*ed to *(blank)*   00   04   0   25
p*ai*ed to George *(blank)*   01   15   0
p*ai*ed for iiij play boyes   00   02   0
                                        Sume is   03   00   6
...

                                                                       30

1604–5

Chamberlains' Accounts   DRO: DC/BFB: Finance: Chamberlains' Accounts
f F9* *(Rendered 10 December)*
...

Theare was freed by the Race this yeare past and nowe accounted for by   35
Iehonadab Sherly then Baylife the Som of xxx li. iiij s. x d. and it apperithe
by his bills, that there was Layde [of] out for the towne that yeare in sewt*es*

15/ apce: *for* a piece *(?)*
17/ lost: l *corrected over* h
22/ 6²: *corrected over another figure*

of Lawe and other busines for the Towne the som of xlj li. xv s. x d. of the
which som he received of the wives at hocti⟨.⟩ xxvj s. vj ⟨.⟩...

...

1606–7
Chamberlains' Accounts   DRO: DC/BFB: Finance: Chamberlains' Accounts
f F11* *(Rendered 2 November)*

The Therteth Daie of March .1607.

This Daie at a generall meetinge of the Bayliffe and Burgesses yt did appere   10
that there was made at the [⟨..⟩pt] Race in mr Machams tyme beinge then
Bayliffe at Shrovetyde 1605. the some of ffifteene poundes cleare of all
charges besides thertie shillinges that was then given by the gentlemen and
distributed by mr Macham amongest the poore of this Towne./
allsoe this present Daie vppon viewinge of the accountes of the last Race   15
beinge at Shrovetyde 1606 mr Harbyn beinge then Bayliffe yt did appere
that there was clered six poundes three shillinges besides an allowaunce made
of fiftie shillinges for a silver beaker of Sir Iohn Rogers and xxxj s. Disbursed
for a chest and thinges lost at the Race. there was allsoe [made] given then to
the poore by the gentlemen xliij s. which vj li. iij s. as yet resteth in mr Bayliffe   20
Harbyns hand. and the xliij s. ys disbursed accordinge to a note therof.

...

1607–8
Chamberlains' Accounts   DRO: DC/BFB: Finance: Chamberlains' Accounts   25
f F12v* *(Rendered 7 November)*

This Daie Iustinian whiteinge and Thomas Pitt beinge Chamberlyns ... haue
recieved for the Towne rentes the some of xxiij li. vij s. vj d. of mr Robert
Swaine for the profett of the Race the last yeare when he was Baylieffe iiij li....   30
...

1608–9
A   *Chamberlains' Accounts*   DRO: DC/BFB: Finance: Chamberlains' Accounts
f B22* *(Rendered 6 November) (Receipts)*   35
...
Receiued of players for playinge in the hall   00   03   4

2/ hocti<.>: *final letter illegible, possibly as result of*   17/ six: s *written over another letter*
attempted correction; for hoctid; *8–9 April 1605*   17/ three: *written over another word*

Rec*eiued* of my vnkell Keynell for monye geatherd on
Hock Monday by the weamen   00   13   3
...

1609–10

A *Chamberlains' Accounts*   DRO: DC/BFB: Finance: Chamberlains' Accounts
f B22v *(Rendered 6 November) (Receipts)*
...

Rec*eiued* of the weomen gathred att hocktyde   01   03   0
...

1610–11

A *Chamberlains' Accounts*   DRO: DC/BFB: Finance: Chamberlains' Accounts
f B23v* *(Rendered 4 November) (Money still owed to the town)*
...

more there is in the handes of Iohn Gawler for monye receiued by
him beeinge bailiffe of the wemminge att hock Munday 1611   *(blank)*

1611–12

Chamberlains' Accounts   DRO: DC/BFB: Finance: Chamberlains' Accounts
f F14v* *(Rendered 2 November)*
...

There was made at Shrovetyde last by the race Iehonadab Sherley
beinge then Baylieffe   xxiiij li.
...

A *Chamberlains' Accounts*   DRO: DC/BFB: Finance: Chamberlains' Accounts
f B24v *(Rendered 2 November) (Receipts)*
...

rec*eiued* more of him gathred by the weamen Hock Mondaye   01   04   0
...

1612–13

A *Chamberlains' Accounts*   DRO: DC/BFB: Finance: Chamberlains' Accounts
f B26 *(Rendered 24 October) (Receipts)*
...

Rec*eiued* of the hockmonye for this yeare   00   15   0
...

2/ Hock Monday: *24 April 1609*
9/ hocktyde: *16–17 April 1610*
17/ hock Munday: *1 April 1611*

30/ him: *Jehonadab Sherlye*
30/ Hock Mondaye: *20 April 1612*
37/ hockmonye: *Hocktide was 12–13 April 1613*

1613–14

A   ***Chamberlains' Accounts***   DRO: DC/BFB: Finance: Chamberlains' Accounts
f B26v* *(Rendered 21 October) (Receipts)*

...

Rec*eiued* of Hock Monye this yeare 1614 geathred by the   5
woemen   00 18 0

...

(Disbursements of Robert Swayne, chamberlain and bailiff)

                                                                                              10
more for the vse of my howse when Mr Sherlye was bailife
at the race   00 13 4
...

1614–15   15

A   ***Chamberlains' Accounts***   DRO: DC/BFB: Finance: Chamberlains' Accounts
f B27v *(Rendered 6 November) (Receipts)*

...

Rec*eiued* of Hock monye from the woemen this yeare   00 19 4
...   20

1615–16

A   ***Chamberlains' Accounts***   DRO: DC/BFB: Finance: Chamberlains' Accounts
f B28v* *(Rendered 4 November) (Receipts of Robert Keynell, chamberlain)*

...   25
Rec*eiued* of Io*h*n Mundes that was p*ai*d by the players
for the hall   00 03 4

...

(Receipts of Thomas Pitt, chamberlain and bailiff)   30

Rec*eiued* att Shroftyde by the *pr*ofet*tes* of a race   07 03 4
...
Rec*eiued* of the weomen w*h*ich thay geat on hock Munday   01 02 10
...   35

5/ Hock Monye: *Hocktide was 2–3 May 1614*
19/ Hock monye: *Hocktide was 17–18 April 1615*
34/ hock Munday: *8 April 1616*

1616–17

A *Chamberlains' Accounts* DRO: DC/BFB: Finance: Chamberlains' Accounts
f B29v *(Rendered 3 November) (Receipts)*

...

Rec*eiued* for hock mony this yeare by the weomen colected   01   02   0   5

...

1620–1

A *Chamberlains' Accounts* DRO: DC/BFB: Finance: Chamberlains' Accounts
f B32v *(Rendered 8 November) (Receipts)*   10

...

Rec*eiued* of players for the vse of the yeeld hall   00   05   0

...

1630–1   15
Chamberlains' Accounts DRO: DC/BFB: Finance: Chamberlains' Accounts
f F23* *(Disbursements)*

...

given vnto the Children of the Revells, that should have acted
a stage playe in the Hall   0.   10.   0.   20

...

BLOXWORTH

1589   25
Dean and Chapter Act Book for Salisbury Deanery WRO: D5/19/12
f 30v *(14 July)*

*Proceedings of a session held in the parish church at Bere Regis before George
Dawkes, LLB, the dean's official, in the presence of Giles Hutchens, notary public* 30

...

Officiu*m* d*o*m*i*ni *contra* paulu*m* Rawlins de Bloxworth
Quo die compar*uit* d*i*c*tus* Rawlins quem d*o*m*inus* iuram*ento* onerauit de
fideli*ter* r*es*pondend*o* ar*ti*cu*l*is &c. deinde exa*m*inatus fatet*ur* that vppon
Shroft Tuisdaie last past⟨.⟩ beinge scholm*aste*r ther for the better exercyse of 35
his scholers did p*ro*cure to play a dialoge w*i*thin the p*ar*ishe Churche of
Bloxworth not any waies in derogation of the lawes established or otherwise

---

5/ hock mony: *Hocktide was 28–9 April 1617*
34/ vppon: v *corrected over another letter*
35/ Shroft ... past⟨.⟩: *11 February 1588/9*

to *pro*phane the Churche vn*de* do*minus* iniunxit q*uo*d agnoscat crimen
pre*dictum* per ip*sum* p*er*petratur cor*am* m*agis*tro Rickman Rectore ib*ide*m
promittend*o* se nu*m*qu*am* in similia relapsur*um* quibus per ip*sum* p*er*actis
do*minus* mo*n*uit eu*m* ad certificand*um* in *pro*ximo ap*u*d Sherborne uel Sar*um*
sub pena iuris/.   5

…

BRIDPORT

1555   10
Robin Hood Ale Account   DRO: DC/BTB: M18/11
f [1]*

…

℃ M*emorandum* of the Accoumpt*es* and Rekenyng of henry waye and Stephen
Shower/ for the Robynhode Ale, made the yere aboue wrytten, as hereafter   15
ensueth

Receipts   ℃ Inprim*is* Made wi*th* the Ale   vij li. xj s.
Item receyved for the Bowth that was solde   xxxij s.
℃   Su*mma* of the hole Rec*eipts* amount to   ix li. iij s.

…   20

1555–6
Cofferers' Accounts   DRO: DC/BTB: M7
f [2]

…   25

It*em* Receyvid of Robyn hod*es* Mony   vij li. vj d.

…

1574–5
Cofferers' Accounts   DRO: DC/BTB: M7/10
f [1]*   30

…

Item paid to Will*i*am Bokerell for a Bull rope   ii s. vj d.

…

Item paid to owyn for the making of Iackalent & his hors hire   iiij s.   35

…

f [1v]*

…

Item to the Mynstrels a maye daye   v s.   40

…

1578–9
Cofferers' Accounts   DRO: DC/BTB: M7/10
single sheet*

…

vnto Loveredge ffor the bulrenge   iij d.   5

…

1592–3
Ale Account for Town Buildings   DRO: DC/BTB: M15/11
ff [2–7]* *(Receipts)*   10

Receipt*es* 1593:   The accompt of Henry Browne and George ffrancke collectors for the
Anno   buyldinge of the m*a*rkett house and scole house of Brydport Then
Elizabethe   beinge Steward*es* for the Ale as Assistant to the said collectors Iohn wey
Regine xxxv°   & Henry Pounde in the yere of the Bayliewike of Iohn Pitt and Gilbert   15
                      holman Baylef*es* of Brydport and henry wey Towne clarke who p*ro*cured
                      the gifte of the free stone for the same buyldinge, of the roght honorable
                      the Lady Stourton. out of Chidioke quarrie as follow*e*th. :1593:

                                          Receved in collections of Townes and   20
                                          p*a*rishes as followeth: & first of.

Brydeporte   Of mr Richarde Russell   ij s. vj d.
              Iohn Swaffilde   ij d.
              mres Ioane Sydwaye   xij d.
              will*i*am Byshop   xij d.   25
              Anthony Browne   ij d.
              Iohn Stronge   ij d.
              mr Iohn wey   xx d.
              Rob*er*t Keate ·   xij d.
              Rob*er*t Myller   vj d.   30
              Mr Henry Pounde   ij s.
              Thomas whithed   vj d.
              Nicholas Hardy   iiij d
              Iohn Goldinge   iij d.
              Thomas Baker   j d.   35
              Richarde Hounsell   vj d.
              mr will*i*am p*a*rker   iiij d.
              Iohn wiles   iij d.
              Steven wey   xij d.
              Rob*er*t Hassarde   iiij d.   40
              chr*is*tofer Davige   xij d.

17/ roght: *for* right

Symonde Colfox	ij d.
mr Iohn Pitt baylie	ij s. vj d.
Iohn Thressher	ij d.
Richard Elworthe Iun*ior*	ij d.
morgan Moone	xviij d. 5
will*ia*m Singleman	xij d.
will*ia*m Shuer	v d.	
The wydow Balstone	vj d.
Steven More	ij d.
Iohn myller	ij d. 10
Samuell mathewe	iij d.
Iohn Wood	ij d.
Richarde Goste	iij d.
Richard Prince	j d.
Richard Hardy	ij d 15
Iohn Russell	iiij d.
Iohn Iames	iiij d.
Ambros Peryam	ij d.
Iohn Balstone	ij d.
Iohn Dollings	ij d. 20
Iames Whetham	vj d.
Richard Colfox	ij d.
Walter hallett	vj d.
Rob*er*t Browne	iij d.
Iohn Coke	iij d. 25
Thomas Triptree	j pecke of malt
Iohn Colfox	j bushell of malt
Will*ia*m Bagge	half b*ushell* of malt
chr*isto*fer Balstone	half b*ushell* of malt
Thomas Browne	j pecke of malt 30
will*ia*m webber	j pecke of malt
mr Henry wade	iij b*ushells* of wheate
mr Iohn Chaplyn	half a b*ushell*
mr Arthur Maynarde	half a b*ushell* malt
Iohn whitmore	j pecke of malt 35
Iohn Nicols	half a b*ushell* malt
Mr Rogers	half a b*ushell* wheat
Iohn Gibbes	j pecke of malt
Richarde Balstone	j pecke of malt
The wydow Colfox	j pecke of malt 40
The wydow Plucknett	ij li. of candels
Rob*er*t Buckerell	j li. of candels
mr Nicholas Stratchlighe	ij li. of bacon

	Summa in mony	xxv s. iij d.
	Summa in malt	v. bushells. j peck
	Summa in wheat	iij bushells di.
	Summa in bacon	ij li.
	Summa in candels	iij li.	5

Porestocke	william wall	iiij d.
	Of Trevys	iij d.
	Of fforde	ij d.
	Of Douche	iiij d. 10
	Of mr knight	iiij d.
	Iohn Douche	iiij d.
	master vicer of porestock	iiij d.
	walter Haywarde	iij d.
	Nicholas Browne	j bushell malt 15
	Edmond Browne	half a bushell malt

	Summa in mony	ij s. iiij d.
	Summa in malt	j bushell di.

20

Chidioke	Of the Lady Stourton and her house	xiij s. ij d.
	Nicholas Gay	iiij d.
	Of his sonne	ij d.
	Iohn Peache	vj d.
	Symonde Bere	ij d. 25
	Richarde Orcharde	ij d.
	Iohn myller	j pecke of malt
	Thold Stone	j pecke of malt
	The wydow myller	di. pecke malt
	Giles wey	half a bushell malt 30
	The wydow waldren	j pecke malt
	Ambros whitt	j pecke malt
	Richarde Olyver	j pecke malt
	The wydow Colfox	di. pecke malt
	mr Iohn Hodder	ij bushells wheat 35

	Summa mony	xiiij s. vj d.
	Summa malt	ij bushells
	Summa wheat	ij bushells	

40

Bradpole	Anne Hardy	j pecke of malt
	Iohn waddon	di. peck malt

Mawde Balson	j pecke of malt
Thomas Luter	j pecke of wheat
Elizabeth wey	a bole of malt
Alice hallett	half a bushell malt
Henry homborne	j pecke of malt 5
Lyonell Browne	half a bushell malt
william Durke	j pecke malt & iij d.
Iohn Taylor	j pecke of malt
Margarett Sewarde	j peck malt
Iohn Browne farmer	vj d. 10
Richarde Newborough gentleman	iij d.

Summa mony	[ix] xij d.	
Summa wheat	j pecke	
Summa malt	iij bushells iij pecke	15

Loders	Robert Larder gentleman	j bushell malt
	Richard Iustee vicer their	j bushell malt
	Iohn Browne	j bushell malt
	The wydow keche	di. bushell malt 20
	Henry Craforde	di. pec malt
	Edmund Rylande	j pec malt
	Robert warren	j pec malt
	Iohn Craforde	j pec malt
	Iohn peache	j pec malt 25
	Iohn marshe	j pec malt
	Iohn Tinker	j pec malt
	Iohn Shipwike	j pec malt
	Iohn mathew	di. pec malt
	The wydow Adams	j pec malt 30
	Iohn warren	j pec malt
	Thomas lane	di. bushell malt
	Robert heare	di. pec malt
	The wydow hallett	di. bushell malt
	Iohn hallett	iiij d. 35
	Nicholas Warren	iiij d.
	Edmond Body	ij d.
	mr Barton	di. bushell wheat
	George Pitfold	di. bushell malt
		40

Summa mony	x d.	
Summa wheat	di. bushell.	
Summa malt	viij bushells. j pecke di.	ǀ

Netherbury & mangerton	Mr Newboroughe promised	di. bushell wheat	
	Ioane Hearne	j bushell malt	
	Iohn Hallett	di. bushell malt	
	Henry Crabbe	di. bushell malt	5
	Summa wheat	di. bushell	
	Summa malt	ij bushells	
Baunton	Robert Mone	(blank)	
	Robert knight	di. bushell malt	10
	Richarde warr	j pec malt	
	Steven Lane	j pec malt	
	Iohn harbor	j pec malt	
	Robert dollinge	j pec malt	
	Mawde Hawarde	j pec malt	15
	Thomas Mynson	j pec malt	
	Richarde hardy	di. pec malt	
	Iohn Stronge	j pec malt	
	William ffloude	j pec malt	
	Steven Hallett	iij pec malt	20
	Iohn Akerman	j pec di. malt	
	Nicholas George	vj d.	
	Steven Austyne	iij d.	
	Summa malt	iij bushells. iij pecke.	25
	Summa mony	ix d.	
Askerswell	Thomas Hardy	j pec di. malt	
	Richard Egerdon	di. bushell malt	
	The wydow Hardy	di. bushell malt	30
	Iohn hardy farmer	di. bushell malt	
	Roger Hardy	di. pec malt	
	christofer darby	xij d.	
	Summa mony	xij d.	35
	Summa malt	iij bushells	
Porestocke	Nicholas Browne	j bushell malt	
	Edmonde Browne	di. bushell malt	40
	Summa malt	j bushell di.	

20/ Steven: S *written over another letter*

Symondsboroughe.	Arthur ffowke gentleman	j bushell wheat	
	Iohn Terrell	j pec wheat	
	Robert dyme	j pec malt	
	Robert Colmer	j pec di. malt	
	Iohn Hounsell	j pec malt	5
	Avice Mynson	di. bushell malt	
	Iohn Crocker	j pec malt	
	Andrew Stevens	j pec malt	
	Iohn hounsell	j pec malt	
	master Docter hounde	j bushell wheat	10
	Iohn Syms	xij d.	
	Thomas Syms	vj d.	
	Mr LLoyde	vj d.	
	Richard Crafte	iij d.	
	Richarde wade	iij d.	15

	Summa mony	ij s. vj d.	
	Summa malt	ij bushells di. pecke	
	Summa wheat	ij bushells j pecke	
			20

Mylton	Iohn Syms	di. bushell malt	
	Symonde donne	j pec malt	
	George Donne	j pec malt	
	Richarde wrixham	j pec malt	
	william Talbott	vj d.	25

	Summa mony	vj d.	
	Summa malt	j bushells j pecke	

Adlington	Luke Iurden gentleman	j pec wheat & a lambe	30
	Richard Baylie	di. bushell malt	
	Thomas Chicke	j pec malt	
	Richarde Payne	vj d.	
	Bastion Pitfold	vj d.	
	The wydow Pitfold	iij d.	35
	william wey	iij d.	

	Summa mony	xix d.	
	Summa malt	iij pecke	
	Summa wheat	j pecke	40

Netherbury	Iohn Charde	j pec of malt	

The wydow Stone   j pec malt
Iohn Games tenant   j pec malt
Thomas Egerdon   j pec wheat
Nicholas Crabbe   j pec malt
Iohn Clare   j pec malt   5
The Wydow Crabbe   di. bushell malt
Horsforde of bowood   j pec malt
Thomas Goudge   j pec malt
The ffarmer mylls   di. bushell malt
Hughe Baylie   di. pec malt   10
Hughe Holt   j pec wheat
Iames Thatcher   j pec malt
Hughe Syms   di. bushell malt
Mr Thomas Gollop   xij d.
master vicer there   xij d.   15
Stone the myller   iiij d.
Thomas Crabbe   ij d.
munden the Smythe   ij d.

         Summa mony   ij s. viij d.   20
         Summa wheat   di. bushell
         Summa malt   iij bushells. di. & di. pecke

Shipton   Roger Knight   di. bushell malt
          william Newton   j pec malt   25
          Richarde whit   j pec malt
          mr walter Gray   xij d.
          Nicholas darby   iij d.

         Summa mony   xvj d.   30
         Summa malt   j bushell

Chilcombe   mystres Byshop   xij d.
          mr Humfry Byshop   iiij s.
          mr Symondes   xviij d.   35
          mr Holman   xij d.
          mr ffoster of pouncknell   xij d.
          mystres Holman   xvj d.
          Iohn Samsome   vj d.
                                         40
         Summa mony   x s. iiij d. |

Burton	mr Iohnson	di. bushell malt
	Iohn Gregory	j pec malt
	Stevens	iij d.
	Richarde Myll	iij d.
	mres Ioane wareham	iiij d. 5
	Ioane Phillips	iiij d.
	mres warehams gentlewoman	ij d.
	Yonge mr wareham	iiij d.
	Hughe myller	ij d.
	Mr Iohn Strode	xij d. 10

	Summa malt	iij pecke
	Summa mony	ij s. x d.

Bemyster	In primis at the Iustices table	xv s. vj d. 15
	Item in the Towne and of Strangers	vj s. viij d.

	Somma mony	xxij s. ij d.

Lyme Regis	Of master mayor	ij s. 20
	mr Belmy	xij d.
	mr Barons	xij d.
	mr Davy	xij d.
	mr Norrys	viij d.
	mr Anthony moone	xij d. 25
	mr Iurden	xij d.
	mr william Barons	xij d.
	mr Hill	xij d.
	mr Greenworde	xij d.
	mres woodrofe	iij pec of salt 30
	mr downe	vj d.
	mr knevett	vj d.
	mres Belmy	viij d.
	mr Ca⌐r⌐penter	vj d.
	mr Syms of charde	vj d. 35
	mr davy	iiij d.
	mr Broake	vj d.	
	Thomas Hyet	xij d.
	Markes Barons	vj d.
	Captaine Cranly	vj d. 40
	Iohn Bellymy	vj d.
	Iohn Shottocke	xij d.

Henry davie   vj d.
Richarde Barons   vj d.
Elizabethe lizerde   ij d.
George plee   iiij d.
Prest the baker   vj d.   5
Iohn Gollop   iiij d.

            Sum*ma* mony   xix s. xj d.
            Som*ma* salt   iij pecke
                                                                        10
Gift*es* of
strangers

mr chr*is*tofer Syms   xij d.
mr Thomas whittle   xij d.
will*ia*m ffushe   ij s. vj d.
Captaine Iordanie   xij d.
Of danby ^⌈2⌉ marynors   ij s.   15
Item on Sunday after may day of strangers wee mett on the way xix d.
Of other strangers the same morninge   iiij d.
mr dowce   xij d.
Of Browne   ij d.
mr Pitt of Blandforde   xij d.   20
mr George   vj d.
Of strangers at the bull   xij d.
Valuntyne the carryer   xij d.
mr Rayndell & his company   iiij s. vj d.
mr Erle   iij s.   25
mr Greenewood of Charde   ix d.
m*aste*r Captaine Moone   ij s.
Of waymouthe Melcombe and in o*u*r way whomewarde
the same tyme   xlv s. viij d.
mr Henry Harbyn   j b*ushel*l wheat   30

            Sum*ma* mony   iij li. x s.
            Som*ma* wheat   j b*ushel*l wheatel

            Receipt*es* on may day   35
In p*ri*mis receved at the Baylief table   v s. iiij d.
Receipt*es* Item at the other table   iij s. x d.
Item on Holyrode day at breakfast   iij s. v d.
Item the same after none for drinke   xij d.

16/ Sunday after may day: *6 May 1593*

Item for ij pott*es* of beare   ij d.
Item the sunday after may day at the bayliefe*s* table   iij s. x d.
Item the same day at breakfast   ij s. ix d.
Item vpon assension day at breakfast   vij s. viij d.

Sum*ma*   xxviij s.

In p*r*imis on whitsonday at breakefast   xvj s. ix d.
Item at dynn*er* the same day   viij s. iiij d.
Item at Supper the same day   xvij s.   10
Item on munday at breakfast   viij s. xj d.
Item more the same daye   xxxj s.
Item on Tuysday at breakfast   vij s. x d.
Item at supper the same day   xxix s. viij d.
Item more at supp*er* the same day   xij s. viij d. 15
Item more of the goodwief ffrancke for drinke   xiiij s.
Item on wensday at dynner   viij li. iiij d.
Item at supper the same day   xxv s.
Item on Thursday at dynner   iij s. vj d.
Item at supper the same day   v s.   20
Item on Satturday at dynner   xxj s. vj d.

Sum*ma*   xviij li. xviij d.

Receipt*es*   Of the p*a*rishe of Symondsboroughe   xxxiiij s.   25
              Of Shipton p*a*rishe   xxiiij s.
              Of Netherbury   xij s.
              Of Bradpole   xij s. ij d.
              Of Porestoke   xxxiij s.
              Of Adlington   xxvij s.   30
              Of mr Iacobb   viij s. iiij d.
              Of mr Richarde Pitt   ij s. vj d.

Sum*ma*   vij li. xiij s. |

                                                                                     35
Trinitie Sunday

Receipt*es*   Item at breakefast   x s.
              Item the west streate spent   xxxiiij s.
              Item the Southe streat spent   xlij s. vj d.

2/ sunday after may day: *6 May 1593*   8/ whitsonday: *3 June 1593*
4/ assension day: *24 May 1593*   36/ Trinitie Sunday: *10 June 1593*

Item the East Streat spent   liij s.
Item the west streate on trinitie munday   x s.
Item more of othe gyuf*tes* then   viij s. vj d.
Item on Tuysday of doctor Iames & others   iij li. ij s. iiij d.
Item on wensday at supper   ix s. x d.   5
Item of mr Iones   iij s. iiij d.

    Sum*ma*   xj li. xiij s. vj d.

    Sum*ma* total*is* malt – 42 b*ushells* at xviij d. *per* b*ushell*   iij li. iij s.   10

    Sum*ma* total*is* wheate – 10 b*ushells* at iij s. *per* b*ushell*   xxx s.

    Sum*ma* total*is* mony   xlviij li. xiiij s. iiij d.
                                                      15

    The totall some of malt wheat & mony   Liij li. vij s. iiij d.

ff [7v–9v]* *(Payments)*

In primis for iij of o*ur* suppers   xvj d.   20
Item for v of o*ur* suppers when we gethered chilcombe   ij s.
Item to will*ia*m webber for heir of his mare   vj d.
Item for iij of o*ur* suppers on thursday   xvj d.
Item for iij of o*ur* suppers on fryday   xij d.
Item paid to Peter for iiij dayes travell   xvj d.   25
Item the next wike on thursday for iij of o*ur* supp*ers*   xvj d.
Item delyu*er*ed mr Baylie Pitt for fursher   v s.
Item for vij calves head*es*   ij s. iiij d.
Item to Browne for ij li. j qu*ar*ter of bacon   ix d.
Item for ij calves head*es* & a chiterlinge on holyrode day   xij d.   30
Item for a pounde of bacon   iiij d.
Item for v of o*ur* suppers when we gethered chidioke   ij s.
Item for iij of o*ur* supp*ers* when we gethered the towne   xij d.
Item for iij mens supp*ers* that made the bower for tow night*es*   ij s.
Item paid to fursher for stones   ij s.   35
Item for viij calves head*es*   ij s.
Item for iiij li. of bacon   xvj d.
Item when we went to Netherbury for v of o*ur* suppers at night   ij s.
Item the next day for iij of o*ur* supp*ers*   xij d.

2/ trinitie munday: *11 June 1593*
3/ othe: *for* other

Item for iij of our suppers on fryday when we gethered Porestocke   ix d.
Item paid to Peter for vj dayes travell   ij s.
Item for iij of our suppers on munday sennight before whitsundaye   xij d.
Item for v calves heades Assension day   xxj d.
Item for vj mackerell   vj d.   5
Item paid to the carpenters for vj dayes worke at taske for iij persons   xvij s.
Item for Peters wages for iiij dayes   xvj d.
Item for a horse for one wyke   xxij d.
Item for our dynners at Bemyster   xij d.
Item for horse meat at Lyme   vj d.   10
Item for a quart of wyne   viij d.

Summa pagine   Lix s. xj d. |

Paymentes   Item paid iij carpenters for iiij dayes worke at taske   ix s. iiij d.   15
Item paid for drayinge of stones   x s.
Item paid to Corbyn and Pullam for ryddinge of the quarrie   iiij s.
Item to Steven hardy for carriage of iij lode of stones from Chidioke   iiij s.
Item to Iohn homborne for vij lode of stones carriage from
Chidioke   ix s. iiij d.   20
Item to Corbyn for ryddinge of the quarrie   ij s. viij d.
Item to Gardyner and Skorche for vj dayes for drayinge of stones   xij s.
Item to wodcock for his wikes worke and iij more with him at taske   xxj s.
Item to Peter for his wages   ij s.
Item to Prince for his horse heir   xvj d.   25
Item for carriage of tymber   vij s.
Item for vij hodgsheddes of lyme   xv s.
Item to the stone drayers   iiij s.
Item to wodcocke   iij s.
Item to Iohn homborne for vj lode of stones carriage from
Chidioke   vij s. viij d.   30
Item to Steven hardy for vj lode of stones carriage from
Chidioke   vij s. viij d.
Item for the carriage of sande   x d.
Item to ij persons for help ladinge of stones   viij d.   35
Item to the stone drayers   ix s. vj d.
Item to buckerell for help ladinge of stones   iiij d.
Item to George ffranck for his horse heir and other charges   ij s. viij d.
Item delyuerd mr Thatcher vpon assumpsit   vj s.

3/ munday … whitsundaye: *28 May 1593*
4/ Assension day: *24 May 1593*

Item for xiiij hodgsheddes of bere at xij s. the hodgshedd to
mr Richard Russell   viij li. viij s.
Item for x bushells of wheat   xxx s.
Item to Thomas Triptree for mutton   xv s. x d.
Item for ij quartes of wyne and suger for master docter Iames   ij s.   5
Item for v quartes of wyne docter Gray had at the east bridge   iij s. iiij d.
Item to Nicholas hardy for fettinge of ij calves   viij d.
Item for a pecke of wheat for cakes   ix d.

Summa pagine   xviij li. vij d. | 10

Paymentes

Item for half a bushell of whe⌈a⌉te my wief bought to make
houshold breade   xviij d.
Item for a calf bought by mr baylie mone   vj s. ij d.
Item to Nicholas hardy for a quarter of beof   xxij s. iiij d.   15
Item paid more for beof   vj s. viij d.
Item for mutton   xvj d.
Item for fetchinge a calf   iij d.
Item paid to Nicholas hardy for iiij lambes   xx s.
Item for viij li. of powder   viij s.   20
Item for lyveryes for the musicions   ij s. vj d.
Item for rushes   xiiij d.
Item for half a calf of Nicholas hardy   iiij s.
Item for a quarter of mutton   ij s. x d.
Item for suger for the kytchin   iij s.   25
Item for xiiij quartes of wine for the Iustices   xij s. vj d.
Item for ij gammons of bacon   iij s.
Item for a rostinge pigge   ij s.
Item spent at Shipton   iij s.
Item spent at Symondsboroughe   iij s.   30
Item for iij [wine] quartes of wyne mr pound called for
when the Iustices were here   ij s. iiij d.
Item to the Coke for his wages   iij s.
Item for a bed of mutton   xviij d.
Item for vj quartes of wine when docter Gray supped here   iiij s. vj d.   35
Item for viij chickinges   xx d.
Item for viij chickinges   xvj d.
Item for ix chickinge   xviij d.
Item for ij capons   xvj d.
Item for butter   iij s. vj d.   40
Item for a capon   viij d.
Item to Iohn Russell for chickinges   ij s. iiij d.
Item for viij chicken   xvij d.

Item for ix chicken   xx d.
Item for iij dozen of trenchard*es*   v d.
Item for vittuels for the musicions from wensday vntyll Sunday   v s.
Item to Nicholas hardy for iij calves   xxx s. iiij d.
Item to Nicholas hardy for half a mutton   iiij s.   5
Item for sending for the bandore   ij s.

Summa pagine   viij li. xj s. ix d. |

Paymen*tes* Item for a capon   viij d. 10
Item to Swete for half a veale   v s.
Item for a q*ua*rter of veale   ij s.
Item to Crabbe for beof   ij s. viij d.
Item for mackerell   ij s. vj d.
Item for butter   iij s.   15
Item for beof   ij s. iiij d.
Item for wyne on satturday after whitsunday for mr Preston   xviij d.
Item to Peter for viij dayes travell in the holidayes   ij s.
Item to chr*isto*fer Snell for a dayes work   viij d.
Item to Prynce for meting S*ir* George Trencharde for o*ur* warninge   iiij d. 20
Item for prewance   ij s.
Item for vij quart*es* of vyniger   xxj d.
Item for iij li. of suger   ij s. vj d.
Item for glasses burste and lost   ij s. vj d.
Item for salt   xij d. 25
Item for viij li. of bacon   ij s. viij d.
Item to mr whithed for v b*ushells* of wheat   xv s.
Item to mr wey for iij b*ushells* wheate   ix s.
Item to Rob*ert* Buckerell for his mare for iiij dayes   ij s.
Item for the colirs of Henry Browne and George ffrancke   xiij s. 30
Item for sope and candels   xij d.
Item for bakinge of breade   xij d.
Item for iij quart*es* of wyne for the kinge of loder   ij s. viij d.
Item to Alforde for beof   ij s.
Item paid and delyu*er*d to George ffrancke for and towardes   35
the buyldinge of the house   x li.
Item more delyu*er*d to mr maynarde by the wief of Henry Browne
to the townes vse   iij li.

17   0   9 | 40

17/ satturday … whitsunday: *9 June 1593*

Charges for vituels when docter Iames
dyned with vs. and other paymentes.

Paymentes

Item for a calf	viij s.
Item for a sholder and a breast of veale	xvj d.
Item for a fatt lambe	iiij s. iiij d.
Item for chicken	ij s. iiij d.
Item for a hocke of veale	xij d.
Item to Clare for a dayes worke	xij d.
Item to williams for her worke	iij s.
Item for tripes	iiij d.
Item to the musicions for there wages	Liij s. iiij d.
Item for there lodginge	ij s.
Item to Locke for mendinge the drome and his worke about the bower	ij s. x d.
Item to Orcharde for his intendance	xij d.
Item to Thomas Buckcombe	iiij d.
Item to George Guyer	vj d.
Item to Robert wey for frethinge the bower	vj d.

Summa   iiij li. xxij d.

1602–3
Town Account   DRO: DC/BTB: M18/10
f [1]*
...

Item for making of Iackalent and for ahorse   iij s. iiij d.

...

f [3]*
...

Item paid more to Mr Tiggins for the yearell of bedfords [m] mens
svpper   ij s.

...

1606–7
Court Leet Proceedings   DRO: DC/BTB: C87, item 2
single mb *(6 October)*
...

pena – iij s. iiij d.

Item that the buttes be sett vp. befor⟨...⟩
And that the highway in the streete⟨...⟩ the bulring: & before the signe of
th⟨...⟩ nexte vpon payne

...

1609–10
Court Leet Proceedings   DRO: DC/BTB: C88
f 23* *(19 March)*

...

Also the said Bailiff*es* haue placed Thomas maniford one of the sones of the   5
said Iohn maniford decessed, w*i*th one Will*ia*m Keele musitian w*i*th him to
dwell & serve as an apprentice from the feast of the Anunciac*i*on of our
Lady the virgin next coming ffor *(blank)* yeres thence following fully to be
complete By and vnder the coven*a*ntes before exp*re*ssed and that the said
will*ia*m shall with due expedic*i*on and assone as the said Thomas shalbe   10
capable thervnto. teach & informe his said app*re*ntice in the art & mistery
of musicke. with gentle vsage & moderate correction.

1613–14
Bill of Complaint in Miller et al v. Maries et al   PRO: STAC 8/214/2   15
mb 4* *(1 June)*

To the King*es* most excellent Ma*i*estie
In humble manner shew and informe vnto yo*u*r most excellent Ma*i*estie
yo*u*r Highnes humble and obedient subiect*es* Rob*er*te Miller Aaron Cooke   20
Nicholas Horsford Angell Churchill Iohn Chard Will*ia*m Whettam Will*ia*m
Colefox Walter Hussey al*ia*s Bayly Inhabitant*es* w*i*thin the Borough Towne
of Bridport in the County of Dors*et* That wheras Your said Subiect*es* having
for many yeares togither now last past inhabited and dwelt w*i*thin the same
Towne of Bridport, haue soe carefully ordered and caried themselves in all   25
their acc*i*ons, and lived w*i*thin the same Towne in such honest and civill
manner that never any iust excepc*i*on was heertofore taken against them nor
any cause by them given wherby any scandale or reproach might any way
arise or grow to blemish their honest fames and reputac*i*ons: Insomuch as
there hath ben a speciall choise made of yo*u*r said Subiect Rob*er*te Miller to   30
execute the Office of a Bailiffe w*i*thin the same Borough w*hi*ch hee hath
discharged w*i*th such faithfull and dutifull service to yo*u*r Ma*i*estie as the same
his office did require. Yet soe it is may it please Yo*u*r most excellent Ma*i*estie
that Will*ia*m Maries of Bridport aforesaid Barber Iohn Lack of Bridport
aforesaid Mercer Iohn Abbott the Yonger of Bridport aforesaid Mercer Iohn   35
Lea of Bridport aforesaid Mercer Anthony Mathew of Bridport aforesaid
yoman Thomas Lack of Bridport aforesaid Shoemaker ˄⌈°Hugh Syms Will*ia*m
Osburne°⌉ and Will*ia*m Marshall of Bridport aforesaid Miller, and diu*er*s
other p*er*sons to yo*u*r Ma*i*est*ies* said Subiect*es* yet vnknowne whose names Your
˄⌈said⌉ Subiect*es* humbly pray may bee by License of this Honorable Co*u*rt   40

12/ with: w *damaged* by small hole

inserted into this Bill of Complaynt when they shall bee knowne, envying
and repyning at the prosperity and good fame of your said Subiectes and of
diuers other Your Maiesties Subiectes Inhabitantes of the said Towne of Bridport
of honest fame and conversacion haue ∧⌈in or about the moneth of Ianuary
now last past⌉ vnlawfully conspired and practized how they might not only   5
soyle and blemish but vtterly extinguish and take away the honest fame and
reputacion of your said Subiectes for ever. ffor which purpose they the said
William Maries Iohn Lack Iohn Abbott Iohn Lea Anthony Mathew Thomas
Lack ∧⌈°Hughe Syms William Osborn°⌉ and William Marshall haue devised
made and contrived ∧⌈in writing⌉ diuers infamous Scandalous & ignomynious   10
Libelles in verse which they have sithence published dispersed and divulged
tending to the traducing of your said subiectes, and of diuers other Your
Maiesties Subiectes Inhabitantes of the said Towne of Bridport, and to the
taxing and upbraiding them for following religious exercises by the Church
of England established and by your Maiesties Ecclesiasticall Lawes enioyned   15
And namely on ⌈or about⌉ the first day of ffebruary now last past the said
William Maries Iohn Lack Iohn Abbott Iohn Lea Anthony Mathew Thomas
Lack ∧⌈°Hugh Syms William Osburne°⌉ and William Marshall, by the
vnlawfull conspiracy and practise aforesaide and in accomplishment therof,
did vnlawfully make, write, and contrive a false scandalous and ignomynious 20
Libell in verse against your said subiectes, and other Your Maiesties Subiectes
Inhabitantes within the said Towne of Bridport which Libell followeth in
these wordes viz. Runne hosford runne Iohn Chard make haste William
Colfox make noe staye, for Miller with his trayne is gonne, make hast therfore
I saie: William Whettam calle Tom Merifeilde Iohn Bishope and the rest,   25
for Baylye and the Angell bright with book are redy prest: Sweete Beniamine
(Camelion lite) make haste I do thee pray, Iames Whettam Balston and Tom
Shutt remember Harry Waye: for Arons howse is fully fraught, with preachers
in greate store, Come quickly then delay noe tyme, make hast I say therfore:
Doe not forgett our sisters deare; for they with vs must pray, and sing a   30
Psalme before they preache, therfore make noe delaye. Lett Baylyes wife call
Beniamins, Alice Wade she will attende, and Whettams wives to Akermans
they forth with speede will sende; In any case lett Buckerelles trulls with
Mris Mullins mayde Call Ostelers wiefe for they will shedd greate store of
teares tis saide, Nell Merifeild calle Angells wife two sisters passinge brave; 35
with Balstons wife and many more whose company wee crave. Proude Agnes
Mris Paynes fyne mayde for marriage she doth looke because shee hath
bestowed some coste, to buy a faire newe booke. Remember likewise speedily
to send for Iohn Wads wife, for shee is calld with Moore tis saide to leade an
honest life: At Iohn Chards howse you shall bee sure your Company to meete,   40

18–19/ by the vnlawfull ... practise: *apparently written over an erasure*

where they with salutations most kindly will you greete; there Cheverell with
Counsell grave instructions will give And Aroun Cooke your Consciences
beinge wounded will relive: When Arons rodd begins to budd, and yeldeth
forth his blosome, these minssinge dames doe think indede, for them tis good
and holesome. The pride of flesh doth often swell his spiritt doth him move   5
and they with him incontinent will enterchange their love. ffor he doth often
walke abroade with them for recreation, It is the only way for soothe for
wenches of theire fashion. Hee is god wate a man of note with them to goe
or ride, his spiritt moves still to their loves at every tyme and tyde: What shall
I saye both night and day their lusts they will fulfill, Therfore tis tyme to   10
end this ryme and leaue them to their Will. finis. Ignoro./ In and by which
Libell they haue maliciously and falsely slaundered your said subiectes and
other honest Inhabitantes within the said Towne, and in coverte termes taxed
them Your Maiesties said subiectes and diuers other Inhabitantes of the said
Towne of Bridport with incontynency and other crymes. And having made   15
or caused to be made contrived and writen the said slaunderous Libell as
aforesaid, they the said William Maries Iohn Lack, Iohn Abbott Iohn Lea
Anthony Mathew Thomas Lack ∧⌜°Hugh Syms; William Osburne°⌝ and
William Marshall on or about the second day of the said moneth of ffebruary
now last past and at diuers and sundry tymes sithence haue maliciously and   20
vnlawfully published the said Libell, by repeating singing and vttering diuers
verses and partes therof And haue dispersed and cast abroade sondry Copies
of the said Libell in sondry places of the said Borough of Bridport, of intente
and purpose to publish the same to the slaunder and wrong of your said
Subiectes. And the said William Maries on or about the Third day of the said   25
moneth of ffebruary now last past came into the Shopp of one Thomas Chard
Mercer in Bridport aforesaid and then and there [in the presence of diuers
Inhabitantes of the said Towne], by the abettement aduise and procurement
of the rest of the said confederates did vnlawfully publishe and reade the said
Libell in the presence and hearing of a greate nomber of your Maiesties loving   30
subiectes then and there presente: wherof your said subiectes having intelligence,
made complaynt of the same to one Mr. Pitt (then and yet one of the
Bailiffes of the said Borough of Bridport) whoe being willing to suppresse the
same scandalous Libell, required the said William Maries to deliuer vnto him
the said Bailiffe the same Libell, but the said Maries (thinking hee should   35
then fayle, of the end hee aymed at viz. ∧⌜the⌝ disgracing Your said subiectes)
yf hee should deliuer the same Libell to the said Bailiffe) refused soe to doe
saying hee would first write a Copy of it. And afterwardes on or about the
same Third day of ffebruary the said William Maries did write a Copy of the
same Libell and the said Mr Pitt repayring againe vnto him the said William   40

36/ subiectes): *closing parenthesis used in error for comma (?)*

Maries required him to deliver the same Libell and the Copy therof (which
hee had writen) vnto him the said Mr. Pitt, and the said Maries deliuered the
said Libell to the said Mr. Pitt but did not deliuer to the said Mr. Pitt the
said Copy which hee the said Maries had soe newly writen/ And after hee
had deliuered away the said Libell, the same day hee the saide Maries having   5
the Copy of the same Libell, did reade the same in the presence and hearing
of sondry Inhabitantes of the said Towne of Bridport at the Shoppe of one
George Waye glover in Bridport aforesaid. And the said William Maries
contynewing still in his malicious course against your said Subiectes did on
or about the Eighth day of the said moneth of ffebruary shew a copy of the   10
same Libell vnto one Thomas Bagge an Inhabitant within the said Towne of
Bridport, and hath sithence given out diuers Copies of the same Libell vnto
other personnes. And the said Iohn Lea on or about the said Third day of
ffebruary did vnlawfully publish and reade in the presence of diuers Inhabitantes
of the said Towne of Bridport the said Libell out of an other Copy which   15
hee had gotten therof: whereof your said Subiect Angell Churchill having
notice repayred vnto him and desired him to deliuer the said Copy vnto him
the said Angell Churchill that he might suppresse it which the said Lea refused
to doe. But in a short space after viz. an hower or theraboutes, the said Iohn
Abbot, one other of the said confederates came into the Shop where Your   20
said Subiecte Angell Churchill and the said Lea were, and then the said Lea
deliuered the same to the said Abbot (whome the said Lea then served) and
the said Abbott did then and there vnlawfully reade and publish the same
Libell openly in the said shop in the presence and hearing of diuers persons
and smyled as hee was reading it, and did well like and allow therof. And   25
the said William Marshall on or about the Sixth day of the said moneth of
ffebruary now last past came into the howse of one Thomas Peirs in Bridport
aforesaid, and then and there in the presence and hearing of diuers of the
Inhabitantes of the said Towne of Bridport did singe certen verses of the said
Libell, and then and there drew out a copy therof out of his pockett and   30
deliuered the same vnto one Iohn Moone gentleman that hee might reade it:
but the said Mr. Moone endeauoring to suppresse the said Libell offered to
cast the same into the fire which the said Marshall perceiving speedily caught
the same away againe, and saide yf Mr. Moone had burned the same, yet
hee had an other copy of the said Libell. And the said William Maries Iohn   35
Lack Iohn Abbott Iohn Lea Anthony Mathew Thomas Lack ˄⌐°Hugh Syms
William Osburne°⌐ and William Marshall in farther prosecucion of their
former malicious and vnlawfull confederacyes and practises against your said
Subiectes and that their purpose of defaming and disgracing Your said
subiectes might the better take effect, on, or about the said ffirst day of   40
ffebruary now last past did vnlawfully make write and contrive, and cause to
be made writen and contrived an other false scandalous and ignomynious

Libell in verse against your said Subiectes and other Your Maiesties subiectes
Inhabitantes within the said Towne of Bridport, which Libell followeth in
these wordes viz. The puritans of Bridporte Towne; I wonder what they meane
to gorge themselves soe full of zeall being out of Charity cleane: I never yet
saw one of them that will small faultes forgive; but yf they haue the vpper   5
hand they countes them selves a sheerve. The lordes praier they forgett, they
doe it not remember as did apeere in towne of late, now in this last December.
A meane man can thou not entreate no not a Iustice of peace; they shewe
their malice what it is, and still doth it increase, Yet now they haue a man in
Towne: as some of them reporte that he an ang⌈e⌉lle is full shewer wherfore   10
they doe resorte, aswell by night as by the day, for they will spare noe tyme
to haue the wordes that hee doth saye, and all to make a cryme; I doe conffese
its verie good the word of god to heare, soe that wee make good vse of it,
and keepe our Conscience cleere. But they soe full of Mallice bee, that all
will not prevaile, although the offence it bee but small, yet needes they must   15
to gaylle; Yet she had bine a woman knowne, and one of their owne minde,
and donne some matter worse then that, they would haue proved kinde:
There was of late as I did heere a matter did befalle as more at large it will
appeer it was in the new hall, of some that shewed littell witt when they came
forth of doore, it seemes that they had neuer a whitt nor yet they bee but   20
poore. Though poore in wealth as I doe meane which is a thing most shewer,
Yet rich to godward may they bee, god graunte it may endewer. An other
matter beyond all this doth make mee much to wonder, how that the cloths
from saddele treese is grone soe far a sounder. Thire is one in towne haue
made reporte although it was but evill, his dearest frinde his father went the 25
next way to the Divill, one yonge man more which in this towne some
hundred marke haue spente, in beer and alle and other thinges yet now hee
doth repente, such a winter as this I never sawe for mildnesse of the weather,
I wonder men should pay soe deere for shewes which bee of leather And hee
that did these verses make Yf you did knowe his name some shame hearof   30
that he mighte take that he doth not the same. And yet hee is a learned man
as by this verse doth showe, yet let hym doe al that he can the crew will not
him knowe, and yet he can the scriptuer Read, and alsoe vnderstand, yet all
the knowledge that hee haue, is out of godes owne hand: me thinke we
shoulde not haue it so a new broome to take place; to put the old broome   35
out of date, beinge comely in the place. The best of vs must haue an end
and soe shall now my Ryme god graunt that we may all amend to morowe
in [the] morning be tyme: Vbi inciperis nole Iuri melier ibi Ensines esse bonas.
In and by which later Libell they haue maliciously and falsely slaundered

38/ Vbi … bonas: *written in display script*

your said subiectes and other Your Maiesties subiectes Inhabitantes within the
said Towne of Bridporte with diuers odious crymes and misdemeanors, but
very covertly and darkly not naming but meaning your said Subiectes, and
diuers other Your Maiesties subiectes Inhabitantes within the said towne of
Bridport. And the said confederates having made and caused to be made   5
contrived and writen the said second slaunderous Libell, they the said William
Maries, Iohn Lack Iohn Abbott Iohn Lea Anthony Mathew Thomas Lack
and William Marshall on or about the said second day of ffebruary now last
past, and at diuers and sondry tymes sithence haue maliciously and vnlawfully
at Bridport aforesaid published vttered repeated and songe the said second   10
Libell. And haue dispersed and cast abroade, and caused to bee dispersed
and cast abroade diuers Copyes of the said second Libell in sondrey places of
the said Towne of Bridport. And to the intent that they might yet bring Your
said Subiectes into more disgrace, the said Anthony Mathew, on or about
the same second day of ffebruary now last past did deliuer a Copy of the   15
said second Libell vnto one Thomas Waye of Bridport aforesaide tellinge the
said Way that hee should haue it bicause it concerned him the said Way, Yet
bound him by an oath to returne the same to him the said Mathew againe,
Which the said Way accordingly did deliuer vnto him the said Mathew. And
afterward ⌄⌈on or⌉ about the ⌄⌈said⌉ Third day of the said moneth of ffebruary 20
now last past the said Mathew deliuered the same second Libell vnto the
said Iohn Lack, one other of the said confederates; and the said Iohn Lack
on or about the ffowrth day of the said moneth of ffebruary now last past
did reade the same second Libell openly in the streete of the said Towne of
Bridport in the presence and hearing of diuers Inhabitantes of the same   25
Borough of Bridport. And on or about the Tenth day of the ⌄⌈same⌉ moneth
of ffebruary now last past the said Iohn Lack deliuered a Copy of the same
second Libell vnto the said Thomas Lack, whoe on or about the said Tenth
day of ffebruary caried the same Lybell vnto one Henry Waye, willing him
to reade it whoe read it accordingly; and whiles hee was reading of a certen   30
verse therin, the said Thomas Lack stroke the said Henry Waye on the
shoulder saying: there is for thee: and when he read and other verse therin,
the said Thomas Lack saide there is for an other, naming one of your said
subiectes, Wherby it appeareth manifestly that hee the said Thomas Lack
knew whoe were meant in and by the said second Libell. Now forasmuch as   35
the making dispersing publishing and publike reading of such slanderous
reproachfull false and ignominious Libelles wherby Your said subiectes heerin
named, and diuers other Your Maiesties loving subiectes, and their good and
honest fame credit and reputacion are traduced taxed slaundered and drawne

32/ and other: for an other

in question, and therby Your said subiectes and the rest soe slaundered, are
left as publike and notorious examples of disgrace obliquy and infamy,
without iust cause given is contrary to the Lawes of this Realme now in force
for the better suppressing of suche enormous offences and misdemeanors.
And forasmuch as daily experience doth witnes, that greate evilles doe spring   5
from this seditious and Divelish course of casting forth Libelles amongst
your Maiesties Subiectes and how dangerous it is to the quiet estate of this
Your Maiesties peaceable gouernment, yf such notorious offendors and
malefactors should escape vnpunished. And forasmuch as the making and
publishing of the said pernicious Libelles by the personnes before named and   10
all other the offences and misdemeanors aforespecified haue ben perpetrated
and committed sithence Your Maiesties ⌈last most gracious⌉ [most] generall
and free Pardon ∧⌈°and are directlie contrarie to diverse your maiesties good
and holesome lawes and ordinnaunces of this your highnes realme of
Englande°⌉ and doe not only deprave Your said subiectes and deprive them   15
of their good name and reputacion (which they hold and esteeme as precious
as their lives and haue formerly received and enioyed much comfort therin)
but alsoe derogate from Godes glory whoe by such abhorred courses and
Divelish practizes is infinitely dishonored and Your said subiectes haue
received and sustayned greate damage and losse therby in their credittes and   20
reputacions wherof they humbly pray reliefe in this Your Maiesties high Court
of Starechamber May it therfore please your most excellent Maiestie to
graunt vnto your humble subiectes Your Maiesties most gratious writt and
writtes of Subpena to bee directed vnto them the said William Maries Iohn
Lack Iohn Abbott Iohn Lea Anthony Mathew Thomas Lack ∧⌈°Hughe Sims   25
William Oburne°⌉ and William Marshall comaunding them and euery of
them therby vpon a certen daye and vnder a certen payne therin to be
lymited ∧⌈& comprised⌉ personally to appeare and bee before your Maiestie
and your highnes most Honourable Counsell in your high Court of
Starchamber then and there upon their corporall oathes to answeare the   30
premisses And farther to stand to and abide suche farther order and censure
heerin as to your Maiestie & your said Counsell shall seeme fitt to bee laide
and inflicted on suche heynous offendors and malefactors And your said
humble subiectes shall ever (according to their bounden duty) pray vnto god
for the contynuance of your Maiesties prosperous and royall Reigne over vs/   35

(signed) Iames More
Francis Ashley

26/ Oburne: for Osburne

Answer of Defendants in Miller et al v. Maries et al   PRO: STAC 8/214/2
mb 2* *(11 July)*

°Iurata vndecimo
die Iulij Anno
duodecimo
Iacobi Regis°

The Aunsweres of Hugh Symes Anthony Mathewe and
William Marshall defendantes to the Bill of Complaynte   5
of Robert Miller and others Complaynantes/

°Harker°

The defendantes by protestacion, not acknowledging nor confesseing any of
the Matters in the said Bill of Complaynte agaynst them exhibited to be
true, in maner, and forme as in the said Bill the same are sett forth agaynst   10
them, And alsoe saveing vnto them ⌈selves⌉ nowe, and at all tymes hereafter
all advantages of excepcion to the vncertenty and insufficyency of the sayd
Bill of Complainte for plea and Aunswere therevnto they saye That longe
before the exhibiting of theire said Bill of Complaynte the Complaynantes
and divers others of the inhabitantes of Bridporte aforesaide to the nomber   15
of one hundred and vpwardes being poore simple people both men weomen
and Maydes often assembled themselves to some of theire owne privatt
howses in ∧⌈the⌉ night tymes and there handled and expounded parcells of
scripture Counterfeyting preaching and Sange Psalmes pretending to professe
a more pure and zealous religion then others And alsoe often tymes gave   20
enterteynment to one Traske a young hot headed and excommunycated
Mynister and one *(blank)* Cheverell a yonge Scholemaster and preacher of
the same sect or oppynion Notwithstanding the Rector and parson of the
same parishe and Towne being a Reverend and learned preacher dothe take
greate paynes with his Charge being most willing to Teache Conferre and   25
give satisfaccion to any desirous to be satisfied in or of Doutfull questions
or poynctes of Religyon, Nevertheles the said Complaynantes and theire
Accomplices vtterly depyse his doctryne; deriding and making a laughing-
game at him and give out in speeches that they had as rather here A dogge
barke as here him preache, and that yf he were dead he would affrighte the   30
devells with many other vnseemely wordes of reproche bothe of him and
others deceassed which theire assemblyes and Conventicles moved divers of
the inhabitantes of Bridporte to suspecte that theire meeteinges were not in
deed to any good purposes, but rather to some evell and licentious ende,
and weare the rather moved to thinke soe because of theire ffeastinge and   35
drinckeing of greate store of wyne at such theire meetinges And theire
assembleyes and Conventicles being contrarye to his Maiesties lawes of this
Realme they the said Complaynantes and divers other of theire said assotiates
were by the Churchwardens of the said towne of Bridporte presented in the
spirituall Courte before doctor Hussey Chauncelor of the diocesse of Bristall   40

28/ depyse: *for* despyse

within which Iurisdiccion they dwell for theire said Assemblyes and
Conventicles And in shorte tyme after theire apparaunces before the said
docter and vppon the generall fame and reporte of theire lascivious vsages
and demeasners at there said meetinges Certen Rymes and verses were written
and Cast abowte the Towne which theis defendantes doe thinke were devised   5
and written by the Complaynantes or some of theire ∧⌈said⌉ Assotiates
purposely in policye that the same might be supposed to have byn written
or invented by the Churche wardens and other well affected persons of the
same Towne thereby to seeke revenge agaynst the said Churche wardeynes
and such others as the said Complaynantes and theire said Complices   10
∧⌈imagyned⌉ to dislike of theire famyliar Assembles and Conventicles, All
which theise defendantes doe thinke the rather for that they have herd, that
a written Ryme was deliuered vnto one Iohn Lea one of the defendantes
mencioned in theire said Bill of Complaynte, An apprentice and servant
vnto one Iohn Abbott Mercer one of the Churchwardens and one of the   15
defendantes likewise in theire said Bill mencioned, and the next morneing
very earlie Angell Churchell a Taylor one of the Complaynantes and one
Thomas Bagge whoe likewise favoreth of the Complaynantes Religion Came
to the shoppe of the said Abbott pretending to buye some of his wares, and
the said Iohn Lea shewed them such wares as they seemed to buye but the   20
said Churchell and Bagg disliked the boyes prices and would not buy of him
but of his said Master, Therevppon the saide Lea wente to his Masters house
distant from the Shoppe and Cawsed the said Iohn Abbott his Master, to come
to the shopp And then the said Churchell, and Bagge made a Cold showe to
buy some of his weares which was not theire occasion but to laye snares and   25
baytes to entrappe the said Iohn Abbott to worke theire malyciouse revenge
vppon him for doeing ∧⌈but⌉ his Office and Dewtye there vppon left the
priceinges of the said wares, And Churchell told the said Abbott that his
boye (meaneing the said Iohn Lea) as he hearde had Certen Rymes written
in paper which he desired to see, the said Abbott ∧⌈aunswered him⌉, he knewe 30
not of yt And there vppon comaunded his boye to deliver them ∧⌈yf he had
any and accordingly the said Lea Deliuered them⌉ to the said Churchell or
Bagge, Then they or one of them desired the said Iohn Abbott to reade
them which he denyed, and they perswaded him yt was noe hurte therefore
earnestly entreated the said Abbott agayne to reade them, vppon whoes greate 35
request the said ∧⌈reade twoe or three lines & Cast yt to the saide⌉ Churchell
and Bagge agayne dislikeing yt, And sithence the Bill exhibited the said
Abbott heareing that he was mencioned a defendant in the said Bill but not
then nor yet served with proces repaired to Miller one of the principall
Complaynantes and demaunded him what reason he and the other   40
Complaynantes had to Charge him vppon the said Bill of Complainte whoe

36/ the said: *for* the said Abbott

neu*er* intermedled with any thing but at the earnest request of Churchell
one of the Compl*aynantes* (as aforesaid) the said Miller aunswered Abbott
that he was verye glad he had occasion to be revenged vppon him and would
be revenged thoughe he spente himselfe to his shirte, And the said said Hughe
Symes one of the defend*antes* sayeth that one will*i*am Reade, a Barber of   5
Bridporte aforesaid one of the Compl*aynantes* assotiatt*es* hath given forthe
that there is a Bayte laide for him the said Symes, what his meaneing is the
said defend*ant* Symes knoweth not, And for further Aunswere and plea vnto
the said Bill of Complaynte theise defend*antes* saye, and eyther and eu*er*y of
them for himselfe seu*er*ally sayeth, That they are not guilty nor eyther of   10
them is guiltye of the deviseing makinge Contriveing writing or devulginge
of the said Lybells in the said Bill of Complaynte menc*i*oned or of any other
the Misdemeanenors in the said Bill expressed in manner and forme as ‸⌈in⌉
the said Bill the same are sett forthe agaynst them, All w*hi*ch Matters theise
defend*antes* are readye to averr and prove as this right honorable Courte shall   15
and will awarde And prayen and eu*er*y and either of them prayeth seu*er*ally
to be dysmyssed out of this honorable Courte with theire reasonable Costes
and Charges by them wrongefully susteyned in this behalfe./

                                                    (signed) Tho*mas* hughes
                                                              Swanton   20

1614–15
Bailiffs' Accounts   DRO: DC/BTB: M2/11
f [1]*

...   25
for a bill of Inditement against the fidlers at Lent assize   ij s. 6 d.
...

Cofferers' Accounts   DRO: DC/BTB: M8/10
f [1] *(Payments)*   30
...
It*em* paied to Beves for paving the Bullring   vj d.
It*em* paied to George Limbert for yron worke for the Bullring   ij s. vj d.
...

                                                                                  35
Answer of Defendant in Miller et al v. Maries et al   PRO: STAC 8/214/2
mb 3* *(28 November)*

Iurat*a* vicesimo   The aunswere of Iohn Abbott one of the Deffend*antes*,
octavo die   to the Bill of Complaynte of Rob*te* Myller Aaron Cooke   40
Novembris

4/ said said: *dittography in* MS   33/ Limbert: t *corrected from* d
16/ prayen: ye *obscured by ink blotch*   40/ Robte: *for* Roberte; *abbreviation mark missing*

Anno
Duodecimo
Iacobi Regis

Nicholas Horsford, Angell Churchell Iohn Charde william whettam
william Colfox & walter Hussey alias Baylie Complaynantes

Harker

The said deffendant, now and att all tymes hereafter, saving vnto himself, all
benefytt, and advantages of excepcion, to the incertentie, and insuffyciencye   5
of the saide Bill by protestacion, first saieth, that he verelie conceaveth, that
the same Bill ys presented against him this deffendant, and thother deffendantes,
(being poore men) in this honorable Courte, with much mallice, and by
incouragement of some others, not named playntiffes in the same, and in
more particuler against this deffendant, yt conteyneth many vntruthes   10
devyzed and sett forth, without any iust cawse, or coullor of any mysdemeanor
comytted or done by this deffendant, Neverthelesse ˄⌈who⌉ for a directe·
aunswere to all the misdemen⟨…⟩ wherewith hee is charged in and by the
same Bill, Doth deny, that hee ys guiltie of them, or any of them, in such
soarte, and manner as in, and by the said Bill they are set forth and alleadged   15
against him, for a farther declaracion, and acknowledgement of soe much of
the matters therein conteyned as hee this deffendant hath ben acquaynted
withall and with the manner thereof ˄⌈hee⌉ further saieth, That abowte
three quarters of a yere nowe last past, hee this deffendant being then, and
yet, one of the Churchwardens, of the Towne of Bridport, in the Countie of   20
Dorset, togeather with one Nicholas Hardey, then thother churchwarden of
the same Towne receaved dyvers messages, sent him this deffendant from
some of thofficers of the ecclesiasticall Courte of the said Countye of dorset,
that then tofore, there were; and had ben dyvers meetinges or conventicles
of dyvers persons both men and women at certen howsses, vsually within   25
the saide Towne of Bridporte at vnseasonable howres in the night tyme, And
that if ˄⌈hee⌉ the saide deffendant, and the said other Churchwardens of the
same Towne, dyd not shortlye presente such offences, being conceaved, and
sayde, to bee contrarie to the lawe, and ponisheable by that Courte, That
then the said Courte would ponishe them the deffendant, and his fellowe   30
Churchwarden, Therevppon the said deffendant and his fellowe said fellowe
Churchwarden, havinge speciall care therein, for the due performance of
theire said office therein conferred togeather thereof, and having consydered
of suche inconvenyency as this Deffendant, and his fellowe Churchwarden
thought might growe or happen by the not presenting of the said Offences,   35
They dyd present such persons inhabitantes within the said Towne, as they
knewe to haue suche meetinges at theire howses, and the howsses of other
persons, in that kynde, and alsoe such as vsed, and frequented such their
meetinges, dyvers of which persons soe presented, are nowe Complaynantes,

---

7/ presented: *3 minims in* MS
16/ for: *erasure before this word obliterated by line fillers*
31/ his fellowe said fellowe: *partial dittography in* MS; *for* his said fellowe

in the said Bill, And thereuppon proces of Citac*i*on were awarded against
thoffenders soe presented, And vppon the said Citac*i*on the same Offenders,
or the moste of them dyd appeere ∧⌈whereof the said Rob*er*te Myller was
one⌉, at a Courte holden at Blandford w*i*thin the said Countye before Iames
Hussey Esquier Doctor of the Cyvell lawe and Chauncellor of the diocesse   5
where the said Offences were comytted, and there, at the said Courte, or
before the said Chauncellor, the saide p*er*sons cyt*e*d, acknowledged theire
offences, and alleadged their estat*es* to be poore & verye vnable to beare theire
expenc*es* of attendans of the said Courte, yt being kept some fower, and
twentye myles from their dwelling places or thereabout*es*, and promysed the   10
⌈said⌉ Chauncellor, that they the said p*er*sons cyted or the most of them,
woulde forbeare from henceforth, to comytt such or the lyke offences any
more or to such effecte, wherevppon the said Chauncellor remytted the
farther ponishem*ent* of theire saide offences, and for that tyme suspended
yt, and sent them home agayne/ principallie in regarde of theire small abilitye 15
in hope of theire reformac*i*on and not for any cleernes w*it*h them of their
said offences, as this deffend*a*nt thinketh And further this deffend*a*nt saieth,
that before thoffences aforesaid were presented, there were certen verses or
rymes made, and cast abroade in the sayde Towne as in the saide Bill ys
alleadged, but whoe devysed or wrote the same verses, or rymes, this deffend*a*nt 20
knoweth not nor knoweth what ∧⌈were⌉ the Contentes of the said rymes, or
verses but by the content*es* of this byll, Saving that yt is true, ∧⌈thatt⌉ abowte
the tyme aforesaid, one paper written w*i*th verses, or rymes, but whether to
the effecte in the Bill menc*i*oned, this deffend*a*nt knoweth not, was delyvered
vnto one Iohn Lea, one other deffend*a*nt, this defend*antes* apprentyce being   25
abowte the age of Sixteene or seaventeene yeres, as he tolde this deffend*a*nt
by one Marye wyllyams, wiefe of Iohn Willyams of Bridporte aforesaide
whoe intreated the said Lea as hee said to readd the same paper or verses,
shee thinkinge as hee said, as the said Lea alsoe saide that yt had ben a *lettre*
sent vnto her, from her daughter, then and yet dwellinge att or neere London   30
but vppon hearing some Parte thereof, yt not falling out, to bee soe, shee
left the same w*i*th the said Lea, as hee alsoe affirmed w*hi*ch beinge made
knowen to the said Angell Churchchell one of the Compl*ay*n*antes* and ∧⌈one⌉
Thomas Bagge, whereuppon, the said Churchell, beinge a tayler and this
deffend*a*nt a mercer early in the morninge then soone after, togeath*er* w*i*th   35
the said Bagge repaired to this deffend*antes* shoppe (being distant from [hi]
his dwelling house a good space) and fynding the said Lea there, and this
deffend*a*nt then, not come thith*er* hee for a fashion and shewe as yt seem⟨…⟩
to shewe him the said Churchell some mercery wares for the said Bagge,

29/ hee: *for* shee *(?)*
32/ the²: *erasure before this word obliterated by line fillers*
38/ seem⟨…⟩: *about 560mm of text area illegible through creasing*

tryfling the tyme in expectac*i*on of this deffendant*es* comyng to his said
shoppe as yt seemed, Sayinge they woulde not buye any of the said wares
vnlesse they mighte buy yt of this deffend*ant*, himself Whereuppon an noth*er*
of this deffend*antes* servant*es* being then, in the said Shoppe went to this
deffendant ˏ⌐when he was⌐ [being] at his house and called him to come to   5
his said shoppe, and this defend*ant* repayred thith*er* accordinglie, and there
found the said Churchell and Bagge, and then after some Little questyoning
abowte the said wares, the said Churchell told this deffend*ant*, that hee had
annother busynes to this deffendant w*hi*ch was, that, hee had heard that this
deffend*antes* said servant, Lea, had a Libell w*hi*ch dyd concerne him the said   10
Churchell, and oth*er*s of the Towne, or vsed wordes to lyke effecte, whereunto
this Deffendant, aunswered the said Churchell that hee knewe yt not. nor
dyd beleeve yt to be true, at w*hi*ch tyme of his this deffend*antes* ⌐said⌐
aunswere, hee this deffend*ant* had never seene, nor readd nor heard of the
same, but receaved the first notyce thereof at that tyme, from the said   15
Churchell, And the said Churchill replyed yt was the better for hym thes
deffend*ant* if hee knewe yt not, And therevppon, this Defend*ant* demaunded
his said Servant Lea for the said paper or verses w*hi*ch are the first intended
Libell as this defend*ant* thinketh but knoweth yt not. And this said Lea, tolde
this Deffendant that hee had certen verses delyu*e*red vnto him by the said   20
Marye Wylliams, in such manner, as ys before, in this aunswere declared,
w*hi*ch hee then delyvered to this deffendant, and this Defendant delyvered
the same, vnto the said Churchell, w*i*thout any p*er*vsall or reading thereof,
or of any parte thereof, not daring to doe yt because the said Churchell, had
called yt a Libell, w*hi*ch Churchell p*er*ceaving, hee said to this Defendant,   25
yow meaning [me] this defendant may read yt, and see what yow delyver, or
wordes to that effecte, yet this deffendant aunswered the said Churchill, that
hee would not read yt for yt woulde bring him this defend*ant* into trouble,
and yet the said Churchill soe p*er*swaded w*i*th this deffendant to reade yt,
Saying eftsoones, that there was no danger in reading of yt, And this   30
Defendant thereuppon alsoe not suspecting that the said Churchill plotted
to intrapp him this defendant, as nowe yt seemes he dyd, dyd take the said
paper in his hand, and turned his face from the said Churchill and Bagge,
and read about fyve, or sixe lynes of the same to himself inwardly or softlye,
and not otherwyse, and the said Bagge looked over this deffend*antes* shoulder   35
vppon the same verses, and said vnto the said Churchill, that those verses
were to the effecte of such as one Will*i*am Maryes one oth*er* of the defend*antes*
to this byll, had And this defendant thereby, and by readinge of the said
fewe lynes p*er*ceaving they were vnnecessarie and vnfytt verses, or rymes left

2/ buye: b *corrected from* p   7/ some: *erasure before this word obliterated by line fillers*

of reading of them any farther, but forthwith delyvered the same to the said
Churchill agayne, Whereuppon Churchill demaunded ⌐of⌐ this defendant
the contentes of the said verses, of purpose, as yt nowe appeereth alsoe to
sifte this defendant & to take advantage against him And this defendant
aunswered, the said Churchill that they were idle verses, and hee which   5
made them was worthie to bee severely ponished for yt or to such effecte,
Sithens which tyme, this defendant doth verely [thinke] beleeve that the
Complaynantes doe presente this suite against him this defendant, in revenge
for presenting the said offences, And moreover this defendant saith, That,
hee is not guiltye of the devysing, making writinge contryvinge or publishinge   10
of the said Libells in the bill mencioned or eyther of them, or of any other
the mysdemeanors or offences wherewith hee ys charged in, and by the said
Bill, in such manner and forme, as in the said Bill of complaynte the same,
are set forthe and declared, All which hee ys ready to averre, and prove as
this moste honorable Courte shall awarde, And praieth to bee dismyssed out   15
of the same with his reasonable ⌐costes⌐ charges and expences, by him moste
wrongefullie susteyned in this behalf.//

                                                        (signed) Hugh Pyne

1616–17   20
Bailiffs' Accounts   DRO: DC/BTB: M2/9
f [3]*
…
[viijd] More to Richard Colfoxe & for ahorse to carrie a Iugler
to Bridwell   ij s. viij d. 25
…

1620–1
Cofferers' Accounts   DRO: DC/BTB: M8/203
f [2v] *(Rendered 25 October) (Payments for Midsummer quarter)*   30
…
More to Henry Parker Sergiaunt for the kinges Plears that were
in Towne   v s.
…

                                                                                 35
1623–4
Bailiffs' Accounts   DRO: DC/BTB: M2/11
f [4v]
…
Item geuen to the Kinges Players to thend they should not playe   x s.   40
…

1624–5
Bailiffs' Accounts   DRO: DC/BTB: M2/9
f [1] *(Rendered 3 November)*

	li.	s.	d.

...

14 of december to the king*es* players   0   5   0

...

1625–6
Account of Thomas Merefeild   DRO: DC/BTB: M13
single sheet *(18 April 1625–19 April 1626)*

...

It*em* for twoo fidlers   viij d.

...

1633–4
Bailiffs' Accounts   DRO: DC/BTB: M2/9
f [2v]

...

Laide fforth the Therteeth day of Aug*us*te vnto the Staige
Plaieares   00   ij s.   vj d.

...

1637
Account of a Sabbath Breaking   DRO: DC/BTB: DE10/3
f [2v]* *(17 July–2 October)*

...

Richard Miller confesseth he was at Willi*a*m dacks house ⟨...⟩ willi*a*m Sweete
⟨...⟩ Avis Namies ⟨...⟩ster willi*a*m th⟨..⟩sters Chr*is*toph*er* holte Richard
niccalle margery Swasey ˄⌈Iohan worth seruant vnto Avys namies⌉ & R*o*bert
Sparke & ther had x single cuppes of Beere at dackes howse at iij of the clock
in [after] the morninge/ being sabeth day & Sweete ⟨...⟩chires & dack sange
wherby the neighbours could not sleepe/

...

1638–9
Bailiffs' Accounts   DRO: DC/BTB: M2/9
f [2]

...

Laide out for amending the bulringe   00   01   00

...

c 1641
Court Leet Presentments DRO: DC/BTB: E2/unnumbered
single sheet*

...

stet   Item wee present will*iam* ffrench of hadstock butcher for killinge a bull   5
without beatinge within this Borrough contrarye to the Anscient Custome
of the towne since the Last Lawe day °am*er*citur ad iij s. j d.°

...

CERNE ABBAS   10

1633–4
St Mary's Churchwardens' Accounts DRO: PE/CEA: CW 1/1
f 20* *(21 April–6 April; rendered 19 April 1635) (Payments)*

...   15

Paid Anth*ony* Thorne & others for taking downe ye Maypole
& making a ˄⌈Towne⌉ Ladder of it   00   03   10

...

CHARLTON MARSHALL   20

1603–4
St Mary the Virgin's Churchwardens' Accounts DRO: PE/CHM: CW 1/1
f 24v* *(24 April–8 April) (Receipts)*

...   25

Item receyved of the weomen at hoctyd   iij s.

...

CORFE CASTLE

      30

1328–9
AC   ***John Stow's Chronicles of England*** STC: 23333
pp 359–60*

...

®King Edvvard   Certaine men of this land, to ye intent to try what friends they had in England, 35
the seconde
bruted to be   craftily deuised that Edward the second king of England was aliue in the
aliue.   Castell of Corffe, but not to bee seene in the daye time, and therefore they
vsed manye nightes to make shewes and maskyng wyth dauncing vpon the
towers and Wals of the Castel, which being perceyued by people of the

---

7/ j d.: j *corrected over another letter*   26/ hoctyd: *2–3 May 1603*

countrey, it was thoughte there had bin some great king vnto whom they
dyd these greate | solemnities: this rumour was spredde ouer all Englande,
to witte, that the olde King was aliue, whence it came to passe, that the
Earle of Kent sente thyther a Fryer Precher, to trye the truth of the matter,
who (as it was thought) hauing corrupted the Porter of the Castell with   5
rewardes, is let in, where he lay all the day in the Porters lodge verye close,
and when night was come, he was willed to put on ye habit of a lay man,
and then was brought into the Hal, wher he saw (as he thought) Edwarde
the Father of the king sitting royally at supper with great maiestie. This Frier
being thus perswaded, returned againe to the Earle of Kente, and reported   10
as he thought, what he saw: wherupon ye Erle saide and affirmed with an
othe, that he would indeauoure by all the meanes he coulde to deliuer his
brother from prison.

...

15

1574–7
Autobiography of Robert Ashley   BL: Sloane MS. 2131
ff 16v–17*

...

Sed cum Patri tunc temporis per Dominum Christoferum Hattonum Regine   20
Elizabethe vicecamerarium demandata esset custodia Corfe Castri in Insula
Purbeck quæ agro Dorsettensi adiacet, eo cum familia illûc transmigrante
vbi Moderator ludi literarij bonam de se famam excitauerat ego ipsius curæ
commendatus facile illius Scholæ princeps evasi vbi memini me ad luctam a
sodali inter ludendum provocatum superiorem evasisse, adeo vt postea laxati   25
inter luctandum cruris redemptionem a me exegerit | Ibi etiam cum ∧⌈in⌉
ferijs Natalitijs Redemptoris nostri ∧⌈celebrandis⌉ Comedia inter no⟨.⟩
actitanda esset principes eius partes quæ alij antea comissæ fueran⟨.⟩ mihi
postea per Magistrum delegatae quâ gloriosâ fortasse mihi nimium placui....
Verum Preceptore Hadriano in Belgiam accito ac preparante ipse Sarisburiam   30
duodecimo ætatis anno inchoato traductus ad studioru⟨.⟩ cursum
continuandum vbi in schola publica Sub Doctore ∧⌈Adamo⌉ Hill Collegii
Bailiolensis quondam Socio literis incubui: Is ingeniorum haud segnis
æstimator currenti præconijs suis calcar addidit, et cum comediæ ∧⌈recitandæ⌉
ac alia solemnia spectacula coram illustrissimo Henrico Comite Pembrooke   35
(qui tu⟨..⟩ in vicinijs habitabat) exhibenda essent mihi primas partes
demandavit.

...

24/ Scholæ: S *written over* s
25–6, 31/ laxati ... redemptionem, duodecimo ... inchoato: *phrases underlined in* MS
26/ Ibi etiam: *also appears on f 16v as catchword following* exegerit

DORCHESTER

c **1603–10**
Prologue for a School Play   Bodl.: MS. Add. B. 97
ff 63–4*

The Prologe to a Presentment of a
Playe before Bishopp Thornburie
& his Chauncellor, in his
Visitacion at Dorchester.
by ye SchoolMaster Sheeke.

Sacrj Senatus Lumen, Ornatissime
Salueto Præsul: tuque Cancellarie,
Iterum benignas quj iocis aures dabis
Salueto, vosque cæterj, nostram quibus
Quæcunque sit dicenda, non visum est grave
Ornare vestrâ fabulam præsentiâ,
Et ludicris res serias postponere.
Nam ludicra audietis, vt moneam prius:
Ne forte quisquam conqueratur postea
Nec digna vestris eruditis auribus. &c.
Sed quis per hoc proscenium affectat viam?
Discede. &c.
          Tragædiam nullam audies &c.
             Hospes: Rumor est tamen.
– Id nostra curat scilicet
Dorcestria, quæ damnat en nos, & tamen
Sunt Histriones maximj.
             Hospes. Comedia igitur?
– At ne istac quidem,
Ne quære, nunquam inveneris. etc.
Captetur vt ne risus? haud Mimj sumus,
Nec agimus Histrioniam, vt tu putas:
Famosj agant, quos omnium leges notant. etc.
             Hospes: Quid *igitur* agetur?
Gratulatur praesulj etc.
– Splendore præstantj viro,
Hic quj sacrato præsidet rector choro. &c.
– Nomen a Spinis tenet,
Omenque, quj per asperas spinas sacrum
Virtutis, & honoris tetigit ipsum Iugum. |

                              Hos*pes* Actores?
Puerj.
                              Hos*pes* Doctissimj.
– O vtina*m* quidem!
At ne quidem doctj at annoru*m* inscij,   5
Et artis etia*m*, Elementa quj primum hauriunt
Gram*m*atica, Corderianj, & Æsopicj leues,
Terentianj, quj salutant literas
A limine ipso vix, imo ne vix quidem.

                                                                     10
At tu tamen, quo pace dicat*ur* tua,
Es curiosus, ista tam subtiliter,
[Fastidiose & quæris, Ad ludu*m* quasi
Ad ⟨…⟩] Hæc vna fuerit causa veniendj tibj.
Aliena curas vereor, excussus tuis. &c.   15

Et curiosos dicunt *es*se garrulos
Quicquid rogabis expedj, at paucis roga. &c.

Virtutis & vitij via*m* exemplo docent,   20
Hanc vt sequat*ur*, alteram vt fugiat Schola:
Sic omne punctu*m* retulit is quj miscuit
Dulcj vtile. &c.

Quid hic agendu*m*, quidue dicendu*m* foret   25
Processera*m* dicturus, at nostro hospitj
Dum vellicatim singula requiret modo,
Dixj omnia, vt sup*er*esse ia*m* possit nihil
                              quod vos deceat: Hic omnes præcor,
Teq*ue* sup*er* omnes (praesul Ornatissime)   30
Patrone Musis, atq*ue* com*m*unis Parens,
Quem nos tenemus Numinis *(blank)* loco
Maiora q*uo*niam haud licuit in praesens darj,
His quæ fatem*ur* parva sunt, ignoscite.
Vtinam apparatus ludos hic dignos daret.   35
Animos volentes & pios habeas tamen.
Sis bonus & almus facilis ô fælix tuis.
Sumus puellj dabimus exactj nihil,
Sumus misellj dabimus eximij nihil,
Sumus pusillj dabimus excultj nihil. | 40
At sj placebunt ista quæ facim*us* tibj
Satis superq*ue* fuerit hoc totu*m* nihil.//

    …

1608
Bill of Complaint in Condytt et al v. Chubbe et al   PRO: STAC 8/94/17
mb 19* *(21 April)*

To the Kings most excellent Maiestye   5
In humble Manner shewe and informe vnto your excellent Maiestye your
humble and Obedient subiectes Iohn Condytt of Dorchester in the County
of Dorset and Elizabeth his wieffe, that wheras your said subiectes having for
many yeares togeather inhabited and dwelt in the same towne of Dorchester
haue so carefully ordered and Carried them selues in all their Accions that   10
ther is not any person as they doe verily thinke in that Borough that can
iustlye taxe or depraue them of anye evell demeanour or offence offered him
in particuler of or of any publick scandall given in generall, the said Elizabeth
behaving her self withall sobrietye decency and woomanhood without any
immodest or light behaviour wherby shee myght iustlye be suspected much   15
lesse censured for incontinencye or any other lewde or loose demeanour And
that whereas Ioh⟨.⟩ White Master of Artes minister and preacher of gods
word and Parson of the Church of the holy Trinitye in Dorchester aforesaid,
Robert Cheeke Master of Artes and Schoole Master of the ffree schole there
and Iohn Aden of Dorchester Merchant being parsons of honest behaviour   20
and living by their seuerall proffessions paynfully and honestlye without
Scandall or offence to any man, Yet so yt is may yt please your excellent
Maiesty, that Mathewe Chubbe of Dorchester aforesaid Marchant and
Margaret his wieffe and Robert Aden of Dorchester aforesaid gentleman
envying and repining at the prosperitye and good ffame of your said   25
Subiectes and of the said Iohn White Robert Cheeke and Iohn Aden and
other parsons of honest and good behaviour haue vnlawfully conspired and
practised howe they might not onlye foyle and blemish but vtterly extinguish
and take away their honest ffame and good Reputacion for euer, for which
purpose they haue devised made and contrived diuers infamous scandalous   30
and ignominious libelles which they haue sithence published dispersd and
divulged tending to the traducyng scandalizing and vniust taxing of your
said subiectes and of the said Iohn White Robert Cheeke and Iohn Aden
and to the stayning of them as much as in them lieth with fowle workes of
perpetuall disgrace obloquie and infamye, And namely on the ffower and   35
twentieth Daye of the Moneth of Iune, in the ffowerth yeare of your
Maiestyes Reigne they the said Mathew Chubb and Margaret his wiffe and
the said Robert Aden did vnlawfully make write and contrive an od⟨..⟩us
and filthie libell against the said Iohn Aden Robert Cheeke and your subiect
Elizabeth Conditt and other of your Maiestyes subiectes, A coppye of which   40
libell is also herevnto filed which beginneth with these wordes, Tall Sturdy

13/ of or of: *first* of *redundant*

Puritan Knaue &c which obscene and filthie lybell not fitt to be rehearsed
in this your honorable Court they the said Mathewe Chubb and Margarett
his wieffe and the said Robert Aden and other persons to your said subiectes
yet vnknowne afterwards vzt: on the twenty sixeth daye of Iune then following
did also vnlawfully dispers(.) and cast the same abroade in seuerall places of   5
the said Burrough of Dorchester and did also themselues read or cause the
same to be read to diuers persons at seuerall tymes both in the howse of the
said Mathewe Chubb and els where in the same Towne of Dorchester and
did often publish the same in seuerall manner both by giuing out verye many
Coppies therof as also the said Margarett Chubb not onlye shewed the same   10
to some persons but did also tell and recompt the substance therof vnto
these persons offering that if they or any friend of theirs would haue a
Coppye therof they should haue yt, And that the said Mathewe Chubb did
make and contriue the same or did cause the same to be made and was
consenting therunto as also to the divulging and publishing therof may   15
appeare for that the said Mathew Chubb in the thirtieth day of the said
moneth of Iune or therabout having conference with a neighbour of his
concerning the said Libell did say and affirme that the sayd Iohn White was
aimed at in one place therof and sayd moreouer that he could find out the
Libeller with a wett finger yf he had listed, which neuerthelesse he did not   20
performe nor discouer the libeller, albehit in respect of his place and office
which he then supplied (being that yeare Bayliffe of the said Borough) he
ought to haue donn especially being charged also by Sir George Trenchard
Knighte so to doe, And the said Chubb having togeather with his other
confederates and associates before named in this manner traduced your said   25
subiectes and the persones before named and others, and taxed them with
the odiouse and hatefull name of Puritans amongst many other sclanders in
the said Libell contryued to bring them into the greater detestacion and
hatred with all men, wheras your said subiectes doe in all poyntes conforme
them selues to your Maiestyes Ecclesiasticall lawe ordeyned to be observed   30
in the Church of England, And not being yet sufficiently satisfied with their
Rude Rayling and hatefull backbiting of your said subiectes and the Rest in
such secreat manner as aforesaid, but the more to add to their divellish
Impietie and to make vpp a full measure of their abhominable invectives
and the more amplye to discover the depth of their hatred conceived against   35
all persons that eyther professe the trueth of doctrine authorized by the Church
of England or doe endeavour to liue religiously and without scandall he the
said Mathewe Chubbe and his other Associates before named haue putt in
execution a more detestable practise then that before mentioned by
publishing reading and divulging out Coppies of his other execrable Lybell   40

9/ manner: *for* manners (?)

made and contrived by them the said Mathewe Chubb and Robert Aden,
conteyning many false and accursed invectives and Rayling termes not only
against your said subiect*es* but eaven by name against that reverend Preacher
Mr William Park⟨…⟩ of Cambridge deceased, who in his liffe tyme was
reverenced of all good men, yet such and so great is the malice of the persons   5
before named that on the ffowerth daye of August in the said ffowerth yeare
of your Ma*ies*tyes Reigne The said Mathewe Chubbe then continewing and
being Bayliffe of the said Towne of Dorchester, did openly at a markett
Crosse in one of the streets of the said Towne read publishe and pronounce
an infamous dampnable and sclanderous Libell against your subiect*es* before   10
named and the said Mr Perkins before that Tyme deceased terming him
among other words of Reproa⟨..⟩ Schismaticall Knaue, Dogg and ympe of
the divell, and most Barbarouslie scandalizing therby the said Mr Parkins
and your said subiects before mentioned and many other your lovying subiects
in dispightfull manner as appeareth in these ver⟨…⟩ vnto these present*es*   15
annexed beginning w*i*th these word*es* You Puritans all whersoever you dwell
&c. wh*i*ch Lybell the said Mathewe Chubb said was found in the streete and
brought him by an other, And having in such manner read the same at the
markett Crosse so publicklye w*i*th a lowde voyce in the presence and hearing
of many persons he offered Coppies therof for money and did after deliu*er*   20
out Coppies of the same, and he the said Mathewe Chubb Margarett his
wieffe and ⟨.⟩obert Aden did at other tymes after reade and publishe the
same in other places And not yet satisfied w*i*th such th⟨..⟩ former slaunders
and abuses but escaping w*i*thout punishm*ent* or rebuke for the same in regard
your said subiect*es* did rather ⟨..⟩deavour to winne them w*i*th Conivence   25
and silence then to procure reformac*i*on by Compl*ain*t they did thervpon
growe more imboldned and in pursuance of their extreame malice against
your subiect*es* They the said Mathew Chubb & Margarett his wiffe and the
said Robert Adin did on the tenth day of October in the said ffowerth yeare
of your Ma*ies*tyes Reigne vnlawfullye make write and contriue a verye false   30
sclaunderous and ygnominious Lybell agaynst the said Iohn White wherin
among other things they terme him by the name of Purytan Prelatte
condempning his doctrine for heresie and doe in their saide Lybell mainteyne
popish doctrine and opinons as maye ∧⌜by⌝ the same vngodly Lybell appeare
wh*i*ch is herevnto annexed, beginning w*i*th this superscriptio*n* and directio*n*,   35
That is to saye, To the Counterfeite Companye and packe of Puritans, in
wh*i*ch they haue also maliciously and falsely slaundered your said subiects
Iohn Condict and Elizabeth his wiffe and other your Ma*ies*tyes subiectes
and in Covert Termes taxed her w*i*th inc⟨.⟩ntinencye And having made or
caused to be made Contrived and Written the said sclaunderous Lybell, they   40

34/ opinons: *for* opin*i*ons; *abbreviation mark missing*

the sayd Mathewe Chubbe and Margarett his wiffe and the said Robert
Aden or some of them did afterwards on the twelfth daye of October then
following and at diuers and sundrie tymes sithence maliciouslye and vnlawfully
disperce and Cast abroade and consent to the dispersing and casting abroad
of the said lybell in sundry places of the Burough of Dorchester, And because   5
they would not be prevented in their intended purpose of sclaundering and
depraving your saide subiectes and the other persons aforenamed who were
but covertlye poynted at in the same Lybell⟨..⟩ But would be suer the same
should be published and come to light and be knowne to be intended agaynst
them. Therfore the said Mathewe Chubb on the eighteenth daye of october   10
then following by the abbetment and consent of his said Confederates did
to divers and sundrye persons of his acquaintance and familiar300000ytye report
and read the said infamouse libell, at which tyme the said Iohn White being
in presence and beyng by the said Mathewe Chubbe informed that the same
Lybell was written against him and some doctrine of his thervpon he desired   15
the said Mathewe Chubb to lett him haue yt as fittest yt was he should
purposing therby to suppresse the same But the said Mathew Chubb thinckinge
that he should then faile of the end he aymed at in disgraceing the said
Mr White and your subiects now Complainantes and others, refused to deliuer
the said Lybell and the more to dispight him and the rest therin scandalized   20
he did then publish and Reade the same him self with lowde voyce in the
presence and hearing of divers persons of good Creditt, And not herwith
contented he the said Mathewe Chubbe and other the afforesaid persons his
confederates before named did afterwards also at many other tymes since
reade the same to others in the presence of much people and haue given out   25
many Coppyes therof Affirming that your said subiectes Iohn Conditt and
Elizabeth his wieffe and the said Iohn White and other persons which nowe
complayne not were intended and ment by the same and that the matters
conceyued in the same libell were true, being indede most sclaunderouse
and false, he the said Iohn White having at no tyme preached taught or   30
defended the poyntes of doctrine in the same mentioned or any other sort
then the same are held by the Church of England, And as the said Chubb
hath bynn opposite to the said Iohn White so hath he also to divers others
his predecessores in that Church and hath bynn euermore quarreling and
wrangling with them and other learned preachers and ministers neere the   35
said Towne of dorchester enviyng in deed more their doctrine then their
persons as may well be presumed, the said Chubb having often mainteyned
and defended publicklye the Popish doctrine of Salvacion by meritts and
other poyntes of doctrine held and maynteyned by the Church of Rome
contrary to the trueth professed in this Church of England, As also that the   40
said Chubb is verie much conuersant and familier with the said Robert Adin
who is well knowne to haue bynn for many yeares past a verye dangerous

Recusant and Convict of Recusancie and so yet contineweth, And moreouer
the said Mathewe Chubb and his partners in the aforesaid vile practizes
finding your said subiectes and other the persons aforenamed still apt to
beare and suffer their indignityes and contumelies they yet ceased not their
infamouse Lybelling and traducing of your said subiects good name and   5
Credditt but they having at other tymes sithence your Maiestyes last pardon
plotted writen and compiled other libels against your said subiects and divers
other persons he the said Mathewe Chubb did in his owne howse read and
publish the same to divers persons to the disgrace and wrong of your said
subiectes which they doe forbeare to vrge further to sett forth in particuler   10
for that they hope the due punishment for those before named wilbe a
sufficient admonition for vndertaking the like vngodly practises in tyme to
come, And wheras further on the Eleventh day of Aprill nowe last past or
therabout they repayered to the said Towne of Dorchester Certene stage
players intituling themselues the servantes of the Lord Barteley who by much   15
intreaty obteyned license to playe in the Common hall of the said Towne
Conditionallye that they shoulde not playe on the Saboth daye, which
neuerthelesse they having an intent to doe by the incouragement of the said
Mathewe Chubbe, the Bayliffe (for that tyme being) sent vnto them the said
players for the Key of the Towne hall which they refused to deliuer but carried   20
the Key to the said Mathewe Chubb who also refused to deliuer yt to the
Bayliffe the same being by them required of him: Whervpon the Bayliffe and
other Burgesses of the towne being assembled and hauing consulted about
the Contempt & insolencye offered by the said playeres they were much
laboured by the said Mathewe Chubbe, to consent that they might playe in   25
the Comon Hall that daye, which they vtterly refusing to assent vnto, the
said Chubbe thervpon peremptorily and disdaynfullye sent them word in
threatning manner that he would be eaven with them and in dispight of the
then Magistrate of the said Towne and other the Burgesses their Assistantes
which formerly withstood him in this behalf did that same Evening of the   30
said Saboth daye him self being a Constable of the said Borough at that tyme
cause and procure the said players to playe at An Inne in the same towne to
the heigh Contempt of Almighty God and his Maiestyes proclamacion to
the Contrarye made, And your said Subiects are also the rather persuaded
that the said Mathewe Chubbe doth knowe who was the auctor and penner   35
of the said Libells because he the said Mathew hath diuers tymes affirmed
that the said Robert Adynn is the Aucthor of them, which happely the said
Chubb reporteth but in policye to shadowe the discouerye of the very aucthor
of them in deed the said Robert Adin being alreadye in so deepe punishment
that much more can not be inflicted he remayning nowe and having so done   40
of longe tyme in the gaoll of Dorchester for recusancie and other misdemeanours
on whom the said Mathewe Chubb presumeth to fasten such a report and

the said Robert Adyn shameth not to take yt vppon him at the instance of
the said Chubbe he being vsually and familiarly conversant with him
notwithstanding he knoweth him not only to be a popish recusante convict
but also to be verie daungerous to the state mutinous and factious in his
proffession, And knowing that the said Robert Adyn shortly after the late   5
Queenes Maiestyes decease offered to sell the sayd Chubb A horse to be paid
for the same when there should be a masse said by Aucthoritye in Ste Peeters
Church in Dorchester and that the said Robert Adyn was punished for the
same by the Iudges of Assize: Nowe for as much as the making dispersing
publishing and publicke reading of such sclanderous reproachfull false and   10
ignominious Lybells Wherby your said subiectes herin mentioned and diuers
others your Maiestyes loving subiectes which fforbeare to complayne and
their good and honest fame Credditt and Reputacions are traduced taxed
sclaundered and drawne in question and therby your said subiectes and the
Rest left as publique and notorious examples of disgrace obloquie and   15
infamye without iust cause given are contrarye to the lawes and statutes of
this Realme and contrarye to divers proclamacions heretofore made and
proclaymed for the better suppressing of such enormous offences and
misdemeanors, And for as much ⟨.⟩s dayly experience doth witnesse what
great evels doe spring from this sedicious and divellish Course of casting   20
forth Lybells amongst your Maiestyes subiects and howe Daungerous to the
quiett estate of this your Maiestyes peaceable gouerment yf such notorious
offendors and malefactors should escape vnpunished, And for as much as
the makyng and publishing of the said pernicious Lybells by the persons
before named and all other the offences and misdemeanors afore specified   25
haue bynn perpetrated and comitted since any generalle pardon which
pardoneth such offences and doe not only depraue your said subiects and
depriue them of their good name and Reputacion which they hold and
esteeme as pretious as their lives and haue enioyed and receyved much Comfort
and sweete contentment therin. But also derrogate from gods glorie who by   30
such abhorred Courses and divellish practises is infinitelye dishonored and
noe Remedye can be given or Condigne punishment inflicted on the said
Offenders and malefactors or meanes is left vnto your subiects by the Comon
lawes of this Realme for the repairing of their Credits fames and Reputacions
so steyned and blemished as aforesaid nor other releifs or remedye can be   35
found or given but by and from your gracious Maiestye, May yt therfore
please your most excellent Maiestye to graunt vnto your said humble subiectes
ˆ⌜nowe complainant⌝ your Maiestyes most gracious writts of Sub pena to be
directed to them the said Mathew Chubbe and Margarett his wiffe and
Robert Adyn comanding them & euerye of them by your maiestyes said   40
writtes vpon a daye and vnder a certeyne payne ⟨…⟩ to be limitted and
Compased to be and personallye to appeare before your Maiestye and your

heighnes honorable Counsell in your heigh Court of Starchamber then and
there to answeare the premisses and further to stande and abide such further
orde⟨.⟩ and censure herein as your Maiestye and your said Councell shall
seeme fitt to be layd and inflicted on such heinous malefactors; And your said
humble subiects shall euer according to their bounden dewtye pray vnto god   5
for the Continewance ⟨...⟩ prosperous and Royall reigne ouer vs.

Exhibits attached to the Bill of Complaint in Condytt et al v. Chubbe et al
PRO: STAC 8/94/17
mbs 20–2*   .   10

                                       °1°

Tall sturdy Puritan knave for soe tearmed was thy name
By playeres whome thou tearmest rogues to thy face spake ye same   15
Thou saiedst by the statutes thou woulds affirme thy talle
which when thou hadst brought them forth thou couldst not at all
Thie mynd is high thie purse is small god knowes it to be trew
ffor were it not for other mens goodes thy state were of bad hue
Yow Puritans count your selves the greatest of men of all   20
But I trust in god ere longe to see all of yow to fall/
Examples two already haue by god of late bynn shewne
By some of your greatest secte the lyke was neuer yet knowen
The one to make yow the more playner to vnderstand & know
is one Lawrence of Steepleton whome all this towne doe know   25
who made himself the vprights man that lived now a daies
& Comended much your deed in the beating downe stage playes
He has to fore most willing byn to lead a quiet lyfe
That now the divell vrgeth him to lye with Condittes wife
or else he sayes he neuer shall recouer his disease   30
She heareinge this a horse did take & rode his mynd to please
Is this the Puritans lyef that all of yow doe professe
Then all your pure lyves are nothing but dissemblinge as I gesse
our savyour Christ foretold that false profettes should arise
that should make shewe of godlines but denie the lord Christe   35
ffor your face and Contenance doth shewe yow dissemblars are
and soe much doth my slender wytt of yow so much Compare
I pray mr lacke pasty take it not in greef what I say
But rather giue me thankes yat would yow haue to leave your bad waies
The Schoolemaster yat was one of them yat stood on your side   40
scaped very hard that he had not bynn forced ye foole to ride
Some of your sect would not yat ringinge we should haue and vse

but other some more better then they will *your* word*es* refuse/
And that soe much as he Rynginge doth so lyke & doth so loue
we wilbe thankfull vnto him as it doth vs behove
O god *prosper* longe our noble Kinge god send him long to raigne
And not to trust the Puritans nor yet the king of Spayne   5
      Post scriptu*m* in Pumbry this 24th of Iune *per* me IA
Adyn yf this Come to thie handes behold and see
do thou not stand against stage plaiers nor Yet trew melody
ffor yf thou doest thou shalt be calld knave and foole
and so shall thy sonne in lawe chicke ye maister of the schoole | 10

°2°

Yow Puritans all wheresoeu*er* yow dwell
ymitateing *your* master the dyvell of hell   15
leaue of your devises the world to delude
least god from his blisse *your* soules do exclude
ffor noe ones so symple that on yow doth looke
but knowes *yat* you liue contrary to *your* booke
yow carry *your* bible gods word to expound   20
and yet in all knavery yow dayly abound
ffor envies hatred & malice great store
in noe creatures lyveinge I thinke is more
as daylie by experience amongst vs we fynd
to mischeef and hatred none more enclynd   25
yea Covetousnes letchery and lijnge for gayne
amongst yow puritans is not Counted vayne
but first w*i*th pride if I should beginn
because it is knowne for a principall synne
a question being asked where doth it abound   30
then in the pure *pre*late *yat* seemes so *pro*found
ffor lardg Cambricke Ruff*es* and laceing great store
bestowed on apparell where doe we see more
I name not french bodies that w*i*th whales bone are Made
for puritans are to holy to meynteyne that trade   35
And many thing*es* more I could now haue spoke
but *yat* some would say I did at them scoffe
w*hi*ch sure I doe not nor meane nothinge soe
yet who crosses their follyes is Counted a foe
oth*er*s there are that are knowne very well   40
w*hi*ch for purenes of lyfe they say they excell
yea *Sainctes* of heaven already Chosen they bee

to iudge the good, and evill of euery degree
yea in this present life they lett not to maynteyne
that their deere frendes are damnd for lyueing vaine
And for theire reward hell fire they haue gained
and thus Parkyns hath said yat his father hath obteynd   5
of his mother he stands doubtfull her to recall
but his sister he is sure shee will neuer fall
But yet for all this when he was forth gonne
the dyvell found his body at play all alone
and taught him to dance the dyvells rownd   10
I could wish he had Parkyns in that pownd
But what a Clowne is this & Rascall Scismatike knaue/
that will iudg his frends such vglie tormentes to haue/
A gratious turne were yt if god had so pleasde
that Cerberus in this world on his bones had ceasde   15
ffor example to others such Counterfaite mates
that will maynteyne Religeon with lyinge prates
yea this Scismaticke dogge and ympe of the dyvell
doth maynteyne that god is the author of evill
Such variety of Religeon amongst vs is vsed   20
that thus is the maiesty of god by them abused
I pray god in mercy forgyue vs our synne
and roote out theis presitions yat newe Religeon beginn
That flocke themselues in Corners both early and late
each knaue makeinge choise of a whoare for his mate   25
& thus vnder Coulor and cloake of good purytie
all villany is Comitted in Corners of obscuritie
In the Church on the sabboth what attention they shew
yf the henn did butt see yt, it would make the cocke crow
when their ghoastlie father to the seat doth repayre   30
after him they flocke as it weare to a fayre
And in such sort there they stand & witnes doe call
that crosse in Baptisme he makes none att all
but if it soe chance out of towne that [yee] ⌈he⌉ bee
then at devine service none of them shall yee see   35
but after him they runne as pigges after a sowe
detesting dyvine service appoynted vs now
To saie they be traytors I hold it noe reason
because traytors are they that Commytt treason
But Rebells I will count them I thinke without blame   40
bycause in disobeyinge the kynge they hold it no shame
for what our kynge Commands that doe they denye

yea praijnge kneeling & standing, all theis they defy
All honest recreacions and mirrymentes they blame
and are not theis Puritans? speake truth for shame
But the spiritt doth them moue their professions to vse
not only to the latten but the kinge to abuse   5
And thus doe I cease their follyes to vnfold
and leaue them to their master which makes them soe bold

> To the execrable Companie [and pack] of Puritans and the
> deepest desemblinge Anabaptistes of this tyme Enymies   10
> to the kynge and state, Lett this I praie thee be
> Delyuered with speed/ |

°3°

To the Counterfait Company & packe of Puritans/   15

Haueinge my self heard a Sermon now of late
preached [by a] in Church by a puritan Prelate
I Could not well conteyne nor hold my penn still
least I should participate in the same ill   20
Though much absurd doctrine that sect hath sowen
which in all former adges hath bynn vnknowne
Yet the matter handled that tyme was so deepe
as the falshood of yt might moue men to weepe
The Saviour of the world Christ Iesus in person/   25
of his sacred death was broughte in question
How that he was not the Sauiour of vs all
But of the elected which cann neuer fall
And how he suffred & did dy for none
but for his people and such as weare his owne   30
O wretch and silly man yf white be thy skynne
yet blacke and defiled is thy soule within
noe mortall man but the dyvell did devise
to cutt & curtaile Christes passion in this wise
ffor Christ our redeemer without all exception   35
for all mankind suffred his passion/
And when of his goodnes he dyed on the tree
his bloud then extended to euery degree/
Such was his Maiestie love, and Charitie
as he would saue those that did him Crucify   40

11/ thee: th *corrected over* y(.)

yf soe he suffred to saue and sett all free
why the worlds savyour ought he not to be
Though all be not saued defect is not his
he performed his loue to giue vs all blisse
who therefore shall publish or holdeth not soe   5
worketh for hell fyre & is our lords foe
But what other fruyt may there be expected
ffrom theis Counterfaite bretheren elected
who wickedly doe hold and so doe professe
that god is the Author of all sinfullnes   10
who likewise affirme yat whatsoeuer chance
Christ is surely theirs and he will them advance/
gods deere children holy Saynctes they are they knowe well
& heaven is their heritage where they shall dwell
As for all other Saynctes that are dead & paste   15
what [they] haue they to do with them or for them to faste
Loe this they will presume because in holy wrytt
they find some authorities for their purpose fytt
but the conditions whereon those are grownded
neuer will they learne least they be confownded   20
Example late on him god would shew noe doubt
Whose ffinger would haue stopt faire Condittes spoute
for god would reveale their liues & manners rude
& shew with what falshood the world they delude
yet lyke most presumptuous and lyke peevish Elves   25
In all their misdeeds they Iustefy themselues
and whosoeuer is not of their Sect a brother
is suer cast awaye and reckoned for none other
But from their false doctryne god keepe me & myne
and that to such errors wee neuer inclyne/   30

Interrogatories for Defendants in Condytt et al v. Chubbe et al
PRO: STAC 8/94/17
mb 17* *(Before 7 May)*

                                                                            35

Interrogatories to be ministred to mathew Chubbe, and margret his wyfe
and Robart Adin defendantes, to ye bill of Complaynt and informacion of
Iohn Conditte and Elizabeth his wyfe Complaynantes/
...

12.

did not certayn stage players which called themselves the Lord Barkleys   40
servantes come vnto the towne of dorchester in or about the moneth of
Aprill in ye yeare of our Lord god 1607. weare they not prohybyted by the

Bayliffes and Magistrates of the sayd towne to play on the Sabbath day, did
not you perswade ye said Bayliffes and magistrates yat the said Stage players
might be licenced or permitted to play in the common hall on the sabaoth
day, did not the said Bayliffs or magistraetes withstand you therein, did not
you thervpon send word to ye sayd Bayliffs officers or Magistrates or some   5
of them that you would be even with them, or some other message to such
effect, And did not the sayd players in the evening of the same day being the
Sabbaoth day by your meanes or procurement play an enterlude at a Common
Inne in the sayd towne of dorchester, weare not you present at such Stageplay
or enterlude, And did not you send for or procure other Company to be at   10
the same enterlude or Stageplay, & what moved you so to doe, weare not
you then or late before an officer in the said towne of Dorchester and what
office did you then beare or supplie./

...

15

Answer of Matthew and Margaret Chubbe, Defendants in Condytt et al v. Chubbe et al   PRO: STAC 8/94/17
mb 18* *(2 June)*

The ioynt and severall aunsweres of Mathewe Chub,   20
Gentleman and Margaret his Wife, two of the
Defendantes, To the byll of Complaynt of Iohn Condytt
and Elizabeth his Wife Complaynauntes.
The said defendantes by protestacion say That they take the said Complaynant
Iohn Condytt not to be a man of any specyall Note, office, credytt or quality   25
eyther within the Towne of dorchester where he dwelleth or in the Common
wealth such as showld be admytted to ympleade and seeke redres in this
high & honorable Cowrt of Starchamber for offences of such kynde as are
pretended in his said Byll/ Also the said Complaynant Iohn Condytt beinge
by his trade a Taylor is not of honest nor iust behavor nor carridge in his trade   30
of Taylorship as theis said defendantes haue crediblye heard & do not dowbt
but will make good & sufficyent prof therof. Likewise there are in the said
byll of Complaynt comprized & set furthe divers matters, supposed Libelles
& surmized offences which concerne not the Complaynantes them selues but
somme others which do not complaine as theis said defendantes do take yt/   35
And therfore the said Complaynantes are not to be receaued to presente their
Complaynt for or concerninge those pretended offences, but they are rather
to be taken them selues to be offenders in producinge & divulginge such
matters as do concerne others, beinge men of estimacion and quality Who
them selues would willingly haue such vnfittinge matters supprest & smothered   40
as theis defendantes do take yt/. Moreouer the said Complaynantes did
heretofore prefer ^⌈into this honorable Cowrt⌉ one other byll of Complaynt
contayninge such or like effect against theis said defendantes and against

Roberte Coker gentleman a goldsmith William Longe Lawrence darby &
william Palmer & others. Therin complayninge of & settinge furth the same
supposed Libelles which are mencioned in their said byll. But before aunswere
was made to that former byll by any of the said defendantes he the said
Complaynant Iohn Condyt compownded with iiij other of the then defendantes   5
namely with the said Roberte Coker william Longe, Lawrence darby and
william Palmer, and he did take of them (blank) the somme of Twelue
poundes for the same composition And in consideracion therof the said
Complaynantes surceased that suite & obtayned that byll to be withdrawen
Synce which agreement the said Complaynantes haue preferred this second   10
Byll into this Honorable Cowrt against theis said defendantes Therin
alleadginge That they theis defendantes with some other vnknowen persons
haue contrived & published the said supposed Lybelles, When as the said
Complaynant Iohn Condyt had formerly compownded with those iiij other
before named Whom they the said Complaynantes do pretend to be the   15
vnknowen persons As theis said defendantes do take yt./ And likewise the
Complaynant Iohn Condyt hath caused offer to be made vnto this said
defendant Mathewe Chub to be likewise dischardged of this newe suite, if
they the said defendantes would but acknolidge that the said defendantes had
wronged the said Complaynant Elizabeth Condyt Which to doe the said   20
defendantes vtterly refused. Wherin the said Complaynantes do much abuse
the worthynes and state of this honorable Cowrt as theis said defendantes do
take yt. ffor all which causes they theis said defendantes do demur in Lawe
& do appleale to the censure of this honorable Cowrt Whether the said
Complaynantes shalbe receaued, or admitted to any farther procedinges in   25
this suite, & whether theis said defendantes shalbe vrged to make any farther
or other aunswere to the same suite in this same Honorable Cowrt./ And
yet neuertheles if this honorable Cowrt shall thinke fitt to order theis said
defendantes to make any farther or other aunswere to the said Complaynantes
Byll Then & not otherwise they theis defendantes (savinge to them selues   30
nowe & at all tymes hereafter all advantages of excepcion to the vncertenty
& insuffityencye of the said Complaynantes byll ffor aunswere they say That
they theis defendantes are chardged in the said Complaynantes Byll to be the
contryvers, publishers, or causers or consenters to the publishinge of three
severall infamows Libelles mencioned in the Byll of Complaint, & which are   35
annexed to the same Byll/. ffor aunswere wherunto they say ffirst as towchinge
the said supposed Libell (beginninge Tall, sturdye Purytan knaue &c) That
a Younge gentleman Namely Iervice Scroope beinge one of the Schollers of
Roberte Chick in the said byll named of thage of xj yeares or therabowte,

---

3/ which: w corrected over another letter   24/ appleale: for appeale
11/ Cowrt: C corrected over B   30–2/ (savinge to … byll: closing parenthesis omitted after byll

and then dyeted or tabled in this defendantes howse did in or abowte the
moneth of Iune in the byll mencioned bringe or deliuer vnto this defendant
Margaret Chub a Paper Wrytinge contayninge somme such matter or the
same as in the said first before mencioned supposed Libell is contayned as a
thinge which he then said he had of a Bowchers boy that fownde yt in the   5
Towne Whervpon this defendant ⌈margaret⌉ in the absence of her said
husband not readinge yt her self did furthwith deliuer the same paper in this
defendantes howse vnto one Mr Oliuer Hayne nowe one of the Bayliffes of
dorchester aforesaid (Who before that tyme had byn in the like office there)
she ⌃⌈supposinge that eyther the said Mr Hayne or one Mr Henry whitle   10
who weare bothe there together was Deputy Bayliff to the said defendaunt
Mathew Chub in his absence. And also she⌉ not knowinge whether yt were
a Libell or not, Neyther doeth she knowe whether Mr Hayne did then reade
yt or not. But she receauinge yt again, did ymmedyatly afterwardes vpon the
comminge home of her said husband deliuer to the defendant mathewe Chub   15
her husband (then beinge one of the Bayliffes of the said Towne) the said
Paper wrytinge. At which tyme also the said defendant mathewe Chub
together with his fellowe Bayliff, and some other of the chief Burgesses of
the said Towne had a privat meetinge at the howse of this said defendant
mathewe Chub to confer of the ratinge of the Subsidye for the Townes men   20
of dorchester/ And this defendant mathewe Chub did then with a loe voyce
read yt, or part therof in the hearinge of his said fellowe Baylif and Burgesses.
Not of any purpose to divulge the wrytinge or to despite or defame the
persons named or aymed at therin, but as thinkinge fit to see the contentes
therof, and to acquaint his said fellowe Officers of the Towne therwith/   25
Vpon readinge wherof at the same tyme he this defendant mathewe Chub
did put yt into his pocket, & did neuer deliuer any copye therof, or otherwise
publishe yt. Neyther did this defendant mathewe Chub to his remembraunce
euer sythence (vntill he had this exhibited Copye out of this Honorable
Cowrt) so much as after againe read yt over. Only at one tyme after (beinge   30
the day followinge) William Willyams Esquier, sonne & heire to Sir Iohn
Willyams knight, and one of your highnes Iustices of the Peace dwellinge
neere to the said Towne beinge at this defendantes said howse did vse or
speake some wordes (as this defendant nowe remembreth) that he had heard
somme thinge of the said supposed Libell, & did desyer (as this defendant   35
nowe thinketh) to see yt in so much that this defendant margaret Chub
(knowinge the said william willyams to be a gentleman of sort & place, &
not likely to breede any scandall or offence therby) did without the knolidge
or consent of the said Mathew Chub her husband fetch the said supposed
Libell furth of this defendantes Chamber in which yt lay, and deliuerd yt to   40
the said william willyams thinkinge he would then furthwith haue redeliuerd
yt againe. But this defendant Mathewe Chub perceavinge the said Mr Willyams

to haue the said wrytinge in his hand, & puttinge yt into his pocket of
purpose to carrye yt away (as yt seemed) the same not beinge then read, he
this def*endan*t mathewe did therfore earnestly require the said mr Willyams
to restore yt againe Which the said mr Willyams then refused, and would not.
Whervpon this said def*endan*t mathewe Chub then chardged him in yo*ur*   5
highnes name to deliu*er* yt to the said S*i*r Iohn willyams his ffather to examyn
the same, he beinge a Iustice of peace as aforesaid/ And theis def*endan*tes do
traverse & deny That they, or eyther of them did envye or repyne at the
pr*o*sperity or good fame of the said Compl*aynan*tes or of the said Iohn White,
Rob*er*te Chick or Iohn Adyn in the said byll named, Or of any other honest   10
p*er*sons of honest or good behavor, or haue to their knolidge conspired, or
practized to foyle extinguishe or take away their honest fame or good
reputac*i*on. Or that they theis def*endan*tes or eyther of them haue made,
wryten, devised, or contrived any infamowes scandalowes or ignominyous
Libell, or haue to their knolidge published, dispersed, or divulged any such   15
supposed Libell as in the said byll of Compl*aynt* is slaunderously surmized
and alleadged./ Only this def*endan*t mathewe Chub did once in privat read the
before menc*i*oned wrytinge at the pr*e*sente receyt therof as aforesaid And the
said def*endan*t margaret did deliu*er* yt to the said mr Hayne and mr Willyams
Not of any evell purpose ˄⌐or⌐ to publishe yt as before is said. And w*i*thout   20
that ˄⌐That⌐ theis def*endan*tes or eyther of them haue geven Copyes therof.
And w*i*thout that That this def*endan*t margaret (to her knolidge) did tell or
recownt the substaunce of the said wrytinge vnto other p*er*sons offeringe
that they or any frind of theirs should haue a Copye therof Savinge that this
def*endan*t margaret to her nowe remembraunce tolde a mayd s*er*vaunt of the   25
said Compl*aynan*tes the same day at night, That there was a Le*tt*re that day
fownd wherin mr Lawrence lightnes in his late sicknes, & her dame were
named In w*hi*ch word*es* this def*endan*t Margaret Chub, meant no evell to
any p*er*son/ And w*i*thout that That this def*endan*t Margaret did make or
contrive the said supposed Libell, or did cause or was consentinge therunto,   30
or to the divulginge or publishinge therof As in the said byll of Compl*aynt*
is surmized & alleadged other then is before menc*i*oned/ And towchinge the
Second supposed Libell menc*i*oned in the said Compl*aynan*tes Byll w*hi*ch
conc*er*neth mr Perkins nowe deceased, he this def*endan*t mathewe Chub for
aunswere doeth say That he this def*endan*t mathewe in or abowte the moneth 35
of August in the ffowerth yeare of yo*ur* highnes raigne, beinge then one of
the Bayliff*es* of the said Towne of dorchester and sittinge at the doore of the
howse of his fellowe Bayliff the forenamed Richard Blachford (w*hi*ch howse was
and is seated neere to the Crosse there) One Thomas ffoy a poore Shoomaker
dwellinge w*i*thin the same Towne did repayer vnto this said def*endan*t   40
sittinge as aforesaid w*i*th his said fellowe Bayliff, & did deliu*er* to this said
def*endan*t mathewe Chub an old fittered pap*er* leafe contayninge such or

the like effect men*ci*oned in the said second supposed Libell wryten on the
outsyde therof You Purytans all &c. and in the inside likewise beginninge
You Purytans all whersoeu*er* you dwell &c. as in the said Byll is set furth.
_∧⌈which foye beinge demaunded then where he had yt aunswered that he
found the same⌉ Wherevpon he this def*endan*t and the said Mr Blachford   5
seinge one Mr Barker (beinge then likewise one of the Constables of the said
Towne) in the streat, before they opened the same did call him vnto them
to heare, & see what the conten*tes* therof was. And then & there at the said
Mr Blachford*es* doore this def*endan*t mathewe Chub did read that wrytinge
in privat betwene them selues w*i*th a loe voyce, and not at the m*a*rket Crosse   10
w*i*th a lowd voyce as in the said byll is surmized. Neyther did this def*endan*t
mathewe Chub knowe or ever see or heare of (to his remembraunce) the
said Perkins men*ci*oned in the same supposed Libell before that tyme. Nor
did vnderstand who was meant by that Perkyns vntyll abowte vj monethes
after that tyme. W*i*thout that, That this def*endan*t did make or contrive   15
the same supposed Libell, or did (to his remembraunce) offer copies therof
for money as in the said byll is likewise surmized./ And towchinge the
Third supposed Libell men*ci*oned in the said Compl*aynantes* byll beg*i*ninge
w*i*th this sup*er*scrip*ci*on Vizt To the Counterfeyt Company and Pack of
Purytans &c, this def*endan*t mathewe Chub for aunswere sayth That such   20
a wrytinge in or abowte the moneth of October in the iiijth yeare of yo*ur*
highnes raigne was fownd in the entrye of this def*endan*tes dwellinge howse
at dorchester aforesaid, at such tyme as this def*endan*t mathewe Chub was at
supper, W*h*ich writinge was folded vp in the manner of a *lettre* sealed and
the sup*er*scrip*ci*on was (as this def*endan*t nowe remembreth) To mr mathewe   25
Chub be theis deliu*er*d W*hi*ch wrytinge beinge so fownde & deliu*er*d to this
said def*endan*t mathewe Chub. (And this def*endan*t beinge then also one of
the Constables of the said Towne of dorchester, and suspectinge yt might be
som*m*e bad matter against him self _∧⌈he⌉ this def*endan*t did then read the
same or p*ar*t therof in the hearinge of mr Richard Blachford his fellowe   30
Constable. And then furthw*i*th fyndinge what yt was, they bothe went
therw*i*th vnto mr Iames Gold then one of the Bayliff*es* of the said Towne to
acquaint him w*i*th yt. At whose com*m*inge to the said mr Gold*es* howse he
this def*endan*t did there finde the said mr Iohn White in the Byll men*ci*oned
in company of the said mr Gold w*i*th others. And bycause the said mr Gold   35
could not him self read the wrytinge, he this def*endan*t did read yt vnto him
in pres*en*ce of the said Iohn white and others. And before or after this def*endan*t
had read yt, he did in deede say to the said mr White, that he this def*endan*t
did think the said White was aymed at in the same writing by cause yt had
in yt (if White be thy skyn &c) At w*h*ich tyme & place the said mr White   40

27–9/ (And this def*endan*t … against him self: *closing parenthesis omitted after* self

desyred to have the same wrytinge Which he this defendant then refused to
deliver, sayinge (as he nowe remembreth) that he beinge an Officer would
keepe yt for his owne dischardge And afterwardes this defendant havinge
hard say that the said Robert Adyn one of the said defendantes was the doer
therof, he this defendant mathewe Chub demaunded of the said Roberte   5
Adyn Whether he did wryte the same, and whether he did cast yt within the
dores of this defendant To whom the said Robert Adyn willingly aunswered
that yt was his owne wrytinge, & that he him self did cast yt into the howse
of this defendant mathewe Chub At which tyme also this defendant did
likewise demaund of the said Roberte Adyn Whether he had not formerly   10
wryten any more, Whervnto the said Robert Adyn aunswered that he had
wryten the Purytans Profession. Which Purytans Profession had byn browght
& shewed to the said defendant mathewe Chub as he remembreth by his
said fellowe Constable longe before. Whervpon he this defendant Mathewe
Chub did make yt knowen aswell vnto Sir George Trenchard knight in the   15
Byll named, beinge then one of the next Iustices of peace to the said Towne,
as also to the said Iohn White & divers others as this defendant remembreth.
And this defendant mathewe Chub likwise sayth that after the readinge of
the same supposed Libell to the said mr Iames Gold and mr White as
aforesaid, he this defendant as he nowe remembreth did neyther read, nor   20
publishe yt Neyther did he deliuer Copye therof nor shewe yt to any other
person Whatsoeuer, vnlesse yt were to ffraunces Ashley Esquier a Iustice of
peace dwellinge in the same Towne of Dorchester (to whom this defendant
deliuered or ⌈shewed⌉ the same) ⌈as he thinketh Vpon the longe sithence
report of the said mr Ashley⌉ but yet not of any malitious purpose towardes   25
the Complaynantes or any others. And this defendant mathewe Chub doeth
traversse & deny that he did at any tyme malitiously or vnlawfully disperce
or cast abroade, or consent to the castinge abroade of the same supposed
Libell in sundry places as in the said byll of Complaynt is likewise slaunderously
surmized & alleadged. And without that That this defendant hath geven out   30
any Copyes of that supposed libell, or did affirme to his remembraunce that
the matters therin contayned are trewe Or that this defendant mathew
Chubbe to his remembraunce hath affirmed that the matters were true, which
are conteyned in the said supposed libell against the complaynantes & other
persones which now complaine not, as in the said bill of complaint is also   35
vntruelie surmised/ °And towchinge the surmise of the said bill, that this
defendant mathew Chubbe hath byn opposite to the said mr White & to
divers other prechers his predecessors in the church of dorchester And that
also this defendant mathewe Chubbe hath been evermore quarrellinge with
them & other learned prechers & mynisters neere the said towne of dorchester   40
enveyenge more their doctrine, than their persones, mayneteyninge &
defendinge publiquelie the popish doctrine of salvacion by merites, this

defendant mathew Chubbe for aunswere saeth that [h] to his remembraunce
hee never quarrelled with anie such precher or mynister, enveyenge their
doctrine, more than ther persones, neither did hee (to his remembraunce)
ever mayneteyne such doctrine of salvacion by merites as in the said bill is
slaunderouslie set forth/ And farder saith with modestie, as beinge provoked   5
thervnto, that noe one within the said towne of dorchester (as this defendant
mathew Chubbe thinketh) hath by manie yeres togither now last past given
so mych yerelie stipend & helpe to the prechers of the said town of dorchester,
as this defendant hath done, And likewise when divers other mynisters,
dwellinge neere to the said towne have come at divers tymes to preach there,   10
this defendant hath not onlie byn vsuallie present at their sermons, but hee
hath also vsuallie enterteyned them at dynner/ Also this defendant abowt
eight yeeres past did at his owne charge, build a convenient dwellinge howse
within the towne of dorchester, for the stipendarie prechers within the same
towne to dwell in rent free & the same howse hath been accordinglie so vsed   15
& enioyed/ And moreouer there havinge latelie risen some difference betwene
the said mr White & this defendant mathew, they the said mr White & this
defendant mathew have sithence mutuallie released either to other all accions
& demaundes/ By all which it may appear (as this defendant conceiveth)
that hee this defendant is not opposite nor an adversary to the prechers nor   20
to their doctrine, as in ye said bill is surmised, & likewise are the said
mathew & Robert Chick frindes as this defendant taketh yt/ And towching
this defendant that hee is mych conversant with the said Robert Adyn the
recusant, hee this defendant mathew Chubbe for aunswere saeth, that the
said Sir Iohn Williams, togither with this defendant were heertofore put in   25
trust, by Iohn Adyn, (brother of the said Robert Adyn) deceassed, & likewise
the admynistracion of the goodes of the said Iohn Adyn hath byn comitted
vnto the said Sir Iohn Williams, to this defendant mathew Chubbe & to the
said Robert Adyn, for which cause & by meanes also of divers suites in law
which the said Robert Adyn now hath & have had in the towne court of   30
dorchester, where the said defendant mathew Chubbe is Stewarde vnder the
said Sir George Trenchard, hee the said [Sir George Tren] Robert Adyn hath
divers tymes resorted vnto the said defendant mathew Chubbes ₐ⌈howse⌉ to
confer of the same busynesses Also towching ye opinion of the said Roberte
Adyn in manie matters of religion this defendant doth vtterlie condempne   35
it/ & this defendant mathew was one of the cheife which principallie gave
evidence against hym before the Iudges of Assize there concerninge the masse
mencioned in the said complaynantes bill, And towching the stage plaiers
mencioned in the said complaynantes bill this defendant mathew Chubbe
for aunswer saeth that some of the same stage plaiers, as this defendant   40
remembreth did at or abowt ye tyme in ye said bill mencioned ask leave of

this def*endan*t beinge an officer, to plaie, *w*ithin ye said towne to whome
this def*endan*t made aunswere, that hee for his p*ar*t was *con*tented they should
play/ also that this def*endan*t to accompanie one *Si*r Adrian Scrope Knight
this def*endan*t being his tenant, did goe to a play at ye In menc*i*oned in ye
said compl*aynan*tes bill where the said knight lodged, but at other tymes this   5
def*endan*t hath verie seldome frequented anie plaies, nor favored plaieres
*m*ore than some others of his place hav*e* don*e* for this def*endan*t for his p*ar*t
hath had of late yeers littel delight to bee p*re*sent at plaies w*i*thowt that ₐ⌜That⌝
this def*endan*t to his remembrance did send word in thretning man*er* to ye
bailives or burgesses of ye said towne that hee would bee even w*i*th them, or   10
that this def*endan*t did ₐ⌜in⌝ dispite p*ro*cure the plaiers to plaie in ye said In,
as in ye said bill of co*m*play*n*t is surmised & aleged And theis def*endan*tes
mathew Chub & m*ar*garet for further aunswere doe saie, & ech of them for
hym & her selfe say y*at* as vnto & cons*er*ning all & singuler the co*n*spiraties
ₐ⌜confederacyes⌝ combinac*on*s, co*n*triving & writing of libels, disp*er*cing,   15
divulging & publishing of libels & all other ye misdemenors & offenc*es*
menc*i*oned & set forthe in ye said bill of co*m*plaint, to have byn done,
comitted or p*ro*cured by theis said def*endan*tes, or either of them, & w*hi*ch
are examinable in this honorable co*ur*tt (other than those & in such man*er*
as theis said def*endan*tes have before acknoledged in theis their said aunsweres)   20
they theis def*endan*tes & everie of them for hym & her selfe severallie saith
that they are not guiltie thereof, nor of anie p*ar*t thereof, in such man*er* &
forme as in the said bill of co*m*plaint is surmised & alleged, All w*hi*ch matters
they theis def*endan*tes & ech of them for so mych as concerneth hym or her
selfe, are & wilbee readie to aver & p*ro*ve, as this honorable co*ur*t shall award,   25
And humblie pray to bee dismissed the same co*ur*t w*i*th their resonable
cost*es* & charg*es* in this beehaulfe susteyned/./°
            (signed) per me Mathew
                        Chubbe   sig*num* Margarete M Chubb
                                                                                  30
                        Supradict*i* defendentes Iurat*i* fuerunt apud
                        dorchester in Com*itatu* Dors*et* Secundo die
                        Iunij 1608. Ad Signu*m* Le George ib*ide*m

coram *(signed)* Th*om*a Barnes Iohn Arnold & Iohanne Geare commissi*onarijs*   35
            1608   Strode

14/ co*n*spiraties: for conspiracies
15/ combinacons: *for* combinac*i*ons; *abbreviation mark missing*
29/ M: *Chubbe has signed with her first initial*

Examination of Matthew Chubbe, Defendant in Condytt et al v. Chubbe et al
PRO: STAC 8/94/17
mb 16 *(2 June)*

The Deposi*c*ion and examyna*c*ion of Mathew Chubbe of dorchester   5
in the Coun*t*ye of dors*et* gent*leman* taken att dorchester aforesaid
the Seconde daye of Iune In the yere of the reigne of our sou*er*eigne
Lord Iames by the grace of god of Englande Scotlande ffraunce and
Irelande Kinge defendor of the faythe &c (That is to saye) of England
ffraunce and Irelande the Sixthe and of Scotlande the one and   10
ffortyeth. Before Thomas Barnes Iohn Arnolde and Iohn Geare
gent*lemen* Co*m*myssion*er*s by vertue of his M*aies*ties Co*m*mission out
of his highnes honorable Courte of Starr Chamber to them and to one
George pope gent*leman* directed, vpon the Interrogatoryes herev*n*to
annexed mynystred on the p*ar*te and behalfe of Iohn Condytt and   15
other Complayn*antes* agaynst the said Mathewe and Margarett his
wife defend*antes* vid*elice*t, The said Mathewe Chubbe beinge sworne
and examyned/

...

20

mb 15

...

12.   To the xij^th Interrogatorie this deponent sayth That to his remembrance the
players mencyoned in the same Interrogatorie did not playe in the evenynge
of the same day therein men*c*ioned by the only means or procurement of   25
this deponent in the said co*m*mon Inne in the said towne Neither doeth this
deponent remember that hee did send or p*ro*cure other company to bee att
the same enterlude, att w*hi*ch ʌ⌈tyme⌉ this deponente was one of constables
of the said towne And touchinge the rest of the same Interr*ogatorie* this
Deponente taketh it, That he hath alredy Aunswered in his said Aunswere   30
[and] ʌ⌈to the bill &⌉ Interrogatories./

...

1608/9
Interrogatories for Defendants' Witnesses in Condytt et al v. Chubbe et al   35
PRO: STAC 8/94/17
mb 2* *(Before 13 February)*

Interrogatoryes to be mynystred v*n*to certeyne Wytnesses
produced on the p*ar*te and behalfe of Mathewe Chubb and   40

28/ of constables: *for* of the constables (?)

Margarett his wife defendant*es* To the bill of Complaynte of
Iohn Cunditt and Elizabeth his wyfe Compl*aynantes*/

...

17   It*em* do you remember the tyme when the lord Barkleys players were at
dorchester in or about Aprill last desiringe to playe in the Towne there did   5
the defend*ant* Mathewe Chub farther and helpe them to playe there on the
Sabboath day, dyd he not rather keepe from them the key of the Towne hall
dyd he att that tyme goe to accompany S*ir* Adrian Scroope his landlord and
att his request, deliu*er* the circu*m*stanc*es* of that which ye knowe or have
credibly hearde and by what occasion touchinge this Interr*ogatorye*/   10

...

Interrogatories for Complainants' Witnesses in Condytt et al v. Chubbe et al
PRO: STAC 8/94/17
mb 7* *(Before 13 February)*   15

Interrogatories to be ministred to witnesses p*ro*duced on the
p*ar*te and behalfe of Iohn Conditte and Elizabeth his wife
Compl*aynantes* against mathew Chub & margret his wife
defend*antes*/   20

...

4./   did not the defend*ant* mathew Chub or margret his wife say vnto Lawrence
Evans or to any other p*er*son to yo*ur* knowledge that mr Iohn white was
aymed at in one place of the said first Libell w*hich* beginneth w*ith* Tall
Sturdie Puritan knave &c./ and that they or one of them Could yf he list   25
finde out the lybeller ^⌈or aucthor therof⌉ w*ith* a wette finger or that they or
one of them vsed word*es* to like effect eyther to ye said Lawrence Evans or to
some other p*er*son, or did you not heare ye said Lawrence Evans say or report
y*a*t the said mathew Chub or margret his wife vsed such word*es* vnto him
and did not the said Lawrence Evans say y*a*t he would depose ye same to be   30
true yf he weare there vnto Lawfully Called, did not mr Chub or margret
his wife or some other p*er*son in yo*ur* hearing say or report y*a*t a song was to
be made of this first Libell./

...

                                                          35

mb 8*

...

21./   did not the defend*ant* mathew Chub in or about the moneth of Aprill A*nn*o
.1607. desire or p*er*swade ye magistrates of the Towne of dorchester y*a*t
certaine Stage players w*hich* called themselues ye Lord Barkleighs servant*es*   40

26/ ⌈or aucthor therof⌉: *interlineation begins in the left margin*

might be permitted to play in ye Comon hall of ye said Towne on ye Sabbath
day when the said magistrates had formerly forbidden them, did not ye
Bayliffes or magistrates withstand his requeste, did he not therevpon send
them word yat he would be eaven with them or such other thretning message,
did not ye said mathew Chub procure ye said players in ye evening of ye same   5
day to play at a common Inne in the Towne, was not ye said Chub present
at ye play himselfe & sent for & procured others also to be at ye same play,
and was not ye said Chub an officer of the said towne at that time, what
office did he then beare./

...   10

1609
Examination of Defendants' Witnesses in Condytt et al v. Chubbe et al
PRO: STAC 8/94/17
mb 3* *(26 April)*   15

Deposycions taken at Dorchester in the Countye of Dorset
the Six and Twentyth daye of Aprill in the yeres of the Reigne
of our souereigne Lord Iames by the grace of god Kinge of
England Scotland ffraunce & Ireland defendor of the fayth &c   20
That is to saye of England ffraunce & Ireland the Seaventh
and of Scotland the Twooe & ffortyeth before Iames fframpton
& Iohn Notley gentlemen by vertue of the Kinges maiesties
Comyssyon to them Iohn Childe & ffrances Hardey gentlemen
directed out of his maiesties most honorable Courte of Starre   25
Chamber ffor the examynynge of wytnesses aswell on the
parte & behalfe of Iohn Cunditt Complaynante as alsoe on
the parte & behalfe of Mathewe Chubbe gentleman & others
defendantes./

...   30

Thomas Buckler servaunt & kynsman to the sayd defendant mr Chubbe
aged Twentye & three yeres or thereaboutes produced to the xiij^th xvij^th &
xviij^th Interrogatoryes onelye and therevppon sworne & examyned./

...

To the xvij^th Interrogatory he sayeth that he Remembreth that the Lord   35
Barkeleys players in the Interrogatory mencyoned were at dorchester about
the tyme in the Interrogatory mencyoned vppon the saboth daye and did
then playe there But whether his master the sayd defendant did further their
playenge there this deponent knoweth not But sayeth that Sir Adryan Scroope
Knight in the Interrogatory named beynge desyrous to see them playe   40

4/ thretning: *4 minims in MS*   5/ evening: *4 minims in MS*

Requested the sayd defendant mr Chubbe to accompanye him thither which
he did to satysfye the Request of the sayd Sir Adryan Scroope And more to
this Interrogatory he doth not depose.

...

mb 4*

...

Hughe haggarde of Dorchester in the Countye of Dorset Butcher aged
ffyftye & ffyve yeres or thereaboutes produced to the xiij^th xvij^th and xviij^th
Interrogatoryes onlye and therevppon sworne & examyned./

...

To the xvij^th Interrogatory he sayeth that he Remembreth that the Lord
Barkeleys players were at Dorchester and as this deponent harde they did
desyre to playe in the Towne hall of Dorchester but the magistrates of the
towne woulde not geve them leave wherevppon Sir Adryan Scroope Knight
beynge at the defendant mr Chubbes howse at supper offered that the sayd
players should playe in his Chamber in an Inne after supper and Requested
the sayd defendant mr Chubbe to goe thither with him which he did
accordinglye And more to this Interrogatory he doth not depose./

...

Answer of Robert Adyn, Defendant in Condytt et al v. Chubbe et al
PRO: STAC 8/94/17
mb 9 *(29 June)*

(signed)
Edward Iones

Iuratus vicesimo nono Iunij Anno Septimo Iacobi Regis
      The Aunswere of Robert Adyn defendant to the Byll of
      Complaynt of Iohn Cundytt and Elizabeth his Wife
      Complaynantes
The said defendant by protestacion sayth That the said Complaynant Iohn
Condytt is a man knowen not to be of any speciall note, office, credyt, or
quality eyther within the Towne of dorchester where he dwelleth or in the
commonwealth suche as should be admitted to impleade and seeke redresse
in this high and honorable Court of Star Chamber for offences of such kynde
as are pretended in his said byll./ Also the said defendant sayth That as he
taketh yt the said three severall matters or supposed Libelles filed to the
Complaynantes Bill of complaynt are not properly to be tearmed or taken
for Libells but are rather Pamphelettes or Invectiues against malefactors and
reputed enemyes to the state such as are the Purytans or Brownistes./ In which
three severall Matters or Pamphelettes the said Iohn Condytt is neyther
named, Nor any wise covertlye decifered or aymed at wherby to fynde him
self aggreved, but to all the said matters (which tend principally against

5

10

15

20

25

30

35

40

Puritanizme and Purytans) he the said Iohn Condytt intrudethe impugneth, and maketh him self both a partie, and a Champion for others (who complaine not) for defence of that cause as more at lardge here under shalbe made manifest./ Moreover the said Iohn Condytt beinge by his trade a Taylor, and a man of very meane reputacion and wealth hath before this tyme (as this 5 defendant dowbteth not well to proue) browght into this honorable Court by vertue of Subpena iiij other severall men of the said borowghe of Dorchester that is to say Roberte Coker william Longe william Palmer and Lawrence darbye) and by his byll of Complaynt then exhibited aswell against this defendant as against them, hath chardged both this defendant and them with 10 the said supposed Libelles specified in this published byll of Complaynt, but before any aunswere eyther by this defendant or by them was therunto made, he the said Iohn Condytt compounded with the forenamed iiij other persons, and for the somme of xij li. by them geven vnto him, procured the said first byll of Complaynt to be withdrawen and cancelled and the said ∧⌈4 recited 15 persons⌉ [parties] to be dismissed. Makinge therby this honorable Court an instrument for his vnlawfull purchase therby to enhable him self to vex and prosecute farther suites against ∧⌈this defendant and⌉ others, Which declareth as this defendant thinketh his vexacion rather to procede of meere covetousnes to gayne, then for any iust cause of offence or grief./ ffor all which causes he 20 this defendant doeth demurr in Lawe, and doth appeale to the graue censure of this honorable Cowrt whether the said Complaynantes shalbe admitted to any farther procedinges in this suite, and whether this defendant shalbe vrged to make any farther or other aunswere to the same suite in this honorable Cowrt And yet neuerthelesse if this honorable Cowrt shall think fit to order 25 this defendant to make any farther or other aunswere to the said Complaynantes byll, then and not otherwise he this defendant, savinge to him self nowe and at all tymes hereafter all advantages of excepcion to the vncertenty and insufficyencye of the said Complaynantes byll for aunswere therunto, and to the said three severall matters or supposed Libelles in the same sayth to 30 euery of them particularly as followeth vizt To the first pretended matter or supposed Libell begininge Tall sturdye Purytan &c and to all the supposed offences mencioned or contayned in the same first supposed Libell or any of them supposed to be committed or don by this defendant, he this defendant aunswereth that he is not giltye therof nor of any part or parcell therof/ To 35 the second pretended matter or supposed Libell begininge thus. you Purytans all whersoeuer you dwell &c and to all the supposed offences mencioned or contayned in the same second supposed Libell, or any of them supposed to be committed or don by this defendant, he this defendant likewise aunswereth that he is not giltye therof nor of any part or parcell therof/ Adding hereunto 40

8–9/ that is … darbye): *opening parenthesis omitted before* that

that the said Complaynantes as this defendant taketh yt, haue herein very
apparantly discovered them selues what they are in the profession of their
religion, in that this said second supposed Libell beinge dedicated and
entituled To the execrable company of Purytans and the deepest desemblinge
Anabaptistes of this tyme enemyes to the Kinge and state &c and beinge in   5
substaunce an Invectiue against Purytans and Innovators of Religion only as
this defendant taketh yt, and neyther of the said complaynantes therin spoken
of, nor so much as by any one word figuratiuely towched or aymed at, yet
they the said Complaynantes do complayne, repyne and take stomake therat
affirminge yt to be an execrable Libell against such as professe the trueth of   10
doctryne aucthorized by the Church of England, and such as endevor to live
religiouslye and without scandall, and that the same contayneth many false,
and accursed invectiues and raylinge tearmes against the said Complaynantes,
as also that the same is very infamowes, damnable, and slaunderowes against
them the said Complaynantes, Wheras in very trewthe the said Complaynantes   15
are in the said second supposed Libell neyther spoken of, nor any wayes
aymed at as aforesaid, nor the Religion aucthorized by the Church of England
in any sort oppugned but mayntayned and defended to the vnderstandinge
of this defendant./ And to the third matter or supposed Libell contayned in
the said byll, begininge thus To the counterfeyt Company and pack of   20
Purytans &c he this defendant for truethe therunto aunswereth That vpon a
Sermon preached as this defendant was credibly enformed, and dowbteth
not but he shalbe well able to proue) by Mr Iohn white in the said byll of
Complaynt named, that Christ was not the Savyor of the whole world, nor
did dye for the synnes of the whole world, but for his elected and chosen   25
people only, and that our said Savyor Christ hath not his fatherly care over
any more then his elected, shewinge the same by a familyar example that as
every Shepherd taketh care and chardge over his owne fflock and no more,
so hath Christ ouer his elected and chosen people and no more, he this
defendant, (not for any privat quarell, grudge or splyne vnto the persons   30
named in the said byll of Complaynt Nor to any other particular person
whatsoeuer, but only in defence of the most meritorious passion of Christ (as
this defendaunt in his vnderstandinge was perswaded) did make the said last
or third matter entituled To the counterfeit company and pack of Purytans,
shewinge therby that Christ was the Savyor and Redemer of all mankynde   35
without all excepcion and that no defect of salvacion was in his said
meritorious passyon. And the said matter so by this defendant framed and
made, he this defendant dispersed and sent furthe three or iiij other copyes
therof to men of good callinge and reputacion the better to consider of suche

22–3/ enformed, and ... proue): *comma used as opening parenthesis*
30–2/ (not for any ... whatsoeuer,: *comma used as closing parenthesis*

doctryne, sealinge the same with severall directions and superscriptions in
forme of Lettres to the said parties, Amongst which mr mathewe Chubbe
had one copye (he this defendant confessinge that with the said mr Chubbe
for good and Lawfull causes he hath byn familyarly conversaunt) And aswell
to the said parties which had those copyes as to the said mr White the   5
preacher he this defendant acknolidged that he did make the same ‸⌈wherof
this defendant as he thinketh shall neede to make no prouf forasmuch as the
Complaynantes themselues in their byll do affirme the same⌉ sayinge that
this defendant shameth not to take yt vpon him. ffor which his so doinge
beinge don to no other intent or purpose he this defendant submitteth him   10
self to the graue and favorable censure of this honorable Cowrt. Without
that, that he this defendant to his knolidge hath in any open or covert tearmes,
slaundered, or geven cause of offence eyther to the said Iohn Condytt, or
Elizabeth his wife, or taxed her of incontynencye, or other lewde demenor.
Or that this defendant hath in any sort depraved the religion established in   15
this Realme of England, or mayntayned popishe doctryne and opinyons
contrary to the said Religion professed as in the said byll of Complaynt is
alleadged/ And as to all other the offences and misdemeanors in the said byll
of Complaynt mencioned, supposed to haue byn don ‸⌈and committed,⌉ by
this defendant which are examinable in this honorable Cowrt, concerninge   20
this defendant, and not herein aunswered, confessed traversed or denyed, he
this defendant sayth that he is not giltye therof, nor of any part therof in such
manner and forme as in the said byll of Complaynt is surmized and alleadged./
All which matters this defendant is, and will be readye to aver and proue as
this honorable Cowrt shall award. And humblye prayeth to be dismissed the   25
same with his reasonable costes and damages in this behaulf sustayned ./.
/
(signed) Mere.

1615

Casebook of Sir Francis Ashley   BL: Harley MS. 6715   30
f 6v* (15 July)

. . .

® Gilbert Reason   *Memorandum* quod .15. die Iulij .1615. I Comitted to ye gaole Gilbert Reason,
who came in ye name of one of ye Princes Players, & for saying to Mr Iohn
Gould ye Chief Bailiff, that he was little better then a traitour for refusing to   35
look on his Comission: And for daring me often to laye him by ye heeles
with other fowle language he was punished within prisone 2 dayes & 2 nights
& then vpon his submission was enlargid.

10–11/ this defendant submitteth him self: *written in left margin and marked for insertion here*
38/ submission: *parts of letters lost by cropping*

1623
William Whiteway's Diary   BL: Egerton MS. 784
f 34* *(4-27 September)*

…

This day we went to London. and returned 23 daies after, hauing staid in   5
London 16 daies. during our abode there, Mr Edward Prichard died. there
came newes of the Prince his arriuall at Portesmouth & ballads were made
of it, but it prooued false, the balladsingers were sent to prison.…

f 35* *(5 October)*   10

…

                                       *

Dr Wright our new B*isho*p kept his visitac*io*n here this yeare in September,
Mr cheeke acted two comedies at the sheerehall for his comming, by his
schollers.   15

…

1630
Borough Court Book   DRO: DC/DOB: 8/1
f 33* *(31 March)*   20

Examinations taken before Mayor Richard Blatchford and William Jolliffe
…

Evan Lewes who sayth he came out of Swanzey with a passe from the Portrive ther to
travall into England to get him service … & cam the next day to this Town   25
⌜of dorchester⌝ monday & stayed ther mo*n*day tuesday & [wensday morning]
lodged [th] at goodman Iefferis house & spent a shilling or two ther & sayth
he was not in any house in the Town but at Cristopher Ienkens & met w*ith*
a fidler of his acquay*n*tance w*ith* a purpose to go to sct Cristophers but left
the fidler & went the wensday morning to Pudlton accompanied w*ith*   30
goodman Iefferis the Tayler & his two daghters.…

f 40 *(5 May)*

Examinations taken before William Jolliffe and William Whiteway, Sr   35
…

Ione Norris daughter of Thomas norris miller of this Borough saith that on
sonday last at night dorathie Allin Georg Gill Thomas the Gardner S*ir* ffrancis
Ashleigh his men ⌜&⌝ Thomas Norris her brother were in the house of her

---

24l Swanzey: *Swansea, Glamorganshire, Wales*   30l Pudlton: *3 minims for* u *in* MS
27l house: *corrected over another word*

ffather within this Borough and they had there two Iugges of beere which
Thomas Norris ⌈her brother⌉ sent and paid for and she seyth that Georg
Gill had an instrument there but there was no dauncing at all this was about
9 of the clok at night. dismissed with Admonicion./

...   5

William Whiteway's Diary   BL: Egerton MS. 784
f 79v* *(5 July)*

...

This day the puppet players craued leaue to play here in this towne, & had   10
a warrant vnder the Kings hand, yet were refused.

1631
Borough Court Book   DRO: DC/DOB: 8/1
f 79* *(9 May)*   15

Cases heard before the mayor and bailiffs
...

Edward Hill   Edward Hill of this Borough blacksmith   xl li.
               Iohn Bayland of the same Glouer in   xx li. ⎫ 2 20
               Thomas Buckler of the same tayler in   xx li. ⎭

               Cognouit   that Edward Hill shall appere at proximas
                                   Sessiones pro Burgo &c and to be of the good
                                   behauier toward [th] all his Maiestis   25
                                   leige people &c

               ...
Edward Hill   for going out of his parish Churche one saboth daye last in the midell of
               seruices to maye
               ...   30

f 96v *(28 October)*

               ...
Richard King   Swareth the name of god blasfemously ∧⌈last night⌉ by his owne Confessing.
paid since   promised to pay it 15 days henceforth;   35
               Song a fythy song that she should lay her legges two yardes asonder ⟨...⟩ hit
               being at 11 of the clock at night. in corse of Anthony edwards: & Robert
               griffin & his wiffe & liddia griffin.
               ...

1/ two: *followed by two horizontal lines, apparently filler*   34–8/ Swareth ... griffin.: *text cancelled administratively*
19m, 28m/ Edward Hill: *in display script and underlined*   36/ fythy: *for* fylthy
23/ Cognouit: *underlined*

Richard King of this Borough Shoemaker in   x li.
          Henry King of the same father to Rychard king in v li.
Cognouit that Rychard King shall apper at the next *Sessions pro* Burgo to
Answer for his lewd song*es* & vnrever*e*nt spech to Authorite
...   5

ff 97–7v* *(31 October)*

Examinations taken before Mayor William Whiteway, Sr, and Richard Blatchford,
bailiff   10
...

William Hutchins whoe saith that about the 21ᵗʰ of September 1631 that
he being a watchman about 10 of the clocke in the night herd a drum*m*
beaten in the street as he conceyveth about the fryery wherevpo*n* this
examinat with Thomas Grudham and Iohn Chaffey watchmen also   15
ₐ⌐went that way⌐ and saw Henry Bridg at his dore in his shirt [wh] of who*m*
this exam*i*nat enquired who beat the drum*m* and he sayd yt was some
downe in the lane [vp] & this exam*i*nat went to Iohn Lie & his dore being
shut knockd at the [dore] ⌐windoe⌐ with his finger and askd who beate
the droom*m* and Iohn Lye Awns*we*red yt was he and this exam*i*nat replyd 20
& s*ai*d yt was not fit to beate a drom*m* in the night & he would be
questioned for yt & so this exam*i*nat & the others dep*a*rted

Iohn Robert*es* constable at that time now exam*i*ned sayth the same night
before being in his owne house after the watch was chargd *willia*m Hutchins 25
& other of the watch came to acquaint him that the*r* was a drom*m*
beaten in the fryery lane by Iohn Lie and shewd this exam*i*nat that they
had bene w*i*th Iohn lye & told him of yt and that *willia*m Hutchins told
him also th*a*t lye would beat [him] the drom*m* agane whervpo*n* this
exam*i*nat went downe & knockd at lyes dore and requird him to op*e*n his 30
dore for he was a const*able* to who*m* Lye Awnswerd th*a*t wer he const*a*bell
or els yf he came [he] to them he woulde sut hem farther and this exam*i*nat
dep*a*rtid aft*er* the const*a*bell then Richard williams & this exam*i*nat went
downe | againe & when we came, we both found him rayling & outragious
saying the constables (& naing [I myself] Iohn Robert*es* and Thomas 35
hyet) were a company of beggerly base fellows at w*hi*ch time the said Iohn
lye swa*r*e 2 oathes blasphemousely by the name of god [as y] and by the

Iohn Lie (left margin, line 13)

Iohn Lie (left margin, line 24)

blod of god as yt was afterward presente at the Lawe day and mor he
sayth not – ther is order given to tak [yt di] ⌜[br]⌝ by distres

Iohn Lie of this Borough in the some of   x li.
Thomas Pouncey Butcher ⎫
Iohn Runney Tucker   ⎭   v li. separatim   5
    Cognouit That Iohn Lie shall appere at the next Sessions pro
    burgo to Awnsre his abuse for beating a dromme in the night
    & abusing the constabls & swearing 2 oathes as aboue
...   10

1632
William Whiteway's Diary   BL: Egerton MS. 784
f 87* *(1 April)*
...   15

This day Dr Buts Vicechancellour of Cambridge hanged himselfe in his
chamber with a Towell: it is said, out of discontent, because the king shewed
much dislike at a play, which he had caused lately to be acted before him in
Cambridge, full of scurrility against the grauest ministers of the Kingdom,
whome they call Puritans....   20
...

1632/3
William Whiteway's Diary   BL: Egerton MS. 784
f 91* *(30 January)*   25
...

        *

...Mr Prin a Counsellor was sent to the Tower for writing a booke against
Stag plaies & dancing, which the Queene tooke to hart, because about the
same time that his booke came forth, she acted her part in a Comedy before   30
the King.
...

1633
Borough Court Book   DRO: DC/DOB: 8/1   35
f 177 *(29 May)*

Examinations taken before Mayor William Jolliffe and William Whiteway, Sr

2 Constables whoe say that on on the one & twentieth day of this instant may [being]   40
examind about coming [about] ⌜betwen x &⌝ Eleven of the clock at night into the George
Gold

40/ on on: *dittography*   41/ coming: *4 minims in MS*

& going vp in the stayers on the back chamber they heard musick & going
into the Roome perceyvid one standing ther in the dark [thet] one of thease
examinates enquird what he was & 2. or 3. tims the fellow mad Awnswer
here was one [a Towne] one of the Towne and pressing him to tell his name
he sayd his name was Gold & one of these examinates askd which Gold &   5
he Awnswerd his name was Gold but discouered no more then before and
[Imediately after these examinates]
And constable Bushrod now farther sayth that this Gold sayd Imediatly after
þat he had heard of vs hertofore but now he perceyvid what he herd was true.
Wherupon this examinat Bushrod ‸⌈askd⌉ wheather he had heard of any   10
dishonestie by [vs] ⌈them⌉ whervnto he Awnswerd [he ment not mee] I
meane not you Mr Constable and this examinat verely beleueth that that yat
which he spake [m] he ment yt by his partner constibl Symondes
                    (signed) Iohn Bushrod
Stephen Gold servant to Rychard Churchill of this Borgh   x li.   15
    Iohn Condit de eadem Tayler in   v li.
    George Panchard de eadem Tyler   v li. separatim
    cognoverunt   that Stephen Gold shall appeare ad proximam
                           Sessionem pro Burgo ad respondendum for his
                           carig toward the constabls   20

William Whiteway's Diary   BL: Egerton MS. 784
f 94* *(22 June)*
…

                                    *
                                                                             25

whitsonales & May games were this yeare much countenanced by speciall
order from the Court in which Sir Robert Philips & Sir Charles Barkley of
Somersetshire were very forward. But Sir Arthur Hopton got a petition
subscribed with the hands of 36. Iustices of that County, to the which the 2.
Knights aforesaid, & Dr. Godwin refused to subscribe: This petition he   30
presented to the King at Woodstocke, where the King conferred with him
about it in priuat, & gaue him such satisfaction, that at his returne he bound
ouer .120. of the Reuellers vnto the Assises. The Sum of the petition was to
set out the dangerous consequents of whitsonales, in which seuerall murthers
had beene this yeare committed in that same county.   35

f 96* *(15 October)*
…
This day Iames Duke of Yorke was borne: & baptised the .24. Nouember.
vpon his birth Mr Prin was released out of the Tower after .9. moneths   40

4/ one … one: *dittography*   12/ that that: *dittography*
9/ þat: *in a blacker ink; apparently a later addition*   17/ Tyler: *for* Tayler

imprisonment for writing a booke against playes and maskes, at which the
Queene found herselfe agreeued.

...

(18 October)   5

The King set forth a booke, to giue liberty vnto sports & pastimes upon
Sunday after Euening praier in confirmation of the like liberty granted to
Lancashiremen in his returne out of Scotland .1617. & required all ministers
to publish it in the Church. which diuerse in conscience refused to do, &   10
many after they had read it shewd that it was against the word of God.

1633/4
William Whiteway's Diary   BL: Egerton MS. 784
ff 98v–9* *(3 February)*   15

...

This day the Gentlemen of the Ins of Court namely the 4. cheife houses,
Inner & midd⟨..⟩ Temple, lincolnes & Grayes in, danced a maske before
the King and Queene in the Banquetting house at Whitehall. Each house
set forth 4. Revelles, & .25. Gentlemen Riders, who rode in great magnificence   20
from Hatton house through the Strand. This maske cost the actors .17. M.
pound⟨.⟩ and did so please the King, that he invited himselfe, the Queene
& Maskers to sup at the Lord Maiors, Sir Ralph fremant the 13. february.
where the Lord Maior spent 3000 s. to entetaine them, in pulling downe
diuers houses betwen his house & Marchantailors Hall, & maki⟨..⟩ a gallery   25
for the King to pass through. The King invited himself to the Lord Maiors,
to make him amends, for the sharp words he had lately giuen him, calling
him old foole, for speaking in the behalfe of the Sopeboilers & Laundresses
of London: which troubled him so that he kept his bed a whole moneth
after it, & was like to dy, had not the Kings message reuiued him. The Queene   30
dancing at the Lord Maiors, strained hir foot⟨.⟩ & was like to haue taken much
hurt. This maske should haue beene danced on Candlemas day which was
Sunday, to countenance the Kings booke, | but at the request of the Gentlemen
of the Ins of Court, as it was thought, it was put off till Monday. The same
night the King gaue a bankett unto all the Maskers, & he & the Queene   35
began to eate first & they would not let any of the lords or ladies tast it, till
the Maskers had done. In this maske the Lady Pie had a foule affront put
upon her, being turned out by the Lord Chamberlaine, because her husband
refused to let his son be one of the Maskers to saue charges.

24/ entetaine: *for* entertaine   37/ Lady Pie: *wife of Sir Walter Pye, attorney of the Court of Wards*
30/ The: *corrected from* Tbe   *and chief justice for Glamorgan, Brecon, and Radnor*

17.th ditto.

Mr william Prin Counsellor of law, hauing beene long imprisoned for a booke
which he wrote against dancing, & masks & enteludes, was now censured in
the Star chamber, fined .5000 li. to the King, to stand in pillory, loose his   5
eares, to plead nor write no more. The aggrauation of his offences, which the
Atturney insisted upon was, that he had let fall some passages, which cast an
aspersion upon the Queene.

...

                                                                                        10

1634
Borough Court Book   DRO: DC/DOB: 8/1
f 210* *(28 March)*

Examinations taken before Mayor Bernard Toup and William Derby   15
...

Buck   The informacion of Elizabeth Membry wife of George Membry of this
Borough Brewer.
who saith that on Sabothday last at night about viij ⌈or ix⌉ of the clock [this
ext] walter Hagge⟨..⟩ lodging in her husband*es* hows & being gone to bed,   20
and this examina*tes* husband this examina*t* was also going to bed. and then
there came into the [⟨.⟩] hous Richard Wale & his wife & Iohn Wyer & his
wife & Anthony Penny & one Buck of ffordington & all went into the said
Haggard*es* chamber who rose out of his bedd. & the said Buck daunced
about the chamber & the said Haggard willed the said Buck to daunce   25
promising him a halfe penny loaf & willed him to shew forth his privy
members to the women then in the chamber which the said Buck did then
the said Wyers wife took a candle and lighted to the said Buckes members
[bu] that they might be seene but this examina*t* saw her not hold the candle
soe neere to hurt him nor did she know that he was hurt there nor did she   30
hear him then complayne of any harme.

...

William Whiteway's Diary   BL: Egerton MS. 784
f 102v* *(13 May)*   35

...

At Glastonbury, while the people were busy setting up of a Maypole, it fell
on th⟨.⟩ head of a son of one of the most forward as he ran out the streete,
& beate out his braines.

...   40

4/ enteludes: *for* enterludes   21/ this²: *for* and this *(?)*
19/ Sabothday last: *23 March 1633/4*   24–5/ Buck daunced ... the said: *underlined in* MS

William Whiteway's Commonplace Book   CUL: Dd.11.73
f 148* *(28 August)*

...

Ignoramus
While this Comedy was acting before *King* Iames in Cambridge, the inventors   5
(to make the *King* an actor in it) caused a post to come gallopping into the
Towne, & When he came upon the Stage, he commanded the Comedians
to forbeare, for that My Lord cheif Iustice Was enformed that they had made
a knavish peice of worke to disgrace the Lawyers, & would haue them appeare
befor him to answere it. The Actors gaue ouer, as if they had not dared to   10
proceed. Whereupon *King* Iames ros out of his chaire, & beckened to them
With his hand, & saying–Goe on Goe on, I Will beare you out. Au*g*ust 28.
1634.

...

15

William Whiteway's Diary   BL: Egerton MS. 784
f 110* *(5 December)*

...

Here came a french woman that had no hands, but could write, sow, wash,
& do many other things with her feet: She had a com*m*ission vnder the seale   20
of the M*aste*r of the Reuelles. not allowed here.

1634/5
Borough Court Book   DRO: DC/DOB: 8/1
f 252v *(2 January)*   25

Examinations taken before the mayor, the bailiffs, and William Jolliffe
...

Iohn Hoskins servant to Iohn Standish confess*eth* that he was at church on
the 28th day of decemb*er* 1634 and went out before pry prayers and   30
sermon wer done ⌈in mor*n*ing⌉ & went to William Churl*es* house to warme
himself being wet and cold & stayd th*er* half an houre th*er* being pr*es*ent
*Willia*m Clark*es* wife & [her children] ⌈Grace Butler⌉ and [at] the same
afternoone he sayth he went to broad close to serve cattlell and met w*ith*
Edward Tewxbury & Rychard Oldish and he sayth th*at* ther was a bull in   35
the ground & he & the oth*er* 2 before namd and a shepherd boy of Iohn
Standish put the bull in pound & set a dog at him and baytid him in the
pound & then he sayth he returnd home & went all three togath*er* into
Church at evening pry*er* time the sermo*n* being begun & continud thear

A warrant
is graunted

8/ My Lord cheif Iustice: *Sir Edward Coke*   34/ cattlell: *for* cattell
30/ pry prayers: *partial dittography*   39/ pry*er*: *for* prayer

all time of [pryer] & sermon and prayer he is ordered to pay [12 d.] for
his absence from church [2 s.] 1 s. within senight or otherwise to be delt
withall

...
                                                                                    5

c 1635
Chronology of Dennis Bond   DRO: D/BOC: Box 22
f 13* *(Inventory)*

The Contentes of Souch houshold   10
stufe I haue Att lutton. waymoth
in my now Dwelling house in Dorchester

                                                                  li.   s.   d.
Imprimis att lutton in ye Halle   15
...
1 pair of virginall   .2   10   00
...

1636   20
Borough Court Book   DRO: DC/DOB: 8/1
f 312v* *(14 October)*

...

William Gosling. coming to this Towne with a license vnder the hand of the
Master of the Revelles signed Henry Herbert & sealed with the seale of   25
the office of Revelles with a Cinque foyle authorizing the said Gosling to
shew the portraiture of the city of Ierusalem dated 15 Iune xij Caroli &
denied to make his shew heere by reason of the dangerous tyme of sicknes.

...
                                                                                    30

f 313* *(19 October)*

Cases heard before Dennis Bond

Gorge Meder wever of Triny parishe [doth being] ⌈giuing⌉ the last night   35
entertaynment vnto Iohn Woodes & Lanslet Gilbert apprentises to Simon
Haslebor & making Woodes drunk: singing of songes.

...

10–12/ The ... Dorchester: *in display script*   27/ 15 Iune xij Caroli: *15 June 1636*
15/ Halle: *in display script*   35/ Triny: *for* Trinity; *abbreviation mark missing*

1636/7
Borough Court Book   DRO: DC/DOB: 8/1
f 331v *(8 March)*

Cases heard before Dennis Bond and Henry Maber   5

Anthony Penny sware 5 oathes by the name of God on friday night last about
   2 or 3 of the clock in the morning in Iohn Durayes howse in Trin*ity*
   p*a*rish ex aff*irmatione* Ioh*ann*is Mory Will*elm*i Parke
   & that [the] at that tyme were *prese*nte there Rob*er*te Bellett hellier Iohn   10
   Gray hellier & Anthony Penny and there they had beere & were drinking.
   And that the same night there was disorder att Iohn Brines dauncing all
   night long. where there was the paviers maide and Duback and diu*er*s
   others of [the] some that were not of the town
...   15

1637
Borough Court Book   DRO: DC/DOB: 8/1
f 335v *(10 May)*
          20
Cases heard before Mayor Dennis Bond and Henry Maber
...

Sarah Vren alias Moore did danse in ye Gaol ye Ester mon*day* & had a fidler
   in the Gaole.
Abigal Serrell the ser*uant* of Mrs: wat*es* for that shee was dansing att the Gaole   25
   is ordered *(blank)*
...

Borough Court Book   DRO: DC/DOB: 8/1
f 337* *(31 May)*   30
...

Robert Powncy maketh oath that Thomas Powncy the younger this weeke
   being at bulbayting did breake the bul kep*er*s head w*i*th his cudgill./

1640   35
Borough Court Minute Book   DRO: DC/DOB: 16/4
f [18v]* *(2 October)*
...

Thomas
Grindham
for his charges

desiring to be allowed 6 s. 4 d. paid the Clerke of the assise for hes [ch]
discharge about imprisoning the fidlers. & ⌈tis ordered the Steward shall   40

7/ friday night last: *3 March 1636/7*   23-4/ & had ... Gaole: *writing cramped because insufficient*
23/ ye Ester mon*day*: *10 April 1637*   *space left between Vren's and Serrell's names*

pay & Grindham is ordered[1] to demaund the 12 s. which he paid the keper
& yf that he cannot recover that the company will take other course for that
mony also

…

FORDINGTON

1617
Casebook of Sir Francis Ashley　BL: Harley MS. 6715
f 22v* *(5 August) (Cases heard at Bridport sessions)*

…

for ye seueral misdemeanors particularlie expressed.
Memorandum yat Nicholas Heyman *alias* Hellier of ffordington was this
daye Comitted till he find suertyes for his good behaviour for keepinge
disorderlie typlinge by a long space without licence: et presertim iustified by
the Constable that on whitsonday last had .6. at least drinckinge & dancinge
in his howse./ And since the pretended tyme of his licence hath harboured
Mr. Cheekes scholers videlicet Mr ffrancis sonne of Weymouth & Mr Harbyns
sonne, who have ben twice there, by their owne Confession, & spent 12 d.
at a tyme, Heyman him selfe being then at home; who would excuse it for
that they came with Ioseph Parkins of dorchester having before denyed yat
ever anie townesman was in his howse
And Mr Pele the Preacher of ffordington enformes that on the Saboth day
last viz. vltima Augusti, there were halfe a dozen drinking there.
　　Et I punisht before Crome & Prower 〈. .〉 drunken in his howse

1635
Churchwardens' Presentments for Salisbury Deanery
WRO: D5/28/35, item 57
single sheet *(24 September)*

…

Item wee present Iulian ffacy for intertaining ffidlers til three or fowre of the
clocke on Sunday morning to the greate disturbance of the neighbors & the
great vnfitting al that were present for the service of God　　contrary to
article 7.8.25

13/ Nicholas … Hellier: *underlined in MS*
25/ 〈. .〉 drunken: *letters and parts of letters lost by cropping*

HALSTOCK

1634
Churchwardens' Presentments for Salisbury Deanery
WRO:　D5/28/34, item 41
f [1v] *(16 July)*

Articell
4.5. All is well sauing that

...

3 Ther haue bin some games or playes vsed in the Churchyard which now
vppon admonicion ar now left of

...

HAYDON

1607
Churchwardens' Presentments for Salisbury Deanery
WRO:　D5/28/10, item 62
single sheet* *(2 December)*

M*emorand*um to call Anne vincent the wiffe of ... vincent of Castleton to
answere certaine ar*tic*les, for that she did one the first daie of December Anno
d*omi*ni 1605 in derision putt one a surplice one her back w*i*th a booke in her
hand & a paire of spectacles one her nose & mett mr. horder vicar of Hadon
& one Richard knight & Edeth whood comeinge from the Church, beinge
then married, by mr. horder

(signed) By me Iohn Horner

...

HINTON MARTELL

1629
Quarter Sessions Orders　DRO: QSM: 1/1
f 199v* *(7–8 July) (Bonds taken for the next assize)*

*Taken at the Shaftesbury sessions before Sir John Croke, judge of King's Bench;
Nathaniel Napier, knight; Gerard Wood, DD; John Whetcombe, DD; and Arthur
Radford and William Whittaker, esquires*

22/　...: *dots used by clerk to indicate omission of name; no editorial excerption in transcription*
24/　1605: *underlined in* MS

transcript*um*

Ad resp*ondendum* hijs
Will*elm*us Scott de Hinton Martell in Com*itatu* Dorsett fidler ten*etur* d*omi*no
Regi in xx li. Will*elm*us Goddard de Toller Ryall in Com*itatu* Wilts' gen*erosus*
in x li. & Thomas ffrye de Ashgroue in Com*itatu* Dorsett pr*edic*to gen*erosus*   5
tenetur eidem d*omi*no Regi in x li.
    pr*o* Comp*arencia* dic*ti* Will*elm*i Scott ad *proximas* Assizes et gen*er*al*em*
    Gaole delib*eracio*nem in Com*itatu* pr*edic*to tenend*as* ad respondend*um*
    sup*er* hijs
...   10

LYME REGIS

c 1544–5
Mayors' Accounts   DRO: DC/LR: G1/2   15
p 81*

Item to my lord[*es*] admyrals pleers   v s. viij d.
...
                                             20

1547–8
Mayors' Accounts   DRO: DC/LR: G1/2
p 23*
  ...
℃ Item payde at Rycherd Leonard*es* towarde the scote when my   25
  Lorde admyrall servant*es* was here w*ith* stockland men   iiij d.
  ...

p 24*
  ...   30
℃ Item payd for bread & beere for the men of stockland when they
  were here   iiij d.
℃ Item payd at Ry*cher*d Leonard*es* house toward my Lord Admyrall*es*
  player*es* by *Maste*r mayor*es* Com*maundement*   xii d.
  ...   35

1548–9
Mayors' Accounts   DRO: DC/LR: N23/2, item 17
f [1]* *(Allowances)*
  ...   40
Item to my lord pr*o*tectors playors   iiij s. ij d.
  ...

c 1552–3
Mayors' Accounts   DRO: DC/LR: G1/2
p 91
...

Ite*m* payd to the kynges plears the xxiij daye of maye   v s. ij d.   5
...

Cobb Wardens' Accounts   DRO: DC/LR: G7/3
f [76]*
...   10
Ite*m* payd vnto the erle of wynswordes players to the merere howsse   iiij s.
...

1558–9
Mayors' Accounts   DRO: DC/LR: G1/2   15
p 152 *(25 March–23 June) (Expenses)*
...

Ite*m* to the quenes ma⟨.⟩estys playeres y*at* playd In the Chvrche   iiij s. v d.
Item for wyne at Crystyn whytt*es* at theyr Comyng   x d.
...   20

1559–60
Mayors' Accounts   DRO: DC/LR: G1/2
p 167 *(25 March–23 June)*
...   25
Ite*m* first I payd to the yeryells of oxfords plyyeres 3 s. 10 d.
more where whasse spend a pone theme 20 d.   v s. vj d. [1 s. 8 d.]
...

1560–1   30
Mayors' Accounts   DRO: DC/LR: G1/2
p 211* *(29 September–24 December)*
...

paid the iiij^th daie of November for a Dyner for Mr pole &
other beyng at my house   v s. viij d.   35
paid the same daie by the advise of Rogere garland Richard
hunt Iohn perot & other to the Duches of Suthfolk*es* plaier*es*
over & aboue that was gatherid   ij s.
...

1567–8
Mayors' Accounts DRO: DC/LR: G1/2
p 140* *(29 September–24 December) (Payments)*
...

17th of desember paid to sherborn players in the churche 2 s. 8 d. 5
...

p 141 *(25 December–24 March)*
...

to Sir thomes nevelles players gave 2 s. 2 d. 10
...

p 262c *(24 June–28 September)*
...

paid the 4th awgust to therle of worsetors players 2 s. 1 d. 15
...

1568–9
Mayors' Accounts DRO: DC/LR: N23/3, item 2
f [1v] *(29 September–24 March) (Expenses)* 20
...

Item paid to hughe of bristowe the 9th of marche for playeing
in the Churche & at my house xvij d.
...

25

f [3] *(25 March–23 June)*

Item to my L Mont Ioyes players iiij s. iiij d.
...

30

f [6] *(24 June–28 September)*
...

Item to the Quenes players the xth of Iulye vj s. viij d.
...

35

1569–70
Mayors' Accounts DRO: DC/LR: G1/2
p 220 *(29 September–24 December)*
...

Item paid to the poppit players xv d. 40
...

23l my: *the mayor's, Robert Davey*   28l L: *for Lord; abbreviation mark missing* p 222 *(25 March – 23 June)*

...

Item to my L of lessetters players　　　　　　　　viij s. xj d.

...

5

1572–3
Mayors' Accounts　DRO: DC/LR: G1/2
p 271 *(24 June–28 September)*

...

pa*i*d my lord montioys playrs　　　　　　　　4 s. 8 d.　10

...

1573–4
Mayors' Accounts　DRO: DC/LR: G2/2
tab 6* *(29 September–24 December)*

15

...

paid the pleyers my L of essetters men　　　　00　02　08

...

tab 10 *(25 December–24 March)*

20

...

paid my lord mont Iois pleyers　　　　　　　00　01　1
paid the quyns pleyers　　　　　　　　　　00　05　8

...

gevyn the quyns Iester　　　　　　　　　　00　03　4　25

...

1577–8
Mayors' Accounts　DRO: DC/LR: G2/2
tab 13 *(Payments)*

30

...

Item to my L of Leicesters players the 17: octobre　　　vij s.

...

Item to my L*or*d monIoyes players 13. decembre　[xii] ij s. vj d.

...

35

3/ L: *for* Lord; *abbreviation mark missing*
17/ L: *for* Lord; *abbreviation mark missing*
17/ essetters: *for* lessetters (?)
22/ 1²: *corrected over* 8
32/ L: *for* Lord; *abbreviation mark missing*
34/ monIoyes: I *corrected over* t

tab 14

...

Item 20 Aprill to certen players iiij s.

...

tab 15

...

Item 6. September. to my L of Sheffeldes players iij s.

...

1583–4
Mayors' Accounts DRO: DC/LR: N23/2, item 51
f [1v] *(Expenses)*

...

li. s. d.

...

Item geven to my Lord bartletes players the 17th of Ianuarye
heare at Lim the Som of ... .5 ..

...

f [2]

...

li. s. d.

...

Item geven to the earle of oxfordes men beinge heare the 4th
of maye ys ... .3 .6

...

1584–5
Mayors' Accounts DRO: DC/LR: G2/2
tabs 23–4* *(Payments)*

...

li. s. d.

...

Item there whas geven to my L of Sesyckes pleeyeres the
26 daye of febyary the Some of 00 03 04

...

Item paid the 25 daye of Maye vnto my L of oxssefords
men the Sume of 00 03 10

...

8, 35, 38l L: *for Lord; abbreviation mark missing*

1586–7
Mayors' Accounts   DRO: DC/LR: G2/2
tab 32 *(Payments)*

...

the 4th of aprell to my L of lessetters players   5 s.   5

...

1587–8
Mayors' Accounts   DRO: DC/LR: G2/2
tab 38 *(Expenses)*   10
...

                                                              li.   s.   d.

...

Item the 28th of Aprell geuen to my *lord* hygh steward
his players the some of   00   06   0 d.   15
...

tab 39
...

Item the iij th of Iune geven to the Queenes playeres by   20
Consent of my Bretheren   00   08   0 d.
...

1588–9
Mayors' Accounts   DRO: DC/LR: G2/2   25
tab 47* *(Expenses)*
...

paid my L exsexe players   0   2   6
paid the quynes tomlers for playe   0   6   6
...   30

tab 49
...

paid the quyenes players Last   0   10   0
...   35

5/ L: *for* Lord; *abbreviation mark missing*
28/ L: *for* Lord; *abbreviation mark missing*

1589–90
Mayors' Accounts   DRO: DC/LR: N23/2, item 58
f [4] *(Expenses)*
...
more paid vnto players which is come to mynd sythens
counteng   00   06   8
...

1592–3
Mayors' Accounts   DRO: DC/LR: G2/2
tab 55*

	li.	s.	d.

...
Item the 9th of december gaue the Erle of worsters plaiers
5 s. 4 d. to furnish 4 s. 8 d. geuen   00   05   04
...
Item deliuered the queenes plaiers the duttons 12 s. 6 d.
vnto 7 s. 6 d. gatherde   00   12   06
...

tabs 56–7
...
Item the 26th of may gaue by consent to my Lord
mountelyes players   00   05   4 d.
...

1593–4
Mayors' Accounts   DRO: DC/LR: G2/2
tab 62 *(Payments)*
...
Item the 16th of october to my lord admeras players   00   05   00
...

1594–5
Mayors' Accounts   DRO: DC/LR: G2/2
tab 73
...
15 aprill gave the quyenes players   15 s. 4
...

32/ admeras: *for* admerals

tab 74

...

p*ai*d the 18th awgust to my Lord egle players   1 s.

...
                                                                         5

1595–6
Mayors' Accounts   DRO: DC/LR: G2/2
tabs 82–3 *(Payments)*

...

Item geven to my Lord Staffordes players   iij s. iiij d. 10

...

1606–7
Churchwardens' Presentments for Salisbury Deanery
WRO: D5/28/9, item 24   15
single sheet* *(20 April)*

...

It*em* we present the maior ffor giving Leaue vnto Certaine Enterlude players
to playe in a scoole howse adioyninge vnto the Church/ being w*i*thin the
Compasse of the Church yerd.   20

...

1608–9
Bill of Complaint in Salter v. Cowper et al   PRO: STAC 8/258/15
single mb* *(17 November)*   25

           To the kings most excellent Ma*ies*tie
Humbly Complayning sheweth and Informeth to yo*ur* highnes, yo*ur* true
and faithfull Subiect Robert Salter of yo*ur* ma*ies*ties Towne of Lyme Regis in
yo*ur* highnes County of dorsett gentleman one of the Officers of yo*ur*   30
ma*ies*ties ffarmors of yo*ur* highnes great Customes of England, That wheras
yo*ur* said Subi*ect* being lawfully appointed and ymployed as one of the said
officers vnder yo*ur* ma*ies*ties said ffarmors, hath dureing all the tyme of his
said ymployment for the space of diu*ers* yeares past, most diligently and
honestlie p*er*formed his best seruices therin, and for the same hath benn   35
very well liked and Comended by yo*ur* ma*ies*ties said ffarmors, Soe it is (yf it
may please yo*ur* highnes) That Beniamin Couper, Richard Harvey, and
Edward Rotheram Inhabitants w*i*thin yo*ur* Ma*ies*ties said Towne of Lyme
Regis and officers also vnder yo*ur* Ma*ies*ties said ffarmor*es*, greatlie maligning
and envying the faithfull demeanor and Carriage of yo*ur* said Subi*ect* in his   40

3/ egle: *for* ogle

said place and function the rather for the said good opinion and liking which
your said ffarmores iustlie Conceiued of him, haue of late very maliciouslie
and often times secretlie and vnder hand detracted slandered and reported
verie ill and Contrary vnto truth of your Subiectes said labores and endeauoures
in his said office, with a full w⟨...⟩ and vppon setled purpose and resolucion   5
therby to bring your said Subiect into great dislike discredit, and disgrace
not onelie amongest your maiesties said ffarmors (vnder whom he long hath
and still doth faithfully bestow his best seruice) but also amongest his
neighbors, frends, and acquaintance to noe small blott and blemishe of his
reputacion and Credit yf your Subiect had not ben the better knowen vnto   10
them for the integritie and sinceritie of his life and Conversacion Synce which
tyme the said Beniamin Couper, Richard Harvey, and Edward Rotheram
perceaving that those their detraccions, slaunders, and reprochfull reports
Could not preuaile to effect soe much in mischeefe against your said Subiect
as they intended and thervppon increasing their malice and purpose to   15
discredit and defame your said Subiect, neither regarding your highnes lawes
against slaunderous Libellers and publishers of Infamous Libells nor the happie
peace and Concord of this your m⟨.⟩iesties kingdome which by such libells ys
often infringed, but vnlawfully Combyning, Conspiring and Confederating
with diuers and sondry other lewd and yll disposed persons and namelie one   20
Susan Harvye wife of the said Richard Harvey, Milicent Tompson, Robert
Hassard thelder, Iohn Hassard, and Ann Hassard his wife, Elizabeth Tasen
alias Tusen spinster, and Iohn Viney all Inhabitants within your maiesties said
Towne, and with diuers others of like disposicion and qualitie to your saide
Subiect as yet vnknowne (whose names he humbly prayeth may be inserted   25
into this bill soe soone as he shall perfectlie knowe them) did for the same
end and purpose, and according to their Combinacion and Confederacy
aforesaid, of late since the first day of Marche in the ffifth yeare of your highnes
raigne of this your Realme of England most maliciouslie, despightfully, and
vnlawfully, devise, make, Contriue, and putt into writting, or Cause and   30
procure to be made, Contriued, and putt into writting against your said
Subiect (vtterlie to ouerthrow his Creditt fame, and reputacion) one most
Infamous, false, slaunderous, scurrill and obscene Libell here following:
That is to saye. Lyme Regis 1607: The first parte of Robert Salter hunting
the Cunney and doo, and shortlie I will the second parte shew. Give eare a   35
while, and listen vnto this newes I shall you tell, of a long meeching fellow
which in the Towne of Lyme doth dwell. his name in breeff I will you tell,
with two syllables you may it spell. A rope and a halter spells Robin Salter,
he is so expert in hunting, in broking, in Cuning matchiuell feates, in
holding his purse from the poore, in studying how to deceiue his neighbor   40
or frend, to make his frend sweare his selfe to the diuell to serue his turne,
and then he will geue him a shake, as the masty Curr doth ouer the litle

dogg till he quake ffor hunting the hayre he did excell, in dorsettshire his
fellow did not dwell, as his wife more playnelie Can tell, with his grayhound
he oftentimes walked abroad about Portland Castle and diuers other places
Eastward he made his abode so that he so feircelie did hunt till his firrett
gott vnder a tuff very ruff into a burro called a {punt / Cunt} But now this meeching   5
hunter in Lyme doth dwell, for polling and for baldery he onelie beares the
bell, as manie Cann tell, he firreted so long he made the Cunney about the
knee to swell; she boulted at potecary ley, then by Salthouse she fledd away,
his firret so cruelly was bent, the Cunney vppon the foote to hunt by the
sent, To a good harbour within two miles of Exmouth this cunney did hye,   10
but this firret did hunt after vppon the foote out of all Crye, and there would
not suffer the poore Cunney to lye, but into the burro the firrett did goe,
and made the poore Cunney to boult the second tyme also. Then the Cunney
to Bridgewater went and ouer into walls she had an intent, but the firret did
pursue her soe fast, that she made a double and Came backe againe in hast;   15
Then throughe manie Coppses and villages this firret hunted her so fast, that
her great belly she was faine to Cast; And after soe done, then this Cunney
Could skipp and runne. If this firret can hunt so well, through brambles and
briers through bushes and thornes, then Potecary Ball and other Craftsmen
take heed of the hornes And after she had fetchd this long race, she was glad   20
to returne for succor into her old place, but yet the firret now and then doth
the Cunney espie neere to burro where she doth lye; At potecary ley the
other day at eleven a Clocke at night this firret was seene a scratching the
Cunney as I heare say her buttockes betweene, But now Potecary ley ys well
you doe watche; this firret and Cunney together you may Catche; ffor yf   25
this firret be suffred vpon your ground still for to hunt, he will make the
Conney swell againe about the {punt / cunt} for thereabouts he will scratch, till
harme he doth Catche. you officers which take this hunting no scorne, keepe
well this Conney out of your Corne, but specially frend Sampford take heed
of the horne, your fences and marces stopp with some force for the firret will   30
in at the porche; But now Ile tell you a wonder yf it be soe; I heare this
Conney is turned into a fatt doo, for heare she goes tripping vp and downe
vpon the toe, the truth it is soe, but neuer a strang dogg that will her Chase
nor once to looke her in the face; but when Salters grayhound doth her espye,
then she ys throughlie chast or else manie doe lye, and yf his firret haue any   35
mind to hunt, he will not be quiet till he haue scratcht her by the Cunt. But
if this Conney or doo, to Salisbury chaunce to goe, the firret will hunt after
the truth it is soe, but yf by the way they chaunce to be spent a Cart will be
prouided thus ys the intent. But gentleman Hassard I hold you in scorne,
that will suffer the Cunney to Continew in your neighbors Corne, and in   40
spending your money so foolishlie in vaine for now the Cunney ys Come
hither in spight of you againe. weele send into walles for some pretty wretch,

that Cuningly this Cunney he may Catche, and so away her fetche, for this
firret and Cunney are growen in such fame, that I feare they will be trobled
with game; But yf Salters firret be so exceeding hott in hunting the Cunney
and doo soe fatt weele send newes to London what thinke you of that, that
he may haue hunting in some other platt, for this Towne of Lyme ys too hott   5
for him to dwell, here Cannot a Conney stay for to sell, but Salters firret will
Catche her by the tayle, before she cann Come to anie saile. finis. I would
haue sett forth some parte of Salters matcheuill feates Conning trickes and
false dealing with manie other vile partes, but that paper is somewhat scant,
but that you shall haue in the second parte with manie trickes and villaynes   10
per me: A.B.C.D. And having thus wickedlie, maliciously, and vnlawfully
devised, Contriued, and putt in writting the said despightfull, slaunderous,
and reprochfull Libell against your said Subiect with a setled resolucion,
intent, and purpose as aforesaid to defame and disgrace him as well among
your Maiesties said ffarmors vnder whom he serued as also amongest others   15
his frends, neighbors, and acquaintance, and vtterlie to ouerthrow his Creditt,
reputacion, and whole estate by publishing and diuulging the said Libell
abroad, The said Edward Rotheram, Beniamin Cooper, Richard Harvye, and
the rest of their Confederats and Conspirators aforesaid as well knowne as
vnknowne, in or about the sixth day of marche in the said ffifth yeare of your   20
highnes said raigne (being then a markett day holden in your Maiesties said
Towne) did most lewdlie and vnlawfully sett vpp, fixe, and fasten the same
Libell, or Cause and procure the same to be so sett vpp fixed and fastened
openlie vppon a boord vnder the Pillory then and yet standing in the most
eminent, Conspicuous and open markett place of your Towne aforesaid to   25
such end and purpose as all sorts of people might then and there publiquelie
and openly behould, read, and peruse the same, And not so Contented the
said Edward Rotheram, Richard Harvye, Beniamin Cooper and their said
other Confederats both knowne and ₍ᵥn₎knowne did with the like intent
and purpose at diuers tymes sithence the said ffirst and sixt day of marche,   30
and in sondry places as well within your maiesties said County of dorsett as
elsewhere within your highnes said Realme of England in like vnlawfull maner
publishe, diuulge, and spread abroad the said infamous Libell ₍ᵃs well₎ by
reading and singing the same, and geving forth Coppies therof, as alsoe by
secret Casting and priuate Convaying of the same Coppies into the dwelling   35
howses of diuers and sondry persons in your said Towne, as likewise by folding
and wrapping vpp diuers Coppies therof in the forme and liknes of letters
sent into your Citty of London and other places some with superscripcions
and indorsementes vnto Certayne of your maiesties said ffarmors, and some
other with like superscripcions vnto diuers other personns of great worth and   40

11/ per me: A.B.C.D.: *written in italic display script*

Creditt who otherwise held a good opinion of your subiect of intent vtterlie
to impayre and ouerthrow your said Subiectes Credit, reputacion, and estate
which hitherto he hath in very honest and good sort vpheld and mayntayned.
In tender Consideracion wherof and for as much as the devising, makeing,
Contriving, writting, reading, and publishing of such lewd, slaunderous and   5
wicked Libells doe directlie tend to the sowing and encreasing of debates,
strifes, and hatred betwixt neighbor[s] and neighbor, to the breach of your
highnes peace and to the vtter vndoeing of your said Subiect, and doe
therefore Condignely deserue to be severlie punished, and hath bin all done
and Comitted since your maiesties last generall pardon. It may therefore please   10
your highnes to graunt vnto your said Subiect your maiesties most gracious
writts of Subpena to be directed vnto the said Edward Rotheram, Beniamin
Cooper, Richard Harvye, Susan Harvye, Milicent Tompson, Robert Hassard
thelder, Iohn Hassard, Ann Hassard, Iohn Craudley, Margarett Craudley
his wife, Elizabeth Tasen alias Tusen, Iohn viney, and to the rest of the said   15
Libelling persons so soone as their names shalbe knowen to your said Subiect
Comaunding them and euery of them therby at a day Certaine and vnder a
Certayne payne therin to be limitted personally to be and appeare before your
maiestie and the Right honorable the Lords of your maiesties most honorable
priuy Councell in your highnes Court of Starr Chamber, then and there to   20
Answere the premisses and to stand to and abide suche further order and
direccion on that behalf as to your maiestie and the said Right honorable Lords
shall seeme to be most agreable to Law and Iustice. And your said Subiect
shall (according to his moste bounden duty) dailie pray vnto god for the
preseruacion of your maiestie long to raigne most happilie ouer vs://   25

(signed) Thomas Hughes

1609
Churchwardens' Presentments for Salisbury Deanery
WRO: D5/28/11, item 24   30
f [1v]*

Presentments made before William Wilkinson, LLD, dean's official

...

29.45

none saue only playing at Cytels in the Church yarde by the cob wardinges   35
Carosing

...

f [2v]

...   40

dominus peremptorie iniunxit inhabitantes ibidem provt patet apud act⟨.⟩†

x 48

wee know no such but that which hath bin presented in the 29th artycle

sauing that ther is a yearly vse and Costom in the toun of chusing kob
wardens on Easter day and going forth with a drom Ancient & flag and
Musycall Instrumentes on whit sunday in the mornyng to fetch in bowes
and so to go the cob howes to breckfast befor morning prayer which wee
tacke to bee a ᴧ⌐profane vse¬ [proffan yous] Contrary to the Ryght sanctify   5
of the lordes day

...

1621–2
Mayors' Accounts   DRO: DC/LR: G1/1   10
p 242
...

Given to the Players not to play heer   vj s. viiij d.

...

                                                                                   15

1623–4
Mayors' Accounts   DRO: DC/LR: G1/1
p 252*
...

Item given to one Iohn Iones whoe had a licence to shew feates   20
of actiuity to depart the Towne by consent of the Company   ij s.

...

1624–5
Mayors' Accounts   DRO: DC/LR: G1/1   25
p 256
...

Given to a messenger sent to Bridport for a Copy of the lettre
to proclayme [the] King Charles   [vj d.] viiij d.
Given to the 2 drummers at the proclayming of the king   xvj d.   30

...

p 257
...

Given to the Lady Elizabeths Players to depart the Towne   35
without playing   v s.

...

5l   sanctify: ify *written over other letters; for* sanctifying (?)
29l   to proclayme ... Charles: *Charles I acceded on 27 March 1625*

1633–4
Mayors' Accounts   DRO: DC/LR: G1/1
p 298

...

Given vnto staige players for sendinge them out of towne   00   05   00   5

...

1635
Churchwardens' Presentments for Salisbury Deanery
WRO: D5/28/35, item 73   10
ff [4v–5]* *(22 September) (Answers to articles about the laity)*

...

8.9. Manie here have on Sundayes or other holydaies made greate bond ffyres
for the Christninge of Apples as they call it causinge thereby greate concurse
of people as allso one William Allford the yonger makinge or callinge himself   15
a Captaine did on Assention day last duringe the tyme of [mor] mourninge
prayer & Exposytion detaine & keepe with him from the Church in a place
called the Millgreene a greate mulltitude of men and youthes there keepinge
Gunninge and drumminge and shootinge & thereby much disturbinge the
minister in divine service & in his Exposytyon or Sermon the saide place   20
beinge neigh vnto the Church & the sounde of the drumbe & Gunnes both
theire in the sayde place & in theire marches to and from the sayde place
out of & into the Towne makinge a lowde sounde into the Church which
allso they continued to doe after notice given them by the Churchwardens
and Constables the divine service was disturbed in the midest ⌊thereof,⌋ | And   25
likely to be broken ofe in regarde of the greatnes of the disturbance which
was continued notwithstandinge earnest Admonitions given them by the saide
officers to decist and William Allford the Elder ffather of the saide William
Allford the yonger beinge a Iustice of Peace of Lyme Regis aforesaide and beinge
himselfe present in the Church at divine service & hearinge the aforesaide   30
disturbance and requested by the Minester & preacher by his authoritie to
appease & suppres the saide tumult did (as we have hearde) for we our seules
were then gone forth to doe our indeavor to appease the aforesaide disorder
in steede of his so doinge vnreverently then & there in the time of divine
service or Exposition speake with an audible voyce and say what a Stirr or   35
what a talkinge or what a pratinge he meaninge or was & is conceived the
Preacher & Minister Mr Iohn Geire (who then was in his Exposyt^⌈i⌉on
maketh he about nothinge (or vsed other words to the like effect

...

32/ seules: *for* selues
37, 38/ (who then ... Exposyt^⌈i⌉on, (or vsed ... effect: *closing parentheses omitted*

MELBURY OSMUND

1622
Bill of Complaint in Gordon et al v. Auncell et al   PRO: STAC 8/153/29
mb 3* *(Before 29 November)*   5

To the king*es* most Excellent Ma*ies*tie
Humbly Complayning showeth and informeth vnto y*our* moste Excellent
Ma*ies*tie y*our* Highnes true loyall faithfull and obedient subiect*es* Iohn Gordon
of Melbury Osmond in y*our* highnes Countye of Dors*et* Clark and Edward   10
ffraunces of Melbury Osmond aforesaid yeoman That whereas y*our* said
subiect Iohn Gordon beinge a gent*leman* descended of an antient house and
beinge educated accordinge to his birth and quality vntill he went to the
Vni*uer*sitye of Abergene ₍ʿin Scotlandʾ₎ where he was Maintayned by his
parent*es* and ffrende*s* in the Studye of the Art*es* and good learninge vntill he   15
was Ma*ste*r of Art*es* and after tooke on him the ffunction of a Minister and
Precher ₍ʿof the word of godʾ₎ in w*hich* Callinge he y*our* said sub*iec*te hath
painefully and Carefully laboured to teach and instructe all such as were vnder
his Cure and Charge (aswell by example of Religious and godlye life as by
doctrine) in the feare of God and obedience to y*our* Ma*ies*ties Lawes and   20
disciplyne of this Church of England and in all thing*es* lyved as befitting his
Callinge in love and Amitye w*ith* all men And whereas also y*our* said Subiecte
Edward ffraunces hath in the whole Course of ₍ʿhisʾ₎ lif lyved in very good
Creditt and estimac*ion* in all places wher he hath fformerly lyved and also in
the place ₍ʿwhereʾ₎ he doth now lyve and hath ever bene of good ffame and   25
reputac*ion* and honest Conu*er*sac*ion* lyvinge in peace and vnitye amongest
his neighbours w*ith*out gyving the least ₍ʿiustʾ₎ offence or Cause of scandall
to any man whatsoever/ and thereby gayned vnto him self the love and good
opinion of all his neighbours and of the whole Country where he lyved and
is knowne to his great Comfort & Content yet Nevertheles Soe it is may it   30
please y*our* most Excellent ma*ies*tie that Christopher Auncell of Wimburne
in y*our* ma*ies*ties said Countye of Dors*et* Tanner Robert Childe*s* Ioan Owen
the wif of Thomas Owen the elder Thomas Owen the younger and Margarett
Abbott the wif of Humfrye Abbott all of Melburye Osmond aforesaid beinge
people of very malicious disposic*ions* and of lewde and wicked behaviour   35
addicted to the sowing of discord and stirringe of Quarrles and debate amongst
their neighbours and to other disorderly and wicked Courses havinge
Conceyved Causeles and secrett malice and displeasure against y*our* said
sub*iec*tes ₍ʿand Elizabeth the wif of your said subiecte ffraunces ʾ₎ and much
envyinge their quiet and peaceable estates, and out of the same their malice   40

14/ Abergene: *for* Aberdene

vnlawfully seeking plotting devising and resolvinge w*i*th them selues by
some meanes or other to bring yo*u*r said sub*i*ectes ˄⌈and the said Elizabeth⌉
into obloquie and disgrace amongst their neighbours and others in the
Countrye where they lyve And to that end and purpose They the said
Christopher Auncell Rob*er*te Child*es* Ioan Owen Thomas Owen ˄⌈the younger⌉   5
and Margarett Abbott did most wickedly and vnlawfully Confederat and
Combyne them selues to and w*i*th dyvers and Sundry other like lewde and
malicious people whose names to yo*u*r sub*i*ectes are yet vnknowen and whose
names yo*u*r sub*i*ectes humbly prayeth may be incerted into this Bill as they
shalbe heareafter [be] discovered. Amongst whom it was most wickedly and   10
maliciously Conspired plotted practized Concluded resolued and agreed that
they the said Confederat*es* should and would by raising and publishinge
false and scandalous and libellous word*es* and slaunder*ous* speeches and
infamous Libells in writting against yo*u*r said sub*i*ectes ˄⌈and against the said
Elizabeth⌉ to wound yo*u*r said sub*i*ectes in their Creditt*es* and reputac*i*ons   15
and to bringe them into Contempt and disgrace amongst their neighbours
and in the whole Countrye where they lyve and also to breed and stirre vpp
strif and Contenti*o*n amongst them selues and Quarrles and debate between
them and their quiet and peaceable neighbours and others inhabitinge w*i*thin
the said Countye of Dors*et*. And for the effectinge of their said wicked and   20
mallicious plott*es* practizes and devises They the said Christopher Auncell
Rob*er*te Child*es* Ioan Owen Thomas Owen the younger Margarett Abbott
and the said other vnknowen Confederat*es* by the Confederacye and
Combinac*i*on aforesaid did in or about the monethes of December and
Ianuary now last past in the xix^th year of yo*u*r Ma*i*esties Raigne most wickedly   25
maliciously and vnlawfully devise Contryve make fframe and writt or cause
to be devised Contryved made framed and putt into writting one most false
scandalous and infamous Libell in most scurrulous Rymes or Verses against
yo*u*r said sub*i*ecte Edward ffraunces and Elizabeth his wif particularly by
name w*hi*ch said false scandalous and infamous Libell ffollow*eth* vizt ffraunces   30
Nedd w*i*th Acteons head doth square vpp [and] and downe his head beinge
hye he doth stye to maister all the Towne and Bes the beare doth swell and
swer she will maister be of all the wyves for hye degree/ And well she may I
tell you trues be Maistres in London of the Stues/ ffor pompe and pride she
beares the bell Shee is as proud as the devill of Hell But her husband I might   35
be I would make her leave her veneree The Country speech doth geather the
sole must hold w*i*th the over leather And bird*es* of a vether will hold together.
In and by w*hi*ch said false slaunderous scurrulous Rymes and Libell they the
said Confederat*es* in the ffirst twoe verses thereof vizt ffraunces Nedd w*i*th
Acteons head doth square vpp and downe his head beinge hye he doth stye   40
to M*a*st*er* all the Towne They the said Confederat*es* most maliciously and
scandalously would intimate and publish that yo*u*r sub*i*ecte was and is a
Cuccold and had Acteons head and by the latter part of the said Libell that

your sub*i*ectes ∧⌈said⌉ wif was or is an infamous woman and fitt to kepe a
Stues or brothrell house w*hi*ch said false scandalous slaunderous and infamous
libell beinge so devised Contryved made and written as aforesaid They the
said Confederat*es* the more to wound ∧⌈and disgrace⌉ your said sub*i*ecte
Edward ∧⌈ffraunces⌉ and his wif did malicio*us*ly publish divulge and disperce   5
abrode the same in dyvers and sundrye places w*i*thin yo*u*r said Countye of
Dorset and in sundry other places w*i*thin this yo*u*r highnes kingdom of
England to dyvers and sundry of yo*u*r Ma*i*esties sub*i*ectes and did ∧⌈deliuer⌉
disperce and Cast abrode dyvers and sundrye Coppies and transcript*es*
thereof and did also read singe repeat and publish the same in dyvers and   10
sundrye Inns Alehouses Taverns in m*a*rkett*es* Townes and other places w*i*thin
yo*u*r said Countye of Dors*et* and else where w*i*thin this yo*u*r highnes Realme
of England to the great disgrace discreditt and scandall of yo*u*r said sub*i*ecte
Edward ffraunces and his said wif. And the said Confederat*es* not hearew*i*th
satisfied but still p*er*sistinge in their wicked and malicious Courses to wound   15
and disgrace yo*u*r said sub*i*ectes in their reputac*i*ons and Credit*tes* They the
said Christopher Auncell Rob*er*te Child*es* Ioane Owen Thomas Owen the
younger Margarett Abbott and the said other Confederat*es* did in the like
malicious and vnlawfull manner in or about the monethes of Iuly and Auguste
last past in this pr*es*ent Twentieth year of yo*u*r ma*i*esties Raigne of England   20
devise Contryve fframe make writt and publish and caused to be devised
Contryved framed made written and published one other false infamous
and scandalous Libell in scurrulous Rymes against all yo*u*r said sub*i*ectes
p*ar*ticularly by name and therein ∧⌈also⌉ scandalously taxinge dyvers and
sundrye other of yo*u*r Ma*i*esties sub*i*ectes of good Creditt and estimac*i*on   25
w*hi*ch said infamous and scurrulous Libell ffollow*et*h in theis word*es* vizt A
badye knott ther be god wott in Melbury Towne doth dwell/ If wee tread the
pathes that they doe lead it will bringe vs all to Hell. If you would know who
they be Look a little further and ther you shall see/ The Parson and his Nurse
Will*i*am Allen and his purse Nedd ffraunces and his beares Mr Gordon and   30
his whores w*hi*ch said last mencioned Libell beinge so maliciously made
Contryved and written as aforesaid they the said Confederat*es* before named
and the other yet vnknowe*n* did in or about the said monethes of [Aug] Iuly
and August and at dyvers tymes sithens publish dyvulge disperce and spred
abroad aswell in the said Towne of Melbury as in dyvers and sundrye other   35
places w*i*thin this yo*u*r Realme ∧⌈of England⌉ and did write or cause to be
written dyvers and sundry Coppies and transcript*es* thereof and did Cast
scatter disperce and deliu*er* the said Coppyes to dyvers and sundrye p*er*sons
aswell in yo*u*r ma*i*esties said Countye of Dorset as in dyvers other Country*es*
and places w*i*thin this Realme and did also read rehearse repeat and interpret   40
the said last mencioned Libell in dyvers and sundrye publicke places as ffaires

11/ Taverns: *for* and Taverns *(?)*

and Markettes and in the streetes Tavernes Alehouses and Inns in publicke
assemblyes in dyvers and sundry Townes and other places of your highnes
Realme as aforesaid and thereby did in most scandalous and Libellous manner
traduce and deprave all your said subiectes with knitting them selues together
in Bauderye and especially your said subiecte Iohn Gordon beinge a minister   5
and precher of godes word as aforesaid to be a whore master or whore hunter
to the great scandall of his profession Callinge and ministrye and to his great
disgrace discreditt and disreputacion and to the stirringe vpp of strif
Contentions quarrles and debates betwixt your subiectes and other their
neighbours and ffriendes wher they lyve And the said Thomas Owen the   10
younger hath not onlye vttered and declared the malicious Venome of his
lewde disposition in partakinge with the other said evill disposed persons in
the vniust scandalizing and traducing of your Maiesties said subiectes by
scurrulous Rymes and odious libells as aforesaid but to make vpp the full
measure of his wickednes he hath also vttered most vnseemlye base and   15
dishonorable wordes Concerning your maiesties brod or great Seale of England
in this manner ffollowing vizt He the said Thomas Owen the younger
Came to the lodging or Chamber of one Iohn Weekes of Melbury aforesaid
labourer and ther the said ^⌈Thomas⌉ Owen holding fourth with his hand a
foul pair of a beastes hornes towardes the said Iohn Weekes said vnto him I   20
doe heare serve thee with the kinges broad Seale and doe require thee by vertue
thereof to appeare at the Gunpowder Mill that I may there make powder
of thy bones In tender Consideracion whereof and forasmuch as the said
conspiracyes confederacies combynacions plottes practices making contryving
and publishing of libells to the scandale and disgrace of your Maiesties   25
subiectes and all other the offences & misdemeanors aforesaid ar contrarye
and repugnant to the good and wholsom Lawes and statutes of this your
highnes Realme of England and were all of them committed perpetrated &
done since your Maiesties last most gracious generall & free pardon & are
not pardoned & deserve to be most sharplye & seuerely punished in example   30
to other like lewde & ill disposed persons to committ the like or greater
offences if thes offendors shall escape with impunitye May it therefore please
your maiestie to grant vnto your said subiectes your highnes gracious writt of
subpena to be directed vnto them the said christopher Auncel Robert Childes
Thomas Owen the younger Ioan Owen Margarett Abbot & the said other   35
vnknowen persons Commaundinge them & every of them thereby at a certayne
day and vnder a certeyne payne therein to be lymited personally to be &
appear before your highnes in your maiesties high Court of Starr chamber
then & there to make particular and direct aunswer to the premisses & farther
to stand to & abyde such order & Iudgment concerning the same offences as   40
to the grave Councell of your highnes said Court shalbe thought meet & are
by the Lawes statutes & ordinaunces of this your highnes Realme to be
inflicted on them & every of them for their said offence or offences And your

said sub*iect*es as neverthelesse in all dutye they are bound shall daylye pray
vnto god for the preservation of your highnes in helth and happines longe to
lyve and Raigne over vs.

(signed) Tho*mas* Cole

Answer of Christopher Auncell, Defendant, in Gordon et al v. Auncell et al
PRO: STAC 8/153/29
mb 1 *(29 November)*

...

Tho*mas* May

The seu*er*all Answers of Chr*istoph*er Auncell
one of the def*endan*tes to the Bill of Informac*i*on
of Iohn Gordon and Edward Franc*es* Compl*ainan*tes

All advantag*es* of excepc*i*on to thincerteinty and insufficiency of the said Bill
of Informac*i*on to this def*endan*t now & at all tymes hereafter saved for
answere vnto so much thereof as anie wayes Concerneth him, he sayth that
he this def*endan*t was heretofore Servant vnto one Thomas Cowp*er* of Melb*er*y
Osmond in the County of Dors*et* Tanner, with whome he *se*rved out an
apprenticehood of seaven years at the said trade of a Tanner And this def*endan*t
hath by the space of these six yeares now last past lived in Wymborne Mynster
in the said County and exercised his trade there for himself as a freeman
And about the moneth of August last this def*endan*t having some occac*i*on
of busines vnto the said Thomas Cowp*er* went to Melb*er*y Osmond with
intent to speake with him Concerning the same But the said Cowp*er* being
from home at the tyme of this def*endan*tes Com*m*ing thither he this def*endan*t
stayed at his howse expecting his retorne In which tyme of his stay this
def*endan*t going towardes the said Cowp*er*s ˄⌈Crowting howse or⌉ Barkehowse
did Casually espy and find on the ground in the backsyde a Certen written
pap*er* which this def*endan*t took vp and went into the said Barkehowse, and
there then being in the said Barkehowse ˄⌈or Crowting house⌉ one Willi*am*
Rookes (a Servant of the howse) [⟨...⟩], this def*endan*t told ˄⌈him⌉ [⟨...⟩]
that he had found a writing in [the backsyde] there Backsyde, and then read
the same vnto [them] ˄⌈him and others⌉, which paper writing conteyned in
substance the matter of the second Lybell menc*i*oned in the Bill beginning
with these word*es* viz a bawdy knot there is God wot &c And this def*endan*t
having so read the same asked the said Rookes what p*er*son the said Gordon
the Compl*ainan*t was who told him that he was a minist*er* wherevpon this
def*endan*t answered to this purpose that it was a fowle peice of worke And
that he would not haue ben the Contriver of it for forty pound*es* And this
def*endan*t having made two nights stay at the howse of the said Cowp*er* to
have spoken with him, who not retorning home in that tyme this def*endan*t
hoped to meet with him at a ffayre which was shortly after to be holden at
Wodbery Hill in the said County of Dors*et*, and so dep*ar*ted from Melbery

Osmand & retorned home to his owne howse in Wimborne Mynster Carying
the said paper with him in his pocket which this defendant did doe ignorantly
not knowing that anie danger or troble might ensue vnto him thereby.
especially for that by his said reading of the said paper, this defendant had
no intent or purpose to scandalize defame or anie wayes traduce the   5
plainantes or eyther of them ∧⌐the said Gordon not being then knowen vnto
this defendant⌐ but rather desyred to haue the Libellers & Contrivers knowne
and punished for their offences In which respect [and also for that] this defendant
hopeth that this honorable Court will not Censure him as a delinquent in
this behalf And as to all or anie the said Conspiracyes Confederacyes   10
Combinacions plotes practises making Contriving & publishing of libells &
all other the offences & misdemeanors aforesaid this defendant sayth that he
is of the same & of euery or anie of them not guilty in ∧⌐such maner & forme
as by the bill of Compleint is enformed⌐ [other manner then in this his
Answere he hath before Confessed] without that that anie other matter or   15
thing in the said Bill of Informacion conteyned materiall for this defendant
to make answere vnto & not herein Confessed & avoyded trauersed or denied
is trew to the knowledge of this defendant All which this defendant is &
wilbe ready to aver & proue as this honorable Court shall Award & humbly
prayeth to be dismissed from the same with his reasonable Costes & Charges 20
in that behalf wrongfully susteyned./

                                                        (signed) Francis Ashley

NETHERBURY

                                                                                  25

1566-8
AC ***Notes from St Mary's Churchwardens' Accounts***   DRO: D/KAT: 7623
f [17v]*

...

In the yeare 1566 the plage was in neitherbury. and then the years folloing   30
viz. 1567.&. 1568 .&. they keept their Church [alls] ale[s] at Whit sundy
and had their Robert hoode and Littell Iohn & the gentle men of the said
parish the cheef acters in it a [⟨.⟩ood] requitalle for gods merscys

c 1568-75   35
AC ***Notes from St Mary's Churchwardens' Accounts***   DRO: D/KAT: 7623
f [18]*

...

memorandum that they keept their al[l]e white sunday and the other sundayes
fowleing as well as on the weecke dayes   40

...

1609
Churchwardens' Presentments for Salisbury Deanery
WRO: D5/28/11, item 31
single sheet

...   5

Item we pre*sente* Iohn Tolly ⌈compar*uit*⌉ for keepinge of [Church] ∧⌈Clerks⌉
ale vppon the whitson holydaies wherby he causeth much disorder by
bulbaytinge & other vnlawful sports:

...

OVER COMPTON   10

1609
Churchwardens' Presentments for Salisbury Deanery
WRO: D5/28/12, item 20   15
single sheet*

...

[⟨.....⟩]   It*em* we pre*sente* will*ia*m masters/ Nicholas Arnold Io*hn* dier Robert Beaton
comparuerunt   Io*hn* Arnold. Nicholas vincent Bartho*l*mew Michell Tho*mas* Michell. iunior
o*mne*s et dimiss*i*   Tho*mas* Michell senior ffrauncis Michell Iames Ham. Henry Gillett Giles   20
                     Beaton Tho*mas* Benton Ralph Bicknell: Samuell dowdall ffrancis Beare
                     Tho*mas* Beare: Bartholmew Eston: Iohn Bicknell [Nicholas] for playeinge
                     at vnlawfull sportes and playes in the Churcheyard:

...

                                                                              25

1617/18
Bill of Complaint in Abington v. Beaton et al   PRO: STAC 8/42/14
mb 9 *(19 February)*

                    To the Kinges most Excellent Ma*i*estie/   30

In most humble manner Complayninge Shewethe and informethe vnto your
most Excellent Ma*i*estie your Loyall faythefull and obedient Subiect Andrew
Abington of Over Compton in your Highnes County of Dorsett Esquier
That whereas your said Subiect nowe is and so for many yeares now last past   35
hathe ben and before him his Auncestors by the space of ffower score yeares
and vpward*es* seised in his and there demesne as of ffee of and in the Mannor
of Over Compton aforesaid with the Right Members and Appurten*ances*
therevnto belonginge *with*in whiche mannor thier now ar and tyme whereof the
Memorye of man is not to the Contrarye there haue ben diuers Coppyhold*es*   40

23*l* sportes and playes: *written over erasure*

Tenement*es* demised and demisable by Coppye of Court Rolle according to
the custome of the said Mannor for one life in possession and one life in
Reue*rs*ion at the will of the Lord of the same Mannor for the tyme beinge,
And allso diuerse other Tenement*es* demised and demisable by leases for life
and lives w*it*hin the said Mannor, And your said Subiect and his Auncestors   5
being so seysed of the said Mannor and p*re*misses There haue ben during the
tyme aforesaid by vertue of Certayne Orders made by the Tennant*es* of the
said Mannor Att seue*r*all Court Barons there holden sundrye exchaunges of
land Meadow and Pasture made aswell by and Betweene the Tennant*es* of the
said Mannor one w*it*h the other as allso Betweene the same Tennant*es* And   10
your said Subiects Auncestors Lord*es* of the said Mannor And lickwiese betweene
the Tennant*es* of the said Mannor and your said Subiect And namely whereas
one ffrancis Beaton one of your said Subiectes Tennant*es* about the Sixteene
yeares last past made an exchaunge w*it*h your said Subiect for one Acre and
halfe of Arable Land*es* lyeng at Cole Easton w*it*hin the said Mannor of Over   15
Compton for the w*hi*ch your said Subiect had of the said ffrancis Beaton
°valuable land*es*° lyenge at *(blank)* °and° *(blank)* w*it*hin the said mannor And
the said ffrancis Beaton exchaunged w*it*h your said Subiect one Close of
Meadowe called dorneford Conteyning by Estimac*i*on ffower Acres and a halfe
and one close of Pasture called middle Easton Conteyning by Estimac*i*on   20
ffower Acres And had for the same of your said Subiect one Close of Meadowe
Called Compton Mill Close Conteyning by Estimac*i*on seaven Acres w*it*hin
the said Mannor of Over Comp⟨...⟩ aforesaid All w*hi*ch said exchaunges
haue ben from tyme to tyme quietly and peaceablely inioyed by your said
Subiect and his Auncestors And the Tennant*es* of the said mannor for the   25
tyme beinge as to the benefitt Com*m*oditie and good Contentment of all
p*ar*ties bothe lord and Tennant*es* Vntill ffower yeares now last past, About
w*hi*ch Tyme Soe it is (May it please your most Excellent Ma*i*estie) That one
ffrancis Beaton Robert Beaton his brother and Henrye Iellett all of Over
Compton aforesaid Husbandmen Three of your Subiectes Tennant*es* of his   30
said Mannor being men of most malicious and p*er*verse disposic*i*ons well
p*er*ceavinge that your said Subiect had bestowed diue*r*se great somes of money
in incloseinge dyking fencinge planting and manuring of the land Meadow
and Pasture ground*es* w*hi*ch had ben taken and Receaued in exchaunge by
your said Subiect and his Auncestors from the said Tennant*es* And by his   35
great care industrye and Charge had muche improued the same The said
Henry Iellett ffrancis and Robert Beaton Envyeng and Repining thereat And
Conceauing som Causelese malice against your said Subiect being thier
Landlord as aforesaid did most Maliciouslye and vnlawfully in or about the
Monethe of August in the Eleventhe yeare of your Ma*i*estie Raigne of this   40
your Realme of England practize Combyne and Confederate together howe

40/ Ma*i*estie: *for* Maiesties

to defeat frustrate and ouerthrowe all the said Exchaunges that formerly had
ben made within the same Mannor during the tyme aforesaid Betweene your
Subiect and his Auncestors and thier Tennantes of the said Mannor vnder
the pretence that the exchaunges were not good in Regard they had Exchaunged
Coppyehold land for parcell of the demeasne Landes of the said Mannor   5
But being vnable of themsealues and by thier owne meanes to Effect the
same without the Assistance and [Col] Contribucion of the Rest of the said
Tennantes the said ffrancis Beaton Robert Beaton and Henrye Iellett to thend
they might Causlesslye incense and stirr vpp the hartes of the Rest of your
said Subiectes Tennantes against hime and sett them all at discord and variance   10
with theire Landlord did most falsely and feynedly bruit abroad and giue
forthe in speaches amongst the said Tennantes That your said Subiect
intended to take from them Certayne Common which they had in ffower
Closes within the said mannor Called Rockeleaze and Somerleaze whereas in
truthe your said Subiect neuer intended any suche thinge By meanes of which   15
said feyned Report the said Confederates did most indirectly drawe and
seduce all or most of the said Tennantes being simple vnlearned people to
yeald and Condiscend vnto thier Vnlawfull plottes and proiectes and to make
a generall Collection and Contribucion of monies amongst themsealues to
defend and mayneteyne as was pretended there Right and interest in and to   20
the said Common within the said ffower groundes Called Rockeleaze and
Somerleaze thoughe indeade wholely to be imployed in suites of lawe aswell
for the ouerthrowinge of the said exchaunges which your said Subiect
peaceablely inioyed as allso for the Vexing and oppressinge of your said
Subiect and the vnlawfull maynteyninge of suche suites as should be iustly   25
Commenced against them or any of them by your said Subiect ffor the
better accomplishment whereof the said Henrye Iellett ffrancis and Robert
Beaton did most vnlawfully plott practize and Combyne to and with one
Iohn Dier Nicholas Clarke alias Kellwaye Ieffery Ham Iames Ham George
Bicknell ffrancis Beere Thomas Michell Iohn Seward alias Clarke Richard   30
Myntorne Zacharye Bicknell Iohn Arnold thelder ˄⌜Thomas Beaton⌝ and to
and with diuers others all Tennantes of the said mannor whoese names ar
yett vnknowne vnto your said Subiect he humblye prayethe may be inserted
into this informacion soe soone as they shalbe known not only to wyne all
thier forces and meanes together to Compasse and effect the dissolvinge of   35
the said exchaunges from your said Subiect [br] but allso to ensnare and
drawe the Rest of the said Tennantes to be Contributorye to them and to
enter into severall bondes and obligacions not only to Contribute vnto them
for the space of seauen yeares after vnder Color of maynteyning thier Common
in the said groundes (beinge a thinge never questioned) but allso never to   40
release vnto your said Subiect nor do any act or thinge without the consent
of the said Confederates, According to which said practize and Combinacion
the said Confederates did frame Contrive and put into writtinge seuerall

bondes or writtinges obligatorye with Condicions to the effect and purpose
aforesaid And amongste others one bond or writting obligatorye dated the
ffifth day of August in the said Eleventhe yeare Wherein the said ffrancis
Beaton together with George Bicknell Richard Mynterne Zacharye Bicknell
ffrancis Beaton Iohn Clark alias Shewer and Iohn Arnold did becom bound   5
vnto the said Robert Beaton and Henry Iellett and vnto one Iohn Carter and
Nicholas Clarke in the som of Twentye poundes with Condicion indorsed
therevppon that the said ffrancis Beaton George Bicknell and the other parties
to the same bond should be at equale Charges with the said Robert Beaton
Henry Iellett Iohn Carter and Nicholas Clarke in the triall of Common of   10
pasture in the said groundes Called Rockeleaze and Somerleaze for seauen
yeares then next ensuinge the date of the same obligacion And allso one other
bonde wherein the said Iohn Carter Robert Beaton Nicholas Clarke and
Henrye Iellett did becom bound vnto the said ffrancis Beaton George Bickenell
ffrancill Beere Iohn Clarke alias Shewer Zacharye Bicknell Richard Mynterne   15
and Iohn Arnold in the som of Twentye poundes with Condicion recitinge
the said former bond and further purportinge That yf the said Iohn Carter
Robert Beaton Nicholas Clarke and Henry Iellett or eyther of them should
doe or suffer to be done any act thing or thinges vnto your said Subiect whoe
as by the said Condicion was pretended, made title vnto the said Common   20
without the consent of the foresaid ffrancis Beaton George Bicknell Richard
Mynterne Zacharye Bicknell ffrancis Beere Iohn Clarke alias Shewer and
Iohn Arnold therein first had and obteyned That then the same obligacion
to be in his full force or to the same intent which said seuerall obligacions
were by the practize and procurement of the said Confederates seald and   25
deliuered by the parties therein eache to other accordingly And the said
Robert Beaton ffrancis Beaton Henry Iellett and the Rest of thier Adherentes
not therewith Contented for the further Strengthening of thier said
Confederacye and Combinacion did about the same tyme most vnlawfully
Contrive and make other bondes and obligacions to the same effect and   30
purpose And namely one other bond or obligacion wherein the said Richard
Mynterne George Bicknell Iohn Shewer alias Clarke and others of the said
Tennantes to the number of Six and Twentye or thereaboutes did becom bound
vnto the said Robert Beaton ffrancis Beaton and others in a great som of
Money with Condicion that they should be at equalle charges and Contribute   35
in the triall of the said pretented Common of Pasture and other thinges
Conteyned in the said Condicion as yet vnknowen vnto your said Subiect
which said bond was lickwiese (thoughe in most seacret manner seald and
deliuered by all the said parties therein mencioned by the only abuse practize

15/ ffrancill: *for* ffrancis   38/ manner: *closing parenthesis omitted after this word*
36/ pretented: *for* pretended (?)

and procurement of the said Confederates which said bondes being so sealed
as aforesaid the said ffrancis Beaton and Robert Beaton by and throughe the
practice and Confederacye aforesaid for the further effecting of thier said
Conspiracye did in or about the monethe of october in the Tewluethe yeare
of your Highnes Raigne Enter vppon and make Clayme vnto som of the   5
groundes which they had formerly exchaunged vnto your said Subiect and did
most vnlawfully disturbe your Subiectes quiet possession thereof, Wherevppon
your said Subiect about the Tearme of Easter in the Thirteenthe yeare of
your highnes Raigne brought Severall acctions of trespasse ˄⌈in your maiesties
court of Comon Pleas at Westminster⌉ against the said ffrancis Beaton Thomas   10
Beaton his Sonne and Robert Beaton for entering in and vppon the same
groundes which they had exchaunged formerly with your said Subiect as
aforesaid Vnto which said accions they all of them appeared and pleaded ye
generall issue of not guilty Whervpon a perfecte issue being ioyned Twoe of
ye said accions wherin ye said Thomas & Robert Beaton were defendantes   15
came to bee tryed by severall wryttes of Nisi prius at ye assizes holden at
Dorchester in & for your said County of Dorsett in sommer then following
when & where ye said accion against ye said Roberte Beaton vpon deliberat
hearing therof before ye Honorable the now lord cheeff Baron then one of
your maiesties Iustices of assize for yat Circuite was found for your said subiecte 20
whervpon ye said other accion was thought fytt to bee stayd in respecte your
said Subiecte was loathe to vse any Courses of rigor & extremity against them,
All which said seuerall accions the said confederates by ye practize aforesaid
& by their generall stock collecion & contribucion amongste them aswell
in the termes at london as at ye said assizes did most vnlawfully by way of   25
vnlawfull maintenance defend & mainteyne And did lay out disburse & pay
All ffees charges & dueties whatsoeuer to Counsellores Attorneys sollicitores
and officeres for & about ye vnlawfull maintenance of ye said accions And
the said Confederates not hearewith satisfied but further plotting and Castinge
about how by Scandalous and infamous Libells to bring your said Subiect   30
his wiefe and Children into publicke disgrace and infamye the said Thomas
Beaton ffrancis Beaton ˄⌈Richard haim Richard Byshop & Iohn clenche⌉
and the Rest of thier said Malicious Adherentes about Three yeares now last
past most wickedly and vnlawfully did frame Contrive and putt into writting
the forme of a Scandalous Libellous and Reprochefull letter in the name of   35

4/ Tewluethe: *for* Tweluethe
8/ Easter: *written over erasure with line filler following*
13–28/ Vnto which said … maintenance of ye said accions: *3 lines of text written in greatly reduced size,*
      possibly by the same hand
16/ Nisi prius: *written in display script*
19/ one: *written over* of

one Thomas Ioyce a person never hard of before and supposed to be by him
written vnto your said Subiect, whiche said letter followethe in these wordes,
Mr Abington seeing you will not bestowe any thing vppon me for godes sake
I pray keepe it and bestowe it vppon your Children and teache them a little
more manner for it seemeth thoughe you ar a gentleman yow bring them   5
vpp licke a sort of vnruly Rigges and vnnurtured squalls who ar better fedd
then taught a great deale I haue seene manye mens Children of good Acount
yet did I never see the licke vnruly and ill mannered Children of a gentlemans
Children as yow ar/ I pray god yow be not so spareing of your money that
yow send your sealfe and your Children to the devill for the loue of it; And   10
even so geuing yow as manye thankes as your Curtesie Comethe vnto I leaue
off to be further troblesome to my sealfe at this tyme Committing you to
the tuicion of your Temptor and Rest youres in what I please Thomas Ioyce
And vppon the backsid of the said scandalous letter or writtinge the said
Confederates did most vnlawfully in further disgrace of your said subiect writt   15
and indorse these wordes following viz: I haue seene Epethapthes written
ouer the doores entering into gentlemens howses yt may be yow would haue
one written over youres yf yow will I pray writt this which followethe for it
is good to putt yow in mynd/ ambitiosus honos opes turpisque voluptas Hæc
tria pro trina numine mundus habet To his very worthye ffrind Mr Abinton   20
at Compton be these deliuered I pray; which said libellous and scandalous
letter the said Thomas Beaton and the Rest of the said Confederates with
full purpose to spread abroad and divulge the Contentes thereof to your
Subiectes great disgrace did by the practize aforesaid lett the same fall in the
vpfeild at Compton aforesaid whereby yt was afterwardes bruited and published 25
abroad/ And the said Confederates themsealues did lickwiese aswell at thier
private meetinges as allso at publicke meetinges in over Compton aforesaid
and other places most maliciouslye and with intent to make your said Subiect
hatefull and Contemptuous recite repeat and publishe the said libellious and
Reproachefull writting And not Restinge there but still persistinge in thier   30
Leawd and wicked Courses the said Iohn dier ffrancis Beaton ⌐Richard haim
Richard Byshop Iohn Clench⌐ and the Rest of thier Complices in or about
the monethe of August in the ffowerteenthe yeare of your Maiesties said
Raigne for the further vilifienge of your said Subiect and his Reputacion did
most Maliciously and vnlawfully by the Combynacion aforesaid frame devise 35
and putt into writting One other most infamous Libell which they most
prophanely and wickedly stiled and intitled your Subiects Commaundementes,

9/ yow¹: for youres
13/ Thomas Ioyce: written in display script
19–20/ ambitiosus honos … mundus habet: 'Ambitious honour, wealth and vile pleasure: the world holds
         these three as a three-fold divinity'; written in display script

which said stile and Libell followethe in these wordes Viz. Heere be Andrew
Abingtons Commaundementes Thou shalt do no Right Nor thou shalt take
no wronge Thou shalt Catche what thou canst that thou shalt paie no man
Thou shalt Committ Adulterye thou shalt beare false wittnes against thy
neyghbor Thou shalt Covett thy neighbors wiefe thou shalt sell a hundred   5
of sheepe to Henrye Hopkines after thou shalt drawe the best of them thou
shalt sell thy oxen twice thou shalt denye thye owne hand which said wicked
false and Scandalous libell the said Confederates by the and throughe the
practize aforesaid and to thend and purpose to make your said Subiect odious
to all his Tennantes Neighbors and frindes by bruiting abroad the said   10
ignominious Libell did most vnlawfully fix and fasten the said Libell vppon
the Churche gate at Trent in your highnes County of Somersett being one
Mile from your said Subiects howse And not therewith satisfied the said
ffrancis Beaton and the Rest of the said Adherentes did not only singe repeat
publishe and divulge the said slaunderous and impious Libell in Innes Taverns 15
and other places in your said Countyes of dorsett and Somersett and elsewhere
did deliuer abroad Coppies thereof But did allso send the same Libell it sealfe
vnto your said Subiect by the said Iohn dier who pretended that he had taken
it that morning betymes from the said Churche gate and out of his good will
had brought it to your said Subiect, whereas in truthe he did it meerely by   20
the practize aforesaid to Notyfie and divulge the same °In tendre Consideracion
whereof And fforasmuch as the said practizes Combinacions Confederacies
vnlawfull maintenances false & scandalous libells & libellous writinges and
the vnlawfull publishing & divulging therof and all other the offences and
misdemeanours aforesaid are Contrary to your Maiesties lawes Statutes and   25
ordinaunces of this your realme of England And have ben all donne &
Committed sithence your Maiesties last generall and ffree pardon And doe
greatly tend to the vtter disgrace of your said Subiecte his family & posterities
And therfor doe Condignely deserue to bee very sharpely & severely punished,
It may therfore please your Maiesty to grante vnto your said subiecte your   30
highnes most gracious wryttes of Sub pena to bee directed to the said ffrancis
Beaton Roberte Beaton Henry Iellett Iohn dyer Nicholas Clark alias Kellway
Ieffrey Haim Iames Haim Georg Bicknell ffrancis Beer Thomas Michell Iohn
Seward alias Clark Richard Minterne Richard Bicknell Iohn Arnold thelder
Thomas Beaton ⌐Richard [Hayyn] Haim Richard Byshopp Iohn Clenche⌐   35
and the rest of the said Confederates soe soone as they shallbee knowne
Commaunding them & euery of them therby at a day Certaine and vnder a
Certaine paine therin to bee lymitted personally to bee & appeare before
your highnes and the Lordes of your Maiesties most honorable priuie Counsell
in your highe Court of Starchamber then & there to answere the premisses   40

23/ libells: *corrected from* libellous

and to stand to and abide such further order & direc*ci*on in y*at* behalfe as to
yo*u*r Ma*ie*sty and the said Lord*es* shall seeme to be most agreeable w*ith* lawe
& Iustice And yo*u*r said Sub*iec*te shall daylie pray for y*our* Ma*ie*sties health &
long life./°   *(signed)* Thom*as* Hughes

POOLE

1508–9
Town Accounts   DRO: DC/PL: CLA P23(1)
p 23 *(15 January–15 January)*
…

It*em* ther*e* resty*þe* mor*e* yn the [chyr] toune boxe of *þe*
money gadyrde by robarde hoode   xvj li. xiij s. iiij d.
…

1509–10
Town Accounts   DRO: DC/PL: CLA P23(1)
p 24 *(15 January–15 January)*
…

It*em* ther restyd more in *þe* towne Boxe *þat* day *þat* Robyn hode & hys
Cu*m*pany gaderyd xx^ti li. x s.
…

1510–11
Town Accounts   DRO: DC/PL: CLA P23(1)
p 25 *(15 January–13 January)*
…

It*em* ther*e* restyd *þat* day in the Town Box   xviij li.
Wher*e* off ther*e* was off Robyn hoders money.   xvj s.
…

1511–12
Town Accounts   DRO: DC/PL: CLA P23(1)
p 26 *(13 January 1510/11–19 January 1511/12)* *(Allowances)*
…

It*em* the Mayre had for Mynstrell*es*   xx s.
…

20/ *þat* day: *15 January 1509/10*
21/ xx^ti li. x s.: *sum underlined in MS*
28/ *þat* day: *13 January 1510/11*

1512–13
Town Accounts   DRO: DC/PL: CLA P23(1)
p 28* *(19 January–17 January)*
…

Item The towne owe*th* vn to rechard hauylon*d* for þe *sergenttys* borde & hys   5
gowne & for þe my*n*strell*ys* & & toward*ys* hys dener [iij li. xiij s. iii]j d. liij s.
iiij d.
…

p 29   10
…

Memorandum that one þ*is* daye be ffor wretyne agreyyd by ffor Ioh*n* Stocker
the*n* beyy*n*ge mayr w*ith* hys bretthers that the Mayr schall haue toward hys
Dener xxvj s. viij d. & for the *sergenttys* borde & hys gowne xl s. & to þe
Mayrys for her kerchevs xx s. & Iff so be þ*at* the kyng my*n*strell*ys* or ffotte   15
me*n* or any other my*n*strell*ys* & players kome to þe towne that the*n* the mayr
schall sende ffor hys bretthers & by ther auysse schall rewarde ‸⌜them⌝ w*ith*
suche money as they thy*n*nge co*n*uenye*n*tt & þ*at* money so geuy*n* for ther
rewarde schall be at þe Townys koste & þe exppe*n*sys done to be at þe meyrys
koste   By me Iohn Stocker   20
…

1515–16
Town Accounts   DRO: DC/PL: CLA P23(1)
p 32* *(14 January–14 January)*   25
…

paide þ*at* day to Cornyssh for þe Mynstrell þ*at* went abowte
þe towne in þe mornyng*es* & þe yevenyng*es*.   vj s. viij d.
…

                                                                                     30
1516–17
Town Accounts   DRO: DC/PL: CLA P23(1)
p 33 *(14 January 1515/16–17 January 1516/17)*
…

payd to the pyper for ys reward þ*at* day for the hole yer goy*n*g   35
mornyg*es* & yeueny*n*g   ij s. viij d.
…

6/ & &: *dittography*
6/ [iij li. xiij s. iii]j d.: *entire sum intended for cancellation*
6–7/ liij s. iiij d.: *sum underlined in MS*
12/ þis daye … wretyne: *17 January 1512/13*
14, 15/ xxvj s. viij d., xl s., xx s.: *sums underlined in MS*

27/ þat day: *14 January 1515/16*
28/ vj s. viij d.: *sum underlined in MS*
35/ þat day: *17 January 1516/17*
36/ mornyges: *for* mornynges; *abbreviation mark missing*

1524–5
Bailiffs' Accounts   DRO: DC/PL: CLA P46(1)
f [5] *(January – January) (Payments)*
…

paid for reward to menstrellys þe 9 day of apryll   ij s.   5
…

paid for a reward to my lord of arrendalles mynstrellys þe
vij day of Iune   iij s. iiij d.
…

paid for a reward to þe kyngys mynstrellys þe 6 day of awgust   iij s. iiij d.   10
…

f [5v]*
…

paid to þe mynstrellys that was at rychard allynys with   15
Master mear and hys bretheryn   viij d.
…

f [6]
…   20
paid to þe kyngys plearys þe xj day of september   vj s. viij d.
…

f [7]*
…   25
paid to þe syngyng man that came to þe towne at þe reqest
of þe Mastarys   ij s. viij d.

1530–1
Town Accounts   DRO: DC/PL: CLA P23(1)   30
p 54 *(27 January–27 January)*
…

Item paide for þe Cokys & other seruentes þat seruyd att Master Mayrez dyner
vj s. viij d. Item paide to þe lord Arundelles players & lord lylez players. vij s.
iiij d. And to þe players þat played att þe Mayrys dyner ij d.   35
…

26/ reqest: *for* request
34–5/ vj s. viij d., vij s. iiij d.: *sums underlined in* MS

1547–8
Bailiffs' Accounts   DRO: DC/PL: CLA P49(4)
f [6v] *(19 January 1546/7–January 1547/8) (Payments)*
...

payd vnto M*aster* mayer/ the xxiiij day off octobar/ 1547/ ffor   5
to pay the kyng mynstryll*es*   viij s.
...

1551–2
Mayors' Accounts   DRO: DC/PL: CLA P51(6)   10
f [4]* *(January–January) (Payments)*
...

the 18 day to s*er*tain players of lorde m*ar*kes dorsett w*hich*
playd in the church and co*m*mawnded by m*aster* mayor
the mayr deput   li. vj s. viij d.   15
...

1552–3
Mayors' Accounts   DRO: DC/PL: CLA PA10
f 12v *(January–January) (Payments)*   20
...

          the 25 day off Maye
Ite*m* payd that day vnto maysther mere the wyche wasse gevyne
vnto the duke off northethomeberelond*es* [pless] pleersse ffore
there Warde by causse the dyd pley   ⟨...⟩ 25
...

f 16*
...

        the 23 day off dessember/ an*n*o/ 52   30
Ite*m* that day vnto maysther mere 5 s. the wyche wasse ffore so
muche money that maysterys merys dyd [paye] ley owthe ffor
me whyllys I wasse att Corfe ffore to paye vnto the kyng*es*
mynsterellsse   5 s.
...   35

1557–8
Town Accounts   DRO: DC/PL: CLA P26(4)
f 57 left*
...   40
Expenc*es* in Lawe and extraordenari charg*es* ow*er* the 3 of Ianivari

1557

13/ the 18 day: *18 June*   14/ mayor: o *written over another letter, possibly* g

anno 1557 //ffor mone paid by Iohn hancok bayle the yer past for
aunseryng of a amont ffor presents gevyn & to prechars & players
&c £5.3.4   v li.⟨...⟩

...

1558–9
Town Accounts   DRO: DC/PL: CLA P26(4)
f 57 left*

...

1558   The 3 of Ianvari anno 1558// ffor so mich paid by mee to havylond
bayle the yer past ffor banketyng of gentyllmen ffor presents geven
them & ffor 10 prechars & in the Lordes players as by his rekening
amont £11.6.5.   xj li.⟨...⟩

...

1559–60
Town Accounts   DRO: DC/PL: CLA P26(4)
f 57 left*

...

//ffor So mich paid by mr godard ffor banketyng of mi Lord &
Lady mon Ioy & others & for presents to them & to players in
reward at all £11   12   xj li. x⟨...⟩

...

1562–3
Bailiffs' Accounts   DRO: DC/PL: CLA PA20(ii)
f 8

...

⟨...⟩se for to ⟨...⟩ wythe Master ⟨...⟩wenes Playres   li.   x s.   d.

1568–9
Town Accounts   DRO: DC/PL: CLA P26(4)
f 10 left* *(September–September)*

...

                                         li.   s.   d.

...

28   Abouesaid// payd the players of brestowe amonte   4   iij

...

37/ Abouesaid: *the month abovesaid, ie, February*

ʃ 14 right*

...

	li.	s.	d.

...

Abouesaid// 3 s. 3 d. & is for somoche p*ai*d to the
players by m*aste*r mayors com*m*andemente   17   iij   iij

...

ʃ 18 right*

...

Abouesaid// 10 s. and is for somoche paid the players
by m*aste*r mayor comandement amonte   19   x   —

...

1569–70
Mayors' Accounts   DRO: DC/PL: CLA P103(60)
ʃ [4] *(September–September)*

...

p*ai*d the 7 daye of Ienuary 1569 to my L*ord* montioyes
plears in Reward   00   03   04d

...

p*ai*d the xj daye of Iully 1570 to my L*ord* of leyseters plears
in Reward./   00   06   ⟨..⟩

...

1570–1
Bailiffs' Accounts   DRO: DC/PL: CLA PA12
ʃ 9* *(October–August)*

...

⟨...⟩yed to the Sargente by ⟨...⟩mandemente w*hi*ch was ⟨...⟩he
Erell of wosters players   ⟨...⟩

...

1573–4
Town Accounts   DRO: DC/PL: CLA P26(4)
ʃ 52 right*

The 30ᵗʰ offe septembar// by Robart nicolas bayle for
So miche he R*eceive*d before that of m*r* Rogers maior
getheryd at hocktyde £2 5 d.   88   ij li. v d.

5/ Abouesaid: *the month abovesaid, ie, July*   39/ hocktyde: *30–1 March 1573*
11/ Abouesaid: *the month abovesaid, ie, September*

The xxvijth of Aperill & xxviij day// by me Iohn hancoke
mayor for So mych Received that tyme hocktyde gethryd
by the whomen xxiij s. iiij d. & by the men getheryd
xviij s. vj d. mont all   111   ij li. j s. x d.
                                                                                          5

1577–8
Mayors' Accounts   DRO: DC/PL: CLA P106(63)
f [4v]* *(September–September)*
...

                          the 25 daie of Aprell 1578   10
Item paid to the Trvmpetor when mayster willforde &
mr newman with the rest of the maysters went to
Broonesey to see the shippe of london   ij s.
...
                                                                                          15

1584–5
Auditors' Accounts   DRO: DC/PL: CLA PA15
f 27*

                                                           li.   s.   d.   20
...

Memorandum   Iohn domyncke az too yelde more ix s. for spoylinge of
            the drvm az in this booke apyerith folio 47   9
...
                                                                                          25

1586–7
Auditors' Accounts   DRO: DC/PL: CLA PA15
f 24v* *(Debts assessed)*

                                                           li.   s.   d.   30
...
Wee fynd that george niclys doth chardge the towne for
a drome which they will not haue   01   10   0⟨.⟩
wee fynd that george niclys doth chardge the towne with the
mendinge of the drome ix s. and wee fynd that hee was spoyld   35
by lendinge owt of the towne by Iohn Domynecke & ther fore
Iohn domyneck oweth ytt   00   09   00
...

2/ hocktyde: *26–7 April 1574*

f 25* *(Payments)*

...

George niclys have payd this xxx s. in his baylys accompt
in the batment*es*   01   10   00

...   5

Letter of Sir Henry Ashley   DRO: DC/PL: CLA P124(81)
f [1]* *(21 May)*

Mas*te*r Mayor I do vnderstande by my Late beinge at my Lo*rd* Marquis that   10
the quenes ma*ie*stis pleasure is shortly vppon whitsontyde to sende down two
gentlmen of her courte as comissione*rs* to vewe all the sea coast*es*, west warde,
and to certefie howe her ma*ie*stis monny is bestowed vppon the repera*cio*ns
of the castles, howe the Bulwarkes, bauners, Trenches diches, and skonces
be maynteyned and made, I praye god that the Bulwarkes & trenches about   15
yo*ur* towne be not fownde in defawlte thoroughe yo*ur* necligence beinge
forewarned specially by me. and by all three deputie Lieutenant*es* at o*ur* laste
beinge at yo*ur* towne More ou*er* I trust youe and the rest of the Iustices of
the towne be not ⟨.⟩gnorant that we be deputie Lieutenant*es* by her ma*ie*stis
ap*p*oyntment vnder my Lo*rd* Marquis for all marcyall affayers, and none   20
else haue to do in yo*ur* towne in those causes; Therefore we [haue] thought
it good to assigne for the ⟨..⟩tter gou*er*nment and the defence of the enemy
Iame Reade to be captayn ou*er* the bande of traynd soldiers whoe according
to his dewtie and myndinge to exercise the shott. did of late cale his bande
together. and sett vpp a Maye poole w*it*h a parret vppon the topp therof and   25
to shoote at him at there own cost*es* and charges without daunger to any
*per*son w*hi*ch is no sup*er*sticio*n*, And as I am informed, youe the Mayor and
mr [M] Newman the Iustice havinge nought to doinge in th*e*is marcyall
affayers haue p*ro*hibitid them to vse there exercise. wherat I marvell that youe
will deale therin, seinge youe haue a Lieutenante appoyntid ou*er* youe whoe   30
hathe comaunded the soldiers to be ⟨..⟩ trayned and exercised accordinge to
the councells comaundement, wherefore I haue willed the sayde captayne to
p*ro*ceed in his device whoe hathe my warrant for the same, And if he be
intervpted agayne, youe will force me to do that w*hi*ch I wold be loathe to
do./ And at my next cominge to the towne w*hi*ch shall be shortly ther sh⟨...⟩e   35
a provest marshall assigned by vs for the better ⟨...⟩ of the captayne/ So for

10/ my Lo*rd* Marquis: *William Paulet, marquess of Winchester and lord lieutenant of Dorset*
14/ bauners: *5 minims in MS*
28/ doinge: *for* do

this tyme I bid youe ⟨...⟩ell, hopinge no more to here of your follys in this
be⟨...⟩id this xxjth of Maye 1587

Your lovinge ffrende
(signed) Harry Asheley

1590–1
Mayors' Accounts   DRO: DC/PL: CLA P119(76)
f [2]* *(September–September)*

...

Iulie
9./

Item mor geuen the Quenes maiestis players that playede
her with the childeren off her maiestis chapell: ther was
gatherell xj s. and I made it xx s. of the townes mony by
the consent of mr madley and mr gregory geuen them a
pers ix s.   000   09   00

...

1601–2
Mayors' Accounts   DRO: DC/PL: CLA P191(A32)
f 1 left* *(September–September)*

...

                                                        li.   s.   d.

...

+   Item mor vj s. geven vnto the Quenes maiestis playeres   000   06   00

...

PUDDLETOWN

1619
Casebook of Sir Francis Ashley   BL: Harley MS. 6715
f 42 *(22 May) (Bonds taken for the assizes)*

...

for bringing a fiddler into Pudletowne in the despite of the Constables when
they had sent him forth: and reviling the .2. Constables.
Thomas Bartlet de Ilsington yeoman tenetur in xx li.

Manucaptores

Richardus Geng de Pudletowne Husbandman et Thomas Stone de eadem
taylor quilibet eorum tenetur in x li.

Exoneratur
primo die Iulij

pro Comparencia dicti Thome Bartlet ad proximam generalem deliberaceonem
ad respondendum ijs &c./

...

2/ 1587: *underlined in* MS   14/ pers: er *written over other letters*
12/ gatherell: *for* gathered

SHAFTESBURY

1311
Bishop Simon of Ghent's Register   WRO: D1/2/1
f 134v* *(6 April)*   5

℃ Littera directa Decano Scheftonie contra exercentes ludos noxios in atrio
conuentualis ecclesie Scheftonie.

℃ Simon permisione diuina Sarum Episcopus? dilecto in Christo filio Decano
Scheftonie salutem graciam & benediccionem Per partes Scheftonie pridem   10
transitum facientes/ inter cetera que nostro auditui fuerant tunc perlata relatu
recepimus fidedigno. quod licet olim circa nostre promocionis auspicia
auctoritate nostra sub penis grauibus fuisset inhibitum & censuris/ ne Atrium
Conuentualis ecclesie loci predicti ludorum turpium & conuenticularum
insolencium excercicio fedaretur aliisque coreis qui ad laciuiam & dissolutam   15
euagacionem miseros concurrencium animos excitant fedaretur. Insuper &
iniunctum quod eiusdem Atrii seu Cimiterij clausura eminens vndecumque
fuisset/ quod brutis animalibus loco deo dicato in quo fidelium corpora
requiescunt/ nullus ad conculcandum pateret ingressus? quidam tamen
contra inhibicionem huiusmodi libertatem & immunitatem ecclesiasticam   20
ledere ac minuere tanquam degeneros filii materni honoris inuidi molientes?
prefatum Atrium seu Cimiterium ausibus temerariis ingredientes/ obsequia
diuina in ecclesia sancte Trinitatis dicto Cimiterio continua aliisque ecclesiis
contiguatis eidem fieri consueta adeo circumstrepunt & ut premittitur coreis
& ludis noxiis perturbant? quod tam ecclesiarum quam Atrii prenotati/ quasi   25
per dies singulos violacio & per consequens interdictum verisimiliter
formidatur. Attendentes igitur quod domus domini decet sanctitudo vt cuius
in pace factus est locus eius/ cultus sit/ cum debita veneracione pacificus
sitque ad ecclesiam humilis & deuotus ingressus quieta conuersacio deo grata
inspicientibus placida/ vt in ea attendantur intentis precordiis sacra sollempnia   30
deuotisque oracionibus insistatur/ cessent eciam in ea eiusque Cimiterio/ &
Atriis deo dicatis conclamaciones ac impetus prophana colloquia & precipue
ludi noxii scurilitates/ & quorumlibet insolencium strepitus conquiescant/
Tibi in virtute sancte obediencie firmiter iniungimus committimus &
mandamus quatinus assumptis tecum si necesse fuerit/ Rectoribus & vicariis   35
ecclesiarum uicinarum dicte ville per dies dominicos et sollempnes omnes
malefactores huiusmodi moneas [&] efficaciter ⌈&⌉ inducas/ quod sub pena
excommunicacionis maioris quam contrauenientes non immerito formidare
poterunt a tam temeraria deinceps presumpcione desistant. Alioquin? cites

---

10/ pridem: *for* non pridem *(?)*   21/ degeneros: *for* degeneres
15–16/ fedaretur … fedaretur: *dittography*   38/ immerito: *6 minims for* imm *in* MS

eos quos rebelles inueneris in hac parte? quod compareant coram nobis vel
Officiali nostro in ecclesia maiori Sarum in proximo Consistorio nostro post
monicionem tuam legitimam de Archidiaconatu Dorsete celebrando nobis ex
officio super hiis & ea tangentibus debite responsuri/ facturi & recepturi
vlterius quod canonicis in hac parte conuenerit institutis. Quid autem feceris   5
in premissis/ ac de nominibus huiusmodi rebellium citatorum nos. Officialem
nostrum seu alium locum suum tenentem aperte certifices die & loco prenotatis
per litteras vestras patentes harum seriem continentos. vale. Data apud
Wodeford. viij. Iduum Aprilis Anno domini .M.° CCC° vndecimo
Consecracionis nostre Quartodecimo.   10

1527

AC   ***Gillingham Manor Court Roll***   Hutchins: *History and Antiquities*, vol 3
p 629* *(6 March)*

...   15

    Memorandum That hit is the custome in the tethinge of Motcombe, usu
longo, time out of remembrance and mynde, that the Soundhey nexte after
Holy Roode day, in May, every yeare, every parishe within the borough of
Shaston shall come down that same day into Enmore greene, at one of the
clocke at afternoon, with their mynstralls and myrth of game; and, in the   20
same greene of Enmore, from one of the clocke till too of the clocke, by the
space of one hole hower theire they shall daunce: and the mayer of Shaston
shall see the quene's bayliffe have a penny loffe, a gallon of ale, and a calve's
head, with a payer of gloves, to see the order of the daunce that day; and if
the daunce fayle that day, and that the quene's bayliffe have not his dutye,   25
then the said bayliffe and his men shall stop the water of the wells of Enmore
from the boroughe of Shaston, from time to time, &c.

...

1614–38   30

AC   ***Gillingham Manorial Court Orders***   JRL: Nicholas MS 69
f 11*

...

A true Copie   Likewise the auncient Custome for the towne of Shaston for the takeing of
of the Recorde   water in the wells or springes in Motcombe within the libertie of Gyllingham   35
hath bin and yet is vsed that the Mayor of Shaston with his Brethren yeerelie
the Sondaye after Holieroode daye in Maye in the afternoone must come
into Enmer Greene in Motcombe where some of the springes of water doe
rise with their games of mirth and musicke and there daunce and sport about
the space of one houre And afterwardes the Mayor is yeerelie to present vnto   40

8/ continentos: *for* continentes

the Bayliffe of Gyllingham in the same Greene a payer of Gloues a calues
heade a gallon of Beere and two penie white loues which is giuen in respect
of their water they take for the vse of their Towne, And yf the Towne faile in
performanc of this Custome they loose the Benefitt of the water/.

5

1626

Depositions in Gower v. Hascoll   DRO: DC/SYB: E102
sheets 61–5* *(Deposition of Thomas Smelgar)*

...

⁵ To the ffifth Interrogatorye this Examinate deposeth and saieth that hee was   10
not present at such time as the said Nicholas Gower in this Interrogatory
named made such demaund for satisfaccion for such fee beofe as hee the
said Robert Hascoll was Charged by the said | Gower to haue taken and
receaved in the time of his Maioraltye and by colour therof of divers Butchers
for selling Bulls fleshe in the said Markett as in this Interrogatorye is alledged   15
nor of his refusing to make satisfaccion for the same to the said Nicholas
Gower, nor did heare that the said Robert Hascoll did afferme or saie that
hee would Iustefie his taking of the said fee beofe by better warrant then the
Barons of the Exchequer could giue | vnto him the said Nicholas Gower for
his the said Gowers taking of fee Beofe in the said markett or ffayer, or   20
wordes to that or the lyke Effect, and therefore canne depose noe more to
this Interrogatorye Saving that hee saieth the said Robert Hascoll tould this
Examinate that there hadd bene some speeches betweene him the said Robert
Hascoll and the said Nicholas Gower concerning Bulls beofe that hee the
said Robert Hascoll hadd taken from the Butchers in the | sayd Markettes   25
And that hee the said Robert Hascoll hadd tould the said Gower therevppon
that some Butchers hadd brought Bulls beofe to the said markett and offred
thee same [not] to sell not being haighted before the same was killed as ought
to be by the Lawes of this Kingdome And that the said Butchers being
Amerced for the same in the Courte of the said Towne hee the said Robert   30
Hascoll hadd taken some of the said Beofe | from the said Butchers and
hadd distributed the same to the poore of the said Towne for their Releife
and saied that as hee conceaved the same belonged to his place as Maior of
the said Towne of Shaftburye to take by vertue of the said Amerceamentes
and not to the said Gower/   35

...

Marginal notes:

°demaund of
satisfaction for
Bulls fleshe°

°mr Hascoll
tooke some
bulls beefe.°

°to ye poore°

41 performanc: *for* performance

1629
Borough Financial Papers   DRO: DC/SYB: C11, item 17
single sheet*

money layed owt abowght the performavnce of owr Coostom the 9 of ⌈may⌉	5
may[y]⌈e⌉ 1629	
first a bowt themakinge of owr besom for Reband and incell	
and penes	ii s. ob.
for a payor of gloves for the bayle of gellingam	iii s. vi d.
for a callves hed	vi d. 10
for to peney white loves	ii d.
for a gallon of the beste alle	vi d.
to William allford for leadinge of the davnce	ii s. vi d.
To Trostrom garves and Iohn ambros for play⌈ei⌉ng in the greene	ii s.
mor for Ther too denors	xii d. 15
Somis xii s. ii d. ob.	

SHERBORNE

c 1505–8   20
All Hallows' Churchwarden's Accounts   DRO: PE/SH: CW 1/1
f [1]*
...

It*em* Rec*eyvyd* of Richard Chepett kyng of the Towne	⟨...⟩
It*em* Rec*eyvyd* of hewe honybrewe for a pott of ale of the	25
Morys daunce	⟨...⟩
...

c 1508–10
All Hallows' Churchwarden's Accounts   DRO: PE/SH: CW 1/2   30
f [1]*
...

It*em* I paid To Iohn Cheselett for me*n*d of the Whurlegog and	
mendyn*n*g of the Shryne	viij d.
...	35

f [1v]*
...

It*em* I paid for rent of the churchhowse & post & ovis	ij s. iij d.
...	40

33/ me*n*d: *for* mendyng (?)

Item I paid for the takyn*n*g downe of te*n*tes and þe carage iiij d.

...

Item for naylys to þe scherne ob.
Item for schafytt tymber xxij d.
Item for þe beryng of þe stage tymber ij d. 5

...

Item for ⌈[e]⌉ þe caryge of þe tentys viij d.

...

f [2] 10

...

Item for þe kepyn*n*g & beryn*n*g of the shryne iiij d.

...

1510–11 15
All Hallows' Churchwarden's Accounts DRO: PE/SH: CW 1/3
mb [1]* *(25 December–25 December) (Receipts)*

...

Item Receyvyd of the kyng Revyll of Iohn Chetknoll vij li. j d. ob.

... 20

mb [2] *(Payments)*

...

Item payed for the beryng of the Shrene on corpus chr*ist*i day
& drynk v d. 25
Item payed to Bartylmew for the kepyng of the same shrene on
corpus chr*ist*i Eue ij d.

...

1512–13 30
All Hallows' Churchwarden's Accounts DRO: PE/SH: CW 1/4
sheet [2] *(25 December–25 December) (Payments)*

...

Item payd ffor thred small naylys for þe shryne iij d. ob.
Item payd ffor beryng off the shryne iiij d. 35

...

Item payd ffor kepyng off þe shryyne on corp*us* chr*ist*i ij d.

...

24/ corpus chr*ist*i day: *19 June 1511*   37/ corpus chr*ist*i: *26 May 1513*
37/ shryyne: *for* shryne

sheet [3]

...

Item payd ffor a kay & mendyng of þe loke ffor þe procession dor   vj d.

...

1513–14
All Hallows' Churchwarden's Accounts   DRO: PE/SH: CW 1/5
single mb *(25 December–25 December) (Rents, sales, and gifts)*

...

...Et de vij li. x s. vj d. receptis de Iohanne yonge Baker. pro ceruisia vendita
vocata Kynges ale hoc anno...

...

(Expenses)

...Et in regardis datis hominibus portantibus la Shryne in festo Corporis christi
hoc anno vnacum filo empto pro dict' Shryne vij d....

...

1514–15
All Hallows' Churchwarden's Accounts   DRO: PE/SH: CW 1/6
single sheet *(25 December–25 December) (Rents, sales, and gifts)*

...

...Et de vij li. xiij s. iiij d. receptis de Roberto Watson pro ceruisia per ipsum
vendita vocata kynges ale hoc anno...

...

(Payments and expenses)

...Et in emendacione la Shryne hoc anno vij d. ... Et in filo & clauibus emptis
pro la Shryne hoc anno iiij d. ... Et in hominibus conductis portantibus la
Shryne hoc anno iiij d. Et soluti Sacriste pro custodiendo la Shryne iij d....

...

1515–16
All Hallows' Churchwarden's Accounts   DRO: PE/SH: CW 1/7
single sheet *(25 December–25 December) (Rents, sales, and gifts)*

...

...Et de Cxvj s. viij d. receptis de Roberto Cookeman ffrunitore pro ceruisia
vocata kyngese ale per ipsum hoc anno vendita...

...

16/ in festo Corporis christi: *15 June 1514*

(Payments and expenses)

...Et in emend*acione* la Shryne hoc anno vj d. Et in ho*mini*bus conduct*is* ad portand*um* la Shryne hoc anno vnacu*m* clau*ibus* & filo empt*is* pro eod*em* xij d....   5

...

1517–18
All Hallows' Churchwarden's Accounts   DRO: PE/SH: CW 1/8
single mb* *(25 December–25 December) (Rents, sales, and gifts)*   10

...

...Et de vij li. viij s. rec*eptis* de Ioh*an*ne pope *pro* ceruis*ia* voc*ata* kyngesalc *per* ips*um* hoc anno vend*ita*...

...

15

(Payments and expenses)

...Et solut*um* pro filo clau*ibus* & vigilac*ione* de la Shryne in festo corp*oris* chr*is*ti Et in ho*mini*bus conduct*is* portant*ibus* dic*tum* Shryne in dic*to* festo vj d....   20

...

1523–4
All Hallows' Churchwarden's Accounts   DRO: PE/SH: CW 1/9
single mb *(25 December–25 December) (Receipts)*   25

...

It*em* Receuyd off wat*er* albon ffor the kyng*es* Ale   vij li. v[ii]j s. viij d.

...

(Expenses)   30

...Item ffor the baryng*e* off the Shryne iiij d. It*em* ffor the trasshe to the Shryne iiij d. Item for the settyng*e* vpp and the takyng*e* downe off the tentte in the Churche yerde iiij d....

...

35

18–19*l* in festo corp*oris* chr*is*ti: *3 June 1518*
19*l* dic*tum*: *written over other letters*

1524–5
All Hallows' Churchwarden's Accounts   DRO: PE/SH: CW 1/10
single mb *(25 December–25 December) (Receipts)*

…

Item Receuyd off Wylliam Meere ffor the kynge Ale   viij li. iij s. iiij d.   5

…

(Expenses)

…Item payd ffor halffe a yerde off bocoram to the banners ij d. … Item ffor   10
makyge the tentt in the chyrche yarde iiij d. … [Item ffor the baryng off the
shryne corpus christi day iiij d.] … Item ffor takyge downe the kynges postes
in the Churchehay ij d.…

…

    15

1525–6
All Hallows' Churchwarden's Accounts   DRO: PE/SH: CW 1/11
single sheet *(25 December–25 December) (Receipts)*

…

Item Receuyd of Wylliam Weddayll for the kynge ale   viij li. iiij s.   20

…

(Expenses)

…for þe tentt iiij d. for packe thred j d. … Item to iiij men þat bayre þe   25
Shryne iiij d.…

…

1527–8
All Hallows' Churchwarden's Accounts   DRO: PE/SH: CW 1/12   30
single sheet* *(25 January–25 January) (Receipts)*

…

In primis Receyuid ⟨…⟩ ⟨..⟩yly late kyng of Shirborne for ⟨…⟩
Churche ale made at Whiȝtsontid Somma   xj li. x s. v d.

…   35

11/ makyge: *for* makynge
12/ corpus christi day: *15 June 1525*
12/ takyge: *for* takynge
34/ Whiȝtsontid: *9–15 June 1527*

(Allowances)

...It*em* paid for packe threde for the shryne ij d. It*em* paid for the makyng of
the Tentte yn the churche yarde iiij d....

...   5

1528–9
All Hallows' Churchwarden's Accounts   DRO: PE/SH: CW 1/13
single mb* *(25 January–25 January)* *(Receipts)*
...   10
...Item he Receyuyd he Receyuid of Harry Sampson laste kyng of Shirborne
for that he made of the churche ale at Whitsontyde Sum*m*a vij li. ix s. v d....
...

(Allowances)   15

...Item paid for the settyng uppe of the tente in the churche yarde iiij d. It*em*
paid for tack*es* & pakthrede for the shryne iiij d....
...

                                                                                                                                     20

1530–1
All Hallows' Churchwarden's Accounts   DRO: PE/SH: CW 1/14
single mb* *(5 February 1529/30–12 February 1530/1)* *(Charges)*
...
...Item paid for settyng vppe of the tente at the Churche dore iiij d....   25
...

1534–5
All Hallows' Churchwarden's Accounts   DRO: PE/SH: CW 1/15
f 9v* *(January/February–January/February)* *(Receipts)*   30
...
Item receuyd of hary albon Yong*e* man Kyng*e* for the cherche   iij li.
Item receuyd of Wyllyam vynssent for the cherche alle   ix li.
...

                                                                                                                                     35

f 13v*

...
Item payd to robert Wattsen for a seme of hurdell*es* for The
kyngg*es* stere yn the cherche howsse   vj d.
...   40

11/ he Receyuyd he Receyuid: *dittography in* MS   12/ Whitsontyde: *31 May–6 June 1528*

Item for the passheon p*art* a corpus crysty day for lynclothe
and the makyng*e* for a netherkaysse y payd   iiij d.
Item for thred and nayll*es* to the shryne y payd   iij d.
Item to the men at bare the shyne y payd them   iiij d.
Item for settyng*e* vpe [and takyng*e* yn] of the tent at þe cherche   5
dore y payd   iiij d.
…

f 14

                                                                               10
Item payd for takynge yn the tent at þe cherche dore   iiij d.
…

f 15v
…   15
Item payd to and androwe massen for makyng*e* of the steyre yn
the cherche howsse   xix s.
Item payd to davy pynchest*er* for makyng*e* of ix stapes of stone
at þe quare for the the howsse   iij s. viij d.
Item payd to that same davy for a lode of asshlere stones for the   20
stere of the cherche howsse at quare   xij d.
Item payd for fechyng*e* of to lode of stones to Iohn sovthe hey
for the stere of the cherche howsse   ij s. iij d.
Item payd to Iohn newman for fechyng*e* of to lode of stones for
the steyre of the cherche howce   ij s. iij d. 25
…

f 16
…
Item payd to Wyllyam adamsse for thre pot*es* of erthe for the stere   30
Warke of þe cherche howsse   xij d.
Item payd to Iohn gowle of burtun for a lode of stons for the
cherche howsse   xvj d.
Item payd to rychard kopere for lyme to þe steyre   xv d.
…   35
Item payd to the to bede men for karyng*e* a way þe robull of The
steyre yn the cherche hows   viij d.
…

1/ corpus crysty day: *4 June 1543*   16/ and androwe: *partial dittography in* MS
4/ at: *for* that *(?)*   19/ the the: *dittography in* MS
4/ shyne: *for* shryne

f 16v

...

Item payd to Rychard elyett for a bosshele of lyme for The steyre
of the cherche hows   iiij d.

...   5

f [17]

...

Item payd for Iohn butleres shope rowme for the kyng alle Whytsontyd viij d.

...   10

1535–6
All Hallows' Churchwarden's Accounts   DRO: PE/SH: CW 1/15
f 2v* *(January/February–January/February) (Receipts)*

...   15

Item receuyd of rogare yngulberd for the charche alle   xiij li.

...

f 5v *(Payments)*

...   20

Item payd for settynge vp and takynge downe of the tent at the
cherche dore to fox and mynterne   iiij d.

...

1536–7   25
All Hallows' Churchwarden's Accounts   DRO: PE/SH: CW 1/16
f 1v* *(January/February–January/February) (Receipts)*

...

Ressaywed of Iohn yonge the yongger that was kyng thes Ere for
the Cherche Alle   xvij li. 30

...

f 4

payde to fox for settynge owppe of the Tente   iiij d. 35
payde to Iohn Adam for berynge of the scrynne   iiij d.
          Item for threde & naylles to ⌜þe⌝ scrynne   iij d.

...

9/ Whytsontyd: *24–30 May 1534*

f 4v

…

Item for hauyng in of the tente j d. & beryng home of the lathers j d.   ij d.

…

1537–8
All Hallows' Churchwarden's Accounts   DRO: PE/SH: CW 1/17
single mb *(28 January–27 January) (Receipts)*

…

…Item Receyuyd of Gervys Aysheley late kyng of Shirborne for that he
brouȝht to the churche clere Summa xvij li. vj s. viij d.…

…

(Allowances)

…Item paid for naylles threde & pynnys to the shryne a corpus christi day iij d.
… Item paid for settyng vppe of the tentte a corpus day & takyng dovne of
the same ayen iiij d./ Item payd for theire dyner that did beare the shryne
vj d.…

…

1538–9
All Hallows' Churchwarden's Accounts   DRO: PE/SH: CW 1/18
f 2* *(27 January–January/February) (Receipts)*

Item Reseued off Roberd coke for the chyrche ale   7 li.

…

f 5 *(Payments)*

payd Iohan botteler for mendyng off the ij torches agenst Wyttsonday   iiij d.
Item payd tomas cardmaker and Wylliam edwardys for settyng op
off the tent In the chyrche yerd   iiij d.

…

f 10* *(Inventory of church goods)*

…Item the cheldes vestmentes with the myter

…

16/ corpus christi day: *31 May 1537*   31/ Wyttsonday: *9 June 1538*

1542–3
St Mary the Virgin's Churchwardens' Accounts   DRO: PE/SH: CW 1/19
f 1 *(Rendered 4 February)* *(Inventory of church ornaments)*

...

...Item the Bysshoppes vestiment*es* Cope and mytere...   5

...

f 2 *(Receipts)*

...

Item receyvyd of Will*i*am Rawlyng*es* for the churche ale   xj li: x s.   10

...

f 3v* *(Payments)*

...

Item paid to henry Clarke for pynnes for the pleyer*es* at   15
Corpus chr*ist*i Day   j d.

...

Item paid to Iohn Butteler*e* for makyng of the kanapy that Thomas
Adampes dyd Sett hym to make   vij s.

...   20

1543–4
St Mary the Virgin's Churchwardens' Accounts   DRO: PE/SH: CW 1/20
mb [1] *(Inventory of church ornaments)*

...   25

...Item the bysshopes vestymentt*es* Cope and mytere...

...

mb [2]* *(Receipts)*

...   30

Item rec*eyuyd* of Iohn oke churche man for this yere   x li.

...

mb [3] *(Payments)*

...   35

...Item paid for caryng a Way of the bord*es* that the player*es* plaid vppon in
the churche ij d....

...

16/ Corpus chr*ist*i Day: *8 June 1542*

mb [4]

...

...Item for Settyng vppe of the tent [of] a Corpuscristy day and for caryng
in a gayne iiij d....

...   5

1544–5
St Mary the Virgin's Churchwardens' Accounts   DRO: PE/SH: CW 1/21
mb [2]* *(Rendered 15 February) (Inventory of church ornaments)*

                                                                            10
...Item the the bysshopes vestymentes Cope and mytere ... Item the bokes
off corpus christi [b] playe...

...

(Receipts)   15

Item receyuyd off Rychard cuppar churche man ffor thys yere   xiiij li.
...

mb [3]*   20
...
Item Receyuyd off Wyllyam calowe ffor the churche ale   xx s. iiij d.
Item Receyuyd off Iohn oke ffor the churche ale   xxvj s. ij d.
...

                                                                          25
1546–7
St Mary the Virgin's Churchwardens' Accounts   DRO: PE/SH: CW 1/22
mb [1] *(Rendered 13 February) (Inventory of jewels and church ornaments)*
...
...Item the Bysshoppes vestymenttes with Cope and myter ... Item the Bokes 30
of Corpus christi...

...

mb [2] *(Receipts)*
...   35
Item of Iohn Sowthey for the Churche alle this yere   xj li.
...

3/ Corpuscristy day: *24 May 1543*   11/ the the: *dittography in* MS mb [5] *(Payments)*

...

Item for gyrdell ij d. Item for paper & pynnes for Corpus
chri*s*ti playe iiij d. ob.   vj d. ob.
Item paid to he*n*ry damper for Settynge vpp & takynge   5
doune of the tentte   iiij d.

...

1547–8
St Mary the Virgin's Churchwardens' Accounts   DRO: PE/SH: CW 1/23   10
mb [1] *(Rendered 29 January) (Inventory of ornaments)*

...

...Item the Bysshoppes vestyment*es* wi*th* Cope & myter*e* ... Item the bokes
of corpus chr*i*sti play...

...   15

mb [2] *(Receipts)*

...

Item re*ceyvyd* of Iohn Sowthey for the Stondynge of peopell
vppon the Churche at the pley   ij s. v d.   20

...

Item re*ceyvyd* of Iohn Adampes for the Churche alle this
yere   xj li. vj s. viij d.

...

                                                                          25

mb [4] *(Payments)*

...

Item paid to the paynter for payntyng of corpus chri*s*ti Garment*tes*   iiij d.

...

                                                                          30

mbs [5–6]*

...

Item paide to henry damper for Settynge vppe of the Tentte   iiij d.

...

Item paid to Iohn Carver for settynge vppe of ye bord*es* before   35
the ij lowe alter*es*   iiij d. |
Item paid to chri*s*toffer harderman for ij yard*es* of [fuschen]
bockerom for Corpus chri*s*ti playe   ix d.

...

1548–9
St Mary the Virgin's Churchwardens' Accounts   DRO: PE/SH: CW 1/24
mb [1]* *(Rendered 17 February) (Inventory of church ornaments)*

...Item the bysshops vestment*es* w*ith* þe coope & myt*er* ... Item the book*es*   5
of Corpus chr*ist*i play...

...

1549–50
St Mary the Virgin's Churchwardens' Accounts   DRO: PE/SH: CW 1/25   10
mb [2] *(Rendered 16 February) (Receipts)*

...

Item rec*eyued* off Thomas gayper and damp*er* at the churche ale   ix s.

...

15

mb [3]*

...

Item rec*eyued* ffor hir*e* off the pleyers clothyng*e*   v s.

...

20

1550–1
St Mary the Virgin's Churchwardens' Accounts   DRO: PE/SH: CW 1/26
sheet [2]* *(Rendered 20 January) (Receipts)*

...

Item re*seyved* of Richarde Chemyll for an alle made for the   25
may*n*teynyg*e* of the palyeng*e* Garment*es*   lij viij d.

...

sheet [3]*

...

30

Item re*seyved* of Iohn yonge for the bysshopes Cope & Chesable   vj s. viij d.

...

Item re*seyved* of Richarde Rogers for alyttell albe   xviij d.

...

35

sheet [7]

...

Item paid to Katerine Walles ffor brusshyng*e* of the Corpus chr*ist*i
Garment*es*   iiij d.

...

40

26l may*n*teynyg*e*: *for* may*n*teyny*n*g*e*; *abbreviation mark missing*   26l lij: *for* lij s.
26l palyeng*e*: *for* playeng*e*

1552–3
St Mary the Virgin's Churchwardens' Accounts DRO: PE/SH: CW 1/28
sheet [2] *(Rendered 26 February) (Receipts)*

Item re*ceyvid* for the hyer of The players Garment*es* x s....   5
...

sheet [4] *(Payments)*
...
...Item for brusshyng of the player*es* Garment*es* iiij d....   10
...

1554–5
St Mary the Virgin's Churchwardens' Accounts DRO: PE/SH: CW 1/30
sheet [1] *(Rendered 17 March) (Receipts)*   15
...
Item re*ceuyd* off Iohn Stevyns this yer*e* ffor the churche ale   xviij li.
...

sheet [3] *(Payments)*   20
...
Item payd to haukyns ffor takyng*e* downe the tent and Iames
ffor caryyng*e* boord & *t*restyll*es* ffro*m* the churche porche   iij d.
...

                                                                                 25
sheet [4]

Item payd to ffooke and Iames ffor bering*e* to churche vj pyc*es*
off ye tent ffro*m* the condytt   ij d.
...   30

1555–6
St Mary the Virgin's Churchwardens' Accounts DRO: PE/SH: CW 1/31
sheet [1]* *(Rendered 9 January) (Receipts)*
...   35
Item re*ceyvyd* of Richarde Chetmyll for the Churche ale this yere   xiij li.
...
...Item re*ceyvyd* of henry Gardener for the player*es* Garment*es* xij d. Item
re*ceyvyd* of the men of yatemester for the same Garment*es* xx d....
...

1556–7
St Mary the Virgin's Churchwardens' Accounts   DRO: PE/SH: CW 1/32
mb [1]* *(Receipts)*

...

...Item receyvyd of Iohn Philippes for the Churche Ale this yere xx li....   5
...Item rec*eyvyd* of men of wyncalton for the players Garment*es* v s. ...

...

1557–8
St Mary the Virgin's Churchwardens' Accounts   DRO: PE/SH: CW 1/33   10
mb [1]* *(Rendered 13 February) (Receipts)*

...

...Item rec*euyd* off Iohn Reed ffor the churche ale this yer*e* x li....

...

...Item rec*euyd* off george churchell ffor lone off vj Ierkens xij d. It*em* ffor   15
lone off belles to martocke xij d. ... Item lone off garme*n*t*es* to castyll cary ij s.
vj d. It*em* rec*euyd* off wynca*n*ton for lone off garment*es* iij s. iiij d. It*em*
rec*euyd* off cawndell ffor lone off the same xvj d....

...

20

1558–9
St Mary the Virgin's Churchwardens' Accounts   DRO: PE/SH: CW 1/34
sheet [1]* *(Rendered 29 January) (Receipts)*

...

...Item rec*eyvid* of Rob*e*rte Wase for the Churche ale this yere xx li....   25

...

sheet [2]

...Item rec*eyvid* of ffuller of Byere for the hyer of Corpuschrist*i* Garment*es*   30
ij s. iiij d....

...

1561–2
St Mary the Virgin's Churchwardens' Accounts   DRO: PE/SH: CW 1/35   35
sheet [1] *(Rendered 1 February) (Receipts)*

...

...Item receyvyd of Thomas Wynnyff for the p*r*ofytt*es* of the Churche ale
this yere xx li....

...   40

6/ wyncalton: *Wincanton, Somerset*   30/ Byere: *probably Beer Hackett, 4 miles from Sherborne*

Item receyvyd of Richarde *(blank)* of yevyll for olde Corpuschr*ist*i Garment*es*
to hym solde v s. ... It*em* Solde to Richarde damper the Sepulker cloth w*ith*
ij Bann*er*clothes xvj d....

1565–6   5
St Mary the Virgin's Churchwardens' Accounts   DRO: PE/SH: CW 1/36
sheet [1]* *(Receipts)*

...

It*em*/ Receauyd of Will*ia*m foster ffor the Churche ale, made
at the ffeast of Pentecost last past./   xxij li. xiiij d.   10

...

1566–7
St Mary the Virgin's Churchwardens' Accounts   DRO: PE/SH: CW 1/37
f 1 *(Rendered 9 February) (Receipts)*   15

...

Receuyd of Iohn Reade, for the churche ale made this
yere   xviij li. xvj s. viij ⟨.⟩

...

                                                                                                                                  20

1567–8
St Mary the Virgin's Churchwardens' Accounts   DRO: PE/SH: CW 1/38
mb [1d]* *(Rendered 15 February) (Receipts)*

...

+ Receuyd of Iohn Dyer for the Rome of the Churche house,   25
to playe his enterludes yn, thre seuerall tymes./   iiij d.

...

mb [3]

                                                                                                                                  30
Receaved of Roberte Albon for the Churche ale this yeare,   xix li. ij s. iij d.

...

1568–9
St Mary the Virgin's Churchwardens' Accounts   DRO: PE/SH: CW 1/39   35
mb [1] *(Rendered 8 February) (Receipts)*

...

It*em* Receued of Iohn Gardnar for the cherche alle this
yeare   xviij li. vj s. vij d. ob.

...   40

1/ yevyll: *Yeovil, Somerset*

1569–70
St Mary the Virgin's Churchwardens' Accounts   DRO: PE/SH: CW 1/40
mb [1] *(Rendered 30 January) (Receipts)*

...

Item Receued of Thomas Maunsell, for the churche alle, this   5
yeare   xv li. ij s.

...

1570–1
St Mary the Virgin's Churchwardens' Accounts   DRO: PE/SH: CW 1/41   10
mb [1] *(Rendered 4 February) (Receipts)*

...

...Item receaued of will*i*am Poope for the churche Ale, thys yeare xviij li.

...

15

1571–2
St Mary the Virgin's Churchwardens' Accounts   DRO: PE/SH: CW 1/42
mb [1] *(Rendered 10 February) (Receipts)*

...

...It*e*m receaved of Will*i*am Rideowte for the Church ale this yere xxij li. x s.   20
⌈over & besydes/ the playsterynge over the highe boorde yn the churche house/
w*hi*ch coste hym xxxiij s. iiij d.⌉

...

mb [3] *(Payments)*   25

...

It*e*m paied to the Quenes plaiers at the Requeste of the Towne   ij s. viij d.

...

mb [4]   30

...

It*e*m paied to Iohn Dier for Makinge and Devisinge garment*es*
Toward*es* Corpus Christi playes   xj s. viij d.
It*e*m paied more for a Cope and Banner Toward*es* the same
playe   xiij s. iiij d.   35
It*e*m paied to Henrye Stephens for Canvas gurswebbe Tinsall
and Neales toward*es* the makinge off the Giant   xiiij s.

...

1572–3
St Mary the Virgin's Churchwardens' Accounts   DRO: PE/SH: CW 1/43
mb [1] *(Rendered 8 February) (Receipts)*

…

…Item Receaued of Robart foster for the church ale this yere xxv li.   5

…

mb [2] *(Church house receipts)*

…

Item Receaued of Robarte cuffe for the roume a gaynste the churche   10
at the corpus Christye playe   x s.

…

mb [3]* *(Receipts)*

…   15

Item Receaued for the stonninge vppon the lydes this yere   xiij s. iiij d.

…

mb [4]*

                                                                                    20

paymentes for | Inprimis paiede To Master knoyle of samforde for Ieaylmes
the corpuschristi | for to make the te[ay]ntes for the corpuscrystie playe   xij s.
playe::

Item payed for the carrayge for iij lode of tymber from samforde   vij s.
Item payed to william hunte for mackynge of a te[ay]nte   viij s.
Item payed to william hunte for mackynge of the heygh te[ay]nte   xij s.   25
Item payed to william hunte for his laubor and his manes laubor
⟨…⟩ to make the scaffouldes   v s. viij d.
Item payed to Poule raulens for mackynge of the players garmentes   iij s.
Item payed to Iohn wheccome for stufe to macke the players
garmentes   xliiij s.   30
Item payed to william redowt for v[ea]ysages for the playeres   xv s.
Item payed to Mr conthe for nayles vij d. ob.
Item payed to william hunte for tackinge downe of the te[ay]ntes   iiij d.
Item payed for a pasment skyne for the playeres   vj d.
Item payed to the carryoure for to brynge Master poyntes regoules   xij d.   35
Item payed to him that dyd playe vpon the trumpite for his paynes   x d.
Item payed for nayeles for the te[ay]ntes   x d.
Item payed for a peacke of wheatten meale for to macke louttes wyfe   vj d.
Item payed to Nayle the carroure for [⟨.⟩] w[ea]youre   xij d.

21/ samforde: *probably Sandford Orcas, 3 miles from Sherborne*
32/ Item … vij d. ob.: *apparently added later by the same hand*

Item payed for bea[y]ringe in of the stufe of the scauffouldes   vj d.
Item payed to Steuens for setteaynge vp of the glase   viij d.
Item payed to Robart coke for broune Paper   iiij d.
Item payed to Iohn Ieaynes for la[⟨.⟩]ce[⟨.⟩] for the players
garmentes   xj d.   5
Item Henrye steauens for thinges to macke the players
garmentes   x⟨.⟩xvij s. ij d.
Item payed to [hunte] for mackinge of a lauder for ye towne   viij d.
            Summa vij li. xjj s. viij d. ob.   Item Receaued of Mr horceay won
                                                  eaylme towardes the mackinge a   10
                                                  teaynt for the corpus christye playe

...

(Payments)
                                                                                  15
Item Payed for the carrayge of a laudder of the gyfte of Mr Mullens viij d.
...

Item payed to Master Steauens a daunseng thursdaye   ij s.
...

Item Payed to [ij] Robarte bute for the sett[ea]ynge vp of the place   20
to put the players garmentes in   xviij d.
Item payed to ij masons a bout the same worke   ij s.
Item Payed to ij Lauberoes a boute the same worke   xiiij d.
...
                                                                                  25
mb [5]

Item Payed to Nycolas kobe for mendynge of the cloke and
for mackynge of a keay for the dowre where as you doo putt/
the players garmentes in   .   xx d.   30
...

[Item Payed to William redowte for vj veaysordes for the playeᣛrᣛs   xv s.]
...

1573–4   35
St Mary the Virgin's Churchwardens' Accounts   DRO: PE/SH: CW 1/44
mb [1] *(Rendered 7 February)* *(Receipts)*
...

Item receaued of Rychard Bampton for the Churche ale this
year/   xx li. vj d. ob./   40
...

9–11/ Item Receaued ... playe: *added later, probably by the same hand*   23/ Lauberoes: *for* Lauberores (?)

mb [2] *(Church house rents)*

...

Item/ receaued of Thomas fuller/ for the ground yn the churche
yarde vppon the playe Daye/   ij s.
Item/ receaved vppon the play daye/ for Standing vppon the   5
leades/   xj s. x d.

...

mb [3] *(Payments)*

...   10

Item/ payd for nayles at the settyng vp of the tentes/ on the play
day/   ij d./
Item/ payde/ for sawynge of two peeces of tymber/ for narrowe
boordes/ to laye/ the lead vppon the churche/ & for the tymber
of the newe seates/   iiij s. iij d. 15
Item/ payde for iij elles/ of Soultwyche/ & iij quarters, of canves/
about the playe/   ij s.
Item/ payde/ for Settinge vp the tentes/ agaynst/ the play daye./   xx d./
Item/ payde for takynge downe of the tentes/ and caryage yn of
the same/   xvj d. 20
Item/ payde/ to Roberte Cooke/ for staynynge/ of Sodom
clothes/   iij s. iiij d.
Item/ payd for brasell/   iiij d.
Item/ payde/ to Iohn dyer/ for gilting of a face/ for the playe/   xviij d.
Item/ payde/ for halffe a hundred of nayles/ occupyed about the   25
corone/ on the play day/   iiij d.
Item/ payd/ for boord nayles aboute/ the tentes/ on the play
Daye./.   iiij d.
Item/ payde/ for ij mennes waiges/ & meate/ & dryncke/ whiche
gave attendance/ about the Leades/ on the play Daye./   xvj d. 30
Item/ payd/ for/ levers to strowe vppon the boordes/ on the
play daye:/   iiij d.
Item/ payd/ to thomas fullers man/ for a dayes worke/ about
the tentes/   iij d.
Item/ payde/ for the new dressyng of Lottes wyffe/   ij d. 35
Item/ payde for laths/ about the playe/   j d.
Item/ payde to two men/ for theire Laboures/ yn settyng vp/
of the backer tentes for the players/ to aray them selves yn./   x d.
Item/ payd vnto paule Rawlynson/ for mendinge/ of iiij^er Ierkyns/
& other thinges of ye play/   vj d. 40
Item/ payd for browne paper/ aboute the playe/   iij d.
Item/ payd for wyne & sugar/ geven to the gentlemen/ at the
muster/ yn horse castell/   ij s. vj d.

Item/ payd for buylding/ of the standinges yn horse castell/ for
the gentlemen to sytt yn/ and for the bearyng yn of the same:/   ij s.
Item/ payde to Thomas Adams/ for makyng cleane of the leades/   vj d.
Item/ payd to henry Rawlynson/ for dyverse thinges/ & necessaries
for the playe/   viij d.   5

...

1574–5

St Mary the Virgin's Churchwardens' Accounts   DRO: PE/SH: CW 1/45
mb [1] *(Rendered 6 February) (Receipts)*   10

...

Item: receaued/ of Laurence Swetnam/ for the churche ale/
this yeare:/   xxj li.

...

15

mb [3]* *(Payments)*

...

Inprimis paide, to william poope/ for clothe and making of the
vyse coote/ that he had forgott/ at his accompt/   xiiij s. xj d.

...   20

1575–6

St Mary the Virgin's Churchwardens' Accounts   DRO: PE/SH: CW 1/46
mb [1] *(Rendered 5 February) (Receipts)*

...   25

Item/ receaued of william Steavens/ for the churche ale this
yeare:/   xxiij li. vij s. iiij d.

...

mb [2]*   30

...

Item receaued/ the playe Daye/ for standinge vppon the churche
Lead*des*/   x s.

...

35

mb [3] *(Payments)*

...

Item/ payd to henry Steavyns/ for nayles/ & clothe/ & other
thyng*es*/ for the play/   iiij s. vj d.
Item/ payd/ to mr Cowthe/ for Gonpowder/   iij s. vj d.   40

Item/ payd to Henry kayes/ for mendynge/ of one/ of the
players cotes/   iiij d.

…

Item/ payd to henry Rawlynson/ for browne pap*er*/ and other
necessaries/ about the play   v s. viij d.   5

…

1576–7
St Mary the Virgin's Churchwardens' Accounts   DRO: PE/SH: CW 1/47
mb [1] *(Rendered 3 February) (Receipts)*   10

…

Item of Will*i*am Cowth for the Churche *(blank)*   xx li.

…

1577–8   15
St Mary the Virgin's Churchwardens' Accounts   DRO: PE/SH: CW 1/49
mb [1]* *(Rendered 9 February) (Receipts)*

…

Item of Briant Cole ffor the Church Ale deliu*er*d the daye of
this Accompte   xx li.   20

…

1588–9
St Mary the Virgin's Churchwardens' Accounts   DRO: PE/SH: CW 1/60
mb [1] *(Rendered 24 February) (Receipts)*   25

…

of the players for the vse of the churche howse   iiij s.

'…

of certaine Straungers to playe in the churche howse   vj d.

…   30

1589–90
St Mary the Virgin's Churchwardens' Accounts   DRO: PE/SH: CW 1/61
mb [1] *(Rendered 15 February) (Rents and other receipts)*

…   35
Item of players in the Churchowse   xviij d.

…

Item of players in the churchowse   ij s.

…

36/ xviij d.: *sum apparently written over erasure*

1590-1
St Mary the Virgin's Churchwardens' Accounts   DRO: PE/SH: CW 1/62
mb [1] *(Rendered 14 February) (Rents and other receipts)*
...
Item of players in the Churchowse   ij s. vj d.   5
...

1597-8
St Mary the Virgin's Churchwardens' Accounts   DRO: PE/SH: CW 1/69
mb [2] *(Rendered 5 February) (Rents and other receipts)*   10
...
of the quenes Ma*ies*tis players for the vse of the churchowse   ij s.
...

1598-9   15
St Mary the Virgin's Churchwardens' Accounts   DRO: PE/SH: CW 1/70
mb [1] *(Rendered 21 January) (Rents and other receipts)*
...
of the queens players for the vse of the churchowse   ij s.
...   20

1599-1600
St Mary the Virgin's Churchwardens' Accounts   DRO: PE/SH: CW 1/71
mb [1] *(Rendered 13 January) (Rents and other receipts)*
...   25
Of the younge men of the Towne for playinge in the Churchouse   xvj s.
...

1600-1
St Mary the Virgin's Churchwardens' Accounts   DRO: PE/SH: CW 1/72   30
mb [3] *(Rendered 18 January) (Rents)*
...
of certaine players for the vse of the Churchowse   ij s.
...

                                                                                    35
1601-2
St Mary the Virgin's Churchwardens' Accounts   DRO: PE/SH: CW 1/73
mb [3] *(Rendered 11 April) (Rents and other receipts)*
...
of Strangers to playe in the church howse   ij s.   40
...

1602–3
St Mary the Virgin's Churchwardens' Accounts   DRO: PE/SH: CW 1/74
mb [1] *(Rendered 29 May) (Rents and other receipts)*

...

of Certayne players for the vse of the Churchowse   iiij s. vj d.   5

...

1603–4
Depositions for the Defendant in Scarlett v. Stocker
PRO: E134/1 James I/Hil 3   10
mb 1*

...

Depositions of witnesses taken at Sherbourne in the County of D⟨.⟩rs*et* the
xxiij^th day of Ianuary in the firste yere of th⟨.⟩ raigne of *our* sou*e*raigne
Lord Iames by the grace of God ⟨.⟩f England ffraunce & Ireland Kinge   15
defender of the faith &c and of Scotland the seauen & Thirtieth before vs
S*ir* Robert Napper knight Iohn ffarewell Esquier and Will⟨...⟩ Wood
gen*tleman,* by vertue of the King*es* Ma*ies*ties Com*m*ission out of his Highnes
Court of Exchequer to vs & others directed for thexa*m*inac*ion* of witnesses
∧ ⌈as well on the p*ar*te & behalf of ffraunces Scarlett clarke pl*ain*t as⌉ on   20
the p*ar*te & behalf of Iohn Stocker Esquier defend*an*t to the bill of Compl*ain*t
of ⌈the said⌉ ffraunces Scarlet Clerk vicar of Sherbourne Compl*ain*ant as
followeth. viz.

...

                                                                             25

(Deposition of Thomas Adams, labourer, aged about 73)

To the eleventh Interr*o*gatory he sayth that he taketh it that the trees growinge
in the said Churchyard doe belonge vnto the owners of the said Parsonage
for he sayth that the late S*ir* Iohn Horsey when he made trunckes for his   30
parad*es* in the Abby garden did for that purpose cut downe ij elmes in the
sayd Churchyard beinge at that tyme ffarmer of the said Parsonage and did
likewise cause one other elme to be felled in the said Churchyard for [in] a
necessary vse for a play in Sherborne called Corpus Christi play ...

...   35

mb 6* *(Deposition of Osmund Forte, parchment maker, aged about 75)*
...

To the eleaventh Interr*o*gatory he sayth that ... the late Sir Iohn Horsey gave
aboue thirty yeres last past as [s] he taketh it a tree to the Churchwardens of   40
Sherborne toward*es* the makinge of a scaffold for a play to be played there

called Corpus Christi playe and thervpon a tree was cut downe in the sayd
Churchyard, which fell out to be hollowe, and thervpon the sayd Sir Iohn
Horsey gave them leave to cut another tree in the sayd Churchyard & so they
did and so they the Churchwardens have both the sayd trees by the good
likeinge of the said Sir Iohn Horsey....   5

...

mb 7* *(Deposition of John Baker, tailor, aged about 80)*

...

To the xjth he sayth that the ffarmers of the Parsonage & Procters have by   10
all the tyme aforesayd had the profites of the trees & shroudes of trees
growinge in the sayd Churchyard: and this deponent sayth that about xxx^{ty}
last past the late Sir Iohn Horsey at the request of the Churchwardens of
Sherborne aforesayd gave a tree towardes the makinge of a stage for the players
for a play to be had called Corpus Christi play & that they felled a tree   15
which was hollowe, & so desired another, & had the first & second for the
vse aforesayd by the direction & appointment of the sayd Sir Iohn Horsey.
and this he knoweth of his certeine knowledge to be trew dwellinge there &
seeinge & knowinge the same.

...   20

1607/8
Somerset Quarter Sessions Roll   SRO: Q/SR 37, pt 2
f 101A* *(13–20 January)*

                                                                             25
°Flagell*atus* et° Relax*atus*
Thomas Nehellyng confesseth he kepeth three fyghting bulls with which he
traveleth to such watches & other places as he ys hyred & sayth since Easter
he hath bynne att Ilton ‸⌜too dayes⌝ att Bakers Churchale & had for his
Bulls fyghting ther xiij s. iiij d. & att Ilchester with Iohn Bowden att a watch   30
which he kept, and att Gregory Stoke with one Trystram Bale who kept a
watch & had ther ix s., he was lykewyse att meere in wilteshire where he
stayde too dayes with his Bulls & had xx s. for his paynes & was lykewyse
att Sturmyster ‸⌜in dorset⌝ att Rafedowne watch where he stayde too dayes
& had xx s. for his paynes & was also att Sherborne Churchale with his Bull   35
& stayd ther one day & had for his Bulls fyghting x s./
°Flagell*andus* & delib*erandus*°

                                                           (signed) Edward Hext:

4/ have: *written over* hath *(?)*

SPETTISBURY

1635/6
Examination of Anne Barter   DRO: PE/WM: CP2/8, item 90
single sheet–single sheet verso *(23 February)*   5

Proceedings of the court held before William Stone, MA, official, in the presence of
Sampson Morice, notary public and deputy registrar
...

Officium domini promotum contra Stephanum Barter et Annam eius vxorem   10
pro incontinencia ante nuptias
Quo die Comparuit dicta Anna et ₍ˆ₎⌜vigore iuramenti sui corporalis alias per
eam prestiti⌝ fassa est that about twelue monethes since this respondent
comeinge from Blandford fayre with Allan Lodge the said Allan perswaded
this Respondent to goe into mr Edmund Bowyers Cony geere neere his house 15
in Spettisbury and then and there the said Allan Lodge had the vse and
Carnall knowledge of her this Respondentes body the first tyme. And further
Confesseth that afterwardes about Whitsuntyde at the setting vpp of a may
pole in Spettisbury in a Close there in the night tyme the said Allan Lodge
had the vse and Carnall knowledge of this Respondentes body the second   20
tyme. And this Respondent likewise Confesseth that Stephen Barter her now
husband had the vse and Carnall knowledge of her body two nightes before
[they] she was marryed vnto him and not before And allso sayth and Confesseth
that noe man besydes the said Allen Lodge and the | sayd Stephen her now
husband [had] ever ₍ˆ₎⌜ha⟨.⟩⌝ the vse and Carnall knowledge of her body   25

The marke   of Anne
Randoll alias   +   Barter.

STOUR PROVOST   30

1621/2
Casebook of Sir Francis Ashley   BL: Harley MS. 6715
f 54v *(14 January) (Bonds taken for the sessions)*
...   35
Commissus per ordinem de Bandford Sessionibus for a scandalous song./

24/ sayd: said *also appears as catchword at foot of recto*
27/ +: *Barter has signed with her personal mark, possibly an attempt to print* Randoll *vertically*
36/ Bandford: *for* Blandford

Will*elm*us Honny de Stower Provost husb*andman* ⎫
Ferdinand*us* Thomas de ead*em* weaver sep*a*ratim ⎬ in xl li.
Edw*ardus* Scot de ead*em* Wheeler ⎫
Will*elm*us Hopkins de ead*em* mason ⎬ vt*erque* in xx li.

    pro compar*ancia* *pre*di*c*torum Honny et Thomas ad *proximas* Sessiones et   5
interim *pro* bono gestu./

Comiss*us* *pro* consimili
Iidem Scot et Hopkins vt*erque* in   xl li.
Et *pre*di*c*ti Honny et Thomas vt*erque* in xx li.   10
    pro compar*ancia* ipsoru*m* Scot et Hopkins ad *proximas* Sessiones et *pro*
bono gestu./
...

STURMINSTER NEWTON   15

1607/8
Somerset Quarter Sessions Roll   SRO: Q/SR 37, pt 2

See Sherborne 1607/8   20

SYMONDSBURY

1634
Henry Burton's A Divine Tragedie   Wing: B6161   25
pp 12–13*
...

1634
                              Example 22.
One good man Paul neer Stoke in Dorcetshire, rejoycing much at the erection
of a summer pole, at a Parish called Simsbury in Dorcetshire, and saying   30
before one of his neighbours, he would go see it, though he went naked
through a quickset hedge: which is a common proverbe they use: Going with
wood in his armes to cast in to the bonfire, where he lived, and using these
words:| Heaven and earth are full of thy glory, O Lord: he was presently
smitten by the stroke of God, and within two or three daies died, and his   35
wife with him. These two last examples are testified by a Minister in his
letter to a brother Minister.
...

WEYMOUTH-MELCOMBE REGIS

1590–1
Mayors' Accounts WM: Sherren MS 177
p 2 *(Payments)*
...

	li.	s.	d.

...
paid to the quenes plleares 00 10 00

...

1596–7
Mayors' Accounts WM: Sherren MS 184
f [2v]* *(Disbursements)*
...

	li.	s.	d.

...
Item paid for a Lyne for the drumbe 00 00 6

...
Item paid Bartholomew Clerke for beatinge the drumbe 00 01 00

...

f [3]*
...

doubt certein [Item geven the Quenes players 00 10 00]
doubte certein [Item bestowed in wine vpon them 00 02 6]

...

1597–8
Mayors' Accounts WM: Sherren MS 185
f [1v]* *(Payments)*
...

	li.	s.	d.

...
Item Mending the drome 000 02 06

...

18/ 6: *numeral obscured by tear in paper*

f [2v]* *(Auditors' supplementary charges)*

...

	li.	s.	d.

...

more mending of the towne drome | 00 | 02 | 06 |

...

1599–1600
Mayors' Accounts   WM: Sherren MS 186
f [2v]*

	£	s.	d.

...

Mor iij s. for a hed for a drom | ... | .3 | .. |

...

More to fipens wyf ij s. a bout the drom | ... | .2 | .. |
More j s. for the snas for the drom | ... | .1 | .. |

...

1603–4
Mayors' Accounts   WM: Sherren MS 190
f [1v]

...

	li.	s.	d.

...

for so moche geven to my Lord sandoies players | – | 05 | 00 |

...

1605–6
Mayors' Accounts   WM: Sherren MS 191
f [1v] *(Disbursements)*

	li.	s.	d.

...

Item giuen vnto the Quenes pleayers | 00 | 10 | 00 |

...

1612–13
Borough Court Minutes   WM: Sherren MS 204
f 6v *(31 August)*

...

vpon this present daye Roberte Stone did take his voluntarie oathe That vpon
ffridaye nighte last Thomas Adams in a very great outrage Comminge out of

41/ Comminge: *8 minims in MS*

his owne howse did sweare that he would sett on fyer his howse and [that he] further vsed theis word*es* or the like in effecte that [s]he dwelt amongest a Company of dogges & Rogues and that he would have all their howses fyered betwene that and the may powle/ oftentimes reiteratinge the same

1615–16

Mayors' Accounts WM: Sherren MS 206
f [2v]*

	£	s.	d.
...			
more given the queens players for not plaing here. by order			
of the aldermen	01	10	..
...			

1617–18

Borough and Borough Court Minute Book WM: MB.O-B
p 130* *(8 August)*
...

      Informac*i*on taken by m*aste*r Mayor from theis sundry p*er*sones herevnder named.
Memorandum that vpon the Nine & twentith day of Iune aboute eighte of the Clocke on the forenoone one Loring aboye of Sixtene yeares olde sounded a drumbe in the Towne aforesaid and being forbidden by m*aste*r Mayor yet w*i*thin an hower after sounded againe. and was forbidden by the S*er*ieant from m*aste*r mayor the second time then somother of theis vndernamed sounded the drombe in a howse the third time and the same daye aforesaid aboute one of the Clocke in thafternoone theis whose names are subscribed w*i*th divers otheres vnknowen being armed w*i*th muskett*es* went forth of the Towne w*i*th a drumbe soundinge a Trumpett and Ancient wherevpon m*aste*r mayor sent vnto them by Iohn Bagg thounger and required them to disolve their Company & retorne backe w*hi*ch messuage being donn to the dro*m*mer he would have retourned but som of the Company affirmed they would beare him oute and soe encoraged him to goe on, after eveninge prayer the Company retorned backe againe into the Towne Armed as before they went forth and vpon Ex*amina*c*i*on of diverse of the p*ar*ties they had bin to fetch a so*m*mer Pole to set vpp on the Towne but broughte none w*i*th them; in the fforefronte of this troope m*ar*ched one Thomas Bascombe with an Axe on his shoulder/
Percivall Gibson dru*m*mer
Mathewe knott Auncient

34/ eveninge: *6 minims in MS*

Angell Lawrence
Ioseph Stephens
Henry Russell
Iacob Vandergozen
Gregory Babbidg   5
Morgan holeman
Nathaniell Allin
Iustinian Bagg
ffabian Hodder
Henry Gawdin   10
Thomas Small
Iohn Small
Thomas Bascombe
William Williames
Thomas Parkins   15
Iohn Harvy
Iohn Shattocke
William Chapple
(*blank*) Boulte
sondry others vnknowen   20

p 132* *(20 August)* *(Constables' presentments to the mayor, recorder, and bailiffs)*
...

Item they present that Percivall Gibson of the Borrough and Towne aforesaid
    Barber Mathew knott of the same Borrough and Towne Sayler Angell   25
    Lawrence of the same Borrough and Towne merchant Nathaniell Allin
    ali*a*s Belpitt of the same Borrough and Towne merchant Gregory Babbidge
    of the same Borrough and Towne merchant Thomas Bascombe of the
    same Borrough and Towne Groome Iohn Harvy of the same Borrough
    and Towne Sayler William Chapple of the same Borrough and Towne   30
    Shoemaker w*i*th diverse other p*er*sons to the number of Twenty p*er*sons
    vpon the Nine and Thirtith day of Iune Anno R*egni* R*egis* Iacobi nunc
    Anglie &c Sextodecimo et Scotie lj^mo aboute eighte of the Clocke in
    the fforenoone of the same day w*i*thin the said Borrough & Towne did
    vnlawfully assemble themsealves haveing w*i*th them swordes Pykes Muskett*es* 35
    and other vnlawfull weapons contrarye to the forme of the statute in such
    case made & pr*o*vided./

...

8/ Iustinian: *5 minims for* ini *in* MS   32/ Thirtith: *for* Twentieth
31/ number: *5 minims in* MS   32/ nunc: *5 minims in* MS

p 134*

...

The day & yeare aforesaid

Percivall Gibson did make oath in Courte that himsealfe Angell Lawrence
  and others being ⟨...⟩ Assembled together vpon *Sain*te Peters day laste   5
  paste vpon a Messuage sent vnto him and others of that assemblye from
  master mayor by Iohn Bagg theyounger to surcesse and retorne backe into
  the Towne the said Percivall Gibson being willing to retorne the said Angell
  Lawrence willed the said Percivall Gibson and the Company to continve
  together and he would beare them oute./.   10

It is ordred att the Sessions by Iohn Pitt Mayor of this Borrough and Towne
  that Angell Lawrence Nathaniell Allin Grigory Babbidge Percivall Gibson
  and Thomas Bascombe shall finde sufficient suerties to appeare att the
  nexte Sessions of the peace to be holden *with*in this Borrough and Towne   15
  then & there to aunswere vnto such matters as shallbee then and there
  obiected againste them for their Comtempte and unseeme and againste
  the king*es* ma*ies*tie and *Maste*r Mayor Comaund

It is ordred att the Sessions aforesaid by *master* Mayor and *master* Baylive 20
  holman that Nathaniell Allin shall finde sufficient suerties to appeare att
  the nexte Sessions of the peace to bee holden *with*in this Borrough and
  Towne then and there to aunswere vnto such matters as shalbee obiected
  againste him and in the meane time to bee of good behavior *which* order
  was made vpon the obraidinge and Contemptious speaches vsed by the   25
  said Nathaniell Allin vnto *master* Mayor in open Courte vidz: that *master*
  mayor did beare him spline and malice

...

p 135   30

Auguste the 25th 1618

Vpon this *present* day Edward Harvy Butcher one of the Searchers sworne
  and apointed for the viewinge and searchinge of Corrupte fflesh killed
  *with*in the Borrough and Towne sayeth and *present*eth vpon his said oath   35
  that Iohn Hingston Boucher here *with*in this Borrough and Towne vpon
  ffridaye beinge the fourtenth day of this instant moneth did kill a Bull
  vnbayted and did put the fflesh thereof vnto sale and there*v*pon he is
  am*er*sed by *master* mayor att iij s. iiij d.

...   40

12/ this: i *corrected over* e

1623–4
Borough and Borough Court Minute Book   WM: MB.O-B
p 304* *(21 September)*
…

Item they present That Thomas Angell of weeke ffidler for playinge on his   5
ffiddle in the howse of the widowe wilforde vpon the Third day of Iune 1624
for which he payed ix d. to the poore

…

Item they present That vpon the xiiij^th day of September 1624 Thomas
Angell of wyke was taken in the howse of katherin Morfell aboute one or   10
Two of the Clock in the morninge playinge vpon his ffiddle and being
druncke for which he sate in the stockes and vpon payement of ij s. vij d. he
was released which monye by the Comaundement of master Mayor was
deliuered back vnto the said Angell
Item they present That Iasper Notley and Iohn Hoare Millers were Tiplinge   15
in the howse of the said katherin Morfell vpon thaforesaid day att the same
howre of the night for which they payed xij d. to the poore
Item they present Thomas Sampson Seruante of ffrances Saunders for being
druncke vpon the same day and time and in the same howse
Item they present William Bagge for Tiplinge in the howse of the said katherin   20
Morfell vpon the day and time aforesaid Contrary to the forme of the Statute
in that behalfe provided.

1625–6
Borough and Borough Court Minute Book   WM: MB.O-B   25
p 321* *(3 October)* *(Presentments by jury of court leet)*
…

Iuratores predicti vlterius dicunt et presentant super sacramentum suum quod
Henricus Backway posuit Cumulum terre Anglice a heape of earthe in loco
vbi le Maypole antehac stet et quod Henricus waltham et Godfrye posuerunt   30
duos Cumulos de le earth & soyle in vico vocato Ste Marye streete Et
preceptum est amovere eosdem Cumulos Citra ffestum omnium sanctorum
proximum sub pena Cuiuslibet eorum delinquentis forisfacere v s:
…

35

1639–40
Borough and Borough Court Minute Book   WM: MB.O-B
p 419 *(7 October)* *(Presentments by jury of court leet)*
…

Ad istam Curiam Richardus Hickes presentat super sacramentum suum quod   40

6/ 1624: *underlined in* MS   31/ Marye: y *corrected over* t

Will*elm*us Barnes ⌈iij s. iiij d.⌉ et Ioh*ann*es Hingston ⌈iij s. iiij d.⌉ occiderunt duos Tauros infra hanc vill*am* citra *proximam* Cur*iam* et non publicè (*blank*) Angl*ice* did not bayte them openly. Ideo vterq*ue* vterq*ue* eor*um* in m*isericord*ia pr*out* sup*er* eoru*m* capita.

1640–1
Borough Financial Records   WM: Sherren MS 243.1
single sheet *(6 February)*

	li.	s.	d.
…			
Payd for the Maypole att Weeke	00	03	00
…			

WIMBORNE MINSTER

1573–4
St Cuthburga's Churchwardens' Accounts   DRO: PE/WM: CW 1/41
p 212* *(14 December–14 December) (Dues received)*
…

Item R*eceyved* for a playe in the Churche howse	vj d.
Item R*eceyved* of Iohn merywether for a playe in the Churchehowse	iiij d.

…

1589–90
St Cuthburga's Churchwardens' Accounts   DRO: PE/WM: CW 1/42
p 31 *(16 December–16 December)*
…

Item Recevid of players that played in the church howse   ij s.

…

1591–2
Churchwardens' Presentments to the Peculiar Court
DRO: PE/WM: CP2/10, item 8
single sheet* *(11 December–11 December)*
…

also we *present* william lucas of ho ⌈l⌉t for playing of a fiddill in the time of gods seruis
…

3*l* vterq*ue* vterque: *dittography in* MS

1595
Churchwardens' Presentments to the Peculiar Court
DRO: PE/WM: CP2/10, item 16
single sheet *(12 June)*

...   5

Item we present william delacourt the sonne of peter delacourt for beating
the drumme in the tyme of service in the Church haye

...

1601   10

Churchwardens' Presentments to the Peculiar Court
DRO: PE/WM: CP2/10, item 51
single sheet *(23 September)*

...

We presente Pike the minstrell for playinge whill Eueni⟨.⟩g prayer was saying: 15
on sonday xx° September 1601

...

We present old bishope and his sonne ˰⌜for⌝ lokeing one Dansers at the time
of Eueing prayer:

...   20

1602
Churchwardens' Presentments to the Peculiar Court
DRO: PE/WM: CP2/10, item 55
single sheet* *(After 24 May)*   25

...

we present hary woodman & his sonne for playing in the time of servis and
sermon in the tithinge of lye the ix^th of maye
we present barnebe dordole for kepping of an Alle the ix^th of maye and much
company in his house in the servis & sermon tim   30
we present Ihon mowlin, Richard meals An noris for beinge at lye at an ale
all servis and sermon time the ix^th of maye

...

1606   35
Churchwardens' Presentments to the Peculiar Court
DRO: PE/WM: CP2/10, item 74
single sheet *(28 April)*

...

Item we present that the widow thringes kepte daunsing in her howse at the   40

18/ time: *3 minims in MS*   29/ kepping: *2 minims in MS*
19/ Eueing: *for* Euening; *abbreviation mark missing*

tyme of evenynge prayer vpon the saboath day, william lukas minstrell, and
Robert homer with others were there daunsinge/

...

1606/7
Churchwardens' Presentments to the Peculiar Court
DRO: PE/WM: CP2/10, item 75
single sheet *(26 February)*

...

In primis we present that Richard Sergent henry fforest Iohn Sergent Iohn
pope vrban Evance and Iohn Swetnam played vppon grene Layne hill
adioning to colehill at the sermon tyme the vij^th day of September or neare
there aboutes/

...

1607–8
Churchwardens' Presentments to the Peculiar Court
DRO: PE/WM: CP2/10, item 82
single sheet* *(22 April–7 April)*

...

entred   we present margaret fuller for kypinge of play at servis & sermon

...

1609–10
Churchwardens' Presentments to the Peculiar Court
DRO: PE/WM: CP2/10, item 92
single sheet*

...

3   We present Thomas moris [& wylliam pottell for] ⌜did kepe mynsterilles⌝
      playng & daunsing in his house the .9th. of Iulye being soundaye at Evninge
      prear
4   Item we present that Richard Moris ∧⌜for daunsynge⌝ & William Pottele for
      playing the Saboth day & doth draw youth from the Church the 9 of Iuly
      ...
8   We present that Britt Minstrele did play at servis one sunday the xvj^th of Iuly
      at Ligh.

...

30/ Evninge: *3 minims in MS*

Churchwardens' Presentments to the Peculiar Court
DRO: PE/WM: CP2/10, item 94
single sheet*

...we present Ioane Etherege for sittinge in the streets at sermon tim on the   5
Saboth day being the i of aprill & maintayning her prentises to play and when
she was gently warned [t] of she abusethe the officers & bad them kisse her
asse twise...

1610–11   10
Churchwardens' Presentments to the Peculiar Court
DRO: PE/WM: CP2/10, item 99
single sheet* *(26 April–16 April)*
...

Item we doe present Iohn Pyeke for playnge on mydsomer day last past being   15
saboeth day as [william] ⌐Iohn⌐ Byshoppe doth affirme one of the sidemen
Iohn Trime⟨.⟩ wife⟨.⟩ h⟨...⟩, daughter margaret/ Elizabeth pitman with
other⟨..⟩ being strangers
...
                                                                                       20

Churchwardens' Presentments to the Peculiar Court
DRO: PE/WM: CP2/10, item 100
single sheet*
...

Item we do present that *willia*m barens of kynson had dansyng in his house   25
vpp on the xv^th day beyng sonday
...

Churchwardens' Presentments to the Peculiar Court
DRO: PE/WM: CP2/10, item 95
single sheet*   30
...

Item we do present bryght the menstrell [for] of holte for playeynge at lye in
the deveyne tyme of serves &
...   35

25/ kynson: *probably Kingston Lacy, in Wimborne Minster parish*
34/ the deveyne tyme of serves: *for* tyme of deveyne serves *(?)*
34/ &: *for* &c *(?)*

1611
Churchwardens' Presentments to the Peculiar Court
DRO: PE/WM: CP2/10, item 93
f [1]*

...

Item we present Richard Corben of Dogdeane for ⌜+⌝ [carying] waching the
Chart and their sommer pole the 13 day of may at Service time & he was
warned to com to the church and to depart the place & he refused it & did
not Com

...

...Item we present Elizabeth Pitman for dauncing out euening prayer time
being the 14 day of aprill. ⌜& being the saboath day.⌝ Item we present
[Elizabeth ⟨....⟩ken for dauncing at euening prayer time being the 14 day]
aprill, Item we present Margaret White the daughter of william white for
dauncing at euening prayer time being the 14 day of Aprill. ⌃⌜& the saboath
day⌝ Item we present Richard king the younger for dauncing at eueni⟨..⟩
prayer time being the 14 day of aprill....

f [1v]*

...Item we present william belten the younger, servant of william Belten
[weuer] ⌜the elder, weuer⌝ for dauncing out euening prayer time the 14 day
of aprill [Item we present] [Item we present Iames ffavin for help drawing a
sommer poole in a carte [at] ⌜at⌝ morning prayer time the 13 day of may.]

...

Item we present Iohn Burte for [disguisinge himself] being at Robert ffulfords
⌜house⌝ with the morrisse dauncers at Sermon time being the 13 ⌃⌜day⌝ of may.

...

1620
Churchwardens' Presentments to the Peculiar Court
DRO: PE/WM: CP2/12, item 60
single sheet *(31 May)*

Ascencion daie nicholas Perham was at a dauncing ⟨.⟩atch at Leigh a drincking
and did much abuse the ⟨...⟩est dauughter of Stiphen Russell. at Evening
prayer time./

...

6/ Dogdeane: g *corrected over* d
12–14/ Item we present [Elizabeth ... day] aprill,: *entire entry intended for cancellation*
35/ Ascencion daie: *25 May 1620*

Ascencion daie old bright with his boy and his daughter played at Cowgrove with their fiddells and Continued there all Evening prayer time with much Companie./

WINTERBORNE KINGSTON

1628
Churchwardens' Presentments for Salisbury Deanery
WRO: D5/28/28, item 92
f [1]* *(3 July)*

An informacion of certayne disorders in Winterborne Kingstone./ Imprimis Iames Gould hath byn heard to sweare most blasphemously, hath lately against Pentecost ioyned with other in collecting mony uppon the sundays for & towardes a Revell Ale or unlawfull meetinge, & uppon the munday in Whitsun Weeke by occasion of this preparacion, neither hee nor scarce any of the yonger men were at divine praier; & hee being a ringer comes often late to praiers uppon the sundayes, & often departes out of the church ere praier & all the service be ended.
. . .

Likewise Iohn Seevier a blasphemous swearer, & one that often laughes or geeres in tyme of sermon, & now about the munday & tuesday in Whitsnweeke was a principall man with other to sing roundes & prophane songes most part of the night.
. . .

WINTERBORNE MONKTON

1616
Casebook of Sir Francis Ashley   BL: Harley MS. 6715
f 15v *(25 May) (Bonds taken for the assizes)*
. . .

for keeping of an Ale and bayting the Bull in tyme of devine prayer hard vnder the Church
Henricus Chepman de Mouncton husbandman   in   40 l.
Iohannes Middleton de eadem yoman et ⎫
Henricus Notley de eadem husbandman   ⎭ 20 li. quilibet
     pro comparencia ad proximas Assisas ad respondendum ijs/

14/ Pentecost: *1 June 1628*
16/ munday in Whitsun Weeke: *2 June 1628*

he being p*ar*tner wi*th* the said Chepman
Ioh*anne*s blanchard de Mo*u*ncton husband*man*   in   40 li.
Iohes Middleton de ead*em* yoman   in   20 l.
Henricus Notley de ead*em* husband*man*   in   20 l.
    p*ro* comp*arencia* ad p*roximas* Assi*sas* ad respond*endum* ijs/   5

...

Wille*l*mus Bartlett d*e* Monckton Clarke   in x l.
    p*ro* comp*arencia* ad p*roximas* Assi*sas* ad dand*um* evidenc*iam* versus
    Henricu*m* Chepma*n* et Ioh*ann*em Blanchard/

...

3/ Iohes: *for* Iohannes; *abbreviation mark missing*

Households

STRANGWAYS OF MELBURY SAMPFORD

1638
Giles Strangways' Account Book   DRO: D/FSI: Box 220
f 6* *(24 June–29 September) (Expenditures)*

...

At oxford ye bill for our supp*er* [⟨.⟩] dinner horsemeate   003   04   10
To ye fidlers there 10 s....

f 10 *(29 September–24 December)*

	ll.	s.	d.
...			
To ye fidlers	000	10	00
...			

f 11

	ll.	s.	d.
...			
At knebworth to ye fidlers 5 s. lost at Tables 10 s.	000	15	00
...			

1638–9
Giles Strangways' Account Book   DRO: D/FSI: Box 220
f 15 *(25 December–24 March) (New Year's gifts)*
...
To ye fidlers 5 s....
...

1639
Giles Strangways' Account Book   DRO: D/FSI: Box 220
f 37v col 2 *(Summary of gifts)*
...

To fidlers bobs I gave   000   10   00   5
...

1639–40
Giles Strangways' Account Book   DRO: D/FSI: Box 220
f 32 *(25 December–24 March)* *(New Year's gifts)*   10
...
... fidlers 5 s....
...

1640   15
Giles Strangways' Account Book   DRO: D/FSI: Box 220
f 57v col 1 *(Summary of trivial expenses)*
...
To fidlers   00   09   06
...   20

1641
Giles Strangways' Account Book   DRO: D/FSI: Box 220
f 74v col 2 *(Summary of trivial expenses)*
...   25
To fidlers. ...   000 02 06: q.
...

APPENDIX 1
Undated Record

Although Murray, *English Dramatic Companies*, vol 2, p 206, dates this visit by the prince's men 'c. End James I,' there is no evidence for even that vague an assignment. The account lacks the conventional heading indicating the author and the year or quarter covered by the account. Internal evidence provides no conclusive evidence for dating of the manuscript. The account registers the cost of presenting Sir George Trenchard with a gift of eels but he was an influential political figure throughout the reign of King James and until his death in 1630. Richard Colfox is repaid for expenses incurred when he went to Axminster on behalf of the borough but the account does not specify what office he held at the time. Similarly, the account notes the receipt of an account from 'Mr. Meller' but fails to specify first, if this is John or Robert Miller and second, if his is a cofferer's or a bailiff's account. The entry in the records is also ambiguous. Are the prince's players those of Prince Henry or those of Prince Charles? Even if we knew that Colfox went to Axminster in his capacity as bailiff of Bridport, we would still have four years in the reign of James; in Miller's case we have five years that might be the year of this account. The gift for Sir George Trenchard suggests that 1630 is the latest possible date for the account and, given the absence of a troupe under the patronage of a prince from March 1625 (when King James died) to December 1631 (when the palsgrave's company became the players of Prince Charles), we can assign the account to the reign of King James but to no specific year or decade within his reign.

See The Documents above (pp 56–7) for a description of the manuscript.

BRIDPORT

Town Account   DRO: DC/BTB: M18/9
single sheet

...   5

Item Gaue the Princes players   x s.   0

...

APPENDIX 2
Post-1642 Records

The fragmentary nature of Shaftesbury's written records makes particularly welcome a 1655–6 account that demonstrates the borough's continued observance of one of its customs during the Commonwealth period. A 1662 agreement to shift Shaftesbury's annual Sunday procession to Motcombe (see pp 248–9) to the Monday before Ascension includes a full description of Shaftesbury's custom; observance of the custom remained essentially unchanged from the early sixteenth century. Records from the Commonwealth and Restoration periods have not been comprehensively searched for this volume.

Account of Richard Harris
Dorchester, Dorset Record Office, DC/SYB: C16b, item 43; 1655–6; English; paper; bifolium; 303mm x 194mm; unnumbered. One of 47 items filed in a manila folder.

Indenture Concerning Enmore Green
See The Documents above (pp 75–6) for a description of Hutchins, *History and Antiquities* and of the Nicholas family's acquisition of Gillingham Manor.

SHAFTESBURY

1655–6
Account of Richard Harris   DRO: DC/SYB: C16b, item 43
f [2] *(25 March–25 March) (Payments)*   5

...

Item To the balie of Gillingham for our accostomed liberty
to fetch water in motcomb 1 payr of gloues at the prœse of
6 s. And a calues head 8 d. in beer 1 s. And bread 2 d.   0 7 10

...   10

1662
Indenture Concerning Enmore Green   Hutchins: *History and Antiquities*, vol 3
pp 629–30 *(1 May)*

...   15

       This Indenture, made the first day of May, in the fourteenth yeere of the

reigne of our soveraigne lord, Charles the Second, by the grace of God, of
England, Scotland, France, and Ireland King, Defender of the Faythe, &c.
annoque Domini one thousand six hundred sixtie-two; Between the honourable
Sir Edward Nicholas, knt. one of his majesties principal secretaries of state,
of his majesties most honourable privy councill, and lord of the manor and   5
liberty of Gillingham, in the county of Dorset, of the one part; and the mayor
and burgesses of the towne and borrough of Shaston in the said countie of
Dorset, of the other part. Whereas the said mayor and burgesses of the said
burrough for the time beeing, and all the inhabitants of the said borrough
for the time beeing, by prescription beyond the memory of man have claymed,   10
used, and enioyed a custome, liberty, and prevelege to take, fetch, and carry
away water, at all times, and upon all occations, from any of the wells and
springs of water in the wast and common ground in the tithing of Motcombe
within the said manor and liberty of Gillingham, to bee used within the said
borough; and likewise to digg, make, repaire, or amend any wells or springs   15
of water within any of the wasts or commons of the Motcombe aforesaid,
within the manor and liberty aforesaid, for the better preservacion of the
said water, for the use of the mayor, burgesses, and other inhabitants of or
within the said borrough for the time beeing; and in consideracion thereof
the said mayor and burgesses, by like prescription, have yeerly on the Sunday   20
or Lord's Day next after the third of May (commonly called Holy Rood
day), payed and performed this custome following, (viz.): the sayd mayor,
accompanyed with some of the burgesses and other inhabitants of the said
towne and borrough, have used to walk out of the said borrough, into the
said manor and liberty of Gillingham, into a place there called Enmore Green   25
(where is a poole of water, and diverse springs and wells), and in that place to
walke or daunce hand in hand round the same green in a long daunce, there
being a musition or tabor and pipe, and alsoe a staffe or besome adorned
with feathers, pieces of gold rings, and other jewells (called a prize besome);
which daunce being ended, the said mayor and burgesses doe, or some one   30
by their appointment doth, tender and deliuer unto the bailiffe of the said
manor of Gillingham for the time beeing one payre of gloves, a calfe's head
raw and undressed, a gallon of ale or beere, and two penny loaves of white
wheat bread; which the said bailiff receiveth and carryeth away to his own
use. The observacion of which custome on the Lord's day occationing some   35
neglect of divine service, and beeinge inconvenient to bee continued; and to
the intent some other day may be now appointed, and for ever hereafter to
bee observed for the payment and performance of the custome and service
aforesaid, without any prejudice nevertheless to the said mayor, burgesses,
and other inhabitants of the said towne and borrough in their custom and   40
liberty of fetching water as aforesaid; itt is hereby agreed, by and between

the said parties to these presents; and the said Sir Edward Nicholas, for himself,
his heyres, executors, administrators, and assigns, doth covenaunt, grant,
promise, and agree, to and with the said mayor and burgesses, and their
successors, that they the said mayor and burgesses, and all other the inhabitants
of the said towne and borrough, shall or lawfully may, from time to time,   5
and at all times for ever hereafter, have and take water for any their occations
to be used within the said borrough from any wells or springs within any
the wastes or common grounds of Motcombe, within the manor and liberty
aforesaid, and have and enjoy like freedome and liberty to digg, repayre, and
amend any wells or springs of water there, as fully as at time heretofore hath   10
been used and accustomed; they the said mayor and burgesses for the time
being yielding, paying, doeing and performing on their parts the said recited
custome and service yeerly, and every year, for ever heereafter, on the Munday
next before the Feast of the Ascension of our Lord God, and in the place
where the same hath been anciently and accustomably performed and done   15
as aforesaid; which shall be as avayleable to the said mayor, burgesses, and all
other the inhabitants of the towne and borrough aforesaid, and as firme and
good against him the said Sir Edward Nicholas, his heyres and assigns, for
the continuance of the said custome and liberty, as if the same had been
done and performed on the day and time anciently used and accustomed, as   20
aforesaid: and that this agreement may for ever heereafter bee observed, kept,
and preserved to posterity in time to come, it is further agreed, that the same
shall bee published and inrolled as well among the rolles of the court of the
manor of Gillingham aforesaid, as among the rolles of the court of the said
borrough of Shaston. In witness whereof, as well the said Sir Edward Nicholas   25
hath to each part of these indentures set his hand and seal, as the said mayor
and burgesses the common seal of the said borrough, the day and year
abovesaid.
Edward (L.S.) Nicholas. Peter (L.S.) King, maior.

Signed, sealed, and delivered, by	Sealed and delivered by the within-	30
the within: named Sir Edward	named mayor of the borrough of	
Nicholas, in the presence of	Shaston, by the assent and consent	
John Nicholas	of the burgesses of the said borrough	
D. Neille.	then present, and in the presence of	
William Legge.	Henry Whitaker.	35
Charles Whitaker.	Richard Greene.	
Joseph Williamson.	William Chaldecott.	
	William Bowles.	
	Thomas Baker.	
	John Young.	40

Gillingham *sessiones* ad cur*iam* manerii ib*ide*m tent*am* primo die Julii, anno regni regis Caroli secundi nunc Angliæ, &c. quarto decimo, hæc indentura irrotulatur in rotulo curiae eodem manerii.

William Yeatman, deputatus scenescalli ibidem,
per Johannem Gibbes, balliuum manerii ibidem.

Lyme Regis Cobb Ale

Annually at Whitsuntide Lyme Regis held the Cobb ale, a custom that probably fostered and confirmed the community spirit of the townsfolk and certainly raised funds for the maintenance of the Cobb and other civic projects. The Cobb, a long dock made of cowstones contained within two curving walls of oak trunks, protected the town from the ravages of the sea and created a port on the activity of which Lyme depended for its livelihood. Constantly battered by the sea the Cobb was constantly in need of repairs, which the Cobb ale helped to finance.

The Cobb ale was the kind of celebration at which one would expect to find performers. The celebrations took place each year at about the same time and lasted between two and three weeks. Besides the several gatherings in the Cobb house, the ale travelled to nearby towns and extended its hospitality to people and ships that happened to visit the borough. The event was administratively complex, requiring considerable time, staff, fuel, food, and (of course) drink. Surprisingly, although records of the ale span a period of fifty-two years, no evidence of performance activity survives. Apart from the feasting the only glimpse we get of the normal activity of the ale comes from the silver whistle donated by William Birret and worn by successive Cobb wardens. Presumably this whistle helped to gather a crowd or to get the attention of a gregarious one rather than to provide or to accompany musical entertainment. In one undated Cobb warden's account book a reward is given to a travelling troupe but its performance need not have been part of an ale (see p 212).

As modern historians have tended to assume that musical and dramatic performances occurred at the Cobb ale, so they have tied payments to players to depart the town without performing to the demise of the ale (at some time after 1606) and attributed both to the rise of Puritanism. For instance, Cyril Wanklyn claims that John Geare, for some time an unlicensed Puritan preacher, 'succeeded in securing the suppression of a celebrated annual festivity, know[n] as the Cobb Ale, [which] had flourished unchecked for two hundred and fifty years before its final disappearance some time after 1610.' With the backing of some influential burgesses of the town such as Robert Hassard, Geare 'succeeded where many might have failed.' According to Wanklyn, 'he started a crusade against this Cobb Ale and he must have had some force of public opinion behind him, because shortly afterwards the institution came to an end' (*Lyme Regis: A Retrospect*, pp 8–9). In *Revel*, Underdown tells essentially the same story but he concludes as follows (pp 57–8): 'In the end the campaign [against the ale] was a failure. Geare had allies in the corporation who won some victories: around 1620, for example, Lyme began making the familiar payments to theatrical companies to leave without performing. But the Cobb was another matter. In 1635 the churchwardens noted that the church porch was in a disgraceful mess, littered with "vessels called tuns which serve for the use of the Cobb".'

Puritanism probably played its part in fostering antagonism to travelling players and to traditional revelry such as that which marked the Cobb ale, but there is no evidence that the ale was centuries old, that Robert Hassard effected its suppression, that John Geare led Wanklyn's 'crusade' or Underdown's 'campaign' against it, or that it survived into the 1630s. Such confident claims depend in part upon blurring the distinction between records of the Cobb and records of the Cobb ale. In 1610, for example, the constables of Lyme Regis were presented for allowing unlawful games to be played at Beaufront on the sabbath as on weekdays (DRO: DC/LR: N23/2, item 82). Similarly, in July 1612, the Lyme Corporation Order Book reports that John Geare had procured an act against the mayor and the Cobb wardens for profane and irreligious abuses (DRO: DC/LR: D1/1 p 42). Although George Roberts and David Underdown note both of these records as evidence of the growing antagonism to the ale (*Social History*, pp 343–4; *Revel*, p 57), neither document ties the proceedings in question to the ale. Underdown's suggestion (quoted above) that the ale proved impervious to Geare's attacks and survived into the 1630s is equally suspect, for it requires that we assume that the tuns creating such a mess in the church porch contained beverages for the ale, but such vessels would have been used in the everyday business of transporting cargo from the Cobb to the mainland. The only record we have of opposition to the Cobb ale per se (also the last record of this custom of the borough) is the churchwardens' presentment of September 1606 noting a kind of bowling in the churchyard ' by reason of a cobbe aell' (p 308). The Cobb ale probably took place for the last time around this year, partly because of the administrative difficulties of managing the event, partly because of the ideological opposition to it on the part of Puritans, and partly because of the alternatives in place for raising funds for the on-going maintenance of the Cobb.

See The Documents above (pp 66–70) for descriptions of the relevant manuscripts.

LYME REGIS

1553–4
Mayors' Accounts   DRO: DC/LR: G1/2
p 95 *(Michaelmas quarter) (Receipts)*
...

Item mor Received off Edward Rodman þe xviij^th off octobir
ye part off pay for þe cobe alle   xxv s.
...

p 121* *(Midsummer quarter)*
...
Item mor Received of Iohn Holcome of þe mony for þe cobe alle   iiij li. x s.
Item mor Received of Edward Rodman for þe cobe alle   xxv s.
...

1555–6
Mayors' Accounts   DRO: DC/LR: G1/1
p 33* *(Receipts)*
…

Rec*eivid* of Thomas Dare & Alexander Davye for the   5
Cob ale   xvj li. xv s. iij d. ob.
…

1558–9
Mayors' Accounts   DRO: DC/LR: G2/1   10
f [19v]* *(Receipts)*
…

Rec*eivid* of Robert Mone in p*ar*te of payment of suche money
as was receivid for the Cob ale   x li.
…   15

1559–60
Mayors' Accounts   DRO: DC/LR: G1/1
p 44* *(Inventory of goods received by new mayor)*
…   20
A whistill of siluer w*ith* a chayne waing xj ownc*es* whiche will*ia*m Birret dyd
give to be warne at the Cob ale and to be delyverid to the nyw wardens at
the Milhill whan they be first chosen
…

25

p 47* *(Receipts)*
…
Item Iohn holcome Mayo*ur* hath receivid in to his Custodie a whistle with a
cheyn of Silver. whiche given by Will*ia*m Birret to be worne yerelie at the
Cob ale. whiche whistle w*ith* the Cheyne weyth xj ownc*es* Troy   30
…

Mayors' Accounts   DRO: DC/LR: G1/2
p 167* *(Receipts)*

35
It*em* more I Reseaved of Iohn hasserd & Mr Recherd hayball
of the Rest of the cobe ayll[ye] – 24 s. 3 d.   xxiiij s. iij d.
…

13–14/ Rec*eivid* … x li.: *entire entry administratively cancelled*

1560–1
Mayors' Accounts   DRO: DC/LR: G2/1
f [36v] *(8 October) (Inventory of goods received by new mayor)*
...

A whistill of silver wi*th* a cheyn wayng xj ounc*es* that Willi*a*m Birret dyd give   5
to be worne at the Cob ale
...

1561–2
Mayors' Accounts   DRO: DC/LR: G1/1   10
p 50* *(6 November) (Inventory of goods received by new mayor)*
...

A whistle of silver wi*th* a cheyn wayng xj ounc*es* which Willi*a*m Birret gaue
to be worn at the Cob ale
...   15

1562–3
Mayors' Accounts   DRO: DC/LR: G1/1
p 54 *(12 October) (Inventory of goods received by new mayor)*
...   20
Item a whistill of silver wi*th* a cheyn weyng xj ounc*es* whiche Willi*a*m Birret
gave to be worne at tyme of the Cob ale
...

1563–4   25
Mayors' Accounts   DRO: DC/LR: G2/1
f [33] *(Inventory of goods received by new mayor)*
...

A whistle of silver wi*th* a cheyne wayng xj ounc*es* that Willi*a*m Birret
gaue   30
...

1564–5
Mayors' Accounts   DRO: DC/LR: G2/1
f [31v] *(Inventory of goods received by new mayor)*   35
...

A whistle of Silver wi*th* a cheyn waing xj ownc*es* which Willi*a*m Beret
gave
...

1565–6
Mayors' Accounts   DRO: DC/LR: G2/1
f [32] *(Inventory of goods received by new mayor)*
...

Item a whistle of silver with a cheyn wayng xj ounces whiche William Birret   5
gave
...

1579–80
Grant of Cobb Kitchen to Borough Corporation   10
DRO: DC/LR: N23/4, item 3
single mb* *(12 October)*

Thys Indenture made the xij^th daye of October in the one and twenteth
yere of the Reigne of our Soueraigne Ladye Elizabethe by the grace of god   15
Queene of England ffrance & Ireland defendor of the faiethe &c Betwene
Richard Baret of Lyme Regis in the Comitye of dorset Merchaunt of thone
partye And Iohn Seward Mayor of the Towne and Borrowghe of Lyme Regis
aforesaid and the Burgesses of the same Towne of thother party. witnesseth
that the said Richard Baret for dyvers good causes and consideracions him   20
especially moving Hathe given graunted demysed and confyrmed and by
theis presentes dothe demyse geve graunt and confyrme vnto the said Mayor
and Burgesses all that parte of his howse called the Cobbe kytchyn nowe or
late in the tennure of Iohn Cogan scituate lieng and being in Lyme Regis
aforesaid in the Corner betwene Richard Davyes howse and the Cobb hall   25
there To haue hold occupy ∧⌈vse⌉ and enioye the same Cobbe kytchyn with
the Comodities thereunto belonging or appertayning. vnto thesaid Maiyor
and Burgesses and their Successors and assignes once euery yere at the feast
of Penthecoste for and during the wholl tyme and so long as the Cobb Ale
and feast for and to the Cobb vse shall contynue and endure ∧⌈so it excede   30
not twenty dayes⌉, and so to vse and enioye thesame in maner and forme
aforesaid yerely, for and during all the tyme and tearme of yeres that thesaid
Richard Baret hathe, might, should or ought to haue in thesame, by any
Conveyaunce way or meane whatsoever/ yelding and paieng therefore yerely
vnto thesaid Richard Baret his executors or assignes at the feast of Saincte   35
Mychaell Tharchangell by the handes of the Mayor of the said Towne for the
tyme being, fyve shillinges of good and lawfull money of England, so long as
thesaid Mayor and Burgesses and their Successors and assignes shall enioye
the said kitchyn and occupacion thereof, by vertue of this Indenture of Lease.
And thesaied Rychard Baret covenaunteth and graunteth for himself his   40
executors heires and Administrators to and with the said Mayor and Burgesses
and their Successors by theis presentes, to warraunt, acquyte and defende

vnto thesaid Mayor and Burgessors and their Successors thesaid Kytchyn
and the occupac*ion* and *v*se thereof for the rente aforesaid and in maner and
forme aforesaid, discharged of all form*er* bargaynes, Sales, graunt*es* and
Incombraunc*es* hertofore com*m*ytted done or suffered by thesaid Richard
Baret or by any other *p*ersonne or *p*ersons by his meanes consent procurem*ent*   5
or abetment whatsoever/ In witnes whereof thesaid Richard Baret to thone
*p*arte of this Indentures remayning w*i*th thesaid Mayo*r* and Burgesses, ha*t*he
putt his Seale And to thother *p*arte of thesaid Indentures remayning w*i*th
thesaid Richard Baret thesaid Mayor and Burgesses haue caused their com*m*on
Seale of thesaid Towne to be sett Geven the day and yere fyrst above writen/   10
(signed) per me Richard Barett

1588–9
Mayors' Accounts   DRO: DC/LR: G2/2
tab 45   15
...
Received of Richard Rosse for the cobbe alle money   15   9   5
...

1591–2   20
Mayors' Accounts   DRO: DC/LR: G1/1
p̈p 140–1*

The Accompte of borrowed money to the purchasinge of the ffee ferme by a
newe Charter/   25
In primis of George Som*er* L li. *which* was paid him agayne
out of Silvester Iurdens cobwardens accompt of the Cob Ale
xxxiiij li.
also by Robe*r*t Hassard out of his Receyvo*urs* accompt [xvj li.]   L li.
xiiij li. v s. vij d.
and out of his Cobb ale money j li. xiiij s. v d.   30
Item borowed to paie the xl li. that
was taken vpp of Robe*r*t Davy viz.
of Iohn Davy   x li.
of Iohn Hayes   x li.   35
of Mr Bellamy & Mr
Barens   } x li.   xl li.
vnd*er* 5 li.
cob ale money
from R hassard.
of mr Elmeston   x li.   40
Item borowed of Iohn Hassard x li.   x li.

1 li. 14 s. 5 d.

1/ Burgessors: *for* Burgesses   31/ and out ... v d.: *apparently added later between existing lines*

of Mr Elesdon xvj li.   xvj li.
of Mr Bydgood lent out of his cob ale money   x li.
Item more layed owt of the Cob ale money by Mr Robert
Hassard in tyme of his Cob ale office   viij li. v s.
      Svmma totalis   jᶜxxxiiij li. v s.⌐ 5

The Accompt pro contra, howe the moneys before in thothre syde, was
repaid; viz.
Inprimis of the Cob ale money. which we accompt
to be the Townes which did growe by George Somer   10
& Siluyster Iurden Anno .1590. and by Robert hassard
& Iohn Bydgood, Anno 1591   Lviij li. xix s. v d.
...

1592–3   15
Mayors' Accounts   DRO: DC/LR: G2/2
tab 59 *(Receipts)*

Receyved of Robert hassard in full account of the cobb alle
at to seuerall tymes   21 li. 07 s. 10 d.   20
...

1595–6
Mayors' Accounts   DRO: DC/LR: G2/2
tab 78*   25
...
Item more of the said William Davy parcell of the Cobb Ale
money iiij li.   iiij li.
...

                                                                    30

1600–1
Cobb Wardens' Accounts   DRO: DC/LR: N23/1, item 63
single sheet–single sheet verso*

  Accompte whiche I haue received the 12 of Iune 1601   35
Item received of mr. fugemes the some of   00   15   00
Item received that wee bagg in brancom and
Item beare and cetton and burport the some of   03   04   00
Item bagge in axmister the some of   00   08   00
Item received of gorge Rocky the some of   00   03   00   40

35/ 1601: *underlined in MS*   38/ cetton: *Seaton, Devon*
37/ brancom: *Branscombe, Devon* 39/ axmister: *Axminster, Devon*

Item receaved of my wiffes bagg in opplam	00	02	06.
Item receaved of the handmayd men	00	11	02
Item receaved of thosse that went not with vs	00	08	00.
Item receaved of my wiffes from charmuth	00	07	01
	05	17	09
Item receaved in wisson that we bagg	01	05	10
Item receaved in colletton and exmuth	01	00	00
Item receaved of the Londerners and of [mr b ⟨…⟩]	00	18	00
	09	01	7
Item the twusdaye Receaved att the cobb howsse			
Item the somme of	16	00	00
Item the wansdaye receaved my self	06	07	00
Item the tirsday receaved att the cobb howsse	02	19	00
Item the ffrydaye receaved att the cobb	02	15	00
Item the saterdaye receaved the some of	01	10	00
Item the sondaye receaved the some of	08	16	00
Item the tudaye receaved the somme of	04	10	00
	52	13	7
Item the saterdaye gorge rockye haue receavd	00	15	4
Item the frydaye gorge rocky haue receavd	00	08	6
Item the sondaye gorge rockye haue receaved	05	06	0
Item the mondaye gorge rockye haue received	08	00	0
	14	09	10
Item receave the frydaye the some of	03	04	00
Item more receaved of thomas whithed ffor a hoset of beare			
and all thinges discharge	00	09	00
Item receaved of tinscom and of coson the some	00	08	00

gorge rocky
haue 10 li.

some is 33 li.   00 s.   09 d.

gorge Rocquey haue Received att the cobb howsse the
some of   14 li. 9 s. 10

1/ opplam: *Uplyme, Devon*
2/ the handmayd: *a ship*
4, 5/ 00   07   01, 05   17   09: *sums underlined in* MS
6/ wisson: *Winsham, Somerset*
7/ colletton: *Colyton, Devon*
7/ exmuth: *Axmouth, Devon*
8/ 00   18   00: *sum underlined in* MS
17/ tudaye: t *written over* d
17/ 04   10   00: *sum underlined in* MS
18/ 52   13   7: *sum underlined in* MS; 2 *and* 3 *corrected from other numerals*
22, 23/ 08   00   0, 14   09   10: *sums underlined in* MS

more owe for 2 hosetz of beare	02		
more haue Receaved in St Mallos	01	00	
more he hathe Receaved hym ad his ⌈wiff⌉	01	10	
more Rest a gilten spone	00	10	
	19	9	10d. ₅
more gorge Rocquey told me thatt his charges came to	06	15	00

1601–2
Cobb Wardens' Accounts   DRO: DC/LR: N23/2, item 75
ff [1–2]*   10

Item
the Accompte of the Coobb ealle for the yeare 1601 deliuer*ed* vnto Mr Robart
hassard meare the 22 daye of febreary 1601

	l.	s.	d. ₁₅
Item Item Receaved of Mr Iohn biggood meare			
Item one easter daye the somme of	04	00	00
Item Item more Receaved by me as appeareth			
Item by *p*articulers the somme of	55	19	01
Som*ma*	59	19	1d. ₂₀

A notte of Suche mony and
charges as I. haue Layd out and
p*ai*d for the Cobb ealle as folowthe

Item p*ai*d in charges as appearethe by the			
Item particullers the somme of	33	19	01 ₂₅
Item Item p*ai*d the 17th of Iune vnto Mr water			
Item harvy by Mr Iohn biggood meare appointement			
Item the somme of	10	00	00
Item Item p*ai*d the 12th of Ianuary 1601 vnto Mr			
Item Robart hassard meare the somme of	04	00	00 ₃₀
Item more deliuer vnto Mr. Robart hassard			
Item meare the 22 daye of febreary 1601 to			
Item ballance this accompte the somme of	12	00	00
Som*ma*	59	19	01

3/ ad: *for* and
4, 5/ 00   10, 19   9   10 d.: *sums underlined in* MS
13/ 1601: *underlined in* MS
14/ 1601: *underlined in* MS
17/ easter daye: *presumably 12 April 1601, when Bidgood was mayor*
19, 20/ 55   19   01, 59   19   1d.: *sums underlined in* MS
33, 34/ 12   00   00, 59   19   01: *sums underlined in* MS

Item more Remayne in mathieu davye
Item handes which he hathe Received in morlays
Item for the Cobb. the somme of   00   17   06

Item more Resting in the wydow Rocquey her   5
Item handes as it maye appeare   *(blank)*
Item made and deliuer vnto Mr Robart hassard
Item meare the 22 daye of febreary. 1601
      by me Iohn Roze |

      \   10

      Item
    Accompte of the mony which I haue Received the 12th of Iune 1601
Item Received of Mr. fugemes the some of   00   15   00
Item receaved when wee went to brancom and
Item to beare and colletton and burport the   03   04   00 15
Item received in axmister the somme of   00   08   00
Item received in charmuthe the some of   00   07   01
Item received of the handmayd men the som   00   11   02
Item received of those thatt went nott with vs att wafet   00   08   00
Item received of my wiffes and of gorge Rocquey wiffes   00   05   00 20
Item received in wisson the somme of   01   04   10
Item received in axmue and other places   01   00   00
Item Received of the Londoners and of mr browne   00   18   00
      9   01   01

Item Received the tusdaye the somme of   16   00   00 25
Item received the wansdaye the somme of   06   07   00
Item received the thirsday the some of   02   19   00
Item received the frydaye the some of   02   15   00
Item received the saterdaye the somme of   01   10   00
Item received the sondaye the somme of   08   16   00 30
Item Received the tusdaye the somme of   04   10   00
Item Received the frydaye the some of   03   04   00
Item Received of thomas whithed for a hoset of beare
Item and paid hyme for his spices and Received of
Item tinscom and colson the some   00   17   00 35
    by me Iohn Roze   Somma 55   19   01|

7/ 1601: *underlined in* MS	18/ the handmayd: *a ship*
11/ 1601: *underlined in* MS	19/ wafet: *Wayford, Somerset*
14/ brancom: *Branscombe, Devon*	21/ wisson: *Winsham, Somerset*
15/ colletton: *Colyton, Devon*	22/ axmue: *Axmouth, Devon*
16/ axmister: *Axminster, Devon*	23/ 00 18 00: *sum underlined in* MS
17/ in: *written over of*	35, 36/ 00 17 00, 55 19 01: *sums underlined in* MS

Item

Accompte of the Charges whiche I haue Layd out
for the Cobb howsse the 12th of Aprill 1601

Item paid for 4 quarts of wyne with a banckett	00	04	00
Item paid for gryning of the maltes the some	00	09	00	5
Item paid for a present vnto Mr fugemes the some of	00	02	02
Item paid for 4 hundreth 1/2 of venisen the some of	00	10	06
Item paid for stivin to brue the somme of	00	07	06
Item paid for 2 tonnes of caske and the houping	01	06	06
Item paid for a busel 1/2 of weathe to brue	00	05	00	10
Item paid vnto gorge Rocquey wiffes the somme of	00	10	00
Item paid for 38 pounds of hopes att 8 d. per pound	01	05	00
Item paid staigge to healpt to brue the some of	00	03	11
Item paid for 88 buselz of maltes whereof 40 buselz			
Item coste 8 s. 2 d. and the other 8 s. amonth	11	18	00	15
Item paid for. 25 pound of butter	00	05	03
Item paid vnto the Rocke to brue the aylle	00	02	00
Item spent att Waffort the somme of	02	02	00
Item paid for. cherimps and 21 chikiyns the somme	00	06	06
Item paid goode tinscom thatt went to bagging	00	00	04	20
Item paid for 1/2 hundreth of faggotz. the some of	00	04	02
Item paid for. cafehenges and other vitels the som of	01	02	02
Item paid for 4 capons the some of	00	03	04
Item paid vnto Richard pamer the some of	00	13	00
Item paid vnto. gorge Rocquey. the some of	01	00	00	25
Item paid luce for 7 dozen of bread the some of	00	07	00
Item paid for. candels. and for. burche the some of	00	05	06.
Item paid for. woud. and waintres the part som of	02	03	06.
Item paid vnto. Lace for vitels that he did buye	00	16	00
Item paid vnto. clatry. for. caks. the some of	00	07	08	30
Item paid ffor. wyne the some of	02	16	04
Item paid ffor 2 venys glasses and 8 other glases	00	04	00
Item paid ffor one spong the some of	00	06	00
Item paid for. 12 coupes. and baikon the some of	00	09	00
Item paid for. beafe the some of	00	02	06	35
Item paid vnto smalling backe agayne	00	05	00
Item paid vnto bery. backe agayne	00	02	06.
Item paid att burport when wee went to bagging	00	04	03
Item paid vnto Iohn piters for his celler	00	06	08.
Item paid for. vitels the some of	00	11	02	40

3/ 1601: *underlined in* MS   40/ 00: *corrected from* 11
15/ amonth: *for* apiece (?)

Item paid for. a plater that was stolle and for vineger		00	03	02	
Item paid for. pouder and for heiring of horses		00	10	00	
Item paid vnto westover the somme of		00	08	06	
Item paid vnto. Iohn Davy. to brue in his bruehowsse		00	10	00	
[by me Iohn Roze] Somma		33	19	01	5

The 17^the of Iune paid vnto Mr water harvy for the cobb.
by. Mr Iohn biggood meare appointement   10   00   00
the 12^the of Ianuary 1601/. paid vnto Mr. Robart hassard
meare   04   00   00
the 22 daye of febreary 1601 paid vnto Mr. Robart hasard   10
meare as doth apeare by another accompte whiche I haue
deliuer hym   12   00   00
                         by me Iohn Roze   26   00   00

1605–6   15
Churchwardens' Presentments for Salisbury Deanery
WRO: D5/28/9, item 59
f [1v] *(11 September)*
...

29. we find that in the week after whitsunday by reason of a cobbe aell then   20
held in the Church yerd was throwing with a bowll to a par of keells for a
spone or otherwise noen/

...

4, 5/ 00   10   00, 33   19   01: *sums underlined in MS*
12, 13/ 12   00   00, 26   00   00: *sums underlined in MS*

Sir John Digby's Embassy to Spain

King James I first sent Sir John Digby as an ambassador to Spain in 1611, when he was to settle the claims of the English merchants in Spanish courts and to negotiate the marriage of Prince Henry to the Infanta Anne. Although she had already been betrothed to Louis XIII of France and Prince Henry would die in 1612, Digby's success in the cause of the English merchants and his discovery of certain forms of corruption used by the Spaniards in their dealings with English officials caused King James to continue to place his trust in his ambassador. As a result, Digby returned to Spain in 1614, 1617, and 1622 in an ongoing effort to negotiate a match between Prince Charles and the Infanta Maria. Digby's efforts must have pleased King James for he gave Digby Sherborne Castle and appointed him vice-chamberlain following his return to England early in 1616, raised him to the peerage as Lord Digby on 25 November 1618 after the second embassy on behalf of Prince Charles, and created him earl of Bristol as a result of the negotiations with King Philip IV in 1622.

Digby's success, which lasted until Prince Charles himself and the duke of Buckingham made their expedition to Madrid to woo the Spanish princess, is worth noting because it stands in sharp contrast to the impression produced by the anonymous report from which the following records of dramatic activity are taken. The author of this report emphasizes that Digby was ineffectual in the early stages of this diplomatic effort because of the arrogance, rudeness, contempt, and inhumanity of the Spanish. This report clearly reveals the author's political bias, that of one staunchly opposed to the Spanish match that Digby was to effect; indeed, the author directs some observations quite explicitly to 'thou ill advised ffavourer of the Spanish partie' (f 3).

Digby might well have felt some frustration at the outset of this embassy. Having landed at Santander, he was only about 100 miles north of Lerma, where the court was to be entertained at the estate of King Philip III's favourite, Francisco de Sandoval y Rojas, marquis of Denia and duke of Lerma. Having relocated to Burgos after two weeks in the poor port town, the earl of Bristol was very close indeed to the court at Lerma but two more weeks passed without any formal greetings from Spain. Given this passage of time, the day on which the Spanish treated Gresley rudely was likely Thursday, 2 October 1617 and the day of the masque-like festivities Friday, 3 October. Digby's experience was not unusual; as J.H. Elliott observes in *Imperial Spain 1469–1716* (New York, 1963), 299, 'Hunting, the theatre, and lavish Court *fiestas* occupied the days of the King and his ministers, so that diplomatic representatives

would constantly complain of the difficulty of obtaining audiences and transacting their
affairs.' The duke of Lerma, though not vigorous in conducting the business of international
diplomacy, aggressively provided for himself, his family, and his friends until he fell from power
in 1618 as a result of a palace coup led by his own son, the duke of Uceda. The prominent
role that the duke of Lerma plays in this anonymous and undated report suggests also that it
recounts the embassy of 1617–18.

As the author of this report remains unnamed, so the date of the report and of the embassy
it describes are not specified. The report must have been written at some time after 1622,
however, because it notes that Digby is now earl of Bristol, a title he received on 15 September
that year. The embassy, however, must be that of 1617–18: Digby held the office of vice-
chamberlain by that time and landed 'at St. Andera; It was (I Call to minde) about the last of
August' (f 1v); he was also vice-chamberlain at the time of his mission to Spain in 1622 but
this journey began in April of that year (see George Roberts (ed), *Diary of Walter Yonge, Esq.*,
Camden Society, vol 41 (London, 1848), 54). The only trip that Digby made from England
to Spain in August was that of 1617 (see Samuel Rawson Gardiner, *Prince Charles and the
Spanish Marriage: 1617–1623*, vol 1 (London, 1869), 107). Cold treatment at the hands of
the Spanish, such as that described in the anonymous report, accords with the foreign policy
of Spain which was in 1617 negotiating with the papacy and jockeying for position as the
Thirty Years War took shape. In 1622 on the other hand, 'the government of Philip IV (who
had succeeded in 1621) was chiefly anxious to gain time, and met Digby in the most friendly
way' (*DNB*, vol 5, p 962). Francis, Baron Cottington, succeeded Digby in Spain in 1616 and
returned to England in the autumn of 1622. Mr. Walsingham Gresley was regularly employed
as a messenger in Spain. Both of these men, in other words, could have attended upon Digby
as the report notes either in 1617 or in 1622.

A transcription of the complete report of Digby's embassy has been published in Walter
Scott (ed), *A Collection of Scarce and Valuable Tracts*, 2nd ed, vol 2 (London, 1809), 501–8.
Scott supplies the material which would have occupied the folios now missing from the
manuscript, folios that were missing when it was in possession of the Acland-Hood family
(Historical Manuscripts Commission, Alfred J. Horwood, 'The Manuscripts of Sir Alexander
Acland-Hood, Bart., of St. Audries, Somerset,' *The 6th Report of the Manuscripts Commission*,
Appendix (London, 1877), 351) and the material lost because of damage to others. For two
reasons it seems unlikely, however, that Scott worked with the Somerset Record Office manuscript before it suffered its damage and losses. First, there are substantial differences in ortho-
graphy and phrasing between Scott's transcription and the SRO manuscript. Second, the foliation,
which ignores the loss of ff 12–14, appears to be seventeenth or eighteenth century, which
implies that the manuscript was incomplete before the time when Scott could have worked
with it. The published version of Digby's complete report, then, derives either from a rather care-
free transcription of the SRO manuscript prior to its damage and losses or from an independent
manuscript account of the embassy, neither of which putative manuscripts has been found.

Taunton, Somerset Record Office, DD/AH 51/3, item A; *c* 1608; English; paper; 21 leaves; 310 mm x
200 mm; foliated 1–11, 15–24 (ff 12–14 now missing, original unfoliated leaves also missing between

ff 2 and 3, 4 and 5, 15 and 16, and 16 and 17); many leaves repaired; modern cover of calfskin and board, on the spine: 'MS. Treatises. Vol. III.' One in a series of letters and speeches from the first quarter of the 17th century bound together in a single volume.

DIGBY OF SHERBORNE

c 1618–22
Reception of Sir John Digby at the Spanish Court
SRO: DD/AH 51/3, item A

f 1

> A Report of the Lord Ambassadors Entertainment in Spaine,
> sent in a Letter written into England, *Sir* Iohn Digbie (now
> Earle of Bristoll) being then extraordinary Ambassador from
> his Maiestie of great Brittaine, King Iames.

> Sir
> Such is my present Charitie as that I Could bee Content to forgiue the Ills
> of Spaine with as good a will as you parted from them, and suffer the blinde
> Policie of the time to haue its Course in Calling black white and Pride Grauitie,
> till Ambition and It fall both into the ditch. yet because of my Promise to
> my friend (in whose Expectacion my Honestie I know is ever present) I will
> noe longer Containe my self in fflatterie, but (laying aside all Court respectes)
> freelie and faithfullie sett downe those Passages that may serue to satisfie
> your selfe, and such other of our friendes as are desirous to know the Certaine
> manner of Master Vice Chamberlaine's Reception and Entertainement in
> the Court of Spaine now at his being last there his Maiesties extraordinary
> Ambassador.

f 2
...

> You know that the King and his whole Court were about this season to
> remoue from Madrid, and to Come ffower daies Iourney as directlie towardes
> his Lordshipp as if hee had Come on purpose to meete him. His occasion
> was, that the Grand ffavourite, the Duke of Lerma had invited his Maiestie
> to the Towne of Lerma, there to recreate him with divers Shewes prepared
> for that purpose....

28/ the King: *Philip III of Spain*   28/ this season: *early September 1617*

f 6v

...Mr Gresley made as much haste to bring back word that at Lerma they
were all very busie in seeing a plaie; soe as hee Could not Come to speake
with any one that vnderstood the businesse...   5

f 7v

...his Lordshipps minde was Changed; and vpon some Caveat or other that
Mr Cottington was seen to whisper in his Eare, he made the boote to bee   10
opened againe, and declared that he was determined to stay there all Night;
Which seemed to some of the Spectators such an Enterlude, as they did
noething envie those that were seeing the Comedie at Lerma....

f 10v   15

...There likewise did Lerma's howse present it selfe to their view; which my
thoughtes regarded, in ∧⌜the⌝ very same manner for all the world as the
refuse People do use the outside of a banqueting howse vpon a Masking
Night, when they Cannot be suffered to goe in....   20

APPENDIX 5
Saints' Days and Festivals

The following list contains the dates for holy days and festivals mentioned in the Records. Exact dates for moveable feasts are included in textual notes. See also C.R. Cheney, *Handbook of Dates for Students of English History*, corrected ed (London, 1996), 84–161.

All Saints	1 November
Ascension Day	Thursday following the fifth Sunday after Easter, ie, forty days after Easter
Candlemas	2 February
Christmas Day	25 December
Corpus Christi Day	Thursday following Trinity Sunday, the eighth Sunday after Easter
Easter Day	Sunday after full moon on or next following 21 March
Easter Monday	Monday following Easter Day
Hock Monday	second Monday after Easter
Hocktide	second Monday and Tuesday after Easter
Holy Rood Day	3 May
May Day	1 May
Midsummer Day	24 June
Pentecost (Whit Sunday)	seventh Sunday after Easter, ie, fifty days after Easter
St Mary the Virgin, annunciation to	25 March
St Michael the Archangel	29 September
St Peter	29 June
Shrovetide	*see* pp 329–30, endnote to DRO: DC/BFB: Finance: Chamberlains' Accounts f B18v
Shrove Tuesday	Tuesday before Ash Wednesday, the start of Lent
Trinity Monday	Monday following Trinity Sunday
Trinity Sunday	eighth Sunday after Easter
Whit Sunday	*see* Pentecost

Translations

ABIGAIL ANN YOUNG

The Latin documents have been translated as literally as possible. The order of the records in the Translations parallels that of the Records text. Place-names and given names have been modernized. The spelling of surnames in the Translations reflects the same principles as used in the Index. Capitalization and punctuation are in accordance with modern practice. As in the Records text, diamond brackets indicate obliterations and square brackets cancellations. However, cancellations are not normally translated; they may be translated when a whole entry is cancelled, especially if it appears that a cancellation may be administrative rather than the correction of an error, or if they seem of special interest or relevance.

Round brackets enclose words not in the Latin text but needed for grammatical sense in English. In accounts of cases heard before ecclesiastical courts, phrases in round brackets may be used to complete formulae suspended with 'etc,' when the remainder of a formula can be deduced with certainty. A word should be said about the prologue, from a Bodleian MS, for a play presented at Dorchester school for the entertainment of guests – including the bishop of Bristol and his chancellor. It presents three particular problems. First, although it is written in the metre of Roman comedy, it has not been translated in verse-form but is presented as continuous English prose. This is partly because the translator is not equal to English iambic verse and partly because, given the way in which syntactic units span more than one line in the original, it could not be rendered into English verse without overstepping REED's guidelines. Second, the regular use of 'etc' by the scribe, possibly to indicate some sort of 'boilerplate' then familiar to those well-versed in this kind of academic exercise, leaves half-lines and clauses hanging, of an uncertain meaning to today's reader. And third, the layout of the MS makes it sometimes hard to detect how many speakers there are (at least two but possibly more) and where the speaker changes. Features such as indented text and MS dashes which might otherwise not have been preserved in the Translations are therefore kept here, on the supposition that they probably signal changes of speaker.

Not all the Latin in the text has been translated here. Latin tags, formulae, headings, or other short sections in largely English documents are either translated in footnotes or not at all. In translated documents containing a mixture of Latin and English, the English sections are normally indicated with '(English)' but in some cases, in which the syntax of English and Latin sections has become entangled, the English text appears in the translation in modern spelling. Individual documents which consist of a single line, or other very short entries, especially those that are part of repetitive annual series, are not normally translated unless they present some unusual syntactic or semantic problem. However, in deciding whether to translate simple Latin formulae in court books, the overall complexity of the entry has been considered. All Latin vocabulary not found in the standard Latin dictionary, the *Oxford Latin Dictionary*, is found in the glossary.

BEAMINSTER

1591–3
Churchwardens' Presentments for Salisbury Deanery
WRO: D5/28/6, item 34
single sheet*

...

Likewise we present that there were stage players played in our parish church. The lord (judge) warned that in future (the churchwardens) should not permit actors to play in the church, etc.

...

BERE REGIS

1590
Deposition Book for Salisbury Deanery   WRO: D5/22/2
ff 47v–8* *(17 December) (Examination of Thomas Howlett, husbandman, aged 30)*

Taken before William Wilkinson, LLD, the dean's official
...

To the second and third articles of the list of charges he deposes *(English)*. And he does not know how to depose any more to these articles as he says.

...

(Howlett's replies to further interrogatories)

To the second interrogatory he replies *(English)*. And otherwise he does not know how to reply to that interrogatory (any more) than he has replied above to the said second and third articles of the list of charges aforesaid.
...

To the fourth he replies *(English)*. And otherwise he is satisfied with the depositions.
To the fifth and the last interrogatories he replies *(English)*.

(Examination of Geoffrey Phipper, husbandman, aged 31)

...

To the second and third articles he deposes *(English)*. And he does not know how to depose any more to these articles as he says.

...

f 48v *(Phipper's replies to further interrogatories)*

To the fourth, fifth, and last interrogatories he replies *(English)*. And he does not know how to reply any more otherwise than he has deposed before.

(Examination of Francis Blundon, shoemaker, aged 21)

...

To the second and third articles he deposes *(English)*. And he does not know how to depose any more to these articles as he says.

...

f 49 *(Blundon's replies to further interrogatories)*

...

To the second, third, fourth, fifth, and last interrogatories he replies *(English)*. And otherwise he does not know how to reply (any more) than he has deposed in his depositions.

...

BLOXWORTH

1589
Dean and Chapter Act Book for Salisbury Deanery   WRO: D5/19/12
f 30v *(14 July)*

Proceedings of a session held in the parish church at Bere Regis before George Dawkes, LLB, the dean's official, in the presence of Giles Hutchens, notary public
...
The lord's office against Paul Rawlins of Bloxworth
Today the said Rawlins appeared. The lord (judge) bound him with an oath to reply faithfully to the articles, etc. Then, when he had been examined, he says *(English)*. Therefore the lord (judge) enjoined that he should acknowledge before Mr Rickman, the rector there, that the aforesaid crime was committed by him, promising that he would never fall again into like (offences). The lord (judge) warned him that, when he had done that, he should certify it on the next (court day) at Sherborne or Salisbury under penalty of law.
...

CORFE CASTLE

1574–6
Autobiography of Robert Ashley   BL: Sloane MS. 2131
ff 16v–17*

...

But since the custody of Corfe Castle in the Isle of Purbeck – which lies next
to the territory of Dorset – had been entrusted at that time to (my) father
by Sir Christopher Hatton, Queen Elizabeth's vice-chamberlain, I moved
there with (my) family, where the headmaster of the grammar school had
earned a good reputation for himself. When I was entrusted to his care, I
easily became the head boy of that school, where I recall that I came out on
top after being challenged to a wrestling match by a schoolmate while we were
playing: so much so that afterwards he demanded a fine from me for the leg
which was weakened in the wrestling. I There too when we put on comedies
during the Christmas celebrations the principal parts, which had previously
been given to another boy, were later assigned to me by the master, with
which glorious (opportunity) I was, perhaps, too pleased....

   But after my teacher Hadrian was summoned to Belgium, and while he was
preparing (to go), I was transferred to Salisbury to continue my course of
study, being then at the beginning of my twelfth year. There I studied in a
public school under Dr Adam Hill, once a fellow of Balliol College. He, no
sluggard at judging genius, added by his reports a spur to my running and
when we recited comedies and put on other solemn shows before the most
illustrious Henry, earl of Pembroke – who was then living in the area – he
demanded that I perform the principal parts.

...

DORCHESTER

c 1603–10
Prologue for a School Play   Bodl.: MS. Add. B.97
ff 63–4*

(English)
Welcome, o most honoured bishop, light of the sacred assembly; and you also,
chancellor, you who again give kindly ears to our jests. Welcome, too, all
you others, to whom it does not seem hard to honour our fable, whatever
might be said, with your presence and to put off serious affairs with ones
that are entertaining (*or* with plays *or* shows). For you will hear pleasantries,
as I shall warn you in advance lest by chance anyone afterwards complain,

nor will they be worthy of your learned ears, etc. But who sets out on a journey by way of this stage? Go forth, etc.

You will hear no tragedy, etc.

Guest: Yet that is the rumour. Indeed our Dorchester, which, lo!, condemns us, fosters it (*ie*, tragedy) and in fact the greatest men are actors (*or* the actors are the greatest *or* they are the greatest actors).

Guest: A comedy then?

– But not even in that way: seek not, you will never find, etc. How indeed can laughter be compelled? We are scarcely mimes, nor do we play the actor, as you may think. Let the well-known do that, whom the laws of all people mark, etc.

Guest: Well, what will be performed? It should please the bishop, etc.

– (Indeed, it should please him), a man outstanding in splendour, who here presides as leader over the consecrated chorus, etc.

– He, who has attained the holy yoke of honour and virtue through harsh thorns, takes his name and sign from thorns. |

Guest: The performers?

Boys.

Guest: Very learned ones?

– O would that they were! Not very learned at all, and inexperienced in years and also in their art: they have taken only the first sip of the elements of grammar and have a nodding acquaintance with the simple letters of Cordier, Æsop, and Terence. (They stand) at the threshold only and hardly even there! But you are still curious how, if you please, this may be so subtly and nicely shown and you are asking about a play as if this were one reason for coming. You have a care for strange things, I fear, shaken by your, etc. And they say that curious people are talkative; I am prepared (to answer) whatever you will ask, but ask in a few words, etc.

They teach in school the way of virtue and vice by example, how to follow the one and flee the other. So he who mixed the useful with the pleasant has reported every point, etc.

Ready to speak, I dealt with what should be done here and what said and I said everything for our guest, while he is now asking each thing one by one, so that nothing can now remain which might become you (to ask). Here I beg you all, and you above all, most noble bishop, patron of the muses and their common parent, whom we hold as *(blank)* in place of a presiding spirit. Forgive the things we say – they are slight – since greater things may not now be given. Would that this preparation would yield worthy plays! Still, you have (before you) willing and respectful souls: may you be good and kindly, approachable by your own, o fortunate one! We are young boys: we will present nothing exact; we are poor and little: we will present nothing exceptional; we are small and weak: we will present nothing refined. | But if the things we put on for you are pleasing, this nearly nothing (of ours) will have been enough and more.

...

1608

Answer of Matthew and Margaret Chubbe, Defendants in Condytt et al v. Chubbe et al PRO: STAC 8/94/17
mb 18* *(2 June)*

(English)
(signed) By me, Matthew Chubbe.   The sign of Margaret M Chubbe.

The aforesaid defendants were sworn at Dorchester in the county of Dorset on 2 June 1608 at the sign of The George there.
Before *(signed)* Thomas Barnes, John Arnold, and John Geare, commissioners. Strode.
1608

HINTON MARTELL

1629

Quarter Sessions Orders DRO: QSM: 1/1
f 199v* *(7–8 July) (Bonds taken for the next assize)*

Taken at the Shaftesbury sessions before Sir John Croke, judge of King's Bench; Nathaniel Napier, knight; Gerard Wood, DD; John Whetcombe, DD; and Arthur Radford and William Whittaker, esquires

Copy
(He is bound over) to reply to these (charges).
William Scot of Hinton Martell in the county of Dorset, fiddler, is bound to the lord king for £20; William Godard of Tollard Royal in the county of Wiltshire, gentleman, for £10; and Thomas Frye of Ashmore in the county of Dorset aforesaid, gentleman, is bound to the same lord king for £10: for the appearance of the said William Scot at the next assizes and general gaol delivery held in the aforesaid county to reply to these (charges).

...

PUDDLETOWN

1619
Casebook of Sir Francis Ashley   BL: Harley MS. 6715
f 42   *(22 May)* *(Bonds taken for the assizes)*

…

(English)
Thomas Bartlet of Ilsington, yeoman, is bound for £20.

Richard Geng of Puddletown, husbandman, and Thomas Stone of the
same, tailor, are each bound for £10.

For the appearance of the said Thomas Bartlet at the next general (gaol)
delivery to answer these (charges), etc.

…

Guarantors

*(The obligation)
is cleared on
the first of July.*

SHAFTESBURY

1311
Bishop Simon of Ghent's Register   WRO: D1/2/1
f 134v*   *(6 April)*

A letter sent to the dean of Shaftesbury against those carrying out unsuitable
pastimes in the churchyard of the conventual church of Shaftesbury.
Simon, by divine permission bishop of Salisbury, to his beloved son in Christ,
the dean of Shaftesbury: greetings, grace, and blessing. While travelling
through the neighbourhood of Shaftesbury not long ago, among other things
that then came to our hearing, we were informed by a reliable report that,
although – in connection with an initiative of our prompting – it had been
formerly ordered under grave penalties and censures by our authority that the
churchyard of the conventual church of the aforesaid place should not be
befouled by the exercise of disreputable plays/pastimes and insolent gatherings and by other dances which arouse the miserable souls of those who come
together (there) to lascivious and dissipated wandering and, moreover, it
was also ordered that the fencing-in of the same churchyard or cemetery be
plainly visible on every side so that there may be no entry for dumb animals to
trample in the place dedicated to God in which the bodies of the faithful
rest, nevertheless some, contrary to this prohibition, striving to diminish and
harm ecclesiastical liberty and immunity, like degenerate sons jealous of
their mother's honour, entering the aforesaid churchyard or cemetery with
rash daring, make such a clamour about and so disturb – as aforementioned
with dances and harmful pastimes – the divine services that customarily occur
in the Church of the Holy Trinity, which forms one joint space with the said

churchyard, and in other churches adjoining the same (churchyard) that we
fear for as it were a daily violation both of the churches and of the afore-
mentioned churchyard and as a consequence probably an interdict (there).
Mindful therefore that holiness befits the Lord's house, so that the worship
of Him in Whose peace the place was made may be peaceful, with due
reverence, and that there may be humble and devout entering into the church,
quiet behaviour pleasing to God and calm for those looking on, so that they
might attend to the sacred solemnities there with intent hearts and persist in
devout prayers, (and) so that they may cease from their outcries and rushing
about in it and its cemetery or churchyards dedicated to God and may quiet
their profane conversations and especially the jeering of a harmful pastime
and the clamours of their insolent behaviour – we firmly enjoin on you by
virtue of your holy obedience, commit to you, and order that you, taking
along with you the rectors and vicars of the neighbouring churches of the
said town if needed, warn all these evildoers on Sundays and holy days and
effectually persuade them under pain of the greater excommunication,
which those who disobey can not undeservedly fear, to desist from such rash
presumption hereafter. Otherwise you shall cite those whom you find to be
rebellious in this regard to appear before us or our official in the greater church
at Salisbury during our next consistory session concerning the archdeaconry
of Dorset to be held ex officio after your lawful warning, ready to respond
to us upon these matters and what pertains to them and ready to do and
receive further what is appropriate in accordance with the canons laid down
in such a regard. You shall certify openly what you have done about the
foregoing and the names of any rebellious persons cited to us, our official,
or another acting as his deputy on the day and in the place aforementioned
by means of your letter patent containing a copy of this (letter). Farewell.
Given at Woodford on 6 April in the year of the Lord 1311 and the fourteenth
year of our consecration.

SHERBORNE

1513–14
All Hallows' Churchwarden's Accounts   DRO: PE/SH: CW 1/5
single mb *(25 December–25 December) (Rents, sales, and gifts)*
…
…And of £7 10s 6d received from John Yonge, baker, for ale sold, called the
king's ale, this year….
…

(Expenses)

…And in rewards given to men carrying the shrine on the feast of Corpus Christi this year, together with thread bought for the said shrine, 7d.…

…

1514–15
All Hallows' Churchwarden's Accounts   DRO: PE/SH: CW 1/6
single sheet *(25 December–25 December) (Rents, sales, and gifts)*

…

…And of £7 13s 4d received from Robert Watson for the ale sold by him, called the king's ale, this year.…

. . .

(Payments and expenses)

…And on the mending (of) the shrine this year, 7d.… And on thread and nails bought for the shrine this year 4d.… And on men hired to carry the shrine this year, 4d. And paid to the sacrist for keeping the shrine, 3d.…

…

1515–16
All Hallows' Churchwarden's Accounts   DRO: PE/SH: CW 1/7
single sheet *(25 December–25 December) (Rents, sales, and gifts)*

…

…And of 116s 8d received from Robert Cookeman, tanner, for the ale, called the king's ale, sold by him this year.…

…

(Payments and expenses)

…And on the mending (of) the shrine this year, 6d. And on men hired to carry the shrine this year, together with nails and thread bought for the same (shrine), 12d.…

…

1517–18
All Hallows' Churchwarden's Accounts   DRO: PE/SH: CW 1/8
single mb* *(25 December–25 December) (Rents, sales, and gifts)*

…

…And of £7 8s received from John Pope for the ale, called king's ale, sold by him this year.…

…

(Payments and expenses)

...And paid for thread, nails, and the watching of the shrine on the feast of Corpus Christi, 6d. And on men hired to carry the said shrine on the said feast, 6d....

...

SPETTISBURY

1635/6
Examination of Anne Barter   DRO: PE/WM: CP2/8, item 90
single sheet–single sheet verso *(23 February)*

Proceedings of the court held before William Stone, MA, official, in the presence of Sampson Morice, notary public and deputy registrar
...

The lord's office promoted against Stephen Barter and Anne, his wife, for incontinence before marriage.

Today the said Anne appeared and on the strength of her corporal oath already taken she acknowledged that *(English)*.

STOUR PROVOST

1621/2
Casebook of Sir Francis Ashley   BL: Harley MS. 6715
f 54v *(14 January) (Bonds taken for the sessions)*
...

Committed by order of the Blandford sessions for a scandalous song.

William Honny of Stour Provost, husbandman	for £40
Ferdinand Thomas of the same, weaver, individually	
Edward Scot of the same, wheeler	for £20 each
William Hopkins of the same, mason	

(Bound) for the appearance of the aforesaid Honny and Thomas at the next sessions and in the meantime for good behaviour.

Committed for the like.

The same Scot and Hopkins each for	£40
And the same Honny and Thomas each for	£20

(Bound) for the appearance of that Scot and Hopkins at the next sessions and for good behaviour.

...

WEYMOUTH-MELCOMBE REGIS

1625-6
Borough and Borough Court Minute Book   WM: MB.O-B
p 321* *(3 October)(Presentments by jury of court leet)*

…

The aforesaid jurors further say and present upon their oath that Henry Backway placed a pile of earth, in English, 'a heap of earth' in the place where the maypole would formerly stand and that Henry Waltham and Godfrye placed two piles of earth and soil in the street called St Mary Street. And they are ordered to remove the same piles before the next feast of All Saints under penalty that each one who is delinquent will forfeit 5s.

…

1639-40
Borough and Borough Court Minute Book   WM: MB.O-B
p 419 *(7 October)(Presentments by jury of court leet)*

…

At this court Richard Hickes presented upon his oath that William Barens – 3s 4d – and John Hingston – 3s 4d – killed two bulls within this town before the next court and not publicly *(blank)*, in English, 'did not bait them openly.' Therefore each of them is under amercement for the sums above their names.

WINTERBORNE MONKTON

1616
Casebook of Sir Francis Ashley   BL: Harley MS. 6715
f 15v *(25 May) (Bonds taken for the assizes)*

…

(English)

Henry Chepman of Monkton, husbandman	for	£40
John Middleton of the same, yeoman and Henry Notley of the same, husbandman		£20 each

For (Chepman's) appearance at the next assizes to reply to these (charges).

(English)

John Blanchard of Monkton, husbandman	for	£40
John Middleton of the same, yeoman and	for	£20
Henry Notley of the same, husbandman	for	£20

For (Blanchard's) appearance at the next assizes to reply to these (charges).

…

William Bartlet of Monkton, clerk   for   £40
For his appearance at the next assizes to give evidence against Henry Chepman
and John Blanchard.

...

Endnotes

119   PRO: SP 16/96   single sheet
Although this document has been published in Stokes with Alexander (eds), *Somerset Including Bath*, vol 1, p 436, we have reprinted it here because it establishes as the precedent for the Somerset action an order for the suppression of ales in Dorset. This is the earliest evidence extant for countywide opposition to such festivities, which are regularly seen, as the visits of travelling performers are, as a focus for increasingly strong Puritan opposition to entertainments.

119–20   PRO: Assi 24/20/140   f 35v
This order was part of the business conducted by a western circuit assize held at Dorchester before Sir John Denham on 21 July 1631. It represents a continuation of the effort to regulate or suppress customary ales and revels on the grounds that they occasioned disorder. The document alludes to an earlier order for the suppression of such events, that of July 1628 when the assizes met at Sherborne. In the same year a group of ministers from Somerset petitioned Sir John Denham to grant an order for the suppression of ales and revels in their home county, an order similar to that made even earlier, in 1627, at 'the last Summer Assises held for the County of Dorsett' (p 119, l.15). For other orders contributing to the effort to regulate, if not eliminate, public ales and revels and for an abstract of the Dorset order of 1631, see Cockburn (ed), *Western Circuit Assize Orders*, pp 33, 46–7.

121   WRO: D5/28/6, item 34   single sheet
The Wiltshire and Swindon Record Office has assigned the bundle of documents including this entry to the years 1591–3; this item, like many others, is not explicitly dated. Although the sheet lists Roger Crabbe and Richard Horsford as churchwardens, in the absence of surviving churchwardens' accounts it is impossible to determine the date more precisely.

121–2   DRO: QSM: 1/1   ff 272v–3
Folio 272v is headed 'de Ordinibus,' and f 273, 'Adhuc de Ordinibus.' The scribe's unusual final 's' is transcribed as a single letter except in 'Maiesties Iustices' (p 122, l.28) where it is a sign for 'es.'
    Thomas Freke (1563–1633) was the son of Robert Freke, teller of the Exchequer and surveyor for Dorset. Robert had married a Blandford girl and set himself up as a country gentleman at Iwerne Courtney. Freke was MP for Dorchester in 1584 and for Dorset in 1604 and 1626 and deputy lieutenant of the county for about thirty years; he and his son owned the largest of the Dorset privateering ships and he lent money to both Sir Walter Ralegh and Lord Burleigh. He was knighted at the coronation of James I. Sir John Strode (d. 1642) of Chantmarle, Dorset, was MP for Bridport in 1620–1. Leweston

FitzJames (*c* 1574–1638) of Leweston, Dorset, was educated at Balliol and admitted to the Middle Temple; he was MP for Bridport in 1597. He was related to the prominent Dorset Trenchard family and had connections with the Hannams of Wimborne Minster. Sir Walter Ralegh complained of his quarrelsome behaviour in 1596 (P.W. Hasler, *The House of Commons, 1558–1603,* vol 2 (London, 1981), 126).

The account of the puppet players is described in Bettey, 'Puppet-Players.' On 5 July 1630, according to the diary of William Whiteway, puppet players had appeared in Dorchester and were refused leave to play although they had Charles I's warrant (see p 200, ll.10–11). Just four years later Beaminster's curate, Mr Spratt, told his parishioners to follow their consciences – not the king – on the sabbath and gave other signs of obdurate Puritanism (Bettey, 'Varieties of Men,' p 847). The puppet players were probably from Lancashire: when William Sands of Preston died in September 1638 he willed to his son John his 'Shewe called the Chaos, the Wagon, the Stage, & all the Ioyners tooles & other ymplem*entes* ... to the said Shewe belonging' (see David George (ed), *Lancashire,* REED (Toronto, 1991), 87 and 334).

122–4 WRO: D5/22/2 ff 47v–8

Thomas Howlett, husbandman, Geoffrey Phipper, husbandman, and Francis Blundon are deposed before officials of the ecclesiastical court in a suit brought for defamation by the minstrel, Thomas Whiffen, and his wife, Eleanor, against Henry Gerrard. Gerrard, the Whiffens, and all the witnesses were from Bere Regis. The depositions, taken on interrogatories proposed by the plaintiffs, were taken before William Wilkinson, chancellor of the diocese of Salisbury, 1591–1613. For Wilkinson's biography, see Brian P. Levack, *The Civil Lawyers in England 1603–1641: A Political Study* (Oxford, 1973), 279. According to Hutchins, David Woodnutt (p 123, l.17) was vicar from 1574 until his death in 1592 (*History and Antiquities,* vol 1, p 155).

125 DRO: PE/BER: CW1 ff 2, 3

Although the presence of the minstrel, Thomas Whiffen, at the 1590 Bere Regis church ale shows that the ale might sometimes attract performers, there is no clear indication – as there is for the Sherborne king ale, for example – that performance or mimetic activity was an intrinsic part of the Bere Regis celebration. Bere Regis ale receipts for the years 1607–8 and 1616–17 are printed in the Records since in those years the parish paid performers who may have played at the ale. Receipts for other years are as follows: £15 in 1608–9 (f 5), £21 2s 6d in 1609–10 (f 6v), £12 in 1610–11 (f 8), £10 5s 3d in 1611–12 (f 10), £11 1s 2d in 1612–13 (f 12), £13 1s 4d in 1613–14 (f 16, repeating the sum recorded in a cancelled account on f 14). Payments to mend the parish drum in 1607–8 (l.36) and for a 'drum Corde' in 1613–14 (f 14) may have had no connection with a specific performance or with the ale. Note that the account of churchwardens Tobias Mead and William Quoke on f 10 is headed 'AD 1612,' which would ordinarily introduce the account for 1612–13; the account on f 12, however, is clearly the 1612–13 account, and a complete account for 1610–11 begins on f 8, so Mead's and Quoke's account must have been for 1611–12.

Two studies referring to the Bere Regis church ale as part of a pattern of local religious controversy and conflict about parish celebration may overstate the Bere Regis evidence. As Underdown states, churchwardens' accounts record church ale receipts in each year until 1614–15, when receipts from the rates are the major source of parish revenue (f 19). He continues, however: 'But there was fierce resistance to the change. The rate produced less than half the amount normally raised by the church ale, there were large unpaid arrears and apparitor's fees "for following the suit against those that do refuse to pay the rate". In 1616 Bere Regis returned to the old ways and held a successful church ale, making a new "vizard for the players". A gap in the churchwardens' accounts obscures the next few years, but by 1624 *the struggle was over*. The 1624 rate raised more than the earlier ales had done, and by now there were increasing revenues from the sale of church seats. Ales were as unnecessary to the repair of the Bere Regis church as they had *at last become unacceptable to its parish élite*' (emphasis added; *Revel,* p 91). Certainly the parish resisted the new levy in 1614 but that seems scant evidence for a 'struggle' in a parish which seems to have made no effort to oust its unsatisfactory vicar, the poet Thomas Bastard, vicar from 1592 to 1618 (Bettey, 'Varieties of Men,' pp 846–7). Similarly, in discussing the impact on local merry-making of 'the demonstration of feeling within Parliament against "profanation" of the Sabbath' early in the reign of Charles I, Hutton says the Bere Regis church ale ended in 1625–6 (*Rise and Fall,* p 189); in fact, the last evidence of an ale at Bere Regis is in 1616–17, a different stage in Hutton's interpretive chronology.

127   DRO: DC/BFB: Finance: Chamberlains' Accounts   f B9
The record refers to the old town hall; the town raised funds to build a new town hall in 1592–3 (ff B13–B13v; see pp 14–15).

127   DRO: DC/BFB: Finance: Chamberlains' Accounts   f B14
Augustine Drake copied these receipts (ll.12–14) below his copy of an original account of 'Monye laied out ... for the towne' by 'Iohn Cleeues,' one of the town stewards for 1594–5. The additional receipts (ll.19–21) are part of Drake's copy, on the same folio, of the reckoning made on 5 November by Cleeves and the other steward, Robert Keynell. They probably represent a summary of the same receipts but are included because they may reflect a separate payment of 7s 6d made by players to Keynell. Drake copies yet another list of receipts for 1595 on f B13v; included is an entry for 7s 6d 'Rec*eiued* of Iohn Cleeues that was Rec*eiued* of the players,' confirming that Trustrum's company and Lord Stafford's and Lord Monteagle's men were players.

John Cleeves (l.10) was an influential Blandford citizen. One of those responsible for the town fund-raising ale in 1591–2, he also served as steward in 1595–6, 1596–7, 1597–8, 1599–1600, 1600–1, 1601–2, 1603–4, and 1604–5 and as chamberlain in 1605–6; he collected money at the 1603/4 Blandford race meeting (p 129, l.24) and was one of three townsmen who loaned money to Blandford in 1600 (ff B10v and B13 and F2, F3, F4, F6, F6v, F7, F8, F9, and F10).

Robert Keynell was again steward in 1595–6, 1596–7, and 1597–8, bailiff in 1600–1, steward in 1602–3, chamberlain in 1613–14, 1614–15, and 1615–16 and bailiff in 1614–15. His brother-in-law, Christopher Comege, left money to the almshouse and to Blandford's poor (ff F2, F3, F4, F7, F12v, F15v, F16, and F16v; see also p 129, l.7 below).

127   DRO: DC/BFB: Finance: Chamberlains' Accounts   f F2
Drake's copy of the original entry occurs on f B15.

127   DRO: DC/BFB: Finance: Chamberlains' Accounts   f B15v
'Gawler' (l.35) may have been John Gawler, a saddler who leased from the town a shop adjoining his house for a twenty-one-year lease ending at Michaelmas 1602; a John Gawler was town bailiff in 1610–11, and the 'widdow Gawler' earned wages during the 1603/4 race meeting. See f F1v and p 132, l.24 and p 135, l.16.

127–8   DRO: DC/BFB: Finance: Chamberlains' Accounts   f F5
Drake's copy of a list of receipts for the same year records that Andrew Pope would pay the town 20s

at the next town reckoning for 'playes played in the yeldhall this yeare past' (f B16v). According to J.H.P. Pafford, Pope was probably a Blandford man ('Blandford Forum,' p 285).

Jehonadab Sherlye (p 128, l.5) was one of Blandford's most prominent citizens between 1590 and 1630. Like John Cleeves, one of those responsible for the ales of the early 1590s that were held to raise money for the new Blandford guildhall, he was steward in 1598–9, 1599–1600, 1600–1, and 1601–2 and – judging by the sum paid him for his expenses – he was one of the more important organizers of the celebrations surrounding the races in 1603–4 (p 132, l.13). He was bailiff in 1604–5, chamberlain in 1606–7, bailiff in 1611–12, and chamberlain again in 1616–17. On 30 May 1615 Blandford's bailiff placed town money in Sherlye's hands; Sherlye was to pay for the use of the money to benefit the poor in Blandford's almshouse. See ff B10v, F4, F6, F6v, F8, F9, F12, F15v, and F17; and p 133, l.36; and p 135, ll.23–4.

128   DRO: DC/BFB: Finance: Chamberlains' Accounts   f B16v

Bailiff Rawlingston (l.12) may have been Thomas Rawlinston who rented the 'play close' from the town in 1600–1 and who sold the town a 'rostinge pugg' for the dinners at the race meeting of 1603–4. The play close was kept available for archery practice; it took its name from the bowling and other unlawful games specifically prohibited in its precincts. See ff B10v and F6 and p 131, l.19.

128   DRO: DC/BFB: Finance: Chamberlains' Accounts   f F6

Pope's payment is for money owed the town for plays in the guildhall in 1598–9 (p 127, l.42–p 128, l.2).

128   DRO: DC/BFB: Finance: Chamberlains' Accounts   f B18v

This is the first reference to the Shrovetide horse race which was an important town fund-raiser between at least 1603–4 and 1615–16; although the Blandford races were celebrated in the eighteenth century, they disappear from the chamberlains' accounts in 1616. The Blandford race meeting, apparently overseen by the town bailiff, may be compared to races at Chester, which had clearer associations with local festive customs. At Chester Shrove Tuesday races dated to 1539–40; the prize for a Shrove Tuesday foot race replaced an earlier guild homage of a football, and a prize for a Shrove Tuesday horse race replaced another homage. In 1610 Chester also began to run a horse race on St George's Day (Lawrence W. Clopper (ed), *Chester*, REED (Toronto, 1979), lii–liii, 41, 234–6). Compiling records for 1608–9 Chester's seventeenth-century antiquarian, David Rogers, states that he believes horse races and other customs are 'yearely vsed' at Chester, 'which is doone in uerye fewe, if anye Citties of Englande' (Clopper (ed), *Chester*, p 238).

In 1603–4 the festivities associated with the Blandford race meeting ran for a week, from Sunday to Saturday. The chamberlains' less detailed accounts for later years specifically assign the race to 'Shrovetide' in 1605–6, 1606–7, 1611–12, and 1615–16; in other years no time of year is mentioned. The relatively large profits of 1604–5, 1605–6, 1607–8, and 1611–12 suggest that at least in those years the race meeting probably ran for a week, as it had in 1603–4; smaller profits in 1606–7 and 1615–16 may reflect less prolonged festivities, less extravagant celebrations, or less well-controlled costs.

Despite the downplaying of Ash Wednesday by Elizabeth it seems unlikely that early Stuart townsmen would have organized seven days of feasting and gambling with Ash Wednesday as the centrepiece of the celebration, particularly with the dietary restrictions which would have obtained on Ash Wednesday and the three days following: the most significant source of revenue in the detailed accounts of 1603–4 are the sums paid the town for dinners and suppers. In years in which the race meeting lasted an entire week the 'Shrovetide' race probably ran from Sexagesima Sunday to the following Saturday, that is, during the week preceding the Monday and Tuesday more commonly called Shrovetide. (For Shrovetide customs before and during the early Stuart period and for the Lenten fast in the reign of James I see Hutton, *Stations of the Sun*, pp 151–7 and 169–70.)

George Harbyn (l.28) occurs in the race meeting accounts for 1603–4; he was bailiff in 1606–7 and chamberlain in 1606–7, 1610–11, 1611–12, and 1612–13. See ff F10v, F12, F14, and F14v and p 132, l.11 and p 134, l.16.

129   DRO: DC/BFB: Finance: Chamberlains' Accounts   f B19
The receipts for the 1603–4 race given here repeat the net profits recorded in the itemized accounts entered on ff B19v–20. John Cleeves and John Roper, town stewards, rendered their account for the same sum on 5 November 1604 (f F9). Roper, or Rooper, was one of the organizers of the town ale in 1592–3, one of the collectors for the poor in 1595–6, and bailiff in 1600–1. Together with John Cleeves and Jehonadab Sherlye, he loaned money to the town in 1599–1600, a debt still unpaid in 1601–2 (ff B11v, F1, F6v, and F8).

129–33   DRO: DC/BFB: Finance: Chamberlains' Accounts   ff B19v–20
The race meeting was probably held 12–18 February 1603/4 (Sexagesima week) rather than 19–24 February, the week which included the days usually referred to as Shrovetide (see pp 329–30, endnote to DRO: DC/BFB: Finance: Chamberlains' Accounts f B18v).

Most notable among the many names in this account are Sir Ralph 'Horssyes' or Horsey (p 130, l.19) and Sir 'Care Rawleigh' or Carew Ralegh (p 130, l.20). A member of one of the most prominent Dorset families, Horsey was lord lieutenant of Dorset as early as 1594 when he was present at one of Sir George Trenchard's dinners with Sir Walter and Carew Ralegh and others, and rebuked Carew Ralegh for loose speeches (G.B. Harrison (ed), *An Elizabethan Journal: Being a Record of Those Things Most Talked of during the Years 1591–1594* (London, 1928), 295). Carew Ralegh (c 1550–1626) was the older brother and lifelong friend of Sir Walter Ralegh. Beginning his career with voyages of discovery he was on a list of captains preparing to defend England against Spain in the 1580s and was vice-admiral for Dorset in 1597. He frequently reaped rewards when his more famous younger brother was in favour with Queen Elizabeth, who knighted Carew in 1601. He became gentleman of horse to Sir John Thynne of Longleat before 1580; after Thynne's death he married the widow, whose Wiltshire connections probably influenced his settlement at Downton House near Salisbury in the late 1590s. During the 1590s he had been one of the set surrounding Ralegh who debated religious topics, and he and his stepson were among those accused before the commission at Cerne in 1594, where the Wyke Regis parson asserted that the Ralegh brothers had confiscated his horse at Blandford three years earlier. When the parson protested that he needed his horse if he were to preach in his parish the next day, Carew is supposed to have answered that 'he might go home when he would but his horse should preach before him.' See 'Sir Walter Ralegh' in the *DNB*; Hasler, *House of Commons*, vol 3, pp 271–3; Harrison (ed), *An Elizabethan Journal 1591–1594*, p 295; G.B. Harrison (ed), *A Last Elizabethan Journal: Being a Record of Those Things Most Talked of during the Years 1599–1603* (London, 1933), 235; and Lloyd, *Dorset Elizabethans*, pp 260–4.

Several prominent Blandford citizens also occur in these accounts. For John Cleeves (p 129, l.24) see p 328, endnote to DRO: DC/BFB: Finance: Chamberlains' Accounts f B14. Hugh Macham (p 131, l.18 and p 132, l.14) was chamberlain in 1610–11, 1611–12, 1612–13, 1621–2, 1622–3, and 1623–4 (ff F14, F14v, F15, F18, and F18v). For Thomas Rawlingston (p 131, l.19) see p 329, endnote to DRO: DC/BFB: Finance: Chamberlains' Accounts f B16v. If 'mr Macham' (p 131, l.23) was not Hugh Macham he may have been the 'mr macham,' bailiff in 1592–3, who took a seven-year lease on the play close (see p 329, endnote to DRO: DC/BFB: Finance: Chamberlains' Accounts f B16v) in the same year (f B10v). Edward Macham was a leaseholder in 1595 (f F1v) and a steward in 1604–5, and 'mr macham' was bailiff in 1605–6 (f F10). The 'mrs keynell' who sold hens to the town (p 132, l.1) may have been the wife of Robert Keynell (see p 328, endnote to DRO: DC/BFB: Finance: Chamberlains' Accounts f B14). Thomas Pitt (p 132, l.9) was chamberlain in thirteen of the years between 1607–8 and 1623–4 (ff F12v–F18v). For John Roper (p 132, l.10), see p 330, endnote to DRO: DC/BFB: Finance: Chamberlains' Accounts f B19. For George Harbyn (p 132, l.11), see pp 329–30, endnote to DRO: DC/BFB: Finance: Chamberlains' Accounts f B18v. For Jehonadab Sherlye (p 132, l.13), see pp 328–9, endnote to DRO: DC/BFB: Finance: Chamberlains' Accounts f F5. Robert Swayne (p 132, l.16) was chamberlain in 1608–9, 1609–10, and 1618–19 and bailiff in 1607–8 and 1613–14 (ff F12v, F13v, F14, F15v, and F17v). The 'widdow Gawler' (p 132, l.24) was probably connected to John Gawler, for whom see p 328, endnote to DRO: DC/BFB: Finance: Chamberlains' Accounts f B15v. Several Pitts were active in Blandford political circles and may, like Thomas Pitt, be proposed as the 'mr pitt' who sold bricks to the town for the kitchen used in the 1603/4 race celebrations (p 132, l.36). In 1591–2 John Pitt 'the youngest' was among those running the ales that raised money for the guildhall and he also guarded almshouse money in 1600. John Pitt the elder kept safe the funds for the guildhall in 1592–3 and he is listed among those holding leases from the town in 1595; he loaned money to Blandford in 1595–6, 1596–7, and 1597–8 and served as steward in 1598–9 (ff B10v, B11v, F1v, F3, F4v, and F6v).

133–4   DRO: DC/BFB: Finance: Chamberlains' Accounts   f F9
Drake's copy of Sherlye's account, including the receipts from the race and the women's hocktide collection, is on f B21v.

134   DRO: DC/BFB: Finance: Chamberlains' Accounts   f F11
The races in this excerpt were probably held 23 February–1 March 1605/6 and 8–14 February 1606/7, if our theory that the week-long race meetings were celebrated during Sexagesima week is correct (see pp 329–30, endnote to DRO: DC/BFB: Chamberlains' Accounts f B18v); if the smaller profits of the 1606/7 race represent a shorter meeting it is possible that the races in that year were held 16–17 February. Sir John Rogers (l.18) was a member of a family prominent in Dorset since the early sixteenth century. See, for example, the entries for Sir John's namesake in S.T. Bindoff, *The House of Commons, 1509–1558*, vol 3 (London, 1982), 208 and in Hasler, *House of Commons, 1558–1603*, vol 3, p 302. Five members of the family were Elizabethan MPs for Dorset or Dorset boroughs (Hasler, *House of Commons, 1558–1603*, vol 3, pp 298–9 and 301–3).

134   DRO: DC/BFB: Finance: Chamberlains' Account   f F12v
In 1595 Justinian Whiteinge (l.28) paid rent to the town for a burgage next to the storehouse he was to retain so long as he remained schoolmaster; he agreed to relinquish the lease of the schoolhouse in 1599–1600 (ff F1v and F6v).

134–5   DRO: DC/BFB: Finance: Chamberlains' Accounts   f B22
The account is that of Thomas Pitt and Robert Swayne; immediately preceding the receipts from the players is the note: 'more that is dew by mee for monye *which* hath been in my hand*es* since the last towne reckoninge,' almost certainly Pitt, since he also served as chamberlain in 1607–8. Thomas Pitt is almost certainly the nephew of 'my vnkell Keynell' (p 135, l.1), probably Robert Keynell (see p 328 endnote to DRO: DC/BFB: Finance: Chamberlains' Accounts f B14).

135   DRO: DC/BFB: Finance: Chamberlains' Accounts   f B23v
A note to the town reckoning for 1612–13 indicates that Gawler had not yet settled the debt (f F15).

135   DRO: DC/BFB: Finance: Chamberlains' Accounts   f F14v
The profits of the race referred to in this excerpt suggest that the race meeting was a week-long celebration. If it was and if we are right that such a celebration would not have overlapped the first days of Lent (see pp 329–30, endnote to DRO: DC/BFB: Finance: Chamberlains' Accounts f B18v), then the race was held during Sexagesima week, 16–22 February 1611/12.

136   DRO: DC/BFB: Finance: Chamberlains' Accounts   f B26v
Swayne's house ('my howse,' l.11) was probably used in the 1611/12 race, the last year when Jehonadab Sherlye was bailiff (see p 135, ll.23–4). The detailed accounts for the 1603/4 race record a payment of £14 15s 8d to Swayne (p 132, ll.16–17) as well as a payment of 2s to a workman for two days work about his kitchen (p 133, ll.1–2).

136   DRO: DC/BFB: Finance: Chamberlains' Accounts   f B28v
This relatively unprofitable race meeting may have been held during Sexagesima week, 4–10 February 1615/16, or just possibly on Shrove Monday and Tuesday, 12–13 February (see pp 329–30, endnote to DRO: DC/BFB: Finance: Chamberlains' Accounts f B18v).

137   DRO: DC/BFB: Finance: Chamberlains' Accounts   f F23
J.H.P. Pafford's transcription of references to players in the chamberlains' accounts omits the reference to the 'Children of the Revells' ('Blandford Forum').

138   DRO: DC/BTB: M18/11   f [1]
Presumably Henry Wey and Stephen Shower were the stewards of the ale and submitted their account as such. Both were later elected to more prestigious civic offices, including that of bailiff (Wey for 1555–6, 1559–60, 1563–4, and 1566–7 and Shower for 1564–5, 1568–9, 1572–3, and 1576–7). Judging from expenses noted in the account, money raised by the ale was spent chiefly on the maintenance of the streets. However, it may be that these expenses were not allowed by the borough, for ff [1] and [1v] have both been cancelled by means of an X running diagonally from corner to corner. One problematic item among the receipts is the booth used by the town to raise funds. The booth was probably a canvas-covered stall from which food was sold to patrons of the ale. The proceeds 'for the Bowth' are so high that they must be from the sale of goods rather than from the sale of the booth itself. Because later records of the Robin Hood ale of Bridport include payments for a bower and because one sense of 'booth' was a temporary dwelling made of the boughs of trees, this booth may have taken that form.

138   DRO: DC/BTB: M7/10   ff [1, 1v]
In the first decade of the seventeenth century the parish registers, extant only from 1600 on, note the baptisms of children of the Buckerell clan and one son of a John Owens; however, no other civic records contemporary with this entry shed light on the biographies of William Buckerell (l.33) or 'owyn' (l.35).
    The Jack-a-Lent (l.35) was a figure of a man, set up in Lent in order to be mocked and pelted; as such it served as a ritualistic scapegoat. In this case the Jack-a-Lent was carried about on horseback. Given the ambiguity of 'making,' it is not clear if 'owyn' fashioned the figure of the Jack-a-Lent or conducted the riding of it.

139   DRO: DC/BTB: M7/10   single sheet
Perhaps this Loveredge was of the same family and trade as the Loveredges noted in early seventeenth-century records, who were reimbursed for supplying iron.

139–53   DRO: DC/BTB: M15/11   ff [2–7, 7v–9v]
To build a market house and schoolhouse required a concentrated fund-raising effort on the part of the citizens of Bridport. Wearing collars as signs of their office (p 152, l.30), Henry Browne and George Francke gathered donations in cash or in kind not only in Bridport but also in almost all the parishes surrounding it. Even the journeys to and from neighbouring parishes proved to be profitable as the collectors appealed to travellers whom they met en route for contributions to the cause. The funds so raised covered the travel expenses of the collectors, the costs of materials and labour for building the schoolhouse and market house, and expenditures for food, drink, and musical entertainment for the major fund-raising events, the drinkings on Holy Rood Day (3 May), Ascension Day (24 May), and May Day (1 May), and throughout the weeks after Whitsunday (3 June) and Trinity Sunday (10 June).

The fact that receipts were registered for each of the main streets of the borough (p 148, l.38–p 149, l.2) suggests that the ales were a fund-raising effort that drew wide public support. In *A Respectable Society*, p 5, Basil Short implies that the giving transcended barriers of class: 'Naturally the citizens of Bridport appear first on the list, about 60 of them contributing amounts varying from a penny, no mean sum at that time, to two shillings and sixpence. Those who did not give money gave malt or wheat, while two gave candles and one bacon. The list is headed by Mr Richard Russell, member of the local family from which sprang the Dukes of Bedford. He gave half a crown as did Mr John Pitt. Smaller gifts came from such people as Symond Colfox, shoemaker, John Thresher, barber, William Shuer, roper, and Thomas Triptree, butcher.' Solid support for the venture came from the leading families of the borough: George Francke, William Byshop, John Wey, Robert Miller, Henry Pounde, Richard Hounsell, Stephen Wey, John Pitt, Walter Hallett, John Colfox, Arthur Maynarde, and Nicholas Stratchlighe all served as bailiffs of Bridport during the last fifteen years of the reign of Elizabeth I or the first decade of the reign of James I. Other donors, such as Robert Hassard, Simon Colfox, Christopher Davige, William Shower, John Miller, and Richard Colfox, were kin of others who served the borough in that capacity (Hutchins, *History and Antiquities*, vol 2, p 10). Morgan Moone was probably related to Gilbert Moone (alias Holman), bailiff with John Pitt at the time of the building ale; Morgan Moone also enjoyed the status of officer in charge of weighing hemp, a product crucial to Bridport's economy (DRO: DC/BTB: PQ/28 p 94).

Lady Stourton (p 141, l.21) was probably Frances, daughter of Sir Thomas Tresham, knight, wife to Edward, tenth Lord Stourton, and lady of nearby Chideock Castle and manor (Hutchins, *History and Antiquities*, vol 2, pp 254, 257–8). She was one of the most generous benefactors of the project. Because of her provision of the stone, taken from her quarries near the top of the hill just west of Bridport, the total cost of the building was approximately £21 (Short, *A Respectable Society*, p 5).

Apart from residents of Bridport, of those contributing to the ale the easiest names to identify are those of well-to-do visitors from the many nearby towns and villages.

The 'vicer of porestock' (p 141, l.13) may have been Henry Browne, presented to the living at Powerstock cum Bampton (now Bothenhampton) in 1567 (Hutchins, *History and Antiquities*, vol 2, p 322). Nicholas Browne and Edmund Browne (p 141, ll.15–16) received a lease for a term of years for a holding called Mappercombe or 'Brown's farm' in Powerstock parish in 21 Elizabeth (1578–9); Nicholas Browne purchased the freehold to the farm for £1367 in the reign of Charles I (Hutchins, *History and Antiquities*, vol 2, p 320).

John Waddon of Bradpole (p 141, l.42) is probably the John Waddon of 'Broppole' whose will was registered in the records of Canterbury for 1599; similarly, a Lionel Browne of 'Brapol' (p 142, l.6) left a will recorded for 1621 (*Calendar of Dorset Wills Proved in the Prerogative Court of Canterbury, Somerset House, London 1383–1700*, George S. Fry (ed) (London, 1911), 15). Richard Newborough, gentleman (p 142, l.11), was probably related to the Newburgh family, who held the manor at Bradpole in the time of Henry VIII (Hutchins, *History and Antiquities*, vol 2, p 155).

Richard Justee (p 142, l.18) is likely the Richard Justice who was instituted as vicar of Loders in 1579 and perhaps held the living until 1596 when William Odell was vicar (Hutchins, *History and Antiquities*, vol 2, p 312). John Browne (p 142, l.19) is probably the gentleman of that village who died in 1597. The inventory of his goods made on 25 March 1597, printed by Hutchins, includes a great deal of livestock and several leases. The total was valued at £455 4s 8d. Robert Larder, gentleman (p 142, l.17), was one of the appraisers of his goods (*History and Antiquities*, vol 2, p 307).

'Mr Newboroughe' of Netherbury (p 143, l.1) may have come from a family of Newburghs of Worth Francis, a holding within the parish of Netherbury; members of the family also came to hold Hurlands, a freehold tenement in the Netherbury manor of Yondover (Hutchins, *History and Antiquities*, vol 2, p 109).

From 1561 to 1639 Richard Egerdon or Eggerdon (p 143, l.29) held a manor and hamlet called South Eggardon about a mile northeast of the little village of Askerswell (Hutchins, *History and Antiquities*, vol 2, p 175); Christopher Darby or Derby (p 143, l.33) was buried in 1603, according to the parish register (Hutchins, *History and Antiquities*, vol 2, p 176); according to Hutchins there are numerous entries in the Askerswell parish register 'relating to a family named Hardy, some of whom lived at the neighbouring hamlet of North Eggerdon in Litton Cheney parish and others at Hembury in this parish' (Hutchins, *History and Antiquities*, vol 2, p 176).

According to Hutchins the parish register of Symondsbury tells us that Arthur Fowke, gentleman (p 144, l.1), married Joan Darby on 5 August 1594 and had a daughter in 1601; Arthur died in 1610 (Hutchins, *History and Antiquities*, vol 2, pp 242–3). Doctor Edmund Hound, DD (p 144, l.10), was presented to the living at Symondsbury 15 February 1583; Hutchins tells us that local traditions say he hanged himself in his cellar; he was buried in 1597 (Hutchins, *History and Antiquities*, vol 2, pp 243–4).

A Thomas Egerdon, gentleman (p 145, l.3), who held the estate of Brodenham in the Netherbury manor of Yondover in 1626, may more tentatively be suggested as the Thomas Egerdon who gave a peck of wheat to the Bridport building ale (Hutchins, *History and Antiquities*, vol 2, p 109). Thomas Gollop, gentleman (p 145, l.14), of North Bowood, near Netherbury, appears in local records associated with different properties in the parish from 1578–9 until his death 7 April 1610 (Hutchins, *History and Antiquities*, vol 2, p 113).

At Chilcombe in 1576–7 Richard Martin was licensed to alienate a moiety of the manor, valued at £7, to John and Humphrey Byshop (p 145, l.34); over the door of the mansion house is carved '1578, John Elnor Bishop' (Hutchins, *History and Antiquities*, vol 2, p 739).

John Hayes, gentleman, was mayor of Lyme Regis (p 146, l.20) at the time of the Bridport ale. Several of the names listed at Lyme Regis may refer to others who served as mayor of the borough: 'mr Belmy' (p 146, l.21), for example, may be John Bellamy, deputy searcher and mayor in 1581–2 and 1591–2; 'mr barons' (p 146, l.22) may have been Robert Barnes, merchant, mayor in 1598–9; 'mr Davy' (p 146, ll.23, 36), may have been John Davey, mariner, and mayor 1589–90 and 1596–7 or Robert Davey, mayor in 1583–4; Richard Norris (p 146, l.24) was mayor in 1597–8 and again in 1605–6; Anthony Moone (p 146, l.25) was mayor in 1608–9; 'mr Iurden' (p 146, l.26) may be either John Jourdain, mayor in 1577–8 and 1584–5, or Silvester Jourdain, Cobb warden in 1590 (see p 366, endnote to DRO: DC/LR: G1/1 pp 140–1). For the most accurate list of mayors of Lyme Regis, see George Roberts, *Lyme Regis*, pp 45–9.

Dr James (p 151, l.5) was likely Dr Francis James, LLD, who was vicar general of Bristol diocese and a Dorset MP (see Levack, *Civil Lawyers*, pp 243–4). Locke (p 153, l.13) was perhaps Thomas Locke, named in 1590 in the list of Bridport tanners and shoemakers. In 1609/10 he (or perhaps his son, or at least his namesake) is listed as a shoemaker in a register of sales of leather (DRO: DC/BTB: O1, art 2) and may be the Thomas Lack of Bridport, shoemaker, named as a defendant in the Star Chamber case of Miller et al v. Maries et al (PRO: STAC 8/214/2; see below pp 154–60). Robert Wey (p 153, l.18) may have been related to John and Gregory Wey, feltmakers; the former, along with two others in the family, Henry and William, held a number of important civic offices in the late sixteenth and early seventeenth century. The 'frethinge' (ie, fretting; p 153, l.18) of the bower suggests that it was a set constructed of lattice interlaced with boughs. This bower may have served the same purpose as the booth (see p 138, l.18 above and endnote) used in the Robin Hood ale.

The king of Loders (p 152, l.33) was probably a summer king, the central figure in a folk custom of Loders, a parish about two miles northeast of Bridport. Although the appearance of this character added to the expenses of the ale, it almost certainly added also to the fun and the profits. So too did the musicians, who received liveries and a generous reward (p 151, l.21; p 153, l.11) probably because they performed on more than one occasion. For further discussion of the various aspects of the ale and the importance of the market house and schoolhouse (which were probably in the vicinity of St Andrew's Church) to the economic and social well-being of the borough, see Short, *A Respectable Society*, pp 4–7.

153   DRO: DC/BTB: M18/10   ff [1, 3]

Although the manuscript has no heading by which to date it, it includes a reference on f [2] to 'Mr. baylie davidge.' According to the Great Red Book of the borough (DRO: DC/BTB: H1, p 364), Richard Davige served as bailiff in 1 James I, from Michaelmas 1602 to the same feast in 1603. King James I acceded on 24 March 1602/3 and he was crowned in London on 11 July, though his royal entry into London was postponed until early the next year. Davige would have been bailiff at the time of the July coronation, which Bridport celebrated with ringing and feasting. 'Mr Tiggins' (l.31) is presumably either Richard Tiggyns, or Tigens, Sr, merchant, or his son and namesake. This family was a prominent one, for a Richard Tiggins (specifically Richard Tiggins, Sr, in 1585) was elected bailiff of the borough ten times between 1552–3 and 1590–1 (Hutchins, *History and Antiquities*, vol 2, p 10).

154   DRO: DC/BTB: C88   f 23

This is part of the settlement of the several children of John Maniford. Thomas' two sisters were bound to masters on the same day although their covenants were concluded and Thomas' was not.

154–60   PRO: STAC 8/214/2   mb 4

Miller v. Maries provides a good illustration of the divisive force of Puritanism in Bridport, for the case pits members of some of the borough's oldest and most powerful families against one another. As John Hutchins' list of bailiffs indicates, several of the litigants had been elected to this important civic office by this time, or would be: of the plaintiffs, Robert Miller (1605–6, 1609–10, 1614–15, 1624–5), Angel Churchill (1634–5), John Chard (1604–5), William Whettam (1618–19, 1623–4, 1634–5), and Walter Hussey, alias Baylie (1633–4, 1636–7, 1640–1); of the defendants, John Lea (1631–2, 1635–6, 1639–40) and Thomas Lack (1617–18); and of those named in the first libel, Thomas Merefeild (1626–7, 1630–1, 1638–9), John Byshop (1622–3, 1626–7, 1629–30, 1636–7, 1641–2), and Christopher Balstone (1619–20) (*History and Antiquities*, vol 1, p 10). An ordinance of 4 January 1631/2 for the wearing of gowns epitomizes the status that many of the men involved in this case would enjoy by that time. The ordinance (DRO: DC/BTB: H5) has been endorsed by William Whettam, John Byshop, Thomas Lack, Walter Baylie, John Lea, Thomas Merefeild, and 'Churchell'; other signatories may have been kin of those involved in Miller v. Maries: Stephen Colfox, William Wey, Thomas Byshop, and John Miller. William Maries, the principal defendant, did not, judging from extant records at least, hold a major civic office but the borough did reward him in 1614–15 for training in the town's armour (DRO: DC/BTB: M8/10 f [2]) and paid him muster wages from the account of William Whettam, cofferer, in 1620–1 (DRO: DC/BTB: M8/203 f [2v]). That William Maries, a major figure in Bridport's muster, should find himself at odds with the town's Puritan faction suggests that we may have in this case what Underdown found in the Star Chamber case of John Condytt v. Matthew Chubbe, both of Dorchester – increasing tension between citizens committed to religious reform and citizens attached to the customary celebrations of their borough; see *Fire from Heaven*, especially pp 23–37, and below pp 161–3.

Although the bill of complaint submitted by Robert Miller and the other plaintiffs does not establish that local ceremonies or celebrations were a basis for conflict, it does make clear that religion, social order, and economics were. The plaintiffs claim that those accused of libel are jealous of their (the plaintiffs') prosperity and accuse the defendants of defying the civic authorities, attempting to contain the dissemination of the writings in question. At the same time the plaintiffs affirm that their religious observances have the approval of the Church of England. The first libellous poem transcribed in the bill of complaint portrays the plaintiffs as a group which, under the cover of a religious gathering, indulges in licentious, adulterous jollity. The mockery of the poem extends to include not only the wives but also, it seems, some of the daughters of the religious reformers; 'Buckerelles trulls' (p 155, l.33) are likely the twin daughters of Richard Buckerell, who were baptized in 1603, according to the parish register. Unlike the first libel, which identifies the subjects of the satire by name, the second poem is far more cryptic. Its central thrust attacks the Puritan faction of Bridport as a whole for their hypocrisy, self-righteousness, and double standards but in its conclusion it takes a distinctive turn when it alludes to the poor quality of cloth and the high cost of shoes. The latter allusion reveals how religious disagreements set shoemaker against shoemaker, defendant Thomas Lack against plaintiffs William Whettam, Thomas Merefeild, and Henry Wey, all of whom are listed with Thomas Lack (not to mention John Lack of Beaminster, tanner, from whom Thomas buys his leather) in the 1609 Register Book for Leather (DRO: DC/BTB: O1, art 2). The involvement of Henry Wey epitomizes the intensity of the religious convictions of some of those involved in this case for on 20 March 1629/30 Henry Wey sailed with his family from Plymouth to Nantucket before settling in Dorchester, Massachusetts (Short, *A Respectable Society*, p 14).

161–3   PRO: STAC 8/214/2   mb 2

This answer of Hugh Syms, Anthony Mathew, and William Marshall occupies mb 2 of the document. The first membrane contains the answer of William Maries and John Lack but it does not elaborate upon the particulars of the case; instead, it asserts the allegations to be groundless and petitions for a dismissal of the charge.

The defence set forth by Syms, Mathew, and Marshall depends upon the social divisions within Bridport. The defendants reaffirm the view expressed in the first libel that the assemblies of the plaintiffs were hypocritical occasions for feasting, drinking, and licentious behaviour. They claim further that the leaders of the faction, Cheverell and Traske, had turned a large number of citizens, many poor and uneducated, against the incumbent parson. Cheverell and Traske were portrayed as the agents of discord. The defendants argue that as there were concerns about Traske, 'a young hot headed and excommunycated Mynister' (p 161, ll.21–2), and about the assemblies at which he preached, the church-wardens of Bridport had presented several of the Puritan faction in the diocesan court. This action of the churchwardens is crucial to the answer of Syms, Mathew, and Marshall, who submit that the libels were written and disseminated by the plaintiffs themselves in order to get revenge against the church-wardens and their associates.

Traske was probably John Traske, a native of Somerset and a schoolmaster there, whom James Montague, bishop of Bath and Wells, judged to be insufficient for ordination. Traske's notoriety increased after he moved to London in 1617, published several works (*Christs kingdome discovered. Or, that the true church of God is in England* (*STC*: 24175.3); *A pearle for a prince, ... Delivered in two sermons* (*STC*: 24176); *The power of preaching. Or, the powerfull effects of the word ... Delivered in one or moe sermons* (*STC*: 24177); *A treatise of libertie from Judaisme, or an acknowledgement of true christian libertie* (*STC*: 24178); and *The true gospel vindicated from the reproach of a new gospel* (*STC*: 24178.5), and ran afoul of the law for preaching that the Jewish sabbath ought to be observed (see Lancelot Andrewes, 'A Speech Delivered in the Starr-Chamber against the Two Ivdaicall Opinions of Mr. Traske,' printed posthumously with other of Andrewes' minor works on pp 63–75 of *Reverendi ... Lanceloti episcopi Wintoniensis, Opvscvla quaedam posthvma* (*STC*: 602)). John Traske was so influential as a powerful preacher and charismatic personality that he was included as the founder of the 'Traskites' in Ephraim Pagitt's *Heresiography*, 6th ed (London, 1662; Wing: P182), 161–97.

163   DRO: DC/BTB: M2/11   f [1]
The Lent assizes normally occurred in February or March each year and the western circuit lasted twenty to thirty days.

163–7   PRO: STAC 8/214/2   mb 3
John Abbot, one of the churchwardens responsible for the presentment of Robert Miller and others of the Puritan faction in the ecclesiastical court, elaborates upon the allegations made by Syms, Mathew, and Marshall that the plaintiffs in this case not only wrote the libellous verses but framed Abbot so as to get revenge against him. Abbot's story clarifies two of the devious methods by which, he alleges, the plaintiffs incriminated him: first, they used persons of lower social status, Mary Willyams, wife of John Willyams, and John Lea, Abbot's apprentice, in order to put the libellous verses into Abbot's hands; second, they used plausible business connections, Angel Churchill being a tailor in need of mercery sold by Abbot, in order to discover the libels in Abbot's possession and to prompt him to read them publicly.

167   DRO: DC/BTB: M2/9   f [3]
Richard Colfox, apparently acting as a serjeant in this case, does not appear elsewhere in the Bridport records. The Colfox family was a very important one, however: Francis Colfox is identified in 1577 as a victualler (DRO: DC/BTB: PQ/28 p 66), Simon Colfox as a shoemaker in 1593 (DRO: DC/BTB: B1/7), John Colfox as a shoemaker in 1609 (DRO: DC/BTB: O1, art 2), and William Colfox, Jr, as a glover in 1635 (DRO: DC/BTB: PQ/28 p 92). John Colfox (specifically John Colfox, Sr, in 1590–1) served as bailiff in 1590–1 and 1594–5. The most distinguished member of the family was Stephen Colfox; he, and/or his namesake, was elected bailiff six times, serving in 1609–10, 1613–14, 1616–17, 1622–3, 1631–2, and 1639–40. Indeed, this payment to Richard Colfox appears in the account of the expenditures made by Stephen. See also pp 333–5, endnote to DRO: DC/BTB: M15/11 ff [2–7, 7v–9].

Bridewell was originally a royal palace built between 1515 and 1520 on the west side of the Fleet River where it joins the Thames in London; the location of Bridewell Palace is shown on the map of

Tudor London reproduced by Roy Porter in *London: A Social History* (London, 1994), 39. In 1553 the city took possession of the property and turned the palace into a prison, hospital, and workhouse. However, the name was extended to other gaols or prisons in the London area and in the provinces (*OED*). In this case, 'Bridwell' (l.25) probably refers to the gaol in Dorchester: in the accounts for 1614–15 Farr and his fellows were paid 3s for carrying a man who stole a horse to the Dorchester prison; this sum, comparable to that which Colfox received, implies that the cost of transporting an offender to London would be much higher.

168   DRO: DC/BTB: DE10/3   f [2v]

The handwriting of this document makes it difficult to ascertain for certain what some of the names are. The range of dates given for this entry in the subheading is based upon the earliest and latest dates recorded on f [2v]. Like others on the page this entry is not exactly dated.

169   DRO: DC/BTB: E2/unnumbered   single sheet

This entry was apparently written after the jurors' names; the last lines are written awkwardly to their right. 'hadstock' (l.5) is probably an error for Halstock, a parish about twelve miles north northeast of Bridport. A similar presentment of nineteen Bridport butchers (including William French, Sr) in 1643 (DRO: BTB/E2/ item 1116) indicates that local butchers persisted in killing unbaited bulls and that the borough strove to have its ancient custom observed.

169   DRO: PE/CEA: CW 1/1   f 20

The heading for the account including this entry is 'The Accompte of William Lock and George Hodges, Churchwardens of the said Town Annis Domini 1633 & 1634, which was made in the parish Church aforesaid, before the Inhabitantes the 19 day of Aprill Anno 1635' (f 18). Since the payment following the entry for the dismantled maypole is for 'a booke intituled The Kings Maiesties declaration' (the Book of Sports, re-issued October 1633), and since accounts for 1633 appear later on the folio, it seems likely that the maypole was dismantled in 1633 or 1634. This is the only reference to the Cerne maypole and it seems too slender evidence to support Underdown's assertion that the Cerne Abbas 'maypole survived the earlier Puritan attack, only to be cut down to make a town ladder in 1635, just when maypoles were reappearing in other places after the second Book of Sports' (*Revel*, p 92). Cerne's maypole may indeed have been a survival; it may also have been a 'reappearance' or an isolated celebration. Maypoles may also have been put up and taken down annually and recycled frequently.

169   DRO: PE/CHM: CW 1/1   f 24v

These accounts have survived only in scraps and it is not always possible to establish the context of receipts or payments. It is possible that an entry for 1600 refers to another hocktide gathering. The entry reads: 'Item Receved of the hoockes xv d.' (f 20v).

169–70   STC: 23333   pp 359–60

Stow situates his peculiar account of the entertainments at Corfe Castle between the names of the mayor and the sheriffs appointed in October 1328 (p 359) and the marginal '1329' (p 360). The regnal year is also noted in the margin of p 360 as 'Anno regis 3' (p 170, l.5m), which ran from 25 January 1328/9 to 24 January 1329/30. We have followed Stow in putting the event within the London civic year, Michaelmas to Michaelmas, but the festivities at Corfe Castle could not have occurred after 13 March 1329/30 when the earl of Kent, Edmund of Woodstock, the youngest son of Edward I, was arrested on a charge of treason. Queen Isabella and Mortimer tricked Kent into revealing his abiding loyalty to Edward II and disloyalty to them by spreading the rumours that the late king was still alive. In other versions of these events a friar who conjured up a devil provided the confirmation that Edward II was still alive. Having received confirmation of Edward II's presence in Corfe Castle, Kent initiated a plot to restore the late king, a plot that would lead to his own indictment, arrest, and execution.

170   BL: Sloane MS. 2131   ff 16v–17

Robert Ashley provides a good example of the educational and sometimes useful nature of dramatic performances. The Christmas performance (ll.26–9) was probably in 1574/5, for it was part of the education Ashley received at Corfe Castle, which preceded his schooling in Southampton. He explains on f 17 that his mother sent him and his younger brother, Francis, to Hadrian à Saravia's school in Southampton when Francis was six years old. That would have been in 1575: Ashley provides the date of his brother's birth as 24 November 1569 (ff 16–16v) and notes that he was at the beginning of his fifth year at that time. Ashley goes on to date the move to Dr Hill's school (see ll.30–4) to the beginning of his twelfth year, which would be the fall of 1576, and he studied there for about a year. Therefore the entertainment of the earl of Pembroke would have occurred some time in 1576–7.

   Christopher Hatton (l.20), a royal favourite at this time, was made constable of Corfe Castle by Queen Elizabeth about 1571. He was later appointed vice-chamberlain of the queen's household on 11 November 1578. Sir Henry Herbert, second earl of Pembroke as of 4 April 1570 (l.35), was an abiding benefactor of Salisbury, even after he became president of the Council in the Marches of Wales and relocated from his home base near Salisbury at Wilton, Wiltshire, to Ludlow Castle. His interest in drama found expression in his patronage of players who performed in the provinces throughout the 1590s (see J.A.B. Somerset, 'The Lords President. Their Activities and Companies: Evidence from Shropshire,' *Elizabethan Theatre* 10 (1988), 93–111).

   Hadrian à Saravia ('Hadriano,' l.30) was a protestant divine who fled to the Channel Islands to escape the religious troubles in Brussels in 1560. After several years as a schoolmaster and assistant minister of St Peter's, Guernsey, he became master of the Southampton grammar school. He returned to Belgium about 1576, according to Ashley, and in 1582 he was appointed a professor of divinity at the University of Leiden and pastor of a reformed church there. He went on to get his DD from Oxford and to hold several important ecclesiastical offices in England. Adam Hill (l.32) studied with Bishop Jewel and attended Balliol College, where he earned a BA in 1569, an MA in 1572, and his BD and DD in 1591. He served as vicar in Westbury, Wiltshire, and Gussage, Dorset, before taking up the offices of prebendary and succentor of Salisbury Cathedral, offices he held until his death in February 1594/5.

171–2   Bodl.: MS. Add. B. 97   ff 63–4

The 'Presentment' is an illustration of plays dubbed as a group, 'Christian Terence.' Though written in the metre of Roman comedy, iambic senarii, the prologue does not appear to be, or to introduce, an adaptation of any of Terence's six extant plays; it is more likely an imitation of Terence in Latin by an English schoolmaster, perhaps Robert Cheeke himself. Allusions to works on the curriculum of the students represent one way in which the entertainment celebrates not only the distinguished guests but also the school itself and its endeavours. Apart from Terence the prologue alludes to the dialogues of Cordier at p 172, l.7 (see STC: 5762 for their English translation). The lines 'Sic omne punctum retulit is quj miscuit | Dulcj vtile. &c' (p 172, ll.22–3) are an adaptation of Horace, *Ars Poetica*, 343–4: 'Omne tulit punctum qui miscuit utile dulci, | lectorem delectando pariterque monendo.' This prologue may also be alluding to the controversies about plays and players current in Dorchester at this time, controversies recorded most fully in the case of Condytt v. Chubbe (see pp 177–80).

John Thornborough (p 171, l.8) was bishop of Bristol 1603–17 and, given the pun on his name (p 171, ll.40–2), it is clear that the entertainment was written for him. Although neither the manuscript of the prologue nor any other Dorset documents specifies the precise date of his visit to Dorchester, he did visit Dorset in 1603, as published visitation articles (see pp 48 and 113) indicate, and again in 1609 (a visitation referred to in PRO: STAC 8/15/19 mb 8). As it seems probable that he would have made a visitation of the school early in his episcopacy the date range 1603–10 has been assigned to this text.

Robert Cheeke ('ye SchoolMaster Sheeke,' p 171, l.11) came to Dorchester in 1595 to be master of the Free School and in 1617 he succeeded William Cheek as rector of All Saints. Puritan in his sympathies he was a generous, well-liked member of the community. He oversaw the rebuilding of the Free School in 1618 and the founding of Trinity School in 1623, the year in which his students presented plays for Bishop Wright during his visitation.

173–9   PRO: STAC 8/94/17   mb 19

The bill of complaint was filed, with an attached copy of the libels as exhibits, on 21 April 1608 but the bill and its attachments must have been composed and written earlier. The original copy of the bill appears on mb 19, that of the libels on mbs 20–2. A second copy of the bill, which occupies mb 10, is incomplete (it deletes the formulaic conclusion, p 178, l.40–p 179, l.6) and is signed by the defendants' attorney; it is probably an administrative copy, to which the second copy of the libels (mbs 12–13) was attached, made for the commissioners who took the formal answers of Matthew Chubbe and other defendants. Because mb 19 served as the outside cover for much of the document when the membranes were joined together and folded for storage, it is more damaged than other membranes. Many words and phrases apparently lost as a result of damage were read under UV light and are enclosed in diamond brackets.

This case of Condytt et al v. Chubbe et al is one of the main sources of information about the social history of Dorchester in the early seventeenth century. The case is fundamental to Underdown's indispensable study of the town, *Fire from Heaven*; see pp 27–37 where he uses the case to establish the character of Dorchester's governors and their milieu. He also draws on the case, specifically the account it gives of the 1607 visit of Berkeley's men to Dorchester, in his broader study of the southwestern counties, *Revel, Riot and Rebellion*, pp 56–8. In Underdown's view, 'The conflict between Chubb and the reformers was one for the town's very soul: for its entire moral and spiritual character' (*Fire from Heaven*, p 38). John Condytt was one of these reformers, 'orthodox members of a protestant Church of England' whose 'beliefs demanded a constant striving after salvation, a refusal to compromise with sin and human fallibility, and required them to press on with building the new Jerusalem, the task that God had marked out, above all others, as their destiny' (p 22). On the other hand, Matthew Chubbe and his circle, according to Underdown, 'stood for an old conception of neighbourliness, of community harmony, of a social order held together by an interlocking network of mutual obligations joining people of all ranks and conditions. At the top, the rich – wealthy burgesses in the towns, prosperous gentry in the countryside – would provide hospitality and charity to whomsoever they chose, in the mythical good old way, not simply to those who were deserving because they were godly and well connected' (p 32). Traditional festivities, local customs, and public performances by travelling players were among the occasions where these opposed forces clashed in early seventeenth-century Dorchester. For the following notes on persons involved in this case we are indebted to the works of David Underdown already noted and to 'Appendix 5: Biographical Notes' of the Dorset Record Society edition of William Whiteway's diary (see Documents, pp 62–3).

The principals in this case were well-established citizens of the borough. John Condytt was a Puritan tailor of Dorchester who was in 1608 on the brink of greater prominence in the borough: constable in

1616, serjeant at mace in 1624, beadle of the company of freemen 1629–30 (in which year he also assisted with the negotiations for the town charter), serjeant at arms 1634 – all of which positions brought him into direct opposition with more festive inhabitants of Dorchester. Matthew Chubbe, goldsmith, was Dorchester's wealthiest man and perhaps its most powerful. One of the burgesses of the town by 1583, he 'was bailiff for the first of several times in 1588, and in the next twenty years he held that and every other possible town office with great regularity' (Underdown, *Fire from Heaven*, p 24). See also L.J. Chubb, 'Matthew and Margaret Chubb,' *SDNQ* 28 (1961–7), 213–18, 230–5, and Underdown, *Fire from Heaven*, pp 23–37, especially p 34. Margaret Chubbe, widow of Matthew in 1617, reaffirmed in her will of 1625 his values, values which included hospitality and philanthropy. She made very generous bequests to the Women's Almshouse (which became known as Chubb's Almshouse) and the New Hospital.

John White (p 173, l.17) was the powerful, influential rector of Holy Trinity parish from the time of his appointment in 1606 until he fled to the Savoy after his house was plundered in 1642. Besides David Underdown, *Fire from Heaven*, passim, see Rose-Troup, *John White*. Matthew Chubbe defends himself against this specific claim that he had quarrelled and wrangled with preachers by adverting to his provision for, and hospitality toward, them, both preachers of the town and visiting ones. He counters the claim that he and John White were at odds by arguing that he and the rector had effected a reconciliation. Underdown remains skeptical of Chubbe's sincerity in these efforts; see *Fire from Heaven*, pp 34–6.

The records of this case refer to two men named John Adyn (p 173, l.20; p 190, l.26). One is a co-complainant with Condytt and others. The other is the late John Adyn, brewer, who was a long-standing member of Dorchester's élite, being a burgess from the 1580s and a bailiff as early as 1582–3. That he was one of Chubbe's circle is evident from the fact that Chubbe and others were trustees for his estate. Robert Adyn, brother of the late John and brother-in-law of Nicholas Vawter, was a Roman Catholic frequently incarcerated in the Dorchester gaol because of his refusal to conform to the religious authorities of the day. Robert Adyn objected to the view that Christ died not for the sins of all people but for those of the elect only. To refute this view and to defend 'the most meritorious passion of Christ' (p 197, l.32) he admits that he wrote 'To the Counterfait Company and packe of Puritans.' Another teaching that divided the parties to this suit appears in the allegation that Chubbe accept the popish doctrine that people could be saved by meritorious works, an allegation he dismisses in his answer to the bill of complaint (p 190, ll.3–5).

Sir George Trenchard (p 174, l.23) of Wolveton, just north of Dorchester, was an important benefactor of the town. A justice of the peace, he sat as Dorchester's MP in 1572 and assumed the office of recorder in 1610.

William Perkins ('Parkins,' p 175, l.4; 1558–1602) was a fellow of Christ's College, Cambridge, from 1584 to 1594. A prolific writer and an influential preacher, he addressed himself to the very issues that, according to this Star Chamber case, divided White and Condytt from Chubbe; see, for instance, *De praedestinationis modo et ordine* (Cambridge, 1598; STC: 19682), translated into English in 1606 (STC: 19683); *A treatise of Gods free grace and mans free will* (Cambridge, 1602; STC:19750); and *A treatise tending vnto a declaration whether a man be in the estate of damnation* (London, c 1588; STC: 19752). For Robert Cheeke, the schoolmaster, see p 339, endnote to Bodl.: MS. Add. B. 97 ff 63–4.

Like other plaintiffs in libel suits, John Condytt and his co-complainants try to prove that the defendants 'published' their libellous works. They 'published' them in the sense of making them public, in this case not through printing and distribution but through the preparation of several manuscript copies of the verses and through the public reading of them. The market cross, like the other sites noted in the bill of complaint (the Common Hall and St Peter's Church), was central to the borough; it stood where South Street widened just before the junction with the main east-west road, West Street. For this and the other locations, see the inset map of the town on the map (p 108). The inn at which Berkeley's men performed (p 177, l.32) was probably the George Inn, Dorchester's 'finest hostelry' according to Underdown (*Fire from Heaven*, p 36). Destroyed by the fire of 1613, the George was rebuilt when Matthew Chubbe, through some shady dealing, acquired its lease in 1617.

179–83   PRO: STAC 8/94/17   mbs 20–2

'Tall sturdy Puritan knave' (p 179, l.14–p 180, l.10) includes the only specific evidence in the Dorset records of direct opposition to players on the part of the Puritan factions. Indeed references to the conflict between Puritans and players provide the structural frame of the piece. The opening lines seem to strike a topical note, as if the author has in mind a published or a performed instance of players calling Puritans 'knaves,' and the conclusion returns to reformist antagonism to 'stage plaiers' and 'trew melody' (p 180, l.8). This last phrase may refer in a general way to the bell-ringing mentioned in the libel, bell-ringing that also seems tied to a particular occasion and a particular dispute setting the author at odds with the schoolmaster, Anglicans with Puritans, indeed Puritans with Puritans. Unfortunately, the records needed to contextualize the apparently topical allusions are not extant. The postscript has been subscribed 'IA'; these initials suggest the possibility that John Adyn, the late brother of Robert Adyn, helped write the verses.

The libels exhibited in this case have little of the salacious humour and explicit bawdy often found in such satires. The attack is chiefly moral: in the second libel ('Yow Puritans all wheresoeuer yow dwell,' p 180, l.14–p 182, l.12) the Puritans, like the Catholics of Spain (p 180, l.5), are mocked for their hypocrisy, pride, treason, and villainy operating under a cloak of purity. Their attire symbolizes the contradictions in their lives for while they shun French bodices stiffened with whale bone, they wear large cambric ruffs, ruffs made of fine, white linen made in Cambray in Flanders (p 180, ll.32–5). Elizabeth Condytt is the chief butt of the satire because of her alleged adulterous solicitude for William Lawrence, clerk, of Winterborne Steepleton. In the 'lightnes' (see p 187, l.27) or delirium that marked Lawrence's illness, presumably he mentioned Elizabeth Condytt and from that mention the libellers created an affair. Besides the mockery found in the libels (evident in localized verbal play such as the punning on John Condytt's/conduit's name near the end of the third libel, 'To the Counterfait Company' (p 183, l.22)), there is some serious engagement with Puritan ideas, such as the idea that the salvific effects of Christ's passion are limited to the elect and the notion that God is the author of evil. The author of the libellous verses argues that belief in these ideas depends upon a highly selective use of the Scriptures and a stubborn refusal to attend to evidence to the contrary.

183–4   PRO: STAC 8/94/17   mb 17

To convict Chubbe of the particular charge made in the bill of complaint, the plaintiffs try to discredit him by attributing to him a wider range of offences. Interrogatory 12 implies that Chubbe failed to observe policies of the borough in his exercise of his offices. Furthermore, the interrogatories imply that he misused the authority of his office and may have used his wealth in order to advance his own causes and friends.

184–91   PRO: STAC 8/94/17   mb 18

The strategy of Matthew and Margaret Chubbe is to distance themselves both from the composition of the libels and from their dissemination. They begin by arguing that they are not the first to be accused of writing these libels. John Condytt, the Chubbes maintain, charged Robert Coker, William Longe, Lawrence Darby, and William Palmer with libel and then, to Condytt's discredit, dropped the charges after receiving £12 from the defendants. The records of Dorchester contain little else about these particular men but all were members of old and fairly prosperous families of the town; the complaint against them does not appear to survive. Matthew and Margaret Chubbe also distance themselves from the discovery of the verses. The first libel, beginning 'Tall sturdy Puritan knave,' provides the most elaborate example of this ploy, for this libel supposedly reached Matthew Chubbe's hands only after it had been found by a butcher's boy, passed on to the young Gervais Scrope, and relayed by him to Margaret Chubbe. Mediating between the origin of the libel and Matthew Chubbe are people different from him in class, age, and gender. That construction of events was, however, understandably biased in the Chubbes' favour. Gervais Scrope was not only a student boarding with the Chubbes but also the son of Sir Adrian Scrope, Chubbe's landlord and his companion at the performance of the play by Berkeley's men. The second libel, beginning 'Yow Puritans all,' was also 'found,' by the poor shoemaker Thomas Foy, who passed it on to Matthew Chubbe. The only libel that Chubbe himself found, that entitled 'To the Counterfait Company & packe of Puritans,' is almost immediately attributed to Robert Adyn, who confesses that he wrote it. Matthew Chubbe counters the claim that he and his wife disseminated the libels by arguing that they passed them on but only to civic officials who would recognize their damaging potential and curtail them. With the second libel, for example, Matthew Chubbe claims that he brought it to the attention of Richard Barker. Barker, constable at this time, was a shoemaker, and a successful one, a burgess of the town in 1593, and a capital burgess by the time of his death in 1621. Similarly with the first libel, the Chubbes report that they retrieved a copy of the libel from the young Mr William Willyams despite resistance on his part and passed it on to his father, a justice of the peace, Sir John Willyams. Sir John Willyams, of Herringston south of Dorchester, was head of an old and influential family with substantial holdings of property in Dorchester. Following his death in 1617 the family clashed with local authorities, a conflict exemplifying the changing relations of townsfolk and gentry; see *Fire from Heaven*, pp 157–8. Matthew Chubbe invokes Sir John Willyams to assist his defence in another way, which depends in part upon establishing his connections with the gentry, particularly those occupying positions of authority, such as Sir John Willyams, JP. Moving in the circles of Sir John Willyams, Sir Francis Ashley, Sir Adrian Scrope, and Sir George Trenchard, Chubbe could hardly be adjudged to be the libellous, heretical malefactor of Condytt's allegations. In response to the charge that Matthew Chubbe facilitated a performance by Berkeley's men, the defendant distances himself from the event by affirming a kind of personal diffidence, a waning desire for stage plays.

192–3 PRO: STAC 8/94/17 mb 2
The interrogatories on mb 2 shed additional light on two aspects of the case. The eleventh interrogatory, for instance, specifies the reason that Margaret Chubbe informed the Condytts' maidservant of a libel in which Lawrence of Steepleton and Elizabeth Condytt were both named; the aim is a good one of course – 'so as the author might the sooner be founde out.' Similarly, interrogatory 18 implies that Matthew Chubbe was not merely diffident about the proposed performance by Berkeley's men but actively opposed, for, he claims, he refused to pass on to them the key to the town hall.

193–4 PRO: STAC 8/94/17 mbs 7, 8
Through their interrogatories the plaintiffs seek to establish evidence of a very different Matthew Chubbe from that in his submissions. Whereas he claimed that he did what a civic officer should do to contain the damage that might be done by the first libel ('Tall sturdy Puritan knave'), the fourth interrogatory

implies that Chubbe looked forward to the song that was to be made of the libel and failed to arrest the perpetrator of it even though he boasted that he could do so 'with a wette finger' (p 193, l.26), that is, easily, as easily as determining which way the wind blows. Whereas Chubbe portrays himself as acting responsibly once the libels reached his hand, interrogatory 8 implies that he acceded to his wife's desire to hear the first libel, fetched it for that purpose, passed it on to a boy (presumably Gervais Scrope), and stood by while he recited all or part of the work. Whereas Chubbe claims that he read the second libel ('Yow Puritans all') in a low voice at Richard Blatchford's house, which happened to be near the market cross (see above, p 187, ll.38–9), interrogatory 12 implies that he read it loudly at the market cross. Whereas Chubbe explains that he had to meet with Robert Adyn because he was the administrator of the goods of Robert's late brother, John Adyn (p 190, ll.26–9), interrogatory 20 implies that Matthew Chubbe and Robert Adyn were kindred spirits and that Chubbe entertained Adyn even when he knew that Adyn was the author of the libellous verses. Whereas Chubbe pretends to indifference concerning the performance by Berkeley's men (see above, p 191, ll.2–8), interrogatory 21 characterizes Chubbe as an energetic sponsor, one prepared to defy both the rules for the proper observance of the sabbath and the civic authorities enforcing them. Finally, whereas Chubbe portrays himself as a generous citizen and a dutiful civic official, interrogatory 23 makes him out to be a usurer, exploitative of others and disrespectful of his social superiors. If these interrogatories were drawn up several months after the bill of complaint and the submission of the defendants' answers, the Condytts' implicit allegation of Chubbe's 'sceasing of horses' (in interrogatory 23) would have been informed by personal experience. Matthew Chubbe was commissioned on 21 August 1607 (5 James I) as constable of Dorchester to conscript horses to help carry provisions to Salisbury for the entertainment of the monarch there. Chubbe used his authority to seize the horse of John Condytt but Condytt, thinking that Chubbe was taking the horse because of a small debt that Condytt owed Chubbe, resisted. As a result Chubbe filed a bill of complaint against Condytt in the Court of Star Chamber (PRO: STAC 8/104/10). In his answer to the charge Condytt argued the plausible case that Chubbe had taken the case to Star Chamber in order to get even for Condytt's earlier libel suit against Chubbe. Concerning Chubbe's usury, see J.H. Bettey, 'Matthew Chubb of Dorchester: Rapacious Moneylender and Benevolent Philanthropist,' *PDNHAS*, vol 112 (1991 for 1990), 1–4.

Robert Adyn, whose answer to the charges appears on mb 9 (see pp 195–8), defends himself more boldly than the Chubbes. He begins by demeaning the Condytts as lower class (the corollary of Matthew Chubbe's effort to cast himself as an associate of civic authorities and leading families) and relatively poor. The second quality coheres with Adyn's accusation that the Condytts profited by charging another group with libel and wished to turn this case to account too. What makes Adyn's defence distinctive is its redefinition of the writings themselves as 'Pamphelettes or Invectiues,' which he claims are directed against enemies of the state and the established church, 'such as are the Purytans or Brownistes' (p 195, l.39). By this construction Adyn appears to be not a dangerous Catholic recusant but a champion of church doctrine and state authorities. His redefinition of the libellous poems also informs his confession that he wrote the third piece, 'To the Counterfait Company & packe of Puritans,' which he sees as his contribution to a debate provoked by a particular sermon by John White.

194–5   PRO: STAC 8/94/17   mbs 3, 4
The testimony of Thomas Buckler (p 194, l.31–p 195, l.3) and that of Hugh Haggard (p 195, ll.8–19) help Chubbe in his defence against the allegation that he facilitated the performance by Berkeley's men. The latter states that Sir Adrian Scrope proposed that the players perform at his room in the inn and invited Matthew Chubbe to attend the performance; the former confirms that Chubbe attended the

interlude to satisfy Scrope's request. Francis Kyrton of Almsford, Somerset, describes on mb 5 a reconciliation between Matthew Chubbe and John White, thereby providing the only corroboration of Chubbe's claim to that effect (p 190, ll.16–19) and countering the evidence to the contrary submitted by witnesses on behalf of the complainants (mb 6).

198   BL: Harley MS. 6715   f 6v
Gilbert Reason is identified as one of the members of Prince Charles' company in its patent of 1610. This record of his work in the provinces antedates those noted by G.E. Bentley in his note on the actor in *The Jacobean and Caroline Stage*, vol 2 (Oxford, 1941), 541–3.

199   BL: Egerton MS. 784   ff 34, 35
In his diary William Whiteway notes a wide range of events that interested him, some of which occurred in Dorset, specifically in Dorchester, and others (such as this arrest of the ballad singers) that took place in London.
     Robert Wright (l.13) was bishop of Bristol from 1623 to 1632. For his entertainment with plays Dorchester had a precedent since Robert Cheeke had directed his boys in a theatrical presentation for Bishop Thornborough; see pp 171–2 for the earlier entertainment and p 180, ll.7–10 for Cheeke's inclusion among the Puritans of Dorchester in the libellous verses attached to the bill of complaint in Condytt et al v. Chubbe et al.

199   DRO: DC/DOB: 8/1   f 33
Lewes visited Dorchester on his second trip into the southwest of England. Six or seven days after Christmas Lewes had set out from Swansea and travelled to Bristol, to Bridgwater, and then on through Devon before returning home by sea. Having borrowed more money from his mother he left Swansea again and travelled into Dorset via Taunton and then proceeded eastward as far as Salisbury. Lewes refers to these events as taking place on 'the next day' and 'monday' (ll.25–6): he had spent the previous Sunday at Beaminster en route from Chard in Somerset to Dorchester.

200   BL: Egerton MS. 784   f 79v
The puppeteers who were not allowed to perform in Dorchester were likely John and William Sands (or Sandes) and company; see pp 121–2 for a fuller account of their conflict with the local authorities at Beaminster.

200   DRO: DC/DOB: 8/1   f 79
Underdown notes that Edward Hill (l.19) was one of the borough's notorious drinkers, one who in his later years would support the royalist cause during the Civil War (*Fire from Heaven*, pp 74, 206).

201–2   DRO: DC/DOB: 8/1   ff 97–7v
William Hutchins (p 201, l.12), a Dorchester butcher, was normally antagonistic to the forces of protestant reform in the borough; on the Hutchins family, see Underdown, *Fire from Heaven*, p 163. 'Thomas Grudham' (p 201, l.15) may be Thomas Grindham; see pp 347–8, endnote to DRO: DC/DOB: 16/4 f [18v].

202   BL: Egerton MS. 784   f 87
Dr William Butts, master of Corpus Christi 1622–32 and vice-chancellor of the university for a third

term, took his own life on Easter Sunday, 1 April 1632, following a performance on 19 March of Peter Hausted's play, *The Rival Friends*. For additional information about the performance, the pressures impinging upon Butts, and the controversy attendant upon the play, see Alan H. Nelson (ed), *Cambridge*, REED (Toronto, 1989), vol 1, pp 637–43 and vol 2, pp 767, 775, 881–3, 920, 960–1, 1024–5, and 1248–50. Whiteway's entry bespeaks his reformist leanings and the religious debates within the universities for it notes only one of the play's several plots, that satirizing the simony and hypocrisy of Sacriledge Hooke.

202   BL: Egerton MS. 784   f 91

William Prynne's book, *Histrio-mastix* (STC: 20464a), came out in 1633 at which time Queen Henrietta Maria herself was engaged in producing and performing in various theatricals (see Stephen Orgel and Roy Strong, *Inigo Jones: The Theatre of the Stuart Court*, vol 1 (London, Berkeley, and Los Angeles, 1973), 51–7). Prynne drew the Inns of Court into the controversy by identifying himself on the title page of his work as an utter-barrister of Lincoln's Inn and by dedicating the volume first to the masters of the bench of that institution. Prynne also included a second dedicatory epistle addressed to the students of the four Inns of Court and to those of Lincoln's Inn in particular.

203–4   BL: Egerton MS. 784   ff 94, 96

Several documents relating to the dispute concerning ales, revels, and May games are extant; see Stokes with Alexander (eds), *Somerset Including Bath*, vol 1, pp 432–47 and vol 2, pp 976–80. Whiteway errs in attributing the leadership of the opposition to such festivities to Sir Arthur Hopton, who was in Spain from 1629 to 1635 according to the *DNB*. A Ralph Hopton and a Robert Hopton, however, do endorse the petition of the Somerset JPs to Charles I (*Somerset Including Bath*, vol 1, p 444).

The 'booke' (p 204, l.7) set forth by King Charles I was *The kings majesties declaration ... concerning lawful sports*, STC: 9254.7, a reissue of King James I's declaration, published in 1617 for Lancashire, in 1618 (STC: 9238.9) for the rest of the kingdom. An excerpt of the issue of 1633 has been published in Stokes with Alexander (eds), *Somerset Including Bath*, vol 1, pp 446–7. For transcriptions of the King's Declaration in full, see George (ed), *Lancashire*, pp 229–31 and Audrey Douglas and Peter Greenfield (eds), *Cumberland/ Westmorland/Gloucestershire*, REED (Toronto, 1986), 366–8. Whiteway goes on to notice in an entry dated 23 November instant (f 96v) the immediate opposition to the declaration. Mr Ignatius Jourdain, probably the mayor of Exeter, brother of Silvester Jourdain (see p 366, endnote to DRO: DC/LR: G1/1 pp 140–1), though not identified as such by Whiteway) wrote to the bishop of Exeter, then in London, asking that he communicate to the king Jourdain's desire that the declaration be revoked. Bishop Hall showed Jourdain's petition to the monarch, weathered the king's displeasure at the challenge to his prerogative, and replied to Jourdain in a letter sharply 'taxing him for his indiscreete zeale.' Whiteway goes on to record the controversy prompted by the order that the book be read in parish churches: he notes on 11 July 1634 (f 104v) disputes in Winchester, in Somerset, and in Dorchester, where, John White refusing to read it, Mr Holliday did so 'on a friday morning 11. July, none being then at Church, but him, & the Clarke & the Churchwardens.' In an entry of 8 September 1634 (f 107), Whiteway returns to the topic observing that all but two of the ministers in Surrey, who had refused to read the declaration, had been reinstated.

204–5   BL: Egerton MS. 784   ff 98v–9

The Triumph of Peace, by James Shirley, was first performed at Whitehall on 3 February 1633/4. The second performance, that at Merchant Tailors' Hall, had been scheduled for 11 February but was postponed until the 13th. For a discussion of the material in Whiteway's diary in the context of other London records of the second performance of the masque, see McGee, '"strangest consequence",' pp 309–42.

205   DRO: DC/DOB: 8/1   f 210
Three of Buck's companions (Haggard, Penny, and Mrs Wyer) were also examined about this case (f 210) but none of them mentions Buck's dancing.

205   BL: Egerton MS. 784   f 102v
In *A Divine Tragedy* (Wing: B6161), Henry Burton includes a story of this fatal maypole at Glastonbury on 13 May 1634; see Stokes with Alexander (eds), *Somerset Including Bath*, vol 1, p 136.

206   CUL: Dd.11.73   f 148
Whiteway relates a story of a performance of George Ruggles' *Ignoramus.* First presented for King James I on 8 March 1614/15, the comedy was so liked by the king that he requested a second performance on 13 May of that year. Whiteway's entry probably refers to the later performance, by which time the play's satire of lawyers had provoked a heated exchange by writers of ballads and broadsides; in this regard, see Nelson (ed), *Cambridge*, pp 861–78. Whiteway probably received a version of the story from his brother Samuel, a student of Cambridge University from 1631 to 1635, who received reports of the incident from others at the university.

206   BL: Egerton MS. 784   f 110
This French woman without hands is almost certainly Mrs Provoe, wife of Adrian Provoe, whom Norwich licensed on 13 July 1633 to perform her feats with her feet; see David Galloway (ed), *Norwich 1540–1642*, REED (Toronto, 1984), 211.

207   DRO: D/BOC: Box 22   f 13
While Dorchester was Dennis Bond's principal seat he had property in Melcombe Regis, his birthplace, Weymouth, and Buckerell. He also had lands in the Isle of Purbeck, Carans Court in Swanage parish, and Lutton (l.11) farm in Steeple parish, which is about sixteen miles west of Corfe Castle.

207   DRO: DOB: 8/1   ff 312v, 313
William Gosling (l.24) also performed in Norwich; see the records of 28 March 1635 (Galloway (ed), *Norwich*, p 219).
   The two apprentices, Gilbert and Woodes, mentioned in the Meder case (ll.35–7), were also questioned (f 313) but did not confirm that the group was singing.

208   DRO: DOB: 8/1   f 337
On the rambunctious Powncys, butchers of Dorchester, see Underdown, *Fire from Heaven*, especially pp 34 and 163–6.

208–9   DRO: DOB: 16/4   f [18v]
Thomas Grindham, a shoemaker with Puritan sympathies, helped constable Gifford Bale incarcerate the fiddlers. According to Underdown, *Fire from Heaven*, p 160, they did so without a warrant and in the process wrongfully imprisoned one of the Gollop family, who sued them for doing so. Given this

suit, Grindham and Bale had high costs to pay and because they did not have the necessary warrant the borough was reluctant to help to defray them.

209   BL: Harley MS. 6715   f 22v
Joseph Perkins (l.21), clothier of Dorchester, became, in Underdown's terms, 'a notorious delinquent' from about this time on. Here he is implicated in misleading youth, drinking, and dishonouring the sabbath; he would end up facing charges of assault, adultery, and rape. See Underdown, *Fire from Heaven*, pp 67–70.

210   WRO: D5/28/10, item 62   single sheet
This presentment is from Haydon, Dorset, not Haydon, Wiltshire. The Dorset parish is within the jurisdiction of the dean of Salisbury's peculiar as the Wiltshire parish is not; moreover Castleton, the home parish of Anne Vincent and her husband (l.22), is also a Dorset parish (in the dean's peculiar) fairly near to Haydon.

210–11   DRO: QSM: 1/1   f 199v
Sir Nathaniel Napier (d. 1635) was sheriff of Dorset, 1620–1, and deputy-lieutenant, 1625–6, and served as MP for Dorset (1625–6), Wareham (1626), and Milborne Port (1628–9) (*William Whiteway*, p 180). John Whittcombe, DD, is probably John Whetcombe (1580–1635), rector of Maiden Newton, 1610–35 and of Frome Vauchurch, 1620–35 (*William Whiteway*, p 183). The charges William Scot had to face are not known but it seems that he had to face them with three other residents of Hinton Martell for Maurice Harris (f 199), Edward Scott, husbandman, and Alban Weare, tailor (both also on f 199v) are all bound over apparently at the same time as Scot. All four men have the same guarantors that they will answer the charges.
    'Ashgrove' (p 211, l.5) is likely an error for Ashmore, a village near Tollard Royal, Wiltshire, home of William Scot's other guarantor. No Ashgrove could be located in Dorset.

211   DRO: DC/LR: G1/2   p 81
For the dating of this item, see The Documents, p 66.

211   DRO: DC/LR: G1/2   pp 23, 24
On the location of Richard Leonard's house (ll.25 and 33) we know only that it was adjacent to that of John Mores (Morris) for the two were ordered in 1551 to repair the gutters between the two properties. Leonard himself is noticed in the borough records, first in 1538 when he paid 6s 8d toward recovery of the town cross and finally in 1562 when he was sworn a burgess and freeman of the borough. He must have died shortly thereafter because he is not named in a list of freemen a year later and in another suit in 1563 Joan Rixer is identified as widow executrix of the last will and testament of Richard Leonard. Although he lost his liberty of the town in 1540 because of a conflict with the mayor he must have been restored to his privileges since he served as a receiver of the Cobb, probably early in the 1550s.
    The payment for the lord admiral's servants (l.26) was probably for food and drink since the charge is the same as that below for bread and beer laid on for the Stockland men (ll.31–2). Elsewhere on p 24 of the account a payment occurs for someone 'to go to stocklond to warne them to cum to make þe bulwarke'; the Stockland men were clearly labourers rather than performers.

211   DRO: DC/LR: N23/2, item 17   f [1]
The heading of the account specifies the date of its rendering as 2 December 3 Edward VI.

212   DRO: DC/LR: G7/3   f [76]
John Battyn and Richard Leonard were receivers of the Cobb at the time of this performance. Although the account is dated 19 December in the heading, the year of Battin's and Leonard's term is not specified. As a result the date of this account book remains tentative. The account books of receivers of the Cobb are no longer in chronological order; for example, following this booklet is one for 1556, then one for 1557, and then one for 1550. Given the evidence of performances in private homes of prominent citizens it is not unlikely that 'the merere howsse' (l.11) is the mayor's house.

212   DRO: DC/LR: G1/2   p 211
Roger Garland, Richard Hunt, and John Perot were all leading burgesses of Lyme Regis; Garland served as mayor in 1549–50 (and died in office 1561–2), Hunt in 1554–5 and 1558–9, and Perot (mistakenly called 'Barratt' by Roberts (*Lyme Regis*, p 46)) in 1555–6.

213   DRO: DC/LR: G1/2   p 140
Wanklyn, *Lyme Leaflets*, p 39, says that the Sherborne players performed in the church in 'the reign of Mary Tudor.' His confusion may have arisen because the quarter book with this entry is located immediately before one for 1558 and Hassard was mayor both in 1557 and in 1567; however, the heading specifies quite clearly 1567.

214   DRO: DC/LR: G2/2   tab 6
Roberts, *Social History*, p 37, reads 'my L of essetters' (l.17) as 'My Lord of Exeter's' and assigns this and the next three entries to 1569. However, there was no Lord Exeter between 1539 and 1605.

215   DRO: DC/LR: G2/2   tabs 23–4
The ornate initial letter of the patron's name makes it difficult to identify the patron but that letter seems to be a capital 'S' and the word a form of Sussex. Halliwell-Phillipps identifies the players as those of Lord Dorset in *Halliwell-Phillipps Scrapbooks: An Index*, J.A.B. Somerset (comp), REED (Toronto, 1979), 55; Wanklyn, *Lyme Leaflets*, p 20, transcribes the name as 'Sesycks' and identifies the patron as Lord Sussex (but as if uncertain of his own transcription, he also notes a performance by Essex's men, a performance for which we have no evidence in surviving accounts).

216   DRO: DC/LR: G2/2   tab 47
Roberts, *Social History*, p 37, assigns the visits of all these performers to 1589 and adds to the list of troupes rewarded by Lyme Regis that year Lord Sherborne's players, of which players there is no record in extant accounts. He may have incorrectly assigned to 1589 the Sherborne players who visited Lyme Regis in 1567–8 (p 213, l.5); this troupe received the same amount that Roberts says the players of Lord Sherborne were given in 1589.

217   DRO: DC/LR: G2/2   tab 55
John Dutton was regarded as one of the best actors in the realm in 1583, when he was recruited from Oxford's troupe to become one of the founding members of the queen's men. Lawrence Dutton, though apparently not among the first list of the actors in Elizabeth's company, was a member no later than 1589. For the touring of a part of the queen's men under the leadership of the Duttons, see E.K. Chambers, *The Elizabethan Stage*, vol 2 (Oxford, 1923; rpt with corrections 1974), 111–12.

218   WRO: D5/28/9, item 24   single sheet
Little information about the schoolhouse survives; see Wanklyn, *Lyme Regis: A Retrospect*, pp 170–1,
who describes the sixteenth-century school as a room that was part of St Michael's Church and accom-
modated ten or twelve pupils. The 'Infant School' shown directly south of the church on a map of 1841
(reproduced opposite p 262 of *Lyme Regis: A Retrospect* and discussed on pp 242–56) is of later construction; having been renovated for flats, it has since been torn down as well.

218–22   PRO: STAC 8/258/15   single mb
The libel transcribed in this bill of complaint, the bawdiest of Dorset's extant early seventeenth-century
libellous poems, does not seem to have been prompted by animosity between religious factions. The
disagreement appears to be an economic one arising from Robert Salter's efforts as a customs officer.
Several prominent townsmen are caught up in the affair, though the nature and extent of their involvement is not established by the bill of complaint: Robert Hassard, Sr (p 219, ll.21–2), had been mayor in
1601–2, John Hassard (p 219, l.22) would be in 1615–16, Richard Harvey (p 218, l.37) in 1616–17.
John Viney (p 219, l.23) never held high public offices but he became an important figure in the next
decade as an ally of the Puritan vicar, John Geare.

222   WRO: D5/28/11, item 24   f [1v]
Normally we have not included the playing of games in the records but given the cross-reference between
the Whitsunday procession and the playing of 'Cytels' (l.35) in the churchyard these two activities may
have been linked; indeed, the game-playing may have been occasioned by the festive 'carosing' (carousing?)
of the Cobb wardens. 'Cytels' is probably skittles, a game that would certainly have disturbed those
attending church services on Whitsunday morning but playing such games at any time in the churchyard was forbidden. It should be noted, however, that it is not the game-playing but the Whitsunday
procession itself that is judged to be a profanation of the sabbath.

223   DRO: DC/LR: G1/1   p 252
John Jones is identified as a player in the record of the baptism of one of his children in St Botolph's
Aldgate, London. When arrested for a performance at Upton on Severn, Worcestershire, he was travelling with a licence (judged by the authorities to be counterfeit) to set forth 'Motion with dyvers storyes
in ytt As alsoe tumbleing vaulteing sleight of hand and other such like feates of Activety…' (see David
N. Klausner (ed), *Herefordshire/Worcestershire*, REED (Toronto, 1990), 394–5 (words quoted are on p 394);
also quoted by Bentley, *Jacobean and Caroline Stage*, vol 2, p 486).

224   WRO: D5/28/35, item 73   ff [4v–5]
Although the christening of apples (l.14) would seem to be a folk custom that should have a long history, this is the only explicit allusion in extant records to the festivity. The mock muster on Ascension
Day (Tuesday 7 May in 1635) had the regular, officially authorized musters for its precedent. The
drumming and shooting would certainly have been heard by the church-goers, for Mill Green (l.18)
was less than 300 yards northwest of the church and, if the march into or out of town took them down
Coombe Street to Monmouth Street to Church Street, the array would have gone right by the western
door of St Michael's. This presentment establishes three divisive issues: the disrespect for the sabbath
by those who celebrate the christening of apples, the disturbance of the Ascension Day service caused
by William Alford, Jr, and his crew, and the failure of William Alford, Sr, who also served as mayor in
1632, to fulfill his responsibilities as a justice of the peace.

225–9 PRO: STAC 8/153/29   mb 3
The bill of complaint, dated before November 1622, indicates that the first libel was composed in December 1621 or January 1621/2 and the second libel in July or August of 1622. Given John Gordon's schooling at the University of Aberdeen and his office as minister and preacher, this case is likely evidence of factionalism in Melbury Osmond arising from Puritanism. Typical of verses satirizing Puritans, the libellous poems in this case assume that the religious gatherings were occasions for sexual indulgence; hence, the mocking accusations of whoring and cuckoldry.

230 DRO: D/KAT: 7623   f [17v]
This and the following entry are taken from a list headed '⟨...⟩ nots taken out of A boock of accounts be gining ⟨...⟩ the yeare of our Lord – one Thovsand five hundreth forty six. 1546 . for the parish of neitherbury' (f [17v]). The notes may be comments on churchwardens' accounts of St Mary's, Netherbury. These entries are almost certainly the source of Hutchins' assertion that there were references in the records of the manor of Yondover (one of three manors associated with Netherbury) to Robin Hood customs at Netherbury (*History and Antiquities*, vol 2, p 108) since other sections of the manuscript excerpt Yondover presentments; the wording Hutchins gives is very close to the phrasing of this passage. The notes include comments that seem to be later interpretations – the antiquary says, for example, that 'in the raigne of ∧⌜King⌝ Edward the 6. The protistant ∧⌜religion⌝ was established wit∧⌜c⌝h went [⟨...⟩] on slowly but in quene marys raine poperry was quickly set vp againe by which we may see how slowly the worck of reformation go∧⌜e⌝s on in all ages' (f [17v]) – and are almost certainly not verbatim transcriptions.

230 DRO: D/KAT: 7623   f [18]
Most of the dated entries in these notes are in chronological order. The entry on f [18] is, however, preceded by an entry dated 1575 and followed by one dated 1568; hence the dating of the entry.

231 WRO: D5/28/12, item 20   single sheet
The record lacks the detail to be sure that these 'playes' (l.23) were theatrical representations rather than games of some sort. Many of the people involved in this case – John Dier, Robert Beaton, John Arnold, Thomas Michell (or his namesake), James Haim, Henry Jellett ('Henry Gillett,' l.20), and Francis Beere – reappear in the dispute that went to Star Chamber, and others – Nicholas Arnold, Bartholomew Michell, Francis Michell, Giles Beaton, Ralph Bicknell, and John Bicknell – were likely relatives of those drawn into the case of Abington v. Beaton et al (see below pp 231–8).

239 DRO: DC/PL: CLA P23(1)   p 28
Richard Havylond was mayor in 1512–13 and 1519–20. The Havylonds were an influential family in sixteenth-century Poole: men with the surname Havylond or Havyland also served as bailiffs of Poole in 1504–5, 1506–7, 1510–11, and 1516–17 and as mayors in 1498–9, 1502–3, 1506–7, 1514–15, 1523–4, 1526–7, 1529–30, 1533–4, and 1534–5 (DRO: DC/PL: CLA P23(1) pp 13, 17, 19, 21, 25, 31, 33, 36, 41, 42, 46, 53, 57, and 58).

239 DRO: DC/PL: CLA P23(1)   p 32
Thomas Cornyssh (l.27), or Cornyssch, was apparently a town servant. He was paid in 1510–11 for transmitting town money and appears in the accounts in most years between 1515–16 and 1522–3; most frequently he was allotted 3s 4d for a load of hay. He may have been the town serjeant, allowed hay for his horse in 1511–12; the mayor was routinely allotted money for the sergeant's board, room,

and dinner in most of these years. A town memorandum of January 1518/19 records Cornyssh's obligation to pay 20s annual rent for a town cellar. See DRO: DC/PL: CLA P23(1), pp 25–38 and 95.

240   DRO: DC/PL: CLA P46(1)   ff [5v, 7]
'rychard allynys' (l.15) probably refers to the townsman who was in charge of the town ale measures in 1518–19 and who, identified as a brewer, served as Poole's bailiff and keyman in 1520–1. In 1524–5 Richard Allyn was controller (DRO. DC/PL. CLA P23(1), pp 35, 37, and 44) This entry falls between dated payments for 22 August (foot of f [5]) and 8 September (foot of f [5v]).

The payment to the 'syngyng man' (l.26) is included since his performance, at the town masters' request, may have been of secular songs in a secular setting. He may also have sung in the parish church of St James: the town book of accounts routinely records sums remaining in the 'church box' and the names of the 'churchmen,' and sometimes lists inventories of the church valuables. See DRO: DC/PL: CLA P23(1). The entry is added beneath the final total of the main account.

241   DRO: DC/PL: CLA P51(6)   f [4]
St James' Church (l.14) was torn down in 1819.

241   DRO: DC/PL: CLA PA10   f 16
If these badly damaged accounts are indeed those of John Notherell, mayor in 1552–3, as seems probable from the contents, then Notherell regularly refers to himself in the third person; in this case, therefore, he reimburses his wife for payments she made to visiting king's minstrels during his absence from Poole. The accounts might also be those of bailiff Nicholas Jordan (who is also referred to – less frequently – in the third person), but it seems more likely that the mayoress would make payments in the absence of her husband than in the absence of the bailiff.

241–2   DRO: DC/PL: CLA P26(4)   f 57 left
The manuscript is numbered with facing pages bearing the same folio number: hence the designation 'f 57 left.' This folio records miscellaneous expenditures for several years indicated in the left margin; there are several such folios in the manuscript, apparently the product of efforts by John Hancoke, mayor in 1573–4, to put Poole's accounts into some order.

242   DRO: DC/PL: CLA P26(4)   f 57 left
The 'Lordes players' (l.12) are probably those of James Blount, Lord Mountjoy, since the next entry is for hogsheads of wine given to Lord and Lady Mountjoy when they first came to Canford. Poole still fell within the jurisdiction of Canford Manor, held after 1553 by the marchioness of Exeter, who demised the manor in 1558 to her nephew, James Blount, Lord Mountjoy, lord lieutenant of Dorset after 1559. In the 1560s Poole paid considerable sums of money to Lord Mountjoy and his servants in the hopes of obtaining his support for the town's efforts to obtain the privileges granted by the queen in 1568 with the Great Charter (Smith, *History of Poole*, vol 2, p 95).

242   DRO: DC/PL: CLA P26(4)   f 57 left
For Lord and Lady Mountjoy (ll.20–1) see the preceding note and Patrons and Travelling Companies.

242–3   DRO: DC/PL: CLA P26(4)   ff 10 left, 14 right, 18 right
The early part of this manuscript represented an attempt on the part of the newly-made county of

Poole to preserve records worthy of the town's new dignity. In addition to careful, calligraphic script, there is an attempt made to preserve consistent double-entry bookkeeping and an effective index. Hence the '4' (p 242, l.37) just before the lower-case Roman numerals refers to the unfinished f 4 right, on which the entry should have been duplicated. The preceding entry on f 10 left is dated 3 February and the subsequent entry is for 7 March.

The numbers '17' (p 243, l.6) and '19' (p 243, l.12) refer to the double-entry duplicate entries on f 17 left and f 19 left.

243   DRO: DC/PL: CLA PA12 f 9
The payment to players was probably made in February or March 1570/1. Entries on the bottom of f 8v are dated in January and later entries on f 9 are dated May through August.

243–4   DRO: DC/PL: CLA P26(4)   f 52 right
John Rogers (p 243, l.39) was mayor in 1572–3, John Hancoke (p 244, l.1) in 1573–4; the entries seem to be in Hancoke's hand and to be a part of his general clean-up of town finance. The number '88' in the first entry and the number '111' in the second refer to the folios where the duplicate entries appear, required by double-entry bookkeeping. Folio 111 lists outstanding transactions between the town and Mayor John Hancoke.

244   DRO: DC/PL: CLA P106(63) f [4v]
Brownsea Island (l.13) dominates the view from the Poole quays; throughout the sixteenth century Poole was responsible for the ordnance and the fort, fighting men, and miscellaneous aspects of Brownsea's maintenance. In Elizabeth's reign Brownsea fell under the jurisdiction of Sir Christopher Hatton, vice admiral of Purbeck (Lloyd, *Dorset Elizabethans*, p 15). 'mr newman' (l.12) is probably William Newman, merchant, who appears frequently in Poole's records; Newman represented Poole to the queen's council in London in 1574–5 and was mayor in 1576–7. Other possible 'mr newmans' are Nicholas Newman, Poole's water bailiff in 1575–6, and John Newman, who aided Nicholas Newman in matters relating to the armaments at Brownsea in 1574–5 (DRO: DC/PL: CLA P24 ff 6 and 7, P26(4) ff 112 right and 115 right, and PA15 p 13). 'mayster willforde' may be John Gillforde, paid 40s on 17 December 1577 to send commissions from London on the town's business concerning the current inquiry into pirates' goods (DRO: DC/PL: CLA P106(63) f [3]), an identification made more likely by Poole's payment of 'mayster willforde's' expenses in the entry following the one printed here. The town was unlikely to pay for the daily expenses of its own citizens unless they were travelling on town business.

244   DRO: DC/PL: CLA PA15   f 27
For the complex foliation and pagination of this manuscript see The Documents, pp 74. This entry is on the bifolium sewn in the back of the booklet and refers to a charge incurred by John Domyneck with respect to his year as bailiff (for which the account no longer survives). See also p 244, ll.34–7 for more on these expenses.

244–5   DRO: DC/PL: CLA PA15   ff 24v, 25
For an earlier reference to the damage Domyneck did to the drum see p 244, ll.22–3.

245–6   DRO: DC/PL: CLA P124(81)   f [1]
A hole in the manuscript has resulted in short gaps in several lines of text.

This document is best understood in the context of Poole's generally testy response to the requests of the English government in the 1580s. The Crown's attempts to suppress piracy in waters near Poole drew Poole's displeasure, for example, because consolidated prosecutions of pirates came into conflict with Poole's claims to admiralty jurisdiction. Poole was reluctant to bear the cost of keeping the armaments and garrison on Brownsea in good order and the Brownsea gunner and the Poole mariners complain of each other in the 1580s. Numerous documents in the borough archives testify to the borough's perhaps unwilling support of troops and transports for the expedition to Flanders in 1585 and their claims against one sea captain who failed to credit one of their payments. Poole particularly resented the restrictions on shipping which kept her ships in port in 1587 and 1588. Sir Henry Ashley, a scion of an old and prominent Wiltshire family, was one of the commissioners under the authority of Francis Hawley, vice admiral for Dorset, who was responsible for seeing to Dorset's maritime and coastal defences against the anticipated Spanish attack. Poole's accounts record regular payments for Ashley's expenses when he came to town for the muster in the 1570s and 1580s (see, for example, DRO: DC/PL: CLA P26(4) f 92 right for 1573). He died in December of 1588 and his son Henry was MP for Poole in 1589. See the calendar of relevant manuscripts in 'Borough and County of the Town of Poole,' *Calendar of Local Archives*, H. P. Smith and Bernard C. Short (comps), vol 1 (Poole, 1958); Sydenham, *History of the Town and County of Poole*, p 276, n (c); Lloyd, *Dorset Elizabethans*, pp 36–8 and 172.

Of greatest interest to REED readers will be the use to which the maypole is put. Instead of the focal point for celebration this maypole is intended only for target practice. For celebratory maypoles attended by semi-military display see the documents describing an incident at Weymouth-Melcombe Regis, below pp 279–81, and episodes at Keynsham (Somerset) in 1619 and at Wells, 1607, in Stokes with Alexander (eds), *Somerset Including Bath*, vol 1, pp 149, 299–301, 347, and 351, and vol 2, pp 493–4 and 720–1.

246   DRO: DC/PL: CLA P119   f [2]
'mr madley' (l.13) is probably Roger Mawdley, mayor in 1588–9 and 1594–5 (Hutchins, *History and Antiquities*, vol 1, p 34).

246   DRO: DC/PL: CLA P191(A32)   f 1 left
Like DRO: DC/PL: CLA P26(4), this manuscript is foliated with facing pages carrying the same number, hence the designation f 1 left. The cross in the left margin refers to an entry for the same payment on f 4 left in a list headed 'wyllyam bramble oweth the corporation as followeth,' a list of Bramble's payments as mayor disallowed by Poole's auditors. Bramble, mayor in 1601–2, was also compelled to reimburse the corporation for moneys he had spent on preaching and on what the auditors considered were excessive rewards to pursuivants and messengers.

247–8   WRO: D1/2/1   f 134v
The plays and uproar in the churchyard and cemetery which Bishop Simon deplores may have been related to Shaftesbury's annual 'custom' of walking in procession to Motcombe. Because of Shaftesbury's inadequate water supply, the town had made an arrangement by the sixteenth century with the neighbouring village and parish of Motcombe, with the consent of the lord of Gillingham Manor. Shaftesbury was permitted to take water from Motcombe's wells and in return Shaftesbury walked annually in procession to Motcombe on the Sunday following 3 May. According to Laura Sydenham the earliest evidence of Shaftesbury's celebration of this date occurs in 1364 when the crowds coming into the abbey church

for early mass disturbed the nuns so much that Bishop Robert Wyvil transferred the chantry of the altar of the Holy Cross from the abbey church to the parish chapel of the church of the Holy Trinity. See Sydenham, *Shaftesbury and Its Abbey*, pp 48–9 and Hutchins, *History and Antiquities*, vol 3, pp 35–6, 44–5, and 629–30.

248   Hutchins: *History and Antiquities*, vol 3   p 629
Although Hutchins implies that Gillingham Manor was held by only three of Henry VIII's queens, Jane Seymour, Catherine Howard, and Catherine Parr (vol 3, p 616), in 1527 Henry was married to Katherine of Arragon. So, unless Hutchins or his source has assigned the wrong date to this entry, the 'quene's bayliffe' (l.23) must refer to Katherine's official.

248–9   JRL: Nicholas MS 69   f 11
The dating is based on an analysis of the manuscript. Cancelled material at the top of f 11 is a continuation of material ending at the bottom of f 2v, the two parts of the text having been separated by other leaves when the original bifolium was bound with others in a booklet. Other material on f 2v was copied from texts of 1614 and the whole booklet was compiled in 1638.

249   DRO: DC/SYB: E102   sheets 61–5
The manuscript is one of several documents in a lawsuit in the Exchequer between Nicholas Gower of Shaftesbury and Robert Hascoll, Shaftesbury's ex-mayor, concerning the mayor's rights to amerce butchers in the market. Thomas Smelgar's response to the fifth interrogatory is printed here. His response to that interrogatory, and to those of Robert Hascoll and Richard Rives, mayor at the time of the lawsuit, are the only passages that raise bullbaiting as an issue. Rives deposes that he knows nothing of Hascoll or any other Shaftesbury mayor taking beef as a fee or of Nicholas Gower demanding satisfaction of Hascoll; he says Hascoll took small quantities of beef from unbaited bulls before the bulls were sold in the market and distributed the beef to the poor (sheets 30–3). Hascoll states that Gower had questioned his authority to take beef and that he had answered he took it 'by waie of Amerciament according to the Lawes and Statutes of this Realme,' whereupon Gower asked if Hascoll's authority was better than 'the Barons Order' and Hascoll retorted that Gower had no such order (sheets 102–3; Gower referred, of course, to the barons of the Exchequer).

250   DRO: DC/SYB: C11, item 17   single sheet
These are payments of the borough of Shaftesbury for the ceremonies associated with the annual procession to Motcombe. The Sunday after Holy Cross Day fell on 10 May in 1629 and on 9 May in 1630. The scribe may have misdated this brief statement of accounts if the contemporary description of Shaftesbury's custom in the Gillingham Manor manuscript quoted above is correct.

Shaftesbury's financial records are fragmentary, and there is no way of knowing whether the expenditures in 1629 (or 1630) were typical. For a listing of expenditures in 1655 and for a description of the custom in the early Restoration period see Appendix 2.

There has been considerable speculation about the Shaftesbury 'besom' or 'bezant' decorated with ribbons and pins in this account. Quoting a nineteenth-century description of 'the original' bezant, Dorset historian, Charles Herbert Mayo, says its tree-like shape 'bears some relation to the tree which, accompanied by a lion and a bird, appears on the seal of the Borough for warrants, 1570.' See Mayo, 'Shaftesbury Bezant,' pp 297–8 (the words quoted are on p 297).

250   DRO: PE/SH: CW 1/1   f [1]

The first three churchwardens' accounts in the series for All Hallows', Sherborne, are undated. According to CW 1/3, John Chetknoll held the 'kyng Revyll' (p 251, l.19) or church ale in that year. An analysis of the dated All Hallows' accounts demonstrates that it was generally customary for the man who held the ale in one year to become churchwarden two years later. He may have served as junior churchwarden in the interim, for after the parish bought and moved into the former Sherborne Abbey church there were usually two wardens: a man held the church ale in one year, became junior warden the next year, and senior warden in the third year, a pattern that was to remain in practice, with few exceptions, from 1542–3 until at least 1585–6. Since John Chetknoll was churchwarden in 1512–13 (CW 1/4 mb [1]), we can safely assign CW 1/3 to 1510–11.

Internal evidence suggests that CW 1/1 and CW 1/2 are earlier than CW 1/3. Some of the same names occur in CW 1/2 and CW 1/3, for example. John Cheselett, paid for mending the whirligig and shrine in CW 1/2 (l.33), is paid for making seats in CW 1/3, for example, and 'bartylmew' keeps the sepulchre in both years. Between 1512–13 and 1528–9 (CW 1/4–CW 1/13) the parish routinely paid 4s annual rent to the master of the almshouse for the church house. 1512–13 was a year of transition in which the churchwarden recorded both the 4s rent for the church house in the churchyard and 2s 9d rent for an earlier church house. In CW 1/2 the warden pays 2s 4d for rent of the church house '& post & ovis' (l.39), a payment suggestively similar to the old church house rent in 1512–13. Such similarities of material in the accounts make it likely that the two are close in date; certainly CW 1/2 is more likely to be before the account of 1511–12, which it resembles, than it is to be the account for 1516–17 or between 1518–19 and 1522–3, the first gaps in the dated accounts.

CW 1/1 records receipts but not payments, just as CW 1/4 records only payments. Most notable in the list of receipts in CW 1/1 is the absence of payments for church seats. Such payments comprise the majority of receipts in 1512–13 (CW 1/4) and are prominent in the receipts after that year. Precise dating of CW 1/1 and CW 1/2 seems impossible but it remains likely that CW 1/1 is earlier than CW 1/2, since CW 1/2 more closely resembles CW 1/3, and that both may be tentatively assigned to 1505–10.

250–1   DRO: PE/SH: CW 1/2   ff [1, 1v]

It is not clear what a 'Whurlegog' (p 250, l.33) was. Sherborne's churchwardens paid for making new ones in 1524–5, 1550–1, 1551–2, 1570–1, 1609–10, and 1610–11 (at least two were constructed in 1550–1 and 1570–1). A carpenter built one in 1524–5, and both timber and iron pins were required in 1550–1 when the beadsman dug holes for the 'horlegoggez,' presumably to anchor them. There are references to locks and rails for the machine in the early seventeenth century and to the construction of a new 'pine' for it in 1619–20; the contraption is mentioned in every year, 1616–21. Perhaps the whirligig was a turnstyle, as Fowler supposes ('Sherborne All Hallows,' SDNQ 23, p 332 n 8 and 'Post-Reformation,' SDNQ 25, p 172 n 17). If so, it probably kept animals from the churchyard, but it might also have been useful for audience control.

The 'post & ovis' (p 250, l.39) are probably ale posts or ale stakes for the king ale in the church house, stakes or poles driven into the ground in front of the building to indicate the holding of an ale. References to tents are reprinted here, although their function is unclear, since tents occur frequently in conjunction with Sherborne's pre-Reformation accounts for Corpus Christi activities (see, for example, p 255, ll.4, 17, 25) and played a role in the elaborate Sherborne Corpus Christi play of the 1570s (p 267, ll.24–5, 33, 37 and p 269, ll.18–20, 27–8).

251   DRO: PE/SH: CW 1/3   mb [1]
For the dating of these accounts see p 356, endnote to DRO: PE/SH: CW 1/1 f [1]. The accounting
year probably ran from Christmas to Christmas, as did the accounting year for CW 1/5–CW 1/11.

253   DRO: PE/SH: CW 1/8   single mb
Churchwarden Robert Cookeman's account dates 'from the feast of Saint Michael, the birth of our lord'
in 9 Henry VIII to the same feast in the following year. The double feast day, some smeared letters, and
the fact that the other accounts in the same period routinely run from Christmas to Christmas suggest
that the scribe intended to erase the reference to Michaelmas and to change it to Christmas and that
the account is for the year from Christmas 1517 to Christmas 1518. Fowler agrees that the scribe
intended to substitute Christmas for Michaelmas. See 'Sherborne All Hallows,' *SDNQ* 23, p 289.

254–5   DRO: PE/SH: CW 1/12   single sheet
In the heading of this account the date of the feast of the Conversion of St Paul (its opening) is mistakenly
given as 15 January rather than 25 January.

255   DRO: PE/SH: CW 1/13   single mb
In the heading of this account the date of the feast of the Conversion of St Paul (its opening) is mistakenly
given as 24 January rather than 25 January.

255   DRO: PE/SH: CW 1/14   single mb
The account is damaged in several places; hence any reference to the king ale is missing. What survives
of the heading indicates that the account ran from the fifth day of an unspecified month to 12 February
1530/1. The heading supplied in the text assumes that the accounting year began and ended in early
February.

255–6   DRO: PE/SH: CW 1/15   ff 9v, 13v
The manuscript contains the undated accounts of churchwardens Harry Sansam (ff 1–8) and John
Haywarde (ff 9–16v). Fowler claims that they are for the years 1533–4 and 1534–5 and that Haywarde's
account is the earlier of the two, citing 'internal evidence' ('Sherborne All Hallows,' *SDNQ* 24, pp 80, 101).
The best available evidence, however, argues for different years. The heading for CW 1/17 declares that
warden John Hill made the account for the year running from the Sunday after the feast of the Conversion
of St Paul 1537 to the same Sunday in the year following. The first receipt in Hill's account acknowledges the turnover of church stock from William Vincent, the previous warden. Vincent's account, clearly
for 1536–7, acknowledges receipt of the church goods from the previous warden, Harry Sansam (CW 1/16
f 2). So Hayward's account is probably for 1534–5 and Sansam's is certainly for 1535–6.
     The early 1530s saw the construction of a new church house. A large upper room was used in Henrician
times for the church ale and rented to players in the reign of Elizabeth. These accounts list the expenses
for building the 'kyngg*es* stere' (p 255, l.39), a massive staircase that led to the upper room, where the
church ale or king revel was held (see p 256, l.16–p 257, l.4; see also pp 39–40, 97, and 101). Apparently the church house construction was unfinished at Whitsuntide in 1534–5 for the parish rented a
room to hold the ale (see below, p 257, l.9).
     The linen 'netherkaysse' (p 256, l.2) was probably a drape on which the shrine rested as it was carried
in a procession like the drape and shrine shown in an initial of the Corpus Christi mass in the Fitzwilliam

Missal of the Use of York (printed as Figure 13 in Miri Rubin, *Corpus Christi: The Eucharist in Late Medieval Culture* (Cambridge, 1991), 254). See Hays, '"Lot's Wife",' p 102.

257   DRO: PE/SH: CW 1/15   f 2v
'rogare yngulberd' or Enghelberd was a native of Cologne. He was churchwarden in 1538–9 (DRO: PE/SH: CW 1/18), and in 1541 his daughter, Alice, married a future steward of Sherborne School (Fowler, 'Sherborne All Hallows,' *SDNQ* 24, p 102 n 5).

257   DRO: PE/SH: CW 1/16   f 1v
Although the scribe writes 'Ih*es*u 1536' in several places, no heading indicates the accounting year. Fowler dates the manuscript to 1535–6 ('Sherborne All Hallows,' *SDNQ* 24, p 121). But the warden for the year was William Vincent, referred to in the accounts for 1537–8 as the 'laste churche warden' (DRO: PE/SH: CW 1/17 single mb). The account probably ran from January 1535/6 to January 1536/7.

258   DRO: PE/SH: CW 1/18   ff 2, 10
In the heading of the account the churchwarden, Roger Enghelberd, says he has received the parish goods from the previous warden, John Hill, 'a*nn*o 1538 the 27 day of Ianuary*e*.' If there were no evidence to the contrary we would assume that this phrase indicated 27 January 1538/9 and that the account was for 1539–40. However, CW 1/17 is clearly dated January 1537–January 1538; the warden, John Hill, states that at the end of the year he handed the church goods, worth £26 16s 9 1/2d, to the next warden, Roger 'engylberde,' the same sum that Enghelberd claims to have received in CW 1/18. Enghelberd died while he was in office; according to Fowler his will was proved in 1538 ('Sherborne All Hallows,' *SDNQ* 24, p 162). So CW 1/18 is properly dated January 1538–January 1539.

The entry on f 10 is the earliest reference to a boy bishop's costume in the Sherborne parish inventories. Inventories are missing for many of the accounts in the 1530s. Although the accounts do not indicate when or why the parish acquired the garments, it is likely that they were purchased from Sherborne Abbey before the monastery was dissolved in March 1538/9, and that the celebration was monastic, not lay. The two preceding entries in the inventory are for ornamented albs 'bowgt from the abbey' and for albs without ornaments. No evidence survives of a boy bishop's procession of the sort described – and attributed to the Sherborne secular parish – in Hutton, *Rise and Fall*, pp 12, 296. The rites were made illegal in a royal proclamation issued in 1541 (*STC*: 7795; printed from a manuscript copy in the Worcester Cathedral Library in Klausner (ed), *Herefordshire/Worcestershire*, pp 537–9), so it is unlikely that Sherborne initiated a new custom, although the boy bishop's vestments remained in the parish stock.

259   DRO: PE/SH: CW 1/19   f 3v
The entry on this folio is the first unequivocal reference to players on Corpus Christi Day at Sherborne. Underdown claims Sherborne (and other communities) 'held elaborate plays annually until about the middle of Elizabeth's reign, and occasionally thereafter' (*Revel*, p 46); Hutton describes a 'single play, performed after the procession' (*Rise and Fall*, pp 41–2). For a somewhat different view of the Sherborne play, arguing that the play replaced an earlier procession, was suspended during the 1550s and 1560s, and was succeeded by a different play in the 1570s, see Hays, '"Lot's Wife",' pp 100–6.

On the same folio the wardens also record a payment of 3s to 'Iohn Carver*e*' and his men for two days' work 'Settyng vppe of the pagentt*es* of the rode lofte' and a payment of 10d for 'nayles & Sprigg*es* for the Same Warke,' payments almost certainly not associated with the play.

259   DRO: PE/SH: CW 1/20   mb [2]
The heading of this account is torn and the rendering date cannot be read. The 'churche man' is submitting the profits of the church ale.

260   DRO: PE/SH: CW 1/21   mbs [2, 3]
In this and later accounts inventories list the book of the Corpus Christi play among the items kept in the church house. The latter was probably used as a storeroom for parish property not used in church services.
    Although two entries for other revenues from the church ale occur on mb [3], Cuppar's receipts (l.17) are almost certainly the main account for the ale in 1544–5. The sum collected is about the usual amount during this period. See the receipts for 1546–7, for example, l.36.

261   DRO: PE/SH: CW 1/23   mbs [5–6]
The 'bordes' set up before the low altars (ll.35–6) may have had nothing to do with the play; the entry is printed here, however, because the players 'plaid vppon' boards 'in the churche' in 1543–4 (p 259, ll.36–7).

262   DRO: PE/SH: CW 1/24   mb [1]
Neither the playbook nor the boy bishop's vestments appears in the inventory for 1549–50 or in later inventories; the inventory for 1550–1 had shrunk considerably as the parish sold forbidden vestments and church vessels (see DRO: PE/SH: CW 1/26 sheet [2]).

262   DRO: PE/SH: CW 1/25   mb [3]
This is the first of Sherborne's several rentals of playing garments between 1549–50 and 1561–2 when the costumes were sold. There is no evidence that Sherborne continued to present the play during these years. Unfortunately, the parish inventories do not mention the playing garments, which were perhaps thought to have little intrinsic value.

262   DRO: PE/SH: CW 1/26   sheets [2, 3]
Although most of the heading is missing – only the rendering date and the name of the junior churchwarden are visible – the account may be safely assigned to 1550–1. The foot of the previous account reports handing £10 11s to 'Iohn Stevyns next wardyn' (CW 1/25 mb [5]) and this account records that the same sum was received from 'Iohn Adampes,' the senior warden for 1549–50.
    The churchwardens sold most of the church vestments in 1550–1, apparently to comply with church policy. Fowler believes the 'lyttell albe' (l.33) also belonged to the boy bishop ('Post-Reformation,' *SDNQ* 25, p 171 n 13).

263   DRO: PE/SH: CW 1/31   sheet [1]
'yatemester' (l.39) is the town of Yetminster half a dozen miles southwest of Sherborne, near Dorset's Somerset border; no Yetminster records confirm this rental.

264   DRO: PE/SH: CW 1/32   mb [1]
The heading at the top of the roll is damaged. The wardens report receiving the church stock from Richard Okeley, warden in 1555–6 (CW 1/31); at the end of the year their balance was £30 14 1/2d, received in turn by the wardens for 1557–8 (CW 1/33 mb [1]), so this is the account for 1556–7. A seventeenth-century hand on the dorse dates the account 1556–7.

264   DRO: PE/SH: CW 1/33   mb [1]

Martock, Castle Cary, and Wincanton (ll.16–17) are in southern Somerset. 'cawndell' (l.18) may be Purse Caundle, Stourton Caundle, or Bishop's Caundle, all small Dorset villages east of Sherborne in the northern part of the county. None of the renters left confirming records of these rentals. Fowler believes the bells lent to Martock were handbells ('Post-Reformation,' *SDNQ* 26, p 7 n 6). The entry, together with the reference to rented 'Ierkens' (l.15), is printed here because Sherborne made few rentals; the only other 'lones' in 1557–8 are of playing garments.

264   DRO: PE/SH: CW 1/34   sheet [1]

This is the last of the churchwardens' accounts printed by Fowler ('Post Reformation,' *SDNQ* 26, pp 49–54).

265   DRO: PE/SH: CW 1/36   sheet [1]

The heading is missing from this account. The Dorset Record Office dates it ' ?1565.' Since William Foster, who ran the church ale, became senior warden in 1567–8, the account may be for 1564–5 or, more probably, 1565–6.

265   DRO: PE/SH: CW 1/38   mb [1d]

The 'Rome' (l.25) in the church house was the large upper-storey room used for the king ale in the Henrician period and rented frequently to players in Elizabeth's reign (see pp 271–3). This is the first such rental. In 1567–8 it was also rented to a scrivener, who taught school there for a fortnight, and to a man who used it to entertain 'thoffycyall*es* and hys companye,' and in ensuing years the room and its equipment were often hired by parishioners for parties and ales.

John Dier rented playing garments from Yeovil in 1566–7, probably to costume the players in his 'enterludes' (ll.25–6; see Stokes with Alexander (eds), *Somerset Including Bath*, vol 1, p 408). Dier's interest in drama probably influenced Sherborne's production of a Corpus Christi play four years later; in 1571–2 the wardens paid him for 'Makeing and Devisinge garment*es* Towar*des* Corpus Christi playes' (p 266, ll.32–3). Although there was also a John Dier active in conjunction with the Robin Hood celebrations in Yeovil, Somerset, and although Yeovil and Sherborne rented or purchased each other's playing garments, the Sherborne and Yeovil John Diers were two different men, as James Stokes convincingly argues (*Somerset Including Bath*, vol 2, pp 970–1).

A John Dier, eighty-eight years old and living in the Sherborne almshouse, was one of the witnesses in a 1603/4 lawsuit (see pp 273–4). Unlike other witnesses in that suit Dier did not testify to the preparations for a Corpus Christi play performance in the 1570s; if the eighty-eight-year-old witness is the same John Dier, however, we know he could have remembered Sherborne's Corpus Christi play of the 1540s. He would have been in his early fifties when he played his interludes in the church house and fifty-six or fifty-seven when he made costumes for the revised parish play.

267–8   DRO: PE/SH: CW 1/43   mbs [3, 4]

Those 'stonninge vppon the lydes' in 1572–3 (p 267, l.16) were, like those who paid for 'Standing vppon the leades' on 'the play daye' (p 269, ll.5–6) in the following year, almost certainly part of the audience for the Corpus Christi play.

The gift of an 'eaylme' (probably an elm tree) from 'Mr horceay' to make a 'teaynt for the corpus christye playe' (p 268, ll.9–11) is almost certainly the gift witnesses swore to thirty years later. In 1603–4 one witness remembered that the tree had been used to construct a scaffold (p 273, l.41), and the eighty-year-old tailor, John Baker, remembered that the tree was used to build a stage (p 274, 1.14). Perhaps the 'teaynts' of 1572–3 were several connected structures like some modern outdoor stages, requiring 'scaffouldes' (p 268, l.1) to support a stage, or a 'heygh te[ay]nte' (p 267, l.25), which may simply have been a high platform to play upon. Other variations in the uses of tents may be seen in the next document (p 269, l.38). 'Mr horceay' is Sir John Horsey, head of the family after his father's death (1564/5) until he died in 1589.

270   DRO: PE/SH: CW 1/45   mb [3]
William Pope (l.18) was junior churchwarden in 1571–2 and senior warden in 1572–3. See DRO: PE/SH: CW 1/42 mb [1] and CW 1/43 mb [1].

270   DRO: PE/SH: CW 1/46   mb [2]
This is the last recorded performance of the parish play although players leased the church house with some frequency during the rest of the sixteenth century.

271   DRO: PE/SH: CW 1/49   mb [1]
This is the last clear reference to the church ale at Sherborne. From 1578–9 to 1584–5 a 'collector' turned in comparable receipts to the parish. By 1588–9 the parish held a street ale, supervised by collectors who reported to and later became churchwardens, thus occupying something of the same position in parish affairs as the men who had presided over the early Tudor king ale. See DRO: PE/SH: CW 1/50 mb [1]; PE/SH: VE1 ff 1–1v, 4; and D/SHA: A118; and DRO: S.235: B1/24, p 2; S.235: C5/2/1; and S.235: C5/2/7–9.

273–4   PRO: E134/1 James I/ Hil 3   mbs 1, 6, 7
In dispute between Sherborne's vicar, Francis Scarlett, and John Stocker, the impropriator of the Sherborne prebend and farmer of Sherborne's parsonage, were the rights to herbage growing in the churchyard and to the shrouds of churchyard trees (the right to cut branches). From the 1540s until Sir Ralph Horsey sold his remaining term in the Sherborne parsonage some time between 1589 and 1603 the Horseys had been farmers of the parsonage. Joseph Fowler explains the lawsuit and its background at some length (*Mediaeval Sherborne*, pp 318–23). Witnesses in the suit testified to incidents showing that 'old Sir John Horsey' (d. 1564/5) or Sir John Horsey (d. 1589) had treated the trees in the churchyard as their property, an indication that Stocker could claim similar rights.

Thomas Adams, labourer, the first witness, said he had lived near the vicarage for about forty-seven years. Adams had felled a tree in the churchyard at the behest of the farmers of the parsonage.

Forte probably remembered the gift of 'won eaylme' made by 'Mr horceay' in 1572–3 (p 268, ll.9–11 and pp 360–1, endnote to DRO: PE/SH: CW 1/43 mbs [3, 4]). The most elaborate productions of the Sherborne Corpus Christi play were in that year and in 1573–4, almost exactly thirty years before Osmund Forte and the other witnesses testified. The accounts for 1572–3 state that Horsey's gift was used to made a 'teaynt,' and perhaps the 'teaynt' required a scaffold. Osmund Forte claims to have dwelt in the churchyard in the house next to the vicarage for sixty years.

Baker's testimony is the only clear suggestion that the actors in the Corpus Christi play in the Sherborne churchyard in the 1570s (about thirty years before the lawsuit of 1603–4) may have performed on a stage.

274   SRO: Q/SR 37, pt 2   f 101A
This document previously appeared in Stokes with Alexander (eds), *Somerset Including Bath*, vol 1,

pp 145–6; that volume also includes an indictment of Nehellyng on 15 September 1607 and what was probably an earlier indictment of April 1607 (vol 1, pp 145 and 200; see also vol 2, pp 910 and 921; Bates (ed), *Quarter Session Records*, vol 1, p 6, also has a transcription of this document).

The document illustrates both the importance of local customs, such as church ales and civic watches, in occasioning performance activity and the existence of local circuits for itinerant entertainers. Nehellyng's route traverses county boundaries, Ilton, Ilchester, and Stoke St Gregory ('Gregory Stoke,' l.31) being in Somerset, Mere in Wiltshire, and Sherborne, Sturminster Newton ('Sturmyster,' l.34), and Ralph Down ('Rafedowne,' l.34) in Dorset.

The Sherborne 'Churchale' in 1607/8 was almost certainly the street ale begun by the parish by 1588/9 (see p 361, endnote to DRO: PE/SH: CW 1/49 mb [1]).

276   Wing: B6161   pp 12–13
In the west corner of Dorset the parish of Symondsbury is just north of Bridport and due south of Stoke Abbott. The clause, 'though he went naked through a quickset hedge' (ll.31–2), is a colloquialism that captures the ardent desire of 'good man Paul,' for, given the speed with which quickset grows and the density of the growth, such hedges were virtually impassable. This example is the second of two which, Burton says, 'are testified by a Minister in his letter to a brother Minister' (ll.36–7). The other case was that of a man of Bothenhampton, Dorset, who was killed when struck in the head by a ball thrown by another bowler.

277   WM: Sherren MS 184   ff [2v, 3]
The payment to Clarke (Clerke) follows a payment to 'two of the porters for caryeing of Iames kinge to dorchester Gaole' and a payment for 'the kepers ffees'; it is possible Clarke beat the drum to accompany the prisoner part of the way to Dorchester. On f [4] the auditors make clear their disapproval of some of the mayor's expenditures; the marginal remarks beside the records of payments to players and for their wine (ll.25–6) indicate this, and the two entries have been cancelled, probably administratively. Other disallowed expenditures include payments for a dinner and for broadcloth for the clerk.

277–8   WM: Sherren MS 185   ff [1v, 2v]
The accounts record moneys paid out on the town's business by John Mockett in 'anno Domini 1597 and in the tyme of his maioraltie anno Domini 1598.' Additional sums due him are recorded by the auditors in 1601.

278   WM: Sherren MS 186   f [2v]
The last date given before these entries is 10 June and so the drums were probably mended in the summer of 1600.

279   WM: Sherren MS 206   f [2v]
The entry occurs after a payment made on 30 May and immediately precedes a payment made 4 July.

279–81   WM: MB.O-B   pp 130, 132, 134
James Stokes, REED editor for Somerset, has pointed out the similarity between elements in the actions of these Weymouth citizens and those embodied in secular processional drama in Somerset. See particularly the records for and his comments on episodes at Wells in 1607 and Keynsham in 1619 (*Somerset*

Including Bath, vol 1, pp 149, 299–301, 347, and 351 and vol 2, pp 493–4 and 720–1). For another maypole with military associations see above, p 245, ll.21–7.

282   WM: MB.O-B   p 304
These entries are from a list of numerous presentments by the constables in the mayoral court. 'weeke' (l.5) is the village of Wyke Regis, up a steep hill from Weymouth and linked to the harbour town by both parish and manorial jurisdiction. Katherine Morfell's common alehouse appears several times in this minute book (on pp 270 and 328, for example) and her licence was evidently not endangered by this wild party.

282   WM: MB.O-B   p 321
According to Weinstock, the maypole stood at the junction of St Mary Street and Coneygar Ditch (modern Bond Street) in Melcombe Regis. See 'Weymouth and Melcombe Regis in Tudor and Early Stuart Times,' *More Dorset Studies,* map facing p 42.

283   DRO: PE/WM: CW 1/41   p 212
The church house had been a chapel of ease, St Peter's, in what is now the town square of Wimborne Minster. In the 1540s it was converted into a parish hall. At that time the building had a fireplace with an iron bar in it and plastered walls; the remodelling required 6,900 bricks, 4,000 tiles, and four loads of Purbeck stone (DRO: PE/WM: CW 1/40 pp 139–40). By the 1560s there were windows with bars and a loft (pp 164 and 166). When the school governors leased the building to a clothier in 1636 they reserved the use of an upper room at the east end of the building 'heretofore vsed by the inhabitants of Wimborne Minster aforesaid for publike meetings' (DRO: PE/WM: GN8/1/3) and that may have been the room rented to players in 1573–4 and again in 1589–90. The parish also rented out space in the church house for brewings and let rooms in the church house to townspeople.

283   DRO: PE/WM: CP2/10, item 8   single sheet
Pencilled dates on the items in this bundle of churchwardens' presentments were probably added by J.M.J. Fletcher, curate of Wimborne Minster, 1906–19, rural dean of Wimborne Minster, 1907–19, canon and prebendary of Salisbury, 1912–40, and principal official of the peculiar of Wimborne Minster, 1915–40. Fletcher arranged the collection of Wimborne Minster documents before their deposit in the DRO.

The pencilled date on item 8 is confirmed by the name of the churchman, Richard Russell, who was one of the churchwardens for the year 11 December 1591–11 December 1592 (PE/WM: CW 1/42 p 43). William Lucas, alias Bright, occurs several times in the Wimborne documents. References to him as 'Britt' or 'bryght' occur in 1609–10, 1610–11, and 1620–1 below. He seems to have been the head of a family of disreputable entertainers: it was probably his boy and his daughter who were the 'Nicholaum Lucas al*ias* Bright' and 'Elionoram Bright al*ias* Lucas alias Haiter' excommunicated for contumacy some time in the 1620s (DRO: PE/WM: CP2/9, item 173). Eleanor was also excommunicated for incontinence with Henry Hayter in 1629 (DRO: PE/WM: CP2/11, item 23). Holt was a village within the large parish of Wimborne Minster, lying to the northeast of the town.

284   DRO: PE/WM: CP2/10, item 55   single sheet
Although Fletcher ascribes this document to 1603, 9 May fell on a Sunday in 1602, not 1603; the

accusations in the presentment are repeated in the acts of the peculiar court for 1601–2 (DRO: PE/WM: CP1/1 pp 64, 72, and 73). 'lye' (l.28) is the parish village of Leigh to the south and east of the town of Wimborne Minster.

285   DRO: PE/WM: CP2/10, item 82   single sheet
The 'play' (l.21) kept by Margaret Fuller may, of course, have been gambling; we have included the entry because its ambiguous language does not exclude drama.

285   DRO: PE/WM: CP2/10, item 92   single sheet
The signatures are those of the wardens or sidesmen from about 1608–9; 9 and 16 July fell on Sunday in 1609. 'fraunces ffrost [& henry Nores] and sweetes other man' were presented for being in an alehouse at 'ligh' (Leigh) during service time on 16 July (item 92v), and 'Britt Minstrele' (l.35) may have been playing there. 'Britt' is probably an alternate spelling for 'Bright,' William Bright or Lucas of Holt.

286   DRO: PE/WM: CP2/10, item 94   single sheet
The document records presentments of several fives players and a player at bowls. The entry is included in the records because it is ambiguous: although Joan's apprentices may have played fives or bowls during the sermon, it is possible their play was dramatic or musical. 1 April fell on a Sunday in 1604 and 1610. The names of the sidesmen, who also sign item 93 (see p 287 and endnote), make it likely that this presentment is for 1609–10.

286   DRO: PE/WM: CP2/10, item 99   single sheet
The presentment is dated by the names of the churchwardens. 'Iohn Pyeke' (l.15) may be the 'Pike the minstrell' (p 284, l.15) presented for playing during evening prayer time in 1601.

286   DRO: PE/WM: CP2/10, item 100   single sheet
There is no reason to question the pencilled date, 1610; many of the same sidesmen who make their marks at the bottom of item 95 (p 286) are also sidesmen in this document (Richard Habgood, William Wilkyinges, Robart Mackrell, John Ellet, Richard Ellet, and James Doll).

286   DRO: PE/WM: CP2/10, item 95   single sheet
The pencilled date 1610–11 appears at the head of the document; this is almost certainly the same year as item 100 (p 286 and endnote).

287   DRO: PE/WM: CP2/10, item 93   ff [1, 1v]
This document presents some dating problems. The churchwardens are not mentioned; listed sidesmen also occur in item 94. Item 93 refers to 14 April as a Sunday and it also refers to morning prayer time and sermon time on 13 May. In 1611 14 April was a Sunday and 13 May was Whit Monday, when there would have been church services. The two dates would have fallen in different churchwardens' years, since the 1610–11 wardens rendered their final account on 16 April. Confirmation that 1611 is correct may also be found in the fact that Elizabeth Pitman and probably Margaret White were cited, probably for dancing, on another occasion in 1610–11 (item 99).

Underdown is probably referring to information calendared from this document when he says that an early Jacobean reform campaign at Wimborne Minster, 'exceptionally energetic in prosecuting absences from church' was not entirely successful; 'sporadic resistance continued, with a maypole and morris dancing in 1608 which led to the usual disorders' (*Revel*, p 56). The only 'disorders' seem to have consisted of frivolous behaviour at service or sermon time or during evening prayer.

288   WRO: D5/28/28, item 92   f [1]
James Gould did not refer to the revel ale at his appearance before the bishop's court on 9 October 1628, saying disingenuously that 'ag*ains*te whitsontyde last he Ioyned wi*th* others of the p*a*rishe to collect some mony toward buying of some drinke ag*a*inst a meetinge of some neighbor p*a*rishioners ∧⌜with⌝ [to] them. but att the meetinge because the Minister was offended as they heard they left off their sport w*h*ich they intended' (WRO: D5/19/31 f 60v).

290   DRO: D/FSI: Box 220   f 6
Giles Strangways regularly rewarded fiddlers when on his travels, as he did ringers, trumpeters, porters, keepers of gardens, officers, and the poor. The earliest payment appears in a list of expenses associated with his visit to Oxford where he toured the chapel of Magdalen College, the grounds and buildings of Wadham College, 'the Physicke schoole,' and one of the libraries (to the curator of which he gave 5s). While he continued to reward musicians who entertained him on his travels, he seems also to have provided a venue for fiddlers at Melbury Sampford, where he registers rewards to these players as annual New Year's gifts. The relatively large sums paid to fiddlers in the summary accounts for 1639, 1640, and 1641 probably cover costs for fiddlers in Dorset and outside the county.

Appendix 3

298   DRO: DC/LR: G1/2   p 121
John Holcombe (l.13), merchant, was elected mayor in 1559 and 1565.

299   DRO: DC/LR: G1/1   p 33
The Davey family was a prominent one in Lyme Regis (see pp 333–5, especially p 334, endnote to DRO: DC/BTB: M15/11 ff [2–7, 7v–9v]) but Alexander (l.5) does not appear to have gone on to hold civic offices. Thomas Dare (l.5), merchant, served as mayor in 1564–5. A draft of this account occurs on DRO: DC/LR: G2/1 f [13].

299   DRO: DC/LR: G2/1   f [19v]
The Moone family, another important local family, had one member serve as mayor; Anthony Moone, gentleman, did so in 1608–9.

299   DRO: DC/LR: G1/1   pp 44, 47
We have included records both of the delivery of the silver whistle and of its receipt partly because these are the earliest records of the whistle and each defines a different use of it: the first indicates that the whistle is a property to be used during the installation of a new Cobb warden, the second that it is to be worn during the ale. Although Roberts, *Social History*, p 336, says that William Birret (l.21) was 'some time mayor,' we have found no contemporary evidence to confirm that he held this office; he may have been the father of Richard Baret (see p 366, endnote to DRO: DC/LR: N23/4, item 3 single mb). A draft copy of part of the account on p 47 appears on DRO: DC/LR: G2/1 f [22].

299   DRO: DC/LR: G1/2   p 167
A member of one of the borough's most influential families, John Hassard (l.36), merchant, served as mayor for terms beginning in 1567, 1572, 1578, 1582, 1588, and 1594.

300   DRO: DC/LR: G1/1   p 50
A draft copy of this account appears in DRO: DC/LR: G2/1 f [34v].

301–2   DRO: DC/LR: N23/4, item 3   single mb
Richard Baret (p 301, l.17) and John Seaward (p 301, l.18) were both merchants; the former twice served as mayor (in 1566–7 and 1573–4), the latter for the year in which this agreement was made. John Cogan (p 301, l.24) appears not to have held public office but he was at least a person of some means at this time: his name appears on a list, which includes many of Lyme Regis' leading families, of donors to the building of the new shambles in 1598 (DRO: DC/LR: N23/1 f 60) and he was reimbursed 13s 4d for a banquet at his house in 1607 (DRO: DC/LR: G7/6).

302–3   DRO: DC/LR: G1/1   pp 140–1
This document reveals the financial importance of the Cobb ale when a crucial legal, political, and economic need had to be met. The importance of the new charter is implicit in the involvement of some of the most powerful men in the borough: Sir George Somers (p 302, l.26), elected MP for Lyme Regis on 25 February 1603/4 and mayor 1604–5; Robert Hassard (p 302, l.29), gentleman, mayor 1601–2; William Ellesdon (p 303, l.1), gentleman, mayor in 1590–1 for the fourth of his five terms; Christopher Elmestone (p 302, l.40), gentleman, mayor in 1599–1600; John Hassard (p 302, l.41; see above, endnote to DRO: DC/LR: G1/2 p 167); and John Bidgood (p 303, l.2), merchant, mayor 1600–1. As Wanklyn notes in *Lyme Leaflets*, pp 118–19, Silvester Jourdain (p 302, l.27) was a member of another of the town's leading families but he forfeited his freedom in 1598 by failing to pay the penalty imposed by the local court. He left Lyme Regis as a member of the expedition, under the leadership of Sir George Somers, bound for the Jamestown colony; they were blown off course by a hurricane and wrecked on Bermuda; for Jourdain's published accounts of his travels, see *A discovery of the Barmudas* (London, 1610; STC: 14816) and *A plaine description of the Barmudas, now called Sommer ilands* (London, 1613; STC: 14817); for Robert Davey, John Davey, John Hayes, John Bellamy, and Robert Barnes, see pp 333–5, endnote to DRO: DC/BTB: M15/11 ff [2–7, 7v–9v].

303   DRO: DC/LR: G2/2   tab 78
A William Davey, merchant, served as mayor 1623–4.

303–5   DRO: DC/LR: N23/1, item 63   single sheet–single sheet verso
This document seems to be a draft of one of John Roze's quarter books during the term as receiver for the Cobb ale; another copy is included as part of Roze's more complete account (below). We have transcribed the draft in extenso because it includes some items that do not recur in the fair copy and some small but potentially significant differences in wording. Although many of the people named in the draft account and in the fair copy cannot be identified, what they provided to the festivity likely implies their occupations as, for instance, brewers or bakers. Roberts says that George Rocquey and his wife were 'the chief cooks' for the ale this year (*Social History*, p 339). 'St Mallos' (p 305, l.2) refers to St Malo, a French port across the English Channel from Dorset. Apparently the collection extended as far as France, to ports from which ships regularly came to Lyme Regis.

305–8 DRO: DC/LR: N23/2, item 75   ff [1–2]

Walter Harvey (p 305, l.26–7), merchant, was elected mayor for four terms, beginning in 1586, 1593, 1602, and 1612. John Roze (p 306, l.9), merchant, became mayor in 1611. The 'mr browne' (p 306, l.23) from whom funds were collected may be George Browne, elected freeman and recorder of Lyme Regis in 1611. The 'Iohn piters' (p 307, l.39) paid for the use of his cellar may well be the John Peters who contributed to the building of the new shambles in 1598 (see p 366, endnote to DRO: DC/LR: N23/4, item 3 single mb). The John Davey whose brewhouse was used for the ale is probably not the same John Davey, mariner and sometime mayor, noted above (pp 333–5, especially p 334, endnote to DRO: DC/BTB: M15/11 ff [2–7, 7v–9v]) along with Robert Hassard and John Bidgood. Further sums received from French ports appear in this account: the 17s 6d received 'in morlays' (p 306, l.2) apparently refer to Morlaix, a port west of St Malo.

CORNWALL

Acknowledgments

We have received much assistance during the years we have been preparing the Cornwall collection and are therefore very glad for this opportunity to say in print how much we appreciate the kind and generous help given us by other scholars, granting agencies, our universities, and colleagues. We are especially grateful to members of the staff in the libraries and record repositories where we have conducted research and are most particularly thankful to the expert librarians and archivists in Cornwall, whom we now value as friends.

Our first and most heart-felt thanks are to O.J. Padel, formerly of the Institute of Cornish Studies, who has given us every assistance possible since the year we started work on this project. A pre-eminent scholar on all things Cornish, he has shared his knowledge and judgment with us unceasingly and has truly been our greatest resource. We are inestimably grateful to him for his help in the last stages of production, for volunteering assistance with the revisions of Appendixes 1 and 2, for researching and writing Appendix 3, and for translating the excerpts from the Cornish play texts. We also wish to thank Margaret Bunt, formerly of the Institute of Cornish Studies, who helped us learn much about Cornwall and who has shown us infinite and ongoing kindness and generosity for many years. Myrna Combellack, also formerly of the Institute of Cornish Studies, was helpful to us in the early years of our work.

Much of our research was accomplished during summers spent largely at the Cornwall Record Office in Truro, where we received invaluable assistance from Peter Hull, Christine North, and David Thomas, and especially from Colin Edwards, who first guided us in our search and, over the years of the project, provided us always with patient and expert assistance. H.L. Douch and Angela Broome of the Royal Institution of Cornwall's Courtney Library have been helpful in the extreme, answering many questions, including some we did not know to ask, and were always unfailingly generous with their knowledge and assistance. Mr M. Veal, of the St Ives Guildhall, in several summers allowed us the use of the mayor's parlour for examining and photographing documents. When the Launceston records were still housed in the Town Hall, Peter Freestone gave generously of his time to make the documents available. A special thanks to Arthur Wills, who welcomed us to Launceston and provided valuable and otherwise unavailable historical resources on the town and information on St Mary Magdalene's Church. Lord Arundell of Hook Manor, Shaftesbury, Dorset, opened his home to us to read the Arundell documents then housed there and provided us a pleasant working area; we appreciate his courtesy and friendship.

We appreciate having received financial support for the research necessary for this volume.

We have been supported in part through major grants awarded to the REED office by the National Endowment for the Humanities and by the Social Sciences and Humanities Research Council of Canada. We are also grateful for the generous support of Father Edward Jackman, o.p., and the Jackman Foundation.

Sally Joyce appreciates funding she received for her research from Miami University, Ohio, and library support from Keene State College. Heartfelt thanks go especially to Sinte Gleska University, Rosebud Sioux Reservation, South Dakota, for encouragement and technical support in the final stages of production of the Cornwall collection.

Evelyn Newlyn is grateful for grants for her research from the American Philosophical Society, the National Endowment for the Humanities, and the American Council of Learned Societies, as well as for funding from the Virginia Polytechnic Institute and State University and from the State University of New York at Brockport. Especially warm thanks must go to David Fowler, whose graciousness in writing many recommendations for grant support literally made her research possible; his kindness, and the advice, information, and support he was always willing to give, will be remembered always. Grant support to her also from the United University Professors PDQWL (Professional Development and Quality of Working Life) Committee of Brockport helped fund photography of the stained glass in St Neot's Church. We wish to thank David Hambly of Liskeard for his excellent photography and for permitting us to publish his photographs of the Creation window of St Neot's Church. Thanks also to the Reverend H.T.C. Olivey, the church's rector, for allowing the photography.

We especially appreciate the assistance given us for many years by the REED staff: Sally-Beth MacLean, Arleane Ralph, William Rowcliffe, Miriam Skey, and Abigail Ann Young; Alexandra F. Johnston gave us much support and assistance in the early years of our research. Their patience and courage in dealing with editors, fine orchestrating of the production of a volume, and never-ending insight are outdone only by their great warmth and friendship. Joanna Mattingly, Honorary Research Fellow at the Institute of Cornish Studies, deserves our deep appreciation for helping us with on-site checking, describing documents and dating, and uncovering additional relevant parish records. Her contribution in the last year and a half leading to final production was scrupulously thorough and painstaking, and her work always exceeded our expectations. We owe special thanks to Robert Tittler, historian and member of the REED Executive Board, for his advice and research direction of final work on the Historical Background section. Professor Tittler and his research assistant, Mark Moody, at Concordia University, Montreal, gave us invaluable help during the late stages of editing this part of the Introduction. Carin Ruff assisted with Appendix 1 and Catherine Emerson provided help with the Latin Translations and the Latin Glossary; we thank them both, along with Subash Shanbhag, cartographer, and William Cooke, English glossarian. Monica Ory was our researcher for the Star Chamber cases included in the Cornwall collection and her considerable effort for us is greatly appreciated. Many others formerly associated with REED deserve recognition for their unfailing support in the early stages of the research: Theodore De Welles, Richard Gyug, Sheena Levitt, Heather Phillips, and Anne Quick.

Many people were especially helpful with advice in the early stages of research or with on-site research in the locations cited, and we appreciate their generous support: Gloria Betcher, the Public Record Office; Claire Breay, the British Library; Mike England and Ken Golding, National Trust, Lanhydrock House; Audrey Erskine, Exeter Cathedral Library; Alan Fletcher, Marsh's Library, Dublin; Michael Hadcroft, St Mary's College Library, Oscott; Michael Heaney, the Bodleian Library; Peter Pool, the Morrab Library; and Diana Wyatt, the Bodleian Library.

We are also grateful for formal permission from the following libraries and repositories or their governing bodies to publish extracts from documents in their possession: the Bodleian Library, University of Oxford; the Board of the British Library; the Cornwall Record Office; the Exeter Cathedral Library on behalf of the Dean and Chapter; the Devon Record Office and the Exeter Diocesan Registry; the National Library of Wales; St Mary's College Library, Oscott; the Public Record Office; the Royal Institution of Cornwall, Courtney Library; and the St Ives Town Council. We also acknowledge the Bodleian Library, University of Oxford, and the National Library of Wales for permission to reproduce the diagrams found in Appendix 2, and the owners of copies of episcopal visitation articles from which we print extracts: Marsh's Library, Dublin, and Lanhydrock House, Lanhydrock, Bodmin.

This collection is for Janet, for her love and patience, and in memory of John Black Bear, a true Lakota man.

Historical Background

When in 926 according to legend the Saxon, Athelstan of Wessex, set the boundary between Cornwall and Devon as the Tamar River, he marked a 1,376 square-mile county of varied and often breath-taking landscape. Haunting moors claim miles near Bodmin and Launceston; sub-tropical and lush vales startle the eye in St Just in Roseland; picturesque sandy beaches curve around towns like St Ives; a rugged, wind-swept coastline surrounds Land's End. Cornwall is a county that stirs the imagination deeply; stone circles and prehistoric remains abound – only Wiltshire has more. Tintagel on the north coast, probably built by Earl Richard in the 1230s, makes us wish it were part of the origins of Arthurian legends.[1] Surrounded on three sides by the Atlantic Ocean and the English Channel, Cornwall has deep estuaries cut into the land: on the Channel, at Helford on the Lizard peninsula, at Pendennis and St Mawes, at Fowey, and at West Looe; on the Atlantic coast, at Padstow. These provide navigable and naturally safe harbours for shipping. On the other hand, Cornwall's rock-bound and reefy shoreline kept it relatively protected from attack. Saxons who invaded may have arrived over land.[2]

Athelstan's boundary also marks the culmination of several centuries of slow domination of the Celtic people in Cornwall. The persistence of Cornish place names in the west of Cornwall testifies to Celtic heritage; here the Old Cornish language (c 800–1200), which had evolved from Brythonic, kept its foothold. Saxon overlords in western Cornwall did relatively little to change the life ways and language of the workers they ruled. Nearly all of the workers – villeins, bordars, and serfs – spoke Cornish, English being the language of a few eastern peasants and some of the upper class, and French, the language of the Norman rulers and those who ruled with but under them. Cornish persisted well into the eighteenth century. In 1339 Bishop Grandisson gave licence to a man named J. Polmarke to assist the vicar of St Merryn near Padstow and to preach in Cornish;[3] in 1595 Cornish was still spoken in St Austell.[4] The Saxon presence did, however, affect the eastern part of Cornwall; the Saxons were attracted there by land more arable than the western uplands. Place names there are thus predominantly English, indicating Saxon influence.[5]

By the time that the Saxon conquest was complete in Cornwall, about 838, the remaining number of Celtic religious sites testified to the roots of its spiritual history. Names of Welsh saints – Petroc, Mawgan, Carantoc, Gulval, Madron, Cleer, Tudy, for example – had become part of Cornwall's hagiography, along with those of saints purportedly from Ireland – Breaca, Etha, Germochus, Gwithianus, and others.[6] Additionally, hundreds of Celtic crosses remain scattered across the Cornish countryside. However, of the more than fifteen Celtic spiritual establishments in Cornwall at the time of the Norman Conquest, all had, by the thirteenth century, either become part of the contemporary religious orders or no longer existed.[7]

At the time of the Conquest the total population of Cornwall was between 20,000 and 30,000, located in the east and along the old trade route from Hayle to Mounts Bay.[8] The Normans seized manors over the entire county but were in the main absentee landlords, interested primarily in exacting the resources of the manors, draining value from a significant number.[9] The Normans also reformed the Cornish religious houses to a stricter rule and subordinated them to grand French monasteries. St Michael's Mount continued as a Benedictine house under Mont St Michel, and another Benedictine house was founded at Tywardreath as a daughter house of Saint Serge of Angers. Augustinian canons arrived in the twelfth century and established houses in Bodmin, Launceston, and St Germans.[10] Ecclesiastics and the barons became partners in rule. The period of fierce baronial rivalry and anarchy that characterized King Stephen's reign (1135–54) was brought to an end by Henry II, who weakened the power of the barons at the same time that he extended the power of his justices in eyre, establishing Launceston as the Cornish site on the assize circuit. Travelling over roads that were often nearly impassible, the justices were 'welcomed neither by the feudal magnates nor by the common people, who, terrified that their misdemeanours would be discovered, took to the woods and moors when the watchman on Launceston church tower announced their appearance on Polston Bridge over the Tamar.'[11]

Economic Development

Henry's centralization of governmental power would prove to be an asset when the revenues from the Cornish stannaries were used to finance Richard I's crusades. In 1198 the stannaries came under the Crown's taxation, making them the most stable, well-established, and lucrative source of revenue in Cornwall for the king.[12] Long before English recorded history, tinners mined in Cornwall and by the close of the twelfth century, Cornwall provided most of the tin for European markets.[13] The long central ridge of rock that runs from east to west, with ramifications that reach out to the sea on either side, makes Cornwall's mining area; streams, flowing for the most part from north to south, provide the necessary water resources for tin mining. Historians believe that as early as 1,000 BC Cornwall may have been involved in tin trading with people from Iberia, Gaul, and Phoenicia; from the fourth to the fourteenth century England was the primary European producer of tin and in the sixteenth century for the western world.[14] Written history of the stannaries begins in 1155–6 with entries appearing in the Pipe Rolls. Because of Cornish tin mining's long history, with its own tradition of stannary administration, Cornish tin miners were higher in status than the ordinary labourer, creating a level of freedom for the Cornish tinner not found in other areas where mining is more recent, as, for example, in the Durham coal mines. The stannaries had their own legal administration – their own laws, enforced by the royal officer, the stannary warden. King John, also the earl of Cornwall, issued the first charter to the stannaries in 1201, recognizing tin mining as central to Cornwall's economy.[15]

Before 1337 the king was the head of the stannary system; after 1337 the head was the prince of Wales, as duke of Cornwall. Below the warden in jurisdiction were the vice-warden and lower stannary courts, with juries and stewards of miners. The charter of 1305 confirmed privileges that had been in place for tin miners for more than a century: privileges of 'bounding' (the right to freely search and dig for tin), of fuel and water to mine, of freedom from ordinary taxation, and of freedom for tinners from all pleas of villeinage, offering complete freedom to any villein who would mine tin.[16] The stannary courts ruled in civil and even criminal matters and miners were exempted from jurisdiction other than that of their stannary court. Even without this charter, so entrenched were the privileges of the tin miners that it had become dangerous for anyone to interfere with stannary rights of jurisdiction.

Population estimates for Cornwall in 1377 indicate that there were about 51,000 people in Cornwall, suggesting that about 10 per cent of the people were occupied at tinning.[17] The number of Cornish tinners in 1300 has been estimated at 2,000, and in 1400, 5,000.[18] The tin industry was carefully controlled; for example, in 1346 the Black Prince ordered that only two pewterers were to work in the duchy, one in the castle of Launceston and the other in the castle of Restormel.[19] Tin mining continued for centuries as Cornwall's chief industry. Tin coinage was the largest single item of revenue and it was against the law to convey or sell uncoined tin; imprisonment, confiscation of metal, and a fine by the prince were common penalties. Technological advances in mining in the fifteenth century affected the growth of towns. Shaft mining, not dependent on streams as the source of tin, was a sixteenth-century 'turning point in the industry,' an important change in technology.[20] This change may have helped stabilize population as miners then located around a shaft area.

Medieval itineraries and descriptions of the county give us a glimpse of the main roads and travel at the time. 'Travel was difficult up to the eighteenth century, one historian reporting that even as late as 1760 there was scarcely a stretch of road in the county fit for wheeled traffic.'[21] Cornish people travelled on foot and on horseback from place to place and hosted travellers from other parts of England. A main road from Exeter to Marazion existed from Roman times, probably the road that appears on the *c* 1360 Gough Map, running through Launceston, Bodmin, and Redruth.[22] Our knowledge of medieval bridge-building is a reliable indicator of often-travelled roads. Henderson and Coates' modern study of early Cornish bridges confirms that while Cornwall remained rural and relatively isolated, it had a network of roads on which people came and went from the Tamar to nearly Land's End.[23] The account of William Worcestre (1478) indicates his travel on part of the old Roman road and on part of a route through Truro to Marazion. His return to Tavistock Abbey in Devon via Fowey and Lostwithiel tells us that there was a road around the Fowey estuary, a route confirmed by Leland's Itinerary in 1538. Leland also travelled on the north coast to Boscastle, then south to Bossiney and Tintagel.[24] Robert Morden's maps of Devon and Cornwall, done for Camden's *Britannia* in 1695, show that there were then three major routes from Exeter through Cornwall. A southern coastal route from Plymouth in Devon into Millbrook in Cornwall went through Looe and Fowey to St Austell; then the road split, a northern route going through Grampound to Truro, and a southern route to the Fal estuary, then to St Erth and on to Marazion and Penzance, finally ending near Land's End. The middle route from Exeter ran from Tavistock through

Liskeard, St Blazey, and St Austell, where it merged with the coastal road. The northern route ran from Exeter to Launceston, then northwest to Davidstow and Camelford, continued near Padstow, and then went southwest to St Columb, Treworga, and Truro.[25]

Cornwall was never as rich in fertile farmlands as other parts of England were. Sizable moors and nearly non-arable areas prevented agriculture from contributing to the county's economy except marginally When Cornwall freed itself from the Forest Law, farming in those tracts of land previously reserved for baronial hunting increased to some extent and the coastal region provided some tracts of fertile land but open field husbandry that was successful in other parts of England, as well as farming in small enclosed fields, was not profitable in Cornwall.[26] Occasionally, struggling farmers and merchants would profit from an unusual agricultural crisis in another part of the country. Cornwall was in such an unusual position during the agrarian crisis, 1315–22. Price inflation and poor harvests from violent weather (such as that of 1315), combined with depletions from war, created famine and a farming crisis throughout England rivalled only by the results of outbreaks of the Black Death in 1348–50 and 1360–1 that reduced the population by one-third. However, the economy of rural Cornwall was not dependent upon wool and corn for its revenues; tin was the main industry. Farmers and merchants in Cornwall may actually have benefitted from the crisis the rest of the country suffered because they brought food to London, given special surety through safe-conduct for travel and, very likely, excellent prices for their usual, small Cornish crops.[27] The outbreaks of the plague affected Cornwall as elsewhere, although it is difficult to know precisely the number of deaths. Nevertheless it seems clear that the decline of population, especially in such boroughs as Bodmin, Helston, Penryn, and Truro, was severe in the late fourteenth and most of the fifteenth centuries.[28]

Unlike other counties in England where long-woolled sheep flourished – counties rich in grasslands, marshes, and fens – Cornwall was not known for exporting high-quality wool for the cloth industry located across Europe. Fine English export wools came from areas like the Cotswolds, Devon, Herefordshire, Shropshire, and Lindsey in Lincolnshire; Cornish wool was coarse and little was exported. Carew described Cornwall's sheep as having 'little bodies, and coarse fleeces, so as their Wooll bare no better name, then of Cornish hayre.'[29]

In the early fourteenth century growth in the trade of Cornish cloth improved local economies. People who were primarily farm workers or fishermen became involved part-time, at least, in the cloth trade, mainly in spinning and weaving in their homes. The west country slowly became more important to the woollen industry; Ireland and Wales sent wool to Cornwall for manufacture. Although Devon and Somerset were primary cloth production centres of manufacture for export, Cornwall too exported cloth known as 'Cornish straights' – a rough, uncoloured woollen cloth.[30] Looe had its own dyeing mill, combs for the industry were made in Liskeard, and many Cornish towns began to have yarn markets.[31] Pewter, made from tin alloy, became a major English export; it was, by the late fifteenth century, second only to cloth in terms of manufactured goods. In Cornwall an underground trade in pewter started in the early fourteenth century, the pewter being made from tin alloy.[32]

During the fourteenth and fifteenth centuries, English shipping in general was hampered by the intermittent Hundred Years' War and Cornish ships bore the brunt of accusations by the French and Spanish of piracy but Cornish crews feared piracy as well. Cornish merchants, eager to profit by the increase in shipping at the ports of Falmouth, Fowey, Looe, Penzance, and St Michael's Mount, were instrumental in developing port capacity. Falmouth Harbour was especially desirable for development, since it is one of the largest in the British Isles, and three major trading towns – Truro, Tregony, and Penryn – were accessible through Falmouth Harbour.[33] In 1427 William Morton of St Michael's Mount successfully petitioned to build a stone pier that would assist in harbouring at least 200 ships of substantial tonnage.[34] Although the tin economy suffered in the late 1400s, the shipping industry from Cornish ports continued to be a major source of income, not only from ports in the Channel but also ports on the Atlantic.[35] At Looe customs records from 1498–9 show typical late fifteenth-century trade between Looe and Irish ports: a ship from Kinsale discharged '150 boards and 12 mantles of Irish cloth' while a ship from Cork arrived with '50 dozen cords, 800 pieces of canvas and 10 pounds of saffron and took away a cargo of blocks of tin, calf-skins, salt and hides.'[36] Dried fish was continually part of Cornwall's trade economy, passing between the Cinque ports and French ports, primarily Bordeaux.

In the sixteenth century Cornwall's dependence on sea trade expanded. Fowey and Looe became involved in the newly-developed trade with Newfoundland by the end of the century as west country ships carried necessary construction materials and provisions for building a settlement there to support the catching and drying of cod on the Newfoundland Banks. Their return cargo of dried cod was taken to Spanish ports. Fruit and salt from Spain were then carried home to Cornwall.[37] These ships passing between Cornwall and Newfoundland, often stopping at other European ports to pick up supplies, were part of a navigation system so consistent that the ships were said to be the training grounds for English seamen of the day.[38]

The movement of mining in a slightly more westerly direction in the early seventeenth century would affect the growth of seaports. Falmouth, Padstow, Penryn, Penzance, St Ives, and Truro would grow while supplying mining with necessities for the industry.[39] Although mining had been for centuries Cornwall's primary industry, as medieval tin markets fluctuated and affected tin production, people concentrated more on agriculture and fishing.[40] New farming strategies improved acreage yields. Cornish coastal lands, once enclosed and treated with seaweed and sand, turned a profit and Cornwall often had surplus corn for export.[41] Traditional seine fishing for pilchards was the county's third economic source, the salted or smoked pilchards exported to continental ports.[42] The increasing need for capital for seine fishing led to greater merchant control of the export markets. Rowse remarks that it was a 'precise example of the Tudor idea of controlling trade in conflict with new economic tendencies – in a word, progress.'[43] Improvements in agriculture and fishing slowly brought economic stability to the county with corresponding growth in population. By the time of the 1641–2 Protestation returns, the population in Cornwall had increased to an estimated 99,000.[44]

Religious History

In the fourteenth century Cornwall felt the upheaval of the Peasants' Revolt, although not to the same extent as was felt elsewhere. Isolated incidents of violence toward the church did occur from time to time. The priest of Poundstock, Penfound, was murdered by parishioners in his chancel in 1357; in 1380 a priest, Walter Sancre, was beheaded in St Hilary parish; and in Crantock in 1382 and Penryn in 1383, clergy were assaulted. Unrest occasionally appeared in members of the clergy themselves. Ralph de Tremur, a former rector from Warleggon on Bodmin Moor who was known for his heretical ideas, was accused in 1354 of denying the 'Real Presence and [having] burnt the consecrated host.'[45]

In general Cornish people were resistant to change. There was a resurgence of devotion in Cornwall once the Hundred Years' War ended and people were able to resume pilgrimages abroad. Further additions to parish churches in the county began, such as the rebuilding in 1469-72 of Bodmin's St Petroc's Church, the largest parish church in Cornwall.[46] Even as late as the 1530s windows were made and put up at St Neot's Church.[47]

By the early Tudor period, however, Cornwall was in a state of political unrest. In 1497 a large contingent of Cornish, angry at Henry VII's levy to support the war with the Scots, rose and marched through Devon and Somerset to London, only to be defeated by royal troops, well armed to crush the insurgency. Many Cornish people were incensed, especially the poor usury-burdened tinners who rebelled against the tax.[48] Hearing of the rebellion the pretender, Perkin Warbeck, seized his opportunity, landing at Whitsand Bay in early September and then proceeding to Bodmin where he proclaimed himself Richard IV. Confronted at Taunton by the king's forces, Warbeck fled, leaving his Cornish followers – common people – infuriated. They took their anger out on the provost of Glasney Collegiate Church (a diligent tax collector for the king), dismembering him in the market square at Taunton. Henry VII enforced the levy, raising £600 from Cornwall.[49] Warbeck was hanged two years later for another conspiracy.

The first half of the sixteenth century brought Henry VIII's separation from Rome and the dissolution of the monasteries. In 1521 Henry VIII was named 'Defender of the Faith,' a title from Pope Leo X in recognition of his opposition to Luther, but by 1534 the Supremacy Act was in place and four years later Henry was excommunicated by the Roman pontiff. On the eve of the Reformation, there was seemingly little in Cornwall to attract the attention of the king and his officials. Religious houses counted but few residents at the suppression: there were nine Augustinian canons at Launceston Priory in 1539 and the same at Bodmin; the Franciscans at Bodmin were nine; St Germans' Augustinians and Tywardreath's Benedictines numbered seven each; Truro's Dominicans numbered eleven.[50] Henry VIII's commissioners were particularly hard on smaller houses such as those in Cornwall with earnings of less than £200. Henry suppressed them first in 1536 and then moved on to the larger houses in 1539. In 1547 Edward VI suppressed the chantries; most collegiate churches, such as Glasney, had been suppressed in 1545.[51]

Although the Cornish people's reputation did not match the reputation of the Welsh for renegade dissent and outright disregard for English law, they held strongly to their beliefs, however quickly changing, and often took action in matters dear to their traditions. In 1548 a proclamation from London stated that parishioners were forbidden to bear candles on Candlemas and to receive ashes on Ash Wednesday, palms on Palm Sunday, and holy bread and water. This was followed by an order to remove all images from churches, which then precipitated a riot at Helston. Led by men mainly from St Keverne, a mob murdered William Body, a layman of

Cornwall who publicly denounced the orders from London. Two days later the conflict worsened, preventing Sir William Godolphin and his justices from holding general sessions in the town. Help came from the king's forces and the riot was quickly quelled.[52]

The Act of Uniformity, passed by parliament under Edward vi in 1549 to enforce the use of the Book of Common Prayer,[53] so angered the Cornish that they demanded a return to the Latin mass that they were used to. In defence of their Cornish language and of the familiarity of Latin in church, they claimed ignorance of the new English, formulating their demands for 'holy bread and holy water made euery sondaye, Palmes and asshes at the tymes accustomed, Images to be set vp again in euery church, and all other auncient olde Ceremonyes vsed heretofore, by our mother the holy Church.' Refusing the new service, they argued that 'it is but lyke a Christmas gamme ... we wyll haue oure olde seruice of Mattens, masse, Euensong and procession in Latten as it was before ... we the Cornyshe men (wherof certen of vs vnderstande no Englysh) vtterly refuse thys newe Englysh.'[54] Marching on Exeter, Cornish rebels initiated the Western Rebellion of 1549, led by some members of prominent households and town officials, and laid seige to the town for five weeks; the Protestant gentry sided with the Crown and troops, reinforced by foreign mercenaries, finally suppressed the rebellion.[55] This suppression tolled a death knell for the Cornish language; scholars of Cornish cite the Reformation as one of the most deciding factors in its demise.[56]

Thirty years later, the people of Cornwall would swing away from their dedication to the old liturgy to a strong opposition to Catholicism. One might assume that the stubborn resistance to change in Cornwall was part of the Cornish personality or Cornish politics rather than an expression of religious conviction but some held fast to their faith. The Arundells of Lanherne remained staunch Catholic leaders, even through the subsequent, more accommodating Protestant reign of Elizabeth and beyond. The family first resisted the Protestant movement under Edward vi; Sir Humphrey was hanged and dismembered for leading Cornish Catholics during the 1549 Western Rebellion. His nephew, Sir Thomas, was also beheaded after conspiring against the earl of Warwick.[57] When Edward's death in 1553 led to the Counter-Reformation under Queen Mary, Thomas Arundell's nephew, John, and other members of the Catholic gentry returned to a more favourable position, at least for a while.[58]

Mounting political tensions leading up to the war with Spain and strong anti-Catholic sentiment proved disastrous in the end for many Catholic families in Cornwall. In 1581 parliament passed an act imposing heavy fines and punishment for attachment to the Catholic church.[59] Many of the leading families were Protestant – the Carews, Edgcumbes, Godolphins, Killigrews, and Treffrys – and many of them had profited by the Protestant Reformation. Some members of the gentry (Sir Richard Edgcumbe, Sir William Godolphin, John Killigrew, Thomas Treffry, and Sir Hugh Trevanion) had served as commissioners, assisting in the spoliation of local churches.[60] Few Catholics outside the wealthy and powerful Arundells of Lanherne were able to withstand the religious and economic persecution that could result in imprisonment, torture and death, or exile and impoverishment. Such was the fate in 1577 of the Douai seminarian and 'last Cornish martyr,' Cuthbert Mayne, lodged at the Tregian family's Golden Manor. The main witness for the prosecution at Mayne's trial, a certain Twigges, claimed that he saw and shared a room with Mayne at Golden, where Mayne divulged his continuing participation in the priesthood. (Twigges entertained at Golden Manor, Christmas 1575; see pp 531–3). Although there are no other known household accounts for Golden Manor that might corroborate the entertainment, Tregian (who was charged with concealing the priest, Mayne) himself offered to provide depositions of at least forty persons present on that occasion to counter the testimony of Twigges, whom Tregian describes as 'a poore parishe Clarke, for hee was no better, runninge aboute the Countrye from place to place, with a balde Enterclude.' Mayne was tried at the 1577 assizes, hanged, drawn, and quartered, and his head impaled at Launceston Castle, one of the most formidable military and penal sites in England.[61]

Many years later Launceston gaol was also the place of imprisonment for a physician, John Bastwick, who was involved in a famous case litigated before Archbishop Laud and the Star Chamber Court. In 1632 or 1633 William Prynne, a lawyer from Lincoln's Inn, published a tract called *Histrio-mastix*, in which he wildly attacked stage players.[62] In 1637 Prynne's friend, John Bastwick, joined in and extended the attack, writing *The Letany of John Bastwick* as an answer to Prynne's work.[63] Bastwick railed against the clergy, deepening the already dangerous situation, saying, 'one would thinke, that hell were broke loose, and that the Deuils in surplices, in hoods, in copes, in rochets, and in foure square cow TVRDS vpon their heads, were come among vs.'[64] Henry Burton, another friend of Prynne, added even more fuel to the fire by attacking bishops as factors of Antichrist, among other insults.[65] On 29 June Archbishop Laud ruled that all three men would lose their ears, pay a fine of £5,000, and be imprisoned for life.[66] Bastwick was imprisoned in August 1637 in Launceston Castle, by then in very poor condition from neglect.

The Duchy of Cornwall

When in 1337 Edward III established the duchy of Cornwall by royal charter he not only created the first duchy in the country but also established a unique political framework for succession to the English throne. Witnessing the results of dynastic conflict over the throne in the death of his father and concerned about succession, Edward proclaimed his seven-year-old son, Edward of Woodstock, the Black Prince, as duke of Cornwall, the highest ranking noble in the realm. Edward's remarkable move linked the title, duke of Cornwall, with the royal succession and made the seisin of the duchy (with its important revenues) of great political interest. By design, the duchy provided substantial income for the duke of Cornwall. The duchy charter stipulated that none of the duchy estates granted by the charter could be broken apart or given up, so that it never passed from the control of the duke of Cornwall.[67] The duchy emerged from the Norman earldom of Cornwall and had been connected to the monarchy since Saxon times.

Entries from the Domesday survey of 1086 tell us something about life in Cornwall just after the Norman Conquest and about the history of landholdings that would become the duchy of Cornwall. Robert, count of Mortain – King William's half-brother and a Norman – was the greatest landholder in England after the king, and the greatest landholder in Cornwall, holding more than two-thirds of the county.[68] The count acquired a good deal of his land from spoliation – seizure through war or pillaging – and ecclesiastical lands were under threat.[69]

The earldom he left as a legacy eventually passed to the second son of Edward II, John of Eltham, and then returned to the Crown in 1336 upon his death.[70] The duchy of Cornwall was created the following year. One of England's largest landed estates even today after centuries of erosion from the selling of manors for various administrative and financial reasons, the duchy and its history play a central role in the economic and political history of Cornwall.

Over the thirty-nine years between 1337 until his death in 1376, Edward the Black Prince became an exemplary duke of Cornwall. He was both charismatic and conscientious, a careful administrator of his Cornish lands. He is acknowledged as epitomizing the best attributes of the Middle Ages — courage, honour, and largesse — and was a national hero in his time.[71]

Edward of Woodstock was given seventeen manors in 1337, including Launceston, Restormel, Tintagel, and Trematon, each of these having a fortress from which the duke of Cornwall could defend himself and deploy his military.[72] The ducal rights and properties extended far beyond the boundaries of Cornwall; the duchy included estates as far away from Cornwall as Knaresborough in Yorkshire, Wallingford in Berkshire, and Kennington in Surrey.[73] The duke of Cornwall had significant political power over Cornwall itself, since he could nominate the high sheriff. A natural administrator, the Black Prince appointed men to control finances and to administer his duchy treasury, and auditors to supervise rents. He held the rights to escheat — the reversion of lands under feudal law to the lord of the fee when legal heirship failed — and control of petty customs. And, most important, he held power over the stannaries. Coinage of tin was a key source of revenue for the duke: 'Each year miners brought ingots to the Duke's coinage halls where their purity was assayed and weighed. A tax was levied based on weight and once this was paid, the ingots were struck with the Duke's emblem or "coined" to indicate that the standards had been met and dues paid.'[74] The duke appointed the warden of stannaries, a royal officer with unprecedented judicial power, as well as a council of advisors to keep him informed about duchy matters but Edward took a great interest in his duchy and ruled it directly.

The duchy did not see the fulfilment of the Black Prince's example in subsequent dukes of Cornwall and suffered fluctuations between mediocre management and benign neglect. Richard of Bordeaux, the second duke and later, in 1377, King Richard II, managing his duchy as haphazardly as he later would his kingdom, significantly reduced duchy land, doling it out as favours to friends and family members.[75] The long and complicated political and economic history of the duchy of Cornwall had begun.

The revenues from the duchy have always played a great part in political manoeuverings of the Crown. Henry VII, after the death in 1502 of Prince Arthur, duke of Cornwall, secured from parliament in 1504 an act which gave his other son, Henry, duke of York, title to duchy revenues as duke of Cornwall.[76] When Henry became king he claimed duchy revenues for his own use, diverting them from the Exchequer. The estimated revenues in 1500 were almost 5 per cent of the Crown's total income and were an attractive source of funds for Henry VIII.[77] The king was not insensitive to power relationships involved with the duchy. Opponents to the Reformation, like Henry Courtenay, marquess of Exeter, who also laid claim to the throne and was executed for treason, were removed. This was a bold move on Henry's part for two significant reasons: the king then became the most important landlord in the southwest when Courtenay's duchy land was transferred to the king, and Cornwall's only member of the House of Lords until the 1600s was the bishop of Exeter. Henry also annexed twenty-eight Cornish manors to the duchy from dissolved monasteries; eight were from Launceston Priory and six from Tywardreath Priory.[78]

When Edward VI succeeded to the throne in 1547 the duchy lands were already attached to the Court of Augmentations that presided over the dissolution of the monasteries, making them an important source of income for the Crown. It was an ironic twist that revenues from Cornish manors were used to crush Cornish people during the Western Rebellion in 1549. Queen Mary controlled Cornish lands through the duchy by appointing Catholic officials. Catholic families, like the Arundells, who had fallen from power under Protestant rule, only temporarily returned to influence through the duchy. This short-lived respite reversed again in 1558 when Elizabeth came to the throne but Elizabeth's policy, at least initially, was one of benign neglect toward the duchy. Ruled through the Exchequer once again, the Cornish duchy lands, despite their important revenues, came to be regarded later in her reign as a bargaining chip for revenue to support the war with Spain.[79] By the time James I came to power in 1603 revenues had dwindled. Recognizing the state of the duchy, Crown officials successfully recovered many formerly sacrificed duchy lands but it was not until Prince Charles, the duke of York and the next king, was affirmed title to duchy control and revenues in 1615 that the future stability of the duchy was secured. John Norden, a cartographer who also provided information on land values, was engaged to survey duchy lands. A wise manager, Charles increased net revenues of the duchy to over 300 per cent, and by 1625 when he became king, the duchy was a viable source of income for him as duke of Cornwall.[80]

From 1337 to 1642 the politics of the duchy determined to a significant extent the fortunes, in both senses of the word, of the great families of Cornwall. The duke of Cornwall's patronage secured their membership and participation in the government of the country and their position in the county. For those on the lower rungs of the social ladder, their opportunities were often determined by the duchy of Cornwall and its relationship to the Crown. The vicissitudes of the Cornish people were well expressed in the words of a Cornishman, who 'complained that a visit from the Duchy rent collector, "was like that of the gospel that when one devil was cast out seven worst came instead of him".'[81]

Boroughs and Market Towns

BODMIN

Located on the west end of Bodmin Moor, Bodmin was commercially and nearly geographically the centre of the county; since about 300 BC it had been a settlement on the north-south trade route across Cornwall from the continent to Ireland and remnants of tin workings have been found dating from before Roman times.[82] Bodmin also has its ecclesiastical claim to primacy. In the sixth century Welsh Saints Guron and Petroc established the abbey/bishropric, Dinuurrin, part of the House of Petroc begun earlier at Padstow, linking Bodmin to one of the most celebrated Celtic saints. By the ninth century Dinuurrin had become the principal house. St Petroc's, Cornwall's largest parish church, was built during the 1130s and the shrine of St Petroc was a major pilgrimage site for the devout who travelled there to venerate the relics of the Celtic saint. At the same time as the building of the parish church and separate from it, the earlier monastery was refounded by Augustinian canons as Bodmin Priory of St Mary and St Petroc. Bodmin was also the home of one of only two Franciscan establishments in Cornwall.[83] Since Bodmin and Truro, where the Dominicans established themselves, were well populated for the time, the friars were attracted there in the early thirteenth century to travel among the people preaching, soon accepting endowments so large that they contributed to church building and to the addition of new monastic buildings rivalling those of the canons.[84] Between 1501 and 1514 Berry Tower of the chantry church of the Holy Rood was built, celebrating the spot where the original town was likely located.[85]

Bodmin may have been a borough as early as the time of the Domesday survey and it was the first recorded coinage site. At the time there were sixty-eight houses and it was the largest town in Cornwall.[86] Up to the fourteenth century, it was mainly the tin trade that helped make Bodmin a busy commercial town. Bodmin regulated trade through its guild merchant, granted in the town's borough charter by Richard, earl of Cornwall (1225–57).[87] Besides regulating trade, a guild merchant had other powers. It could, for example, 'grant a town's liberty to a runaway serf who had hidden within its bounds for "a year and a day"... A licence for such power was payable annually to the monarch and, when in 1179/80 a raid was made on un-licensed guilds of the south western shires, Bodmin burgesses were fined for keeping a guild without royal warrant.'[88] County assize courts were held in Bodmin only three times during the thirteenth and fourteenth centuries: sometime between 1227 and 1272, 1310–11, and 1330–1.[89] Although we know little about local government of the time, we do know from early schedules to Chancery submitted by the sheriff of Cornwall the names of burgesses elected and members of parliament. Bodmin made returns to parliament from 1295 on.[90]

Bodmin Priory, one of Cornwall's pilgrimage sites and a great centre of devotion, was a powerful landlord in the Bodmin area. Large tracts of land from Bodmin to Padstow belonged to the church: on one side of the Camel River the land belonged to the priory; on the other, to 'the bishop, with the livings in the hands of the dean and chapter.'[91] Until the Dissolution the prior was lord of the borough but the mayor and burgesses often quarrelled over rights.[92] The growing dissatisfaction with the church and clergy in the sixteenth century was more pronounced and extended at Bodmin, in part because of Bodmin's large population, twice that of any other town at the time. The once flourishing Franciscans at Bodmin surrendered to the Dissolution in poverty in 1538, £16 in debt, their numbers reduced to a warden, nine friars, and some lay brothers.[93]

Bodmin's formal charter of incorporation in 1563 provided for a mayor and twelve capital burgesses and councillors; a common council would also be selected, composed of twenty-four.[94] Like many other towns Bodmin gained the right to run its town government, something their previous attachment to Bodmin Priory did not fully allow.[95] Two annual three-day fairs and a Saturday market were granted and one more three-day fair was added in 1594.[96] One of the three-day fairs granted by the 1563 charter was held around 6 December, with pie powder jurisdiction.[97]

In the early fourteenth century Bodmin lost its central position as a tin town when the tin trade fluctuated but a trade in leather goods developed in its place. Town records preserve names of the Skinners' and Glovers' guilds, and the Salting Pool near the Launceston Road is believed to be the place where hides were salted. Lime for removing hide hair was brought in from Padstow.[98] Today's Rhind Street appears in fifteenth-century parish accounts as 'Rynestrete,' probably referring to the 'rind' or the 'tree bark which was milled to obtain tanic acid to convert raw hides into leather for Bodmin's principal industry from the middle ages to c. 1860.'[99] Fishing also played a significant part in the local economy. The nearby Camel River provided abundant, high-quality fish for local use and for sale to nearby communities, so abundant that the prior's arms were comprised of '3 salmon fish,' signifying his jurisdiction over the Camel waters, a control contested by the burgesses up to the Dissolution.[100]

Extant records from 1469–72 show that Bodmin had over forty guilds by the fifteenth century; five were trade guilds and many were religious guilds, some attached to St Petroc's Church or to chapels in the area.[101] They were housed on 'almost every street of the old town, the principal Hall being in Fore Street.'[102] The guildhall on the southern side of the street was probably the 'House of Petroc' that appears in the Bodmin records, as well as the 'Hall House' that appears in the 1563 charter. The present-day Guildhall possibly incorporates parts of the meeting place of St Petroc's guild of Skinners and Glovers.[103] Many guild activities were directed toward church construction in the fifteenth and early sixteenth centuries in Cornwall, especially in the years just before the Reformation. At Bodmin thirty guilds and 'ten other groups raised two-thirds of the total sum of £196 7s 4 ½d,' probably for the south aisle and south porch of the church.[104] Groups contributing the most were associated with the parish church or major chapels: these included the Erasmus guild, the Corpus Christi guild, and the five trade guilds. The guilds of St George and St Thomas had their own chapels.[105]

During the Western Rebellion Bodmin, 'as it had been in the time of Flamank and Warbeck, was the natural centre of resistence.'[106] In 1549 Bodmin's Mayor Boyer was hanged as a rebel leader but a subsequent shift in local religious opinion found Bodmin displaying a quarter of Cuthbert Mayne's dismembered body as a warning against the practice of Roman Catholicism in 1577.[107]

There are no population figures surviving from the poll tax of 1377 for Bodmin but it was the largest town in Cornwall during the Middle Ages and beyond.[108] In 1602 Carew remarked that Bodmin was a lively town with the greatest weekly market in Cornwall, 'the quarter Sessions for the East diuision, and halfe yeerely faires.'[109] On the basis of the 1642 Protestation returns, the population of Bodmin has been estimated at 1,473.[110]

LAUNCESTON

Originally the Celtic settlement Lanstephan, often appearing in historical accounts as Lan Stefanton, Launceston was founded on the site of St Stephen's Priory in Newport, today a suburb of the town. Dunheved, site of the Norman castle, became a district of Launceston.[111] By the late Middle Ages there were three separate townships: Launceston (St Stephen), Dunheved, and Newport. Newport grew up around Launceston Priory in the early Middle Ages and although it never received a royal charter it did have some township privileges. Although no evidence has been discovered for support, Newport claimed that the township was granted a market and a fair in 1557. Newport was under the lordship of Launceston Priory until its dissolution when Newport was annexed to the duchy of Cornwall. Little is known about Newport's administration under the duchy but the township had a mayor and two reeves, probably elected from the burgesses. Newport returned two members to parliament first in 1529 and perhaps even earlier. The name of the borough varies on the six surviving indentures: in 1545 and 1553 it is 'Launceston'; later, in 1553, it is 'Launceston' with 'alias Newport' crossed through; in 1554 it is 'Newport' with 'iuxta Launceston' inserted; in 1555 it is 'Newport alias Launceston.'[112] Municipal records from Newport for our period are not extant.

Dunheved, the oldest borough in the group now called Launceston, grew up around Launceston Castle, the site of the original Celtic hillfort across the River Kensey from Launceston (St Stephen). Robert, count of Mortain, after building the castle on the hill at Dunheved but before 1086, moved the market from the older St Stephen to Dunheved. The confusion increased after 1529 when both Newport and Dunheved returned writs under the name 'Launceston.' Dunheved had earlier done the same but then reverted to its ancient name, Dunheved. Elizabethan returns and Crown office lists usually distinguish between Newport, the area around the priory, and Dunheved, but increasingly after the sixteenth century scholars and other commentators often have not separated the two, and even more often use 'Launceston' to mean any of the three districts.[113] Henceforth here, we use the name 'Launceston' to mean Launceston and Dunheved unless clarification is specifically available. Surviving borough accounts from Dunheved at the Cornwall Record Office are identified as Launceston records.

Located between Dartmoor and Bodmin Moor, Dunheved was chiefly a military settlement on Old Street, probably the ancient Roman road running from Exeter to Marazion.[114] It was important throughout the Middle Ages, the 'strategic key of the peninsula,' only two miles from the Devon border, guarding the approaches to Cornwall.[115] The Norman Count Robert of Mortain held court and administered his land from Launceston and it was as a judicial centre for the shire that Launceston would come to claim itself as the major town in Cornwall. It was the site of the county assizes and often an inconvenient spot for officials from other parts of Cornwall, given the town's location so near the Tamar. Occasionally the assizes were held at Bodmin or Lostwithiel, more convenient locations, until Launceston complained about the loss of trade from the assizes; a 1386 charter granted Launceston the permanent benefit of the assizes, although even after a guarantee, they sometimes were held at other towns.[116]

Launceston is the only known medieval walled town in Cornwall, highly defensible in the early thirteenth century when the six-foot-thick walls were in top condition soon after the town wall was joined to the castle wall.[117] Launceston Castle was one of the fortifications given to Edward the Black Prince as part of duchy holdings in 1337. In 1369 he brought the castle up to full garrison strength, renewing its military power.[118] He also improved the buildings of the castle, adding a chapel and assize hall; it was repaired again in 1461.[119] Carew in 1602 commented on Launceston Castle, saying that it was 'an ancient Castle, whose steepe rocky-footed Keepe, hath his top enuironed with a treble wal, and in regard therof, men say, was called, Castle terrible.'[120] The castle was used as a gaol well into the seventeenth century.

Launceston had a market at the time of the Domesday Book. It later received a borough charter under Reginald, earl of Cornwall between 1141 and 1167.[121] As a free borough Launceston could elect a mayor. Rather than having a provost or portieve, elected by burgesses but answerable to the lord of the manor, Launceston's mayor was answerable to the burgesses who elected him, an important distinction for free boroughs.[122] In the early fourteenth century Launceston had eight aldermen and twelve burgesses who elected a mayor, probably just before the official year began on the feast of St Katherine, 25 November. According to a 1302 assize court record, both Launceston and Dunheved had their own burgesses and disputes arose between them concerning their mutual rights and liberties. A merchant guild is recorded for Dunheved, and markets on Tuesdays and Saturdays, with an annual fair in Whit week.[123] Like four other early boroughs (Bodmin, Liskeard, Tregony, and Truro), Launceston sent two members to parliament from 1386. Travelling 'some three hundred miles of medieval road' from Cornwall to London, the members from the county usually served only one term and were paid 2s a day, including travel time.[124] In the late thirteenth century a guildhall was begun in the Dunheved district.[125] Surviving borough accounts indicate that in 1487 the guildhall was used for elections, and probably even earlier.[126] The guildhall occupied a place on the present High and Church Streets and perhaps part of the nineteenth-century bank location.[127]

Borough accounts from the fifteenth and sixteenth centuries indicate fifteen guilds in Launceston, some associated with St Mary Magdalene's Church and eight with St Thomas.'[128] The St Mary Magdalene guild, a trade or municipal guild, may be the same as the unnamed guild of 1334, one of the earliest mentions of a guild in Cornwall. Launceston's minstrels were part of a confraternity attached to St Mary Magdalene's Church; St Thomas' parish had the All Hallows' guild at Tregadillett, about two miles from Launceston, probably founded in 1479. Around 1500 All Hallows' guild accounts note that half of the thirty members were women, although women are only twice recorded as officers of the guild, in 1491 and 1497. Although membership fees are not common in extant guild accounts, we know that the guild of St Mary Magdalene charged sons of freemen 16d and outsiders, 6s 8d. Many rural Cornish guilds accepted lambs as payment (worth about 10d each in the 1540s); the All Hallows' guild accepted lambs, and Mattingly suggests that it may have been a shepherds' guild or connected to sheep stores. Chapels were often supported by guilds; Tregadillett may have had a chapel of ease supported by the All Hallows' guild. 'Mornspeches,' morning meetings held several times a year to discuss non-parish business, are recorded in 1530–1; there may be a connection between these 'mornspeches' and the 'speche howse' that appears in the Launceston borough accounts in 1540 and 1577.

Although St Stephen's is considered the 'mother church' of Launceston, the first parish church was actually built about 1080 within the castle walls and was dedicated to the Virgin Mary. The present parish church of St Mary Magdalene was dedicated in 1524.[129] Launceston Priory was dissolved in 1539, when John Tregonwell reported to the king that all things were in good order. The priory income at the time was £354. Although the priory was later demolished, parts of the foundation can still be seen near the Kensey and the priory's Norman doorway remains as the entrance to the White Hart Hotel on the market square.[130]

After the Dissolution many boroughs procured new charters of incorporation confirming their rights and privileges. Launceston's in 1555/6 indicated the right to elect a mayor and to appoint eight aldermen who had the right to admit burgesses and freemen at their discretion.[131] A yearly fair was granted 'on the vigil of the day, feast, and morrow of the exaltation of the Holy Cross' and 'a market within the town of Newport ... on every Wednesday in each and every week ... and also a Court of Piepoudre within the fair time.'[132] Income to maintain bridges and roads, to pave streets, to repair churches and the guildhall, and to pay other municipal fees came from land the town owned within the borough and from outside commons.[133] The local economy, supported as elsewhere by tin works such as the nearby Radmore tin works, was supplemented by domestic industry.[134] Cornwall is also naturally rich in granite and slate and Launceston borough accounts contain many references to local quarrying. From the fifteenth century on, improvements in pasture and selection of stock helped produce better wool. Local sheep raising provided wool for spinning and weaving in homes, as well as hides for tanning.[135]

Launceston was a busy town throughout the Middle Ages and Renaissance because of the castle gaol and assize courts held there. Carew noted that Launceston's prosperity in his time came from 'more use, and profit of faire lodgings, through the Countie Assizes.'[136] Launceston remained otherwise a smaller town throughout our period.[137] Never the size of Bodmin's, the town population has been estimated at only 882 in 1642, according to the Protestation returns of that year.[138]

LOSTWITHIEL

Located on the Fowey estuary, Lostwithiel began under the patronage of the lords of the manor of Bodardle (who lived in Restormel Castle) although neither Lostwithiel nor Restormel appear in the Domesday Book. In 1194 Richard I received ten marks from Robert Cardinhan, lord of the manor, in payment for a market at 'Lostwetell'; about the same time Lostwithiel earned its first charter.[139] The charter recognized that the town had burgesses but Cardinhan and his bailiffs would still be judges in the borough court. The burgesses were allowed to elect one of their own as provost or reeve to represent their interests. Town businesses were protected from outsiders since aliens were forbidden to set up a shop or tavern unless the town representatives agreed.[140]

Richard, earl of Cornwall, bought Restormel Castle in about 1268 from Isolda de Cardinhan, granddaughter of Robert, and with it the town of Lostwithiel, including its three mills and a fishery. Restormel Castle, located on a hill less than two miles from Lostwithiel, overlooks the Fowey River valley. The keep was probably built by Robert Cardinhan about 1200. In the late thirteenth century stone buildings were added for halls and chambers, as well as a large gateway and chapel. Remnants of what was once the outer wall were discovered earlier in this century. During the late thirteenth century, Edmund, earl of Cornwall, made Restormel his main place of residence but he was the last lord of Cornwall to reside there. The castle was a favourite place to stop for Edward, the Black Prince, and was so 'modern' for the time that it had piped spring water, a luxury feature. He stayed at Restormel twice: 20 August to 4 September 1354 and around Easter, 1363.[141] The glory days of the castle ended soon after the death of the Black Prince in 1377. During the Reformation Henry VIII made pastureland of the great park. In modern times the ruins were used as a quarry. The only remaining buildings at Restormel are those that were inside the great keep: a hall, chapel, three chambers, and three upper chambers, all now under the care of the Office of Works.[142]

The purchase of Restormel Castle forged a link between town and castle, the future duke of Cornwall and the duchy, and the monastery, Tywardreath. Richard granted Lostwithiel a charter in 1268, giving it a measure of independence as a free borough. Besides exempting the burgesses from tolls throughout Cornwall, the town could regulate its commerce by means of its guild merchant; it was granted a yearly three-day fair at the feast of St Bartholomew (24 August) and a weekly Tuesday market.[143] As a borough Lostwithiel first sent two burgesses to parliament in 1305.[144] Lostwithiel's charter gave the townspeople an unusual amount of power in local government; while many charters exempted townsmen from their hundred courts they were still subject to the court of the shire. Townsmen in Lostwithiel, however, were subject only to their borough court, presided over by their lord and his bailiffs.[145] Lostwithiel and the duchy palace in the thirteenth century therefore 'was to Cornwall what the Palace of Westminster was to London and the country as a whole, the seat of government.'[146]

Lostwithiel's economy, as in much of Cornwall, depended on the tin trade and shipping. Besides being a market town Lostwithiel was an inland port like Truro and its role in tin coinage and in being the site of a stannary court until the eighteenth century brought people into the town on business, mercantile and legal. By the early sixteenth century its prosperity eroded because the silting up of the Fowey estuary made its port no longer suitable for shipping tin from the Bodmin Moor works.[147]

Lostwithiel had two religious guilds: Corpus Christi, first mentioned in the 1368 will of John Dabernon, and St George's, dating from 1414.[148] St George's guild was of some importance; it had its own chaplain and probably maintained its relative exclusivity through admittance fees, 20d for married couples and 3s 4d for outsiders. St George's guild, like other religious guilds, was responsible for dirges for the dead on its patronal festival, for annual masses the day following, and for supporting and attending funerals of guild members. Accompanying feasts and entertainments sponsored by the guild were intended to raise money for the parish church.[149] The parish church, St Bartholomew's, was founded in the late twelfth century, probably in 1180, but the main part of the church was built in the fourteenth century. St Bartholomew's, along with St Nicholas', the parish church at nearby Fowey, belonged to Tywardreath Priory until the Dissolution.

The Benedictine monastery at Tywardreath, founded c 1088, was never a prosperous house and never an attractive pilgrimage site like Bodmin Priory. Although Edmund, earl of Cornwall and brother of Henry III, spent a great deal of time at Restormel, made Lostwithiel the capital of the county, and spent a good amount of money on the town, the monastery at Tywardreath did not interest him – the abbey of Hailes in Gloucestershire was his primary focus.[150] The small monastery struggled along, falling apart until it drew attention, as all Cornish monasteries did, when the Reformation began. The prior and six monks were warned by Bishop Veysey to change their behaviour, say matins according to the Rule, and close 'all windows and doors by which women might enter.'[151] Thomas Treffry, friend of Cromwell and no friend to the prior of Tywardreath – since the prior was still 'nominal lord of the borough of Fowey' and a thorn in tenant Treffry's side – drew the king's attention to the village of Fowey and Tywardreath.[152] As a result Tywardreath was one of the first Cornish monasteries to be dissolved in 1536, its income at the time only £123.[153] Carew says of Tywardreath Monastery: 'A little beyond Foy, the land openeth a large sandie Bay, for the Sea to ouer-flow, which, and the village adioyning, are therethrough aptly termed Trewardreth, in English, The Sandie towne. Elder times, of more deuotion then knowledge, here founded a religious house, which, in King Henrie the eights raigne, vnderwent the common downefall.'[154]

The sense of autonomy that had developed in Lostwithiel since the time of Robert, count of Mortain, made itself apparent in economic and financial strategies employed to resist the Crown Exchequer's keen awareness of sources of income. The Chantry Act of 1547 confiscated chantry endowments and lesser endowments for fraternities and guilds.[155] The Chantry Certificates of 1546 and 1548 registered only one fraternity in Cornwall, although many more existed, suggesting the kind of evasion that occurred in Lostwithiel.[156] Rowse recounts a Court of Augmentations case where 'the mayor and burgesses of Lostwithiel had concealed from the Crown the lands with which the gild [of St George's chapel] was endowed. We learn that the chapel was "defaced immediately upon the last [Commotion]" by order of the mayor [Richard Hutchings]. Sir William Coles, former gild priest, deposed that the gild was "only maintained by the devotions of them that were and would be brethren and sises of the same…" Coles denied that there were any lands belonging to the gild, and said that he had "never heard it called St. George's chantry till now of late by the adversaries of the said mayor and brethren". From this we may infer two things – that he had been got at by the mayor, and that there were two factions in the town. For other witnesses deposed that there were lands belonging to the gild: St. George's mills, for example, and St. George's closes. There were also lands of St. Bartholomew, patron saint of the parish church.'[157] While its status as an actual chantry might be in question, extant records from the steward of the guild, 1536–7, indicate that the guild did make payments for rent of ground that belonged to St George's mills and St George's close, called 'Beades Parke.'[158] In spite of attracting a good deal of attention for its nearby Restormel Castle and stannary, Lostwithiel remained a small town in comparison to Bodmin. Lostwithiel received a charter of incorporation, providing for a mayor and aldermen, in 1608.[159] At the start of the Civil War Lostwithiel's population, on the basis of the 1642 Protestation returns, was 393.[160]

PENRYN

Located on the Fal estuary, Penryn is first recorded in 1236 when the town was granted a charter by the bishop of Exeter but its enfranchisement was confirmed only in 1547.[161] As is true for small towns in the shire, we know little about its town government except that in the sixteenth century Penryn's municipal administration was headed by a mayor or portreeve, with the help of bailiffs and burgesses.[162] In 1547 the borough began sending two members to parliament and was incorporated in 1621, during the reign of James I.[163] A weekly Monday market and a fair on the vigil, feast, and morrow of St Thomas the Martyr (29 December) were granted 8 January 1258/9 and a fair on the morrow of St Vitalis (28 April) and two days after was granted in 1311.[164] Penryn was also an important port for trade between Cornwall and France and Spain. It was close to the sea – closer than Truro – and foreign trade helped Penryn develop into one of the busiest ports in the county. In 1602, however, Carew was little impressed with the town, commenting that Penryn was 'rather passable, then noteable, for wealth, buildings, and Inhabitants.'[165] But there was considerable wealth nearby. The fortune of the Killigrew family, for example, came in part from trade at Penryn.[166] The Killigrews, who owned the land near where the port town of Falmouth would develop – about two miles from Penryn – achieved significant political power in the sixteenth century, in part because of Sir Henry Killigrew's friendship with the Cecils. Arwennack, their home, was rebuilt in 1567 for over £6000 – lavish for the time.[167]

In 1377 there were about 300 people in Penryn.[168] Three centuries later, when Walter Ralegh, lord warden of the stannaries, visited Falmouth Harbour, he commented that only Arwennack and a few other houses were there.[169] But foreign trade and the use of Penryn as a port increased so significantly that the population, many of whom were not native to Cornwall, had more than tripled by 1642 when 1,143 have been estimated as resident in Penryn.[170]

Penryn had no parish church but was part of the parish of St Gluvias, the mother church, dedicated in 1318. A chapel of St Mary Magdalene in Penryn existed in the town before 1322 and Penryn paid yearly to the altar at St Gluvias for the chaplain, who was elected by the town burgesses but approved by the vicar.[171] Penryn was best known for the Collegiate Church of St Thomas at Glasney (Glasney College), a college of secular canons situated just south of the town. Founded by Bishop Bronescombe in 1267, it was the 'most flourishing and richest institution in Cornwall' up to the Dissolution.[172] Glasney's local power came from the land it owned in Penryn and from tithes and patronage income from sixteen local parishes.[173] Glasney's connection to the Cornish play, the *Ordinalia*, has long been the subject of scholarly speculation, many believing that the play was written there.[174] The church was a likely place for entertainments and attracted residents as no other establishment in Cornwall could. For many rectors, living in rural parishes was a lonely life. Travel was long and difficult and they were unlikely to have many educated visitors; books were few. So attracted to Glasney were they that in 1372 Bishop Brantingham 'wrote to the Provost of the College complaining that some rectors absented themselves from their parishes and resided in the College where they consumed the provisions and were a greater burden to the College than honour to God.'[175]

Glasney did have its moments of less-than-virtuous history. Bishop Grandisson chastised Glasney in his 1360 prohibition, specifically directed to its provost and chapter, threatening excommunication, against 'silly and harmful pastimes,' holiday entertainments, and plays (see pp 503–4).[176] In injunctions issued after his visitation of 1387, Bishop Brantingham called upon the warden and chapter at Glasney to take particular care to avoid certain occasions of misbehaviour. These included singing the offices irreverently and improperly, disobeying their rule, associating with suspicious women, and not looking after the books and vessels belonging to the collegiate church.[177] Although scholars believe that in general the behaviour of the canons at Glasney was good, in 1400 Bishop Stafford at his visitation again found problems: the vicars and canons were charged with seriously neglecting their sacred duties.[178]

Glasney was suppressed in 1545. About 1815 a document was discovered at Penryn stating that the town was owed 'a moidore [a gold coin] a year for the loss of Glasney College.' In 1865 the antiquarian, C.R. Sowell, feared that 'the claim had lapsed.'[179] The remains of the collegiate church were then described as 'inconsiderable but interesting.' Some tracery remained, door jambs and sills, stones that had been used in local building, part of a chapel mullion, and some sections of foundation masonry.[180] Today, only fragments remain.

ST IVES

When Carew travelled to St Ives in the hundred of Penwith he was not very impressed with this little fishing port. The town and port, he said, are 'both of meane plight, yet, with their best meanes, (and often, to good and necessarie purpose) succouring distressed shipping. Order hath bene taken, and attempts made, for bettering the Road with a peere, but eyther want, or slacknesse, or impossibilitie, hitherto withhold the effect: the whiles, plentie of fish is here taken, and sold verie cheape.'[181] At the Conquest, St Ives, along with nearby Lelant and Towednack, was part of the great manors of Ludgvan Leaze (Luduham) and Connerton, the 'paramount manor of the Hundred of Penwith.'[182] Lelant, where the parish church was located, was the main village in the area and in the early Middle Ages was an important port and market town.[183] St Ives had no parish church of its own until the early fifteenth century but did have a small Norman chapel of ease under the mother church in Lelant. For services, baptisms, purifications, and burials the people of St Ives had to travel between two and four miles to the mother church, often over nearly impassable roads. St Ives was, however, a recognized parish for revenues, for debts, and for civic matters by the fourteenth century. In 1408 and 1409, in two separate petitions, the St Ives inhabitants requested their own parish church but it was not until 1428 that the chapel enlargement was completed and a church was dedicated to St Andrew and consecrated by Bishop Lacy of Exeter for the performance of all sacraments, although St Ives had no cemetery until 1542.[184]

Through most of the fourteenth century St Ives was a small fishing hamlet with a few houses and shelters for fishing boats. In fact the 1327 subsidy roll records forty-seven taxpayers at St Ives.[185] But slowly St Ives grew mainly because it was central to sea trade to and from Ireland and Brittany. As Lelant's harbour gradually became choked with silt, St Ives benefited from increased trade traffic and growing population. Eventually St Ives would struggle with silting as well and in 1538 Leland wrote that sand from storms had 'sore oppressid' houses in St Ives and a 'fair pere [was] sore chokid with sande.'[186]

The first fair on record in the area is for Lelant. William Bottreaux, lord of the manor of La Nant (Lelant), was granted a Thursday market by Edward I in 1295; the same charter allowed two fairs, one on the Purification of the Virgin (2 February) and one on the Assumption (15 August).[187] In 1487 King Henry VII granted Lord Willoughby de Broke of Ludgvan

Leaze a weekly Saturday market and two yearly fairs.[188] We know from the extant St Ives borough records beginning in 1570 that the town government was run by a portreeve, twelve councilmen, and twenty-four burgesses.[189] From 1558 on, the year of its enfranchisement, St Ives returned two members to parliament.[190] Town officials also had power that burgesses of other towns closer to the Tamar did not; 'though expected to pay its full quota of national taxes it was largely autonomous in the management of its own affairs. Therefore the "12 and 24 men," as they were styled, had to deal with all manner of business   repairing the church, controlling the fisheries, looking after the parish paupers, upholding the law and punishing offenders, enforcing public health regulations, collecting harbour dues, running the market, and also, most importantly in those warlike times, when the coast was always liable to attack by French, Spanish and Turkish vessels, taking active measures for the defence of the town.'[191] A long way from London – St Ives is only sixteen miles from Land's End – St Ives' relative isolation is probably the main reason for the persistence of its entertainments and customs, recorded long after other towns had given up those that the Reformation discouraged.

Fishing was the primary source of income for St Ives for centuries with both seine fishing and drift net fishing practised. These methods were described thoroughly by Carew, including the fortunes of both the seiner and the pilchard merchant. Pilchards, said Carew, 'at first carried a very lowe price, and serued for the inhabitants cheapest prouision: but of late times, the deare sale beyond the seas hath so encreased the number of takers, and the takers iarring and brawling with one another.... The Sayners profit in this trade is vncertayne ... but the Pilcherd Marchant may reape a speedy, large, and assured benefit.'[192] As everywhere in Cornwall merchants had begun to control the trade market. There was also extensive mining in the St Ives area. Although the Godolphins were not actually from St Ives, they lived only about ten miles away and were economically and politically influential in the hundred of Penwith. The family's interest in developing mining techniques affected the St Ives economy since the Godolphins made use of St Ives' harbour. The Godolphins also hired German master miners to develop the mining for them near Marazion and Mounts Bay. St Ives prospered additionally from mining innovation since both foreign visitors and supplies came into their port. In 1593, for example, The Hart of St Ives brought charcoal and oaks from Milford Haven for Sir Francis Godolphin's tin works.[193] There was a growth in the late sixteenth century of the tin shipping trade with South Wales, so that the 'collaboration between Cornish metal and South Wales smelting, which was such a notable feature of the Industrial Revolution of the eighteenth and nineteenth centuries, was anticipated in the Tudor age.'[194] Two surveys to determine the county's resources, done in 1570 and 1582, indicate the increase in foreign shipping at the time, which helped to increase the general population in St Ives as well. A subsidy roll from the reign of Henry VIII shows what was true in nearly every Cornish port town – that there were foreigners who lived and worked among the Cornish. In St Ives, for example, there were '23 foreigners, all Bretons, of whom 4 are tailors, 7 labourers, 9 fishers and 3 smiths.'[195] In 1327 there had been fewer than fifty taxpayers in St Ives; by 1642 there were over 1,800 people by estimation.[196]

The Dissolution did not touch St Ives as much as it did less isolated areas of the county. But the institution of the English Prayer Book and the change from the Latin mass disturbed people in St Ives and throughout Cornwall. Leaders from St Ives joined in the 1549 Western Rebellion and the town's portreeve, John Payne, was eventually hanged on the gallows in St Ives for his participation.[197] In fact, St Ives was one of the few towns in western Cornwall that did not support the monarchy during the growing unrest before the Civil War. St Ives instead supported parliament and the Commonwealth, partly because Sir Richard Grenville with his persecutions of Roundheads was unpopular – even detested – but mainly because local influential leaders of the time were Puritans and they supported the Revolution.[198]

St Ives did not become incorporated until 1639 when a mayor replaced the portreeve. The twelve aldermen and twenty-four burgesses continued and the town gained a recorder and a town clerk. St Ives would also have its first grammar school. The new charter from Charles I specified a Wednesday and a Saturday market and four fairs: 10 May, 20 July, 26 September, and 3 December.[199] The last of these is probably the 'Pig Fair' that Matthews says happened around 30 November, the feast of St Andrew, the patron saint of the parish church, and was still celebrated in the nineteenth century. It was called the 'Fairy-mow,' an anglicization of the Cornish 'Fàr-a'-Moh,' meaning 'Pig Fair.'[200] Pigs were brought into the town in great numbers and kept in 'pigs towns' at nearby Breakwater and Porthmeor; pork was sold at booths at the fair, and according to popular legend, a mock mayor was elected.[201]

Private Households

Cornish gentry, whose wealth would come mainly from the tin trade, included the pre-Conquest families of the Carmynows, claiming descent from King Arthur, the Cosworths, the Polwheles, and the Trevelyans. Other medieval families were of Norman descent: the Arundells of Lanherne and Trerice, the Bassets, the Bodrugans, the Carews, the Chamonds, the Champernownes (resident mainly in Devon), the Edgcumbes, the Grenvilles of Stowe, the Killigrews, the Pomerays, the Reskymers, the Roscarrocks, the St Aubyns, the Tregians, and the Trevanions. By the fifteenth century the Godolphins rose to fortune too, through control of the stannaries, becoming perhaps the richest family in Cornwall during the sixteenth century.[202] Like important families of the gentry all over England the Cornish gentry intermarried with one another, creating a network of power and interpersonal influence that affected social and economic conditions throughout our period. The Arundells of Tolverne, Carews, Edgcumbes, and Godolphins were related by marriage; the Arundells of Trerice were intermarried with the Carnsews, Cosworths, and St Aubyns; and the Godolphins were further intermarried with the Killigrews.[203] Cornwall, somewhat isolated and far from the locus of national power, no doubt lost many men aspiring to wealth and position to London but the loss from the shire connected the gentry to the Crown. There had always been a strong link between Cornwall and the Crown, ever since the Conquest; William and Robert, the count of Mortain and earl of Cornwall, who was given vast holdings in the county, were half-brothers.[204]

The Killigrews and the Godolphins were typical of the Cornish gentry, families involved in the economy and local government of the shire. The Killigrews, with their great household at Arwennack near Penryn and Falmouth Harbour, had interests in both trade and tin mining. The Killigrews filled positions in the administration of the duchy, were members of parliament, and participated in local government. John Killigrew became governor of Pendennis near Falmouth and was also a commissioner when the new Prayer Book was introduced. The family had long-standing connections with St Mawes Castle, built in 1543. The castle was an important military fortification protecting the harbour at Falmouth, one of the crucial artillery forts during the reign of Henry VIII.[205] But the Killigrews, like others of the gentry, fell upon hard times. They often lived beyond their means, building their grand home, Arwennack. To maintain their lifestyle they turned to piracy. In 1555 the Killigrew brothers, John and Thomas, pursued Spanish ships, confiscating cargo.[206] Their brother, Peter, was imprisoned in the Tower for privateering with the French.[207] The family also held influence in other towns in Cornwall. William Killigrew, brother of Sir Henry, was constable of Launceston Castle from 1576 and through his relatives, the Cecils, was instrumental in securing positions for various people from Dunheved in parliament during the years 1558–97.[208]

The Godolphins from Godolphin near St Michael's Mount were involved in the tin industry and introduced many innovations to mining. Sir William Godolphin, during the reign of Henry VIII, was a prominent man who increased his estates over the years through rewards for loyalty to the king and to subsequent protestant rulers. The Godolphins had under Henry been supportive of the dissolution of the monasteries; Sir William and his son were 'granted in survivorship the office of steward of the Somerset lands in Cornwall and of the King's lands in Alverton, Penzance, and Tywarnhayle.'[209] Sir Francis Godolphin was the family member who particularly gave all of his energy to the shire, in both public administration and mining development.[210] He served as receiver-general of the duchy under Elizabeth and supervised military fortifications on the Scilly Isles; he was a major military leader in the war against Spain.[211] Documents pertaining to the households of the Killigrews and the Godolphins are not extant.

Of the great families extant records of dramatic activity and musical activity have been located only for the Arundells, the Carews of Antony, and the Pomerays of St Neot. The wealthy and powerful Arundell family of Lanherne in Mawgan parish was Cornwall's most prominent.[212] The Arundells attracted attention both for their hospitality and for military and civic affairs. One of the many Sir John Arundells was a fleet commander for Henry V and at the Reformation Humphrey Arundell became a governor of St Michael's Mount. He led an army in the 1549 rebellion. The Wardour Castle, Wiltshire, branch of the Arundell family was founded by Sir Thomas Arundell who was executed in 1552.[213] One of Cornwall's major families for more than 400 years, the Arundells gathered an archive of documents pertaining to their vast holdings in Cornwall, Devon, Dorset, and Wiltshire, dating from the twelfth century to nearly the present day.[214] Richard Carew's comments about Cornwall contained in his 1602 *Survey of Cornwall*, appear under the relevant boroughs and parishes. Thomas Pomeray's will appears under St Neot.

Drama, Music, Dance, and Popular Customs

The historical records from Cornwall, while fewer in number than we suspect originally existed, provide evidence of an extended pattern of popular entertainment and dramatic performance across the county, giving us a picture of rural social life that well illustrates Cornish pride in their traditions. This picture, of course, is dependent upon the survival of documents and therefore a lack of information in the Records about performance in a particular town does not mean that factors prevented drama, music, and dance there but rather that records and references testifying to such performance have not been found. While the people and the institutions in Cornwall were subject to the decisions of the monarchy and to ecclesiastical mandates from Exeter, the county's relative isolation may have protected local entertainment longer than in areas closer to London or the ecclesiastical see. A selection of the historical records, discussed below, demonstrates that despite exterior impositions by church and Crown, and interior difficulties such as poor travel conditions, political turmoil, and a limited economy, a richness of entertainment occurred in Cornwall in the period right down to 1642.

Drama

Cornish people enjoyed a rich variety of drama, including cycle plays, a saint's play, Robin Hood plays, a 'Susanna' play, and other plays unnamed in the records but sometimes called 'interludes' or 'miracles.'[215] Like the drama itself, records of performance of some of these plays are dispersed throughout the county, connected to individual parishes, towns, and manors. In addition to the historical records, we are fortunate to have, even if all are not complete, extant dramatic texts in Middle Cornish. The 'Charter Interlude,' a fragment, is one character's part in a play about matchmaking, and as such is an important example of early secular drama in Britain.[216] The *Ordinalia* is a cycle drama containing plays for three days, the extant manuscript focusing on Christ's Passion and the legend of the Oil of Mercy. Another version of a cycle drama, the *Creacion*, seems to be the first day's play from a longer cycle and has repetitions in its beginning that are related to the first day's play of the *Ordinalia*. *Beunans Meriasek*, a saint's play intended for performance over two days, concerns the life and miracles of Camborne's patron, St Meriasek. (For these last three plays see Appendix 2.)

No texts remain, however, for the Robin Hood plays so popular in Cornwall or for the other dramatic performances, by travelling troupes or local groups of players, that are noted in historical documents. Additionally unfortunate is that the known historical records make no specific reference to the plays for which there are extant texts; thus, no certain complementarity can be asserted between the surviving play texts and the historical references to performance, although some of the historical records, such as those for St Ives, are extremely suggestive. That the Cornish tradition of drama was long-standing, however, may be attested by a reference in Cornish to a comedic entertainer, found in the twelfth-century 'Old Cornish Vocabulary'; this early document, which translates Ælfric's Latin/Old English vocabulary into Cornish, includes terms for musical instruments, singers, and dancers (see Appendix 1).

Although failing to refer to the extant plays, the historical records do testify to Robin Hood plays, interludes, and a drama called a 'miracle' play. The Penheleg manuscript, declaring the royalties of John Arundell of Lanherne, records a 'Mirable' play at Sancreed, where a murder occurred (see p 520); since a plain-an-gwary existed at Sancreed, the play may have been performed there. The bailiff's hearing was concerned with the 'Royalties' of Sir John Arundell of Lanherne and his ancestors within the hundred of Penwith and contains testimony regarding the Arundell family's historic claims and privileges. In a case confirming their criminal jurisdiction in the area, the manuscript recounts the statement of an elderly man who, with other men, witnessed a murder when he was a boy, perhaps around 1500, at 'a Mirable Play at Sanckras Parish' in 'the Place' there. Perhaps testifying to the audience's interest in the play, the murderer was bound and held until the play's end, when he was taken to prison and eventually hanged. The Penheleg manuscript remains the only record of a performance called a 'miracle' play in Cornwall; however, since the meaning of the word 'miracle' is uncertain and might refer to a variety of different works, such as a saint's play or a cycle play, for example, the precise nature of that drama performed in Sancreed is unknown.

Drama in Cornwall was also associated with Corpus Christi Day, one of the most popular celebrations throughout England during the fifteenth and early sixteenth centuries; this celebration occurred on the Thursday after Trinity Sunday, falling between 23 May and 24 June. Corpus Christi plays in Cornwall, as they are recorded for Bodmin between 1494–5 and 1566, appear to have been, in contrast to the cycle drama, smaller productions similar to the Corpus Christi plays in other areas of England.[217] Although historical records indicate that Corpus Christi guilds were located in Bodmin and Lostwithiel, no specific records attest those guilds' direct involvement in dramatic performance.[218] The Bodmin Receivers' Accounts therefore provide much of what we know about Corpus Christi celebrations in Cornwall. The General Receivers' Accounts from Bodmin note, for example, payments for materials such as tinfoil, linen and satin cloth, leather, and other items used to make clothing and crowns for the Corpus Christi play, including materials for the costume for Jesus. The accounts for 1514–15 record a payment of 6s 6d for a purple satin garment stipulated to be for Jesus.

Two inventories from Bodmin's St Petroc's Church also contain references to costumes that suggest the performance of religious drama. One now-missing record, the 1539 inventory from St Petroc's Church, is fortunately preserved in the antiquarian *Bodmin Register*, written in the first part of the nineteenth century. The *Register* describes two costumes for Jesus and four coats for 'tormeteris.' Although torturers play significant parts in both the *Ordinalia* and *Beunans Meriasek*, no certain evidence exists that the garments were used for productions of these particular plays.[219] The 1539 inventory further observes that, at the time of its writing, these costumes for 'tormeteris' were in the hands of four named men, probably the actors playing those roles. The account also confirms the recycling of ecclesiastical garments for the drama: the coat then kept by Richard Corant was 'made of a sewt of vestyments for goode frydayes.' A second Bodmin inventory, of 1566, notes three costumes for Jesus, two made of 'red wosterd' and one of 'red bocrom,' along with three 'tormenttowers' costumes 'of satyn of bryddes of yolo & blue,' as well as two costumes for devils and two crowns, one of them black. Although devils are present in the *Ordinalia*, again connections between records and texts can only be speculative.

While the Bodmin accounts may suggest a Corpus Christi play focused on the Passion,[220] the St Ives Borough Accounts suggest performance of the cycle drama, with entries indicating both payments for, and receipts from, drama. The St Ives accounts list receipts in 1571–2 for several days, at an unspecified time, from 'the first daye of the playe' to the sixth day, as well as additional income 'for drincke monye after the playe.' The meaning of the references to six days of a play is unclear, given the many ways the phrase could be interpreted. Payments in these accounts are clear, however, for a variety of expenses associated with the play, including wages for the 'pypers,' money spent to purchase hurdles and a line, wages for the carpenters who 'made hevin,' and funds for unspecified 'thinges for the playe.' Two different payments are also recorded for lambskins, one for six skins and one for two dozen; since a stage direction in the play of the *Creacion* requires 'Adam and Eva aparlet in whytt lether,' the lambskins may have been for their costumes.

In 1572–3 St Ives also received money for an interlude; although Matthews speculated that John Clarke's payment was for a play manuscript, the amount is fairly large, £1 11s, suggesting that the sum may instead have been received for admissions.[221] Since a plain-an-gwary existed at Stennack in the parish of St Ives, a play on a large scale could well have been presented there.

Entries in Cornish records also document the performance of Robin Hood plays during the last half of the sixteenth century and may help to confirm the belief that interest in Robin Hood grew during the late 1500s.[222] A champion of the oppressed, the figure of Robin Hood flourished from when it was mentioned in Langland's *Piers Plowman*, and Robin became a folk hero who appealed to the common people interested in social justice. As a figure of the 'outdoor life and the greenwood,' he is often associated with spring and Whitsuntide, or summer games.[223]

Several entries concerning drama, which usually refer to Robin Hood plays, are preserved in the antiquarian copy of the churchwardens' accounts for the parish of Antony. The 1555–6 accounts name, in a single entry, both the actor playing Robin Hood and a woman from among the 'maydyns' who turned over receipts. Between 1553–4 and 1558–9 a series of such receipts appears in the Antony records from 'Robyn Hodde & the maydyns,' for a fairly constant amount, usually between 40s and 50s. However, whether a connection exists between the maidens and the Robin Hood play is not clear. We know that at this time a number of churches had guilds for young women and possibly the collections from the maidens were for the feasting that commonly accompanied celebrations around Robin Hood, although the association of Robin Hood and a maidens' guild is not usual. Moreover, even if 'maydyns' does refer to a young women's guild, the occasions for which money was received from 'Robyn Hodde' and from the maidens may have occurred at entirely different times. Another possibility is that the term 'maydyns' may refer to part of Robin Hood's company. In any case the accounts confirm that within a period of six years, five different performances of a Robin Hood play were held in the same location.

The Stratton church also received money for Robin Hood plays; accounts for 1535–6 name I. Greby as the actor who played Robin Hood while the 1536–7 accounts name the company's leader, John Mares, who might himself have played the part of Robin Hood.[224] Since both the rood loft and the new chancel at St Andrew's were built at this time, donations from the plays may have been used for rebuilding inside the church.[225] In subsequent years in Stratton Robin Hood plays were also performed, in 1538–9 and in 1543–4. On the latter occasion the church may have made money by selling stage sets since the accounts note that two people paid the church 'for the wode of Robyn hode is howse.' Extant documents from across England indicate that a house or arbour was often built for Robin Hood, a temporary structure used for feasting that symbolized Robin Hood's Sherwood Forest revels.[226] A record of St Breock may allude to a similar structure; the entries for 1573–4 note two different amounts received, one sum from 'Robyn hoode & hys Cumpanye' and the second sum from the players for wood.

Costumes for Robin Hood plays are mentioned in the churchwardens' accounts for St Columb Major, which indicate ownership of various sorts of costumes that the church apparently rented to performers. Inventories of parish goods for 1584–5 and 1585–6 include a 'ffryers Coate' that was probably a costume for a Robin Hood play, since the accounts for the year 1587–8 include a sum the church received 'for the lont of the Robbyn hoddes clothes.' The 1594–5 account similarly notes a debit 'of Robyn hoodes monyes,' perhaps also for the rent of the costumes, which sum was to be paid 'at our ladye day' by several men who are listed as owing 'for ye same.'

Historical documents from Cornwall such as these from St Columb contain a significant number of entries attesting the performance of Robin Hood plays, performances that not only provided a popular form of entertainment but that also contributed in a variety of ways to small local economies. In St Ives, for example, two records for different years indicate that funds were both earned from, and disbursed for, the performance of a Robin Hood play: in 1583–4 St Ives received income from a Robin Hood play, while four years later, in 1587–8, the town disbursed payment to a Robin Hood from St Columb Major. Given the role of such performances in Cornwall's local economy, it is doubly unfortunate that no texts exist for the Robin Hood plays performed there.

PLACES OF PERFORMANCE

Drama in Cornwall in the period prior to 1642 seems to have been presented in a number of conventional settings such as church and guildhalls: the church house at Stratton was rented to various groups of entertainers, including 'Egyppcions,' for example, and the Bodmin Guildhall hosted Harry King's travelling company in 1504–5. While many parish churches remain, few guildhalls exist today in their entirety. In Launceston, for example, the hall no longer survives except in parts that have been discovered in adjacent buildings (see p 388). Bodmin is an exception, the present-day hall incorporating parts of the medieval building (see p 386). In addition to these usual settings for drama, at least some of Cornwall's major plays were presented in the round, in an open-air amphitheatre called in Middle Cornish a plain-an-gwary, from the Cornish words 'plen,' meaning 'arena' or 'field,' and 'guary,' meaning 'play.'[227] Performance in such a theatre is suggested by stage diagrams and directions in the manuscripts for both the *Ordinalia* and *Beunans Meriasek*; by Cornish place-names; by references in historical documents; and by existing structures.

The Plain-an-gwary

Caution is necessary in drawing conclusions about existing ancient structures in Cornwall which appear to be dramatic playing places. The presence of a round, flat area surrounded by a sloping bank of earth and/or stone, where people could have stood or sat, and that looks like an amphitheatre, does not in itself imply the existence of a plain-an-gwary or the performance of drama. Some confusion can occur if the term 'round' is used interchangeably with the terms 'playing place' and 'plain-an-gwary.' The fact that the structure at Perranzabuloe is referred to as 'Piran Round' does not help matters.

While a plain-an-gwary does imply a 'playing place' of some sort, the term 'round,' correctly used, refers instead to prehistoric, Roman, or early British camps or strongholds; the remains of these level, circular areas enclosed by earth and stone walls are scattered across Cornwall. Jenner in 1911 estimated the existence in Cornwall of eighty or ninety 'rounds.'[228] Although archaeological field work has found in West Penwith alone, the most westerly part of Cornwall, many more than that number of possible 'rounds,' in only a few instances can these 'rounds' be, with any confidence, associated with drama, since such an association would require the evidence of an historical document or a place name.[229]

A similar caution is recommended when considering references in the historical documents to an event called 'play.' As used in Cornwall in the period of early drama, the term 'play' did not refer solely to drama but was also used in connection with various sports and games. The plain-an-gwary at St Just in Penwith, for example, may have been used for the 'play' of hurling.[230] The slogan associated with hurling in St Ives illustrates this use of the term: 'Guare wheag, yw Guare teag' ('Fair play is good play').[231] Leland provides another example of varying usage of the word 'play'; in describing a ruined castle near Truro, Leland remarks that the area was then being used 'for a shoting and playing place.'[232] The term 'playing place' here may thus refer to an arena for games and sports rather than for drama, although such a place could, of course, have been employed for multiple uses (see p 559 for terminology concerning playing places).

In at least one instance, at Castilly, an ancient structure does seem to have been remodeled in the early Middle Ages into a plain-an-gwary.[233] Similarly, the existing structures at Perranzabuloe and St Just in Penwith, each known as a plain-an-gwary, may also have been constructed for some other purpose and then used for drama.[234] In essence, however, a 'round' is usually only a 'round'; and a plain-an-gwary or a 'playing place' is a location where drama may have been performed. In Appendix 3, O.J. Padel provides the names of ancient parishes where a surviving name indicates a former playing place.[235] Of course, other playing places may have existed, whose names have not survived or are yet to be found.

Documentary Evidence of Dramatic Performance in the Plain-an-gwary

Although performance of Cornwall's drama in a plain-an-gwary is suggested by staging diagrams in the play manuscripts and by Cornish place names, none of the historical records offers absolute evidence of performance in those amphitheatres. The St Ives records, however, may be referring to a plain-an-gwary in records that mention 'ye playing place.' Not only were receipts recorded in 1571–2 for a major dramatic event in St Ives that may have occupied six days (see p 513), but payments also were made for items that might well have been needed in a plain-an-gwary, such as hurdles and a line. In the following year, when St Ives earned another fairly large sum for the 'enterlude,' other money was earned from the sale of 'six score and thre foote of elme bordes in ye playing place.' Again, the Penheleg manuscript seems also to refer to a plain-an-gwary as it recounts the quarrel in Sancreed *c* 1500 that started 'in the Place before the Play began' and continued when the two combatants 'went out of the Play' and pursued their argument to the death. An existing place name in Sancreed, 'Plain Gwarry,' further attests the presence in earlier times of a plain-an-gwary at that location.

Carew discusses the plain-an-gwary in his 1602 history, although a number of his comments on the plays and their production, as well as on the physical details and construction of the plain-an-gwary, are of uncertain interpretation. Carew states that the 'Guary miracles' were presented in an amphitheatre forty or fifty feet in diameter, which he says the people 'raise' in an 'open field' for the purpose of presenting plays to the public.[236] Perhaps Carew means to imply a temporary structure since the two existing amphitheatres, each of which is called a plain-an-gwary, are considerably larger. The playing place at St Just in Penwith, for example, is 126 feet in diameter[237] and that at Perranzabuloe is '143 feet across on the north-south axis, and 135 feet on the east-west,'[238] which is more than twice the size of the playing places Carew describes. Playing places may not have been uniform in size, of course, even if originally built for theatrical performance. Moreover, since playing places came into existence in a variety of ways, their ultimate size probably depended in part on whether they resulted from construction or reconstruction. Perhaps most problematic in Carew's account, however, is the implication of crudeness and carelessness in production, implied in his assertion that the Cornish actors did not memorize their parts but repeated them after an on-stage prompter (see p 537). Even if Carew's account is authentic rather than apocryphal, his sixteenth-century commentary is not necessarily applicable to fourteenth-century presentation, and he may also have been generalizing from a single performance; his remarks, then, probably should not be construed as having widespread application to all of the Cornish drama.[239]

Antiquarian Descriptions of the Plain-an-gwary

William Borlase's two mid-eighteenth-century descriptions of the playing places at St Just in

Penwith and Perranzabuloe are of considerable value in understanding the sites as they were in earlier times. At the time Borlase was studying and measuring these sites, certain features were evident which time has since eroded; therefore, his valuable descriptions and his drawings of the two existing playing places are included here.

In his 1754 work, *Observations on the Antiquities, Historical and Monumental, of the County of Cornwall*, Borlase records his comments on the playing place at St Just in Penwith (see fig 1):

> In these continued Rounds, or Amphitheatres of stone (not broken as the Cirques of Stones-erect) the Britans did usually assemble to hear plays acted, to see the Sports and Games, which upon particular occasions were intended to amuse the people, to quiet and delight them; an institution (among other Engines of State) very necessary in all Civil Societies: these are call'd with us in Cornwall (where we have great numbers of them) Plân an guare; viz. the level place, or Plain of sport and pastime. The benches round were generally of Turf, as Ovid, talking of those ancient places of sport, observes:
>> In gradibus sedit populus de cespite factis,
>> Qualibet hirsuta fronde tegente comas.
>
> We have one whose benches are of Stone, and the most remarkable Monument of this kind which I have yet seen; it is near the church of St. Just, Penwith; now somewhat disfigured by the injudicious repairs of late years, but by the remains it seems to have been a work of more than usual labour, and correctness....
>
> It was an exact circle of 126 feet diameter; the perpendicular height of the bank, from the area within, now, seven feet; but the height from the bottom of the ditch without, ten feet at present, formerly more. The seats consist of six steps, fourteen inches wide, and one foot high, with one on the top of all, where the Rampart is about seven feet wide. The Plays they acted in these Amphitheatres were in the Cornish language, the Subjects taken from Scripture History, and 'call'd Guirimir, which Mr. Lluyd supposes a corruption of Guari-mirkl, and in the Cornish dialect to signify a miraculous Play, or Interlude. They were compos'd for the begetting in the common people a right notion of the Scriptures, and were acted in the memory of some not long since deceased.'
>
> In these same Cirques also, were perform'd all their Athletary Exercises, for which the Cornish Britans are still so remarkable; and when any single combat was to be fought on foot, to decide any rivalry of Strength or Valour, any disputed Property, or any Accusation exhibited by Martial Challenge; no place so proper as these inclosed Cirques.[240]

In his *Natural History of Cornwall*, published a few years later in 1758, Borlase similarly describes the playing place called Piran Round, located at Perranzabuloe (see fig 2):

> But to return to the interludes: The places where they were acted were the *Rounds*, a kind of amphitheater, with benches either of stone or turf. Of the former sort that exhibited in the Antiquities of Cornwall ... served this purpose; but a much larger one, of higher mound, fossed on the outside, and very regular is the amphitheater in the

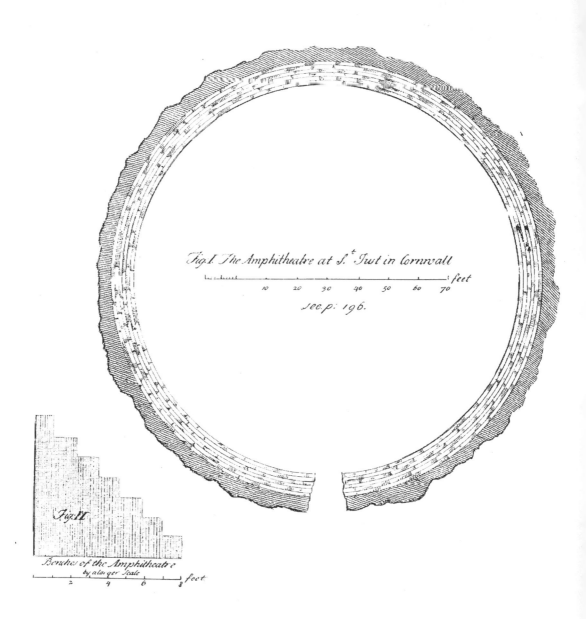

Fig.I. The Amphitheatre at S.t Just in Cornwall

10   20   30   40   50   60   70   feet

see.p. 196.

Fig.II

Benches of the Amphitheatre
by a larger Scale

2   4   6   8   feet

Figure 1: Amphitheatre of St Just in Penwith. Borlase, *Observations*, plate xvi

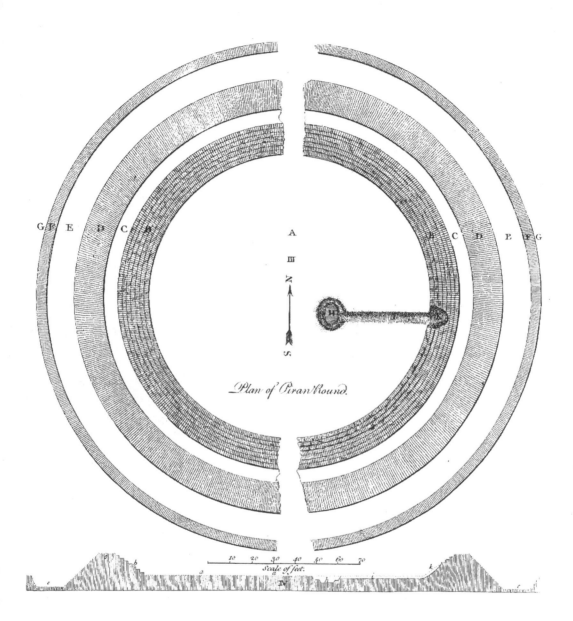

Figure 2: Plan of Piran Round. Borlase, *Natural History of Cornwall*, plate xxix.

parish of Piran-sand, which, as it has some peculiarities, I have here planned ... with the following references.

A, the area of the amphitheater, perfectly level, about one hundred and thirty feet diameter; B, the benches, seven in number of turf, rising eight feet from the area; C, the top of the rampart, seven feet wide; D, the outer slope of the rampart; E, the foss; F, the slope of the foss; G, the level of the hill on which the work is formed; H, a circular pit, in diameter thirteen feet, deep three feet, the sides sloping, and half way down a bench of turf, so formed as to reduce the area of the bottom to an ellipsis; I, a shallow trench, running from the pit H nearly east, four feet six inches wide, and one foot deep, till it reaches the undermost bench of the amphitheater A, where it is terminated by a semi-oval cavity K, eleven feet from north to south, and nine feet from east to west, which makes a breach in the benches....

This is a curious and regular work, and is formed with the exactness of a fortification, but the visible benches within, the pit, the trench, and cavity, and the foss having no esplanade beyond it, determine it in its present figure to the uses of an amphitheater. The greatest difficulty is to account for the pit H, and the trench and cavity I K, which are appendixes to it. Now it must be observed, that the scenary part of these performances was much worse than the composition; that the subject being taken from Scripture-History, the persons of the Deity brought upon the stage from above, and the infernal spirits from below, they thought it necessary to appropriate peculiar places to actors of such different characters; accordingly I find by their interludes that they had a place in their *Rounds* which they called Heaven, and I infer from thence that they had another called Hell; and from these two places the different beings were to proceed when they came to act, and withdraw to, when their parts were finished: I conjecture therefore, that as K might represent the upper regions, so the pit H might be allotted to the infernal. In the interlude of the resurrection also, the pit H might serve for the grave; the trench, and the cavity might be designed to exhibit the ascension into Heaven. How proper these wild expedients were to raise the admiration, affections, and piety of the beholders, the judicious reader will easily guess, and lament the age of ignorance, when by mutual consent of Laity and Clergy, (for without both they could not take place) the people were to have every truth set before their eyes by memorials, scenes, and symbols, though the most incoherent, unedifying, and absurd.

These interludes obtained not only in Cornwall (where they were called *Guare-mir*, or Miracle Plays, and the place of acting *plaen an guare*, but elsewhere, and lasted sometimes more than one day, and were attended not only by the vulgar, but by people of the highest condition, and were remembered, says Bishop Nicholson, by the last generation.[241]

TRAVELLING PERFORMERS

Even with the uncertainty of Cornish roads during this period, companies of players travelled within and outside Cornwall, although determining entertainers' 'circuits' is nearly impossible.[242] A few examples of records, however, can indicate some of the distances that local performers traversed within the county. Some distances travelled were not terribly long; the 'enterlwd players' of St Dennis travelled to St Breock to perform, about eight-and-a-half miles, the players from Milton Abbot were only seven miles from home when they performed at Launceston, and those from Germoe were around nine miles from home when they visited St Ives (see pp 506, 495, 516). Considerably greater distance, about twenty-seven miles, exists between the home base of a Robin Hood company from St Columb Minor and St Ives where they played.[243] Such companies may, of course, have been on tour, travelling shorter distances between their playing locations. Dancers also travelled within Cornwall to perform, as discussed below (p 411).

Cornish players also travelled outside the county to perform. Records from the neighbouring county of Devon note that in 1534–5 Barnstaple paid the 'players of Cornewall.' Perhaps these players came from Liskeard, since Liskeard players are known to have travelled to Barnstaple four years later, in 1538–9.[244] Another performer from Cornwall who travelled outside the county, a juggler said to be 'seruant to sir Iohn arrundell the yonger knyght,' was also rewarded the same year in Plymouth, Devon.[245]

Players from outside the county similarly travelled into Cornwall to perform. In the years 1470–1, for example, the Launceston records refer to wine and a reward given to 'Thomas le Stulstus,' the earl of Warwick's servant, who was performing as a fool. Much later in Launceston, in 1520–1, a 'Iogeler' identified as a servant of the king performed, earning both wine and a payment.

Travelling companies that may have come from outside Cornwall include the 'venesicians,' who played at Launceston in 1572–3, and the 'Egyppcions,' who rented the Stratton church house once in 1522–3 and three more times between 1559 and 1562. More certainly from outside the county were the 'kynges enterluyd plaers' who performed at Poughill in 1550–1, receiving dinner as well as payment for their entertaining. Lord Stafford's company of 'Enterlude players' performed in Launceston in 1575–6, perhaps on the same tour that took them to Exeter in the same year.[246] The players who came to Liskeard 'with Commissions' twice in 1631–2 may also have been licensed professional groups from outside Cornwall. Travelling groups seem to have found work in the great houses of Cornwall, since an Arundell family record indicates a payment in 1504 to 'egypcians' who danced.

Because many entertainers appearing in the records cannot be identified by location, their status as local or touring performers cannot be known in the absence of additional information. To cite just a few examples, no home base is recorded for the company led by Harry King that played in the Bodmin Guildhall in 1504–5. Similarly unknown is the identity of the 'Enterlude players' who performed in Launceston on 1 September of 1574–5. In some instances, however, the circumstances of a record can lead to a tentative suggestion regarding a group's origin: for example, a sum received in Bodmin in 1470–1 from 'the players yn the church hay William mason and Iis felowis' is found in the 1469–72 accounts for the rebuilding of the Bodmin church, suggesting that Mason and his companions may not have been a travelling company but a local troupe that donated some of its proceeds to the rebuilding.

Regrettably, no origin is known for the performers discussed in Heywood's *Apology for Actors*, whose play frightened the Spaniards from attacking and thus saved the Cornish town of Penryn. According to Heywood this event, which he suggests occurred around 1600, took place one night in Penryn when the noise of a mock battle on stage, complete with trumpets and drum, so alarmed the attacking Spaniards that they fled in disarray to their ships. Describing the players as 'strangers,' Heywood declares the company to be 'of the same quality' as the players of the earl of Sussex (see p 505).[247]

Since none of the Cornish records seems to indicate that travelling players were turned away, they may have been generally welcome visitors to the county whose citizens appreciated their amusements.

DRAMATIC PERFORMANCE AND STAINED GLASS ICONOGRAPHY IN ST NEOT'S CHURCH

An historical record of the drama that may be singular in the way it tells us about medieval play production is the stained and painted glass in St Neot's Church, Cornwall. Built between 1480 and 1530,[248] the church presents in one of its earliest windows a series of Old Testament scenes which in content and manner of presentation seem connected to the Middle Cornish plays, the *Ordinalia* and the *Creacion*. The five trefoil-headed main lights of the church's east window in the south aisle, the Creation Window, contain fifteen scenes illustrating material from Genesis. In many of the subjects treated in the fifteen scenes in its five primary lights, St Neot's Creation Window is like the narrative stained glass of other churches. Several scenes, however, seem to indicate the influence of Cornwall's dramatic performances upon the presentation of scriptural narrative by the glaziers and stained glass artisans.

In the window's seventh scene on The Temptation, for example, the drama's impact seems evident in the figure of the serpent, clearly depicted as a human being dressed in a snake suit (see fig 3a). Covered by a garment made to look like green snakeskin, the serpent has human form and human limbs with which it clings to the tree. This kind of costume was necessary for the actor portraying the serpent in both the *Ordinalia* and the *Creacion*, since both plays require the serpent to move about, descend and ascend to and from the loca, and in general use its arms and legs to climb, reach, and walk.

The drama's influence on the window appears most persuasively in the fourteenth scene, reflecting not only the legend of the Oil of Mercy but that legend as presented in the Cornish drama (see fig 3b).[249] Depicting the death of Adam, the scene shows on the right the tree from which Seth received the seeds representing the Oil of Mercy, with the Christ-child in the tree's branches. In the foreground Adam lies on the near side of a large canopied bed while on the far side Seth leans forward to put the apple-pips in his father's mouth and nostrils. The puzzling stage direction in the *Creacion* that at his death Adam 'falleth upon a bead' becomes clear when we see St Neot's window and understand 'bead' as a variant spelling of 'bed.'[250]

The stained and painted glass in St Neot's Church is a record vastly different in kind from written historical documents. However, the scenes presented in the glass clearly suggest some of the ways in which performance of the Cornish drama influenced the stained glass artists' understanding and vision, and therefore their depiction of biblical figures and events. In thus reflecting that influence the St Neot's church windows contribute particularly to our understanding of the Cornish drama's staging, costuming, and set design.

Figure 3b: The Oil of Mercy

Figure 3a: The Temptation

The Creation Window of St Neot's Church. Photographs by David Hambly

Music and Minstrels

Since the three major play manuscripts, the *Ordinalia, Beunans Meriasek,* and the *Creacion* all refer to pipers who performed at each play's end, we know that music was certainly a part of Cornwall's dramatic presentations. The text of the *Ordinalia* also contains an extensive list of musicians and instruments: the musicians include minstrels, drummers, harpists, and trumpeters, while the instruments range from the recorder to the viol and from nakers (kettledrums) to organs.

Payments for musicians associated with drama are found in both the churchwardens' accounts from Camborne for 1549–50 for a 'pyper yn the playe,' and the St Ives Borough Accounts for 1571–2, for 'pypers for there wages.' In Liskeard in 1582–3, Mayors' Accounts note payments to interlude players and to 'Parre the Minstrell,' but there is no way of knowing if the two entertainments were linked.

References to other minstrels and musicians, public and private, also appear in the records for our period. For example, Bodmin accounts for 1503–4 note 4s paid to an unspecified number of waits in the early sixteenth century and Devon records mention two Cornish men, John Gadgcombe and Samuel John, who were chosen waits for the city of Exeter in 1639–40.[251] The importance of the minstrels associated with the church of St Mary Magdalene, Launceston, is confirmed by the indulgence of forty days that Bishop Lacy granted on 16 June 1440 to those contributing to the minstrels' support (see p 491); exterior wall carvings on the church associate the minstrels with the church and the feast of Mary Magdalene, 22 July. The Launceston records of 1573–4 partially identify two of the paid musicians, 'Robyn the synger' and 'a singing man' who travelled from 'south Tawton.'

Household documents from Cornwall contain references to minstrels in private performance, and to valued musical instruments as well. The 1466–7 stewards' accounts for the Arundells of Lanherne record the purchase of 'ij whit Bonett*es* for mynstrell on Newe yere ys day,' along with cloth at the same time. Indicating the importance of musical instruments, Cornish wills and inventories occasionally list them in household accounts or mention them as bequests. The 1586 household inventory from Trebelzue Manor, St Columb Minor, records a white and black bone lute, covered with red velvet, and lute strings; in Edward Arundell's will, proved in November 1586 before the inventory, the lute is labelled his 'best lute' and is bequeathed to his nephew for the nephew's wife. Richard Clere of Calstock, in his will of 1601 that was proved in 1606, also carefully disposes of his musical instruments by bequeathing his harps to two blind boys and his trumpet to a 'meheamed' man.

Music also figures in another class of historical records found to contain material relevant to Cornwall. A few documents from Star Chamber cases are included among the records here because the charges in those cases were based on libellous statements and stories about an individual, usually on matters sexual and sometimes on matters excretory, that were in some instances put to music and sung. Those persons who made the complaint, thereby claiming injury from the circulation and performance of slanderous statements and songs, were usually of some prominence, leading one to speculate that there was probably considerable local interest in hearing these stories and songs. The Star Chamber cases thus provide insight into another kind of musical entertainment that was based in part on the undercutting of someone, usually in a superior social position.

Dance

A number of records from the sixteenth century note the popularity in Cornwall of morris dancing; although traditionally attached to Whitsuntide, this dancing occurred at other times as well. Robin Hood, the maypole, lords of misrule, mock courts, and the lord and lady of summer games all appear connected to morris dancing, often because dancing occurred at church ales, which sometimes had special themes; Robin Hood was a favourite, and because in addition to being a player in a dramatic performance he was also sometimes a dancer, references to him in historical documents may be unclear as to which of these arts he was in a particular instance performing.[252]

The sixteenth century saw an increase in morris dancing as a way for parishioners to raise money for their parish church[253] and some of the entries in Cornwall's records may testify to this. Early in the century, in 1505–6 for example, dancers from St Erme, Boscastle, and Minster visited Bodmin. That entries seem less frequent at the middle of the century may reflect the growing discouragement of morris dancing and dancing in general then, particularly from 1547–53, during the reign of Protestant Edward VI.[254] However, even though existing records across England show that church prosecutions rose from 1601–30 and, with that rise, a decline in morris dancing occurred, the records from Cornwall indicate that dancing in general persisted in the seventeenth century.[255]

In the latter half of the sixteenth century, churchwardens' accounts for St Breock note that dancers from Ludgvan visited in 1565–6 and performed for payment, as did dancers from Grampound two years later, in 1567–8. Since a few years later, in 1574–5, St Breock also rewarded dancers from St Eval and from Phillack, St Breock may have been a regular stop for travelling dancers during the time encompassed by these records. Towards the end of the century, in 1595–6, Camborne's churchwardens' accounts note payment to two different companies of travelling morris dancers, from St Levan and from Gunwalloe 'in lesid' (the parish of Landewednack in the Lizard).

St Columb Major had its own troupe of morris dancers; churchwardens' inventories of parish goods over several years mention morris costumes. In 1584–5 the church possessed five coats for dancers along with a 'ffryers Coate,' twenty-four 'dansinge belles,' and a streamer. In the 1587–8 inventory the five coats are specifically identified as 'morrisshe Coates' but by then the bells had diminished to twenty. An additional morris coat was added in 1589–90 to make six but by 1594–5 these costumes had aged into 'syxe old moryshe cotes' and a 'newe moryshe Coate' had been acquired. The church inventory for 1596–7 contains the last mention of these seven costumes for the dance.

Writing at the turn of the century, Carew defended dancing in part because it was enjoyed by the country's leaders. Carew refers to dancing in the dialogue he repeats, wherein another person cites dancing and minstrelsy as abuses at church ales. Carew counters this charge by asserting that 'sober and open dauncing' should be allowed until it is also 'banished from mariages, Christmas reuels, and (our Countries patterne) the court,' indicating the prevalence of dancing throughout the country and his belief that the court should provide an example of behaviour in amusements as well as in rule (see p 537).

Local Customs

RIDINGS

Popular outdoor activities in Cornwall began as soon as spring weather. One of the earliest processions was a riding in Lostwithiel in celebration of St George. St George had become increasingly popular in Cornwall after the 1415 battle of Agincourt and guilds named after the saint are found in nine places in Cornwall, including Lostwithiel.[256] Another example of his popularity is a window, from around 1500, at St Neot's Church, which depicts St George and his armour.[257] The legend of St George also appears over the porch of St Mary Magdalene's Church in Launceston, which was dedicated in 1524.[258]

Lostwithiel's riding, held on St George's Day, was sponsored by the religious guild of St George at St Bartholomew's Church.[259] The guild chose a member to represent St George and he led the procession through the streets. Discussions of Lostwithiel's riding often refer to St George as a mock prince since he ruled for the day and paraded on horseback with crown, sceptre, and sword.[260] Great care was given to his armour in preparation for the procession: the 1536–7 accounts note as much as 13d paid for the scouring of the armour and 4d for grease and oil as well as 4d for 'two dowsen ˄⌐of poinctes⌐' for the armour's maintenance. Music surely accompanied the riding since a piper was paid 12d for his labour. According to Carew, after the person representing St George was received by the curate and divine service was held at the parish church, he was feted at a special house erected for the occasion where he received all the honours of a prince of Cornwall (see pp 500–1). Since the dukes of Cornwall had a palace at Lostwithiel, of which some remains exist, there would have been some local familiarity with such honours. The Lostwithiel riding accounts for the same year also note 3s allowed for the dinner on the day of the riding.

Bodmin riding, celebrated on or near 7 July each year, first appears in the records for 1469, although the tradition is said to be much older.[261] The riding is not the same as the beating of the bounds celebration, held yearly on Rogation Days.[262] The riding, some believe, purposely coincided with the feast of St Edgar, the Saxon king who is said to have gilded St Petroc's Shrine in 963.[263] During the three-day event, riders gathered flowers and leaves to make garlands to present to the Bodmin Priory.[264] Citizens of the town partook in the riding ale, when the ale brewed the previous October was itself honoured in procession; funds were collected for church repairs and rebuilding. Several riding guilds are listed in the Bodmin records and the Bodmin 1583 ordinance for the Shoemakers' Guild required church attendance of members at the time of the riding.[265]

During the second and third days of the festivities, sports, especially wrestling, occurred in an area called Halgavor, outside the town, where a mock court was held (see p 474).[266] Carew's *Survey of Cornwall* discusses Halgavor as a place where pranks occurred, including trials for slovenliness before the mock court. Carew also discusses combat with a dragon said to lurk in the area (see p 474). Bodmin still has, in fact, a place called 'Dragon Pit'; the name may be a remnant of the legend relating that in the sixth century St Petroc encountered a dragon there, or it may be a relic of the custom of Halgavor play, or both.[267] The diary of William Carnsew of Bokelly may or may not refer to Halgavor entertainment when he records that on 29 July 1576 he attended the 'bodman playes.' Since Carnsew goes on to remark that he spent there a total of 12s, five of those shillings given to wrestlers, the 'playes' may very well refer to summer sports held later than the early July Halgavor games. Bodmin may also have had another custom that was popular, the election of a mock mayor, an instance similar to Launceston's and St Ives' legendary elections of the mayor of the Pig Market.[268]

MAY DAY CELEBRATIONS AND SPRING AND SUMMER GAMES

May celebrations were also popular and probably ancient Cornish pastimes. The Launceston borough records note a payment in 1431–2 for expenses for 'le may' and celebrations are later noted in 1574–5 payments to players on 'May daie'; whether the tradition was continuous over the centuries or whether the later event was a revival is not known. Therefore, most of what we know for certain about such spring and summer celebrations and games in Cornwall comes from the records for St Ives, where festivities included a maypole and an annual king and queen, or lord and lady, of the games. The king and queen probably appeared in costume since the 1578–9 account from St Ives notes payment for 'Cadwellye' (cloth) given to 'the dyer when he was kynge.' Beginning in 1571–2 many of the existing borough accounts record the names of the annual king and queen, or in a few instances the names of their fathers, as well as the amount of money the king and queen collected, sometimes for charity – as when the lord and lady for 1633–4 'deliuered to the overseers of the poore' the amount gathered. The St Ives accounts may not be consistent in the terms referring to the rulers over the may and summer games. It is impossible to know if 'king and queen' and 'lord and lady' are synonymous terms and if the references to both sets of titles mean that the king and queen presided over games at more than one time during their yearly tenure, or if there was more than one set of rulers. In his history of St Ives, Matthews infers that the king and queen would have had duties at various times during the year and suggests that the king and queen would have presided in particular over 'sports at the maypole, on Saint John's Day and at Christmas time.'[269] On the other hand the St Ives accounts for 1590–1 refer to two different kings; one, the son of Thomas James, is listed as 'Sommer kinge,' while another, 'william Stirrie,' is identified as 'kinge of the maye game this yere.' Perhaps the references are to kings for two different years, or perhaps different people were chosen to preside over games held at different times of the year.

The maypole is mentioned specifically in connection with the king and queen and the summer games in 1615–16, when a sum from the lord's and lady's receipts pays for the making of a maypole. Because the leaf for the 1615–16 accounts is torn and lost at the edge, only tantalizing bits of words remain. In 1684–5 the maypole was removed to the 'Sawpitt.'[270]

THE 'OBBY 'OSS

The annual revel of the Padstow 'Obby 'Oss is another popular spring custom still celebrated in Cornwall, a tradition associated with May Day and said to be of great antiquity.[271] The 'Obby 'Oss and its accompanying dancers perform variously, the horse dancing, touching women (which some consider lucky), gathering money, and seeming to die symbolically only to be 'reborn.' While the tradition of the 'Oss' dance through the streets is an element of the custom that is probably unchanged, other parts of the ritual are undoubtedly rather different from older practice. The earliest historical reference to the custom, at least in Cornwall, appears in the late-fifteenth-century play *Beunans Meriasek*, the text referring to a Hobby Horse and its 'pair';[272] the word 'pair' is the name still given today to the 'Oss' accompanying dancers in Padstow. The Cornish towns of Helston and Newlyn may also have had hobby horses, as may other Cornish villages where the custom has not survived.[273]

FLORA DAY AND THE 'FURRY DANCE'

No documentary evidence exists in the records to corroborate the ancient nature of another Cornish custom, the Helston 'Furry Dance,' performed in that town on its 'Flora Day,' usually 8 May. Like the 'Obby 'Oss of Padstow, the Helston Furry Dance is associated with spring, and since its origins are unknown, various possibilities have been proposed, including the suggestion that the custom may be pre-Christian; most likely, perhaps, this was a May Day custom that was transferred to the celebration of St Michael, Helston's patron saint.[274] While St Michael's feast day is 29 September, 8 May is the day celebrating his apparition at Monte Gargano in Italy.[275] In the Furry Dance a long line of specially-selected dancers weaves in and out of houses and gardens, symbolically 'driving out evil and darkness to let in goodness and light.'[276] The Hal-an-Tow song, celebrating spring but also mentioning Robin Hood, St George, St Michael, invading Spaniards, and 'Aunt Mary Moses,' is also associated with Flora Day; the Hal-an-Tow song, some say, is the oldest part of the Flora Day celebration.[277]

ANIMAL SHOWS AND SPECTACLES

Animal spectacles and torments were also considered entertainment and are documented in Cornwall in the sixteenth century and beyond. The Bodmin General Receivers' Accounts for 1504–5 record a payment to a 'Berewarde' in Bodmin and the Stratton churchwardens' accounts report an apparent trade-off in 1526–7 when the parish paid out for 'a bhare' the same amount as it received from the bear-keepers for 'rome yn the churchhowse.' The 1582–3 payment in the West Looe Mayors' Accounts to 'Colakote' in order 'to goe to the showes' may also refer to an animal display. An antiquarian comment on a copy of this record refers to 'a merry tale' about a man in the time of Elizabeth (1558–1603) who had a licence to show an ape and who tricked the government officials of Looe into paying to see it as the 'queen's ape' (see Appendix 6); the antiquarian's comment suggests that the 'showes' that 'Colakote' was given money to see in 1582–3 were a similar animal exhibit.

Although in some instances animals seem to have been simply displayed, more commonly they were teased or made to fight in contests on which people probably wagered. Only two references to cockfighting appear in the extant Cornish records for this period but the scarcity of documentation may mean nothing about the activity's extent or length of history in Cornwall. Cockfighting certainly took place in Bodmin, as indicated by a 1603 lease noting the location of a cockpit on the relevant piece of ground, and the Liskeard Mayors' Acounts record cockfighting in that town in 1635–6, when 'Sir Willyam Wrey and diuerse other gentlemen' were provided both money and wine for this event.[278] Evidence appears in the Cornish records for bullbaiting as well; Goulding's antiquarian record of the Stratton stockwardens' accounts for 1568–9, for example, notes payment to John Cotell 'for the bull ryng.' In 1572–3 Launceston recorded payments for hooks and eyes and for mending 'ye bull chayne,' with expenses noted the following year 'for mending the Bull ring'; a workman was paid in 1574–5 for setting rings in the 'brode stone' and another paid for a rope 'to ty the bull.' Justice for the bull may have prevailed some time later, if only temporarily; a 2 January 1640/1 notation details payments 'for a dayes woorke for settin peeces for ye yarncleyers' and 'for timber and setting in the long peeces which the bull tore vp in the corne markett house.'

CHURCH ALES

Another favourite form of entertainment in Cornwall was church ales; most if not all parish churches held church ales, selling drink to make money for the parish or for parish guilds. Stratton's High Cross parish guild, for example, was supported by fees, gifts, and a yearly ale.[279] Although specific references seldom appear in the records, Carew's comments indicate the probability that entertainment was regularly a part of the medieval church ale; he describes these gatherings as a source of much pleasure, even though corrupted by 'a multitude of abuses, to wit, idlenes, drunkennesse, lasciuiousnes, vaine disports of minstrelsie, dauncing, and disorderly night-watchings' (see pp 535–6). Since the quantity of food purchased can suggest the potential size of the audience for entertainments, the records of expenses for church ales at Kilkhampton in two different years are included in Appendix 5.

Private Household Entertainment

A few words about private entertainments should be said to complete this discussion. In addition to the public performances that occurred in Cornwall, private performances took place in households of important families. At Christmas in 1575, for example, Francis Tregian of Golden Manor hosted an interlude in his home, an event that proved significant in Tregian's trial and conviction (see pp 531–3). More specific information concerning private entertainments is found in the 1466–7 accounts for the manor of Lanherne, which confirm dramatic performance as well as music and dance. Records enumerate purchases for 'disgysynges,' including paper, cloth, glue, colouring materials, and gold foil. The household also purchased cloth in connection with a visit to 'lord sstafford.' The Arundell family of Lanherne provided for morris dancers as well, the same household accounts noting payment for four dozen bells for morris dancing. This payment may be, in fact, one of the first recorded references to actual morris dancing.[280] These accounts suggest that the Arundell household may have engaged in preparations during the year for a variety of amusements that included drama and dance.

The Documents

The descriptions of the documents from which the records are drawn are given in chronological order under five headings: Diocese, Boroughs and Parishes (arranged alphabetically), Monasteries (which contains a single monastic record), Households (alphabetically by family name), and County of Cornwall. Within those boroughs with more than one class of documents, ie, Bodmin, Launceston, and St Columb Major, civic records are listed first, followed by parish records, legal records, and then miscellaneous documents. Antiquarian records are treated at the end of the document class to which they belong. Shelf-marks and titles given are according to the preference of the individual record offices and libraries where the documents are held. The description of a document yielding entries for more than one place is located under the first relevant borough or parish.

Diocese of Exeter

Ecclesiastically, Cornwall formed an archdeaconry within the diocese of Exeter; thus it was subject to both the bishop of that diocese and his subordinate, the archdeacon of Cornwall. Statutes, such as those of Bishop Quinel, and visitation articles drawn up for the diocese as a whole pertain equally to Cornwall and to the neighbouring county of Devon, which was also part of the same diocese and the site of its cathedral. The registers of two of Exeter's most active medieval bishops, Grandisson and Lacy, also contain documents relevant to Cornish entertainment but the registers used are described below under the specific locations to which they refer, the parishes of Launceston and Penryn and the monastery of Tywardreath.

STATUTES OF BISHOP PETER QUINEL

Although the original manuscript is no longer extant, thirteen manuscript copies of Bishop Quinel's statutes survive from the fourteenth and fifteenth centuries. None of these MSS was suitable to be used as a base text. Exeter D & C MS 3549A is described here because it was not known to the editor of the standard edition of these statutes. For a full discussion of the statutes and their MSS, see the endnote to this entry (pp 593–4). John Wasson (ed), *Devon*, discusses the extant manuscripts of Bishop Quinel's statutes on pp xxxi and 437–9.

Exeter, Exeter Cathedral Library, Exeter D & C MS 3549A; 15th c. copy of Bishop Quinel's statutes of 1287; Latin; parchment and paper; ii + 116 + ii; 170mm x 245mm (100mm x 173mm); 1⁷, 2–7⁸, 8⁴; modern pencil foliation; frequent blue initial letters surrounded by red penwork, rubricated section headings and some slight rubrication of text, catchwords; 16th c. (?) binding of dark brown leather on wood.

BISHOP JOHN WOOLTON'S VISITATION ARTICLES

Articles to be in- | quired of, within the Diocesse of Ex- | *on, in the visitation of the reuerende* | father in God, John Bishop | of Excester. | *In the .xxi. yeare of the reigne of our most* | gracious soueraigne Lady Elizabeth, by the | grace of God, Queene of Englande, Fraunce, | and Ireland, defendresse of the | fayth . &c. | [device] | Imprinted at London, by | *Thomas Purfoote.* | Anno. 1579. STC: 10203.

ARCHDEACON WILLIAM HUTCHINSON'S VISITATION ARTICLES

[Device] | ARTICLES TO BE | ENQVIRED OF BY THE | CHVRCH-WARDENS AND SWORNE- | *men within the Archdeaconry of Cornewall in the* | visitation of the Right Worshipfull, WIL- | LIAM HVTCHINSON Doctor of Diui- | nitie, Archdeacon of the said Arch- | deaconrie of CORNEVVALL. | *Anno Domini.* | 1613. | [device] | LONDON | Printed by *William Stansby.* | 1613. STC: 10190.5.

[Device] | ARTICLES | To be enquired of by | the Churchwardens and sworne-men | *within the Archdeacony of Cornwall* | in the Dioces of EXCETER: | In the visitation of the worshipfull Mr. | *William Huchenson* Doctor of Diuinity and | *Archdeacon of the sayd Archdeaconry.* | Holden in the yeere of our Lord God, 1614. | [device] | LONDON, | Printed by IOHN BEALE. 1614. STC: 10190.7.

VISITATION ARTICLES DURING VACANCY

ARTICLES | TO BE ENQVIRED | of in the trienniall Visita- | tion of the Diocesse of | EXETER. | *Holden Anno* 1627. | By authority of the most Reuerend | Father in God, GEORGE Lord Archbishop | of CANTERBVRY His Grace, Primate | of all ENGLAND and | Metropolitan | [rule] | [device] | [rule] | Imprinted at LONDON | 1627. STC: 10206.

Boroughs and Parishes

ANTONY

St James Collectors' and Churchwardens' Accounts (A)

The top of the first page of the antiquarian copy notes: 'Iste liber pertinet Ecclesie Sancti Jacobbi Maria de Antony.' However, the original documents are no longer there. The CRO comments in its catalogue, 'Accts of collectors and churchwardens 1538 to 1584 and 1570–1582 with list of goods … of Antony Church 1637. In July 1952 only this transcript was seen by Miss M.J. Groombridge, County Archivist. At that time the original was said to be in Antony Church.

It was not seen in July 1976. It is not at Antony House and its whereabouts was not known at the rectory of St. John.' This antiquarian account is therefore known to be before 1952 but the writer is unknown. The antiquarian copy indicates the original pagination parenthetically in the left margin. The accounting term for these accounts appears to be February/March– February/March until 1548–9 at least. By 1555–6 the accounts definitely run from August– August. The arrangement of entries in the accounts for 1553–4 and 1554–5 also suggests an August–August account year.

Truro, Cornwall Record Office, P/7/5/1; early 20th c. antiquarian copy of collectors' and churchwardens' accounts for 1538–84; Latin and English; paper; 2 gatherings: (1) Accounts of Collectors and Church- wardens, 1538–84; 66 + i; 262mm x 200mm (225mm x 173mm); (2) Churchwardens' Accounts, 1570–82, with list of goods and possessions of Antony Church 1637; ii + 15 + ii; 253mm x 201mm (220mm x 135mm), average 24 long lines; contemporary pagination; (1) has single leaves sewn and (2) has single sheets with a metal fastener; no decoration; 20th c. binding in black cloth, pressed diamond pattern on covers, with a brown cardboard folder around manuscript, beneath binder.

BODMIN

Records for Bodmin come from a rich variety of sources and contain references to a range of activities. Records that include entries for dramatic activity are comprised of church inventories; general receivers' and town receivers' accounts; a lease referring to a pit for cockfighting; the mid-fifteenth-century accounts for rebuilding the parish church, St Petroc's; the early sixteenth- century accounts for building the Holy Rood chantry steeple; and a portion of Carew's *Survey of Cornwall* on Halgavor games at Bodmin.

Civic Records

General Receivers' Accounts

These are a badly deteriorated sequence of accounts from 1473 to 1541 with some gaps. Il- legible readings in B/Bod/314/3/10 are supplied from an extant draft version (B/Bod/314/3/5). Lysons and Lysons, *Magna Brittania*, vol 3, p 35, contains the earliest antiquarian record of the travelling company's 'disportes' in Bodmin which are recorded in B/Bod/314/3/21. Read- ings no longer legible in the manuscript are supplied from Lysons and Lysons.

Truro, Cornwall Record Office, B/Bod/314/3/10; 1494–5; English; parchment; single membrane, originally numbered '2' and stitched at both ends as second mb in a continuous roll; 483mm x 370mm (440mm x 350mm); receipts written on back; left margin damaged.

Truro, Cornwall Record Office, B/Bod/314/3/20; 1503–4; English; parchment; single membrane, originally stitched at both ends as part of a continuous roll; 396mm x 382mm (285mm x 255mm); receipts written on back; left margin damaged.

Truro, Cornwall Record Office, B/Bod/314/3/21; 1504–6; English; parchment; single membrane, originally numbered '21' on back and stitched at both ends as part of a continuous roll; 680mm x 333mm (655mm x 280mm); receipts written on back; damage to both margins to a depth of 100mm on left edge.

Truro, Cornwall Record Office, B/Bod/314/3/22; 1505–6; English; parchment; single membrane, originally stitched at both ends as part of a continuous roll; 615mm x 340mm (575mm x 280mm); receipts written on back; both margins damaged to a depth of 100mm on left edge. A continuation of B/Bod/314/3/21.

Truro, Cornwall Record Office, B/Bod/314/3/26; 1509–10; English; parchment; single membrane, originally numbered '17' and probably part of a continuous roll; 680mm x 310mm (650mm x 235mm); receipts written on back; both margins damaged, ink faded, and parchment soiled.

Truro, Cornwall Record Office, B/Bod/314/3/31; 1513–14; English; parchment; single membrane, originally stitched at both ends as part of a continuous roll; 128mm x 280mm (115mm x 230mm); receipts written on back; faded ink, both margins damaged, with loss of payments on right.

Truro, Cornwall Record Office, B/Bod/314/3/32; 1514–15; English; parchment; fragment of membrane, probably part of a continuous roll; 222mm x 272mm (210mm x 225mm); written all in one direction with receipts on back; poor condition.

Truro, Cornwall Record Office, B/Bod/314/3/39; 1519–20; English; parchment; single membrane, originally stitched at both ends as part of a continuous roll; 245mm x 270mm (180mm x 215mm); receipts written on back; poor condition, left margin damaged.

Truro, Cornwall Record Office, B/Bod/314/3/51; 1529–30; English; parchment; single membrane, originally stitched at both ends as part of a continuous roll; 640mm x 303mm (620mm x 210mm); receipts written on back; poor condition, left margin heavily damaged.

Town Receivers' Accounts

These manuscripts are in very poor and incomplete condition. The fragments were at one time stored in a box of miscellaneous Bodmin records but have recently been repaired and catalogued.

Truro, Cornwall Record Office, B/Bod/314/2/15; c 1501–13; Latin; parchment; single membrane; 666mm x 330mm (500mm x 270mm); faded writing, top half of membrane missing.

Truro, Cornwall Record Office, B/Bod/314/2/12; c 1514–39; Latin; parchment; single membrane; 190mm x 220mm (170mm x 190mm); numbered '2' in 19th c. ink; manuscript incomplete and has several holes.

Truro, Cornwall Record Office, B/Bod/314/2/3; 1537–8; English; parchment; single membrane; 558mm x 543mm (350mm x 470mm); top of membrane missing.

Parish Records

St Petroc Church Building Accounts

St Petroc's Church, like other churches in Cornwall rebuilt during the later Middle Ages, experienced renewal in the fifteenth century. From 1469–72, the St Petroc Church Building Accounts list funds gathered from various church guilds and fund-raising activities. Many entries concern the Bodmin riding, sponsored by five trade guilds called the riding guilds: St John's for Drapers and Tailors; St Loy's for Smiths; St Petroc's for Skinners and Glovers; St Anyan's for Shoemakers, and St Martin's for Millers. CRO: B/Bod 243, the 1583 Shoemaker's Order, also mentions the Bodmin riding (Munn, *Bodmin Riding*, pp 11–12). See p 439 for a discussion of the relevance of Bodmin riding records for this collection.

Truro, Cornwall Record Office, B/Bod/244; 1469–72; Latin and English; paper; 19 single mounted leaves; 300mm x 205mm (text area inconsistent), some leaves have 2 columns; paginated; fragments and leaves are mounted and contained in mounted paper cover with title in ink on front: 'A List of all those who | gave voluntarily to | the building of the church of | BODMIN | 1469 to 72.'

Berry Tower Building Receipts

The Berry Tower Building Accounts concern the building of the tower on the chantry church of the Holy Rood, a chantry built to celebrate the place where the original town may have been, and where St Petroc's remains were returned on the feast of the Holy Rood after being taken to Brittany in 1177. This manuscript is one of many scraps and badly deteriorated leaves of varying sizes from a sequence of accounts, 1501–14 with some gaps, which were at one time stored in a box of miscellaneous Bodmin records and now are repaired and catalogued.

Truro, Cornwall Record Office, B/Bod/314/1/6; 1505–6; English; parchment; 2 separate membranes which were originally stitched together as part of a continuous roll with receipts on one side and payments on the back; 510mm x 315mm (482mm x 240mm) combined; numbered '5' in 19th c. hand; membranes torn and faded.

St Petroc Inventory of Church Goods

Truro, Cornwall Record Office, B/Bod/233; 6 October 1566; English; paper; single sheet; 225mm x 304mm (180mm x 285mm), 23 long lines; much mutilated; torn edges, holes in bottom, faded areas.

Antiquarian Records

St Petroc Inventory of Church Goods (AC)

An antiquarian transcription published in John Wallis' *The Bodmin Register* (1827–38), pp 39–42, is the earliest extant copy of a 1539 church inventory that refers to costumes for the drama that were made from ecclesiastical garments. Snell, *Edwardian Inventories of Church Goods for Cornwall*, also prints these records (pp 29–32), saying that he consulted Mr E.W. Gill, town clerk of Bodmin, who was 'certain that these documents are not now among the Corporation records.' They 'were apparently preserved amongst the Corporation of Bodmin records until the 19th century, but have now disappeared' (p xxii). See also Whitley, 'The Church Goods of Cornwall.'

John Wallis (ed), *The Bodmin Register; Containing Collections Relative to the Past and Present State of the Parish of Bodmin* (Bodmin, published in numbers, from 1827 to 1838).

Legal Records

Lease to William Collier

This is a ninety-nine-year lease from the mayor and the burgesses of the borough of Bodmin to William Collier, a saddler, of land called Friarys Park.

Truro, Cornwall Record Office, B/Bod/20; 1603; English; parchment; single membrane; 270mm x 314mm (213mm x 289mm); the phrase 'This indenture made' and the words 'B⟨.⟩tweene' and 'witnesseth' are in display script; poor condition, a hole in the centre of the manuscript and several small holes throughout account for lost text; endorsed by William Collier, same hand as text; seal is missing.

Miscellaneous Records

Richard Carew, *Survey of Cornwall*

Richard Carew of Antony House was born in 1555 into an old and powerful family, inter-married with the Edgcumbes of nearby Plymouth, the Arundells, and the Godolphins, three of Cornwall's most prominent families. Educated at Christ Church, Oxford, Carew was well-connected to the literary circles of his time and was a friend of Sir Philip Sidney. He was admitted to the Middle Temple, the Inn of Court of the Carews, in 1574, followed by his brother George in 1577. As part of the Tudor gentry, Carew participated in the legal and political administration of Cornwall, fulfilling his duties during the last decades of the reign of Elizabeth I. In 1581 he began serving as justice of the peace and was appointed sheriff of Cornwall in 1582; in 1584 he represented Saltash in parliament. In 1594 Carew translated John Huarte's *Examen de Ingenios* (*The Examination of Men's Wits*) from the Italian version into English and Tasso's *Godfrey of Bulloigne*, and published in 1598 'A Herring's Tale,' the first long English poem in rhyming hexameters. Carew died in 1620.[281]

In 1602 Carew published his *Survey of Cornwall*, an important early history and description of the county in the tradition of Leland and of Carew's contemporary and friend, William Camden; although Leland and Camden intended to survey and discuss all of Britain, Carew limited himself to the county of Cornwall. In his book, Carew first discusses various aspects of the county as a whole, including its climate, mineral deposits, people, topography, and history. He then considers each of the nine hundreds in Cornwall, in this case discussing the Halgavor celebrations at Bodmin. He combined his survey of Cornwall with personal observations, experiences, and opinions. Carew also provides the much-quoted story of the forgetful and recalcitrant actor who mischievously repeated aloud the prompter's chastisements, to the great amusement of the audience. Carew discusses as well such Cornish entertainments as shooting and hurling; those entries are included in Appendix 4. See also under Lostwithiel and County of Cornwall, pp 500–1 and pp 534–8.

THE | SVRVEY OF | CORNWALL. | *Written by Richard Carew* | *of Antonie, Esquire.* | [Stafford's framed device showing Opportunity standing on a wheel which floats at sea] | LONDON | Printed by s. s. for Iohn Iaggard, and are to bee sold | neere Temple-barre, at the signe of the Hand | and Starre. 1602.; some printed decoration at book endings and beginnings, and initial letters of 2 books have scroll work decoration; topic headings cited marginally; catch-words printed at bottom. *STC*: 4615.

CALSTOCK

Will of Richard Clere

Truro, Cornwall Record Office, AP/C/118/1; 22 August 1601; Latin and English; paper; single sheet; 334mm x 304mm (103mm x 281mm).

Inventory of Richard Clere

Truro, Cornwall Record Office, AP/C/118/2; 19 September 1606; English; paper; single sheet; 305mm x 211mm (179mm x 138mm).

CAMBORNE

In addition to these churchwardens' accounts, extant Camborne parish records include parish registers beginning in 1538, deeds from the fourteenth century onward, accounts of the overseers of the poor from 1648 onward, and 1628 estate rental accounts.

St Meriadocus and St Martin Churchwardens' Accounts

These manuscripts are comprised of different kinds of wardens' accounts: those of churchwardens (ff 7, 14), parish wardens (ff 31, 39v, 41), poor wardens (f 102), and stock wardens (f 111). This variety may account for the diversity of accounting terms in the records transcribed here. Early churchwardens' accounts may relate to the feast of St Meriasek (Meriadocus) (7 June) but insufficient accounts survive to give a clear picture. About the surviving Camborne documents, David Thomas remarks that 'specific documents have survived for crucial periods, so allowing us to construct an almost continuous record. Beginning with the early years, we have the superb set of Wardens' (and early Guild) Accounts, covering the years 1535–1657, only discovered in 1968' ('The Wardens of Camborne Church and Parish, 1534 to 1980, with Guild and Chapel Wardens, 1534 to 1558,' *Cornish Studies* 6 (1978), 53). Thomas explains that these records show that Celtic saints persisted alongside newer Roman ones and St Meriadocus was not simply supplanted by St Martin. The use of the name 'Meriasek' in the accounts starting in 1554 is a result of church reform going on at the time (pp 54–5). Excerpts on the game of hurling from CRO: PD/322/1 are included in Appendix 4.

Truro, Cornwall Record Office, PD/322/1; 1535–79; English; paper; iv + 103 + iv; 310mm x 207mm (275mm x 182mm approximately), average 28 long lines, some leaves have 2 columns; modern pencil foliation; all leaves have been mounted, some loss of words due to deterioration, perhaps from water; modern blue cloth binding, no title.

Truro, Cornwall Record Office, PD/322/2; 1581–1628 (but lists churchwardens to 1663); English; paper; ii + 107 (+ 14 fragments) + iii; 315mm x 215mm (text area varies), average 41 long lines; modern pencil foliation continued from volume 1; all leaves have been mounted on modern paper; modern blue cloth binding, no title.

FOWEY

Bill of Complaint in Rashleigh v. Kendall et al

Kew, Public Record Office, STAC 8/249/4; 3 November 1614; English; parchment; single membrane (mb 4 in bundle) attached by sewing to mbs 1–3 and with parchment label in top left corner; 760mm x 817mm (740mm x 817mm); mb 4 endorsed: 'Rashley *versus* Kendall & al*ios* M. 12° I*acobi* R*egis*' and 'Iovis Tertio Die Novembris Anno Duodecimo Iacobi Regis | I Parker.'

JACOBSTOW

Bill of Information in Stawell v. Mapowder et al

Kew, Public Record Office, STAC 8/27/10; 15 July 1617; English; parchment; single membrane (mb 2 in bundle) sewn to mb 1 at left hand side; 405mm x 664mm (389mm x 635mm); mb 2 endorsed in different hand: 'Attorn*atus* R*egis* Versus Mapowder et al*ios* Trin' 15° I*acobi* R*egis*' and 'Mercur*ij* nono die Iulij An*n*o xv° I*acobi* R*egis* | I Parker.'

LAUNCELLS

Bill of Complaint in Painter v. Yeo

Kew, Public Record Office, STAC 8/236/29; 12 October 1612; English; parchment; single membrane (mb 2 in bundle) attached by sewing to mb 1 and with parchment label at top left corner; 389mm x 579mm (370mm x 540mm); mb 2 endorsed: 'Paynter versus Yeo M' Decimo I*acobi* R*egis*' and 'Lune Duodecimo die octobris Anno Decimo Iacobi Regis | Th*omas* Mynatt.'

LAUNCESTON

Launceston is the name used today for three medieval boroughs: Launceston (originally Lan Stephen or St Stephen); Dunheved (the site of the old Celtic hillfort that became Launceston Castle); and Newport, now a district of Launceston. The history of the development of the tri-borough area can be found on pp 386–9. The borough accounts, many of them from Dunheved, are identified as Launceston documents at the Cornwall Record Office and we use their shelf-marks here.

A large body of documents in various states of preservation exists for the borough of Launceston. Ranging from the thirteenth to the nineteenth century, these documents include bundles of rolls, fragments fastened or boxed together, and bound volumes.

Some of the earliest churchwardens' accounts come from St Thomas' Church, in the section of Launceston previously known as Newport. The accounts include interesting details about criminals executed in Launceston at the gaol but contain no material on dramatic activity. Entries that refer to the minstrels (musicians) from St Mary Magdalene's Church come not from the parish records but from borough accounts, since the minstrels regularly accompanied the mayor on civic and social occasions.

Civic Records

Borough Accounts

Truro, Cornwall Record Office, B/Laus/135; 1404–5; Latin; parchment; 6 membranes attached at the top with original parchment attachment; 200mm x 55mm (110mm x 55mm); unnumbered.

Truro, Cornwall Record Office, B/Laus/137; 1431–2; Latin; parchment; single membrane; 750mm x 220mm (face 690mm x 185mm, dorse 180mm x 190mm); some writing faded.

Truro, Cornwall Record Office, B/Laus138; 1445–6; Latin; paper; 3 leaves folded in half and 1 half-sheet sewn, making 7 leaves; 219mm x 153mm (206mm x 132mm); no foliation.

Truro, Cornwall Record Office, B/Laus/139; 1449–50; Latin; paper; 8 sheets folded in half and sewn, several blank pages; 219mm x 143mm (199mm x 123mm); no foliation.

Truro, Cornwall Record Office, B/Laus/141; 1450–1; Latin; parchment; single membrane; 598mm x 242mm (face 585mm x 213mm, dorse 364mm x 210mm); top is faded and deteriorated from damp and eaten away by mice. '

Truro, Cornwall Record Office, B/Laus/143; 1459–60; Latin; parchment; single membrane; 655mm x 293mm (face 619mm x 279mm, dorse 546mm x 254mm); some discoloration from damp, some holes; some headings written large.

Truro, Cornwall Record Office, B/Laus/153; 1465–6; Latin; parchment; single membrane; 670mm x 270mm (face 635mm x 225mm, dorse 445mm x 220mm); badly torn at top, mildewed, eaten away.

Truro, Cornwall Record Office, B/Laus/158; 1466–7; Latin; parchment; 2 membranes, attached serially; 1244mm x 285mm (1214mm x 240mm); unnumbered; dorse writing begins on last membrane.

Truro, Cornwall Record Office, B/Laus/160; 1469–70; Latin; parchment; 2 membranes, stitched together; 1000mm x 150mm (960mm x 150mm); unnumbered; left half of MS missing and the rest torn and stained. Supplied readings for CRO: B/Laus/160 are from the Seneschals' Accounts (CRO: LR/140), an eighteenth-century antiquarian copy of the records from 1334 to 1543; the antiquarian provided full copies and partial copies of the originals.

Truro, Cornwall Record Office, B/Laus/147; 1470–1; Latin; parchment; 3 membranes attached serially; 1475mm x 240mm (face 1375mm x 205mm, dorse 1150mm x 205mm); unnumbered; hole at edge of manuscript, 9mm x 15mm.

Truro, Cornwall Record Office, B/Laus/162; 1476–7; Latin; parchment; 3 membranes, attached serially; 1591mm x 207mm (1408mm x 174mm, some large spaces); unnumbered; dorse writing begins on last membrane of roll; some water damage and holes at start of first membrane.

Truro, Cornwall Record Office, B/Laus/164; 1478–9; Latin; parchment; 2 membranes, attached serially; 1574mm x 261mm (1397mm x 227mm); unnumbered; written only on face; some faded, worn, and damp-marked spots.

Truro, Cornwall Record Office, B/Laus/170; 1520–1; Latin; parchment; 2 membranes, attached serially; 1471mm x 255mm (face 1471mm x 202mm, dorse 1223mm x 202mm); unnumbered; dorse writing begins on last membrane; some damp marks on edges of roll and places eaten by mice, some mildew.

Truro, Cornwall Record Office, B/Laus/171; 1530–1; Latin; parchment; 2 membranes, attached serially; 1238mm x 155mm (half missing, impossible to judge original measurement); unnumbered; dorse writing begins on last membrane; right half of the membrane is missing due to damp and mice.

Truro, Cornwall Record Office, B/Laus/172; 1543–4; Latin; parchment; 3 membranes, attached serially, with stitching in original format; 2568mm x 269mm (face 2503mm x 267mm, dorse 595mm x 242mm); unnumbered; dorse writing begins at bottom of third membrane; headings and some letters written large; excellent condition except for some deterioration at top of first membrane.

Truro, Cornwall Record Office, B/Laus/179/2/1; 17th c.; paper; an unnumbered bundle of 23 un-numbered scraps of varying sizes at one time rolled and held together with a thin strip of parchment (now lost) which includes the following:

2 January 1640/1; English; single sheet; 203mm x 196mm (102mm x 168mm); endorsed by William Kever, mayor (different hand from text). The fragment is annotated in the top left corner in a different hand with a later date: 'x: 3°: 1643.'

23 January 1640/1; English; single sheet; 132mm x 198mm (122mm x 99mm); endorsed by William Kever, mayor (different hand from text).

Borough Expense Book

Truro, Cornwall Record Office, B/Laus/173–78; 1571–7; English and Latin; paper; 40 (+ 12 fragments) + ii; 315mm x 205mm (text area varies), average 36 long lines; no foliation; ragged edges, some fading, 12 leaves torn out at end, before fly-leaves; some large capitals, some headings written large; bound in original parchment cover with title on front: 'The Booke of All the necessarye Exspences Layd owte for the towne or Borowghe of Donneheuyd Alias Launceston 1572.'

Miscellaneous Records

Register of Bishop Edmund Lacy

The manuscript description of the Register of Bishop Edmund Lacy is from Wasson (ed), *Devon*, p xxx. Wasson comments there that Bishop Lacy's Register contains 'many mandates for good crops, success of the English in war ... for the success of Bishop Beaufort at a peace conference, and the like.'

Exeter, Devon Record Office, Chanter 11; 1420–55; Latin; parchment; 340mm x 250mm; 581 leaves; foliated j to cccclxxxxv by scribe, continued in modern ink from 496 to 581 (these last pages consisting of wills and ordinations and probably originally bound separately); 19th c. binding in board and half-calf.

LISKEARD

In 1836 documents, papers, and other articles belonging to the borough of Liskeard were passed on to the incoming town clerk. With these items was a list of the surviving Liskeard records at that time: they included charters, constitutions, parchment court rolls from 1392 to 1586, and mayors' accounts from 1444 to 1733.[282]

At present extant records for Liskeard include royal charters and deeds from the mid-thirteenth century forward; borough court books and court rolls from 1331 onward (with gaps); fifteenth-century ecclesiastical notifications for additions to the parish church; a 1507–8 tax collectiana by street; borough constitution books from 1588 forward; a 1561–2 settlement of a legal dispute with Bodmin regarding trade; fifteenth-century reeves' accounts; a rent book beginning in 1581; and late seventeenth-century Quaker accounts.

Mayors' Accounts

Truro, Cornwall Record Office, B/Lis/266; 1575–6; Latin and English; parchment; 2 membranes attached at top, probably the result of repair; (1) 783mm x 321mm (668mm x 270mm), (2) 385mm x 321mm (face 340mm x 270mm, dorse 335mm x 270mm); unnumbered; no decoration except headings written larger.

Truro, Cornwall Record Office, B/Lis/267; 1582–3; Latin and English; parchment; 2 membranes attached at side with original parchment strips; (1) 356mm x 313mm (face 285mm x 275mm, dorse

265mm x 270mm), (2) 664mm x 231mm (face 590mm x 185mm, dorse 410mm x 152mm); unnumbered; no decoration except headings written larger and flourished initials.

Truro, Cornwall Record Office, B/Lis/268; 1604–6; Latin and English; parchment; 2 membranes sewn together at top, the smaller first, probably result of repair; (1) 374mm x 328mm (face 340mm x 328mm, dorse 325mm x 280mm), (2) 603mm x 333mm (500mm x 302mm); unnumbered; no decoration except headings written larger.

Truro, Cornwall Record Office, B/Lis/270; 1606–7; Latin and English; parchment; 2 membranes attached at top with original strips of parchment; (1) 413mm x 365mm (face 368mm x 365mm, dorse 310mm x 365mm), (2) 540mm x 254mm (face 413mm x 203mm, dorse 205mm x 183mm); unnumbered.

Truro, Cornwall Record Office, B/Lis/272; 1608–9; Latin and English; parchment; 2 membranes attached at top with original strips of parchment; (1) 330mm x 431mm (330mm x 423mm), (2) 521mm x 260mm; unnumbered.

Truro, Cornwall Record Office, B/Lis/284; 1629–32; Latin and English; parchment; 2 membranes attached at top with original braid of parchment; (1) 292mm x 397mm (face 272mm x 397mm), (2) 393mm x 215mm (330mm x 197mm); (1) 3 entries on dorse, (2) no writing on dorse; unnumbered; ink blotches across top face of (1).

Truro, Cornwall Record Office, B/Lis/288; 1635–7; Latin and English; parchment; 2 membranes attached at top with the smaller first, result of repair; (1) 477mm x 342mm (face 420mm x 285mm), (2) 675mm x 310mm (face 565mm x 275mm); unnumbered; both written on only one side, account begins on larger membrane (2) and continues on smaller membrane (1) which has been placed and attached on top; no decoration except capitals written larger.

LOSTWITHIEL

Surviving civic records for Lostwithiel at the CRO include borough charters beginning as early as 1194; receivers' accounts beginning in the thirteenth century; deeds from the fourteenth century forward; charity records beginning in 1584; and seventeenth-century borough court and maritime court books. Parish records include registers from 1609 onward.

St George's Guild Steward's Accounts

St George's guild, which sponsored the Lostwithiel riding, was a religious guild, responsible for various church activities and for caring for a fixed shrine, probably a chapel and lands in the surrounding area that were dedicated to St George.[283] The Steward's Accounts, kept by Richard Curteis, were incorporated into the Augmentation depositions as part of the evidence in a Chancery case regarding the guild's property near Lostwithiel. The charge against town officials concerned concealment from the Crown of endowed lands. The case revealed the town's factions, one of them certainly continuing to support traditional mumming ceremonies on

St George's Riding Day.[284] Material in the accounts omitted from the Records in this collection include liturgical expenses, mass pence for St George's, rent money, annual allowances for St George's dirges, offering payments, and various rents for the lands dedicated to St George, that is, all payments not specifically for the St George's riding.

Kew, Public Record Office, E 315/122; 1536–7; Latin and English; paper; bifolia of 8 leaves mounted on guards; 301mm x 207mm (280mm x 130mm approximately), single column; modern ink foliation. Bound as ff 19–26 into a leather guard book with a tooled border on cover and gilt title on spine: 'Augmentation Office. Court of Augmentation Depositions. Hen. 8–Edw. 6. 112.'

Richard Carew, Survey of Cornwall

See under Bodmin (pp 422–3) for *STC*: 4615.

MANACCAN

Bill of Complaint in Webber v. Kindsman et al

Kew, Public Record Office, STAC 8/304/38; 29 October 1604; English; parchment; single membrane attached by modern sewing to STAC 8/304/1–45 and with parchment label for all in top left corner; 442mm x 613mm (369mm x 568mm); endorsed: 'Lune Vicesimo Nono Octobris Anno Sec*un*do Regni Iacobi Regis &c l Willi*a*m Mill.'

PENRYN

Episcopal Order to Glasney Collegiate Church

John Wasson (ed), *Devon*, xxix–xxx, comments on the registers of Bishop Grandisson, finding them 'in many ways the most interesting of the Exeter bishops' registers. They contain numerous calls for public processions, which do not appear in the present collection, and record the constant efforts by Bishop Grandisson to reform the clergy and to prevent insolencies by boy-bishops and choristers.'

Exeter, Devon Record Office, Chanter 3; 1331–60; Latin; parchment; i + 221 + ii; 305mm x 225mm; foliated j to ccxxj by scribe; 19th c. binding in board and half-calf.

Thomas Heywood, An Apology for Actors

Thomas Heywood (d. 1650?) from Lincolnshire was a well-known actor and playwright. He was a member of the lord admiral's company and one of the theatrical retainers of Henry Wriothesley, the third earl of Southampton. Heywood was also a member of the earl of Somerset's company of players, who were later servants of the queen under James I; Heywood attended her funeral in 1619 as 'one of Her Majesty's players.' He wrote his first play in about 1585 and wrote in other genres as well. He claimed to have either written or helped write over 200 plays, and he composed for the lord mayor's pageants in London up to 1640. Heywood's defence of the profession of acting includes a reference to a specific performance in Cornwall.

ᴀɴ | APOLOGY | For Actors. | Containing three briefe | Treatises. | 1 Their Antiquity. | 2 *Their ancient Dignity.* | 3 *The true vse of their quality.* | Written by *Thomas Heywood.* | *Et prodesse solent & delectare* – | [horizontal rule] | *LONDON,* | Printed by *Nicholas Okes.* | 1612. | [all within compartment showing masks at top and sides, and a nightingale in a thornbush at foot]. *STC*: 13309.

POUGHILL

St Olaf Churchwardens' Accounts

This St Olaf Churchwardens' Account does not specify the accounting term; what evidence there is in the later accounts of the period covered by this MS suggests that early to mid-February was the normal accounting term.

Truro, Cornwall Record Office, P/192/5/1; 1525–98; Latin and English; paper; iv + 100 + ii; 306mm x 200mm (250mm x 108mm approximately), average 24 long lines; 19th or 20th c. pagination; much torn, water-marked leaves are mounted and repaired; bound in cream leather (1894), title on spine in gold on red background: 'Poughill St. Olaf | Churchwardens Accounts | 1528–1598.'

ST BREOCK

St Briocus Churchwardens' Accounts

From 1565–6 onward the accounting year for the St Briocus Churchwardens' Accounts was from the eve of Ascension Day in one year to the same in the next.

Truro, Cornwall Record Office, P/19/5/1; 1529–98; English; paper; iv + 58 + iv; 285mm x 192mm (text area variable), average 42 long lines, some columns; modern foliation; 5 gatherings of approximately 10 folios, repaired and mounted on paper and rebound, and 1 loose leaf consisting of a mounted fragment (150mm x 180mm); modern binding of green cloth and tan leather.

ST COLUMB MAJOR

St Columba the Virgin Churchwardens' Accounts

St Columb Major records have been extensively transcribed by Thurstan Peter, 'The St. Columb Green Book.' Serjeantson, 'Church and Parish Goods of St. Columb Major,' p 345, also transcribes some records but assigns the 1588 inventory to 1587. Excerpts on hurling from the St Columb Major accounts are included in Appendix 4.

Truro, Cornwall Record Office, P/36/8/1; 1584–1909; English; paper; x + 229 + i; 410mm x 272mm (400mm x 220mm, plus marginalia), average 43 long lines; contemporary foliation partial and inconsistent; 30 gatherings of approximately 8 folios, some leaves have been trimmed about an inch, some folios mounted; no decoration, larger writing for headings and marginal notes; bound in green vellum with 2 engraved brass clasps.

Bill of Complaint in Webber v. Kindsman et al

See under Manaccan (p 429) for PRO: STAC 8/304/38.

Bill of Complaint in Lawry v. Dier et al

Kew, Public Record Office, STAC 8/202/30; 22 June 1615; English; parchment; single membrane (mb 3 in bundle) attached by sewing to mbs 1–2 and with parchment label in top left corner; 431mm x 477mm (402mm x 434mm); mb 3 endorsed: 'Lawrey I vers*us* I Dyer et al*ios* Tr' 13° Ia*cobi* R*egis*' and 'Iovis vicesimo secundo Die Iunii Anno Decimo t*er*cio Iacobi R*egis*. I I Parker.'

ST IVES

Borough Accounts

The two volumes of records for St Ives, citing the usual payments and receipts and making a number of references to plays, note a variety of special expenses related to the quay, including money given to soldiers and poor people sailing from Ireland. The St Ives accounts also record the king and queen of the summer games and their profits. Transcriptions of many of the borough accounts are included in Matthews' *History of St. Ives* but Matthews' dating of records is not always considered reliable. Discrepancies are recorded in endnotes where they occur.

In cases where the original document headings have been lost, we have relied on the dating decisions given by R. Morton Nance in his annotated copy of Matthews' *History of St. Ives* held in the Royal Institution of Cornwall (the Nance Collection, no shelf-mark) and have indicated this in the relevant endnotes where applicable. The St Ives Borough Accounts have no shelf-marks because they are stored in the Mayor's Parlour in the St Ives Guildhall. Excerpts on hurling from the St Ives Borough Accounts Book II appear in Appendix 4. The account year for Borough Accounts I is Michaelmas to Michaelmas; the accounts transcribed from Borough Accounts II run from All Saints to All Saints.

Borough Accounts I

St Ives, Guildhall, no shelf-mark; 1570–1638; English; paper; ii + 93 + ii; 301mm x 192mm (variable text area), average 31 long lines, some folios have 3 or 4 columns; modern pencil foliation; leaves once edged in gold now repaired and mounted in tightly bound MS, title page decorated with a large (105mm x 108mm) letter A, interlaced and with leaves, first 3 lines of title larger, with flourished letters, 40mm border, straight double lines; bound in 19th or 20th c. cream-coloured leather, gold on black line all around top and bottom boards close to edge, on spine 6 gold bars and title in gold on black: 'RECORD | BOOK | OF THE | PARISH | OF | ST. IVES.'

Borough Accounts II

St Ives, Guildhall, no shelf-mark; 1638–1830; English; paper; ii + 219 + v, approximately 10 gatherings, 356mm x 235mm (335mm x 195mm approximately), average 43 long lines; some modern pencil and ink foliation; leaves have been trimmed and mounted; some enlarged initials, flourished leaf decoration, title page decorated with heavy lines around 3 initial words, and a decorative border (195mm long); brown leather binding with tiny embossed leaf border on boards, vine and flower embossed across spine but no title.

ST KEVERNE

Bill of Complaint in Webber v. Kindsman et al

See under Manaccan (p 429) for PRO: STAC 8/304/38.

ST NEOT

Inventory of Thomas Pomeray

Although the inventory is available the will itself is no longer extant. The Pomerays were an old Norman family who built their castle at Tregony on the Fal River.[285]

Truro, Cornwall Record Office, AP/P/245/2; 6 May 1611; English; paper; single sheet; 202mm x 163mm (141mm x 139mm).

SANCREED

Deposition of John Veal et al (A)

The Penheleg manuscript from 1760 is an antiquarian copy of a book written in 1578–80 that detailed the historic rights and privileges of the Arundell family in the period from 1500 to 1580. It was compiled by John Penheleg, a servant of the Arundell family of Lanherne and bailiff of the hundred of Penwith, of which the family was overlord, and contains a geographical description of the hundred of Penwith with listings of parishes, tithings, and boundaries. Witnesses testifying to the Arundell family's jurisdiction over criminals also referred to dramatic activity in Sancreed.

Truro, Cornwall Record Office, X/50/5; 1760; English; paper; ii + 16 + ii; 319mm x 195mm (289mm x 157mm), average 35 long lines; 18th c. pagination; leaves are mounted, no decoration except some headings in larger letters; 18th c. brown leather binding, tooled with diamond pattern, title in gold on top of front board: 'A BOOK DECLARING THE ROYALTIES WHICH | SIR JOHN ARUNDELL of LANHERNO KNIGHT | AND HIS ANCESTORS | HAVE HAD WITHIN THE HUNDRED OF PENWITH' and on the bottom of the front board in gold: 'BY JOHN PENELEG GENTLEMAN.'

STRATTON

Parish Records

St Andrew Churchwardens' Accounts

These accounts are parish guild records, made by the wardens of the stores of the High and Holy Cross of St Andrew's Church. These parish guilds were made up of men and women who collected the money made from 'stores.' These stores usually consisted of dairy and grazing animals or bee colonies, which parishioners rented or the wardens maintained. Profits were given to the church.[286] The High Cross churchwardens' accounts begin and end in the week after Candlemas and the Stockwardens' Accounts in the week after the feast of St Martin. The British Museum purchased these manuscripts, now BL: Additional MS. 32243 and 32244 from William Maskell, former vicar of St Andrew's Church, 23 February 1884.

London, British Library, Additional MS. 32243; 1512–77; Latin and English (headings in Latin); parchment and paper; ii (+ original cover) + 103 + iii; 312mm x 219mm (274mm x 173mm approximately), average 28 long lines; 1884 pencil foliation; quarto gatherings, leaves repaired and mounted (f 58 cut; ff 60, 60v, 61, 61v faded; ff 101v, 102 blank); modern binding in blue-green leather, title on spine: 'High Cross | Wardens' | Accounts of | Stratton. | *County* Cornwall. | 1512–1577,' and on the original cover the title in large letters: 'The Counte Boke | of | The hye Crosse Wardenys of | Stratton | *anno domi*ni | m° ccccc xij.'

London, British Library, Additional MS. 32244; 1532–48; Latin and English (headings in Latin); paper and parchment; ii (+ vellum wrapper) + 20 (+ vellum wrapper) + ii; average 335mm x 212mm (average 275mm x 180mm), average 24 long lines; 1884 pencil foliation; leaves are mounted; original covers are decorated as follows: title on the recto of the original front vellum wrapper: 'liber compet Gen*eral* Recepto (..) *Sanct*i andrie de Stratton,' and on the recto of the vellum wrapper at the end of the MS are drawn in ink groups of figures, among them the 3 dead, 2 figures wearing crowns, and a group of 3, 1 of which appears to be a jester and another appears to have a halo; the verso of the vellum wrapper has a figure which appears to be a knight (perhaps St Christopher or St George) holding a child-sized king (perhaps Christ); modern blue-green leather binding, title in gold on spine: 'Churchwardens' Accounts | of Stratton, *County* Cornwall, | 1532–1548.'

Antiquarian Records

St Andrew Stockwardens' Accounts (A)

R.W. Goulding (comp), *Records of the Charity known as Blanchminster's Charity in the Parish of Stratton, County of Cornwall, until the Year 1832* (Louth, Stratton, and Bude, 1898).

TRURO

John Leland, Itinerary

As Carew would do later in the sixteenth century for his *Survey of Cornwall*, John Leland, the king's librarian, travelled through England between 1534 and 1542 and intended to write a survey of the various counties. Although he died before completing his task his notes on Cornwall survive. His observations on the landscape and Cornish towns in the mid-sixteenth century provide details not otherwise available and he often visited prominent people, like William Carnsew of Bokelly, writer of the Carnsew Diary, remarking upon them as friends and commenting on their homes.[287] Leland's Itinerary, when he records his tour through Cornwall, refers to a site where plays may have been performed.

Oxford, Bodleian Library, MS. Top. gen. e.10; *c* 1535–43; English; paper; iii + 106 (includes half-leaves 26b, 68b, 87b, 91b, 95b) + ii; 207mm x 152mm average, several wider pages folded on right margin (text area variable), average 30 long lines; modern pencil foliation; small tears, right edges and bottom edges frayed, some damage from damp, many leaves repaired; bound in contemporary gray-brown suede, with title on upper spine: 'LELAND'S | ITINERARY,' on lower spine: 'VOL | II,' and at the bottom: 'MS.Top. Gen. e.10.'

WEST LOOE

West Looe borough records include a 1574 charter, leases from 1573 and later, and seventeenth-century accounts of constables and overseers of the poor as well as records relating to the borough court, the appointment of borough officials, and parliamentary elections. Parish records include registers, churchwardens' accounts, overseers' accounts, and charitable deeds, all beginning in the mid-to late-seventeenth century.

Mayors' Accounts

A note written in an antiquarian copy of CRO: B/WLooe/12/1 concerns a tale of the queen's ape, which we include in Appendix 6.

Truro, Cornwall Record Office, B/WLooe/12/1; 1582–3; English; paper; single leaf; 304mm x 239mm (165mm x 165mm), average 27 long lines; leaf numbered '1' and recently mounted; endorsed, but no decoration or seals. The leaf is included with other single leaves in a bundle, some of which may have been from a single account book.

WHITSTONE

Bill of Complaint in Robins v. Vosse et al

Kew, Public Record Office, STAC 8/246/13; 15 November 1620; English; parchment; single membrane (mb 3 in bundle) attached by modern sewing to mbs 1 and 2 in top left corner; 480mm x 557mm

(467mm x 542mm); mb 3 endorsed: 'Robins *versus* Vosse et al*ios* | Mich' 18ˢᵒ Ia*cobi* Reg*is*' and 'M*ercurij*
Decimo Quinto Novembr*is* Anno Decimo octavo Ia*cobi* Reg*is*. | I Parker.'

Monasteries

EPISCOPAL LICENCE TO THE MONASTERY OF TYWARDREATH

This licence, like the prohibition directed to the collegiate church of St Thomas the Martyr at
Glasney in Penryn parish (see pp 503–5), is drawn from the registers of Bishop Grandisson and
the description below is taken from Wasson (ed), *Devon*, p xxix. The monastery, dedicated to
St Andrew, was founded at Tywardreath, near Lostwithiel, in the eleventh century by Richard
fitz Turold, chief baron of Cornwall.

Exeter, Devon Record Office, Chanter 4; 1333–60; Latin; parchment; 242 + v; 305mm x 225mm;
foliated j to ccxlij by the scribe; 19th c. binding in board and half-calf.

Households

Cornwall has many great houses. While some still retain their ancient documents, in other
instances family and household documents have been placed in public repositories. Only a few
of these documents yielded records for this collection.

ARUNDELL OF LANHERNE

The Arundell family records from the manor of Lanherne in Mawgan include an account
of household expenses enumerating supplies purchased for plays, dances, and other amusements. The Stewards' Accounts from Lanherne, housed at the Royal Institution of Cornwall
in Truro, are among a large number of documents discovered by Charles Henderson and bequeathed at his death in 1933 to the Royal Institution, the major archival repository at the
time. The Stewards' Accounts were edited by H.L. Douch, 'Household Accounts at Lanherne.'
Other accounts of the Arundell family were in private hands until 1991 and are now at the
CRO in Truro.

Sir John Arundell's Stewards' Accounts

The Sir John Arundell in these records is the eleventh Sir John Arundell of the elder Roman
Catholic branch of the family, who lived at Lanherne in St Mawgan. He was likely the Sir John
who became vice admiral of Cornwall in 1447 and who married Catherine, daughter of Sir
John Chideock of Dorset in 1451.[288]

Truro, Royal Institution of Cornwall, Courtney Library, HK/17/1; 1466–7; Latin and English; parchment and paper; 2 paper sheets folded, making 4 leaves, and attached to parchment with thread; paper

215mm x 145mm (text area variable), parchment 190mm x 430mm (160mm x 265mm approximately); no foliation; 2 paper leaves badly torn and frayed at ends; unbound and wrapped in modern paper translation.

Sir John Arundell's Household Account Book

This household book probably belonged to the twelfth Sir John Arundell (d. 1557), who was active in the Prayer Book Rebellion. Sir John was imprisoned in 1550, along with his brother Thomas, who was accused of plotting against the earl of Warwick. Sir John was married first to Elizabeth, whose inventory is included below. By the time of the twelfth Sir John Arundell, Lanherne was a home of great status and prosperity: it was 'one of the earliest "improved" houses of the Tudor period in Cornwall, ranking for magnificence with Stowe, Place, and Cotehele.'[289]

Truro, Cornwall Record Office, AR/26/2; 1503–7; Latin and English; paper; 68 leaves (+ fragment sewn to f [19]); 208mm x 137mm (text area varies), average 32 long lines; modern foliation omitting blank leaves; 5 gatherings, some blank leaves and some uncut in last gathering; excellent condition; paper leaves are bound into a heavy parchment envelope-type cover with a thick leather strip attached at the spine with 4 braided strips, on front, in contemporary hand: 'Iohn Arundell' and in pencil in a later hand: '1504.'

Inventory of Elizabeth Arundell

Elizabeth Arundell was married to the twelfth Sir John Arundell of Lanherne (d. 1557), the Sir John imprisoned in the Tower of London in 1550 with his brother Thomas. Elizabeth Arundell recorded the contents of the rooms at Lanherne – twelve chambers and nine additional rooms, including a nursery.[290]

Truro, Cornwall Record Office, AR/21/16/1; 1564; English; parchment; 2 membranes attached at the top with thin green ribbon; 157mm x 566mm (106mm x 548mm); unnumbered; no decoration except headings written larger.

Will of Edward Arundell

Edward Arundell (d. 1586) of Trebelzue is the son of the twelfth Sir John Arundell (d. 1557) and Elizabeth Arundell (d. 1564).[291]

Truro, Cornwall Record Office, AR/21/21/2; 16 October 1586, proved 10 November 1586; English; parchment; single membrane with Latin probate attached to will by seal tag; 494mm x 625mm (455mm x 525mm); decorated initial letter; fragment of archbishop of Canterbury's seal; possible contemporary endorsement: 'John Arundell his last will & Testament 1586,' later endorsement (19th c.?) depicting pedigree of Arundells named in will.

Inventory of Edward Arundell

Truro, Cornwall Record Office, AR/21/22; 1586; English; paper; 16 leaves, 1 gathering of 7, plus 2 leaves at end (original gathering of 9?); approximately 100mm x 307mm (94mm x 300 approximately); no foliation; paper leaves tied with a string.

CARNSEW OF BOKELLY

Diary of William Carnsew

William Carnsew was part of a family with great mining interests in Cornwall, linked to other prominent Cornwall and Devon families by marriage. He was a member of parliament from Penryn in 1559. Besides managing his estates, Carnsew travelled widely in Cornwall and was interested in national affairs, writing and receiving many letters in keeping abreast of political events. His diary, covering all of 1576 and two months of 1577, includes many references to his friends and current events. He remarks upon his activities, his efforts at practising medicine, his travels and visits to friends, and his entertainment. Carnsew was a Puritan who read extensively, as his diary shows; it has been suggested that his membership in parliament in 1559 was because protestants were needed, and may have been arranged by one or the other of Cornish protestant families, the Grenvilles, the Carews, or the Killigrews.[292] Made for his own information, the diary is often difficult to read, since Carnsew wrote in a small hand, often using abbreviations to accommodate the small space he allotted for each entry.[293] When William Carnsew died in 1588, his son Richard inherited Bokelly. Although knighted and a public servant of some reputation, Richard Carnsew lived extravagantly and died in debt. Chancery proceedings were initiated against him and the Carnsew papers, including William Carnsew's diary, became part of the Public Record Office holdings.[294]

Kew, Public Record Office, SP 46/16; 1576–7; English; paper; 16 leaves; 208mm x 154mm (195mm x 120mm), average 27 long lines; modern pencil foliation in diamond-shaped brackets; slightly frayed edges, mounted on paper. Now bound as ff ⟨37⟩–⟨52⟩ with other papers in a modern volume with modern red leather and cloth binding, spine decorated with seven gold bars and title: 'State Paper | Domestic Supplementary | Vol. 16.'

TREGIAN OF GOLDEN

Francis Tregian of Golden Manor, near Tregony on the Fal River, was a member of the recusant Tregian family. He was the son of John Tregian, who married the daughter of John Arundell of Lanherne; Francis Tregian also became more closely linked to the Arundell family when he married Mary Stourton, Lady Arundell's daughter by a previous marriage. The Tregian family, like the Arundells of Lanherne, were recusants, and Francis Tregian was zealously involved in his religion; he was also well known at court as an accomplished courtier and as a man ready to defend his faith.[295] Tregian came under protestant scrutiny because of a variety of factors, not the least of which was his rejection of Queen Elizabeth's personal attentions. When Sir

Richard Grenville, who played a major role in the protestant movement in Cornwall, went to Golden Manor ostensibly searching for a fugitive named Bourne, he discovered Cuthbert Mayne, Devon man and Douai seminarian, ordained in 1575. Mayne returned to England in 1576 and became steward of Golden Manor.[296] The privy council subsequently found Cuthbert Mayne guilty of treason for publishing a Catholic tract at Golden, guilty for defending Rome and the pope, and guilty for being in possession of an *Agnus Dei*, as well as for other charges.[297] Mayne was hanged and dismembered in Launceston in 1577. In 1578 Francis Tregian was tried at Launceston for harbouring Mayne. Tregian was found guilty of sheltering a traitor and was imprisoned in the Marshalsea. For a more detailed account of the circumstances and witnesses at the trial, see p 610, endnote to St Mary's College Library, Oscott: MS 545.

Treatise on the Trial of Francis Tregian

The full title on the Oscott manuscript is: 'The great and long Sufferings for the Catholic Faith of Mr. Francis Tregian Esquire of Golden in Cornwall together with the Martyrdom of Mr. Cuthbert Mayne at Launceston, in the same county, the proto-martyr of Douay College and consequently of all our English Seminaries.' This title reflects well the contents of the manuscript, which also includes the prison life of Tregian from 1579–93. The manuscript was written by Charles Tregian, the son of Francis Tregian. The history of the manuscript and its transmission to the Oscott Library is uncertain but Boyer and Lamb suggest the likely possibilities.[298] The account of Tregian's trial from Oscott 545 is printed in John Morris (ed), *The Troubles of Our Catholic Forefathers*, first ser (London, 1872), 110–12. *The Mirror of Heroes*, a Latin biography of Tregian by his grandson, Francis Plunket, was published in 1665.[299]

Sutton Coldfield, West Midlands, St Mary's College Library, Oscott, MS 545; 20 July 1593; English; paper; vii (including title-page on recto of second leaf) + 86 + vii; 105mm x 160mm (80mm x 130mm); first and last 12 pages blank, except for title page, all 172 pages ruled, 148 pages covered with writing, contemporary ink pagination (1–148); first leaf of text and last fly-leaf damaged, some fading; leather binding fragile, 17th c. (?), spine worn away, gold line tooled on front and back covers 4mm from edge. Several endorsements in various hands on the recto of the title page, on the first page of the text, and on the verso of the last leaf, record progressive ownership of the manuscript.

County of Cornwall

RICHARD CAREW, SURVEY OF CORNWALL

See under Bodmin (pp 422–3) for *STC*: 4615.

Editorial Procedures

Principles of Selection

In accord with the goal of the REED project we have attempted to find and present all known material concerned with performance of drama, secular music, and dance in Cornwall before 1642. We have also aimed to gather here records of folk customs such as May festivals and maypoles, fooling, juggling, puppet shows, animal displays and torments, and ridings with such mimetic features as a mock mayor or prince-for-a-day. Material concerning performance includes not only specific references to plays, dancers, or musicians but also references to related matters such as costumes for actors or morris dancers and stage properties such as Robin Hood's house. It also includes legal documents such as those of Star Chamber cases where defendants answer allegations of performing slanderous ballads and verses in public places.

In keeping with REED practice we have not included entries pertaining to Midsummer bonfires, perambulations of civic boundaries, Rogation Days, and standard bell-ringing; nor have we dealt with civic rituals such as musters or feasts, or with entries that seemed specifically to concern liturgical performance, such as payments to a musician for singing in the choir. The word 'play' has been interpreted generously, however, and when context or other evidence supports interpreting an ambiguous notation as relevant, we have chosen inclusion. As an example, William Carnsew's entry in his diary that he met an acquaintance at the 'bodman playes' (see p 531) is, when viewed in isolation, ambiguous because the word 'playes' might not refer solely to drama; however, since the Halgavor celebration in Bodmin at that time included performance activities, the entries may refer to drama and so we present it here. In another example, since we know that music was an important part of the feast of St Mary Magdalene in Launceston, we regularly include expenses for the feast even though a particular year may not specifically cite musical activity. Similarly, we include entries under Lostwithiel pertaining to the riding on St George's Day where someone was costumed and paraded in the guise of St George; entries for Lostwithiel also list payments for preparing for St George to make his ride, such as the cleaning of his armour. On the other hand, although John Maclean, *Parochial and Family History of Trigg Minor*, vol 1, p 227, refers to later instances in Bodmin history when guild riding there may have involved processing with a decorated pole, musicians, and a 'Riding tune,' evidence of related mimetic activity before 1642 was never uncovered in the records examined and thus the material was excluded.

The many references in Cornish historical documents to church ales are not included in the Records in the absence of clear indications of any related performance activity; however, since the contemporary historian Carew writes that dancing and minstrelsy occurred at church ales in Cornwall (see p 535), we include in Appendix 5 sample expenses from Kilkhampton for such events. Also, documentary references to hurling, an ancient 'game' with many levels of significance, are presented in Appendix 4; other games of skill and chance have been excluded. Additional documentary materials which did not qualify for inclusion in the main records text but which are important to the goals of the volume are also located in the Appendixes. Appendix 1 contains the 'Vocabularium Cornicum' that translates Latin-Old English word pairs for musical instruments and performers into Cornish. Appendix 2 presents speeches and staging diagrams from the manuscripts of the three major plays in the Cornish language, including a list of musical instruments from one of the plays, and several passages referring to entertainment to be held after the conclusion of a day's play, entertainment that evidently included performing by minstrels, piping, and dancing.

In determining the relevance of some items we have necessarily focused on context and in several instances have excluded records in the absence of context suggesting performance activity in Cornwall. The following list concerns specific items that were carefully considered before exclusion from the Cornwall collection:

1/ a payment to 'Rogues of Exceter' in CRO: P/167/5/1, late sixteenth-century churchwardens' accounts for the Cornwall-Devon border parish of North Petherwin. While the term 'rogues' sometimes designated a touring group of actors paid to perform, it was also applied to a variety of travelling people; in the absence of other evidence, we did not include such items. Unlike these 'Rogues,' references to Egyptians or gypsies which appear in the Stratton Churchwardens' Accounts (see pp 521–2) and in a household account book of Arundell of Lanherne (see p 530) are included in the volume because evidence suggests these were entertainers.

2/ an examination taken in Banbury, Oxfordshire, in 1633 of the members of Richard Bradshaw's acting company (who, incidentally, are cited as 'wandring Rogues' for allegedly travelling under false letters patent) in which Richard Whiting, a member of Bradshaw's acting company, testifies to meeting his father in Cornwall. The document (PRO: SP 16/238) does not, however, mention any performances in Cornwall by this company. The Bradshaw document will be part of forthcoming REED volumes for counties where the troupe actually performed.

3/ a 1344 account (PRO: C/66/212, mb [30d]) of a disturbance at a Cornwall stannary in Redruth involving men with the surnames of 'Pipere' and 'Taborer' and a man named 'Robertus Hodyn.' Although in fourteenth-century Cornwall surnames are usually assumed to designate occupation, there is no indication that the professions of these men had any bearing on the nature of the incident. Furthermore as these names were listed as part of a complaint, it is possible the individual who gave as his name a variant form of 'Robin Hood' was using a pseudonym.[300]

4/ a 1583 Bodmin Shoemakers' Guild Ordinance (CRO: B/Bod/243) threatening fines upon any master suffering 'anye Iornaye man to Rune in skore in there house for typlyng or playe above xij d.' where the context of a running debt clearly allows us to read 'playe' in the sense of gaming and gambling.

For the most part, the material included here is transcribed from the original historical documents; pertinent references now extant only in antiquarian copies are noted as such. Usually we have transcribed only relevant excerpts rather than the whole document, except for those instances where context was considered important as with some of the Star Chamber cases where, in fact, the entire document seemed pertinent. We have tried to do as complete a search as possible of those records generally found to be fruitful, such as parish churchwardens' accounts and borough accounts of mayors or receivers, but we have not made a full search of diocesan documents or records of the Star Chamber; we include here the results of an examination limited to those cases assigned to the subject categories of defamation, offences against religion, sedition, and riot, rout, and unlawful assembly; such cases often involve libellous plays, poems, and songs, and other popular pastimes of interest to us. Similarly we have not exhaustively researched wills and inventories but include examples with pertinent information brought to our attention by archivists or found in printed sources.

More references to performance in private households may well exist in documents still contained in family muniment rooms in Cornwall. The Arundell archive, formerly held by the owner at Hook Manor, is an example of such a collection; the Cornwall Record Office's 1991 acquisition of that archive makes much more accessible that large collection of valuable documents and the accounts, wills, and inventories that are included in this volume may indicate the kind of material still privately held. The Royal Institution of Cornwall acquired the Trelawny collection in 1994, formerly privately held. Examination of the more than 450 documents is nearing completion, according to the Courtney Library Report from the Royal Institution. Future explorations in other such collections as they may become available for study will perhaps result in additional information about dramatic performance in Cornwall.

Although in the past few years the Cornwall Record Office has acquired some important documents, in the early years of our research several collections reposed in their original locations – in town buildings and in private hands; these collections had been very minimally catalogued and often were available for perusal only at limited times. In consequence, our efforts to find relevant material have at times been undertaken in unusual circumstances; for example, before the deposit of one large set of documents in the Record Office, which deposit was in large part the result of an editor's urging, those documents had to be researched from the boxes in which they were stored in the basement of the town hall. In other instances where documents were not conveniently located in libraries and record offices, we have learned how simultaneously to stand on a chair, hold a document in one hand at the edge of a window, and with the other hand take a photograph at the precisely calculated moment that the sun would appear briefly from clouds. We have done our best to present here all known and accessible records, and we look forward to reading the work of other scholars who will expand or amend the product of our efforts.

Dating

Dates of accounts are based on evidence within the documents unless otherwise indicated in the accompanying notes. Documents usually have a double date, such as 1466–7, that reflects the accounting year, which often began at Michaelmas (29 September). Entries dated between 1 January and 24 March in the documents and in accord with the contemporary calendar, which did not begin a new year until Lady Day (25 March), are represented by a split year date, for example, 1 February 1466/7. When documents were dated with regnal years, which is often the case, those dates have been translated into calendar years. Record subheadings show the limits of the accounting period but only in cases where the fiscal year is not the customary Michaelmas to Michaelmas range. Additionally, any specific dating information (for example, the date a letter was written or a will was probated) that does not appear in the text of the record itself is supplied in the subheading. Customarily, financial records do not specify dates of performance or related activity but give dates when payments were made. If the date of an event is determinable on the basis of internal evidence this is discussed in an endnote. Readers can find details of the accounting terms of individual runs of accounts discussed on a case by case basis in The Documents section. Specifics on the character of the records and gaps in the extant materials are also provided there.

Editorial Conventions

We have attempted to reproduce as much as possible the appearance of the original manuscripts in regard to layout. Transcriptions of excerpts from the extant Cornish plays, the *Ordinalia*, *Beunans Meriasek*, and the *Creacion*, which appear in Appendix 2, required an altered format designed to approximate the system of indentations and ordering within the stanzas in the manuscript; this is explained in the appendix itself (see p 546). Left marginalia in original documents appear in the left margin of the edited text, as close as possible to that original position; right marginalia are also set in the left margin but are indicated as such by the symbol ®. Routine headings and marginalia are indicated in editorial subheadings. Material from antiquarian collections or compilations is also indicated by an A or AC to the left of the record heading.

Original paragraphing has in all instances been preserved. A document's lineation has also been reproduced except in material excerpted from continuous prose; in those prose passages, a change of page or folio is marked by a (|). A caret accompanying a raised interlineation in the original is reproduced in the edited text, and those interlineations above the line are indicated by upper half brackets (⌐ ¬). Where textual material has decayed, been lost, or is illegible because of some other damage, that illegibility is attested by diamond brackets ⟨ ⟩; when the number of letters lost can be reasonably conjectured, dots within those diamond brackets indicate the number of letters lost: one dot for one letter, two dots for two letters, three dots for three or more lost letters. Cancellations in the original are placed within full square brackets [ ]. An obvious blank space left in the manuscript, where the scribe apparently intended to supply additional material, is indicated by *(blank)*.

The edited text preserves original capitalization, punctuation, word-division, and spelling. Thus 'I' and 'J' have not been distinguished and for each we have routinely used 'I.' The form 'ff' for a modern 'F' has also been retained. Those entries from printed sources follow the spelling and punctuation in those sources. Manuscript braces have been reproduced in necessary instances but otiose fillers and flourishes have not. Virgules are indicated by / and //. Dittography and such obvious scribal errors are mentioned in footnotes. Superior letters have been silently lowered except for those used with numerals. Most abbreviations in the documents have been expanded and those expansions are indicated in italics. Abbreviations not expanded include those for sums of money and for terms still in common currency (eg, 'St,' 'Mr,' 'vizt' or 'viz,' 'etc'). The abbreviations 'Xpi' and 'xpi' are expanded as 'Chr*isti*' or 'chr*isti*,' and 'Ihc' as 'Ie*sus*.' Where expansion of an abbreviation was not obvious or the case and number of a word was ambiguous, an apostrophe signals the abbreviation.

Notes

1   Charles Thomas, *Arthur and Archaeology* (London, 1993), 12.
2   See further Malcolm Todd, *The South West to AD 1000* (London and New York, 1987), 1–6.
3   Hingeston-Randolph (ed), *The Register of John de Grandisson*, pt 2, p 910.
4   Crysten Fudge, *The Life of Cornish* (Redruth, 1982), 11–13. Most scholars agree that in western Cornwall Cornish was spoken longer than in eastern areas of the county. Martyn F. Wakelin remarks that 'it may be noted that John Trevisa, himself a Cornish-man, makes no reference whatever to the language in his famous interpolations on the language of Britain in his translation (1387) of Higden's *Polychronicon*, obviously feeling that it was not worthy of special mention' (*Language and History in Cornwall* (Leicester, 1975), 94).
5   An important social record of Bodmin under Saxon rule is preserved in the tenth-century Bodmin Gospels. The Gospels record the names of those who were freeing slaves, the slaves' names, and the witnesses to the manumissions. From about 950–1050, 122 slaves were freed. The majority of the slaves were Cornishmen, with Cornish names, eg, Brenci, Freoc, Riol, and Rumun; the rest of the slaves were Saxon, except for twelve whose names were biblical, so not identifiable as either. The owners were both. See Fudge, *Life of Cornish*, p 9. The Bodmin Gospels are preserved in BL: Additional MS. 9067 and edited by Whitley Stokes, 'The Manumissions in the Bodmin Gospels,' *Revue Celtique* 1 (1870–2), 332–45; see also Henry Jenner, 'The Bodmin Gospels,' *JRIC* 21, pt 2 (1923), 113–45, and 'The Manumissions in the Bodmin Gospels,' *JRIC* 21, pt 3 (1924), 235–60.
6   Nikolaus Pevsner, *Cornwall*, 2nd ed (New York, 1970), 15–18.
7   *Monastic Britain*, Ordnance Survey (Southampton, 1978), 7.
8   Norman J.G. Pounds, 'The Population of Cornwall before the First Census,' *Population and Marketing: Two Studies in the History of the South-West*, Walter Minchinton (ed) (Exeter, 1976), 13. See *VCH: Cornwall*, vol 2, pt 8, p 53 for a breakdown of the population.
9   Halliday, *History of Cornwall*, p 109.
10 David Knowles and R. Neville Hadcock, *Medieval and Religious Houses: England and Wales* (London, 1971), 148, 162–3, 172.

11 Halliday, *History of Cornwall*, p 113.

12 *vch: Cornwall*, vol 1, pp 524–5; Ronald F. Homer, 'Tin, Lead and Pewter,' *English Medieval Industries: Craftsmen, Techniques, Products*, John Blair and Nigel Ramsay (eds) (London, 1991), 57–80; for an account of the stannaries under Edmund, earl of Cornwall, see L. Margaret Midgley (ed), *Ministers' Accounts of the Earldom of Cornwall 1296–1297*, Camden Society, 3rd ser, vol 66 (London, 1942), xxiv–ix and John Hatcher, *English Tin Production and Trade before 1550* (Oxford, 1973), 20. The five stannary towns were Bodmin, Helston, Liskeard, Lostwithiel, and Truro.

13 Ray Millward and Adrian Robinson, *The South-West Peninsula* (London, 1971), 117–24.

14 Although the Domesday survey does not mention tin mining, Saxon coins have been found in many Cornish towns – St Austell, for instance. In 1774 miners found a buried collection of coins in St Austell from the reigns of twelve Saxon rulers, probably hidden during a Danish incursion (*vch: Cornwall*, vol 1, pp 375, 378). See further, Hatcher, *English Tin Production*, p 16.

15 Hatcher, *English Tin Production*, p 20.

16 Hatcher, *English Tin Production*, p 48.

17 Pounds, 'Population of Cornwall,' p 13.

18 Hatcher, *English Tin Production*, p 67.

19 *Register of Edward the Black Prince*, pt 1 (London, 1930), 26–7.

20 Rowse, *Tudor Cornwall*, p 55.

21 Halliday, *History of Cornwall*, p 279.

22 Frank Stenton, 'The Road System of Medieval England,' *Economic History Review* 7 (1936), 7–19. See also the reproduction in E.J.S. Parsons, *The Map of Great Britain, c. A.D. 1360, Known as the Gough Map* (Oxford and London, 1958), 16–37. We are indebted to Gloria Betcher for her as yet unpublished analysis of the roads in Cornwall for our period ('Minstrels, Morris Dancers, and Players: Tracing the Routes of Travelling Performers in Early Modern Cornwall,' paper given at the International Medieval Congress, Leeds, 1996).

23 Charles Henderson and Henry Coates, *Old Cornish Bridges and Streams* (London, 1928).

24 William Worcestre, *Itineraries*, John H. Harvey (ed) (Oxford, 1969), 12–13, 39 and John Leland, *The Itinerary of John Leland in or about the Years 1535–1543*, Parts 1–3, vol 1, Lucy Toulmin Smith (ed) (Carbondale, 1964), 173–211, 315–26.

25 William Camden, *Camden's Britannia Newly Translated into English with Large Additions and Improvements* (London, 1695; Wing C359).

26 *The Agrarian History of England and Wales*, Edward Miller (ed), vol 3 (Cambridge, 1991), 303–23; and Joan Thirsk (ed), vol 4 (Cambridge, 1967), 71–8.

27 Ian Kershaw, 'The Great Famine and Agrarian Crisis,' pp 85–132. See also John Hatcher, *Rural Economy and Society in the Duchy of Cornwall 1300–1500* (Cambridge, 1970), 80–101.

28 Miller (ed), *Agrarian History*, vol 3, 722–3.

29 Carew, *Survey of Cornwall*, sig G3 verso; see also Peter J. Bowden, *The Wool Trade in Tudor and Stuart England* (London, 1962), 33–4.

30   Rowse, *Tudor Cornwall*, p 67; see also J.L. Bolton, *The Medieval English Economy 1150–1500* (London, 1980), 287–304.

31   John Keast, *A History of East and West Looe* (Chichester, 1987), 27.

32   Homer, 'Tin, Lead and Pewter,' pp 69, 73.

33   James Whetter, *The History of Falmouth* (Redruth, 1981), 9–10.

34   Halliday, *History of Cornwall*, p 149.

35   See Hatcher, *English Tin Production*, table X, p 127.

36   Keast, *History of East and West Looe*, p 21.

37   Keast, *History of East and West Looe*, p 23.

38   Keast, *History of East and West Looe*, pp 23–4.

39   Martyn F. Wakelin, *Language and History in Cornwall* (Leicester, 1975), 71.

40   Miller (ed), *Agrarian History*, vol 3, pp 732–5; Thirsk (ed), *Agrarian History*, vol 4, pp 74–5.

41   Rowse, *Tudor Cornwall*, p 75.

42   Halliday, *History of Cornwall*, pp 206–7.

43   Rowse, *Tudor Cornwall*, p 69.

44   Pounds, 'Population of Cornwall,' p 16. Pounds reaches this estimate by raising the figure from the list of signatories (30,645) to 33,000 to include boroughs and parishes that had been omitted, by doubling it to include women, and by adding 50 per cent for the young who were not likely included.

45   H. Miles Brown, *The Church in Cornwall* (Truro, 1964), 36.

46   Munn, *Introducing Bodmin*, p 82.

47   Newlyn, 'Stained and Painted Glass at St. Neot's Church,' p 95.

48   Anthony Fletcher, *Tudor Rebellions*, 2nd ed (London, 1973), 14–17; Rowse, *Tudor Cornwall*, p 64, explains that a 'species of usury ran throughout the industry, from the great merchant buyers at the top – chiefly the London pewterers – through the dealers and the lesser merchants, to the small tinners at the bottom sustaining the burden.' Great families controlled the tin industry and were backed by stannary court decisions: 'The stannary parliament of 1588 divided all tinners into two classes: manual labourers, "spaliers" and "pioneers" as they were called, and gentlemen who shared in tin works or received toll tin as landlords, owners of bounds with all other workers required in the industry, smiths, blowers, smelters' (p 65).

49   Halliday, *History of Cornwall*, pp 166–7; see also Julian Cornwall, *Revolt of the Peasantry 1549* (London, 1977), 41–7.

50   Knowles and Hadcock, *Medieval Religious Houses*, pp 162, 148, 223, 122, 79, 219.

51   See Lawrence S. Snell, *The Suppression of the Religious Foundations of Devon and Cornwall* (Marazion, 1967), 61–106.

52   Rowse, *Tudor Cornwall*, pp 257–8.

53   For 2 & 3 Edward vi c.1 (1548–9) see *The Statutes of the Realm*, vol 4, pt 1 (London, 1819), 37.

54   'A copye of a Letter contayning certayne newes, and the Articles or requestes of the Deuonshyre and Cornyshe rebelles' (London, 1549; STC: 15109.3), sigs B vi verso and

B vii. See also Joyce Youings, 'The South-Western Rebellion of 1549,' *Southern History* 1 (1979), 99–122.

55 Cornwall, *Revolt of the Peasantry*, pp 100–13.

56 See, for example, Fudge, *Life of Cornish*, p 25. In 1602 Carew noted that Cornish was fading, 'for the English speach doth still encroche vpon it, and hath driuen the same into the vttermost skirts of the shire' (*Survey of Cornwall*, sig P4).

57 Cornwall, *Revolt of the Peasantry*, pp 232–3.

58 S.T. Bindoff (ed), *The House of Commons 1509–1558*, vol 1 (London, 1982), 333–4.

59 For 23 Elizabeth c.1 (1580–1) see *The Statutes of the Realm*, vol 4, pt 1, p 657.

60 Halliday, *History of Cornwall*, p 186.

61 P.A. Boyan and G.R. Lamb, *Francis Tregian, Cornish Recusant* (London, 1955), 56–60.

62 William Prynne, *Histrio-mastix. The players scourge* (London, 1633; *stc*: 20464). Some years later, in 1648, Prynne became a member of parliament for the town of Newport (Launceston).

63 John Bastwick, *The Letany of John Bastwick* (London, 1637; *stc*: 1572).

64 Bastwick, *Letany*, p 114.

65 Henry Burton, *For God and the King. The summe of two sermons* (London, 1636; *stc*: 4141) and *An apology of an appeale* (London, 1636; *stc*: 4134).

66 The Star Chamber account appears in *A New Discovery of the Prelates Tyranny, in their late prosecutions of Mr. William Pryn, an eminent Lawyer; Dr. John Bastwick, a learned Physician; and Mr. Henry Burton, a reverent Divine* (London, 1641; Wing: P4018).

67 Hatcher, *Rural Economy and Society*, pp 3–6.

68 *vch: Cornwall*, vol 2, part 8, p 57.

69 Of the twenty-six manors held by St Petroc's, Bodmin, de Mortain took seven outright, and seven others were occupied by him or his followers under the lordship of the church in name only. See G.A. Kempthorne, 'Notes on the Cornish Priories,' *Old Cornwall* 2.10 (1935), 5.

70 Graham Haslam, 'Evolution,' *The Duchy of Cornwall*, Crispin Gill (ed) (London, 1987), 23. See also Hatcher, *Rural Economy and Society*, pp 3–7.

71 John Harvey, *The Black Prince and his Age* (London, 1976), 15, 48, 87. See also Richard Barber, *Edward, Prince of Wales and Aquitaine: A Biography of the Black Prince* (London, 1978), passim.

72 Haslam, 'Evolution,' p 24.

73 Rowse, *Tudor Cornwall*, p 79.

74 Haslam, 'Evolution,' p 28.

75 Hatcher, *Rural Economy and Society*, p 7.

76 Haslam, 'Evolution,' p 30.

77 Haslam, 'Evolution,' p 31.

78 Haslam, 'Evolution,' pp 31–2.

79 Graham Haslam, 'The Elizabethan Duchy of Cornwall, an Estate in Stasis,' *The Estates of the English Crown, 1558–1640*, R.W. Hoyle (ed) (Cambridge, 1992), 110–11.

80 Haslam, 'Evolution,' pp 34–40.

81   Haslam, 'Evolution,' p 40.

82   Todd, *The South West*, pp 4, 109.

83   Munn, *Introducing Bodmin*, pp [ii–iii], 81.

84   Halliday, *History of Cornwall*, pp 136–7.

85   Munn, *Introducing Bodmin*, p 5. The Berry Tower was built by the Holy Rood guild and local people paid for most of the building according to the Berry Tower Building Accounts, making contributions such as a silver spoon, a silver girdle, and a cow hide. See Robert Whiting, *The Blind Devotion of the People: Popular Religion and the English Reformation* (Cambridge, 1989), 107.

86   *vch: Cornwall*, vol 2, pt 8, p 69; see also H.C. Darby and R. Welldon Finn (eds), *The Domesday Geography of South-West England* (Cambridge, 1967), 335–6.

87   J.S. Roskell (ed), *The House of Commons 1386–1421*, vol 1 (Stroud, 1992), 295.

88   Munn, *Bodmin Riding*, p 95.

89   Roskell (ed), *House of Commons, 1386–1421*, vol 1, p 303. Thereafter the assizes were held at Launceston.

90   Roskell (ed), *House of Commons, 1386–1421*, vol 1, p 297.

91   Rowse, *Tudor Cornwall*, p 161.

92   Roskell (ed), *House of Commons, 1386–1421*, vol 1, p 296.

93   Knowles and Hadcock, *Medieval Religious Houses*, p 223 and Halliday, *History of Cornwall*, p 169.

94   Martin Weinbaum (ed), *British Borough Charters 1307–1660* (Cambridge, 1943), 13.

95   See Robert Tittler, 'The Incorporation of Boroughs, 1540–1558,' *History*, ns 62 (1977), 24–42.

96   Munn, *Introducing Bodmin*, pp 78, 82.

97   Munn, *Introducing Bodmin*, p 37. 'Pie Powder' (from the French 'pied poudreux' jurisdiction, meaning 'dusty of foot') referred to a jurisdiction where itinerant merchants or traders could sell their wares but were subject to the judgments of the summary court who administered justice during the fair.

98   Munn, *Introducing Bodmin*, p 1.

99   Munn, *Introducing Bodmin*, p 23.

100 Munn, *Introducing Bodmin*, p 28.

101 Mattingly, 'Medieval Parish Guilds,' p 293. The guilds of St Leonard and the Trinity were attached to the chantry chapel of St Leonard; other chapels with guilds included the St Thomas Becket Chantry and St Anne's Chapel. Munn, *Introducing Bodmin*, pp 67, 23, 28.

102 Munn, *Introducing Bodmin*, p [i].

103 Munn, *Introducing Bodmin*, p 17. A medieval fireplace was found in a building adjacent to the existing Guildhall on Fore Street. Munn adds, 'Stained glass windows in the council chamber depict the arms of the U.K., Cornwall, Bodmin and the Priory; a circular window between the chamber and main hall depicts the borough seal; a 15th century bell hangs in the main hall; 12-holed stocks are in the lobby.'

104 Mattingly, 'Medieval Parish Guilds,' p 303.

105 Mattingly, 'Medieval Parish Guilds,' pp 298–9. Mattingly notes that the guilds are sometimes called in the records names like 'the maidens,' blurring the distinction between guilds and other groups of parish contributors.

106 Halliday, *History of Cornwall*, p 180.

107 Cornwall, *Revolt of the Peasantry*, pp 202–3; Munn, *Introducing Bodmin*, p 82.

108 Roskell (ed), *House of Commons, 1386–1421*, vol 1, p 296.

109 Carew, *Survey of Cornwall*, sig Ii3 verso.

110 Peter Clark, Kathy Gaskin, and Adrian Wilson, *Population Estimates of English Small Towns 1550–1851*, Centre for Urban History, Working Paper No. 3 (Leicester, 1989), 17. A contemporary list of householders at the end of the Bodmin church building accounts (1472) indicates 460 householders. Mattingly estimates 4.5 people per household, totalling 2,070 people ('Medieval Parish Guilds,' p 308).

111 Roskell (ed), *House of Commons, 1386–1421*, vol 1, p 303.

112 Bindoff (ed), *House of Commons, 1509–1558*, vol 1, p 56.

113 Roskell (ed), *House of Commons, 1386–1421*, vol 1, pp 303–6.

114 Betcher, 'Minstrels, Morris Dancers, and Players.'

115 Roskell (ed), *House of Commons, 1386–1421*, vol 1, p 303.

116 Roskell (ed), *House of Commons, 1386–1421*, vol 1, pp 303–4. Launceston remains the site of the Feudal Dues ceremony, begun under Richard, earl of Cornwall, discontinued, and revived under the current Prince Charles. According to a 1324 account, the dues consisted of contributions from various Cornish manors and towns: among other things, a grey cape, valued at 16d, from St Neot; one pound of pepper and 100 shillings from Launceston; a 'bow de arburne' (alder) from Truro; a brace of greyhounds for Elerky in Veryan; gilt spurs from Penvose in St Tudy; a salmon spear and a daily carriage of wood in the form of 'ashen faggot' from Stoke Climsland; and 300 puffins from the Scilly Isles (Venning, *Book of Launceston*, p 40).

117 P. Sheppard, *Historic Towns of Cornwall: An Archaeological Survey* (Truro, 1980), 75.

118 Roskell (ed), *House of Commons, 1386–1421*, vol 1, p 303.

119 Sheppard, *Historic Towns of Cornwall*, p 75.

120 Carew, *Survey of Cornwall*, sig Gg4.

121 Adolphus Ballard and James Tait (eds), *British Borough Charters 1216–1307* (Cambridge, 1923), 379.

122 Halliday, *History of Cornwall*, p 154.

123 Roskell (ed), *House of Commons, 1386–1421*, vol 1, p 304.

124 Halliday, *History of Cornwall*, p 129. Some accounts report that Dunheved made returns to parliament as early as 1295 (see Roskell (ed), *House of Commons 1386–1421*, vol 1, p 304).

125 Halliday, *History of Cornwall*, p 126.

126 Roskell (ed), *House of Commons, 1386–1421*, vol 1, p 304.

127 Peter and Peter, *Histories of Launceston and Dunheved*, pp 74–5.

128 St Mary Magdalene's Church: Assumption of the Blessed Virgin Mary; St Christopher; St George; Holy Cross; Jesus; St John Baptist; St Mary Magdalene; and a guild of min-

strels. St Thomas' Church: All Hallows at Tregadillett; St Anthony; St Blaise; St Christopher; St John; St John Bridlington (may be the same as St John); St Peter; St Thomas (Mattingly, 'Medieval Parish Guilds,' p 314). All material on guilds in Launceston comes from Mattingly's 'Medieval Parish Guilds,' pp 291–329.

129   Peter and Peter, *Histories of Launceston and Dunheved*, p 311.

130   Halliday, *History of Cornwall*, pp 170, 173.

131   The letters patent made the mayor and aldermen initially Crown appointees. While the office of mayor was an annual one, the mayor elected from among the aldermen, the position of alderman itself was for life (*Calendar of the Patent Rolls*, Philip and Mary, vol 3, *1555–1557* (London, 1938), 174–7.)

132   Peter and Peter, *Histories of Launceston and Dunheved*, p 55.

133   Rowse, *Tudor Cornwall*, p 97.

134   Peter and Peter, *Histories of Launceston and Dunheved*, p 177, citing mayor's account of 1521–2.

135   Carew, *Survey of Cornwall*, sigs G3–G3 verso.

136   Carew, *Survey of Cornwall*, sig Oo2.

137   The total population of the medieval parliamentary borough may have been no more than 500; see Roskell (ed), *House of Commons, 1386–1421*, vol 1, p 303.

138   Clark et al, *Population Estimates of English Small Towns*, p 17.

139   Charles Henderson, *Essays in Cornish History*, A.L. Rowse and M.I. Henderson (eds) (Oxford, 1935), 44–5; see also Adolphus Ballard (ed), *British Borough Charters 1042–1216* (Cambridge, 1913), xxx.

140   Ballard (ed), *British Borough Charters*, p 217.

141   Henderson, *Essays in Cornish History*, p 52.

142   Henderson, *Essays in Cornish History*, p 52.

143   Henderson, *Essays in Cornish History*, p 46; Ballard and Tait (eds), *British Borough Charters*, pp 5, 248, 250, 266. A second weekly market on Thursday was granted in 1325 (*Calendar of the Charter Rolls preserved in the Public Record Office*, vol 3 (London, 1914), 479).

144   Roskell (ed), *House of Commons, 1386–1421*, vol 1, p 312.

145   Roskell (ed), *House of Commons, 1386–1421*, vol 1, p 312.

146   Halliday, *History of Cornwall*, p 119.

147   Bindoff (ed), *House of Commons, 1509–1558*, vol 1, p 54.

148   Mattingly, 'Medieval Parish Guilds,' pp 291, 315.

149   Mattingly, 'Medieval Parish Guilds,' pp 297, 300–1.

150   Knowles and Hadcock, *Medieval Religious Houses*, pp 79, 120.

151   Cited by Halliday, *History of Cornwall*, p 169.

152   Halliday, *History of Cornwall*, p 169.

153   Halliday, *History of Cornwall*, pp 168–9.

154   Carew, *Survey of Cornwall*, sig Mm4 verso.

155   For 1 Edward VI c. 14 (1547) see *Statutes of the Realm*, vol 4, pt 1, p 24.

156   Mattingly, 'Medieval Parish Guilds,' p 295.

157   Rowse, *Tudor Cornwall*, p 296, discussing and quoting a case in Augmentations, Miscellaneous Books 122, PRO: E 315/122, ff 15–28. See also Mattingly, 'Medieval Parish Guilds,' p 327 n 129.

158   PRO: E 315/122, ff 20v, 21.

159   Bindoff (ed), *House of Commons, 1509–1558*, vol 1, p 54.

160   Clark et al, *Population Estimates of English Small Towns*, p 19.

161   Ballard and Tait (eds), *British Borough Charters*, pp xcviii, 46, 55, 95; Bindoff (ed), *House of Commons, 1509–1558*, vol 1, p 57.

162   Bindoff (ed), *House of Commons, 1509–1558*, vol 1, p 57.

163   Weinbaum (ed), *British Borough Charters, 1307–1660*, p 17.

164   *Calendar of Charter Rolls*, vol 2 (London, 1898), 16, and vol 3, p 183.

165   Carew, *Survey of Cornwall*, sig Qq2 verso.

166   Rowse, *Tudor Cornwall*, p 76.

167   Sir Henry Killigrew was an able diplomat and the brother-in-law of William Cecil. See Amos C. Miller, *Sir Henry Killigrew: Elizabethan Soldier and Diplomat* (Leicester, 1963), 13, 248. Arwennack is mentioned in the first section of the *Ordinalia*, 'Origo Mundi,' along with other Cornish place names near Penryn – Enys, Penryn woods, and Bohellan fields. See Gloria J. Betcher, 'Place Names and Political Patronage in the Cornish *Ordinalia*,' *Research Opportunities in Renaissance Drama* 35 (1996), 122–4.

168   Halliday, *History of Cornwall*, p 126.

169   J. Whetter, *The History of Falmouth* (Redruth, 1981), 10.

170   Clark et al, *Population Estimates of English Small Towns*, p 19.

171   Charles Henderson, *The Cornish Church Guide* (Truro, 1964), 74, 156–7.

172   Henderson, *Cornish Church Guide*, p 157.

173   Nicholas Orme, *Education in the West of England 1066–1548* (Exeter, 1976), 167–8.

174   See, eg, Brian O. Murdoch, 'The Cornish Medieval Drama,' *The Cambridge Companion to Medieval English Theatre*, Richard Beadle (ed) (Cambridge, 1994), 211–39.

175   Roland J. Roddis, *Penryn: The History of an Ancient Cornish Borough* ([Truro], 1964), 43.

176   To clarify for scholars who may find reference to a 'Bishop Beaupre' in connection with Glasney or dramatic performances around 1360, we could not confirm a title of bishop. But a Sir John Beaupre appropriated St Just in Penwith to Glasney in 1355, an aisle of the church was called the Beaupre aisle, and two priests prayed daily in the chapel for the well-being of the Beaupre family. See Sowell, 'Collegiate Church of St Thomas,' pp 24–5.

177   F.C. Hingeston-Randolph (ed), *The Register of Thomas de Brantyngham, Bishop of Exeter, (A.D. 1370–1394)*, pt 2 (London, 1906), 671–3.

178   See F.C. Hingeston-Randolph (ed), *The Register of Edmund Stafford (A.D. 1395–1419)* (London, 1886), 112–13.

179   Sowell, 'The Collegiate Church of St Thomas,' p 33.

180   Sowell, 'Collegiate Church of St Thomas,' pp 29–30.

181   Carew, *Survey of Cornwall*, sig Rr2.

182   Henderson, *Essays in Cornish History*, p 85.

183   Henderson, *Essays in Cornish History*, p 84.

184   Henderson, *Essays in Cornish History*, pp 88–9.

185   Matthews, *History of Saint Ives*, pp 48, 50.

186   Bodl.: MS. Top. gen. e.10, f 7v.

187   Matthews, *History of Saint Ives*, p 46. St Ives, Towednack, and Lelant were under the manors of Ludgvan Leaze at the time of the Domesday survey. For a discussion of the different areas of the parish and the history of their possession, see Henderson, *Essays in Cornish History*, pp 80–7.

188   Henderson notes that he derived this information from a 1722 manuscript of the history of St Ives by Thomas Hicks, now lost (*Essays in Cornish History*, p 91).

189   P.W. Hasler, *The House of Commons, 1558–1603*, vol 1 (London, 1981), 135.

190   Bindoff (ed), *House of Commons, 1509–1558*, vol 1, p 58.

191   Cyril Noall, *The Book of St Ives: A Portrait of the Town* (Chesham, 1977), 20.

192   Carew, *Survey of Cornwall*, sig K1 verso.

193   Rowse, *Tudor Cornwall*, p 75.

194   Rowse, *Tudor Cornwall*, p 58.

195   Matthews, *History of Saint Ives*, p 117.

196   Matthews, *History of Saint Ives*, pp 48, 50; Clark et al, *Population Estimates of English Small Towns*, p 21.

197   Cornwall, *Revolt of the Peasantry*, p 202.

198   Matthews, *History of Saint Ives*, pp 194–5.

199   Matthews, *History of Saint Ives*, p 193; Weinbaum (ed), *British Borough Charters*, p 17.

200   Matthews, *History of Saint Ives*, p 397.

201   Noall, *Book of St Ives*, p 104;

202   Halliday, *History of Cornwall*, p 156.

203   Richard Carew, *Survey of Cornwall*, F.E. Halliday (ed) (London, 1953), 311–13.

204   Rowse, *Tudor Cornwall*, p 77.

205   Rowse, *Tudor Cornwall*, p 247.

206   Halliday, *History of Cornwall*, p 188.

207   Rowse, *Tudor Cornwall*, p 318.

208   Hasler (ed), *House of Commons, 1558–1603*, vol 1, p 126.

209   Rowse, *Tudor Cornwall*, p 231.

210   Rowse, *Tudor Cornwall*, pp 54–5.

211   Rowse, *Tudor Cornwall*, pp 86–7.

212   Early deeds and charters attest to 327 properties owned by the Arundells in Devon, Dorset, and Cornwall. Lanherne Manor, the bishop of Exeter's property at the time of Domesday, came to the Arundells through the marriage of Alice Lanherne to Sir Remfry de Arundell in 1231. See V.L. Vivian, *The Visitations of the County of Cornwall comprising the Herald's Visitations of 1530 and 1620* (Exeter, 1887), 2.

213   Information supplied by O.J. Padel.

214   Surveyed by the Royal Commission on Historical Manuscripts in 1871, the archive

has since been apportioned; the Cornwall portion – 15,000–20,000 items – is now housed at the CRO. See Christine North, 'The Arundell Archive,' *JRIC*, ns II, vol 1 (1991), 49–51 and McCann, *Introduction to the Arundell Archive.*

215 To spare other researchers one particular wild goose chase, we note that L.E. Elliott-Binns, in *Medieval Cornwall* (London, 1955), 403–4, states that 'in 1428 a certain Cornishman, Jakke Trevaill by name, is said to have presented various plays and interludes before Henry VI,' and credits 'William Sandys (Uncle Jan Trenoodle) *Specimens of Cornish Provincial Dialect*'; however, the Sandys book does not contain references to documents concerning such drama.

216 For an edition of the 'Charter Interlude' see Lauran Toorians (ed), *The Middle Cornish Charter Endorsement* (Innsbruck, 1991); for analysis see Evelyn S. Newlyn, 'The Middle Cornish Interlude: Genre and Tradition,' *Comparative Drama* 30.2 (1996), 266–81.

217 Gloria J. Betcher, 'Makers of Heaven on Earth: The Construction of Early Drama in Cornwall,' *Material Culture and Medieval Drama*, Clifford Davidson (ed), forthcoming.

218 Betcher, 'Makers of Heaven on Earth.'

219 See Sally Joyce Cross, 'Torturers as Tricksters in the Cornish *Ordinalia*,' *Neuphilologische Mitteilungen* 4.34 (1983), 448–55.

220 V.A. Kolve, *The Play Called Corpus Christi* (Stanford, 1966), 44–9.

221 See Matthews, *History of Saint Ives*, p 144 and Nance's comments in his annotated edition of Matthews' *History of Saint Ives*; the Courtney Library of the Royal Institution of Cornwall in Truro holds Nance's edition of Matthews in the Nance collection, no shelf-mark.

222 David Wiles, *The Early Plays of Robin Hood* (Cambridge, 1981), 54.

223 Wiles, *Early Plays of Robin Hood*, p 17.

224 For a brief discussion of the accounts for 1535–6 and 1537–8 see N.M. & A., '"Howde Men": Robin Hood's Men,' *Notes and Queries*, ser 11, vol 2 (1910), 16.

225 Mattingly, 'Medieval Parish Guilds,' p 305.

226 Wiles, *Early Plays of Robin Hood*, p 17.

227 O.J. Padel, *Cornish Place-Name Elements*, English Place-Name Society, vol 56/57 (Nottingham, 1985), 114, 186–7.

228 Henry Jenner, 'Perran Round and the Cornish Drama,' *The Seventy-Eighth Annual Report of the Royal Cornwall Polytechnic Society*, ns 1.3 (1911), 38–44.

229 Vivien Russell, *West Penwith Survey* (Truro, 1971), 41–7.

230 A. Ivan Rabey, *Hurling at St. Columb and in Cornwall* (Padstow, 1972), 5.

231 Borlase, *Natural History*, p 300.

232 Bodl.: MS. Top. gen. e.10, f 11v.

233 Thomas, 'The Society's 1962 Excavations,' pp 3–14.

234 For a discussion of the plain-an-gwary at St Just in Penwith, see A. Guthrie, 'The Plain-an-Gwarry, St. Just, Cornwall: Report on an Exploratory Excavation,' *Proceedings of the West Cornwall Field Club*, ns 2.1 (1956–7), 3–7.

235 An earlier version of Padel's list of ancient parishes where a plain-an-gwary may have existed appeared in Evelyn S. Newlyn, *Cornish Drama of the Middle Ages: A Bibliography* (Redruth, 1987), 8–10.

236 Carew, *Survey of Cornwall*, sig T3 verso.

237 Borlase, *Observations*, p 196.

238 Although Borlase, in his *Natural History* of 1758, stated the diameter of the playing place at Perranzabuloe to be 130 feet (p 298), Higgins provides these larger dimensions of '143 feet across on the north-south axis, and 135 feet on the east-west' in his *Medieval Theatre in the Round*, p 29.

239 William L. Tribby, 'The Medieval Prompter: A Reinterpretation,' *Theatre Survey* 5 (1964), 73. Philip Butterworth revisited this issue, arguing for Carew's account as evidence, in 'Book-carriers: Medieval and Tudor Stage Conventions,' *Theatre Notebook* 46 (1992), 15–28.

240 Borlase, *Observations*, pp 195–6; Borlase documents the quoted material as follows: 'Bishop Nicolson's Letter to Dr. Charlett, Nov. 14, 1700. pen. Mr. Ballard of Magdalen College, Oxford.'

241 Borlase, *Natural History*, pp 297–9.

242 Betcher, 'Minstrels, Morris Dancers, and Players.'

243 See Betcher, 'Minstrels, Morris Dancers, and Players.'

244 See Wasson (ed), *Devon*, pp 38–9.

245 Wasson (ed), *Devon*, p 228.

246 See Wasson (ed), *Devon*, p 155.

247 Since Heywood's *Apology* was published in 1612 and he states that this event took place 'some 12 yeares ago, or not so much,' the play was perhaps performed around 1600.

248 Patricia Bourke, 'The Stained Glass Windows of the Church of St. Neot, Cornwall,' *Devon and Cornwall Notes and Queries* 33 (1974–8), 65.

249 On that legend, see F.E. Halliday, *The Legend of the Rood* (London, 1955) and Esther Casier Quinn, *The Quest of Seth for the Oil of Life* (Chicago, 1962). For a fuller discussion of the drama's possible influence on St Neot's glass, see Newlyn, 'The Stained and Painted Glass of St. Neot's Church,' pp 89–111.

250 See Paula Neuss (ed and trans), *The Creacion of the World: A Critical Edition and Translation* (New York, 1983), 160 for stage direction. See also R. Morton Nance, 'Painted Windows and Miracle Plays,' *Old Cornwall* 5 (1955), 244–8 for a discussion of its meaning.

251 Wasson (ed), *Devon*, pp 204–5.

252 Michael Heaney, 'Kingston to Kenilworth: Early Plebian Morris,' *Folklore* 100.1 (1989), 89.

253 Heaney, 'Kingston to Kenilworth,' p 89.

254 Heaney, 'Kingston to Kenilworth,' pp 96–7.

255 John Forrest and Michael Heaney, 'Charting Early Morris,' *Folk Music Journal* 6.2 (1991), 177.

256 Mattingly, 'Medieval Parish Guilds,' p 305.

257 Robert Whiting, *The Blind Devotion of the People: Popular Religion and the English Reformation* (Cambridge, 1989), 203.

258 Robbins, *Launceston, Past and Present*, p 75.

259 Munn, *Bodmin Riding*, pp 82–6. The town of Liskeard customarily held a riding but records do not exist. Carew, *Survey of Cornwall*, sig Nn1 verso, tells us that the celebration of St George occurred on Little Easter, which is Pentecost or Whitsunday, the seventh Sunday after Easter. St George's Day is 23 April. In years when Easter falls on 16 April, the following Sunday would be St George's Day and Little Easter.

260 See Robert Whiting, '"For the Health of My Soul": Prayers for the Dead in the Tudor South-West,' *Southern History* 5 (1983), 72; and Mattingly, 'Medieval Parish Guilds,' p 302.

261 Munn, *Bodmin Riding*, p 10.

262 Although the date of the Bodmin riding is not certain, in 1700 Edward Lhuyd claimed that the riding festivities took place on the two Mondays right after St Thomas' Day (his translation was celebrated on 7 July). At the time Lhuyd wrote, the Bodmin riding no longer included mandatory church attendance (Lhuyd is quoted in Munn, *Bodmin Riding*, p 20). Rogation Days, when processions or perambulations occurred, crops were blessed to ensure a good harvest, and plagues were forestalled with prayers, are the three days before Ascension Day (Holy Thursday). The 'mayor, corporation and inhabitants, preceded by sergeants and town crier in regalia, followed the borough boundary on horseback. Upon reaching certain landmarks such as a Celtic cross or bridge, the gathering halted and the crier announced "thus far extends the ancient borough of Bodmin"; and, in order to further impress the limit upon youngsters, buns and coins were hurled into nearby pools or streams for them to recover.' This probably Anglo-Saxon tradition is recorded in the borough's 1563 charter (Munn, *Introducing Bodmin*, p 77).

263 Munn, *Introducing Bodmin*, Appendix 3, p 81.

264 Munn, *Introducing Bodmin*, introduction, np. Munn also suggests that the figure on the borough's seal may be Edgar.

265 CRO: B/Bod/243, printed in Munn, *Bodmin Riding*, p 13.

266 Historians often refer to a riding air and a fife and drum band but they may not have been part of the riding during our period.

267 St Petroc is said to have had two encounters with a dragon but the first occurred at Padstow. In the second, when a dragon who had some wood in its eye came, hoping for a miracle cure, to the temple where St Petroc was praying, the saint healed the dragon. See Gilbert H. Doble, *Saint Petrock, Abbot and Confessor*, 3rd ed (Shipston on Stour, 1938), 17, 21.

268 Munn, *Introducing Bodmin*, pp 46, 79. The Parish Church Rebuilding Accounts (CRO: B/Bod/244, 1469–72) list the various riding guilds and moneys received for the church. The Shoemakers' Ordinance is held at the CRO: B/Bod/243. The term 'jantacle' is used for the riding and sports. Part of the Rebuilding Accounts and the Shoemakers' ordinance are reprinted in Munn, *Bodmin Riding*, pp 11–14.

269 Matthews, *History of Saint Ives*, p 145.

270 Matthews, *History of Saint Ives*, p 258.

271 Thurstan Peter discusses early stories about the tradition and what he terms 'aetiological myth' in 'The Hobby Horse,' *JRIC* 19 (1912), 241–73.

272   See National Library of Wales: Peniarth MS. 105, p 39, ll.1061–2: 'me a pe ȝen hebyhors / hay cowetha' ('I will pay to the hobby-horse and its pair.'); see also Whitley Stokes (ed and trans), *The Life of Saint Meriasek, Bishop and Confessor: A Cornish Drama* (London, 1872), 61.

273   Donald R. Rawe, *Padstow's Obby Oss and May Day Festivities*, enlarged ed (Padstow, 1982), 12, 14.

274   H. Spencer Toy does not see the connection asserted by others between the Helston Furry Day and Roman festivals; see his *The History of Helston* (London, 1936), 368–79. For a broad discussion of the various customs associated with this celebration, see R. Morton Nance, 'Helston Furry Day,' *JRIC*, ns 4 part 1 (1961), 36–48.

275   Edward M. Cunnack, *The Helston Furry Dance* (Helston, 1957; new ed 1972), 7; see also David Hugh Farmer, *The Oxford Dictionary of Saints* (Oxford, 1978), 277–8.

276   Jill Newton, *Helston Flora Day* (Bodmin, 1978), 31–2. See also E.M. Cunnack, *Helston Flora Day* (Helston, 1951; new ed 1972), passim and Peter's discussion in 'The Hobby Horse,' pp 258–9.

277   Toy, *History of Helston*, p 15.

278   R. Polwhele, *The History of Cornwall*, vol 1 (London, 1803; rpt Dorking, 1978), 53. Polwhele notes that the 'fighting of cocks was more the sport of gentlemen than the common people,' which may explain both the probability of wagering and the providing of refreshments.

279   Whiting, 'For the Health of My Soul,' p 71.

280   See Michael Heaney and John Forrest, *Annals of Early Morris* (Sheffield, 1991), 14, and 'Charting Early Morris,' pp 169–86.

281   F.E. Halliday (ed), *The Survey of Cornwall* (New York, 1969), 15–71.

282   Allen, *History of the Borough of Liskeard*, p 24.

283   For discussion of the St George's Guild activities see Whiting, *The Blind Devotion of the People*, pp 106–7 and Mattingly, 'Medieval Parish Guilds,' pp 301–2.

284   Rowse, *Tudor Cornwall*, p 296.

285   Halliday, *History of Cornwall*, pp 111, 123.

286   Mattingly, 'Medieval Parish Guilds,' p 290.

287   Halliday, *History of Cornwall*, pp 174–5.

288   J. Jackson Howard, H. Farnham Burke, and H. Seymour Hughes (eds), *Genealogical Collections Illustrating the History of Roman Catholic Families of England. Based on the Lawson Manuscript* (London, 1887–92), part 3, p 224 and North, 'The Arundell Archive,' p 53.

289   North, 'The Arundell Archive,' p 54. See Rowse, *Tudor Cornwall*, pp 253–90, for an account of Arundell's participation in the Prayer Book Rebellion.

290   North, 'The Arundell Archive,' p 54.

291   Rowse, *Tudor Cornwall*, p 343.

292   Hasler (ed), *House of Commons, 1558–1603*, vol 1, p 557.

293   Pounds, 'William Carnsew of Bokelly and His Diary,' pp 22–3.

294   Pounds, 'William Carnsew of Bokelly and His Diary,' p 15.

295 Boyan and Lamb, *Francis Tregian*, pp 22–6.

296 Boyan and Lamb, *Francis Tregian*, pp 28–35, 42–4.

297 Boyan and Lamb, *Francis Tregian*, p 49.

298 Boyan and Lamb, *Francis Tregian*, pp 140–3.

299 For *Mirror of Heroes*, see Boyan and Lamb, *Francis Tregian*, Appendix 2, pp 139–40.

300 The *Calendar of the Patent Rolls of Edward III*, vol 6 (London, 1902), 401, summarizes the commission of oyer and terminer looking into this incident. Commissions of a similar nature are found in vol 5, p 553, and vol 6, p 71. PRO: JUST. I/117a mb [2], a 1302 assize roll pertaining to Mousehole, is another example of a record containing personal identification by occupation. In this document, Osbertus Le Pibith, Richardus Le Pybyth, and Martinus Le Webbe, all of Mousehole, brought a writ of novel disseisin at the assizes against David Le Dysener concerning holdings in Mousehole. 'Pybyth' is the Cornish word for piper. In another example, *The Register of Edward the Black Prince*, part 2 (London, 1931), 110–11, the names 'Richard Horn' and 'John Tabourer' appear.

Select Bibliography

This select bibliography cites articles and books with transcriptions of the records as well as some useful reference materials. No attempt has been made to include all works mentioned in the Introduction, textual footnotes, and Endnotes.

Allen, John. *The History of the Borough of Liskeard* (London and Liskeard, 1856).

Badcock, W. *Historical Sketch of St. Ives and District* (St Ives, 1896).

Bakere, Jane E. *The Cornish Ordinalia: A Critical Study* (Cardiff, 1980).

Borlase, William. *The Natural History of Cornwall* (Oxford, 1758).

– *Observations on the Antiquities, Historical and Monumental, of the County of Cornwall* (Oxford, 1754).

Browne, Austin L. *Corporation Chronicles: Being Some Account of the Ancient Corporation of East Looe and of West Looe in the County of Cornwall* (Plymouth, 1904).

Carew, Richard. *The Survey of Cornwall* (London, 1602; *STC*: 4615, fac ed Amsterdam, 1969).

Chambers, E.K. *The Mediaeval Stage.* 2 vols (Oxford, 1903).

Chandler, John. *John Leland's Itinerary: Travels in Tudor England* (Stroud, 1993).

Couch, Thomas Q. 'Popular Antiquities: Bodmin Riding, and Halgaver Sports,' *JRIC* 1 (1864), 56–60.

Cox, J. Charles (ed). *Churchwardens' Accounts* (London, 1913).

Dalton, J.N. (ed). *Ordinale Exoniensis.* Vol 1. Henry Bradshaw Society, vol 37 (London, 1909).

Douch, H.L. (ed). 'Household Accounts at Lanherne,' *JRIC*, ns 2, pt 1 (1953–4), 25–32.

Dunstan, G.R. (ed). *The Register of Edmund Lacy, Bishop of Exeter, 1420–1455.* 5 vols. The Canterbury and York Society (in conjunction with the Devon and Cornwall Record Society), vols 60, 61, 62, 63, 66 (Torquay, 1963–72).

Fowler, David C. 'The Date of the Cornish "Ordinalia",' *Mediaeval Studies* 23 (1961), 91–125.

Goulding, R.W. (comp). *Records of the Charity known as Blanchminster's Charity in the Parish of Stratton, County of Cornwall, until the Year 1832* (Louth, Stratton, and Bude, 1898).

Halliday, F.E. *A History of Cornwall,* 2nd ed ([London], 1975).

Hatcher, John. *Rural Economy and Society in the Duchy of Cornwall 1300–1500* (Cambridge, 1970).

Henderson, Charles. *St. Columb Major Church and Parish* (Long Compton, [1930]).

Higgins, Sydney. *Medieval Theatre in the Round: The Multiple Staging of Religious Drama in England* (Camerino, 1995).

Hingeston-Randolph, F. C. (ed). *The Register of John de Grandisson, Bishop of Exeter* (A.D. 1327–1369): Part 1, 1327–1330, with Some Account of the Episcopate of James de Berkeley (A.D. 1327) (London and Exeter, 1894); *Part 2, 1331–1360* (London and Exeter, 1897); *Part 3, 1360–1369, together with the Register of Institutions* (London and Exeter, 1899). 3 vols (London and Exeter, 1894–9).

— *The Registers of Walter Bronescombe* (A.D. 1257–1280), and Peter Quivil (A.D. 1280–1291), *Bishops of Exeter, with Some Records of the Episcopate of Bishop Thomas de Bytton* (A.D. 1292–1307) (London and Exeter, 1889).

Lysons, Daniel, and Samuel Lysons. *Magna Britannia*. Vol 3, *Cornwall* (London, 1814).

Maclean, John. *The Parochial and Family History of the Deanery of Trigg Minor in the County of Cornwall*. 3 vols (London and Bodmin, 1873–9).

— *Parochial and Family History of the Parish and Borough of Bodmin* (London, 1870).

Matthews, John Hobson. *A History of the Parishes of Saint Ives, Lelant, Towednack and Zennor* (London, 1892).

Mattingly, Joanna. 'The Medieval Parish Guilds of Cornwall,' *JRIC*, ns 10, pt 3 (1989), 290–329.

McCann, Lucy. *Introduction to the Arundell Archive* (Truro, 1996).

Munn, Pat. *Bodmin Riding and Other Similar Celtic Customs* (Bodmin, 1975).

— *Introducing Bodmin: The Cornish Capital* (Bodmin, 1973).

Murray, John Tucker. *English Dramatic Companies 1558–1642*. 2 vols (New York, 1963).

Nance, R. Morton. 'Helston Furry Day,' *JRIC*, ns 4 (1961), 36–48.

Newlyn, Evelyn S. 'The Stained and Painted Glass of St. Neot's Church and the Staging of the Middle Cornish Drama,' *Journal of Medieval and Renaissance Studies* 24 (Winter 1994), 89–111.

Noall, Cyril. 'The St. Ives Borough Regalia,' *The Borough of St. Ives 1639–1974* (Penzance, 1974).

Peacock, Edward. 'On the Churchwardens' Accounts of the Parish of Stratton, in the County of Cornwall,' *Archaeologia* 46.1 (1880), 195–236.

Peter, Richard, and Otto Bathurst Peter. *The Histories of Launceston and Dunheved in the County of Cornwall* (Plymouth, 1885).

Peter, Thurstan (ed). 'The St. Columb Green Book,' *JRIC*, supplement to pt 1, 19 (1912), 1–89.

Polwhele, Richard. *The History of Cornwall* (Falmouth, 1803; rpt 1987).

Pool, P.A.S. (ed). 'The Penheleg Manuscript,' *JRIC*, ns 3 (1959), 163–228.

Pounds, N.J.G. (ed). 'William Carnsew of Bokelly and His Diary, 1576–7,' *JRIC*, ns 8 (1978), 14–60.

Powicke, F.M. and C.R. Cheney (eds). *Councils & Synods with Other Documents Relating to the English Church*, vol 2, A.D. 1205–1313, pt 1, 1205–1265; pt 2, 1265–1313 (Oxford, 1964).

Robbins, Alfred F. *Launceston, Past and Present: A Historical and Descriptive Sketch* (Launceston, 1888).

Rowse, A.L. *Tudor Cornwall: Portrait of a Society* (London, 1941).

Serjeantson, R.M. 'The Church and Parish Goods of St. Columb Major, Cornwall,' *The Antiquary* 33 (1897), 344–6.

Snell, Lawrence S. (ed). *The Edwardian Inventories of Church Goods for Cornwall.* No 2 (Exeter, [1955]).

Southern, Richard. *The Medieval Theatre in the Round.* 2nd ed (London 1975).

– *The Staging of Plays Before Shakespeare* (London, 1973).

Thomas, Charles. 'The Society's 1962 Excavations: The Henge at Castilly, Lanivet,' *Cornish Archaeology* 3 (1964), 3–14.

Wallis, John (ed). *The Bodmin Register; Containing Collections Relative to the Past and Present State of the Parish of Bodmin* (Bodmin, 1827–38).

Wasson, John M. (ed). *Devon.* Records of Early English Drama (Toronto, 1986).

Whitley, H. Michell. 'The Church Goods of Cornwall at the Time of the Reformation,' *JRIC* 7 (1881–2), 92–135.

Wilkinson, John James (ed). 'Receipts and Expenses in the Building of Bodmin Church, A.D. 1469–1472.' *Camden Miscellany*, vol 7. Camden Society, ns 14 (London, 1875).

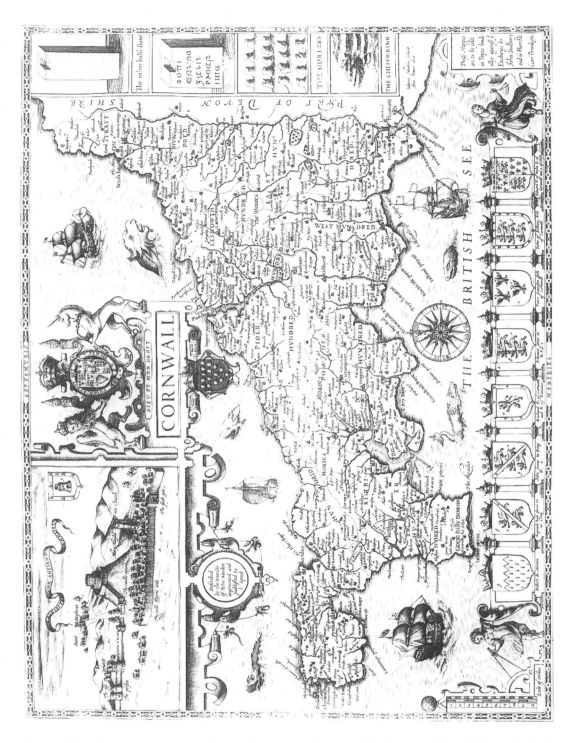

Cornwall with Launceston inset from John Speed, *Theatre of the Empire of Great Britaine* (1611).
This item is reproduced by permission of The Huntington Library, San Marino, California.

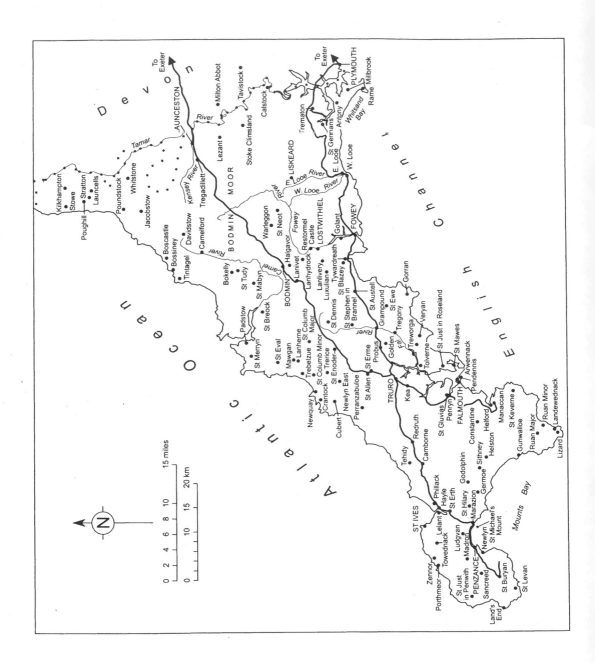

Cornwall with principal Renaissance routes

Diocese of Exeter

1287

Statutes of Bishop Peter Quinel
(16 April) (Chapter thirteen) *

…

Ne in ecclesijs vel cimiterijs earum mercata vel placita secularia teneantur vel   5
edificia secularia construantur xiij

…Et quia in cimiterijs dedicatis multa sanctorum & saluandorum corpora
tumulantur quibus debetur omnis honor & reuerencia, sacerdotibus
parochialibus districte precipimus vt in ecclesijs suis denuncient publice ne
quisquam luctas coreas vel alios ludos inhonestos in cimiterijs exercere   10
presumat precipue in vigilijs & festis sanctorum cum huiusmodi ludos
teatrales & ludibriorum spectacula introductos per quos ecclesiarum

Collation: 5 Ne] De *ABCHP*   5 in] *omitted in ACP*   5 vel¹] & *DN*   5 earum]
-rum *abbreviation sign damaged in F,* eorum *G*   5 secularia] *ending obscured in L*
5 teneantur] *omitted in B*   5 vel³] ⌐vel⌐ *N or N²,* et *GJ*   5–6 vel³ … construantur]
B or B² adds in margin   6 edificia] edificata *J*   6 secularia] seculiaria *H*   6 xiij] *D or*
D² adds 12. capitulum *in margin, F adds* xiiij *in margin, J adds* .Capitulum .xiii. *in margin,*
13. *K, omitted in ABCGHLNP*   7 cimiterijs] cimitererijs *H*   7 multa] multorum
K, multo *N, followed by blot that may represent attempted correction; N adds stroke,*
possibly a cancelled minim, before multo   7 &] ⌐&⌐ *C, omitted in H*   7 saluandorum]
soluendorum *ACP, omitted in H*   7 corpora] corpa *F,* corporum *K, H corrects* corporora
to corpora *by expunction*   8 quibus] *N or N² corrects to* -i- *over* -e-   9 parochialibus]
parochialis *J*   9 precipimus] *second* -i- *and part of* -m- *written over erasure by N or N²*
9 vt] nec *F*   9 denuncient] *D² corrects to* denuncient *over erasure,* denunciant *H*
9–10 ne quisquam] *N or N² adds in margin*   9 ne] nec *F*   10 luctas] ludas *H; J*
adds vel *after* luctas   10 coreas] choreas *EFGL,* correas *K*   9–11 ne … precipue]
omitted in E   10 cimiterijs] *D or D² corrects to* cimiterijs *over erasure*   10–11 exercere
presumat] presumant excercere *G*   10 exercere] excercere *CDHP, N or N² corrects to*
ex∧⌐c⌐ercere   11 presumat] *D² corrects to* presumat *over erasure,* presumant *BFHL*
11 precipue] presipue *J*   11 & festis sanctorum] sanctorum & festis *DN*   11 &] *H*
adds in *after* &   11 cum] *omitted in K*   12 teatrales] theatrales *FGP,* teaturales *K*
12 &] *B or B² adds* ad *in margin after* &, *N or N² adds* ∧⌐ad⌐ *after* &   12 spectacula]
spectalia *ACP,* spectaculum *B*

coinquinatur honestas, sacri canones detestentur. Quod si aliqui post factam denunciacionem ludos huiusmodi, quamquam improprie dictos eo quod ex eis crimina oriuntur, exercuerint, predicti sacerdotes eorum nomina loci archidiacono vel ipsius officiali denuncient vt per ipsos pro suis demeritis canonice puniantur.   5

(Chapter seventeen)
...

De vita & honestate clericorum xvij   10
...Item clerici modesti sint & sobrij abstinentes se a crapula & ebrietate. Nam vt ait beatus Gregorius, 'Guloso nichil turpius, cuius fetor in ore, pallor in facie, tremor in digitis, & in cuius corde nullum latet secretum.' Et vt inter clericos & histriones (sicut est) ita & appareat omnibus dispar professio, districte precipimus quod ad conuiuia non accedant, maxime sacerdotes, nisi   15
a domino domus specialiter sint inuitati. Quod si inuitari contigerit, sese non ingurgitent sed protinus post prandium ad propria sobrij reuertantur.

Collation continued: 1 coinquinatur] conquinatur *H*   1 sacri canones] sacri ordines *ACEFGHJKLP, D or D2 erases a word after* canones   1 detestentur] detestantur *EHK*   1 aliqui] aqui *H*   1 factam] sanctam *E*   2 denunciacionem] denun⟨...⟩ionem *H*, denunciaonem *JK*   2 quamquam] *B or B2 corrects* quamquam *to* quamuis *in margin*   2 quod] *A adds* [quod] *or* quid *after* quod, *CP add* quid   2 ex] *omitted in E*   3 exercuerint] excercuerint *GH, omitted in D, but D2 adds* exercerunt, *omitted in N*   3 predicti] *omitted in D but D2 adds; J adds* [sacerdotibus] *after* predicti   4 archidiacono] archidiaconi *K*   4 ipsius] eius *N*   4 officiali] officialis *K*   4 denuncient] denunciet *G,* de nuncierit *K*   4 per] *omitted in HL*   5 canonice] *omitted in E*   5 puniantur] pₐ⌜u⌝niantur *E*   10 honestate] honeste *E*   10 clericorum] clerum *P*   10 xvij] .16. *D, F adds* xviij *in margin, rubrica H, J adds* Capitulum .xvij. *in margin,* 17. *K, omitted in BCGN*   11 sobrij] sobriij *A*   12 beatus Gregorius] *underlined in a lighter colour of ink in P*   12 beatus] *omitted in H*   12 Gregorius] *apparently rubricated in B*   12 Guloso] Gulose *A,* Gulosi *C,* gulo *H,* Gloso *K*   12 nichil] mihi *C*   12 turpius] *DEHN add* est *after* turpius   12 fetor] *DHKN add* est *after* fetor   13 tremor ... secretum] *omitted in J*   13 tremor] terrmor *E*   13 &] *omitted in BEH*   13 cuius] *omitted in DKLN*   13 Et] *omitted in H*   13 vt] *K adds* ait *after* vt   14 clericos] *B adds* est *after* clericos, *expunged by B or B2*   14 &2] *omitted in BDHLN*   14 appareat] appariat *C,* apparet *H, DHJLN add* in *after* appareat   14 omnibus] *omitted in K*   14 dispar] disse *G*   14 professio] prosessio *C*   15 districte] Distrite *H, N or N2 corrects* -tri- *over erasure*   15 ad] *omitted in K*   15 conuiuia] conuiuium *E, J reads* conuiua, *but gives* conuiuia *as catchword,* -ia *corrected by N or N2 over erasure*   15 accedant] *K adds* & *after* accedant   16 specialiter] spiritualiter *KN, corrected to* spiritualiter *over erasure by N or N2*   16 sint] fuerint *EH,* sicut *K, omitted in ABCFGJP*   16 inuitati] *N or N2 corrects over erasure*   16 Quod] quos *DKN, omitted in B*   16 si] *omitted in B*   16 inuitari] imitari *A, omitted in B*   17 ingurgitent] ₐ⌜in⌝gurgitent *B, D or D2 corrects over erasure*   17 ad propria] *omitted in G*   17 sobrij] sobriij *A, omitted in K*   17 reuertantur] reuertentur *ACFGHP,* reuertant *DE, K corrects* -entur *to* -antur

Nusquam tabernas excerceant nisi peregrinacionis causa in itinere constituti
sed ita modeste & sobrie semper viuant vt in omni tempore inter sanctum
& prophanum, mundum & immundum, discernere sciant & valeant sicut
decet. Item quia omnis voluptuositas per quam ad dissolucionis materiam
deuenitur est in clericis precipue detestanda, precipimus quod clerici   5
histrionibus & ioculatoribus non intendant? ad aleas vel taxillos non ludant?
nec alijs ludentibus sint participes aut inspectores nec ad spectacula publica
spectandi gracia presumant accedere? non auibus nec canibus vtantur venatorijs.
Hec & alia quam plurima sunt clericis interdicta quorum conuersacio a
laicorum actibus est remota quos sicut loco ita religione debent precellere.   10

…

1579
Bishop John Woolton's Visitation Articles   STC: 10203
sig Biij verso   15

…

60 Whether the Minister and Churchwardens haue suffered anye Lordes of
mysrule, or Summer Lordes or Ladyes, or any disguysed persons or others,
in Christmasse, or at Maygames, or any Morice dancers, or at any other
time to come vnreuerently into the Church, or Churchyarde, and there to   20
daunce, or playe any vnseemely partes, wyth scoffes, ieastes, wanton iestures,
or rybaulde talke, namely in the tyme of common prayer. And what they be
that commit such disorder, or accompany or maintaine them?

…

Collation continued: 1 Nusquam] Numquam *FG* 1 tabernas] *H adds* non *after*
tabernas 1 peregrinacionis causa] causa peregrinacionis *DEN* 1 in] *dittography J*
1 itinere] itnere *G*, itenere *P* 2 modeste & sobrie] sobrie & modeste *BE* 2 semper
viuant] viuent semper *H*, viuant semper *KL* 2 semper] *omitted in DN* 2 viuant]
D2 corrects from viuantur 2 vt] et *H* 2 in] *omitted in BE* 2 sanctum] *B or B2*
corrects secundum *to* sanctum *by expunction* 3 prophanum] pphanum *F* 3 &
immundum, discernere] *B or B2 corrects from* discernere & immundum 3 discernere]
discerne *L*, decernere *G*, discernre *K* 3 sciant & valeant] valeant & sciant *B* 3 &3]
vt *K* 3 valeant] veleant *P* 4 ad] *omitted in ACKP* 4 materiam] materia *ACP*
4–5 Item … detestanda] *omitted in H* 5 detestanda] deₐ⌐te⌐standa *G* 6 histrionibus]
histrioribus *K* 6 ioculatoribus] iaculatoribus *K* 6 non intendant? ad aleas] *omitted*
in E 6 intendant] intendunt *F* 6 ad aleas vel taxillos non ludant] *omitted in G*
6 aleas] alias *B*, alas *K* 6 vel] vel ad *EH* 6 taxillos] taxillas *D*, taxilles *F*, *N or*
N2 corrects to -os *over erasure* 7 alijs] alienis *G* 7 sint] sicut *F* 7 aut] nec *E*
7 inspectores] inspectatores *L* 8 presumant accedere] accedere presumant *N* 8 non]
omitted in ABCEFGHJLP 8 nec] vel *EK*, vero *J* 8 vtantur venatorijs] venatorijs non
vtantur *ABCEFHL*, uenatorijs vtantur *G*, venatoribus non vtantur *J*, venatorijs non
vtantantur *P* 9 &] atque *K* 9 plurima] plura *DEFJN* 9 interdicta] interducta *H*
9 a] *omitted in K* 10 laicorum] laicis *L* 10 loco] locor *A*, locorum *C*, loca *J*, loquor
P, *N or N2 corrects to* -o *over erasure* 10 ita] *J adds* & *after* ita 10 debent] debet *H*

1613
Archdeacon William Hutchinson's Visitation Articles   STC: 10190.5
sig A2 *(Articles concerning the church)*
...

    4 Whether hath there beene any fighting, chiding, brawling, or quarrelling   5
in your Church, or Churchyard, and by whom, or any interlude beene
played in your Church, or wares sold by chapmen, in your Churchyard on
the sabaoth and holidaies?
...

    10

sig A2v *(Articles concerning the clergy)*
...

    6 Whether is your Minister a Preacher, or contrariwise is he a sower of
discord, a haunter of Tauernes, or Alehouses, a common hunter, hawker,
dicer, carder, swearer, or dancer, or is suspected to liue incontinently, or   15
doth frequent any suspected places, or giue euill example of life?
...

1614
Archdeacon William Hutchinson's Visitation Articles   STC: 10190.7   20
sig A2 *(Articles concerning the church)*

    3 Whether hath there beene any fighting, chiding, brawling, or qarrelling,
any playes, feasts, temporall Courts, or Leets, laye Iuriers, musters, or other
prophane vsage in your Church or church-yard, any Bels superstitiously   25
rung on Holidaies or their Eeues, or at any other time without good cause
allowed by the Minister and Churchwardens? haue any Trees beene felled in
your Churchyard, and by whome?
...

    30

sigs A4–4v *(Articles concerning the clergy)*
...

    33 UUhether doth your Minister resort to anie Tauerns, or Alehouses,
except for his honest necessities, or doth he boord or lodge in anie such
place, doth he vse anie base or seruile labor drinking, riot, dice, cardes, tables   35
or anie other vnlawful games: is he | contentious, a hunter hawker swearer
dauncer suspected of incontinencie or giue euill example of life?
...

23/ qarrelling: *for* quarrelling   24/ Iuriers: *for* Iuries

1627
Visitation Articles During Vacancy   STC: 10206
sig B4

...

13 Whether haue you or your Predecessors Churchwardens there suffered   5
any Playes, Feasts, Banquets, Churchales, Drinkings, or any other profane
playes to bee kept in your Church, Chappell or Churchyard, or Bells to be
rung supersticiously on Holydayes or Eues, abrogated by the Booke of
Common Prayer?

...   10

Boroughs and Parishes

ANTONY

1548–9

A **St James Collectors' and Churchwardens' Accounts** CRO: P/7/5/1
p 12* *(February/March – February/March) (Payments)*

...

Item payd to the players of Melbroke   xij d.

...

1553–4

A **St James Collectors' and Churchwardens' Accounts** CRO: P/7/5/1
p 18* *(August–August) (Receipts)*

...

Item recevyd of Robyn Hodde & the maydyns   xl s. viij d.

...

1554–5

A **St James Collectors' and Churchwardens' Accounts** CRO: P/7/5/1
p 20* *(August–August) (Receipts)*

...

Item recevyd off Robyn Hode & off the Maydens
                Sum   xlj s.

...

Item recevyd off Robyn Hode & off the maydens   xlj s.

...

7/ Melbroke: *Millbrook*

1555–6

A ***St James Collectors' and Churchwardens' Accounts*** CRO: P/7/5/1
p 23 *(11 August 1555–17 August 1556) (Receipts)*

…

Item recevyd of Robert Hode Iohn Rowye & of ye maydyns 5
Elzaberth Serell   xlvij s. v d.

…

1557–8

A ***St James Collectors' and Churchwardens' Accounts*** CRO: P/7/5/1 10
p 28* *(Remembrances)*

…

A rembrans the xvj of Iuly anno lviij that Robyn Hode & ye madyns
delevered to Robert Gache & Wyllyam Charke collectorys   xl s.

…   15

1558–9

A ***St James Collectors' and Churchwardens' Accounts*** CRO: P/7/5/1
p 29 *(13 August–5 August) (Receipts)*

…   20

Item recevyd of Robyn Hode & ye maydyns   xl s.

…

BODMIN

25

1470–1
St Petroc Church Building Accounts CRO: B/Bod/244
p 6 *(Receipts)*

⟨…⟩ the players yn the church hay Will*iam* mason and Iis felowis v s.   30

…

1494–5
General Receivers' Accounts CRO: B/Bod/314/3/10
single mb *(4 October–4 October) (Payments)*   35

…

⟨It*em* payed to⟩ Wyllyam Carpynt*er* for sylu*er* and the makyng of ⌈a⌉
Garnement and for colours ocupyed for dyademys & crownys & such od*er*

30/ ⟨…⟩: MS *torn at edge*
37/ ⟨It*em* payed to⟩: *illegible; transcribed from* CRO: B/Bod/314/3/5, *a draft version*

⟨longyng to Cor…⟩ Chr*ist*i game and for tynfoyle that
Iohn Wythyall had of Rafe Stayn*er*   iij s.

…

c 1501–13   5
Town Receivers' Accounts   CRO: B/Bod/314/2/15
single mb* *(Payments)*

…

…⟨.⟩ad Minstrall' de Exon*ia* …

…   10

1503–4
General Receivers' Accounts   CRO: B/Bod/314/3/20
single mb *(4 October–4 October) (Payments)*

…   15
Item I payde in Rewarde onto the waytes   iiij s.

…

1504–5
General Receivers' Accounts   CRO: B/Bod/314/3/21   20
single mb *(4 October–4 October) (Payments)*

…
Item I paide & yevyn in Rewarde onto harry Kyngge and his
Cumpaney for ther disportes in the Ilde halle   v ⟨s.⟩
…   25
Item I paide & yevyn onto a Berewarde for a Rewarde   v ⟨s.⟩

…

1505–6
General Receivers' Accounts   CRO: B/Bod/314/3/21   30
single mb *(4 October–4 October) (Payments)*

…
Item in Rewarde I yevyn to the Ministrell*es* of My lord of
devynshire is   iij s. viij ⟨.⟩
…   35

1/ ⟨longyng to Cor…⟩: *illegible; transcribed from* CRO: B/Bod/314/3/5
1/ Cor…⟩ Chr*ist*i: *18 June 1495*
24/ ⟨s.⟩: *damaged; read by Lysons*
26/ ⟨s.⟩: *damaged; read by Lysons*

General Receivers' Accounts   CRO: B/Bod/314/3/22
single mb *(4 October–4 October) (Payments)*
…

Item I paide and yevyn to a daunce Seynte Erme Botrescastelle
and mynstre   iij s. iiij d.   5
…

Berry Tower Building Receipts   CRO: B/Bod/314/1/6
mb [1]* *(4 October–4 October) (Receipts)*
…   10

Item Rec*eived* of Robyn hoode and his felowys of ther gaderyng ⟨..⟩ ^⌐the⌐
makyng of the Bery stypelle ix s. ⟨…⟩
…

mb [2]*   15
…

Item Rec*eived* of Roby⟨.⟩ hoode and h⟨.⟩s felowys at anothe⟨.⟩ ⟨…⟩e of
goode ⟨.⟩oney and badde…
…
                                                                           20
1509–10
General Receivers' Accounts   CRO: B/Bod/314/3/26
single mb *(4 October–4 October) (Payments)*
…

Item I paide to Iohn Whyte for ⌐cloth⌐ the ⟨…⟩yng of a g⟨…⟩ for Ie*sus*   25
agayne the showe of Corporis Chri*sti* ⟨…⟩
Item I paide for Richard B⟨.⟩yg⟨..⟩ xx d. Item I paide to Iohn he⟨…⟩
Item I paide to Iohn hoyge and Cristofer paynter x⟨…⟩
Item I paide to William Taylor for the makynge of garment*es*   vj d.
…   30
Item I paide to Mich*ael* Coran⟨…⟩ for staynynge of garneme*ntes*   xvij d.
Item I paide to william sagemore for v yard*es* of lynnyn clothe
at Corporis Chri*sti* shewe   ij s.
…

4/ Botrescastelle: *Boscastle*   27/ B⟨.⟩yg⟨..⟩: *MS illegible 24 mm*
25/ g⟨…⟩: *MS torn at edge*   27/ he⟨…⟩: *MS torn at edge*
26/ Corporis Chri*sti*: *30 May 1510*   28/ x⟨…⟩: *MS torn at edge*
26/ ⟨…⟩: *MS torn at edge*

1513–14
General Receivers' Accounts   CRO: B/Bod/314/3/31
single mb* *(4 October–4 October) (Payments)*

…

Item I paide in a Reward yevyn to ∧⌈a⌉ Bereward of the Kynges   ⟨…⟩ 5

…

⟨…⟩aid to Berew⟨…⟩

…

1514–15   10
General Receivers' Accounts   CRO: B/Bod/314/3/32
single mb *(4 October–4 October) (Payments)*

…

Item I paide for a garment of p*u*rpelle satyn Reversy and the
makynge of the ⟨…⟩ for Ie*su*s   vj s. vj d. 15

…

Item I paide for leder and the makynge of the thyng*es* for the
showe ⟨…⟩or*is* cristi day hit amounteth to   iiij s. iiij d.

…

                                                                                              20

c 1514–39
Town Receivers' Accounts   CRO: B/Bod/314/2/12
single mb* *(Allowances)*

…

…Item D*e* xvj d. dat*is* ludi de Treourdraith Item D*e* xvj d. ⟨…⟩pud*io* de   25
launevett Item D*e* xij d. dat*is* tripud*io* de seynte mabyn ⟨.⟩tem D*e* xij d. ⟨…⟩
tripud*io* de la⟨.⟩hydr⟨…⟩…

…

1519–20   30
General Receivers' Accounts   CRO: B/Bod/314/3/39
single mb *(4 October–4 October) (Payments)*

…

Item I paide in reward to the waytes this yere ⟨…⟩

                                                                                              35

5/ ⟨…⟩: *MS torn at edge*
7/ ⟨…⟩aid: *MS torn at edge*
7/ Berew⟨…⟩: *MS torn at edge*
15/ ⟨…⟩: *letters worn and illegible*
18/ ⟨…⟩or*is*: *letters worn and illegible*
18/ ⟨…⟩or*is* cristi day: *7 June 1515*
25/ ludi: *for* ludo *(?)*

25/ Treourdraith: *possibly Tywardreath (?)*
25/ ⟨…⟩pud*io*: *MS torn at edge 17 mm*
26/ launevett: *probably Lanivet*
26/ ⟨…⟩: *MS torn at edge 10 mm*
27/ la⟨.⟩hydr⟨…⟩: *possibly Lanhydrock*
34/ ⟨…⟩: *MS torn at edge*

1529–30
General Receivers' Accounts   CRO: B/Bod/314/3/51
single mb *(4 October–4 October) (Payments)*

...

Item paide for the makynge of the barrys a corpor*is* chri*sti* day   5
at the shewe this yere   iiij d.

...

1537–8
Town Receivers' Accounts   CRO: B/Bod/314/2/3   10
single mb *(4 October–4 October) (Payments)*

...

...Item in reward*es* to S*ir* perys Egecomb is mynstrell*es* xij d. Item in reward*es*
to my lorde lyole is mynstrell⟨.⟩ v s. Item in reward*es* to my lorde pr*in*ce is
mynstrell*es* ⟨...⟩ ...   15

...

1539
AC **St Petroc Inventory of Church Goods**   Wallis: *The Bodmin Register*
pp 41–2* *(5 October)*   20

...

...It*em* one Jesus cotte of purpell sarcenett. It*em* a Jesus cotte *(blank)* It*em* a
sewte of vestyments of cremsyn velvett ... I of the gyft of docter Tregonwell.
... It*em* 4 tormeteris cotes, inkepyng one w*ith* John Vyvyan, a noder w*ith*
Thomas Bligh, the 3d w*ith* Nicholas Opy, and the 4th w*ith* Richard Corant,   25
made of a sewt of vestyments for goode frydayes.

...

1566
St Petroc Inventory of Church Goods   CRO: B/Bod/233   30
single sheet* *(6 October)*

...

...sencer of latten toe lent Clothes for ye Comun*i*on tabell ij polys one of
brasse & a nother of yron ij newe vant Clothes [& a nold] iij sacryng bell*es*
iij Cruat*es* iij Iesus cot*es* ij red wosterd & one of red bocrom iij tormenttowers 35
Cot*es* of satyn of brydd*es* of yolo & blue ij cappes of sylck toe devel*es* cotes
wherof one ys newe [toe saudyers Cot*es* of whyte] a Croune of black a nother
for ⟨...⟩...

...

5/ corpor*is* chri*sti* day: *16 June 1530*   24/ tormeteris: *for* tormenteris
15/ ⟨...⟩: *hole 10 mm*   38/ ⟨...⟩: *MS torn at edge 42 mm*

1602
Richard Carew, Survey of Cornwall   STC: 4615
sigs Kk2–2v

...

® Halgauer

    The youthlyer sort of Bodmyn townsmen vse sometimes to sport themselues,   5
by playing the box with stra*n*gers, whome they summon to Halgauer. The
name signifieth the Goats moore, and such a place it Is, lyIng a litle without
the towne, and very full of quauemires. When these mates meete with any
rawe seruingman, or other young master, who may serue and deserue to make
pastime, they cause him to be solemnely arrested, | for his appearance before   10
the Maior of Halgauer, where he is charged with wearing one spurre, or going
vntrussed, or wanting a girdle, or some such like felony: and after he hath
beene arraygned and tryed, with all requisite circumstances, iudgement is
giuen in formal termes, and executed in some one vngracious pranke or other,
more to the skorne, then hurt of the party condemned.   15

    Hence is sprung the prouerb, when we see one slouenly appareled, to say,
He shall be presented in Halgauer Court.

    But now and then, they extend this merriment with the largest, to the
preiudice of ouer-credulous people, perswading them to fight with a Drago*n*
lurking in Halgauer, or to see some stra*n*ge matter there: which concludeth   20
at least, with a trayning them into the mire.

...

1603
Lease to William Collier   CRO: B/Bod/20   25
single mb

This Indenture made the first daye of September in the Raigne of oure
gratious sovereigne Lorde Iames by the grace of god king of Englande
Scotlande ffraunce & Irelande defendor of the feith: &c that is to saye in   30
the firste yere of his Reigne of Englonde, fraunce, & Irelande, & the xxxvij^th
of Scotland B⟨.⟩twene the Maior & Burgesses of the Borough of Bodmyn in
the Countie of Cornewall of the one p*ar*tie, & william Collier of the seide
Borough of Bodmyn Sadler of the other p*ar*tie witnesseth that theseid Maior
& Burgessis for & in Consideration of the rent*es* & services hereafter specified   35
& declared haue demysed graunted & to ferme letten & by these present*es*
do for them & there successors with there whole & full consent de⟨..⟩se &
gr⟨...⟩ & to ferme lett vnto theseide william Collier one plott or pece of
grounde w*i*thin theseide Borough & towne ⟨...⟩duryn in a place there lying
in the Southeaste parte of theseide towne called the ffryers Conteynyng   40
liiij^or foote in bredth ⟨...⟩tie one f⟨.⟩ote in length: vpon some parte wherof
there is nowe a Cocke pitt built & made at the cost*es* & chardges of thesaid

w⟨....⟩am Collier w*hich* plotte or pece of grounde afforseid is bounded there w*i*th the kings high waye of the north p⟨...⟩, the land ⟨.⟩f the seid maior & burgessis of the east, west, & sowth part*es* thereof. ...

...

CALSTOCK

1601
Will of Richard Clere   CRO: AP/C/118/1
single sheet *(22 August; proved 15 December 1606)*

...

...I geue & bequeath vnto one blynde boy one harpe & vnto an other blynde boye an other harpe & vnto a meheamed man a trumpett *y*at canne vse ye same...

...

1606
Inventory of Richard Clere   CRO: AP/C/118/2
single sheet *(19 September)*

...

It*em* ij harpes & one trumpett   xlij s.

...

CAMBORNE

1539–40
St Meriadocus and St Martin Churchwardens' Accounts   CRO: PD/322/1
f 7* *(June–June; rendered 13 June) (Receipts)*

...

It*em* receuyd of the yong men of ther Tavern clere   xxvij s. iiij d.

...

It*em* receuyd of Thomas Iohn harvy that he recevyd at the
pley that the yong men mad   iij s. viij d.

...

1542–3
St Meriadocus and St Martin Churchwardens' Accounts   CRO: PD/322/1
f 14* *(June–June; rendered 12 June) (Receipts)*

...

It*em* furst they recevyd of the yong me*n* is mony by the hand*es*
of Richard Crane   xj s. vj d.

...

1549–50
St Meriadocus and St Martin Churchwardens' Accounts   CRO: PD/322/1
f 31 *(December–December; rendered 7 December) (Payments)*
...

Item payd to a pyper yn the playe   iiij d.   5
...

1555–6
St Meriadocus and St Martin Churchwardens' Accounts   CRO: PD/322/1
f 41 *(3 March–16 February) (Receipts)*   10
...

ffyrst Resevyd of the yowng men   vij li.
...

1577–8   15
St Meriadocus and St Martin Churchwardens' Accounts   CRO: PD/322/1
f 102 *(4 August 1577–27 September 1578) (Poor wardens' payments)*
...

Item in primis for expences payed to the interlude players   iij s. j d.
...   20

1582–3
St Meriadocus and St Martin Churchwardens' Accounts   CRO: PD/322/2
f 111 *(23 November 1582–27 November 1583) (Stockwardens' payments)*
...   25

Item paid to the Interlude in ye parish   xiiij d.
...

1595–6
St Meriadocus and St Martin Churchwardens' Accounts   CRO: PD/322/2   30
f 129* *(Payments)*
...

Item peayd to the morishe daunce of sent leven   xii d.
...

Item peayd to the morishe daunce that was out of gannwla   35
in lesid   xii ⟨.⟩
...

35/ gannwla: *Gunwalloe*

FOWEY

1614
Bill of Complaint in Rashleigh v. Kendall et al   PRO: STAC 8/249/4
mb 4* *(3 November)*   5

    To the Kings moste excellent Maiestie
In all humble manner Complayning sheweth and informeth vnto your
Maiestie your true and faythfull subiect Iohn Raisheleigh of ffoye in your
highnes Countye of Cornewall Esquier That whereas the makeing contriuing   10
or publishinge of any scandalous libells, letters, Rolles; escrowes schedules or
other writings contayning any libellous scandalous and infamous matter rumor
or reporte tending to the disgrace contumely or repro∧ˈaˈche of any your
Maiesties most loving Subiectes and especially ∧ˈthe same beingˈ composed
or compiled by such as bee preferred by your highnes to any places of   15
Magistracy and authority where they dwell ∧ˈand thatˈ [but cheifly] to the
obloquie discreditt and slaunder of such persons as your Maiestie hath
likewise putt and constituted in the like functions, and administracion of
Iustice in their Countryes hath by the most iuste and honorable sentence of
your Maiesties highe Courte of Starr chamber, bynn from tyme to tyme with   20
publicque and exemplarye Censure seuerely punnished, as a common and
greeuous offence in this age and very daungerous to the peaceable gouerment
of this your Realme of Englande; And whereas your saide subiect doth and
all his life tyme hath lived in good creditt accompte and reputacion in your
County of Cornewall where hee dwelleth, and hath for the space of tenn   25
years laste paste and vpwardes bynn and yett is one of your Maiesties Iustices
of peace in your saide Countye, And hath likewise heertofore by your highnes
bynn elected and chosen vnto the office of highe shirrife of the saide Countye
which hee duly and sincerely executed to the best of his vnderstandinge skill
and knoweledge, without any note or aspercion of any notorious Crime or   30
other misbehauiour iustely imputed or obiected againste him, yet neuertheless
Soe it is (if it maye please your most excellent Maiestie) That Sir Anthonye
Rowse knight, and one Ambrose Rowse Esquier two of your Maiesties
Iustices of your peace of your saide Countye, togeather with Edwarde Hearle
Esquier, and one Thomas Kendall heertofore one other of your Iustices of   35
peace in your saide Countye, But sythence for sundry misdemeanors and
outrages committed by him lately censured and fyned in your highnes saide
Courte of Starrchamber and nowe iustely displaced and putt out of your
Maiesties Commission of your peace in the same Countye, All of them
extremely maligning and envyinge the prosperitye reputacion and Creditt of   40
your saide Subiect And deviseing with themselues howe they might out of
their malitious desire of revenge caste some notorious Calumniacion reproache

and obloquie vpon your saide Subiect to his [irreparable] ‸⌜irreparable⌝
disgrace and infamye did to that end and purpose diuers and sundry tymes
in the Eleventh and Twelueth yeares of your Maiesties Raigne ouer this your
saide Realme (and since your Maiesties laste gracious, generall, and free
pardon) vnlawfully and malitiously combyne confederate conspire and plott   5
[together] aswell with and amongste themselues as also with divers other
malitious persons, and namely with Iohn Hunkyn, Charells Barrett, Peter
Hitchins, walter Truboddye, Robert Venton, Walter Barrett, Margarett
Peirse, the wife of Thomas Peirse, Alice Skirret, the wief of Launder Skirret,
daughter of the said Margaret Pearse ‸⌜Richarde Lillicrapp Sara Lillicrapp   10
the wief of the saide Richard Lillicrapp Iohn Barret Margaret Lympincot⌝
and with many other loose and dissolute persons (whose names so soone as
your saide Subiect shall know[e] he humbly prayeth maye bee heere inserted)
howe and by what wayes and meanes they might best and moste easilye
effect and bringe to passe their saide wicked desire & determinacion, againste   15
your saide Subiect, Immediatly after which conspiracye confederacy plott
and combinacion so entred into, for the intent & purpose aforesaid all the
saide confederates aswell knowne as vnknowne by the malitious abettment
procurement & instigacion especially of the saide Sir Anthonye Rowse
Ambrose Rowse, Thomas Kendall, Charells Barrett, walter Barrett, and   20
Edwarde Hearle, did in or aboute the tymes and yeares aforesaide ‸⌜and since
your Maiesties last gracious generall & free pardon⌝ vnlawfully devise frame
contriue, and publishe in divers places in your saide Countye divers and
soundry infamous and scandalous libells, letters, Rolles, and escrolles, in
writing tending to the greate disgrace and slaunder of your saide Subiect, in   25
the course and manner of his life and conversacion, therein moste malitiously
scandolously, and falslye, slaundering and taxeing your saide Subiect with
incontinency, adultery, incest and of other great and haynous offences of
that nature; Among which scandalous libells lettres Rolles & escrowes, being
very many in number of moste odious spightfull & infamous qualitye The   30
saide Confederattes within the tyme aforesaide did firste moste wickedly and
unlawfully devise frame contriue and write, in divers longe Rolles & escrowes
aswell of paper as of parchement, one most false scandalous and infamous
libell, stuffed and cloyde vpp with many fowle immodest and vnciuell termes
and speeches conteyning both in matter and manner divers grosse and filthy   35
wordes, factes, attemptes & enterprises, vnfitt and vnseemely to bee heere att
large expressed, thereby supposed to haue benn committed by your saide
Subiect moste falsely purporting & conteyning in Substance and effect amonge
many other things farr worse and fowler then are fitt to be heere litterally
sett downe as followeth, vizt That your saide subiect for two & twentye or   40

41 since: *added in left margin*

three and twentye yeares togeather, and more hadd bynn and was a marryed
man and hadd a wief who liued with him farr aboue twentye yeares though
with much trouble and discontent till aboute some five yeeres since or little
more, and that then shee being ouercome with thought and greif for his
lascivious incontinency, and filthy course of life, with very care and sorrowe ⁵
for the same dyed And that your saide subiect being a marryed man for soe
longe tyme as aforesaide vizt in the seuerall yeares of our Lorde God one
thowsande five hunndred nyntye fower, one thowsande five hundred nyentye
five, one thowsand five hundred nyentye seauen, one thowsande five hundred
nyenty eight ∧⌈and also since [in the yeeres] his said wifes death viz in the ¹⁰
yeares⌉ one thowsande six hundred and tenn, one thowsande six hundred
and Eleven did acquaynte himselfe with sundry lewde and dishonest weomen,
and for bribes and rewardes giuen vnto them hadd committed many notorious
& infamous incontinencyes, adulterye, and incestes, with them ∧⌈as⌉ [and]
namely with Pascall Hickes, dorothy Parkett, Margaret Lympencote, ¹⁵
Katheryne Leekes, a daughter of one Hunnys, Anne Bease, Marye Hitchins,
Alice Badcocke, Elizabeth Mondaye, Alice Cocke alias Skirrett, Sara Hill,
Ioane ffarme, Katheren Lukers, Sara Lambe, Thomasyn Langdon, Thomasyn
Stevens, Agnes whitter, Grace Bachewell, Ioane Saunders, debora Parnecote,
Agnes Persed, Agnes Allen, Ioan Pomery, Alice Crabb, Thomasyn Moone ²⁰
Paschas Moone Agnes Packett her sister besides the thyrd sister to them
Agnes Harrys, Cicely Lendon, Ioan Ienkyn, Alice Standen, Katheren Beale,
Margery Commons, Lowdy Hearle, Agnes Beale, Ioan Webb, Mary Webb,
one *(blank)* Porthe, Margarett *(blank)*, Thomasyn Tynker, dorothye Taylor,
And with the seuerall wives of william Pherrys, william Byrde, william ²⁵
Hendye, Michaell Vyan, and his ∧⌈wiefes⌉ daughter, And further that your
saide Subiect as hee hath hadd many concubynes att his commaundement,
soe hath hee hadd likewise many Baudes, whome hee hath imployde for his
filthy luste, and namely the saide Paschall Moone, Iohn Beale, George Cowley,
Henry Cooke, Iohn Kittowe, william webb, Arthure Tremeere, Sampson ³⁰
Lethby, Iohn Hambly, Iohn Crabb, william Hendy, Nicholas Bearne, Michaell
Vyan, and divers others And that they haue bynn and still bee imployed by
your saide Subiect for the bringing of such weomen to his Backe, as hee
desired to haue the Companye of, And that they had brought divers ∧⌈woomen⌉
especially of those [formerly] abouenamed vnto him to bee abused by him, ³⁵
And that your saide Subiect being in Commission of the peace within your
saide Countye hath for all the tyme aforesaide threatned and terrefyed the
Churchwardens of his parishe that they haue not dared to present him for
his saide Crymes, but hath hither vnto escaped punnishment for the same,
and that thereby hee is become a meere scandall both to the Church of God, ⁴⁰
and alsoe to all good Christyans thereaboutes, And lastlye that your saide
Subiect hadd dealt with and perswaded divers of the saide weomen to belieue,

that to committ incontinency adultery, or incest, with him was noe synn
nor offence before God / The which saide moste scandalous disgracefull and
infamous libell, in substance and effect as aforesaide but amplifyed and
aggrauated with vniust and odious contumelious and spightfull Circumstances
ₐ⌜and⌝ sett fourth and expressed with broader fowler and immodester tearmes   5
wordes and phrases then your saide Subiect thinketh meete to bee heere
litterally sett fourth & specifyed being so contriued [framed &] ₐ⌜framed &⌝
putt into writing, in divers & sundrye Rowells, escrowes, and schedules some
in paper, and some in parchment, The saide confederates caused soone after
to bee turned out of prose into Rymes & verses, and aswell the verses as also   10
the prose to bee written and sett downe both in paper and ₐ⌜in⌝ parchment,
in many & sundry Coppyes and transcriptes, of mere intent & purpose to
scatter dispirse divulge & publishe the same ⟨...⟩ as many hands and places
& ₐ⌜vnto⌝ [into] the notice of as many persons as they coulde, ffor the further
effecting of which their saide malitious purpose, the saide confederates of   15
late in divers and sundry places within your saide County of Cornewall devon,
London, and elswhere within your Realme of Englande aswell by themselues
as by divers & sundry other persons by them therevnto procured as yet
vnknowne vnto your saide Subiect (whome when hee shall happen to knowe
hee humbly prayeth maye bee heerein also inserted) did in very great   20
assemblyes & meetings not only in divers generall Sessions of your Maiesties
peace in your saide seuerall Countyes But also in sundry Tauernes, Innes,
Alehowses, & other publique & common places within this your saide Realme
reade pronounce publish repeate and singe the saide false & scandalous libells,
lettres Rolles & schedules, both in prose and verse in moste disgracefull &   25
ignominious manner, thereby of purpose to inure a perpetuall blemish spott
& infamy, vpon your saide Subiect, They and euery of them dayly &
continually laughing, scoffing Iesting & sporting att the contentes of the said
libell and taking great pleasure and delight therein, & spreading dispersing
and castinge abroade sundry Coppyes thereof, to soe many persons by lettres   30
messages & otherwise as they could possiblye by all ₐ⌜their⌝ meanes invente
or devise, to the intollerable scorne contempt & dirision of your saide subiect,
And to the detracting deprauing & traducing of your Subiectes good name
creditt & reputacion, and to the making of him odious & hatefull not vnly
in your saide County of Cornewall, but alsoe in all your Maiesties Realme of   35
Englande ... In and by which articles your saide Subiect is moste falslye
charged to haue committed incest, Adultery, and incontinency, with all the
weomen ₐ⌜named⌝ in the saide infamous libell aboue mentioned whereas in
truthe moste of them weare such as your Subiect did neuer speake withall
nor did euer see or knowe to the vtmoste of his remembrance By meanes of   40
all which practices your Subiectes creditt and estimacion is like to receaue a
perpetuall stayne and blemishe to the greate scandall and obloquie of him &

his posterity for euer, Vnlesse it bee by your Royall Maiestie and your
honorable Counsell prevented; and the offenders aforesaide dulye punnished;
In tender consideracion whereof and for asmuch as all and singuler the saide
practizes, Combinacions, Confederacyes, making contriving & publishing
of libells, libellous and infamous writings, vnlawfull examinacion of witnesses,   5
Corrupt briberyes, libellous letters, and all other the offences and misdeameanors
aforesaide, are very daungerous and enormious in soe peaceable and well
gouerned a Monarchy, And are growne vnto that bouldnes and impudence,
As that they will dare approache into your highnes Courte and presume
with their virulent and venomous aspercions, to touche even the best and   10
noblest of your worthy and honorable state, Vnlesse the Censure of Iustice
and rigor of the lawe, doe speedily take houlde of them, And for that they
haue benn all downe and committed since your Maiesties laste generall
gracious and free pardon It maye therefore please your Highnes to graunte
vnto your saide Subiect Your Maiesties most gracious writtes of Subpœna to   15
bee directed vnto the saide Sir Anthony Rowse ⌃⌐knight⌐ Ambrose Rowse
Edwarde Hearle and Thomas Kendall Esquieres Charells Barrett Walter
Barret Peter Hichins Iohn Hunkyn Walter Truboddye Robert Venton
Margaret Peirce the wief of Thomas Peirce Alice Skirret the wief of Launder
Skirret Richarde Lillicrapp Sara Lillicrapp the wief of the saide Richard   20
Lillicrapp Iohn Barret and Margaret Lympyncote commanding them and
euery of them the persons before named to bee and personally to appeare
before your Maiestie in your highnes Courte of Starrchamber att a certeyne
daye and vnder a certeyne payne therein to be conteyned then and there to
make aunsweare vnto the premisses layde to their charge and further to stande   25
to and abide such order censure and punnishment therein as to your Maiestie
and your Highnes honorable Counsell of that Courte ⌃⌐shall seem meete⌐
And your saide subiect shall as hee is euer bounden praye for your Maiesties
longe and happy raigne ouer vs.

Francis Bacon   30
Thomas Rychardson
Thomas Hughes

JACOBSTOW

35

1617
Bill of Information in Stawell v. Mapowder et al   PRO: STAC 8/27/10
mb 2* (15 July)

To the kinges most excellent Maiestie   40

Sheweth and informeth your highnes Sir Henry Yelverton knight your

Maiesties Attorney generall That wheras Iohn Stawell of Iacobstowe in the
County of Cornewell esquier and Loer Stawell daughter of the said Iohn
Stawell Emanuell Sheere one of the Attorneyes of your Maiesties Court of
Comon pleas Ellis Spiller of Iacobstowe afforesaid gentleman and Thomasine
his wiefe Iane Prowse daughter of the said Thomasine Henry Verchill of   5
Iacobstowe afforesaid Clerke Martin Vdye of Iacobstowe afforesaid yeoman
Iohn Noy of Iacobstowe afforesaid gentleman Thomas Lamerton servant to
the said Emanuell Sheere Ienkyn Benalleck and Margarett his wiefe beinge
all Inhabitantes within the said parishe of Iacobstow are all persons of ˄⌈honest
fame & report & of⌉ good quallitie & esteeme & haue byn soe carefull in   10
theire severall courses of liefe that they haue alwayes hertofore liued in peace
& amitie & in good credytt and reputacion amongest their neighbors and
free from all Imputacion of Scandall Infamie or reproach Yet now so it is if
it shall please Your most exellent Maiestie one Emanuell Mapowder of
Iacobstowe aforesaid Marie his wife Margaret ffetherstone late of Iacobstowe   15
aforesaid and diuerse others vnknowne persons and whose names Your said
Attorney prayeth may be incerted into this Informacion as they shall happen
to be knowne being all most malitious & envious persons and maligning in
generall the Amitie and peace of the Inhabitantes of the parish of Iacobstowe
aforesaid but especiallie the good name and reputacions of the said persons   20
before mencioned did most wickedlie and vnlawfullie out of the Wickednes
of their owne Corrupt hartes and without anie occation given or offered vnto
them by the said persons before named or by anie other the Inhabitantes of
the said Parrish most malitiouslye wickedlie and vnlawfullie plott practise
and Agree together to scandalize and reproach [all] the good names Creditt   25
& reputacion of all the said persons before mencioned by publishing and
divulging generallie false and vntrue Imagined matter of infamie and reproach
against them. And to thend thessaid false and vntrue matters of infamie
and reproach might take the deper roote and impression in the myndes of
the Common and vulgar sorte of people within the said parish and thereby   30
make the said before named Inhabitantes of the said parish the more ridiculous
and scorned at they the said Emanuell Mapowder Marie his wife Margaret
ffetherstone and the said other vnknowne persons did fu⌈r⌉ther malitiouslie
and vnlawfullie Conclude and agree together after they had raised and
diuulged such false and forged matters of Infamie and reproach as aforesaid   35
to reduce the same into [riding] Rimes in the nature of a Libell and then to
publish and divulge the same: And in execucion thereof they the said
Emanuell Mapowder Marie his wife Margaret ffetherstone and the said other
vnknowne persons well knoweing that the Churchwardens and eight other
persons sidemen and Assistantes to the said Churchewardens of the said   40

16/ others: *for* other (?)

parishe had vpon Due Consideracion of the state and quallities of the said
Iohn Stawell Emanuell Sheere Ellis Spiller and Martin Vdye placed some of
them to sytt in the tyme of divine servise in an Ile ∧⌈in⌉ [f] the said ∧⌈parishe⌉
Church of Iacobstowe aforesaid called Suttcott Ile they the said Confederates
and the said other vnknowne persons to drawe them into scorne and reproach   5
for being placed there malitiouslie and vnlawfullie gaue fourth manie false
and vntrue reportes taxing the said Iohn Stawell Emanuell Sheere Ellys Spiller
and Martin Vdye with greate pride and Insolencie for making suit to be so
placed in the said Ile whereas in Truth they were propounded to sitt there
vpon the mere mocion of the said Churchwardens and sidemen. And they   10
did lykewise most falselye and malitiouslie publish and divulge that the said
Henrie Verchill a graue & learned preacher out of a malitious disposition to
the other Inhabitantes of the said parishe would beare parte of the Chardge
of the said seate and beare as they termed it one end of the Chardge thereof
And that the said Loer Stawell daughter of the said Iohn Stawell had a   15
loathsome Infirmitie and that the said Iane Prowse daughter of the said
Thomasine Spiller had liued incontinentlie with the said Noy, and that the
said Thomasine Spiller and Ienkin Benalleckes wife and ∧⌈one⌉ Sapience
Hogd had allso liued incontinentlie, and haveing with manie Cunning and
Subtill deuices raised and divulged the said seuerall slanders and false   20
disgracefull reportes and reproaches as aforesaid they the said Emanuell
Mapowder Marie his wife Margarett ffetherstone and the said other vnknowne
persons in further execucion of their said wicked and vnlawfull plott practise
and Agreement did most malitiouslie and vnlawfullie deuise frame and wryte
diuerse [rydyng] Rimes in the nature of a Scandelous Libell most iniuriouslie   25
and falselye taxing all the before named Inhabitantes and diuerse other
persons of honest and sober Conversacion with such matters as they the said
Conspiratores had so falsely and malitiouslie divulged against them as
aforesaid which said [ryding] Rimes doe follow in these wordes (vizt.) Quoth
Mr Sheere, I praye You give care, and hearken vnto me, I am placed full   30
lowe, as all you doe knowe, a shame it is to see but if you will, now vse the
Skill, that I shall take in hand, I will haue a place, with a greater grace, as
you shall vnderstand, Suttcott Ile, will make me smile, If I may come therein,
I doe not Doubt but putt them out, if I doe once beginne, for they who sytt
there, they are so bare, and of so lowe a degree I dare to sweare, they are so   35
bare, they will not wage Lawe with me, I will haue my Chaire placed fast by
the wall but I will not come vpp ⌈vn⌉till the right order doe me call Austine
Midland was to a [⟨.⟩] greate Coste and besides that he hath taken a greate
cost but who shall take this matter in hand, but the lypping Master and
loppyng man vpp then Martyn Vdye arose with his read nose well dyed   40

19/ Hogd: for Hodg (?)

with Alehowse Can give me my right for I am kyn[⟨.⟩]e to a knight, and will
sytt there if I can This is ill doon said Iohn Heydon for this ∧⌈will⌉ Cause
much strife, quoth the ould Squire it is my desyre, to sytt there by my wife,
Then after followed his fine daughter somthing leged lyke an Auter who if
she should staye in the Churche too long she will there shed her water, but   5
whether it be could or hott Thomas Baglehole will bring her a Chamber
Pott. Then spake Iohn Iuiiiu as he was wonte he had no money to spend,
quoth the ould Sir Harrie the seate I will Carrie and thou shalt beare the
one end The game is begun said Iohn Collyn and Spiller is sett vpp alofte
and his wife Cutt, comes ietting vpp well lyke a thing of nought. Then   10
followed after her fine daughter well leged lyke a Crane said Mr Noy though
I seme Coye yet I haue layen with Your daughter Iane. Iane Spiller is to London
gone, and gon she is aroaye with her father, but she hath made a thred bare
squire yt had bene better she had gone awaie rather. Goe pick a Sallet said
Ienkin Benalleck though my wife be but a Iade, she shall Compare with   15
Spillers mare for they be both of one Trade. Sapience Hodge weares her
masteres badge and she must runne for a wager, she is a foule mare none for
her doth Care, bycause she is a trayned souldior./ And the said Emanuell
Mapowder Marie his wife Margaret ffetherstone and the said other vnknowne
persons having so made Contriued and wrytten the said false and scandalous   20
Rimes and verses as aforesaid in the forme and Nature of a Libell as aforesaid,
the said Marie Mapowder Margarett ffetherstone and the said other vnknowne
persons by and with the privitie and Consente of the said Emanuell Mapowder
most malitiouslie and vnlawfullie did saye singe repeate and publish the said
false and scandalous verses and libell to diuerse and sundrie persons vizt. to   25
one Richard Mondaye and one dyer ∧⌈and to one Roberte Coke Roberte
Ryell⌉ and to diuerse other persons within the said parishe of Iacobstowe
aforesaid. And afterwardes did Cause diuerse Coppies of the said Libell to be
made and wrytten and then did malitiouslie and vnlawfullie divuldge and
Cast abroade the said Coppies thereof in diuerse places in the said Countie   30
to the greate discredytt scandall & reproach of the said Iohn Stawell and of
Loer Stawell his daughter Emanuell Sheere Ellis Spiller Thomasine his wife
Iane Prowse daughter of the said Thomasine Henrie verchill Martin vydye
Iohn Noy Thomas Lamerton Ienkin Benalleck & his wife and of diuerse
others to the greate offence of all other the Inhabitantes of the parishe. And   35
your said Attorney further informeth Your Maiestie That the said Ellis Spiller
being so placed to sytt in the said Ile called Suttcott Ile as aforesaid did

10/ ietting: *first* t *corrected over* y
17/ masteres: *possibly* misttes

therevpon build a new Pewe in the said Ile, where he his wife and familie
did Afterwardes sytt to heare divine servise in the said Churche. But now so
it is further yf it shall please your Maiestie the said Emanuell Mapowder Marie
his wife Margaret ffetherstone associating vnto them ∧⌜selues one Tobias
ffetherstone &⌝ diuerse other vnknowne Riotous and disorderlye persons to   5
the nomber of six persons ∧⌜whose names your said Attorney humbly de⌜si⌝reth
may be inserted into this Informacion as they shall herafter be discouered
and⌝ being all of them Armed arrayed and prepared with swordes staves
barres of Iron Axes Hatchetes sawes & such other instrumentes and weapons
about the Moneth of September last past in most riotous and vnlawfull   10
manner entered into the said parish Churche of Iacobstowe and then &
there Riotouslie and vnlawfullie in greate furie & outrage did breake downe
deface hew & Cutt in peices the said seate so sett vpp and erected by the
said Ellis Spiller as aforesaid to the greate terror and Affrightment of all
Your Maiesties loveing subiectes inhabiting thereaboutes. In tender Consideracion 15
whereof And forasmuch as the said w⟨..⟩ked & malitious plottes practises &
Agreementes and the said making Contriuing and publishing of the said
scandalous and infamous libell verses and Rimes the said Riott in the Churche
and all and singuler the said offences and misdemeanors [and] ∧⌜are⌝ directlie
Contarie to diuerse the good and wholsom lawes and Statutes of this your   20
Maiesties Realme of England and haue bene all perpetrated Committed and
doon sithence your Maiesties last gratious and generall & free pardon, and
that it would bee a greate incouragement to other lyke evill disposed persons
to Comitt the lyke offences if theis soe foule greate heynous and notorious
offenders should escap vnpunished May it therefore please your most excellent 25
Maiestie to graunte your highenes ⟨..⟩ most gracious writtes of subpena to
bee directed to the saide Emanuell Mapower Mary his wife & Margarett
ffetherstone Comaundinge them and every of them thereby at a certayne
daie & vnder a Certayne payne herein taken by your Highenes sett downe
and lymitted personallye to ⟨...⟩ee and appeare before your Maiestie and the   30
Lordes of your highenes most honorable [pryvie] Councell in your Highenes
most honorable Courte of Starchamber there to answere the premisses And
further to stand to and abide such order direccion & sentence ⟨...⟩en as to
your Maiestie and the said Lordes of your said Counsell shall seeme fitt. And
your said Attorney shall praie &c./   35

                                 Henry yeluerton.
                                 Iohn Giles   Higgons

30/ before: b *corrected over* w

LAUNCELLS

1612
Bill of Complaint in Painter v. Yeo   PRO: STAC 8/236/29
mb 2* *(12 October)*   5

                    To the Kings most excellent Maiestie
In most humble manner Complayning shew and informe vnto yor most
excellent Maiestie; yor loyall faithfull and obedient Subiectes Richard Painter
of Launcells in yor highnes Countie of Cornewall yeoman and Marie wise   10
of Launcells aforesaid single woman; That whereas yor said Subiectes haue
from their seuerall infancies and Childhoodes allwaies lived in good Creditt
and reputacion and honestlie Carried and demeaned themselves in their life
and Conversacion to the generall approbacion and good likeing of all the
neighbours and inhabitants thereabouts without anie the least spott blemishe   15
or ymputacion of anie vnchaste lewd and incontinent living yet Soe yt is (maie
yt please yor most excellent Maiestie) That one Richard Mill of Pyworthie
in yor highnes Countie of devon having for a long tyme without anie iust
Cause or occasion Conceaved and borne a verie deepe and irreconcileable
hatred and malice against yor said Subiects did in or about the moneth of   20
Maie now last paste in this present Tenth yeare of yor highnes Raigne over
this yor Realme of England most vnlawfullie and maliciouslie Combine
Conspire plott practize and Confederate to and with one Ioane Yeo the wife
of Iohn Yeo thelder Iohn Yeo the Younger their sonne Richard Vowler *alias*
ffowler all of the parishe of Launcells aforesaid in yor said Countie of   25
Cornewall being all of them lewd loose and disordered persons and whollie
addicted and accustomed to make and Contrive scandalous and infamous
libells vpon those against whom they haue Conceaued anie the least
displeasure and with diuerse others such like malevolent and ill affected
persons whose names yor said Subiectes as yet knowe[th] not But humblie   30
praye[th] they maie haue libertie to inserte them soe soone as they shall be
knowne and discouered how and by what wicked vngodlie and vncharetable
meanes to Caste a perpetuall staine and blemishe vpon yor said subiects their
Creditts good names and reputacions and vtterlie to disgrace and disparage
them in their advauncements by waie of mariage (being both single and   35
vnmaried persons; And for the better effecting of suche their lewd and
vngodlie practizes and Confederacyes The said Richard Mill and the rest of
his said malicious adherents did diuerse and sondrie tymes in the foresaid
Moneth of Maie meete together in Alehouses and other places in the parishe
of Launcells aforesaid And there did most lewdlie and wickedlie Consulte   40

36/ persons;: *semicolon for closing parenthesis*

Conferre and advise how they might disgrace impeache and scandalize yor said
subiectes lives and Conversacions in the fowlest and most infamous manner
that mought be And after manie and sondrie Conferences and Consultacions
on that behalf The said Richard Mill Ioane Yeo Iohn Yeo Richard ffouler
alias Vowler and the rest of the said Confederats in or about the said moneth   5
of Maie did for the better wreakeing and executing their malicious intents
and purposes aforesaid make frame Contrive and putt or cause to be putt
into writting One most false infamous scandalous and scurrill libell in these
words following vzt. Scribibo Scribing omnibus vobis I thought it fitt to
write vnto you all in a few talls, that all of you must remember the mowheis   10
pals; how Richard Penter and Marie Wise when they were at yeo to the
feast; begin yf you will know the 29 of November, he proued himself a veri
cometimber, But yf there ⌃⌐be⌐ anie that are willing to know, let them aske
of dick Voller or els of Iohn Yeo; and the will tell you in plaine tals, that the
found them two out by the mowheis pals, the pals are bad and verie ferking   15
but the ould abed but a litle gerking, Then saith dick Vowler and asked what
they meane; then said dick Penter here is Charlamens weane, and where haue
doun his mead they could not tell, then saith they she ⌃⌐is⌐ gone downe indle
the hill; then saith dicke Penter let vs goe D⟨..⟩e noe saith the you haue had
a good chance & when the had danced but once about the flore Ther ⟨..⟩   20
Comes the mayd into the fore dore & what the did there the Could not tell,
some saith the did ile some said the did well But as I thinke the [⟨.⟩] mean'd
noe harme the said it was out against the barne and thervpon he mad a breche
because her bodi he did not tiche, & manie such as he doth vse such dealinges
it is as bad as any healinge to bringe a maide in such a fame & not to giver   25
the hole screame; If anie man aske how made this rime, yt was Steven
Cockcrum in a drinkinge time. And haveing thus wickedlie maliciouslie and
vnlawfullie deuised Contriued and putt into writting the said despightfull
slaunderous reprochefull and opprobrious libell against yor said subiectes
with a full and setled resolucion intent and purpose as aforesaid to defame   30
disgrace and discreditt them amongest their frends neighbours and
acquainttance and vtterlie to overthrowe their Creditts reputacions and whole
estates by dispersing divulgeing and publishing the said libell abroade; The
said Richard Mill and the rest of his said libellous adherents did in the said
Moneth of Maie and at diuerse other tymes before and since as well in the   35
house of the said Iohn Yeo thelder as in diuerse Tavernes Alehouses and other
places within yor said Comitie of Cornewall read singe repeate publishe and
divulge the said disgracefull and reprochfull libell [⟨.⟩] against yor said subiects
and did likewise on their Alebenches and in other places in most scoffinge
lewd and obscene manner interprett and expound the said libell against yor   40

12/ begin: for being (?)   24/ did: first d written over m or w (?)

subiectes to their intollerable disgrace and infamie and noe lesse greeff both
of them and their freindes; And yet not satisfied therwith But further Coveting
to publishe and disperse their wicked and vngodlie invencions in some more
disgracefull manner to thend the whole Country therabouts might take notice
of it; The said Richard Mill, Iohn Yeo the younger Richard ffowler alias   5
Vowler and the rest of the said Confederats as well knowne as vnknowne, not
regarding yor highnes lawes against slaunderous libellers and publishers of
infamous libells nor the happie peace and Concord of this yor Maiesties
Kingdome which by such libells is often infringed did by and throughe a
mutuall practize Confederacie and Conspiracie betweene them in or about   10
the said Moneth of Maie before mencioned fould and wrappe vp the said
libell soe contrived and made in manner as aforesaid in the forme and likenes
of a letter and did indorse the same and directe ^⌐it⌐ to yor subiecte Marie
Wise with this superscripcion vpon the backe side thereof vizt To her loving
frend Marie Wise deliuer this with as much speed as maie be spedd; And   15
haveing soe folded and indorsed the same The said Iohn Yeo the younger by
the practize aduise and procurement of the said other Confederats and by
and throughe the Confederacie aforesaid did in or about the same moneth
of Maie repaire vnto a Certaine watermill neer vnto Launcells aforesaid where
he had knowledge that yor said subiecte Marie Wise was, and Cuninglie   20
insinuating himself into her Companie, and vpon some Coulorable surmizes
and pretences did earnestlie request and entreate yor said subiecte Marie to
spare and lend him her horse to ride home thereon; which being obteined;
He the said Iohn Yeo the Younger did ride the said horse vnto a Certaine
stile in the waie to Launcells aforesaid where he knew that yor said subiecte   25
Marie must needes passe from the said Mill; And there allighting The said
Iohn Yeo the Younger according to the former dirreccions instruccions and
appointment of his said libellous Complices by and throughe the practize
and Confederacy aforesaid did then and there leaue the said horse tyed to
the said stile and the said libell soe folded vp in the manner of a letter as   30
aforesaid and directed vnto yor said subiecte Marie with the said indorsement
and superscripcion before mencioned to the open view of all such passengers
as had occasion to goe that waie to the great and manifest disgrace discreditt
and reproche of yor said subiectes In tender Consideracion whereof; And
ffor as much as the said Confederacies Combinacions practizes makeing   35
Contriving and publishing of scandalous and infamous libells are contrarie
to yor Maiesties lawes statutes and ordinances of this yor Realme of England
and doe tende to the sowing of strife and dissention betweene neighbour and
neighbour and are verie heinous and enormious in soe peaceable and well
gouerned a Comon wealth and haue bin all donn and Comitted sithence   40

36/ contrarie: co *written over another letter*

yor Ma*iesties* last gen*er*all and free p*a*rdonn and doe therfore Condignelie
deserve to be verie sharplie and seuerlie punished. It maie therfore please yor
Ma*ie*stie to graunte vnto yor said sub*iectes* yor Ma*iesties* most gracious writts
of Subpena to be directed vnto the said Richard Mill, Ioane Yeo, Iohn Yeo,
Richard ffowler al*ias* Vowler and the[r] rest of the vnknowne Confederats   5
soe soone as they shalbe knowne Comaunding them and eu*er*ie of them
therby at a daie Certaine and vnder a Certaine payne therin to be lymitted
p*er*sonallie to be and appeare before your Ma*ie*stie and the lords of yor Ma*iesties*
most ho*nourabl*e privye Counsell in yor highe Courte of Starr Chamber then
and there to Aunswere the premisses and to stand to and abide such further   10
order and dirrecc*i*on on that behalf as to yor Ma*ie*stie [⟨.⟩] and the said lords
shall seeme to be most agreable w*i*th lawe and Iustice And yor said Sub*iectes*
will dailie praie for yor Ma*ie*stie.

Tho*mas* Hughes

15

LAUNCESTON

1404–5
Borough Accounts   CRO: B/Laus/135
mbs [2–2d]* *(Travelling expenses)*   20

	ap*u*d Tauystoke p*rim*a nocte	
C	In ludis in cena	ij. d.
C	In vino & c*er*uis*ia*	iij d.
C	In fena & p*r*obend*a*	vij d. 25
C	In ferr' eq*uorum*	ij d.
C	It*em* in vino	v. d.
C	It*em* in vino	ij. d.
C	In oblac*i*onib*us*	ij d.
		30
	ap*u*d plympton	
C	In prandio	[iiij d.] vj d.
C	In equis	vijj d.
C	In copia p*r*ocess*us*	ij d.
		35
	ap*u*d Tauystoke domorsu*m*	
C	In cena	vj d.
C	In equis	vj d.
C	In pane & vino ad iantaculum	ij. d. ob.
C	In vino dato domi p*er* Maiorem	ij d. ob. 40

33/ equis: e *corrected over* a

℃   In ij c!aponibus emptis   iiij. d.

    Summa .v. s.

    Secundo vice In I capone   ij d.   5
℃   In carne vitulorum   ij d.
℃   In cena apud Tauystok   xv d.
℃   In equis   xvj d.
℃   In ludis   iiij d.
℃   In iantaculum mane iij d.   10

    apud plympton
℃   In prandio x d. ob.
℃   In equis xvj. d.
℃   In cena domi cum I capone xviij d. ⌈ob.⌉   15

    Summa plus extra |

℃   In vino potato eundo foras   iij d. ob.
℃   In v. caponibus   x. d. ob. 20

    [Summa]
    [Summa totalis]

℃   In vino dato Roberto heye per Maiorem: causa essendi bonus   25
    amicus in Curia de Tremeton   v d.

                                        Summa viij s. x d.
                                        Summa totalis xiij s. x d.
                                                                          30
℃   Tertia vice &c
℃   In oblacionibus   ij d.
℃   In vino   xij d.
℃   In equis   xix d.
                                                                          35

1431–2
Borough Accounts   CRO: B/Laus/137
single mb* *(25 November–25 November) (Necessary expenses)*
…
…In expensis circa le may xj s. vij d.… In xij d. datis Willelmo Crese pro   40
pone' le beris [intus] in domo sua
…

1440
Register of Bishop Edmund Lacy   Devon Record Office: Chanter 11
f ccxiii verso *(16 June)*

Indulgencia   Item xvj^to die Mensis predicti Anno domini supradicto ibidem Dominus   5
concessit omnibus vere penitentibus & confessis qui ad sustentacionem
confratrie Ministrallorum beate Marie Magdalene Launceston aliqua de bonis
sibi a deo collatis contulerint legauerint seu quouismodo assignauerint grata
caritatis subsidia quadraginta dies Indulgencie
...   10

1445–6
Borough Accounts   CRO: B/Laus/138
f [7]* *(25 November–25 November) (Expenses for wine)*

...In I lagena vini data Waltero Colle capellano in die Marie Magdalene ⌈horn⌉   15
viij d. In iij lagenis & quarteria [d] vini expensis per Maiorem et socios in
nocte Marie Magdalene ⌈horn⌉ ij s. ij d. In pane idem tempus ⌈horn⌉ I d....

1449–50   20
Borough Accounts   CRO: B/Laus/139
f [5]* *(25 November–25 November) (Expenses for wine)*

[...In vino expensis in nocte Marie Magdalene [xix] inter Maiorem &
mynstrall' xix d....]   25

1450–1
Borough Accounts   CRO: B/Laus/141
single mb* *(25 November–25 November) (Necessary expenses)*
...   30
...In expensis per Maiorem & socios in nocte Marie Magdalene vij d....

single mb dorse *(External expenses)*
...
...In argento Dato Brown pyper iiij d....   35
...

8/ quouismodo: *2 minims for* ui
16/ capellano: no *corrected over other letters*

1459–60
Borough Accounts   CRO: B/Laus/143
single mb dorse *(25 November–25 November) (Expenses for wine)*
…

…In expens*is* fact*is* in vigil*ia* Marie Magdalene ⌈die &⌉ *pro* crastin*o* p*er*   5
Maiore*m* & so[c]cijs *suis* p*ro* iiij lagen*is* vini & I potell*o* & pane xix d.…
…

1465–6
Borough Accounts   CRO: B/Laus/153   10
single mb* *(25 November–25 November) (Expenses for wine)*
…

…In pan*e* expens*o* circa maior*e* & soc*ijs* suis ac mynstrell' in vig*ilia* be*a*te
m*a*r*ie* magdalane I d. ob. In iij lagen*is* & I q*ua*rt*eria* vin*i* exp*ensis* circa Maiore
& soc*ijs* suis ac eciam Mynstrell' id*em* temp*us* xviij d. ob.   15

1466–7
Borough Accounts   CRO: B/Laus/158
mb [2] *(25 November–25 November) (Expenses for wine)*
…   20

…In pan*e* empt*o* Petr*o* Pyke p*ro* maiore & soc*ijs* suis in vigil*ia* *sanct*e m*a*r*ie*
magdalane ij d. In I lagen*a* & I potell*o* vini rubij empt*is* Petr*o* Pyke id*em*
temp*us* xij d. In I q*ua*rt*eria* & I lagen*a* vini albi empt*a* eid*em* Petri id*em*
temp*us* vij d. ob.…

1469–70   25
Borough Accounts   CRO: B/Laus/160
mb [2]* *(25 November–25 November)*

…In reward*o* dat*o* Ministrall' …   30
…
… ⟨..⟩ior' & soc*ijs* suis in vigil*ia* *sanct*e m*a*r*ie* magdalane xiiij d.…
…

1470–1   35
Borough Accounts   CRO: B/Laus/147
mb [1]* *(25 November–25 November) (External expenses)*
…

…In reward*o* dat*o* p*er* maiorem ad le Bere hurde Com*itis* Warwici xx d. In
reward*o* dat*o* Thome Stultu*m* R*i*card*i* Com*itis* Warwici xvj d.…   40

6/ so[c]cijs *suis*: *for* socios suos   40/ Stultu*m*: *for* Stulto *(?)*
23/ eid*em* Petri: *for* eodem Petro *(?)*

mb [2]*

...In rewardo dato Roberto Walkere vno seruienti Georgio duci Clarencie
vocato le Berehurde xx d....

5

(Expenses for wine)

℃   In vino dato ad le Berehurde Comitis Warwici vj d. In pane idem tempus ob.
In vino dato Maiori & socijs suis pro le searchyng de Campanis iij d. In pane
idem tempus I d. In vino dato vno seruienti Ricardi Comitis Warwici vocato   10
Thomas le Stulstus idem tempus vj d.... In expensis circa Maiori & socijs
suis & le Mynstrall' in vigilia Sancte marie magdalene ij s. iij d. In I lagena
vini data *(blank)* Croght & *(blank)* Commissariis domini Regis idem tempus
vij d. In I quarteria vini albi data Willelmo Parker & Iohanni Davy Canonico
& alijs Cantaribus in ffesto marie magdalene I d. ob....   15

1476–7
Borough Accounts   CRO: B/Laus/162
mb [2] *(25 November – 25 November) (External expenses)*
...   20
...In expensis circa Maiore & socijs suis in vigilia marie Madgalene xx d....
In rewardo dato seruienti domini principis vocato le Berehurde idem tempus
xx d. In rewardo dato iij^bus Mynstrallis de domino Chaunceler hoc anno xij d....
...
25

1478–9
Borough Accounts   CRO: B/Laus/164
mb [1] *(25 November–25 November) (External expenses)*
...
...In rewardo dato vno Ioculatore ludendo coram maiore & Socijs suis viij d....   30
In expensis maioris & Communitatis in vigilia beate Marie Magdalane iij s....
...

1520–1
Borough Accounts   CRO: B/Laus/170   35
mb [1]* *(Rents paid)*
...
...Et in redditu resoluto Ministral' pro tenemento in boriali vico per annum ij d. ob....
...

3/ vno: *for* vni   21/ Madgalene: *for* Magdalene
10/ vno: *for* vni   22/ idem tempus: *the summer assizes*
11/ Maiori: *for* Maiore   30/ vno Ioculatore: *for* vni Ioculatori

mb [2] *(Gifts of wine)*

...Et solut*i pro* vino dat*o* seruient*i* dom*i*ni Reg*is* viz a Iogeler illuc ven*ient*i hoc a*n*no vj d.

...Et solut*i pro* vino empt*o* in vigilia b*eat*e Marie Magdalene hoc anno xij d....

(Necessary expenses)

...Et solut*i pro* pane & seruic*i*a empt*is* cu*m* candel*is* in vigilia b*eat*e Marie Magdalene hoc anno in Gilda Aula xij d....

(External expenses)

Et in regard*o* dat*o* Custod' vrsor*um* dom*i*ni Reg*is* illuc ven*ient*' hoc a*n*no iij s. iiij d.... Et in regard*o* dat*o* seruient*i* dom*i*ni Reg*is* videlic*et* a Iogeler. illuc venient*i* hoc anno iij s. iiij d. Et in regard*o* dat*o* conseruator' vrsor*um* Duc*is* ˄⌈de⌉ Southfolke illuc ven*ient*' hoc anno viij d. Et in regard*o* dat*o* conseruator' vn*ius* bestie voc*ate* a Camele hoc a*n*no xvj d.... Et in regard*o* dat*o* diu*er*sis lusorib*us* de plymouth & launceston ij s....

...

1530–1

Borough Accounts   CRO: B/Laus/171

mb [2]* *(External expenses)*

...

⟨...⟩ in Regard*o* dat*o* iij Ministrall*is* Domini R*egis* illuc ⟨...⟩ Ricard*o* Dyngle Organist*e* in ffesto Mar*i*e Magdale⟨...⟩ Greynfild Vicecomit*is pro* Copia Commiss*ionis* taxa⟨...⟩ solut' histrioni D*o*m*i*ni R*egis* illuc venient*i* hoc anno ⟨...⟩...

...

1542–3

Borough Accounts   CRO: B/Laus/172

mb [2] *(Rents paid)*

...

...Et solut*i* Minnstrell' alt' redd' de lyan' *pro* ten*emento* in quo Rob*er*tus Skynn*er* modo inh*a*bitat iiij d....

...

27/ ⟨...⟩: *right half of* MS *torn away*

mb [3] *(Necessary expenses)*

...Et solut*i* p*ro* pane s*er*uicia & vino in vigilia marie magdalene hoc anno
xj d. ob....

...   5

(External expenses and rewards)

...Et in regard*o* dat*o* Ministrall' D*omi*ni Reg*is* ib*ide*m hoc anno iij s.
iiij d....   10

1572–3
Borough Expense Book   CRO: B/Laus/173–78
f [12]* *(Payments)*

...   15

Item p*ai*d to the venesicians that were here & plaid here whereof
there was gathered   vij s.

...

f [17] *(Payments)*   20

...

Item for hook*es* and eyes & for mending ye bull chayne   iij s. iiij d. ob.

...

1573–4   25
Borough Expense Book   CRO: B/Laus/173–78
f [18] *(Payments)*

...

Item geiven the players of Mylton   ij s.

...   30

Item geiven Robyn the synger by m*aste*r mayor   vj d.

...

f [19]

...   35

Item p*ai*d vnto a singing man w*hi*ch came frome south
Tawton   ij s.

...

29/ Mylton: *probably Milton Abbot, seven miles from Launceston, in Devon*
36–7/ south Tawton: *South Tawton, Devon*

f [19v]

...

Item paid the Beere hearde   vj s. viij d.

...

5

ſ [22]

...

Item for mending the Bull ring   iij d.

...

10

1574–5
Borough Expense Book   CRO: B/Laus/173–78
f [24] *(Payments)*

...

Item to Robart Shere the xvij[th] of Ianuary for playing on the   15
drums two markett daies   iiij d.

...

Item to the players one May daie   x s.

...

20

f [24v]*

...

Item to Thomas Laurens for setting the rynges in the brode
stone   xiij d.
Item for iiij rynges for the same stone   xv d. 25

...

f [25v]

...

Item to the Enterlude players i september   x s. 30

...

Item to poppet players   x s.

...

f [26v]*   35

...

Item to William Seymor for a rope to ty the bull   x d.

...

1575–6
Borough Expense Book CRO: B/Laus/173–78
f [38v] *(Payments)*
...

Item paid to the Enterlude players viz my L*ord* Stafford*es* men   5
by m*aster* maiors comaundemt   xiij s. iiij d.
...

1640/1
Borough Accounts CRO: B/Laus/179/2/1   10
single sheet* *(2 January) (Payments)*
...

                                                              s. d.

...
for a dayes woorke for settin peeces for ye yarncleyers   2–0   15
for timber and setting in the longe peeces w*hic*h the bull tore
vp in the corne markett house   1–6
...

single sheet* *(23 January) (Payments)*   20
...
ffor 4 ffore lockes ffor the Bull chine   01–0
...
ffor 5 new lenthes ffor the Bull chene   02–6
ffor a pine ffor the Bull chen   00–4   25
...

LISKEARD

1575–6   30
Mayors' Accounts CRO: B/Lis/266
mb [2] *(Payments)*
...
Item vnto nyne Enterlude players this yere   vj s. viij d.
...   35
Item more vnto certen Enterlyde players this yere   ij s. iiij d.
...

6/ comaundemt: *for* comaundement

1582–3
Mayors' Accounts   CRO: B/Lis/267
mb [2] *(Payments)*
...
Item geiven to Parre the Minstrell   ij s.   5
...
Item gave to certen Enterlude players   iij s. iiij d.
...

1604–5   10
Mayors' Accounts   CRO: B/Lis/268
mb [2] *(Payments)*
...
Item paid to players   xx s.
...   15

1606–7
Mayors' Accounts   CRO: B/Lis/270
mb [2] *(Payments)*
...   20
Item geiven to Players this yere   xij s.
...

1608–9
Mayors' Accounts   CRO: B/Lis/272   25
mb [1] *(Casual receipts)*
...
...Et de xij s. receptis de Petro Hambly et Iohanne Harell pro licencia
ad vendendum potum et ludendum in Guilhalda die Penticostis hoc
anno...   30
...

1631–2
Mayors' Accounts   CRO: B/Lis/284
mb [2]* *(Payments)*   35
...
Geiven to the players that Come with Commissions at two
severall tymes   xx s.
...

1635–6
Mayors' Accounts   CRO: B/Lis/288
mb [2]* *(Payments)*

…

Item given to S*ir* Willyam Wrey and diu*er*se other gent*lemen*   5
at the first Cockfistinge in wyne   vj s. viij d.

…

Item bestowed on S*ir* W*illya*m Wrey and diu*er*se other gentlemen
at the Cockmatch   iij s. iiij d.

…   10

LOSTWITHIEL

1536–7
St George's Guild Steward's Accounts   PRO: E 315/122   15
f 19v* *(Receipts)*

…

Item Receaued of Straungers in the day of the Rideng and the
morowe vppon   ix s. ij d.

…   20

f 20v* *(Payments)*

…

Item for the Skowring of St George's harnes   v d.

…   25

f 21*

Item paied for a paire of hose against St Georg*es* rideng   xx d.
Item for allowance for the dynn*er* on St Georg*es* rideng day   iij s.   30
Item paied to the vicar of lanleu*ery* for the pr*i*vie ffines of
St Georg*es* milles and to the Shryne   xv d.
Item paied to the piper for his labor at St Georg*es* rideng   xij d.
Item paied for two dowsen ˄⌜of poinct*es*⌝ for the tieing vp of
St Georg*es* harnes   iiij d.   35
Item paied to the Reckening at Robert Allens   viij d.
Item paied for the Skowringe of the harnes   xiij d.
Item for his boarde for iij daies   xj d.
Item I axe allowance for a chese   iiij d.
Item I offered at the masse of Req*ui*em the morowe after the Rideng   j d.   40
Item paied for bred at the latter ende of St Georg*es* rideng   [j d.] iiij d.

Item I axe allowance for oyle & grece for St George*s* harnes   iiij d.
Item paied for Skowgens at St George*s* Rideng   viij d.

...

f 22*   5

Item paied for nayles to Nicholas the britton for fastneng of
St George*s* harnes   viij d.

...

Item paied for two Crockes for to hange a Coverlet befor   10
St George[s] [rideng da] in the rideng day   ij d.

...

1602
Richard Carew, Survey of Cornwall   *STC*: 4615   15
sigs Nn1–1v

...

® Lostwithiel.

Lostwithiel should seeme to fetch his originall from the Cornish Loswithiall,
which in English, soundeth a Lions tayle: for as the Earle of this prouince
gaue the Lyon in armes, and the Lions principall strength (men say) consisteth   20
in his tayle; so this towne claymeth the precedence, as his Lords chiefest
residence, & the place which he entrusted with his Exchequer, and where his
wayghtier affaires were managed. Maioralty, markets, faires, and nomination
of Burgesses for the Parliament, it hath common with the most: Coynage of
Tynne, onely with three others; but the gayle for the whole Stannary, and   25
keeping of the County Courts, it selfe alone. Yet all this can hardly rayse it
to a tolerable condition of wealth and inhabitance. Wherefore I will de- | tayne
you no longer, then vntill I haue shewed you a solemne custome in times past
here yeerely obserued, and onely of late daies discontinued, which was thus:
Vpon little Easter Sunday, the Freeholders of the towne and mannour, by   30
themselues or their deputies, did there assemble: amongst whom, one (as it
fell to his lot by turne) brauely apparelled, gallantly mounted, with a Crowne
on his head, a scepter in his hand, a sword borne before him, and dutifully
attended by all the rest also on horseback, rode thorow the principall streete
to the Church: there the Curate in his best beseene, solemnely receiued him   35
at the Churchyard stile, and conducted him to heare diuine seruice: after
which, he repaired with the same pompe, to a house foreprouided for that
purpose, made a feast to his attendants, kept the tables end himselfe, and was
serued with kneeling, assay, & all other rites due to the estate of a Prince: with
which dinner, the ceremony ended, and euery man returned home again.   40
The pedigree of the vsage is deriued from so many descents of ages, that the
cause and authour outreach remembrance: howbeit, these circumstances

offer a coniecture, that it should betoken the royalties appertaining to the honour of Cornwall.

...

MANACCAN

1604

Bill of Complaint in Webber v. Kindsman et al PRO: STAC 8/304/38 single mb* *(29 October)*

To the kinges moste excellent Maiestye

In all humblenesse complayninge sheweth and enfourmeth your most excellent Maiestie your dutifull and obedient subiectes Matthew webber clarke and Suzan his wyfe That whereas your said subiectes by all the tyme of their entermarriage togeather haue liued in good name fame reputac*i*on and Credict amongst their neighbours w*i*thin the Countie of Cornewall and amongst others of your highnes good and lovinge sub*iec*tes of great accompte w*i*thout anye taint or towche of Infamye adulterye deceipte or breache of your highnes lawes statutes or ordynaunces Neuerthelesse one Iohn Snellinge of St keveren in the said Countye of Cornewall Sampson Roswarne of Sainct Columbes & one Iohn kynsman of Mannacken being men of badd lewde contentious and slaunderous disposic*i*on knowing the premisses to be true and consorting and confederatinge w*i*th diuers persons of lyke lewde disposic*i*on to your said S*u*biect as yet vnknowne whose names your said Subiect most humbly praieth maye be inserted into this Bill when they shalbe Learned & knowne did for all the tyme of one whole yeare now last paste vnlawfullye and maliciously Combyne practize and confederate togeather How and by what meanes they might vniustlye impeache Blemishe slaunder and drawe into question the good names Credictes honest and vnspotted reputac*i*ons of the said [Peter] ⸢Matthew and⸣ Suzan your highnes said Subiectes And for that purpose by vnlawfull Confederacy aforesaid They the said Iohn Snellinge Sampson Roswarne and Iohn kindsman not havinge the feare of God before their eies nor anye dutifull regimen of your Ma*ies*tyes good and godlye Lawes and Statutes haue for the space of one yeare now last past daylye of their p*re*pensed mallyce sediciously Contryved made and written published Caste & spread abroade a most faulse and sedic*i*ous Lybell of and againste your said Subiectes thereby to defame and discredit them w*i*th and amongste all oth*er*s your good & Lovinge sub*iec*tes and also to provoke and stirre vp dissenc*i*on and disagreement betweene them your said sub*iec*tes tendinge to the seperac*i*on of them a sonder And to make your said subiectes odyous and infamous to all people The tenor of w*hi*ch faulse sclaunderous and sedic*i*ous libell or Ryme so made and published and in reioycing manner

songe and said in diuers places and before diuers persons by the said Snelling,
Roswarne, and kindsman, of and againste [the] your said subiectes [which
said libell] is herevnto annexed which said sedicious libell or Ryme so beinge
wickedly faulselye and maliciouslye contryved and made by the said Snelling
Roswarne and Kindsman They the said Snelling Roswarne and kyndsman   5
did there by entende and meane and for all the tyme aforesaid haue expounded
the said libell to and against your said subiectes and haue published songe
said dispersed and spread abroade the said libell in diuers and sondrye places
and vnto diuers and sondrye of your Maiesties subiectes and haue likewise
giuen and deliuered Copies thereof to diuers persons, poinctinge at your   10
said subiectes as the parties meant by whome the said libell was made and
published entending thereby to make odyous and infamous your said subiectes
with all your Maiesties Subiectes and amongst all their ffreindes neighbours
and acquaintance and also to procure and worke dislyke discontentment and
seperacion betweene them the said Matthewe webber & Suzan your said   15
subiectes All which are vnfitt to be suffred to passe without impunitye in this
your highnes well governed common wealthe And they the said malicious
Conspiratours [Hughe] Snellinge Roswarne and kyndsman not satisfyed
with their said malicious makinge Contryvinge publishinge and dispersinge
of the said sedicious libell and Ryme against your said Subiectes to thentent   20
aforesaid But being reprooved by diuers persons of good sort & quallity for
their said slaunderous contryvinge and publishing of the said Rymes or
libells still perseueringe their mallicious and wicked purposes therein Haue
threatned and given owt in publique speaches that they would be reuenged
of all those persons eyther by beatinge woundinge or killinge of them that   25
did reprooue them the said libellours for then so doinge Or that should
disclose their said Conspiracyes & practizes And to that end and purpose by
the Confederacie aforesaid [the] your said Subiectes haue diuers tymes since
the last generall pardon threatned beaten miscalled and misvsed diuers of
your Maiesties said Subiectes for the cawses aforesaid By reason of which   30
said lewde & sedicious libells and Rymes the good names fames Credictes
and Reputacions of your said Subiectes is much impaired slaundered and
impeached: In tender consideracion whereof and for that all suche libellours
and Rymeres and the publishers and spreaders abroad of the same sclaunderous
libelles and Rymes should not escape vnpunished for their so wicked offences   35
and misdemeanours the same beinge all done and Comitted within two yeares
last past & since your Maiesties ˄⌈last⌉ gracious free & generall pardon And
for that also the same do tend to the Disturbance of your louinge & dutyfull
subiectes And are against your highnes moste godlye Lawes statutes and
ordynaunces royall estate & prerogatiue to graunte vnto your said Subiect   40

28/ your: y *corrected over* s

your highnes moste gracious Writtes of Su*b*pena to be dyrected to the said
Iohn Snellinge Sampson Roswarne and Iohn Kinsman Comaundinge them
and euerye of them thereby at a certayne daye and vnder a certayne paine
therein to be limitted personallye to appeare before yo*u*r Ma*ie*stye in your
highnesse most highe Co*u*rte of Starchamber at westminster then and there   5
to aunsweare the premysses And to abyde suche further order and dyrection
therein as to the Lo*rde*s and oth*er*s of yo*u*r highnesse said co*u*rte shalbe
thought meete and Convenyent And your said Sub*iecte*s shall daylye praye
vnto almightie God for yo*u*r Ma*ie*styes longe and happie raigne over vs./

R. Sturdye 10

PENRYN

1360–1
Episcopal Order to Glasney Collegiate Church   15
Devon Record Office: Chanter 3
ff ccviii verso – ccix verso* *(10 December)*

...

Inhibic*io*
Ep*iscop*i de
lud*is* i*n*honest*is*

...Ioh*ann*es miserac*i*one di*u*i*n*a Exoniens*is* Ep*iscop*us? dilec*t*is in chr*ist*o
filij*s* .. Custodi & Capit*u*lo ecclesie collegiate *sanct*e Marie de Otery 〈.〉os*t*re   20
fundacionis patronat*us* & dioc*es*is? Salutem & mor*um* cl*er*icalium honestatem.
Ad n*os*tram non sine gra*u*i cordis displicencia & stupore? p*er*uenit noticiam
qu*o*d annis pr*e*terit*is* & quibusdam pr*e*cedentib*us* in sacratissimis do*m*inice
Natiuitatis ac *sanct*orum Steph*an*i Ioh*ann*is ap*osto*li & euangeliste, ac
Innocencium sollempnijs q*ua*ndo om*ne*s chr*ist*i fideles diuinis laudib*us* &   25
officijs ecclesiasticis, deuocius ac q*u*iescius insistere tenent*ur*, aliqui pr*e*dic*t*e
ecclesie n*os*tre Ministri, cu*m* pueris, nedu*m* matutinis & vesp*er*is ac horis
alijs? sed qu*o*d magis detestandu*m* est, intra missar*um* sollempnia, ludos
ineptos & noxios honestatiq*ue* cl*er*icali indecentes, quin v*er*ius cultus diuini
ludibria detestanda infra ecclesiam ipsam inmiscendo co*m*mittere, diuino   30
timore postposito, p*er*niciso, quar*un*dam ecclesiarum exemplo tem*er*e
pr*e*sumpserunt, vestimenta & alia ornamenta ecclesie non modicum eiusdem
ecclesie n*os*tre & n*os*tru*m* da*m*pnum & dedecus, vilium *scilicet* scenulentor*um*que
sparsione multip*l*ic*iter* det*u*rpando, Ex quor*um* gestis scurilib*us* & cachinnis
derisorijs nedu*m* p*o*p*u*lus more catholico illis potissime temporib*us* ad   35
ecclesiam co*n*ueniens a debita deuocione abstrahit*ur*, sed & in risum
incompositum ac oblectamenta illicita, dissoluit*ur* cultusque diuin*us* irridet*ur*
& officium p*er*peram impedit*ur*. Sicq*ue* quod ad excitandum & augendu*m*
fidelium deuocionem fu*er*at pr*i*mit*us* adinuentum, ex talium insollencijs in

---

20/ 〈.〉ostre: *for* nostre *or* Nostre   32/ non: *3 minims for first* n *in* MS
31/ p*er*niciso: *for* pernicioso   34/ cachinnis: *7 minims in* MS

dei & *sanctorum* irreuerenciam & contemptu*m* non sine reatu blasphemie co*n*uersum *vel* pocius est *per*uersum. Nequeuntes igit*ur* vlterius sana consciencia, abusiones tam nephandas s*ub* dissimila*ci*one absq*ue* remedio p*er*transire, vob*is* Iniungim*us* & mandam*us* s*ub* pena suspensionis & excommunica*ci*onis quatin*us* ab hui*usmodi* insollencijs & irrisionib*us* deceter*o* total*iter* desistatis, & nulla talia exn*unc* in eadem ecclesia fieri quo*modo*libet *per*mittatis. *Sed* ad explendu*m* dlulnum ufficiu*m* p*r*out ip*sorum* dieru*m* exig*it* reuerencia deuocius solito intendatis. Et ne ex ignorancia quisquam exn*unc* vnq*uam* in hac p*ar*te se valeat excusare: vobis .. Custodi precipimus q*uod* presentes litteras *n*ostras ante instans festu*m* Natal*is* domi*n*i in presencia omniu*m* Ministroru*m* sollempni*ter* publicetis eademq*ue* li*tt*eras *n*ostras ne in obliuione*m* | transeant in quatuor vel q*u*inq*ue* libris ecclesie magis vsualib*us* transcribi fideli*ter* faciatis. Si qui *v*ero contra *p*resens mandatu*m* *n*ost*rum* venire *p*resumpserint citetis seu citari faciatis *per*emptori*e*, q*uod* comp*ar*eant coram nob*is* *ter*cio die iuridico post lapsum d*ictarum* festiuitatu*m* sup*er* tam tem*er*aria *p*resump*ci*one responsuri, & condignam penitenciam recepturi. De die *v*ero recep*ci*onis presenciu*m*, & quid in hac p*ar*te fec*er*itis: nos citra festu*m* Circumcisionis domi*n*i *cer*tificetis *per* vestras patentes li*tt*eras haru*m* seriem continentes. sigillo vestro commu*n*i consignatas. Dat*a* in Manerio *n*ostro de Chuddelegh: decimo die mens*is* Decembr*is* Anno domi*n*i Millesimo .CCC.ᵐᵒ Sexagesimo. Et Consecr*a*cionis *n*ostre, xxxiiijᵗᵒ....

(7 January)

℃ Emanarunt consimiles li*tt*ere paucis *v*erbis mutatis .. decano .. Precent*ori* & .. Cancell*ario* ecclesie cath*edralis* Exon*iensis* .. Cantori & Capit*u*lo ecclesie collegiate *sanct*e Crucis Cryditon/ ac .. Preposito & Capit*u*lo ecclesie collegio *sanct*i Thome martiris Glasneye ... Et hoc modo fuit certificatu*m* p*er* .. Prepositu*m* & Capit*u*lum ecclesie colleg*iate* *sanct*i Thome Martiris Glasneye. Reu*er*endo in ch*r*isto p*at*ri ac d*omi*no/ domino Ioha*n*ni dei gra*ci*a Exon*iensis* Ep*iscop*o: sui humiles & deuoti .. Preposit*us* & Capit*u*lum ecclesie vestre collegiate *sanct*i Thome M*art*ir*is* Glasneye obed*ienci*am & reu*er*encia*m* debit*am* tanto p*at*ri cu*m* om*n*i subiectione & honore: Mandatu*m* vestru*m* reu*er*endu*m* in vigilia Nat*alis* domi*n*i recepim*us* in hec *v*erba. Ioha*n*nes &c. vt s*up*ra exceptis paucis *v*erbis mutatis. Cuius auc*t*orita*te* mandati vestri reu*er*endi: om*n*ia in d*ic*to mandato *v*estro contenta in d*ic*ta vigilia: Ego .. p*re*posit*us* anted*ic*tus in presencia omniu*m* Ministroru*m* d*ic*te ecclesie p*r*out mandat*ur* publicaui/ & ne talia in d*ic*ta ecclesia a*m*modo fiant: publi*c*e & sollemp*n*iter inhibui/ eademq*ue* li*tt*eras *v*estras reu*er*endas/ in missali/ Martiligio & Collectario feci t*r*anscribi/ et mandatu*m* *v*estru*m* originali libro

27/ collegio: *for* collegiate

statutor*um* *dicte* ecclesie annexui/ Et nullu*m* Ministror*um* *dicte* ecclesie *vestre*⸳
contra mandatu*m* *vestrum* in aliquo venientem inueni. Et *sic* mandatu*m*
vestr*um* reu*er*endu*m* in omnibus sum*us* plene & reu*er*|enter executi. Da*ta*
Glasneye in crastino Epiphanie d*omi*ni. Anno d*omi*ni supradicto

...   5

c 1600
Thomas Heywood, An Apology for Actors   STC: 13309
sig G2*

...   10

® A strange
accident
happening at a
play.

    As strange an accident happened to a company of the same quality some
12 yeares ago, or not so much, who playing late in the night at a place called
Perin in Cornwall, certaine Spaniards were landed the same night vnsuspected,
and vndiscouered, with intent to take in the towne, spoyle and burne it, when
suddenly, euen vpon their entrance, the players (ignorant as the townes-men 15
of any such attempt) presenting a battle on the stage with their drum and
trumpets strooke vp a lowd alarme: which the enemy hearing, and fearing
they were discouered, amazedly retired, made some few idle shot in a brauado,
and so in a hurly-burly fled disorderly to their boats. At the report of this
tumult, the townes-men were immediatly armed, and pursued them to the 20
sea, praysing God for their happy deliuerance from so great a danger, who by
his prouidence made these strangers the instrument and secondary meanes
of their escape from such imminent mischife, and the tyranny of so remorceless
an enemy.

...   25

POUGHILL

1550–1
St Olaf Churchwardens' Accounts   CRO: P/192/5/1   30
p 89* *(Payments)*
...

payd to the kyng*es* enterluyd plaers & for there dener   viij s. ij d.
...

35

ST BREOCK

1557–8
St Briocus Churchwardens' Accounts   CRO: P/19/5/1
f 6v* *(Receipts)*   40

The daunsers   Made ther accou*n*te & hath payed in clere gaynys   iij li. ij s. iij d.

Svsanna ys
Playe

Chrystoffer Rychard made hys accounte & hath payed to the
store clere   xxxvj s.

...

1565–6
St Briocus Churchwardens' Accounts   CRO: P/19/5/1
f 17v *(30 May–22 May) (Payments)*

...

payed to lydwan dauncers   iij s.

...

1566–7
St Briocus Churchwardens' Accounts   CRO: P/19/5/1
f 19 *(22 May–7 May) (Payments)*

...

Item payed to an enterlwd players of Saint denys   iij s. iiij d.

...

1567–8
St Briocus Churchwardens' Accounts   CRO: P/19/5/1
f 20v *(7 May 1567–18 May 1568) (Payments)*

...

Item payed to a daunce of gramputh   iiij s.

...

1571–2
St Briocus Churchwardens' Accounts   CRO: P/19/5/1
f 28* *(23 May–14 May) (Payments)*

...

payed to a dawnce of the west partyes besydes hys gatheryng   viij d.

...

1573–4
St Briocus Churchwardens' Accounts   CRO: P/19/5/1
f 32* *(29 April 1573–19 May 1574) (Receipts)*

Received off Robyn hoode & hys Cumpanye   vj s. vj d.
Received off Robyn hoode & hys Cumpanye for wd   xv s.

...

9/ lydwan: *probably Ludgvan*
16/ enterlwd: *for* enterlewd *(?)*

23/ gramputh: *probably Grampound*
38/ wd: *for* wood; *abbreviation mark missing*

1574–5
St Briocus Churchwardens' Accounts   CRO: P/19/5/1
f 35 *(19 May–11 May)* *(Payments)*
...

payd to the dawnce off sent Evall	xvj d.	5
payd to the dawnce off fylleck	ij s. vj d.	

...

1590–1
St Briocus Churchwardens' Accounts   CRO: P/19/5/1
f 51* *(27 May–12 May)* *(Payments)*   10
...

Item given by Consent of the parish vnto the players of
Robyn Hoode that Came from St Cullombe the Lower   v s.
...   15

1591–2
St Briocus Churchwardens' Accounts   CRO: P/19/5/1
f 54v *(12 May–3 May)* *(Payments)*
...   20

Item gaue vnto the Robyn hoode of Maugan   v s.

ST COLUMB MAJOR

1584–5   25
St Columba the Virgin Churchwardens' Accounts   CRO: P/36/8/1
f [10]* *(30 November–30 November)* *(Parish goods)*
...

Theare are belonginge to this parisshe die et anno ut supra a *(blank)* Ladder
v Coates for Dancers/ A ffryers Coate. 24. dansinge belles/ A streamer of   30
Red moccado and [Boc] Locram. vj yardes of white wollen clothe
...

1585–6
St Columba the Virgin Churchwardens' Accounts   CRO: P/36/8/1   35
f [14]* *(30 November–30 November)* *(Parish goods)*
...

Suche churche goods and parisshe goods as is this daye belonginge to this
parisshe and are as ffolloweth.... 5 coates for dancers/ 1 friers coate/ 24

14/ St Cullombe the Lower: *St Columb Minor*

dansinge bell*es*/ a streamer of Red moccado and Locram/ 6 *yards* of white
wollen clothe...

...

1587–8
St Columba the Virgin Churchwardens' Accounts   CRO: P/36/8/1
f [18] *(30 November–30 November) (Receipts)*

...

Rec*eaved* for the lont of the Robbyn hoodes clothes xviij d....

f [19] *(Parish goods)*

...

The Churche goods and other goods belonginge to this p*a*rish and vewed this
daye are as followith ... 5. morrisshe Coates 20 dancinge bells/ 1 streamer
of Red moccado and Locrum...

...

1588–9
St Columba the Virgin Churchwardens' Accounts   CRO: P/36/8/1
f [21v] *(30 November–30 November) (Parish goods)*

...

The Churche goods and other thing*es* belonging to this p*a*rish and vewed
this daye and deliu*e*red to the wardens of the yere now ensewith ... 5. morrishe
Coates/ 20 dancing bells/ A streamer of Red moccado an locru*m*...

...

1589–90
St Columba the Virgin Churchwardens' Accounts   CRO: P/36/8/1
f [23v] *(30 November–30 November) (Parish goods)*

...

The olde wardens do this daye deliu*er* vnto Marke Retallacke and Iohn peirs
the said goods in p*a*rcells as followeth.... 6. morrisshe Coates/ 20 dansing
belles/ A streamer of red moccado And Locrum....

...

1590–1
St Columba the Virgin Churchwardens' Accounts   CRO: P/36/8/1
f [24v]* *(30 November–30 November) (Parish goods)*

...

The olde wardens do deliver this daye vnto Sampson Bray and willi*a*m

23/ the wardens: *John Nuttell and Stephen Hurvye*
31/ Marke Retallacke and Iohn peirs: *newly elected wardens 1589–90*

Cocke the said goods in parcells as ffollowethe ... 6 morishe cootes/ 20
daunsing bells/ A Streamer of red moccado & loccrum...

...

1594–5   5
St Columba the Virgin Churchwardens' Accounts   CRO: P/36/8/1
f [28v] *(30 November–30 November) (Debts)*

...

Rychard beard owethe to be payd at our ladye daye in lent x s./ of Robyn
hoodes monyes   10
Robert calwaye owethe ∧⌈for ye same⌉   ij s. viij d.
ffrances Bennye owethe x s. [⟨...⟩ ij d.]/ Iohn lae owethe   iij s.
wyllyam Tryscot owethe vj s. ij d./ Iohn Pers owethe xij d.

(Receipts)   15

Thomas Braben hathe brought in hys dancyng Coate

...

(Parish goods)   20

There Remaynethe in ye paris wardens kepyng ... syxe old moryshe cotes &
a newe moryshe Coate with ye wardens...

...

                                                                               25

1595–6
St Columba the Virgin Churchwardens' Accounts   CRO: P/36/8/1
f [29v] *(30 November–30 November) (Parish goods)*
...
Ther is deliuered into the hands of Robert Darr and Io Trobelfold the wardens ...   30
seven morishe Cotes...

...

1596–7
St Columba the Virgin Churchwardens' Accounts   CRO: P/36/8/1   35
f [30v]* *(30 November–30 November) (Parish goods)*
...
There is delivered vnto Thomas Dara and martin Rowe wardens of the
parishe for this the parishe goods viz ... Seaven morishe Cottes...
...   40

p 508, l.40–p 509, l.1/ Sampson Bray and william Cocke: *newly elected wardens 1590–1*

1604
Bill of Complaint in Webber v. Kindsman et al   PRO: STAC 8/304/38

See Manaccan 1604

5

1615
Bill of Complaint in Lawry v. Dier et al   PRO: STAC 8/202/30
mb 3* *(22 June)*

To the King*es* most excellent Ma*ie*stie   10
In all humblenes Complayning doe shewe and informe vnto your most
excellent Ma*ie*stie: your Ma*ie*sties loyall and obedient Subiect*es* Hugh Lawry
of St Collombe in the County of Cornwall Carpenter and Mary his wief
That whereas your said Subiect*es* now are and from the tymes of their seuerall
nativities hetherto respectiuely haue byn of modest and honest fame and   15
Conversac*i*on and euer since their intermariage haue lived soberly and lovingly
together as becommeth Man and wief to their owne Mutuall Content*es* and
the good example of others And whereas there is nothing that doth more
iniuriously blemish the reputac*i*on of your Ma*ie*sties loving Subiect*es* nor tend
more to the breach of your Ma*ie*sties lawes and peace and the disturbance of 20
your highnes most happy gouernement then the Contriving and publishing of
infamous obscene and scandalous libells and the stirring vpp and nourishing
of discorde and debate betwixt Man and wief Yet so it is Most gratious
Souereigne the p*re*misses notwithstanding That on or neere about the ffirst
day of Aprill in this Thirteenth yeere of your Ma*ie*sties most happy Raigne   25
ouer this your highnes Realme of England One Iohn dier of St Collombe
aforesaid yoman Beniamyn Strangman of the same yeoman, Iohn Strangman
the younger of the same yoman, Honor Strangman of the same, and Iunyfer
Benny of the same: together with diuerse other p*er*sons to your said subiect*es*
yet vnknowne and whose names your said Subiect*es* desire may be inserted   30
into this Bill when they shalbe knowne: At St Collomb aforesaid did most
vnlawfully plot practise Combyne and Consult together how they might
blemish the reputac*i*ons of your said Subiect*es* and more especially the
reputac*i*on of your said Subiect Mary and also how they might stirr vpp and
nourish discord betweene your said Subiect*es* by some such libell as aforesaid 35
And then and there by the Combynac*i*on and to the intent aforesaid, they the
said Iohn dier, Beniamyn Strangman, Iohn Strangman, Honor Strangman,
and Iunyfer Benny some or one of them with the previtie abetment and
approbation of the rest of them as also of the said p*er*sons vnknowne did
falsly and maliciously invent contriue and write a most infamous, scurrilous, 40
obscene and slaunderous libell or writing contayning most filthy and

reprochful Matter of slaunder and disgrace secretly ment and intended to
and agaynst both your said Subiect*es*, more especially agaynst your said
Subiect Mary by and vnder the name or discription of a Wench, of a Mayden
become a wief, and in and by the said libell supposed or intimated to lie at
the said Towne of St Colombe Where your said Subiect*es* are indeede resident   5
and abiding, And agaynst your said Subiect Hugh by and vnder the name of
a Carpenter in and by the same libell most obscenely supposed or intimated
to haue had Carnall Company With the said Mary being become a wief, the
tenor or effect of which said libell here followeth in these words Viz.: yf there
be any Man that can tell me quickelye a Medicyne for to Cure a wench that   10
is greeued sore and sicklye, let him Come at St Collomb Towne and there he
shall haue newes, where lyes this wench oppressed sore as it will make you
muse, the ground of this here is as I haue heard it spoken, shee alwayes doth
bedue her sheat*es* her flood hatch it is broken, and the streame of it runneth
through the brooke as shee lies sleeping, her vilme was broken with a thrust   15
for out her pisse doth flye, which greef of hers to help full many hath assaide,
but all their labor was in vayne they could not cure the Mayd, then shee
thought on an other trick shee needs would Change her lief, shee sold away
her Maydenhood and is become a wief, and then there came a Carpenter
who thought sure with a Pyn, to mend her floodgate and thereby to kepe   20
her water in, he tooke great Payne and wore his flesh and loked thin and
pale, but all his labor was in vayne he could not good at all, then out shee
Cries most bitterly and still the tyme doth Curse, that shee the Chamber
pott should hold and ope her neither purse, wherein dispaire entred and off
the strapps rented, which brooke her gate and spilde her state which runneth   25
like a vent, yf soone shee be not cured great Pynnes will beare greate price, a
greate Pyn for a Chamber pott because shee will not rise, then shee a Mayde
p*er*force must hire the Chamber pott to sett, which still will stand her a
greate Pynne els shee bedd must weatt, but I haue heard her say of late such
vertue is in myse, they are very good for the disease so they be bake in pies,   30
first they must stripp away the skyn and afterwards them bake, and for full
three dayes after no other meate must take, and then they must take the skins
and heate them good and warme, uppon a Chaffer dishe and coles least Cold
should doe her harme, and clapp some on her breast and some vppon her
hall, butt lett her put most p*ar*te of them vppon her what I call, therefore all   35
you good farmers when you doe turne your corne, saue vpp all the myse you
catch for M*ist*ris and bring downe vnto her house, it shalbe for your gayne
for shee will content you for your cost and payne, but if this will not serue a
lack what shall I saye, some other phisick lett take her greef for to allay, if

26/ will: i *written over another letter*

Phisick will not helpe then lett goe with speede, and take some heare and
sue her geare and bite away the threade, :. And farder so it is most gratious
Souereigne that the said libell being so invented contriued and written as
aforesaid, they the said Iohn dier Beniamyn Strangman, Iohn Strangman,
Honor Strangman and Iunyfer Benny some or one of them with the *previtie*   5
abetment and approbation of the rest of them as also of the said *persons*
vnknowne at St Cullombe aforesaid by the Combynation aforesaid and to
the intent aforesaid on or about the said ffirst day of Aprill and at diuerse
dayes and tymes since haue written and deliuered or caused to be written
and deliuered to very Many of your Maiesties loving Subiect*es* the Neighbors   10
frindes and acquayntance of your said Subiect*es* and vnto diuerse others
diuerse Copies and transcript*es* of the said libell, and haue likewise both
vppon the said ffirst day of Aprill and at sundry tymes since in the hearing
of such others of your Maiesties loving Subiect*es* as aforesaid at St Colomb
aforesaid by the Combynac*ion* and to the intent aforesaid openly and with a   15
lowde voyce read rehearsed spoken vttered sunge *proc*laymed published and
divulged in most scoffing and disgracefull Manner the word*es* Matter and
effect of the said libell affirming the same to be true and saying with all that
they would iustifie the Matter thereof and cause the boyes of the said Towne
of St Colombe publiquely and openly to singe the same allowde in the   20
street*es* of the same Towne or to the like effect, All which plott*es* practises
Combynations and Consultations and other offences and misdeameanors
aforesaid were had contriued and executed since your Maiesties last most
gratious generall and free Pardon and are to the high displeasure of Almightie
godd and contrary to your Maiesties lawes and peace and to the euell example   25
also of your Maiesties well disposed Subiect*es* if the same should passe without
some exemplary punishment And to ₐ⌈the⌉ greate scandall and disgrace of
your said Subiect*es* as aforesaid and are examinable and punishable by and
before your Maiestie and the Lords of your Maiesties most Honorable privie
Counsell in your Maiesties High Court of Starr Chamber May it therefore   30
please your Maiestie to graunt vnto your said Subiect*es* your highnes most
gratious writes of Subpena to be directed vnto them the said Iohn dier
Beniamyn Strangman Iohn Strangman the younger Honor Strangman and
Iunyfer Benny and to euery of them thereby Commaunding them at a certen
day and vnder a certen payne therein to be lymitted *per*sonally to be and   35
appeere before your Maiestie and the Lords of your Maiesties most honorable
privie Counsell in the high Court of Starr Chamber Then and there to
aunswere the *pr*emisses and to receaue such punishment as shall stand with
iustice and their demerit*es* And your highnes said Subiect*es* according to their
bounden duties will hartilie pray vnto god for your Maiesties most happy and   40
prosp*er*ous Raigne long to Continue.

Ioh*n* Glanuill:.

1615–16
St Columba the Virgin Churchwardens' Accounts   CRO: P/36/8/1
f [48] *(30 November–30 November) (Receipts)*

...

And geiuen by the young men of the parish which plaide   5
a stage play   iij s. iiij d.

...

ST IVES

10

1571–2
Borough Accounts 1   St Ives Guildhall
f 3* *(Names of officials)*

...

Iames huchin ⎤   15
                        kinge & Quen⟨...⟩ somme⟨...⟩s.
Ienat ootes ⎦

...

f 3v* *(Receipts)*

...   20
Item receiued the first daye of the playe   xij
Item receiued the seconde daye which amounteth to   j   xij   ij
Item receiued the thirde daye which amounteth to   iiij   x   xj
Item receiued the fourthe daye which amounteth to   j   xix   vj
Item receiued the 5 daye which amountethe to   iij   ij   25
Item receiued the sixt daye which amountethe to   iij   j
Item more receiued for drincke monye which amounteth   j   ij
Item more receiued of william trinwith in the churche yeard
whiche amountethe to   j   xvj   ij
Item receivyd for drincke monye after the playe   ij   viij 30
Item receiuyd ⟨...⟩he churche wardons to bestowe upon poore
pe⟨..⟩le which mr Coswarthe gave   vij
Item receiuyd for ⟨...⟩ xiiij pounde of tithe butter   v   x
Item receiuyd of ⟨...⟩ wardons of the market house
Item r⟨....⟩ued of ⟨...⟩ wardons of the Keye   iij   xix   x   35
⟨...⟩d ⟨...⟩es huchine for the somer games   xiiij   vj
⟨...⟩ wardens of the eyle   xviij

...

15/ ⟨...⟩ somme⟨...⟩s.: MS torn 17mm and 16mm   36/ ⟨...⟩d ⟨...⟩es: MS torn 33 mm and 13 mm
31, 33, 35/ ⟨...⟩: MS torn 8 mm   37/ ⟨...⟩: MS torn 57 mm
34/ ⟨...⟩: MS torn 11 mm

f 4* *(Payments)*

...

Item payd to mr laynyane for iiij trees	j
Item payd to the pypers for there wages	⟨...⟩
Item payd to william barreat for xiij pound of hops	ij
Item payd to Iohn goman for a barell of drink	iiij
Item payd to one of the Carpenters	ij

5

...

f 4v* *(Payments)*

10

	li.	s.	d.

...

⟨...⟩ to a man of earthe for making hurdels	iiij	ij
⟨...⟩ to carveddris for mr bears dinner		xj
⟨...⟩ to thomas hickes to deliver mr trinwithe ⟨...⟩yd			15
thinges for the playe		iij

...

⟨...⟩ for halfe a dosin of white lambes skyns	ij
⟨...⟩d to Tregerthar for cutting the trees	iiij
⟨...⟩yd to standlye for a lynge when the ⟨...⟩ were about the playne	x

20

...

⟨...⟩ payd to martine goodall for ij dosin of lams skynes	
which amountethe to	iiij

...

Item spent vpon the carpenters yat made hevin	iiij

25

...

1572–3

Borough Accounts *1*   St Ives Guildhall
f 6* *(Names of officials)*

30

...

Harrie sterrie ⎫	
Iane walshe ⎰	Kinge & Quene of ye sommer ga⟨...⟩

...

4/ ⟨...⟩: MS torn at edge 14 mm; since pound
   column is visible but there is no sum there, we
   know the pipers' payment was in shillings or pence
13/ ⟨...⟩: MS torn at edge 27 mm
13/ earthe: St Erth
14, 15/ ⟨...⟩: MS torn at edge 25 mm

15/ ⟨...⟩yd: MS torn at edge 22 mm
18/ ⟨...⟩: MS torn at edge 22 mm
19/ ⟨...⟩d: MS torn at edge 17 mm
20/ ⟨...⟩yd: MS torn at edge 15 mm
20/ ⟨...⟩: MS torn at edge 16 mm
22/ ⟨...⟩: MS torn at edge 10 mm

f 6v* *(Receipts)*

	li.	s.	d.
...			
Item receiuyd of Iohn Clarke for ye enterlude	j	xj	5
Item receiuyd of william Trinwith for six score and thre			
foote of elme bordes in ye playing place		vj	
Item receiuyd of harrie hayne for 3 bordes		j	vj
...			
Item receiued of the kinge and quene for the somer games	j		iiij 10
...			

f 7* *(Payments)*

...

Item payd to Iohn william for thinges which he delyueryd aboute the laste   15
playe ⟨...⟩
Item more paid to mr thomas trinwith to paye co⟨...⟩
of Trewro for lyneclothe ⟨...⟩
...

20

1573–4
Borough Accounts *i*   St Ives Guildhall
f 7v *(Names of officials)*
...

Iohn ootes ⎫
margaret hockin ⎬ kinge & quene of ye sommer game   25
...

1578–9
Borough Accounts *i*   St Ives Guildhall   30
f 10* *(Receipts)*
...

Item Recevyd of Thomas Eva & Elizabeth amys kynge and
Quene of the somer game   vij s. vj d.
...
35

16/ ⟨...⟩: MS torn at edge 34 mm
17/ co⟨...⟩: MS torn at edge 38 mm
18/ ⟨...⟩: MS torn at edge 44 mm

f 11* *(Payments)*

...

Item payd for Cadwellye w*hich* was gevyn the dyer when he
was kynge by order gevin me   iiij s. vj ⟨.⟩

...   5

1583-4
Borough Accounts *1*   St Ives Guildhall
f 13 *(Names of officials)*

...   10

gregor*ie* polkenhorne ⎫
mary nancothan   ⎬   kinge & quene of the som*m*er game
                    ⎭

f 13v* *(Receipts)*

                                                          li.   s.   d. 15

...

Item Rec*eived* of Iamis pormantor for the Roben houde   xvj
Item Rec*eived* of harry stery att twelth efe   vj

1585-6
Borough Accounts *1*   St Ives Guildhall   20
f 56* *(Names of officials)*

...

harrye heck*es*   ⎫
Elyzabeth cockyn   ⎬   kyng & quene of the summer game
...   ⎭   25

f 56v *(Receipts)*

...

Item Receved from the king and quene   xxij   30
...

1586-7
Borough Accounts *1*   St Ives Guildhall
f 16* *(Payments)*   35

...

Item paid the players of Germal which gathered for yeir church   ij s.
...

17l Item ... xvj: *a sketch of a pointing hand is in left margin of this entry*
30l Item ... xxij: *a sketch of a pointing hand in different ink is in left margin of this entry*
37l Germal: *the parish of Germoe*

1587–8
Borough Accounts ı   St Ives Guildhall
f 17v* *(Receipts)*

…

Item Received of Thomas candrowe ffor thacompe of yonge   5
candrowe beinge the kinge of the maye game   0 . 04 . 4

…

(Payments)

…   10
Item gave the·Robin howde of St colloms the lower by
thapointment of mr tregera   0 . 05 . 0

…

1590–1   15
Borough Accounts ı   St Ives Guildhall
f 22* *(Receipts)*

…

Reseved of Thomas Iames his sonn being Sommer kinge   x s.

…   20
Reseved of william Stirrie kinge of the maye game this yere   xiij s. vij d.

…

1591–2
Borough Accounts ı   St Ives Guildhall   25
f 24v* *(Receipts)*

                                                              li.   s.   d.

…
Item receiued of Ioell hicks for sommer games   0 – 18 – 0

…   30

1594–5
Borough Accounts ı   St Ives Guildhall
f 5* *(Receipts)*

…   35
Item for the Sommer games of Iohn hosear   xix s. iiij d.

…

11/ St colloms the lower: *St Columb Minor*
21/ this yere: *written in over accounting line*

1595–6
Borough Accounts I   St Ives Guildhall
f 19* *(Names of officials)*

...

Nyclys Hick*es* ⎤
Iane sterrye ⎦   lord & Ladie of þe som*er* games   5

...

1596–7
Borough Accounts I   St Ives Guildhall   10
f 51* *(5 December) (Receipts)*

...

Item Rec*eyve*d of Stephen Barbar for p*ar*te of the profitt made
by the Sommer games remayninge in his hand*es*   vj s.

...   15

1615–16
Borough Accounts I   St Ives Guildhall
f 61* *(Rendered 20 October) (Receipts)*

...   20

More Iames Stearye rec*eive*d of ⎫   wherof p*ai*d [him] ⌈henrye⌉
henrye Shapland and Eliz*abeth* ⎬   S⟨...⟩ ij to helpe make a m⟨..⟩
Taylor lorde & ladye att ⎬   x s.   pole–vnto a la⟨..⟩ & viij s to
the Sommer games ⎭   paye s*er*gea⟨..⟩ maior: ⟨...⟩

...   25

1633–4
Borough Accounts I   St Ives Guildhall
f 79* *(Receipts)*

...   30

Collected by Io*h*n the sonn of Henrie Stephens and Margerie the
daughter of Edward Ham*m*ande be Chosen Lord and Ladie the
sum*me* of xiiij s. and by them deliu*e*red to the overseers of the
poore for this yere   xiiij s.

22/ S⟨...⟩: MS *torn at edge*
24/ ⟨...⟩: MS *torn at edge*

1639–40
Borough Accounts *II*   St Ives Guildhall
f 3v* *(1 November–1 November) (Payments)*

	li.	s.	d.

...

memorandum given to mr Robert Arundle when he brought
the Cupp given by his Maister to our Towne   02 // 00 // 00
memorandum more att that tyme att mr Hammande*s* spent   00 // 16 // 00

...

1640–1
Borough Accounts *II*   St Ives Guildhall
f 4* *(1 November–1 November) (Payments)*

	li.	s.	d.

...

memorandum more received from the Lord and Ladie last
yeare past   00 – 08 – 00

...

ST KEVERNE

1604
Bill of Complaint in Webber v. Kindsman et al   PRO: STAC 8/304/38

See Manaccan 1604

ST NEOT

1611
Inventory of Thomas Pomeray   CRO: AP/P/245/2
single sheet *(6 May; proved 29 April 1612)*

...

Item a Harpe   iij s. iiij d.

...

SANCREED

1568
A ***Deposition of John Veal et al***   CRO: X/50/5
pp 26–7* *(20 June)*

...

        Men Sworn touching the liberties of Conerton and the
            Hundred of Penwyth appendant to the Manor

Iohn Veal of Boriane Gentleman of the age of 78. Sworn at a Court holden
at Pensance the 20th. Day of [the] Iune Anno decimo Elizabethe by William
Gilbert under Steward of the Hundred Court of penwyth being upon his
Oath Examined Touching the Liberties of Connerton and the Hundred of
penwyth appendant unto the same Manor saith that when he was a Boy of   5
good Remembrance his Grandfather and his Father both dwelling than at
Sanckras within the hundred of Penwyth did see one Sir Iohn Trevrye knight
a Sanctuary Man at St. Borians which had committed some great offence
then against the King and thereupon Comitted to the Tower & by means of
a servant which he had, broke prison & came into Cornwall to Saint Borian   10
and claimed the priviledge of the Sanctuary: It fortuned within a while after
there was a Mirable Play at Sanckras Parish divers Men came to the play
amongst whom came a Servant of this Mr. Trevrye – named Quenall and (in
the Place before the | Play began) the said Quenal fell at Variance with one
Richard Iames Veane & so both went out of the Play and fought together   15
the said Quenall had a sword & a Buckler, and the other had a single Sword
the said Quenall was a very tall Man in his Hight; the other gave back and
fell over a Mole Hill and e're he could recover himself: the said Quena⟨..⟩
thrust his sword through him and so immediately dyed and Quenall taken
and bound to the End of the Play: and before the Play was done his Master   20
hearing thereof came to the Place with other Sanctuary Men and by force
would have taken him away from his said Grandfather Mr. Veal and others
but he was not able so to do but with a Suffitient Guard he was Carried to
Conertone Goal Where he was after hanged on the Gallows in Conerton
Down and so was more in his Time for there was no prisoner then Carried   25
to Launston Goal

Davyc Parkin Parson of Redruythe of the age of 80. Years Sayth as Mr. Veal
hath said
Richard Gossen of the age of 78. Sayth as Mr. Veal hath said   30
William Rawe of the age of 87. Saith as Mr. Veal hath said
Iames Cook of the age of 90 *(blank)*
...

12/ Mirable: *written over an erased word which may have begun with* M *and ended with* y *or* g
18/ Quena⟨..⟩: *edge trimmed*

STRATTON

1522–3
St Andrew Churchwardens' Accounts   BL: Additional MS. 32243
f 12* *(10 February–8 February) (High Cross wardens' receipts)*
...
Item rece*v*yd of the Egyppcions for the church howse   xx d.
...

1526–7
St Andrew Churchwardens' Accounts   BL: Additional MS. 32243
f 14v *(5 February–3 February) (High Cross wardens' receipts)*
...
Item rece*v*yd of the ber*e*hurd*es* for to haue rome yn the churchhowse   ij d.
...

f 15 *(High Cross wardens' payments)*
...
Item p*ai*d for a bhare   ij d.
...

1535–6
St Andrew Churchwardens' Accounts   BL: Additional MS. 32244
f 4* *(16 November–14 November) (Stockwardens' receipts)*
...
Item rece*v*yd of I Greby w*hi*ch was callyd Robynhode & of
hys felows   xij s. iiij d.
...

1536–7
St Andrew Churchwardens' Accounts   BL: Additional MS. 32244
f 5v *(15 November–12 November) (Stockwardens' receipts)*
...
Item rece*v*yd of Iohn Mar*es* & of hys company þ*at* playd
Robyn hoode   xxxviij s. ⌈iiij d.⌉
...

1538–9
St Andrew Churchwardens' Accounts   BL: Additional MS. 32243
f 32v *(4 February 1537/8–9 February 1538/9) (High Cross wardens' receipts)*
...
Item rece*v*yd of players at þe church howse   ·   iiij d.
...

St Andrew Churchwardens' Accounts   BL: Additional MS. 32244
f 6v *(13 November 1538–18 November 1539) (Stockwardens' receipts)*
…
Item rec*evyd* of Robyn hode & of hys men   iij li. x d.
…

1539–40
St Andrew Churchwardens' Accounts   BL: Additional MS. 32243
f 34 *(10 February–7 February) (High Cross wardens' receipts)*
…
Item rec*evyd* of players for þe church howse   j d.
…

1543–4
St Andrew Churchwardens' Accounts   BL: Additional MS. 32244
f 13 *(13 November 1543–18 November 1544) (Stockwardens' receipts)*
…
Item rec*evyd* of mathe Rose & margaret martyn for the wode of
Robyn hode is howse   iij s. v d.
…

1559–60
St Andrew Churchwardens' Accounts   BL: Additional MS. 32243
f 62* *(6 February–3 February) (High Cross wardens' receipts)*
…
Item Recevid of Iewes ⌐°Ieptyons°¬ for the churche howse   ij s. vj d.
…

1560–1
St Andrew Churchwardens' Accounts   BL: Additional MS. 32243
f 63v* *(4 February 1559/60–9 February 1560/1) (High Cross wardens' receipts)*
…
Item Receuyd of þe Iepsyons one ny3th y*n* the church howsse   iiij d.
…

1561–2
St Andrew Churchwardens' Accounts   BL: Additional MS. 32243
f 65* *(10 February–8 February) (High Cross wardens' receipts)*
…
Item R*ecevyd* of the Iepcyons for the chvrchehouse   iiij d.
…

1562–3
St Andrew Churchwardens' Accounts   BL: Additional MS. 32243
f 68 *(9 February–7 February) (High Cross wardens' payments)*

Item paid to a mynyster to helpe playe & syng   iiij d.   5
...

1568–9
A   *St Andrew Stockwardens' Accounts*
Goulding: *Records of the Charity known as Blanchminster's Charity*   10
p 68 *(Payments)*
...

paid to John cottell for the bull ryng x d.
...
15

TRURO

c **1535–43**
John Leland, Itinerary   Bodl.: MS. Top. gen. e. 10
f 11v
20
...

...The˄ᶜr is aˡ castelle a quarter of a mile by West out of Truru longging to
the eˡrˡle of Cornwale now clene doun/ the site ther˄ᶜofˑ is ˑnowˑ usid for a
shoting and playing place
...
25

WEST LOOE

1582–3
Mayors' Accounts   CRO: B/WLooe/12/1
p [1]* *(Rendered 29 September) (Payments)*   30
...

Item to Colakote tow shellinges to goe to the showes
...

35

WHITSTONE

1620
Bill of Complaint in Robins v. Vosse et al   PRO: STAC 8/246/13
mb [3]* *(15 November)*
40

To the Kinges most Excellent Maiestie./

In most humble wise Complayninge sheweth vnto your most Excellent
Maiestie your Highnes loyall and obedient subiect Grace Robins the naturall
daughter of Walter Robins and of Alice his wife of Whitsone in your Highnes
County of Cornewall yeoman, That wheras your Highnes said subiect from
her [marriage] ∧⌈maturitie⌉ hitherto hath been of Honest virtuous and Chast   5
life and Conuersacion and so hath been allwayes reputed and accompted
amongst your Maiesties lovinge subiectes being the Neighbours freindes and
allyes of your Highnes said subiect to the great Comfort of the said parentes of
your Highnes said subiect who haue not only to their great Charges bestoued
great somes of monie in the honest Ciuile and vertuous Iducacion of your   10
said subiect But allso haue now of late offered a great porcion of monie in
marriage with your said subiect for her better advancement and preferrement,
And wheras Richard Vosse of Whitson aforesaid in the said County of
Cornewall yeoman degorye Congdon of the said parishe and Countye
yeoman [⟨…⟩] Roger Gere yeoman Thomas Rowe Alexander Milton Iohn   15
Cullacott the yonger Iane Vosse & Margarett Randall haue of longe tyme
booren an inveterate and Cawselesse mallice and displeasure against your
Highnes said subiect and envyinge her prosperous estate Ciuill carryage and
vertuous chaste and Commendable manner of life and behauiour and seekinge
and vnlawfully indeavoring by all waies and meanes to ouerthrowe the good   20
estate of your Highnes said subiect or at least wise vtterlie to depryue her of
her said good name fame and Reputacion did att or before whittsunday now
last past maliciouslie vnlawfully and most falselie frame deuise Contryue
and make and cawse to be framed devised Contryued and made in wryting
a most infamous scandalous and false libell concerninge your said subiecte   25
therby vtterlie to discreditt and blemish the good name and fame of your
Highnes said Subiecte And falsely to cawse her to be reputed for A whoore
and to haue Committed fornicacion with seuerall persons in the said Libell
secrettlie and maliciouslie intimated And they the said Richard Vosse degorie
Congdon [⟨…⟩] Roger Geare Thomas Rowe Alexander Milton Iohn Cullacott   30
the younger Iane Vosse and Margarett Randall together with other persons of
their confederacie yet vnknowen to your Highnes said subiect whose names
your said subiect most humblie praieth may be inserted into this her bill of
Complaint when they are Discouered maliciously and greedily longinge and
thirstinge for the vtter ruine and ouerthrowe of your Highnes said subiecte   35
and of her said good name fame and estimacion did on the said Whitsonday
now last paste at whitson aforesaid in your Highnes said County of Cornewall
maliciouslie and vnlawfully cast and lay downe or cawse to be cast and laid

---

1/ Complayninge: *4 minims for* ni *in* MS   16/ Randall: *rest of line, about 120 mm, covered by line filler*
3/ Whitsone: *for* Whitstone   31/ Randall: *followed by about 110 mm of line filler at start of next line*
13/ Whitson: *for* Whitston   37/ whitson: *for* whitston

downe the said most infamous scandalous and false libell aforesaid in wrytinge
in a seate of the Church of Whitsone aforesaid the tenor wherof followeth
in these word*es*

Robins grace hath left her place   5
And as it did hap on the priest*es* bell she tooke a nap
but there she made no long staye
for w*i*th a Roule she meant to plaie.

And for the vse of her other thinge   10
on her finger he putts a Ringe.

That very Roule beshrew his poull
Keepes Robins grace and A Whore
he keepes Grace Robins and now no more.   15

Good my freinds behold him well
without he amend he is a sainct for Hell
and he for wante of other fuell
mak*es* Robins Grace his other Iuell.   20

But now there is hoape he will repent
for he loues mens wyues
And to whorish maid*es* he doth assent
for as he did beginne   25
He meanes to end in Sodoms sinne.

Theres an end quoth Mariery daw
he that keepes a such a Whore
Can dispence w*i*th the Lawe   30

This for the first part publiched
the second follos then imparted

⟨..⟩ of march
1619   35
By me Mary Boborough

In and by w*hi*ch said libell the said confederat*es* by the names Robins Grace
and Grace Robins did maliciously ∧⌈& slaunderously⌉ intend and meane
yo*ur* said subiect and sought and indeauored therby to p*ro*cure her to be
suspected and defamed [according] according to the further purport of the   40

2/ Whitsone: *for* Whitstone

said libell, And they the said malicious vnlawfull & sclanderous persons
thinking that they haue not sufficientlie slandered & blemished the good
name fame and reputacion of your Highnes said subiect by casting of the
said slanderous & infamous libell in the said parish Churche of Whitsone
aforesaid in manner as aforesaid haue diuers and sundry daies & tymes   5
sithence the said feast of whitsonday now last past at whitsone aforesaid in
your Highnes said county of Cornwall and in diuers other places eswhere
within the said county most vnlawfully maliciously & slanderously diuulged
and published the said false infamous and sclanderous libell vnto diuers of your
Maiesties loving subiectes by reading saying and singing of the said slanderous   10
and malicious libell to the great and vtter ouerthrowe and wounding of your
Highnes said subiectes estate and of her good name and fame and to the great
greife and discomfort of her said parentes and of all her alliance and freindes
wherfore for asmuch as the said manner of offence of libelling is against your
Maiesties most wholsome lawes and doth tend to the great disturbance of   15
your Maiesties most peaceable and happie gouerment and is thoccasion of
many slaughters murders and outrages amongst manie your Maiesties most
loyall and peceable subiectes May it therfore please your excellent Maiestie the
premisses considered to graunt vnto your Highnes said subiect his Maiesties
most gracious writt of subpena to be directed to the said ᴧ⌈Richard Vosse   20
Degory Congdon⌉ [⟨…⟩] Esq Roger Gere Thomas Rowe Alexander Milton
Iohn Cullacot the yonger, [Thomas Vosse] Iane Vosse [his wife] ᴧ⌈&⌉
Margarett Randall and to euerie of them therby commaunding them and
euerie of them at A certayne daie and vnder a certaine paine ⌈therin to be
limitted⌉ personally to appeare before your Maiesty and your Maiesties most   25
honorable [privie] privy councell in your Maiesties high Court of Starre chamber
then and there to answere the premisses and further to stand to and abide such
order as by your Maiestie and your Maiesties most honorable privy Councell
in that behalf shalbe thought meet & requisite, And your Maiesties said
subiect according to her bounden duty will dayly praie vnto God for your   30
Maiesties most happy raigne ouer us long to Continue./

                                                        Iohn Glanuill:/

4/ Whitsone: *for* Whitstone   13/ freindes: *followed by one and two-thirds lines of line filler*
6/ whitsone: *for* whitstone   15/ doth: th *corrected over* e
7/ eswhere: *for* elswhere

Monasteries

TYWARDREATH

1338
Episcopal Licence to the Monastery at Tywardreath
Devon Record Office: Chanter 4   5
f ccxiii verso* *(18 April)*

…

lic*encia* Tylwardreith mora*m* trahendi in aliq*u*a ecc*les*ia *vel* Cap*ell*a eoru*m*
Mon*a*sterio apropriata†

℃ I*oh*annes &c Dilec*tis* filiis Priori & Con*uen*tui de Tylwardreith *n*ostre dioce*s*is   10
sal*utem* gr*a*ciam & ben*ediccionem.* necnon constanciam in adu*er*sis? Cum
sicut nob*is* expon*ere* curauistis/ & al*ias* id patens *v*eritas manifestet. *propter*
hostiles piratar*um* insidias & incursus vob*is* hiis dieb*us* plus solito iminentes
nequeatis in Mon*a*sterio *v*estro pre*dic*to supra litus maris situato/ & *p*ericulis
tam alienigenar*um* hostium/ q*u*am, eciam indigenar*um* vos asserencium   15
suspectos. eo q*uo*d estis de regione alia oriundi/ multiplicit*er* expo*s*ito absq*ue*
graui *p*ericulo a*n*imar*um* & corporu*m* residere? nos deuocionis *v*estre precib*us*
inclinati/ *v*t cum & quociens *p*ericula huiusmodi eueniant. ad ecc*les*iam
aliqua*m* *vel* Capellam *v*estro Mon*a*sterio apropriata*m* in *n*ostra dioce*s*i a mari
remociorem & con*t*ra insultus huiusmodi tuciore*m* *p*ersonalit*er* accedere   20
valeatis & ibidem moram trahere? licenciam & auctoritate*m* tenore p*re*senciu*m*
impertimur/ Ita ta*m*en q*uo*d in loco huiusmodi ad que*m* vos declinare
contigerit a mu*n*danis spectaculis & lasciuiis separati/ om*n*i euagandi &
discurrendi occa*s*ione sublata in diuinis officiis tam diurnis q*u*am noct*ur*nis
insistatis assidue/ deuote/ debite & honeste/ ac om*n*ia obser*u*etis & faciatis/   25
que si in Mon*a*sterio *v*estro *p*ersonalit*er* essetis obseruare & fac*er*e teneremini/
iux*t*a regularis obser*u*ancia*m* discipline. Cur*e*tis eciam *v*t scandalu*m* euitetis
corda & corpora *v*estra in om*n*i castitate & *sanct*imonia tam domi q*u*am

---

13/ iminentes: *6 minims in* MS

loco huiusmodi custodire prouiso/ quod in fraudem more claustralis/ quesito
figmento aliquo nichil fiat quodque presenti nostra licencia cum vrgeat
necessitas dumtaxat vtamini quousque votiua pacis serenitas arriserit/
cooperante Rege pacifico & excelso/ Data apud Clist octauodecimo die
Mensis aprilis/ anno domini supradicto./   5

...

Households

ARUNDELL OF LANHERNE

1466–7
Sir John Arundell's Stewards' Accounts   RIC, Courtney Library: HK/17/1
f [3v]* *(Expenses)*   5
...

Item di. li. vermelon of Betty   xij d.
Item di. li. orsedy of Betty   xij d.
Item viij quayeres paper for disgysynges   ij s.
...   10

f [4]*

Item ij whit Bonettes for mynstrell on Newe yere ys day of Betty   xvj d.
Item ij ellis of holond cloth for Melionek the same day   xxij d. 15
Item iiij dosyn Bellis for the Moruske of Betty   iij s.
Item ij quayers paper for the Moruske of Betty   vij d.
Item v ellys of holond cloth for disgysynges whan ye wer avysid to
go to my lord sstafford of Betty wheche was delyueryd to my lady   ij s. vj d.
Item di. li. glewe of Betty for the Moruske   ij d.   20
Item iij yerdis blak Bokeram whan ye wolde to my lord w⟨...⟩
disgisyng whech y delyuerid to my lady of Betty   ⟨...⟩d.
Item j li. of Rede lede of Thomas Wotton   ⟨...⟩
Item j li. of [Red] of whyt lede of Thomas Wotton   ⟨...⟩

20/ Moruske: *hole 10 mm follows but no text lost*   23/ ⟨...⟩: MS *torn at edge 45 mm*
21/ w⟨...⟩: MS *torn at edge 20 mm*   24/ of [Red] of: *dittography*
22/ ⟨...⟩d.: MS *torn at edge 35 mm*   24/ ⟨...⟩: MS *torn at edge 48 mm*

Item j li. of Glewe of Tho*mas* Wotton   ⟨...⟩
Item verdigres of Thomas Wotton   x⟨...⟩d.

...

Item ij dosyn & iij levys of gold foyll of Thomas Wotton   xiiij d.
Item ij quayers pap*er* of Thomas Wotton   vj d.   5

...

1504–5
Sir John Arundell's Household Account Book   CRO: AR/26/2
f 19* *(Payments)*   10

...

It*em* the xiiijth day to the egypcians when they davnsyd afor*e* me   xx d.

...

1564   15
Inventory of Elizabeth Arundell   CRO: AR/21/16/1
mb [2] *(17 October)*

...

®.iiij li.

                                        In the norcery
Item iij fetherbeddes ij bolsters ij Coverlet*es* ij bedstedd*es* a cofer one stoole   20
& a payre of virgynall*es*

...

1586
Will of Edward Arundell   CRO: AR/21/21/2   25
single mb *(16 October; proved 10 November)*

...Item I give him my best lute to ⟨...⟩wed on his wieffe, w*hi*ch lute is white
and blacke, and the case crimson velvett imbrodered all over w*i*th golde...

                                                                                                    30

Inventory of Edward Arundell   CRO: AR/21/22
p [1]* *(12 December)*

...

                        in [one of] ye forsaid trouncke[s]
j lute of white ⌈20 s.⌉ & blacke bone covered w*i*th crimsen vellet   35
j littell gilt boxe ⌈12 d.⌉ for to hold ring*es*
j pap*er* of lute ⌈1 d.⌉ stringes
ij p*ar*e of gloves ⌈6 d.⌉

...

1/ ⟨...⟩: MS *torn at edge 33 mm*   28/ him: *John Arundell, a nephew*
2/ x⟨...⟩d.: MS *torn at edge 10 mm*   28/ ⟨...⟩wed: *hole in* MS
12/ the xiiijth day: *of November*

CARNSEW OF BOKELLY

1576
Diary of William Carnsew   PRO: SP 46/16
f [9]* *(29 July)*   5

...

G 29   I am wrytyn to to meett mr mohan att bodman playes spente ther 12 s.
wherof I gaue wrastlers 5 s....

...

     10

TREGIAN OF GOLDEN

1593
Treatise on the Trial of Francis Tregian
St Mary's College Library, Oscott: MS 545   15
pp 89–94* *(20 July)*

...

     Some other as impertinente proofes hee powred foorth, but that which
seemed to searue for the twist of his woorke was a most detestable and neuly
deuised examinatione of a lewde fellow, subordened for the purpose, named   20
Twigges, which mantayned that the same good fellow, forsoothe, had sundry
tymes resorted vnto Golden mr Tregians house, where hee saw *Cuthbert*
Maine, and diuerse others to repaire often vnto Mr Tregians chamber, and
therto remayne so | longe a space as a mass myghte well bee sayed, further
that hee comminge vnto Golden with an Enterclude at Christe masse in the   25
yeare of our Lord 1575. was then lodged with the sayde *Cuthbert* Maine, at
which tyme Maine told him that hee was a preiste, that hee had been at Rome,
that hee brought from thence diuerse Agnus Dei, and wee know not what,
that hee had greater authoritye then any minister in England, that this
world was naughte, and would not amende vntill this lande wer inuaded by   30
Spanniardes, as it should bee shortely, and I know not who.
     Much more good stuff to the like effect was contayned in the same
examinatione which the sayde TWigges, beeinge caled foorth, did with a
pale countenaunce, tremblinge handes and staggeringe tounge (signes of a
guilty conscience) on his othe affirme to bee true: all which if it had been   35
true, as it was most false, had it yet been very littel to the purpose to have
proued mr Tregian guilty of the crime where of hee was accused.|
     But in trothe althoughe with one limde twigge they intended then to take tow
birdes, yet this examinatione was not newly deuised, neither now produced so

---

7m/ G 29: *a small penned flower in the margin signalled Sunday 29 July*
7/ I: *same hand but smaller and cramped*

much against Mr Tregian as therby to giue out to the worlde some colourable
shew besydes bare woordes, which at first through ouermuch hast was omitted,
that *Cuthbert Maine* forsooth, who now had been executed, almost a yeare
beefore, with out all doubte was ⌐not⌐ a very good man but an enymy to
the state, and vnwoorthy of lyfe, that hee hadd been at Rome, and brought   5
from thence bulls, Agnus Deis and such other stuffe, wherof with out any
proofe or colour of proofe most maliciously and wickedly hee had been
beefore accused and condemned, soe that which first through the furye of
blinde malice was vndiscretly omitted, was now, as they thought, vpon
mature deliberatione very politikely amended, and in truth if this euidence,   10
thoughe most vntruth, had been deuised and produced when first *Cuthbert*
Maine was arrained, their | proceadinges, then vndoubtedly would not haue
seemed altogether soe maliciously intended, as now they plainely appeare to
bee most wicked dealinges, which by noe colour can bee defended.

    After the euidence was once ended mr Tregian beesides many other, after   15
tryall, speeches deliuered in the defence of his Innocency, declared that no
man, as hee hoped, whoe was indued but with common sence, would thinke
it lykely that a poore parishe Clarke, for hee was no better, runninge aboute
the Countrye from place to place, with a balde Enterclude, should bee lodged
with *Cuthbert* Maine, beeinge stewarde of his howse, and how in truth, was   20
by him well vsed, and lodged, and of whome of all other his seruantes, no
one excepted, hee made most accompte, beesydes, admittinge that Twigges
had layne with him, yet hee well hoped it woulde also bee thought as vnlikely
that Cuth*bert* Maine beeinge both wise and lear-|ned, would vnto a meere
straynger, and one whome hee neuer saw beefore that howre, imparte matters   25
of so greate importance, as which by the lawes of the Reaulme, and throughe
the hatred conceaved of his functione, whereof hee was not ignorante, shoulde
either haue coste him the loss of his life, or at least the depriuaunce of his
liberty, moreouer this good Twigges beeinge demaunded by Mr Tregian in
what parte of his house *Cuthbert* Maine was lodged, what manner of chamber   30
it was, what windowes were in it, what fashione bedd he laye in, where the
chimnye stood, and such like, ouertaken by meanes of his ignoraunce therin,
after hee had muttered a woorde or two very vnaptelye and indirectely to the
first proposed questione, hee was inforced to answere the rest with shamefull
silence, which the Iudge who was chiefe in commissione perceauinge with   35
out any blusshinge, commaunded him foorthwith not to answere one woorde
more as hee termed it vnto such vaine and friuolous questions; but | after to
putt the matter out of all doubte, mr Tregian offered ther presently to prooue
in the face of the courte, by the depositione of at least 40 credible persones,
that the same Christemasse, when this good fellow played the interclude in   40
his house, for hee neuer played any, but that one alone, *Cuthbert* Maine was
not there, nor as yet had been receaued into his seruice, nor almost eyghte

monthes after, neither in truth was hee then in England, but at Doway in
flanders, who came ouer into this reaulme the Easter followinge, but by no
meanes possible hee could bee permitted to produce any one of his wittenesse
for proofe of the same, for if the depositione of this honest companione,
which they had for their purpose, soe cunningly contryued and politykely   5
procured, had been playnely descryed, and publikely disprooued, their fine
fisshinge woulde haue proued but a foolishe frogginge, all the fatt had fallen
into the fire, and the whole frame of their intended and Babilonicall buildinges,
had been vnioynted.

County of Cornwall

1602
Richard Carew, Survey of Cornwall   STC: 4615
sigs S4–T4*

...

® Recreations.

But let me lead you from these impleasing matters, to refresh your selues   5
with taking view of the Cornish mens recreations, which consist principally
in feastes and pastimes.

Their feasts are commonly haruest dinners, Church-ales, and the

® Feasts.

solemnizing of parish Churches dedication, which they terme their Saints
feast. | 10

Haruest
dinners.

The haruest dinners are held by euery wealthy man, or as wee terme it,
euery good liuer, betweene Michaelmas and Candlemas, whereto he inuiteth
his next neighbours and kinred, and though it beare onely the name of a
dinner, yet the ghests take their supper also with them, and consume a great
part of the night after in Christmas rule: neither doth the good cheere   15
wholly expire (though it somewhat decrease) but with the end of the weeke.

Church-ale.

For the Church-ale, two young men of the parish are yerely chosen by
their last foregoers, to be Wardens, who deuiding the task, make collection
among the parishioners, of whatsoeuer prouision it pleaseth them voluntarily
to bestow. This they imploy in brewing, baking, & other acates, against   20
Whitsontide; vpon which Holydayes, the neighbours meet at the Church
house, and there merily feed on their owne victuals, contributing some petty
portion to the stock, which by many smalls, groweth to a meetly greatnes:
for there is entertayned a kinde of emulation betweene these Wardens, who
by his graciousnes in gathering, and good husbandry in expending, can best   25
aduance the Churches profit. Besides, the neighbour parishes, at those times
louingly visit one another, and this way frankely spend their money together.
The afternoones are consumed in such exercises, as olde and yong folke
(hauing leysure) doe accustomably weare out the time withall.

When the feast is ended, the Wardens yeeld in their account to the   30
Parishioners, and such money as exceedeth the disbursments, is layd vp in

store, to defray any extraordinary charges arising in the parish, or imposed
on them for the good of the Countrey, or the Princes | seruice. Neither of
which commonly gripe so much, but that somewhat stil remayneth to couer
the purses bottome.

®Saints feasts.

The Saints feast is kept vpon the dedication day, by euery housholder of the   5
parish, within his owne dores, each entertayning such forrayne acquaintance,
as will not fayle when their like turne commeth about, to requite him with
the like kindnes.

Of late times, many Ministers haue by their ernest inuectiues, both
condemned these Saints feasts as superstitious, and supressed the Church-   10
ales, as licencious: concerning which, let it breed none offence, for me to
report a conference that I had not long since, with a neere friend, who (as I
conceiue) looked heerinto with an indifferent and vnpreiudicating eye. I do
reuerence (sayd he) the calling and iudgement of the Ministers, especially when
most of them concurre in one opinion, and that the matter controuersed,   15
holdeth some affinity with their profession. Howbeit, I doubt, least in their
exclayming or declayming against Church-ales and Saints feasts, their
ringleaders did onely regard the rinde, and not perce into the pith, and that
the rest were chiefly swayed by their example: euen as the vulgar, rather
stouped to the wayght of their authoritie, then became perswaded by the   20
force of their reasons. And first touching Church-ales, these be mine assertions,
if not my proofes: Of things induced by our forefathers, some were instituted
to a good vse, and peruerted to a bad: againe, some were both naught in the
inuention, and so continued in the practise. Now that Church-ales ought to
bee sorted in the better ranke of these twaine, may be gathered from their   25
causes and ef-|fects, which I thus rasse vp together: entertaining of Christian
loue, conforming of mens behauiour to a ciuill conuersation, compounding of
controuersies, appeasing of quarrels, raising a store, which might be conuerted,
partly to good and godly vses, as releeuing all sorts of poore people, repairing
of Churches, building of bridges, amending of high wayes; and partly, for   30
the Princes seruice, by defraying at an instant, such rates and taxes as the
magistrate imposeth for the Countries defence. Briefly, they tende to an
instructing of the minde by amiable conference, and an enabling of the
body by commendable exercises. But I fearing lest my friend would runne
himselfe out of breath, in this volubilitie of praising, stept athwart him with   35
these obiections: That hee must pardon my dissenting from his opinion,
touching the goodnesse of the institution: for taken at best, it could not bee
martialled with the sacred matters, but rather with the ciuill, if not with the
profane; that the very title of ale was somewhat nasty, and the thing it selfe
had beene corrupted with such a multitude of abuses, to wit, idlenes,   40
drunkennesse, lasciuiousnes, vaine disports of minstrelsie, dauncing, and
disorderly night-watchings, that the best curing was to cut it cleane away. As

for his fore-remembred good causes and effects, I sawe not, but that if the
peoples mindes were guided by the true leuell of christian charity & duetie,
such necessary and profitable contributions might stil be continued gratis,
& the country eased of that charge to their purse and conscience, which
ensueth this gourmandise. His reply was, that if this ordinance could not   5
reach vnto that sanctity which dependeth on the first table, yet it succeeded
the same in the next | degree, as appertayning to the second. Mine exception
against the title, he mockingly matched with their scrupulous precisenes, who
(forsooth) would not say Christmas, nor Michaelmas, as other folk did; but
Christs tide, and Michaels tide: who (quoth he) by like consequence must   10
also bind themselues to say, Toms tide, Lams tide, and Candles tide. But if
the name of ale relish so ill, whereas the licour it selfe is the English mans
ancientest and wholesomest drinke, and serueth many for meate and cloth
too; he was contented I should call it Church beere, or Church wine, or what
else I listed: mary, for his part hee would loqui cum vulgo, though hee studied   15
sentire cum sapientibus. Where I affirmed, that the people might by other
meanes be trayned with an equall largesse to semblable workes of charitie,
hee suspected lest I did not enter into a through consideration of their nature
and qualitie, which he had obserued to be this: that they would sooner depart
with 12. pennyworth of ware, then sixepence in coyne, and this shilling they   20
would willingly double, so they might share but some pittance thereof againe.
Now in such indifferent matters, to serue their humors, for working them to
a good purpose, could breed no maner of scandall. As for the argument of
abuse, which I so largely dilated, that should rather conclude a reformation
of the fault, then an abrogation of the fact.   25

For to prosecute your owne Metaphore (quoth hee) surely I holde him
for a sory Surgeon, that cannot skill to salue a sore, but by taking away the
lymme, and little better then the Phisicion, who, to helpe the disease, will
reaue the life of his Patient from him. Abuses, doubtlesse, great and many |
haue, by successe of time, crept hereinto, as into what other almost, diuine, or   30
ciuill, doe they not? and yet in these publike meetings, they are so presented
to euery mans sight, as shame somewhat restrayneth the excesse, and they may
much the sooner bee both espied and redressed. If you thinke I goe about to
defend Church-ales, with all their faults, you wrong your iudgement, & your
iudgement wrongeth mee. I would rather (as a Burgesse of this ale-parliament)   35
enact certaine lawes, by which such assemblies should be gouerned: namely,
that the drinke should neither be too strong in taste, nor too often tasted:
that the ghests should be enterlarded, after the Persian custome, by ages, yong
and old, distinguished by degrees of the better and meaner: and seuered into
sexes, the men from the women: that the meats should be sawced with   40
pleasant, but honest talke: that their songs should be of their auncestours
honourable actions: the principall time of the morning, I would haue

hallowed to Gods seruice: the after-noones applied to manlike actiuities: and
yet I would not altogether barre sober and open dauncing, vntill it were first
thoroughly banished from mariages, Christmas reuels, and (our Countries
patterne) the court: all which should be concluded, with a reasonable and
seasonable portion of the night: and so (sayd hee) will I conclude this part   5
of my speach, with adding onely one word more for my better iustification:
that in defending feasts, I maintayne neither Paradox, nor a conceite in
nubibus, but a matter practised amongst vs from our eldest auucestours, with
profitable and well pleasing fruit, and not onely by our nation, but, both in
former ages, by the best and strictest disciplined com- | mon wealth of the   10
Lacedemonians, who had their ordinary Sissitia, and now in our dayes, as
well by the reformed, as Catholike Switzers, who place therein a principall
Arcanum imperij.

...

Pastimes to delight the minde, the Cornish men haue Guary miracles,   15
and three mens songs: and for exercise of the body, Hunting, Hawking,
Shooting, Wrastling, | Hurling, and such other games.

Guary miracle. The Guary miracle, in English, a miracle-play, is a kinde of Enterlude,
compiled in Cornish out of some scripture history, with that grossenes,
which accompanied the Romanes vetus Comedia. For representing it, they   20
raise an earthen Amphitheatre, in some open field, hauing the Diameter of
his enclosed playne some 40. or 50. foot. The Country people flock from all
sides, many miles off, to heare & see it: for they haue therein, deuils and
deuices, to delight as well the eye as the eare: the players conne not their
parts without booke, but are prompted by one called the Ordinary, who   25
followeth at their back with the booke in his hand, and telleth them softly
what they must pronounce aloud. Which maner once gaue occasion to a
pleasant conceyted gentleman, of practising a mery pranke: for he vndertaking
(perhaps of set purpose) an Actors roome, was accordingly lessoned (before-
hand) by the Ordinary, that he must say after him. His turne came: quoth   30
the Ordinarie, Goe forth man and shew thy selfe. The gentleman steps out
vpon the stage, and like a bad Clarke in scripture matters, cleauing more to
the letter then the sense, pronounced those words aloud. Oh (sayes the
fellowe softly in his eare) you marre all the play. And with this his passion,
the Actor makes the audience in like sort acquainted. Hereon the prompter   35
falles to flat rayling & cursing in the bitterest termes he could deuise: which
the Gentleman with a set gesture and countenance still soberly related, vntill
the Ordinary driuen at last into a madde rage, was faine to giue ouer all. Which
trousse though it brake off the Enterlude, yet defrauded not the beholders,

8/ auucestours: *for* auncestours

but dismissed them with a great deale | more sport and laughter, then 20. such Guaries could haue affoorded.

They haue also Cornish three mens songs, cunningly contriued for the ditty, and pleasantly for the note.

...   5

® Three mens songs.

APPENDIX 1

'Vocabularium Cornicum': Old Cornish Translation of Ælfric's Glossary

British Library: Cotton MS. Vespasian A. XIV is a copy made in Wales *c* 1200 of a twelfth-century Cornish original that translated Ælfric's Latin/Old English glossary into Old Cornish, arranging words by subject. Kenneth Jackson, *Language and History in Early Britain: A Chronological Survey of the Brittonic Languages, 1st to 12th c. A.D.* (Edinburgh, 1953; rpt Dublin, 1990), 60–1 (based partly on Max Förster, *Der Flussname Themse und Seine Sippe* (Munich, 1941), 286 and 289), gives the date of the original as *c* 1100; this seems based on the mistaken belief that Ælfric's Old English original would not have been understood much after *c* 1100. From the Cornish forms shown in it, a later date would be preferable and it is now accepted that Old English continued to be understood by scribes rather later than Jackson and Förster believed. The dating of the vocabulary falls on the margin between Old and Middle Cornish but is usually classed with Old Cornish. Containing some additional Cornish words not also found in Ælfric, the manuscript has a number of entries pertaining to musical instruments and to performers.

Eugene Van Tassel Graves edits and discusses in detail the 'Vocabularium Cornicum' in 'The Old Cornish Vocabulary,' PhD dissertation (Columbia University, 1962). In addition to providing a linguistic and topical discussion, Graves includes for each Latin-Cornish word pair the Latin-Old English word pair from Ælfric's glossary. The 'Vocabularium Cornicum' is arranged by subject headings, typical of glossaries of the time, such as 'Heaven, Earth, Man, Animals, Plants, Houses.' The entries on f 7, the performers 'Cantor: cheniat' and 'Cantrix: canores' are grouped with ecclesiastical pairs such as 'Her∧⌐e⌐mita: ⌐h⌐ermit . Nonna: laines.' or 'lector: redior . lectrix: rediores.' indicating that these were performers in the church or church-related activities. They are included here because it is interesting that the church evidently used female singers. The entries from f 7v follow the list of ecclesiastical personnel and, although the grouping has no heading, the words appear to be secular. Immediately preceding the excerpted list of instruments and performers are the two words 'gigas,' glossed 'enchinethel' (giant, alien) and 'Nam*us*: cor.' (the former a misreading of the Latin 'nanus') for 'dwarf,' and following the excerpted list is 'Mercator *vel* Negotiator: Guiegur.' for 'merchant or trader,' suggesting that the glossary has here provided a list of secular entertainers. Graves remarks on 'Liticen: keniat co*m*bricam.' saying that it is 'the hornpipe, an obsolete British wind-instrument, played at rural gatherings and among sailors' (p 124). The Latin 'Mim*us vel* Scurra,' translated to the Cornish 'barth,' rather than 'bard or poet' actually meant 'entertainer or buffoon.'

While 'bard' may have had loftier associations in Wales, Graves argues that in Ireland and Cornwall it referred to a secular performer, often one engaged in comedic entertainment (p 125). The word pair 'Subtularis: ꝑibanor.' on f 9v, where the Latin word means 'shoe' but the Cornish word means 'piper,' appears as an unusual entry in a household inventory. It may be the result, Graves says, of a misreading of the Old English 'swiftlere' (shoe) as 'hwistlere' (p 345).

The Old Cornish Vocabulary is incorporated in Robert Williams, *Lexicon Cornu-Britannicum: A Dictionary of the Ancient Celtic Language of Cornwall* (London, 1865), and printed in Edwin Norris (ed), *The Ancient Cornish Drama*, vol 2 (1859; rpt London, 1968), 309–435. Julius Zupitza includes Ælfric's glossary in his critical edition, *Aelfrics Grammatik und Glossar* (Berlin, 1880), 297–322. There is also an Italian edition of the Vocabulary in Enrico Campanile, *Profilo etimologico del cornico antico* (Pisa, 1974).

For the purpose of translation, readers are directed to Graves' dissertation and to R. Morton Nance, *A New Cornish-English Dictionary* (St Ives, 1938; rpt Redruth, 1990) which incorporates words from the Vocabulary; for the Latin, see the Latin Glossary where the terms are glossed in accordance with the guidelines described there (p 628).

London, British Library, Cotton MS. Vespasian A. XIV; *c* 1200 copy made in Wales of a 12th-c. original; parchment with paper leaves (where bound); v + 179 + ii; 203mm x 152mm, average 35 lines; modern pencil foliation; some enlarged letters in red, green, and blue; relatively modern binding in brown cloth and leather, gold scroll decoration on spine, written on spine: 691 | LIVES OF | THE WELSH | SAINTS, ETC | BRIT. MUS | COTTON MS. | VESPASIAN | A.XIV.

12th century
Old Cornish Translation of Ælfric's Dictionary
BL: Cotton MS. Vespasian A. XIV
f 7

5

… Cantor: cheniat . Cantrix: canores …

f 7v

… Fidis: corden . Citharista: Teleinior . Cithara: telein . Tubicen: barth hirgorn . 10
Tuba: hirgorn . Tibicen: piꝑhit . Musa: pib . Fidicen: harfellor . Fidicina: fellores . Fiala: harfel . Cornicen: cherniat . Cornu: corn . Fistula. ꝑibonoul . Liticen: keniat *combricam* . Linthuus: tollcorn . Poeta: pridit . Mim*us vel* Scurra: barth . Saltator: lappior . Salta*trix*: lappiores…

15

f 9v

… Subtularis: ꝑibanor…

APPENDIX 2

Cornish Plays and Their Evidence for Performance

Extant Texts of Three Cornish Plays

Four texts are extant of plays written in the Cornish language: 'The Charter Interlude,' the *Ordinalia, Beunans Meriasek,* and the *Creacion of the World.* The 'Charter Interlude' is a piece of dramatic verse written on the back of a Cornish land deed dated 1340 and the forty-one lines on the deed appear to be the speeches for one actor in a popular type of interlude concerned with matchmaking. Because the *Ordinalia, Beunans Meriasek,* and the *Creacion* offer some useful information about the presentation of drama in Cornwall, passages from those three texts are included here. Manuscripts for the *Ordinalia* and *Beunans Meriasek,* for example, both contain stage diagrams attesting performance in the round and all three texts refer to activities after the plays such as minstrelsy, dancing, and drinking.

THE *ORDINALIA* MANUSCRIPT

The *Ordinalia,* Cornwall's counterpart to the cycle drama, is one of Cornwall's earliest surviving dramatic texts; its manuscript, MS. Bodl. 791, dates from the fifteenth century but the text of the play from the fourteenth (see Fowler, 'Date of the "Ordinalia",' pp 91–125, P.P. Harris, 'Origo Mundi,' pp 8–14, and Jenner, *Handbook of the Cornish Language,* pp 27–8).[1] Although precisely determining a place of composition for the *Ordinalia* is impossible, the manuscript does provide internal clues in references to minor place names near Penryn (see Bakere, *Cornish Ordinalia,* pp 32–3; Crawford, 'Composition of the Ordinalia,' pp 144–52; and Murdoch, 'Place-Names in the Cornish *Passio Christi,*' pp 116– 18; see also, Betcher, 'A Reassessment,' pp 436–53, who argues for a provenance in Bodmin). Moreover, since the composer or compiler possessed knowledge of both literature and theology, the play has been presumed to have been written by someone associated with Glasney Collegiate Church, built at the edge of Penryn by Bishop Walter Bronescombe (see p 392).

Written in the Middle Cornish language but with stage directions in Latin, the *Ordinalia,* like the cycle plays in Middle English, presents chronologically scenes from Christian legend and Scripture and, also like the English cycles, it was performed over several days. Unlike the

---

1 *References cited in Appendix 2 are given in full below, pp 557–8*

English cycles, however, the *Ordinalia* as it is extant focuses more narrowly on the Passion and Resurrection of Christ, with special attention to the legend of the Oil of Mercy (see Halliday, *Legend of the Rood*, pp 12–14; Longsworth, *Cornish Ordinalia*, pp 46–71; Murdoch, *Cornish Literature*, pp 89–90; and Quinn, *Quest*, pp 2–3). And unlike the English cycles that usually link past and present with the future by concluding with a play on the Last Judgment, the text of the *Ordinalia* stops short of Judgment Day and ends with Christ's Resurrection and reception in Heaven.

Stage diagrams and other information in MS. Bodl. 791 indicate that the *Ordinalia* was presented over three days. In contrast to the English cycles' structure of a large number of relatively short and discrete plays that each focus on a specific story, the *Ordinalia* has three large plays, each containing a number of different but connected stories. For example, 'Origo Mundi,' the first day's play, begins with the Creation of the World and tells of Adam and Eve, Noah, Abraham, Moses, David and Bathsheba, Solomon's building of the temple, and the protomartyr Maximilla, and ends at the time of Solomon. The second day's play, 'Passio Christi,' begins with the Temptation of Christ, presents several stories traditionally associated with the Passion, and ends after the Crucifixion with the Deposition and Entombment. 'Resurrexio Domini,' the third day's play, begins with the message to Pilate of Christ's Resurrection and ends with Christ in Heaven; in addition to such traditional elements as the Harrowing of Hell and Thomas's doubting, 'Resurrexio Domini' contains uncommon elements such as the death of Pilate.

The existing manuscript of the *Ordinalia* may, however, be part of a longer play, since the last lines of 'Origo Mundi' contain an alternative ending, suggesting that on some occasions a Nativity play followed 'Origo Mundi' instead of 'Passio Christi.' The alternative ending is present in a word, 'flogholeth' (childhood), written above the word 'passyon' (Passion), and in the words 'a Iesus hep gorholeth' (of Jesus, without bidding) written at the end of the verse and with a line drawn to the place where 'flogholeth' is interlineated. This alternative ending, which appears to invite the audience to see on the next day a Nativity play, adds further weight to the suggestion that the extant parts of the *Ordinalia* were once part of a longer and fuller cycle play.

The *Ordinalia* is not as accessible as one might wish. Only 'Origo Mundi,' the first part of the *Ordinalia*, is available in a modern scholarly edition, Harris' PhD dissertation for the University of Washington. Norris' *The Ancient Cornish Drama* offers a complete but earlier (1859) scholarly edition of the *Ordinalia* with a somewhat stilted translation but extensive editorial apparatus. Markham Harris offers a modern popular translation in *The Cornish Ordinalia: A Medieval Dramatic Trilogy* (1969).

Included here from the *Ordinalia* is a speech by King David in 'Origo Mundi,' the first day's play, when he has gone to cut the three rods that in legend connect Adam and Christ; delighted at finding the rods, he commands various musicians to perform and lists a number of musical instruments. King Solomon's speech at the end of that first day's play attests to the presence of minstrels who will then pipe for the audience and contains as well the alternative ending alluding to a Nativity play at some time performed as part of the *Ordinalia*. Undoubtedly because of the nature of the play, the ending of 'Passio Christi,' the *Ordinalia*'s second play, has no reference to music and so we do not include it here. The Emperor's speech at the end of 'Resurrexio Domini,' the third day's play, blesses the audience and urges the minstrels to play for dancing. These speeches are found respectively in Norris, *Ancient Cornish Drama*, vol 1, ll.1995–2000 and 2825–46, and vol 2, ll.2631–46.

Ordinale de Origine Mundi

Oxford, Bodleian Library, MS. Bodl. 791; *c* 1400–1500; Cornish and Latin; parchment and paper; ii + 94 + i; 260mm x 170mm (225mm x 160mm), average 32 long lines; contemporary foliation 1–84, later (perhaps modern) foliation 85–90; some mice holes or erosion near bottom of f 1, some mold and water damage to parchment flyleaves; pricking noticeable on many leaves; each of the 3 plays is followed by a circular stage plan locating the chief characters on the stage (ff 27, 56v, and 83); bound in brown leather, with 'BODL. | 791' at bottom of spine.

THE *BEUNANS MERIASEK* MANUSCRIPT

Cornwall's particularized saint's play, *Beunans Meriasek*, is one of only three such extant plays in Britain. The other two plays, both in Middle English, concern Mary Magdalene and St Paul, while the Cornish play focuses on the life and miracles of Meriasek, the patron saint of Camborne. Saints' plays are also extant in Brittany and bear comparison with *Beunans Meriasek*. Although the sole manuscript of *Beunans Meriasek* (National Library of Wales: Peniarth MS 105) is dated 1504, the play may have been composed in the latter part of the previous century. When Whitley Stokes saw the MS in the nineteenth century the date was visible; Stokes supplies a plate showing the colophon with the date (see Stokes, *Meriasek*, pp v, 264, and plate opposite page xvi). While the play's author is unknown, the colophon at the end of the manuscript reveals the scribe to have been one 'Had Ton' or 'Rad Ton,' the letters of the first name unclear and still a matter of dispute. Thomas, *Christian Antiquities*, p 23, who suggested 'RADTON' instead of Stokes' 'HADTON,' mentions a 'Sir Ric. Tone, prest,' who was buried in Camborne in 1547 and who may have been the scribe.

The first ten pages (271 lines) are in a different hand (see R. Morton Nance, manuscript notes on *Beunans Meriasek*, *c* 1930, Royal Institution of Cornwall, Truro), and this hand can hardly be earlier than *c* 1550, judging by the late form 'bedneth' (for 'blessing'), which occurs three times in these pages (Stokes, *Meriasek*, ll.198 and 224–5), contrasting with the earlier term 'banneth' in the remainder of the play (and also with earlier 'ben(n)eth,' 'bennath,' and 'banneth' in the opening pages themselves). Presumably the first ten pages needed to be replaced, owing to wear or weathering, fifty years after being written and a copy was made and bound with the older remainder.

The play was presumably written for performance in Camborne since the only dedication in Cornwall to St Meriasek occurs at Camborne parish church. Two further factors support this: first, one scene takes place in the Camborne area, with references to local landmarks, which might not have meant much outside of the parish (see Thomas, *Christian Antiquities*, pp 22–36); second, there are references in the play to 'Mary of Camborne.' However, it is not impossible that it was also performed elsewhere. There is no firm evidence of a plain-an-gwary in Camborne parish but such evidence might not have survived or could yet be discovered; in any case, it is not certain that productions occurred only in such amphitheatres. A connection between Camborne and Glasney College, Penryn, shortly before 1504 suggests a possible place of composition (see Thomas, *Christian Antiquities*, p 23). Written in Cornish, the play has stage directions in both Latin and Middle English; all of the English directions and some of the Latin are added in a different hand (see Stokes, *Meriasek*, pp v–vi).

Like the *Ordinalia*, *Beunans Meriasek* was intended to be performed in the round and over a period of two days, as attested by the manuscript's staging diagrams. During those two days the scenes concerning St Meriasek range between Cornwall and Brittany, while other scenes concerning St Silvester, the fourth-century pope, and set in Rome, expand the chronological and geographical range of the play. Such saints' plays were also sometimes called 'miracles' but the term might have been used for several kinds of drama. A reference in the antiquarian Penheleg manuscript states that a 'Mirable' was performed in the plain-an-gwary at Sancreed (see pp 519–20) but any kind of drama may have been performed there.

At present, the only scholarly edition of *Beunans Meriasek* is that of Whitley Stokes, *The Life of St. Meriasek* (1872), which is not always readily accessible. Myrna Combellack edited and translated the play as her PhD thesis for the University of Exeter, 'A Critical Edition of *Beunans Meriasek*' (1985), and also prepared *The Camborne Play*, a performance translation. Perhaps most available is Markham Harris' popular translation, *The Life of Meriasek: A Medieval Cornish Miracle Play* (1977).

Included from *Beunans Meriasek* is the last portion of the Duke of Cornwall's speech at the end of the first day's play wherein he states that the enemy Teudar has been defeated; the Duke urges the audience to drink and the minstrels to pipe after the play and invokes upon them the blessing of Mary of Camborne. The Earl of Vannes' speech, of similar content, ends *Beunans Meriasek*'s play for the second day. In Stokes' *Meriasek* these are ll.2505–12 and 4557–69 respectively.

Ordinale de vita sancti mereadoci episcopi et confessoria

Aberystwyth, National Library of Wales, Peniarth MS 105; 1504; Cornish, English, and Latin; paper; 90 leaves, (half-sheet marked '91a, 91b,' inserted before the 46th leaf); approximately 200mm x 150mm (text area varies); modern pencil pagination 1–180 (also modern foliation in pencil at top right and antiquarian foliation in ink at bottom left of each folio); pp 98 and 180 have diagrams of stage plans; bound in brown leather and labelled on back: '310. Cornish Mystery.'

THE *CREATION* MANUSCRIPT

In addition to the *Ordinalia*, Cornwall possesses a later, incomplete cycle drama, the *Creacion of the World*, sometimes known as *Gwryans an Bys*. The earliest manuscript of the *Creacion*, MS. Bodl. 219, is dated 12 August 1611; it may have been composed slightly earlier, though the state of the language cannot be earlier than the second half of the sixteenth century. For the best discussion, see Neuss, *Creacion of the World*, pp lxx–lxxiv, who tentatively suggests a date in the 1550s or later.

The *Creacion* appears to be the first part of a longer work intended for performance over more than one day. Not only is the *Creacion* subtitled 'The First Day of Playe' but also at the end of that play the character of Noah invites the audience to return the next day to see Redemption; unfortunately no manuscript of that next day's play survives. Noah also encourages the audience to remain and to dance to the music of minstrels after the play, observing that this is customary.

The *Creacion* is written in Late Cornish but the stage directions are all in English, reflecting the later date of the *Creacion* compared with the *Ordinalia* and *Beunans Meriasek*. While the manuscript of the *Creacion* is nearly two centuries later than that of the *Ordinalia*, the two plays correspond word-for-word in a number of passages within their first thousand lines, causing speculation that initial sections of the *Creacion* resulted from an actor's mnemonic reconstruction of his lines; the *Creacion* echoes the speeches of Deus Pater in the *Ordinalia*, along with the lines of those characters with adjacent speeches (Neuss, *Creacion of the World*, pp xxxvii–xlix).

We cannot determine the length of that larger work of which the *Creacion* was a part or the days required for performance. The members of the audience are told that they will see Redemption on the next day; if the entire work followed the model of the *Ordinalia* and ended with the Resurrection then that larger work may have required only two days. On the other hand, since the *Creacion* expands the corresponding segment of the *Ordinalia* and also ends earlier in scriptural time than does the first part of the *Ordinalia* – with Noah rather than with Solomon – the fuller play may have required more than two days for an entire performance.

The manuscript of the *Creacion* also differs from that of the *Ordinalia* in containing no diagrams for staging in the round, which does not obviate such performance. In fact, stage directions in the *Creacion* refer often to action in the plain; Lucifer's rebellion, for instance, requires 'every degre of devylls of lether and sprytys on cordys ruining into the playne' (Neuss, *Creacion of the World*, p 26). However, the attention in the *Creacion*'s stage directions to facial expression might suggest a theatre smaller than the two plenys-an-gwary existing in Cornwall, as might the mechanical contrivances the *Creacion* requires (Neuss, *Creacion of the World*, pp lxii–lxiii). On the other hand the plain-an-gwary Carew describes is only forty to fifty feet in diameter and a theatre that size might have offered the staging the *Creacion* requires. The structures at Ruan Major and Ruan Minor, as described in 1803, were also relatively small, being respectively sixty-six feet and ninety-three feet in diameter (see Polwhele, *History of Cornwall*, vol 2, p 192).

The *Creacion* is readily accessible in Neuss' modern scholarly edition, which includes a good translation and introduction. Stokes' earlier edition and translation, *Gwreans an bys: The Creation of the World* (1864), is also useful. Hooper edited Nance and Smith's edition of the play in Unified Cornish with translation. Rawe's published translation, *The Creation of the World* (1978), was revised and refined from the text used for the production of the play at Piran Round in Cornwall in 1973. Noah's speech transcribed here is found in Stokes, *Creacion*, ll.2531–48, and in Neuss, *Creacion of the World*, ll.2532–49.

The Creacion of the World, the first daie of playe

Oxford, Bodleian Library, MS. Bodl. 219; 12 August 1611; Cornish and English; paper; xxiv + 74; 300mm x 200mm (text area variable), average 38 long lines; modern foliation of flyleaves, contemporary foliation 1–74; gatherings of 10–12 (f ii, a half page with ll.2083–93 copied in a later hand, is pasted on to f i); no decoration; bound in white parchment with gold ornamentation in the shape of a cross, gold stamped lines, and initials 'I K ' on board, title on spine, in ink: 'Arch I B 33,' '31,' and '219.' Folios 1–27 contain the text of the play; ff 28–74 are blank.

The manuscripts of the Cornish play-texts use a curious layout, which is easy to follow if the manuscript is being read in extenso but is difficult to reproduce in print and hard to comprehend if reproduced. Rather than attempting an exact reproduction, we have devised a system of indentation which gives the intended text, though not the layout, of the manuscripts. The manuscript layout was designed to display the rhyme schemes of the stanzas, often *aabccb*; this was achieved by placing the rhyming pairs (*aa* and *cc*) below one another, with the pair of non-adjacent rhyming lines (*b ... b*) offset to the right, each of these lines of poetry attached by a drawn line to the couplet which it was intended to follow. This general pattern is followed, with variations, in the manuscripts of both the *Ordinalia* and *Beunans Meriasek*. Sometimes a more complex rhyme scheme was used, for example, with an additional line of poetry, intended to come at the end of a six-line stanza, offset even further to the right and joined to the whole stanza by an additional drawn line (see, for example, the 'Speech of King Solomon,' transcribed below). The conventional method of printing the stanzas, followed here, is to print the lines in the order in which they were intended to be understood, while indenting the lines which are offset to the right, and then indenting further those lines which in the manuscript are offset further to the right.

> ### Ordinale de Origine Mundi   Bodl.: MS. Bodl. 791
> f 18v *(Speech of King David)*
> ...
> Whethoug menstrels ha tabours
> trey hans harpes ha trompours   5
>   cythol crowd fylh ha savtry
> psalmus gyttrens ha nakrys
> organs inweth cymbalys
>   recordys ha symphony
> ...   10
>
> f 26 *(Speech of King Solomon)*
> ...
> a tus vas why rewelas
> fetel formyas dev an tas   15
>   nef ha nor war lergh y vrys
> woge henna y fynnas

adam eua dre y ras
   ys gruk haual sur keffrys
      thotho deffry
ol an beys a ros thetha
may hallons ynno bewa   5
hagh a fleghys vynytha
   a theffo a nethe y
y vennath theugh yn tyen
keffrys gorryth ha benen
   an guary yv dve lymmyn   10
ha the welas an flogholeth
awothevys cryst ragón passyon
   avorow devg a dermyn
      hag ens pup dre
a barth an tas . menstrels a ras . pebough w⌈h⌉are   15
a Iesus hep gorholeth

f 82 *(Speech of the Emperor)*
...

a tus vas why re welas . a thasserghyens crist del fue   20
porthow yfarn a torras . yn mes adam hag eue
kemmys a wruk both an tas . ys gorras the lowene
the vap den y tysquethas . pur wyr mur a kerenge
hag yn ban the nef then ioy . ihesu a wruk yskynne
worth an iaul hay company . rak as guytho yn pup le   25
hay vennath theugh pup huny . lemmyn ens pup war tu tre
now menstrels pybygh bysy . may hyllyn mos the thonssye
...

Ordinale de vita sancti mereadoci episcopi et confessoris   30
National Library of Wales: Peniarth MS. 105
p 71 *(Stage direction)*
...

°And Iohn ergudyn aredy a horse bakke þat was þe Iustes with constantyn
[with a] ffor to play þe marchont°   35
...

10/ an ... lymmyn: *beginning with this line, the rest of 'Origo Mundi' is in a different hand*
11/ flogholeth: *part of an alternative ending*
16/ a ... gorholeth: *this line, though placed at the end of the text in the MS, is also part of the alternative ending; a drawn line connects this material to line 12*
24/ hag: *added in left margin, cramped*
34/ ergudyn: *Nance, 'Folklore,' p 133 suggests that the name in Cornish means 'snow-lock' (white hair)*

p 97 *(Speech of the Duke)*

...

Evugh oll gans an guary
ny a vyn ag*es* pesy
 alue*n* golo*n*   5
wy ag*es* beth gor hagruek
banneth c*r*ist ha m*er*yasek
 banneth maria cambron
pybugh menstrels colonnek may hyllyn donsia dyson

             10

pp 178–9 *(Speech of the Earl of Vannes)*

...

Dywhy banneth m*er*yasek
ha maria cambron wek
 banneth an abesteleth   15
Evugh oll gans an guary
nyavyn ag*es* pesy
 kyns moys an plaeth |
pyboryon wethugh in scon
nyavyn ketep map bron   20
 moys t⟨...⟩
Eugh bo tregugh
wolcu*m* vethugh
 kyn fewy syt⟨...⟩

             25

  ffinit*ur* p*er* d*omi*num ⟨......⟩
  anno d*omi*ni M^l v⟨...⟩

The Creacion of the World, the first daie of playe Bodl.: MS. Bodl. 219

f 27 *(Speech of Noah)*   30

...

An kethe Iorna ma ew de // 3en tase dew rebo grassyes
why a wellas pub degre // leas matters gwarryes
ha creac*i*on oll an byse /

             35

In weth oll why a wellas
an keth bysma consumys

21/ t⟨...⟩: text illegible; the donsya *in Stokes,* Meriasek, *p 264*
24/ syt⟨...⟩: *text illegible;* sythe*n* o*m*ma *in Stokes,* Meriasek, *p 264*
26/ d*omi*n*um* ⟨......⟩: *text illegible;* d*omi*num HADTON *in Stokes,* Meriasek, *p 264*
27/ M^l v⟨...⟩: *text illegible;* M^l v^c iiij *in Stokes,* Meriasek, *p 264*

der lyvyow a thower p*ur* vras.
ny ve vdn mabe dean sparys
 menas Noy y wreag hay flehys

dewh a vorowe a dermyn   5
why a weall matters p*ur* vras
ha redemp*ci*on grauntys
der vercy a thew an tase
 Tha sawya neb es kellys.

                10

Mynstrells grewgh theny peba
may hallan warbarthe downssya
 del ew an vaner han geys

heare endeth the Crea*ci*on of the worlde: 15
w*i*th noyes flude: wryten by william
Iordan: the xii^th of August: i6ii

Stage Diagrams in the Play Manuscripts

Stage diagrams in the *Ordinalia* and *Beunans Meriasek* offer convincing evidence that Cornish drama was presented in a theatre in the round (see figures 4–8). Five stage diagrams appear in the play texts, one for each of the three days of the *Ordinalia* and one for each of the two days of *Beunans Meriasek*. A list of characters along with a notation of their number of speeches appears in each day's play. Useful for a variety of purposes, this check-list may have been intended as a guide for apportioning more than one part to an actor (Nance, 'The Plen an Gwary or Cornish Playing-Place,' p 209). When considered in conjunction with the stage directions in the play manuscripts and with the action indicated in the plays, the stage diagrams mandate an outdoor area large enough for battles and for actors to ride around on horseback, with raised *loca*, sometimes known as 'stations' or 'mansions,' on the periphery, to and from which actors would ascend and descend. The plain-an-gwary fills these requirements well, its sloping sides suitable both for those stations demanded by the texts and for the audience to stand or sit for clear viewing.

INDICATIONS OF STAGING IN THE *ORDINALIA*

The first day's play, 'Origo Mundi,' is followed in the manuscript by a diagram (see figure 4) that positions eight stations around a circular open 'plain' in which free-standing structures and props would be placed as required by the text. Two of those eight peripheral stations, for 'celu*m*' (Heaven) and for the 'tortores' (torturers), were fixed in the same location for all three days of the *Ordinalia*. Assuming Heaven, placed at the top of each diagram, to be in the east for all three days, then 'infernu*m*' (Hell), as indicated in diagrams for 'Origo Mundi' and

'Resurrexio Domini,' would be located in the north, with the station for the torturers in between Heaven and Hell. Beginning at the top of the diagram for 'Origo Mundi' and moving clockwise around the playing place, stations on the circumference are designated for 'celum,' 'episcopus,' 'Abraham,' 'Rex salamon,' 'Rex dauid,' 'Rex pharao,' 'infernum,' and 'tortores.'

The diagram for the Ordinalia's second play, 'Passio Christi,' again has eight stations (see figure 5), but since this day's play does not require a station for Hell, that location in the north is given to the 'Doctores.' Clockwise from the top, stations are assigned for 'celum,' 'centurio,' 'Cayphas,' 'princeps annas,' 'herodes,' 'pilatus,' 'Doctores,' and 'tortores.' On the third day of the Ordinalia Hell is again in the north for the play 'Resurrexio Domini' (see figure 6). Beginning at the top of the diagram, the stations are for 'celum,' 'milites,' 'Nichodemus,' 'Iosep abarmathia,' 'Imperator,' 'pilatus,' 'infernum,' and 'tortores.'

Directions given to the actors in the first scenes of the Ordinalia suggest something of the nature of its 'celum,' which consisted of a topmost level for Deus Pater and the angels, and a somewhat lower level for 'paradys' (Norris (ed), Ancient Cornish Drama, vol 1, l.75), where Adam and Eve first live and where Seth later seeks the Oil of Mercy. This two-tiered structure is implicit in the stage direction that, following his opening speech, 'descendit Deus de pulpito' (Norris, vol 1, l.48.1) and then he creates Adam. While on that lower level, Deus Pater instructs Adam to lie down upon the earth, where the deity creates Eve. Stage directions and dialogue thus suggest at least two levels between which Deus Pater, Adam, Eve, angels, and devils all moved.

Since stage directions to actors in other parts of the Ordinalia also indicate that stations were raised, most or perhaps all of the loca designated in the play's diagrams may have been situated on the sloping bank. Episcopus, Abraham, Rex Solomon, and Rex David, for example, are all directed to descend from or ascend to their stations. The locations for Hell and for the torturers were probably also on the bank, since Lucifer, Satan, Beelzebub, and the torturers are all told at various times to descend or ascend between their particular stations and the platea.

In addition to attesting raised stations, the manuscript of the Ordinalia indicates action requiring an arena large enough to allow considerable spectacle and a fairly wide range of movement. Such characters as Cayphas, Herodes, Pilatus, Annas, and Lucifer are at various times directed to 'parade,' apparently with considerable freedom for individual interpretation; stage directions to Herodes and Lucifer, for example, indicate 'pompabit si voluerit herodes' and 'pompabit lucifer si placet' (Norris, vol 1, ll.1676.1 and 1906.1). Character movement in other parts of the play also requires a fairly large arena. In the segment on David and Bathsheba, for instance, David rides horseback in the plain, as do Uriah and the messenger when they go off to war.

Other directions and plot elements in the Ordinalia may also signal a connection between the plays and the plain-an-gwary, since several actions, such as the creation of Eve and the earth's rejection of Pilate, seem to require of the platea a concealed pit that is accessible from the theatre's side. Such a pit and a connecting ditch appear to have been part of the still existing plain-an-gwary at Perranzabuloe. As Borlase, Natural History, p 298, described it in 1758, that playing place, now known as Piran Round, contained an elongated depression in the plain,

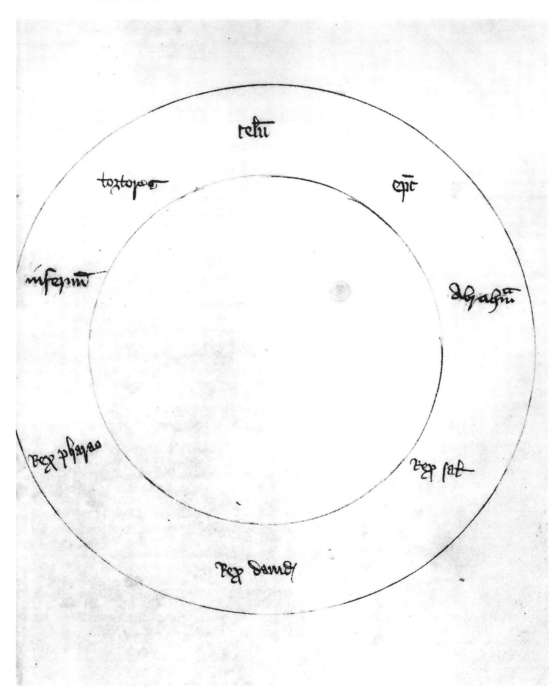

Figure 4: MS. Bodl. 791, f 27. Reproduced by permission of the Bodleian Library, Oxford.

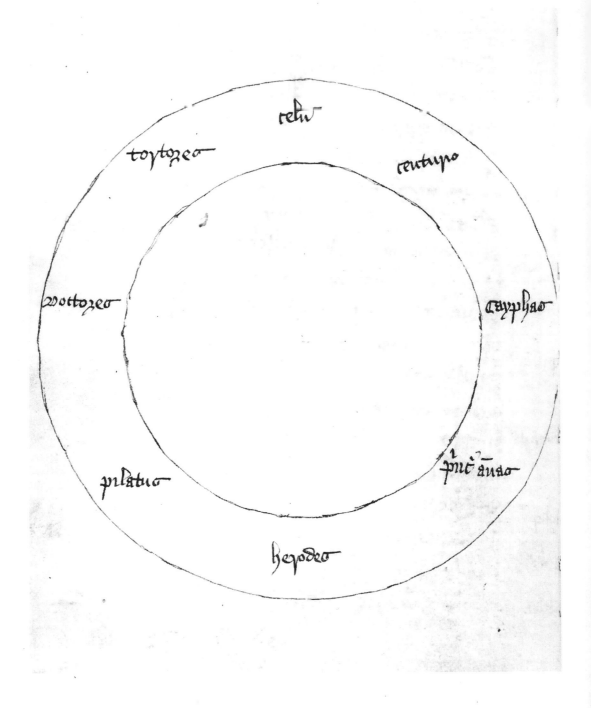

Figure 5: MS. Bodl. 791, f 56v. Reproduced by permission of the Bodleian Library, Oxford.

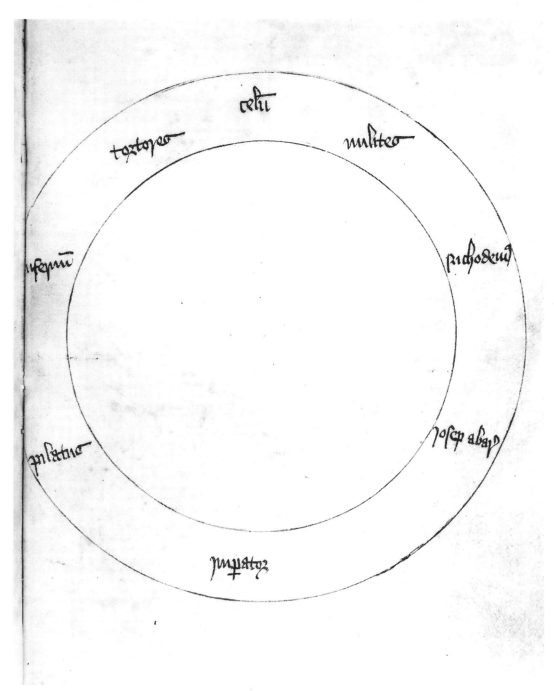

Figure 6: MS. Bodl. 791, f 83. Reproduced by permission of the Bodleian Library, Oxford.

running from an opening in the amphitheatre's east bank to a circular pit in the platea, thirteen feet in diameter, with a turf bench (see pp 403, 406). This indentation, known because of its shape as the 'Devil's Spoon,' is still visible, although the depredations of time and weather have made it less evident. Halliday, *Legend of the Rood*, pp 29–32, argues that the stage directions and the 'Devil's Spoon' are connected; Holman's assertion in 'Cornish Plays and Playing Places,' p 54, that the 'Devil's Spoon' was merely a cooking trench has not been generally accepted.

INDICATIONS OF STAGING IN *BEUNANS MERIASEK*

The diagram for the first day of *Beunans Meriasek* has twelve stations noted clearly, with additional incomplete markings around the edges (see figure 7). A 'Capella' is located in the centre of the plain and arranged around the periphery, beginning at the top and proceeding clockwise, are stations for 'Celum,' 'Siluester,' 'Magister,' 'Episcopus kernov,' 'Dux britonum id est pater mereadoci,' 'Rex Conanus,' 'Constantinus' (located at the bottom directly opposite Heaven), 'Tevdarus Imperator,' 'Dux Cornubie,' 'Comes rohany,' 'Exulatores,' and 'Tortores,' underneath which is a notation for 'Infernum.' Including the station for Hell, the first day's play in *Beunans Meriasek* has thirteen stations.

The second day's section of *Beunans Meriasek* seems to have had even more stations, perhaps fifteen altogether (see figure 8). However, because a large piece is missing from the left side of this manuscript leaf and therefore from the upper left arc of the circular diagram, the names of all of the stations are not now visible. Fortunately, the complete titles for some names now missing, such as the First and Second Dukes Magus and the Bishop of Pola, are provided by Whitley Stokes, *Meriasek*, p 266, an early editor who saw the manuscript in a more complete condition. Beginning at the top and proceeding clockwise are 'Celum,' 'Siluester,' 'ij Episcopus,' 'Episcopus ke⟨r⟩nov,' 'Comes vennete⟨n⟩sis,' 'Rex massen,' 'Imperator Constantinus,' 'Tirannus Imperattor,' 'Comes globus,' '⟨Primus Du⟩x Magus,' '⟨Secundus⟩ dux Magus,' 'Ep⟨iscopus⟩ Pol⟨y⟩,' 'ffilius Mulieris,' 'infernum,' and 'Tortores.'

Stage directions in *Beunans Meriasek*, as in the *Ordinalia*, imply raised *loca* and characters in the plays for each of the two days are required to move up and down between their particular stations and the platea. Moreover, directions requiring that a number of actors move between levels at one time indicate that these stations may have been of considerable size if, for example, Dux Cornubiae descends with twenty armed men from one station, or if Tevdarus descends with fifteen from another station.

Like the *Ordinalia*, *Beunans Meriasek* requires a large, open acting space. Characters must ride about on horses, parade grandly, and engage in battle on a relatively large scale, as when the forces of Tevdarus engage those of the Dux Cornubiae. Also necessitating a large central arena are the structures required in the plain, which include a hill on which characters can stand, a chapter house, and a 'capella.'

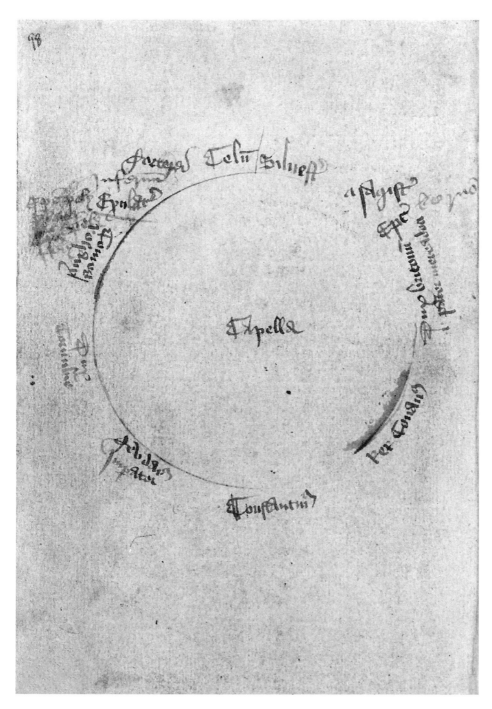

Figure 7: Peniarth MS 105, p 98. Reproduced by permission of the National Library of Wales.

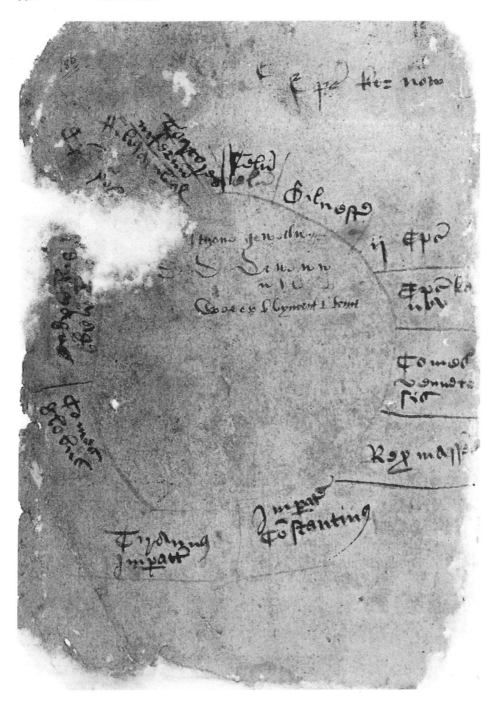

Figure 8: Peniarth MS 105, p 180. Reproduced by permission of the National Library of Wales.

References

Bakere, Jane A. *The Cornish Ordinalia: A Critical Study* (Cardiff, 1980).

Betcher, Gloria J. 'Place Names and Political Patronage in the Cornish *Ordinalia*,' *Research Opportunities in Renaissance Drama* 35 (1996), 111–31.

– 'A Reassessment of the Date and Provenance of the Cornish *Ordinalia*,' *Comparative Drama* 29 (1995–6), 436–53.

Borlase, William. *The Natural History of Cornwall* (Oxford, 1758).

Campanile, Enrico (ed and trans). 'Un frammento scenico medio-cornico,' *Studi e Saggi Linguistici* 3 (1963), 60–80.

Combellack, Myrna (ed). *The Camborne Play: A Verse Translation of Beunans Meriasek* (Redruth, 1988).

– 'A Critical Edition of *Beunans Meriasek*.' PhD thesis (University of Exeter, 1985).

Crawford, T.D. 'The Composition of the Cornish Ordinalia,' *Old Cornwall* 9 (1980), 144–52.

Fowler, David C. 'The Date of the Cornish "Ordinalia",' *Mediaeval Studies* 23 (1961), 91–125.

Halliday, Frank. *The Legend of the Rood* (London, 1955).

Harris, Markham. *The Cornish Ordinalia: A Medieval Dramatic Trilogy* (Washington, DC, 1969).

– *The Life of Meriasek: A Medieval Cornish Miracle Play* (Washington, DC, 1977).

Harris, Phyllis Pier (ed). 'Origo Mundi, First Play of the Cornish Mystery Cycle, *The Ordinalia*. A New Edition.' PhD dissertation (University of Washington, 1964).

Hawke, Andrew. 'A Lost Manuscript of the Cornish *Ordinalia*?' *Cornish Studies* 7 (1979), 45–60.

Holman, Treve. 'Cornish Plays and Playing Places,' *Theatre Notebook* 4.3 (1950), 52–4.

Hooper, E.G. Retallack (ed). *Gwryans an Bys or Creation of the World.* R. Morton Nance and A.S.D Smith (trans) (Redruth, 1985).

Jenner, Henry. 'Descriptions of Cornish Manuscripts – II: The Fourteenth-Century Charter Endorsement, Brit. Mus. Add. Ch. 19491,' *JRIC* 20.1 (1915), 41–8.

– 'An Early Cornish Fragment,' *Athenaeum*, no 2614 (1 December 1877), 698–9.

– *A Handbook of the Cornish Language Chiefly in Its Latest Stages with Some Account of Its History and Literature* (London, 1904).

– 'Perran Round and the Cornish Drama,' *The Seventy-Eighth Annual Report of the Royal Cornwall Polytechnic Society*, ns 1, pt 3 (Penryn, 1912).

Longsworth, Robert. *The Cornish Ordinalia: Religion and Dramaturgy* (Cambridge, Mass, 1967).

Murdoch, Brian. *Cornish Literature* (Cambridge, 1993).

– 'The Place-Names in the Cornish *Passio Christi*,' *The Bulletin of the Board of Celtic Studies* 37 (1990), 116–18.

Nance, R. Morton. 'Folklore Recorded in the Cornish Language,' *The Ninety-First Annual Report of the Royal Cornwall Polytechnic Society*, ns 5, pt 2 (1924), 124–45.

– 'New Light on Cornish,' *Old Cornwall* 4.6 (1947), 214–16.

– 'The Plen an Gwary or Cornish Playing-Place,' *JRIC* 24.3 (1935), 190–211.

Nance, R. Morton (ed and trans). 'The Charter Endorsement in Cornish,' *Old Cornwall* 2.4 (1932), 34–6.

Neuss, Paula (ed and trans). *The Creacion of the World: A Critical Edition and Translation* (New York, 1983).

Newlyn, Evelyn S. (ed). *Cornish Drama of the Middle Ages: A Bibliography* (Redruth, 1987).

– 'The Middle Cornish Interlude: Genre and Tradition,' *Comparative Drama* 30.2 (1996), 266–81.

Norris, Edwin (ed). *The Ancient Cornish Drama.* 2 vols (1859; rpt London, 1968).

Padel, O.J. 'Notes on the New Edition of the Middle Cornish "Charter Endorsement",' *Cambrian Medieval Celtic Studies* 30 (Winter, 1995), 123–7.

Polwhele, Richard. *History of Cornwall.* 2 vols (Falmouth and Truro, 1803–8; rpt Dorking, 1978).

Quinn, Esther Casier. *The Quest of Seth for the Oil of Life* (Chicago, 1962).

Rawe, Donald R. (trans). *The Creation of the World (Gwryans an Bys)* (Padstow, 1978).

Sandys, William. 'On the Cornish Drama,' *JRIC* 1.3 (1865), 1–18.

Stokes, Whitley (ed). 'The Fragments of a Drama in Add. Ch. 19,491, Mus. Brit.,' *Revue celtique* 4 (1879–80), 258–62.

– (ed). *Gwreans an bys: The Creation of the World* (London, 1864).

– (ed). *The Life of St. Meriasek, Bishop and Confessor: A Cornish Drama* (London, 1872).

Thomas, Charles. *Christian Antiquities of Camborne* (St Austell, 1967).

– 'Piran Round and the Medieval Cornish Drama,' *Piran Round Souvenir Programme* (Newton Abbot, 1969).

Toorians, Lauran (ed). *The Middle Cornish Charter Endorsement: The Making of a Marriage in Medieval Cornwall* (Innsbruck, 1991).

APPENDIX 3

Ancient Parishes with Possible Examples of the Plain-an-gwary

O.J. PADEL

At the following locations there may have been a playing place, or plain-an-gwary. In some instances the evidence for the use consists solely in the place name; occasionally the evidence is instead, or additionally, local memory. Grid references to Ordnance Survey maps are given where possible but in some instances the name is now lost and the exact site cannot be determined; such names are in italics below. Further field-work and work on sources in the Cornwall Record Office, Truro, may succeed in locating some of the lost sites and may also produce further instances. The sites below are listed according to their ancient parishes in alphabetical order.

Many of the references to these playing places come from the check-lists of archaeological sites, parish by parish, published by various authors in *Cornish Archaeology* yearly from 1962 to 1980 and by Vivien Russell in her *West Penwith Survey* (1971); these are cited in abbreviated form, as '*CA* [vol], [page],' or as 'Russell, [page],' which in either case refers to the check-list of the parish in question; further references to the individual sites will be found in those check-lists. When the source is not a parish check-list another source is given, eg, CRO and LHA for the Lanhydrock Atlas, Lanhydrock, Cornwall; other references are cited below.

A fair number of playing places are situated on the glebe-land of the church. In other cases a playing place was a reused 'round,' that is, an Iron-Age or Romano-British fortified farmstead; however, the majority of such 'rounds' were not used as playing places. Again, a site called a playing place is not automatic proof of the performance of plays; such arenas may have been used also, or instead, for the playing of sports.

References Cited:

Cornish Archaeology 2 (1963)
  Warner, Richard, 'Parochial Check-List of Antiquities: Parish of Perranzabuloe,' pp 67–72
Cornish Archaeology 3 (1964)
  Warner, Richard, 'Parochial Check-List of Antiquities: Parish of Kea,' pp 95–7
  – 'Parochial Check-List of Antiquities: Parish of St Allen,' pp 97–9
Cornish Archaeology 5 (1966)
  Dowson, Edith, 'Parochial Check-List of Antiquities: Parish of Constantine,' pp 80–2
  Sheppard, Peter, 'Parochial Check-List of Antiquities: Parish of St Goran,' pp 74–6

Cornish Archaeology 6 (1967)
  Dowson, Edith, 'Parochial Check-List of Antiquities: Parish of Grade-Ruan,' pp 102–5
  Sheppard, Peter, 'Parochial Check-List of Antiquities: Parish of St Ewe,' pp 98–101
  Tangye, Michael, 'Parochial Check-List of Antiquities: Parish of Redruth,' pp 90–5
Cornish Archaeology 7 (1968)
  Dowson, Edith, 'Parochial Check-List of Antiquities: Parish of St Keverne,' pp 101–6
Cornish Archaeology 9 (1970)
  Dowson, Edith, 'Parochial Check-List of Antiquities: Parish of Landewednack,' pp 155–6
  Sheppard, Peter, 'Parochial Check-List of Antiquities: Parish of St Stephen-in-Brannel,' pp 144–9
  Thomas, Charles, 'Parochial Check-List of Antiquities: Parish of Camborne,' pp 136–44
Cornish Archaeology 15 (1976)
  Sheppard, Peter, 'Parochial Check-List of Antiquities: Parish of Probus,' pp 103–9
Cornish Archaeology 19 (1980)
  Appleby, Cedric, 'Parochial Check-List of Antiquities: Parish of Sithney,' pp 89–94
Cornish Archaeology 20 (1981)
  Beagrie, Neil, 'Parochial Check-List of Antiquities: Parish of Luxulyan,' pp 209–14
Douch, Henry Leslie. *Cornish Windmills* (Truro, 1963).
Picken, W. M. M. 'Trezance, Lahays and the Manor of Cardinham,' *Devon and Cornwall Notes and Queries* 26 (1954–5), 203–8.
Polwhele, Richard. *The History of Cornwall.* 7 vols (Falmouth and Truro, 1803–8; rpt Dorking, 1978).
Russell, Vivian. *West Penwith Survey* (Truro, 1971).
Smith, Lucy Toulmin (ed). *The Itinerary of John Leland In or About the Years 1535–1543.* 5 vols (London, 1906–10; rpt 1964).
The Victoria History of the Counties of England. *The Victoria History of the County of Cornwall.* Vol 1. William Page (ed). (London,1906; rpt 1975).
Whitley, H. Michell. 'Cornish Rounds or Playing Places,' *Devon and Cornwall Notes and Queries* 7 (1912–13), 172–4.

List of Locations

Camborne (possible)
Race, SW 634410 approx: CA 9, 141

Constantine
1/ Trebah, SW 765272 approx: CA 5, 81
2/ Lower Treglidgwith, SW 738294?: CA 5, 81

Cubert
The Playing, c 1696: LHA vol 1, p 40

Golant
a Playing Place c 1670 (report of *c* 1740), SX 121551 approx: CRO: R/5438

Gorran
The Plains, SX 002428: *CA* 5, 76

Kea
Playing Place, SW 814419: *CA* 3, 97: Whitley, 173

Landewednack (possible)
Cross Common, SW 708126 approx: *CA* 9, 156; Polwhele, vol 2, p 192

Lezant
Playing Park, 1680: CRO: ARD/TER/68

Ludgvan (possible)
Churchtown, SW 503329: Russell, 75

Luxulian (possible)
Castilly, SX 031627: *CA* 20, 210

Newlyn East ('modern')
VCH, 457

Padstow
The playing place: Douch, 51–2

Perranzabuloe
Piran Round, SW 778544: *CA* 2, 72

Probus
1/ Trewithen, SW 912479 approx: *CA* 15, 107
2/ Candor (possible), SW 875494: *CA* 15, 106

Rame
Place, SX 425492 approx: Picken, 206

Redruth
Plain-an-Gwarry, SW 698425: *CA* 6, 92

Ruan Major (possible)
Churchtown, SW 703163 approx: *CA* 6, 104; Polwhele, vol 2, p 192

Ruan Minor
Plain-an-quarry, SW 715155: *CA* 6, 104; Polwhele, vol 2, p 192

St Allen
Plyn en Gwear, SW 805527?: *CA* 3, 99

St Buryan
Pendrea, SW 405250 approx: Russell, 71

St Columb Major ('modern')
VCH, 457

St Enoder
The Playne place or Fayre Parke, early 17th century: CRO: ARD/TER/194

St Erme
Whitley, 173–4

St Ewe
Plenaguary, SW 986461: *CA* 6, 100

St Hilary
Plain-an-gwarry, SW 533314

St Ives
Stennack, SW 513402 approx: Russell, 72

St Just in Penwith
Churchtown, SW 370314: Russell, 73

St Keverne
1/ Laddenvean (possible), SW 788213: *CA* 7, 105
2/ Tregoning, SW 793213: *CA* 7, 105

St Mabyn
The pleinge place, 1613: CRO: ARD/TER/304

St Stephen in Brannel
Churchtown, SW 944534: *CA* 9, 147

Sancreed
Plain Gwarry, SW 419295: Russell, 78

Sithney
Plain an Gwarry, SW 643287: *CA* 19, 91

Stoke Climsland
The playing close, 1601: CRO: ARD/TER/394

Truro (Kenwyn)
Truro Castle, SW 823450: Smith, vol 1, p 198

The Hurling Game in Cornwall

The game of hurling continues to be one of Cornwall's most popular customs. The origins and original meaning of this game can now only be surmised from sixteenth- and seventeenth-century extant records, although it appears connected with rites of spring and ancient ceremonies. Hurling's ceremonial and ritualistic elements suggest that its origins and practices may have roots in the impulses and desires that are represented by the king and queen of May and summer games, and so we include records of the practice here.

Because the game has inevitably changed over time, we cannot assume the authenticity of current hurling practices, but in essence the game takes place between two teams of Cornish people who attempt to move the ball to a goal by throwing it to a teammate or by running and carrying it. Two early references to receipts and expenses relating to the hurling game or ball are found in the churchwardens' accounts of Camborne (CRO: PD/322/1) and St Columb Major (CRO: P/36/8/1). Borough accounts of St Ives, a Cornish town with a long history of hurling, afford a single seventeenth-century hurling expense.

The three- to four-inch hurling ball was likely made of silver over a wooden core; records from St Columb Major in 1592–3 and from St Ives in 1638–9 refer to the ball as silver. However, the records from St Columb Major for 1593–4 refer in one entry to the ball as silver and in another entry to the ball as 'sylver ball gylt,' the latter description suggesting that a ball of silver was covered with gold. The substance of the ball may, of course, have varied in different times and in different areas of Cornwall.

Richard Carew's *Survey of Cornwall* (1602) offers a contemporary account of the hurling game. If Carew is correct the game existed in two forms. One, 'hurling to goales,' was conducted in a relatively confined area, perhaps even a plain-an-gwary, with a limited number of players per side (see p 567). Carew observes that this version of the game was 'mostly vsed at weddings,' where the guests would take on 'all commers,' inviting conjecture about the symbolic value of the hurling. Equating the gold ball that was used in medieval times with the sun, A. Ivan Rabey, in *Hurling at St. Columb and in Cornwall: A Study in History and Tradition* (Padstow, 1972), 7, explains that the ball would bring 'luck, fertility and health' and still does when the contemporary ball is 'handled in turn by would-be lovers, sick people, youths and men in their prime.' Rabey asserts that this use of the ball in the game incorporates 'the remnants of a Spring Festival as old as any in the world.' Whatever the symbolic significance of the ball and the games, the first of these two versions of hurling was governed, according to Carew, by 'many lawes,' in contrast to the second, freer version of the game.

Carew explains the second version of the game, called 'hurling to the Countrey,' as 'more diffuse and confuse' than 'hurling to goales.' Since this second version of the game took place between two or more parishes per side, countless players might be involved. Because the goals were three or more miles apart, the play ranged widely over the countryside, in Carew's words, 'thorow bushes, briers, mires, plashes and riuers whatsoeuer.' Contemporary games of hurling similarly involve large and irregular numbers of players and take place throughout the town streets as well as in the country.

Other early historians of Cornwall also mention hurling. In his Speculi Britanniae Pars (*c* 1603), Norden discusses wrestling and hurling, those 'sharpe and seuere' activities of Cornish men, and observes that while the first is 'violent,' the second is 'daungerous.' Norden links the hurling game to the stones on the edge of Bodmin Moor called 'The Hurlers,' finding them arranged in a 'straglinge manner' corresponding to the positions and posture of Cornish men engaged in the sport. Camden, in the 1610 translation of his history and description of Britain, also discusses the stones, recounting the legend that the stones are the remains of impious young people who were turned to stone for their blasphemy.

For descriptions of CRO: PD/322/1, CRO: P/36/8/1, the St Ives Borough Accounts II, and Carew's *Survey of Cornwall*, see 'The Documents' pp 423–4, 430–1, 431–2, and 422–3. Norden's Speculi Britanniae Pars and Camden's *Britain* are described below. The former is dated 1603 by William Ravenhill, 'The South West in the Eighteenth-Century Re-mapping of England,' *Maps and History in South-West England*, Katherine Barker and Roger J.P. Kain (eds) (Exeter, 1991), 5; it is dated *c* 1604 in the facsimile edition of *Joel Gascoyne: A Map of the County of Cornwall 1699*, William L.D. Ravenhill and O.J. Padel (eds) (Plymouth, 1991), 11n.

John Norden, Speculi Britanniae Pars
London, British Library, Harley MS. 6252; *c* 1603; English; paper; ii + 76 + iiii; 302mm x 208mm (218mm x 122mm), average 43 long lines, some columns; modern pencil foliation; includes coloured maps and drawings of artifacts and monuments, title page is decorated and some letters in gold, catchwords usually used; bound in brown leather with gold stamping, title on spine: 'JO. NORDEN | SPECULI | BRITANNIAE | PARS | CORNWALL,' 'MUS. BRIT. | BIBL. HARL.,' and '6252 | PLUT. LXV B.' Some words, especially proper nouns and terms specific to hurling, are in display script.

William Camden, *Britain*
[Ornament.] | BRITAIN, | OR | A CHOROGRAPHICALL | DESCRIPTION OF THE MOST | flourishing Kingdomes, ENGLAND, | SCOTLAND, and IRELAND, and the | *Ilands adioyning, out of the depth of* | ANTIQUITIE: | BEAVTIFIED WITH MAPPES OF THE | *severall Shires of* ENGLAND: | Written first in Latine by *William Camden* | CLARENCEAUX K. of A. | Translated newly into English by *Philémon Holland* | Doctour in Physick: | Finally, revised, amended, and enlarged with sundry | Additions by the said Author | [armorial device] | LONDINI, | *Impensis* GEORGII BISHOP | & IOANNIS NORTON. | M. DC. X.. STC: 4509.

CAMBORNE

1554–5
St Meriadocus and St Martin Churchwardens' Accounts   CRO: PD/322/1
f 39v *(24 February 1553/4–3 March 1554/5) (Receipts)*

...

Item Resevyd of Mr william crane for the horlyng   xij d.

...

ST COLUMB MAJOR

1592–3
St Columba the Virgin Churchwardens' Accounts   CRO: P/36/8/1
f [26v] *(30 November–30 November) (Debts)*

...

Iohn Menheere owith for a silver ball delivered to Tobye at his instance and
vpon his worde x s.

...

1593–4
St Columba the Virgin Churchwardens' Accounts   CRO: P/36/8/1
f [27] *(30 November–30 November) (Debts)*

...

Iohn Menheere Restethe owyng as by the last accompt for a sylver ball gylt x s.

...

f [27v] *(Receipts)*

...

Receaved of Toby Bennet for the silver ball for which I⟨..⟩n Menhere
within is charged and thus discharged   x s.

...

COUNTY OF CORNWALL

1602
Richard Carew, Survey of Cornwall   STC: 4615
sigs V1v–V3v

...

Hurling   Hurling taketh his denomination from throwing of the ball, and is of
two sorts, in the East parts of Cornwall, to goales, and in the West,
to the countrey.

. For hurling to goales, there are 15. 20. or 30. players more or lesse, chosen
out on each side, who strip themselues into their slightest apparell, and then
ioyne hands in ranke one against another. Out of these ranks, they match
themselues by payres, one embracing another, & so passe away: euery of
which couple, are specially to watch one another during the play.   5

After this, they pitch two bushes in the ground, some eight or ten foote
asunder; and directly against them, ten or twelue score off, other twayne in
like distance, which they terme their Goales. One of these is appoynted by
lots, to the one side, and the other to his aduerse party. There is assigned for
their gard, a couple of their best stopping Hurlers: the residue draw into the   10
midst betweene both goales, where some indifferent person throweth vp a
ball, the which whosoeuer can catch, and cary through his aduersaries goale,
hath wonne the game. But therein consisteth one of Hercules his labours:
for hee that is once possessed of the ball, hath his contrary mate waiting at
inches, and assaying to lay hold vpon him. The other thrusteth him in the   15
brest, with his closed fist, to keepe him off; which they call Butting, and
place in weldoing the same, no small poynt of manhood.

If hee escape the first, another taketh him in hand, and so a third, neyther
is hee left, vntill hauing met (as the Frenchman sayes) Chausseur a son pied,
hee eyther touch the ground with some part of his bodie, in wrast-|ling, or   20
cry, Hold; which is the word of yeelding. Then must he cast the ball (named
Dealing) to some one of his fellowes, who catching the same in his hand,
maketh away withall as before; and if his hap or agility bee so good, as to
shake off or outrunne his counterwayters, at the goale, hee findeth one or
two fresh men, readie to receiue and keepe him off. It is therefore a very   25
disaduantageable match, or extraordinary accident, that leeseth many goales:
howbeit, that side carryeth away best reputation, which giueth most falles in
the hurling, keepeth the ball longest, and presseth his contrary neerest to their
owne goale. Sometimes one chosen person on eche party dealeth the ball.

The Hurlers are bound to the obseruation of many lawes, as, that they must   30
hurle man to man, and not two set vpon one man at once: that the Hurler
against the ball, must not but, nor hand-fast vnder girdle: that hee who hath
the ball, must but onely in the others brest: that he must deale no Fore-ball,
viz. he may not throw it to any of his mates, standing neerer the goale, then
himselfe. Lastly, in dealing the ball, if any of the other part can catch it flying   35
between, or e're the other haue it fast, he thereby winneth the same to his
side, which straightway of defendant becommeth assailant, as the other, of
assailant falls to be defendant. The least breach of these lawes, the Hurlers
take for a iust cause of going together by the eares, but with their fists onely;
neither doth any among them seek reuenge for such wrongs or hurts, but at   40
the like play againe. These hurling matches are mostly vsed at weddings, where
commonly the ghests vndertake to encounter all commers. |

The hurling to the Countrey, is more diffuse and confuse, as bound to few of these orders: Some two or more Gentlemen doe commonly make this match, appointing that on such a holyday, they will bring to such an indifferent place, two, three, or more parishes of the East or South quarter, to hurle against so many other, of the West or North. Their goales are either those Gentlemens houses, or some townes or villages, three or foure miles asunder, of which either side maketh choice after the neernesse to their dwellings. When they meet, there is neyther comparing of numbers, nor matching of men; but a siluer ball is cast vp, and that company, which can catch, and cary it by force, or sleight, to their place assigned, gaineth the ball and victory. Whosoeuer getteth seizure of this ball, findeth himselfe generally pursued by the aduerse party; neither will they leaue, till (without all respects) he be layd flat on Gods deare earth: which fall once receiued, disableth him from any longer detayning the ball: hee therefore throweth the same (with like hazard of intercepting, as in the other hurling) to some one of his fellowes, fardest before him, who maketh away withall in like maner. Such as see where the ball is played, giue notice therof to their mates, crying, Ware East, Ware West, &c. as the same is carried.

The Hurlers take their next way ouer hilles, dales, hedges, ditches; yea, and thorow bushes, briers, mires, plashes and riuers whatsoeuer; so as you shall sometimes see 20. or 30. lie tugging together in the water, scrambling and scratching for the ball. A play (verily) both rude & rough, and yet such, as is not destitute of policies, in some sort resembling the feats of warre: for you shall | haue companies layd out before, on the one side, to encounter them that come with the ball, and of the other party to succor them, in maner of a fore-ward. Againe, other troups lye houering on the sides, like wings, to helpe or stop their escape: and where the ball it selfe goeth, it resembleth the ioyning of the two mayne battels: the slowest footed who come lagge, supply the showe of a rere-ward: yea, there are horsemen placed also on either party (as it were in ambush) and ready to ride away with the ball, if they can catch it at aduantage. But they may not so steale the palme: for gallop any one of them neuer so fast, yet he shall be surely met at some hedge corner, crosse-lane, bridge, or deepe water, which (by casting the Countrie) they know he must needs touch at: and if his good fortune gard him not the better, hee is like to pay the price of his theft, with his owne and his horses ouerthrowe to the ground. Sometimes the whole company runneth with the ball, seuen or eight miles out of the direct way, which they should keepe. Sometimes a foote-man getting it by stealth, the better to scape vnespied, will carry the same quite backwards, and so, at last, get to the goale by a windlace: which once knowne to be wonne, all that side flocke thither with great iolity: and if the same bee a Gentlemans house, they giue him the ball for a Trophee, and the drinking out of his Beere to boote.

The ball in this play may bee compared to an infernall spirit: for whosoeuer

catcheth it, fareth straightwayes like a madde man, strugling and fighting
with those that goe about to holde him: and no sooner is the ball gone from,
but hee resigneth this fury to the | next receyuer, and himselfe becommeth
peaceable as before. I cannot well resolue, whether I should more commend
this game, for the manhood and exercise, or condemne it for the boysterousnes   5
and harmes which it begetteth: for as on the one side it makes their bodies
strong, hard, and nimble, and puts a courage into their hearts, to meete an
enemie in the face: so on the other part, it is accompanied with many dangers,
some of which doe euer fall to the players share. For proofe whereof, when
the hurling is ended, you shall see them retyring home, as from a pitched   10
battaile, with bloody pates, bones broken, and out of ioynt, and such bruses
as serue to shorten their daies; yet al is good play, & neuer Attourney nor
Crowner troubled for the matter.

...
                                                                                  15

c 1603
John Norden, Speculi Britanniae Pars   BL: Harley MS. 6252
ff 28v–9

...

wrestling &
Hurling
cornish
actiuityes

The Cornish-men as they are stronge, hardye and nymble. so are their   20
excercises, violent. two especially wrastling, and Hurling. sharpe and seuere
actiuities, and ⌐in⌐ neither of theis doth any countrye exceede or equall them.
In the first they haue | in all places the commendation, In the seconde the
peculiaritie: Because els-where it is not in manner vsed. Thowgh the Deuonshire
man standeth muche vpon the firste, and somethinge on the seconde. The   25
®wrestling and
hurling in two
sortes
firste is violent, But the seconde is daungerous. the firste is acted in two sortes,
by Holdster (as they call it) and by the Coller. The seconde likewise two wayes,
as Hurling to goales, and Hurling to the Countrye. The manner mighte be
declared but the vse is not of necessitye.

...
                                                                                  30

f 70v

The Hurlers. c.18. certayne stones raysed and sett in the grounde. of some
6. foote high and 2 foote square, some bigger some lesser. and are fixed in   35
suche straglinge manner, as those Countrye ⌐men⌐ doe in performinge that
pastime Hurlinge. the manner of the standinge of theis stones is as followeth.
Hurlers   ...

2/ from: *for* from him *(?)*
34/ The: *T is in gold*
37/ the standinge ... as followeth: *watercolour of 30 stones, tinted light brown, on green ground, follows*

This monumente seemeth to importe an intention. of the memoriall of some matter done in this kinde of excercise. thowgh time have worne out the maner.

...

1610
William Camden, Britain   STC: 4509
p 186
...

And yet is Cornwall nothing happier in regard of the soile, than it is for the people; who as they were endued and adorned with all civilitie, even in those antient times; (For by reason of their acquaintaince with merchants sailing thither for tin, as Diodorus Siculus reports, they were more courteous toward strangers:) so they are valiant, hardie, wel pitcht in stature, brawny & strong limmed: such as for wrastling, (to speak nothing of that manly excercise, & feat of hurling the Ball which they use) so farre excell, that for slight and cleane strength together, they justly win the prize and praise from other nations, in that behalfe...

...

p 192

Hard by, there is a number of good big rockes heaped up together, and under them, one Stone of lesser size, fashioned naturally in forme of a cheese, so as it seemeth to be pressed like a cheese, whereupon it is named, Wring-cheese. Many other Stones besides in some sort foure square, are to be seene upon the plaine adjoyning; of which seven or eight are pitched upright of equall distance asunder. The neighbour Inhabitants terme them Hurlers, as being by a devout and godly error perswaded, they had beene men sometimes transformed into Stones, for profaning the Lords Day, with hurling the ball. Others, would have it to be a Trophee (as it were) or a monument, in memoriall of some battell: And some thinke verily they were set as meere stones or land marks, as having read in those authors that wrote of Limits, that stone were gathered together of both parties, and the same erected for bounders...

...

Hurling.

Wring cheese.

Hurlers.

12–14/ (For by ... strangers:): *Diodorus Siculus*, Bibliotheca, *5.22.1–5*

ST IVES

1638–9
Borough Accounts II   St Ives Guildhall
f 2 *(1 November–1 November) (Payments)*

	li.	s.	d.
...			
me*morandum* for a silver Bale that was brought to Towne	00 // 06 // 6		
...			

APPENDIX 5
Sample Church Ale Expenses at Kilkhampton

The churchwardens' accounts for Kilkhampton included here indicate somewhat the scope of a church ale, at which there was often music and entertainment. The accounting year begins and ends on the Sunday before the feast of St Andrew the Apostle (30 November).

St James Churchwardens' Accounts
Truro, Cornwall Record Office, P/102/5/1; 1563–1603; English; paper; iii + 80 (2 leaves have leather covers affixed) + ii; 309mm x 215mm; modern pencil foliation, with another set of higher pencilled numbers indicating volume previously bound with something else, making a whole of at least 146 leaves; leaves repaired and remounted onto new sheets; bound in modern red cloth with title stamped in gold on spine: 'Kilkhampton–Churchwardens' Accounts–1563–1604.'

1593–4
St James Churchwardens' Accounts   CRO: P/102/5/1
f 59 *(25 November–24 November)* *(Payments)*
...

Item layd out for malte & hoppes	xxxvij s.	5
Item layd out for ij bushelles of wheate	xij s. viij d.	
Item payd for iiij Dosen of Trenchers	vj d.	
Item payd for ij pounde of Reasons	viij d.	
Item payd for fyshe against ganmonday	v s.	
Item payd for apples then	xiiij d.	10
Item payd for woode	ij s. viij d.	
Item payd for butter & other necessarys and vyctelle for the parishe	xliiij s.	
Item for washinge of the clothes dyverse tymes	iiij d.	
Item payd for saffron & peper	viij d.	15

...

9/ ganmonday: *6 May*

1594–5
St James Churchwardens' Accounts   CRO: P/102/5/1
f 60v *(24 November – 23 November) (Payments)*

Item payd for breade at ganmondaye	xiiij s. viij d.	5
Item payd for fyshe then	iiij s. iiij d.	
Item payd for veniger	vj d.	
Item payd for Reasons & Spice	xiiij d.	
Item payd for xiiij pounde of butter	iiij s. viij d.	
Item payd for vitelle	xxvj s.	10
Item payd for vj pound of bacon	ij s.	
Item payd for three pounds of hoppes	ij s.	
Item payd for woode	xvj d.	
Item payd to the Cooke for his paynes	xij d.	
Item payd for a halfe bushelle of wheate	iiij s.	15
Item payd for caridge of our drinke	xij d.	

...

5/ ganmondaye: *26 May*

A Merry Tale of the Queen's Ape in Cornwall

'A Merry Tale' came to our attention through a note written in CRO: B/WLooe/58/3, part of CRO: B/WLooe/58/1–4, a bundle of antiquarian MS notes and transcripts, including some by Richard Peter. CRO: B/WLooe/58/3 is an antiquarian copy of B/WLooe/12/1, where 2s are paid 'to Colakote … to goe to the showes' (see p 523). An asterisk appears in the antiquarian account after the word 'showes' and the word is underlined. Below, the unknown transcriber has commented: 'See "A Merry tale" page 281 Bond's history of Looe.' Although this note has been attributed to Richard Peter, the note is not his but the transcriber's; Peter does make an unrelated comment on the foot of the page, probably leading to the misattribution. 'Bond's history' is Thomas Bond's *Topographical and Historical Sketches of the Boroughs of East and West Looe in the County of Cornwall* (London, 1823), and the tale, quoted below, appears on pp 281–5. A.L. Rowse, in *St. Austell: Church: Town: Parish* (St Austell, 1960), Appendix a, pp 132–3, reproduces Bond's headnote and 'A Merry Tale' nearly verbatim, the few changes in wording having no effect on the meaning of the text.

A MERRY TALE.

I have now nearly exhausted my subjects. As a faithful Historian, however, I cannot help inserting the following story, which I have seen in print, for the mere purpose of gravely contradicting the slurs which are thereby intended to be imposed on one or other of the two Looes. Similar jokes have been made on other Cornish Boroughs, but all of them create more mirth than mischief, whatever their authors intended. This story is printed at the end of an old edition of Æsop's Fables, and runs thus:

'A MERRY STORY.

'Having been conversant with birds and beasts, I will add one true story thereon, which demonstrates that stupidity and ignorance possess some human souls to such a degree, that they seem to have no more knowledge than the beasts that perish.

'In the reign of Queen Elizabeth, a fellow who wore his hat buttoned up on one side, and a feather therein, like a tooth-drawer, with the rose and crown on his breast for a badge, had obtained a licence from the then Lord Chamberlain, to make a show of a great ape about the country, who could perform many notable tricks; and by going to markets and fairs, his master picked up a great deal of money. | The ape usually rid upon a mastiff dog, and a man beat a drum before him. It happened that these four travellers came to a town called Loo in Cornwall, where, having taken an inn, the drum beat about the town to give notice, that at such a place was an admirable ape, with very many notable qualities, if they pleased to bestow their money and time to come to see him; but the towns-people being a sort of poor fishermen who minded their own employments, none of them thought it worth their while to see this worthy sight, at which the fellow being vexed, resolved to put a trick upon them whatsoever came of it, and therefore he contrives a warrant which he sends to the Mayor to this effect:

'These are to will and require you and every one of you with your wives and families, that upon sight hereof, you make your personal appearance before the Queen's Ape, for he is an ape of rank and quality, and is to visit all her Majesty's dominions, that by his converse and acquaintance with her loving subjects, he may be the better enabled to do her Majesty service in discovering their fidelity and loyalty. And hereof fail not, as you will answer the contrary at your utmost peril.'

This warrant being brought to the Mayor, he sent for a shoemaker at the farther end of the town to read it, which when he had heard, he assembled his brethren the Aldermen to the Common-hall, to consult of this weighty affair. Being met, they all sate silent | at least a quarter of hour, no man speaking a word, not knowing what to say; at length a young man who had never served any office said, 'Gentlemen, if I might speak without offence, and under correction of the Worshipful, I would give my opinion in this matter.' 'Pray, neighbour, speak freely,' quoth the Mayor, 'for though you never yet bore any office, yet you may talk as wisely as some of us.' 'Then,' says the young man, 'I am of the mind that this ape-carrier is an insolent saucy knave, who designs to make our town ridiculous to the whole kingdom; for was it ever known that a fellow should be so audacious to send a warrant without either name or date to a Mayor of a town, who is the Queen's Lieutenant, and that he and his brethren, their wives and children, should be all commanded to appear before a jackanapes; therefore, my counsel is that you take him and his ape, with his man and his dog, and whip the whole tribe of them out of the town, which will be much for your reputation and credit.' At which words, a grave Alderman, being much disturbed, replied, 'Friend, you have spoken little better than treason; remember it is the Queen's Ape, and therefore be careful what you say.' 'You speak true, brother,' quoth the Mayor. 'I wonder how that saucy fellow came into our company; pray, friend, depart; I think you long to have us all hanged.' The young man being put out of doors, 'Well now, brethren,' says the Mayor, 'what is to be done with this troublesome business?' 'Marry,' quoth another old se- | nior, 'we may see by the feather in his cap, and the badge he wears, that he is the Queen's man, and who knows what power a knave may have at Court, to do poor men in the country an injury? therefore, let us e'en go and see the Ape, it is but two-pence apiece, and no doubt the Queen will take it well, if it come to her ear, and think that we are very civil people to show so much duty to her Ape; what may she imagine we would do to her bears if they should come hither; besides 'tis above two hundred miles to London, and if we should be complain'd of and fetched up by pursivants or messengers, I'll warrant it would cost us at least ten groats a man, whereas we now come off for twopence apiece.' This wise speech was though so pertinent, that the whole drove of townsmen with their wives and children went to see the Ape, whom they found sitting on a table with a chain about his neck, to whom Mr. Mayor put off his hat, and made a leg to show his respect to the Queen's Ape; yet pug let him pass unregarded; but Mrs. Mayoress, coming next in a clean white apron with her hands laid upon it, she, to show her breeding, makes a low curtsie to him; and pug, like a right courtier, though he did not mind the man, yet, to shew his respect to the woman, put out his paw to her, and made a mouth; which the woman perceiving, 'Husband,' quoth she, 'I think in my conscience the Queen's Ape mocks me;' whereat pug made another wry face at her, which Mr. Mayor observing, grew very angry, cry-|ing, 'Thou sirrah ape, I see thy sauciness, and if the rest of the courtiers have no more manners than thou hast, I am afraid they have been better fed than taught; but I'll make thee know, before thou goest out of town, that this woman is my wife, an antient woman and a midwife, and one that for her age might be thy mother;' and then going in a rage to the door, where the ape's tutor was gathering in his pence, 'Sir,' says he, 'do you allow your ape to abuse my wife?' 'No, by no means,' quoth the fellow. 'Truly sir,' quoth the Mayor, 'there be sufficient witness within that saw him make mops and mows at her, as if she were not worthy to wipe his shoes.' 'Sir,' said the fellow, 'I will presently give him severe chastisement for his impudence;' and thereupon taking his whip, and holding Jack by the chain, he gave him half a dozen smart lashes, that made pug's teeth chatter in his head like virginal jacks; which Mr. Mayor espying, runs to the fellow, and holding his hand, cried out, 'Enough, enough, good Sir, you have done like a gentleman; let me intreat you never to give correction in your wrath; and pray, Sir, when the play is done, be pleased to come along with your ape to my house, and both of you take a small supper with me and my wife.'

APPENDIX 7
Saints' Days and Festivals

The following list contains the dates for holy days and festivals mentioned in the Records. All days are entered under their official names but unofficial names occurring in the Records are also given in parentheses and repeated in their alphabetical place as required. Only feast days themselves are listed; if the night or eve of a feast or its tide or season (likely the feast day itself with its octave) is referred to, its date may be inferred from that of the feast. Exact dates for moveable feasts are included in textual notes. See also C.R. Cheney, *Handbook of Dates for Students of English History*, corrected ed (London, 1978), 84–161.

Cornwall also possessed its own saints, Meriasek being perhaps the best known. Some of the entertainments noted in these records may have been associated with those Cornish saints, who are listed and discussed by Charles Henderson, *The Cornish Church Guide and Parochial History of Cornwall* (Truro, 1925; rpt 1964), and by B. Lynette Olson and O.J. Padel, 'A Tenth-Century List of Cornish Parochial Saints,' *Cambridge Medieval Celtic Studies* 12 (1986), 33–71.

Candlemas	2 February
Christmas	25 December
Circumcision	1 January
Corpus Christi Day	Thursday after Trinity Sunday (eighth Sunday after Easter)
Easter	Sunday after the first full moon on or following 21 March
Epiphany (Twelfth Day)	6 January
Gang Monday	Monday after Rogation Sunday (fifth Sunday after Easter)
Good Friday	Friday before Easter
Holy Innocents' Day	28 December
Lady Day	25 March
Lammas Day	1 August
Little Easter	see Pentecost
May Day	1 May
Michaelmas (St Michael)	29 September
New Year's Day	1 January
Pentecost (Whitsunday, Little Easter)	seventh Sunday after Easter, ie, fifty days after Easter

St George	23 April
St John the Apostle	27 December
St Mary Magdalene	22 July
St Stephen	2 August
St Thomas	21 December
Twelfth Day	6 January
Whitsunday	see Pentecost

Translations

ABIGAIL ANN YOUNG

The Latin documents have been translated as literally as possible. The order of records in the Translations parallels that of the Records text. Place names and given names have been modernized. The spelling of surnames in the Translations reflects the same principles as used in the Index. Capitalization and punctuation are in accordance with modern practice. As in the Records text, diamond brackets indicate obliterations and square brackets cancellations. However, cancellations are not normally translated; they may be translated when a whole entry is cancelled, especially if it appears that a cancellation may be administrative rather than the correction of an error, or if they seem of special interest or relevance.

Round brackets enclose words not in the Latin text but needed for grammatical sense in English. Not all the Latin in the text has been translated here. Latin tags, formulae, headings, or other short sections in largely English documents are either translated in footnotes or not at all. Individual documents which consist of a single line, or other very short entries, especially those that are part of repetitive annual series, are not normally translated unless they present some unusual syntactic or semantic problem. All Latin vocabulary not found in the standard Latin dictionary, the *Oxford Latin Dictionary*, is found in the glossary.

The Cornish play-texts appearing in Appendix 2 (pp 546–9) have been translated below (pp 590–2) by O.J. Padel. See p 546 of the headnote to that appendix for a discussion of manuscript layout as it pertains to rhyme scheme.

DIOCESE OF EXETER

1287
Statutes of Bishop Peter Quinel
*(16 April) (Chapter thirteen)**

...

That markets or secular pleadings shall not be held in churches or their churchyards nor secular buildings be constructed (there). 13.

...And because many bodies of the saints and of those worthy of salvation, to whom all honour and reverence is due, are buried in consecrated churchyards, we strictly command parish priests to announce publicly in their churches that no one shall presume to practise wrestling, round dances, or other improper pastimes in churchyards, especially on the eves and feastdays of the saints, since the sacred canons (*ie*, canon law statutes) loathe for such stage-plays and shows of derision to be introduced, by which the decency of churches is polluted. But if, after the announcement has been made, any have practised pastimes of this kind – although they are improperly so-called, since (only) crimes arise from them – the aforesaid priests shall report their names to the archdeacon of the district or his official so that they may be punished canonically by those (officers) for their faults.

...

(Chapter seventeen)

...

Of the life and integrity of clerics. 17.

...Likewise, clerics should be decent and sober, abstaining from excessive intoxication and drunkenness. For, as blessed Gregory says, 'Nothing is more disgusting than an overindulgent person: a stench lurks in his mouth, pallor in his face, a tremor in his fingers, and in his heart no privacy lies.' And so that the way of life of clerics may appear in every way to be different from that of entertainers – as in fact it is – we strictly order that priests in particular not attend dinner parties unless they have been specially invited by the master of the house. But if they happen to be invited, they should not drown themselves in drink but should return sober to their homes immediately after the meal. They should never frequent inns unless they are on a trip by reason of a pilgrimage but they should always live in so decent and sober a fashion that at all times they know how, and are able, to tell the difference between the sacred and the profane, the clean and the unclean, just as is fitting.

Likewise, because all indulgence in pleasure, through which one attains the raw material for dissolute behaviour, ought particularly to be shunned among clerics, we order that clerics not attend to entertainers and jugglers, play dice and knucklebones, nor be onlookers of or sharers with those who are playing, nor presume to attend public shows in order to watch (them), nor employ hunting birds or dogs.

These, and very many other things are forbidden to clerics, whose way of life is removed from the activities of the laity, whom they ought to excel in devotion as much as in station.

...

BODMIN

c 1514–39
Town Receivers' Accounts   CRO: B/Bod/314/2/12
single mb* *(Allowances)*

...

...Likewise of 16d given to the play from (*or* of) Tywardreath. Likewise of

16d ⟨given⟩ to the dance from (*or* of) Lanivet. Likewise of 12d given to the dance from (*or* of) St Mabyn. Likewise of 12d ⟨given⟩ to the dance from (*or* of) La⟨n⟩hydr⟨ock⟩....

...

LAUNCESTON

1404–5
Borough Accounts CRO: B/Laus/135
mbs [2–2d]* *(Travelling expenses)*

At Tavistock the first night

On the plays at supper	2d
On wine and beer	3d
On hay and fodder	7d
On horseshoe/s	2d
On wine	5d
On wine	2d
On alms	2d

At Plympton

On dinner	6d
On horses	8d
On a copy of the proceedings	2d

At Tavistock on the way home

On supper	6d
On horses	6d
On bread and wine at breakfast	2½d
On wine given at home by the mayor	2½d
On two capons bought	4d

Sum 5s

On a second occasion on one capon	2d
On veal	2d
On supper at Tavistock	15d
On horses	16d
On plays	4d
On breakfast in the morning	3d

At Plympton

On dinner	10½d

On horses   16d
On supper at home with one capon   18½d

Sum more elsewhere |

On wine drunk when going out of doors   3½d
On five capons   10½d

[Sum]
[Sum total]

On wine given to Robert Heye by the mayor for his being a
good friend in the court of Trematon   5d

                                                          Sum 8s 10d
                                                     Sum total 13s 10d

On a third occasion, etc.
On alms   2d
On wine   12d
On horses   19d

1431–2
Borough Accounts   CRO: B/Laus/137
single mb* *(25 November–25 November) (Necessary expenses)*
...
...On expenses for the May, 11s 7d.... In 12d given to William Crese for
putting 'le beris' in his home.
...

1440
Register of Bishop Edmund Lacy   Devon Record Office: Chanter 11
f ccxiii verso *(16 June)*

Indulgence

Also on the sixteenth day of the aforesaid month in the year of the Lord
abovesaid, the same lord (bishop) granted forty days indulgence to all who
were truly penitent and had confessed who gave, bequeathed, or in any way
assigned any of the goods given them by God as free alms to the support of
the confraternity of minstrels of St Mary Magdalene at Launceston.
...

1445–6
Borough Accounts   CRO: B/Laus/138
f [7]* *(25 November–25 November) (Expenses for wine)*

...On one gallon of wine given to Walter Colle, chaplain, on (St) Mary
Magdalene's Day (paid by *?*) Horn, 8d. On three gallons and a quart of wine
consumed by the mayor and his fellows on (St) Mary Magdalene's Night
(paid by *?*) Horn, 2s 2d. On bread at the same time (paid by *?*) Horn, 1d....

1449–50
Borough Accounts   CRO: B/Laus/139
f [5]* *(25 November–25 November) (Expenses for wine)*

[...On wine consumed on (St) Mary Magdalene's Night among the mayor and
the minstrel/s, 19d....]

1450–1
Borough Accounts   CRO: B/Laus/141
single mb* *(25 November–25 November) (Necessary expenses)*
...
...On expenses (incurred) by the mayor and his fellows on (St) Mary Magdalene's
Night, 7d....

single mb dorse *(External expenses)*
...
...On silver given to Brown, (a) piper, 4d....
...

1459–60
Borough Accounts   CRO: B/Laus/143
single mb dorse *(25 November–25 November) (Expenses for wine)*
...
... On expenses incurred on (St) Mary Magdalene's Eve (and) Day (*or* on
(St) Mary Magdalene's Eve during the day) and for the morrow by the mayor
and his fellows for four gallons and one potell of wine and for bread, 19d....
...

1465–6
Borough Accounts   CRO: B/Laus/153
single mb* *(25 November–25 November) (Expenses for wine)*
...
...On bread used about the mayor and his fellows and the minstrel/s on

St Mary Magdalene's Eve, 1½d. On three gallons and one quart of wine used about the mayor and his fellows and also the minstrel/s at the same time, 18½d.

1466–7
Borough Accounts   CRO: B/Laus/158
mb [2] *(25 November–25 November)(Expenses for wine)*
...
... On bread bought by Peter Pyke for the mayor and his fellows on St Mary Magdalene's Eve, 2d. On one gallon and a potell of red wine bought by Peter Pyke at the same time, 12d. On one quart and one gallon of white wine bought by the same Peter at the same time, 7½d....

1469–70
Borough Accounts   CRO: B/Laus/160
mb [2]* *(25 November–25 November)*

...On a reward given to minstrel/s...
...
⟨...⟩ mayor and his fellows on St Mary Magdalene's Eve, 14d....
...

1470–1
Borough Accounts   CRO: B/Laus/147
mb [1]* *(25 November–25 November) (External expenses)*
...
...On a reward given by the mayor to the earl of Warwick's bearward, 20d. On a reward given to Thomas, fool of Richard, the earl of Warwick, 16d....

mb [2]*

...On a reward given to Robert Walkere, a servant of George, duke of Clarence, called the bearward, 20d....

(Expenses for wine)

On wine given to the earl of Warwick's bearward, 6d. On bread at the same time, ½d. On wine given to the mayor and his fellows for the searching of the fields, 3d. On bread at the same time, 1d. On wine given at the same time to a servant of Richard, earl of Warwick, called Thomas the fool, 6d.... On expenses (incurred) about the mayor and his fellows and the minstrel/s on St Mary Magdalene's Eve, 2s 3d. On one gallon of wine given to *(blank)*, Croght, and *(blank)*, commissioners of the lord king, at the same time, 7d.

On one quart of white wine given to William Parker and John Davy, canon, and the other singers on the feast of (St) Mary Magdalene, 1½d....

1476–7
Borough Accounts   CRO: B/Laus/162
mb [2] *(25 November–25 November) (External expenses)*
...

...On expenses (incurred) about the mayor and his fellows on (St) Mary Magdalene's Eve, 20d.... On a reward given to the lord prince's servant called the bearward at the same time. On a reward given to three minstrels of the lord chancellor this year, 12d....
...

1478–9
Borough Accounts   CRO: B/Laus/164
mb [1] *(25 November–25 November) (External expenses)*
...

...On a reward given to a jester playing before the mayor and his fellows, 8d.... On the expenses of the mayor and the community on St Mary Magdalene's Eve, 3s....
...

1520–1
Borough Accounts   CRO: B/Laus/170
mb [1]* *(Rents paid)*
...

...And in rent paid by minstrel/s for a holding on North Street annually, 2½d....
...

mb [2] *(Gifts of wine)*

...And paid for wine given to the lord king's servant, that is, a juggler, coming there this year, 6d.
...And for wine bought on St Mary Magdalene's Eve this year, 12d....

(Necessary expenses)

...And paid for bread and ale bought, together with candles, on St Mary Magdalene's Eve this year in the guildhall, 12d....

(External expenses)

And in a reward given the lord king's bearward/s coming there this year, 3s
4d.... And in a reward given to the lord king's servant called a juggler coming
there this year, 3s 4d. And in a reward given to the duke of Suffolk's bearward/s
coming there this year, 8d. And in a reward given to keeper/s of one beast
called a camel this year, 16d.. And in a reward given to various players of
Plymouth and Launceston, 2s....

...

1530–1
Borough Accounts   CRO: B/Laus/171
mb [2]* *(External expenses)*
...
⟨...⟩ in a reward given to three minstrels of the lord king there ⟨...⟩ to Richard
Dyngle, organist, on the feast of (St) Mary Magdalene ⟨...⟩ Greynfild, sheriff,
for a copy of the commission of taxation ⟨...⟩ paid to an entertainer of the
lord king coming there this year ⟨...⟩ ...

...

1542–3
Borough Accounts   CRO: B/Laus/172
mb [2] *(Rents paid)*
...
...And paid by minstrel/s for another rent 'de lyan' for the holding in which
Robert Skinner now lives, 4d....

...

mb [3] *(Necessary expenses)*

...And paid for bread, ale, and wine on (St) Mary Magdalene's Eve this year,
11½d....

...

(External expenses and rewards)

...And in a reward given to the lord king's minstrel/s in the same place this
year, 3s 4d....

...

LISKEARD

1608–9
Mayors' Accounts   CRO: B/Lis/272
mb [1] *(Casual receipts)*

…

… And of 12s received from Peter Hambly and John Harell for a licence to sell drink and to play in the guildhall on Pentecost this year…

…

PENRYN

1360–1
Episcopal Order to Glasney Collegiate Church
Devon Record Office: Chanter 3
ff ccviii verso–ccix verso* *(10 December)*

…

The bishop's prohibition of dishonourable pastimes

…John, by divine mercy bishop of Exeter, to his beloved sons in Christ, .., warden, and the chapter of the collegiate church of St Mary at Ottery, of our foundation, patronage, and diocese (sends) greeting and decency of clerical behaviour. It has come to our notice – not without serious displeasure of heart and consternation – that in past years and on some previous most holy solemnities of Christmas and of Sts Stephen and John, the apostle and evangelist, and of the Holy Innocents, when all the faithful in Christ are bound to attend more devoutly and more tranquilly to divine praises and the ecclesiastical offices, some ministers of our aforesaid church, together with the choirboys, not only during matins and vespers and the other (canonical) hours but – what is more worthy of detestation – also during the solemnities of the masses, have rashly dared, putting aside the fear of God out of the pernicious example of some (other) churches, to carry out silly and harmful pastimes unbecoming to clerical decency – nay rather more truly mixing in detestable mockeries of divine worship in the church itself – while disfiguring the vestments and other ornaments of the church in many ways, indeed with the spattering of low and muddy things, no small loss and shame to our same church and to us. By their scurrilous deeds and derisive laughter not only are the people gathered at church at those times in particular out of catholic custom drawn away from their due devotion but they even burst into disorderly laughter and illicit mirth, divine worship is mocked and the divine office is basely hindered. And so what had originally been devised to rouse and increase the devotion of the faithful has been converted, or rather perverted, into irreverence and contempt for God and the saints by the insolence of such (practices), not without commission of blasphemy. Therefore we, unable any longer to pass over with a clear conscience such unspeakable abuses under (this) disguise without a remedy, enjoin and order you under pain of suspension and excommunication that you utterly desist hereafter from insolencies and mockeries of this kind and that from now on you do not permit any such activities to occur in the same church in any way, but that you take care to carry out the divine office with more devotion than usual as the reverence of those days requires.

And, lest anyone ever hereafter be able to excuse himself in this regard out of ignorance, we order you, .., warden, solemnly to publish our present letter before Christmas coming in the presence of all the ministers and – lest our same letter be forgotten – I to have it faithfully transcribed in four or five frequently-used books of the church. But if anyone presumes to go against our present order, you shall cite them – or cause them to be cited – peremptorily to appear before us on the third court day after the end of the said festivals, ready to answer for such rash presumption and to receive suitable punishment. Inform us of the day of receipt of the present letter and what you have done in this matter by your letter patent containing a copy of this letter and sealed with your common seal before the feast of the Lord's Circumcision. Given at our manor of Chudleigh, 10 December AD 1360 and in the thirty-fourth year of our consecration....

Similar letters, with a few words changed, have been issued to .., the dean, .., the precentor, and .., the chancellor of the cathedral church of Exeter; to .., the chanter, and the chapter of the collegiate church of the Holy Cross at Crediton; and to .., the warden, and the chapter of the collegiate church of St Thomas the Martyr at Glasney.... Certification was made by .., warden, and the chapter of the collegiate church of St Thomas the Martyr at Glasney in this way:

To the reverend father in Christ and their lord, Lord John, by the grace of God, bishop of Exeter, his humble and devoted (sons), .., warden, and the chapter of your collegiate church of St Thomas the Martyr at Glasney (send) their obedience and the reverence due to so great a father, with all subjection and honour. We received your revered order on Christmas Eve in the words, 'John, etc' – as above with only a few words changed. On the authority of this, your revered order, I, .., the beforesaid warden, made all the contents of your said order known openly on the said Eve in the presence of all the ministers of the said church, as is ordered, and – lest such things happen in the said church hereafter – I forbade them publicly and solemnly. I have also had your same revered letter copied in our missal, martyrology, and collect-book and have attached your order to our original statute book of the said church. And I have not found any minister of your said church violating your order in any way. And so we have carried out your revered order fully and respectfully | in every way. Given at Glasney on the morrow of the Lord's Epiphany, in the abovesaid year of the Lord.

...

TYWARDREATH

1338
Episcopal Licence to the Monastery at Tywardreath
Devon Record Office: Chanter 4
f ccxiii verso *(18 April)*

...

A licence for Tywardreath, to stay in some church or chapel appropriated to their monastery.†

John, etc, to his beloved sons, the prior and convent of Tywardreath in our diocese (wishes for) your safety, grace, and blessing, and also constancy in your adversity. As you have been careful to explain to us – and the truth of it shall show openly in other ways – because of hostile raids by pirates and attacks threatening you more than usual these days you are not able without grave danger to your souls and bodies to stay in your aforesaid monastery, located by the sea shore and exposed in many ways to the dangers of foreign foes as well as those of native enemies who assert that you are suspect because you come from another region. We, moved by your devoted prayers, grant permission and authority by the tenor of the present (letter) for you to go personally to some church or chapel in our diocese appropriated to your monastery which is farther from the sea and more safe from attacks of this kind and to stay there for the duration of this danger. Nevertheless, you shall, in this place to which you happen to move, attend assiduously, devoutly, duly, and honourably to the divine offices, both day and night, remaining apart from worldly and dissolute shows (and) putting aside every occasion for wandering or rushing about, and you shall observe and do everything which you would be bound to observe and to do if you were personally in your own monastery. So as to avoid scandal, take care also to keep your hearts and your bodies in all chastity and sanctity, whether you are at home or in this new place, provided (also) that you do nothing for any sought-after excuse to deceive the way of life of the cloister and that you use our present licence only so long as necessity demands, until the longed-for serenity of peace has arrived, with the peaceful and lofty king as your co-worker. Given at Clist on the eighteenth day of the month of April in the aforesaid year of the Lord.

...

APPENDIX 2

Ordinale de Origine Mundi   Bodl.: MS. Bodl. 791
f 18v *(Speech of King David)*

...

Blow minstrels, and drums,
three hundred harpers, and trumpeters,
dulcimer, fiddle, viol, and psaltery,
shawm, zithers, and kettle-drums,
organs, also cymbals,
recorders and hurdy-gurdy.

...

f 26 *(Speech of King Solomon)*

...

Good people, you have seen
how God the Father created
heaven and earth, according to his will.
After that He desired
Adam (and) Eve, through His grace:
He made them indeed similar, moreover,
to himself, truly;
He gave them the whole world,
that they might live in it,
and their children, for ever,
who may come from them.

His blessing to you, entirely,
male and female likewise.
The play now is done;
and to see the passion   *or*   and to see the childhood
which Christ suffered for us   of Jesus, without bidding,
come on time tomorrow.
And let everyone go home,
in the name of the Father.
Minstrels, of (your) grace,
pipe immediately.

f 82 *(Speech of the Emperor)*
...

Good people, you have seen how it was concerning Christ's resurrection.

He broke the gates of hell; Adam and Eve outwards,
(and) as many as did the Father's will, he brought them to joy.
To the Son of Mankind He showed, very truly, much love,
and upwards to heaven, to joy, Jesus ascended,
so as to guard them against the devil and his company, in every place.
His blessing to you, every one: now let everyone go homewards.
Now minstrels, pipe diligently, so that we can go to dance.

...

Ordinale de vita sancti mereadoci episcopi et confessoris
National Library of Wales: Peniarth MS. 105
p 97 (Speech of the Duke)
...

Drink, all, with the play (or players?):
we shall entreat you with a full heart.
You shall have, man and woman,
the blessing of Christ and Meriasek, the blessing of Mary of Camborne.
Pipe, hearty minstrels, so that we can dance straight away.

pp 178–9 (Speech of the Earl of Vannes)
...

To you the blessing of Meriasek,
and of sweet Mary of Camborne,
(and) the blessing of the Apostles.
Drink, all, with the play (or players?),
we shall entreat you,
before going from the (playing-)place. |
Pipers, blow, at once:
we shall, every mother's son,
go to dance.
Go or stay,
you shall be welcome,
though you be here for a week.

It is finished, by Sir Rad. Ton,
AD 1504.

The Creacion of the World, the first daie of playe
Bodl.: MS. Bodl. 219
f 27 (Speech of Noah)
...

This same day is done, to the Father God be thanks.

You have seen, every rank (of you), many matters played,
and the creation of the whole world.

You all have also seen
this same world destroyed
by very great floods of water.
Not one human being was spared,
except for Noah, his wife, and his children.

Come tomorrow on time:
you shall see very great matters,
and redemption granted,
through the mercy of God the Father,
to save anyone who is lost.

Minstrels, do pipe for us,
so that we can dance together,
as is the manner and the custom.

(English)

Endnotes

463–5   Statutes of Bishop Peter Quinel   Chapter thirteen
These statutes survive in thirteen known manuscripts. Twelve of these were examined for the collation and edition prepared by Frank Barlow for Powicke and Cheney, *Councils & Synods*, vol 2, pt 2, pp 982–1059. The thirteenth manuscript not used by Barlow was brought to the attention of Wasson by the archivist of the Exeter Cathedral Library, Mrs Audrey Erskine. Its shelfmark is Exeter Cathedral Library: Exeter D & C MS 3549A.

As no one of the thirteen manuscripts could be preferred as a base text, the text – first printed in Wasson (ed), *Devon*, pp 4–6 – represents a full collation and recension of all the available manuscripts and contains the best readings to be found in them. The critical apparatus of alternate readings found there has been included in this volume. See Wasson, pp 437–9, for a full discussion of the collation and recension of the manuscripts.

The manuscript sigla assigned by Barlow in the introduction to his edition (pp 982–4) have been used here. The additional manuscript not examined by Barlow has been designated as *P*. A list of the sigla is provided below, together with remarks specifically relevant to the sections used in this volume. For a fuller description of the manuscripts, their affiliations, and the place of these statutes in the general history of English canonical collections, see Barlow's introduction.

A: Exeter Cathedral Library: D & C MS 3522. Chapter 13, title p 37, REED section p 38; chapter 17, title p 41, REED section p 44.

B: Exeter Cathedral Library: D & C MS 3523. This chapter has been corrected by the scribe or another contemporary hand (*B2*). Chapter 13, title f 15, REED section f 15v; chapter 17, title f 17, REED section ff 17v–18.

C: Exeter Cathedral Library: D & C MS 3524. Chapter 13, title f 35v, REED section, f 36; chapter 17, title f 38, REED section ff 39–9v.

D: BL: Harley MS. 220. This manuscript has been corrected by the scribe or by another contemporary hand (*D2*). There are heavy marginal notes of a legal character, none of which pertains to the sections used here. There is a marginal hand pointing to the quotation from Gregory the Great in chapter 17. Chapter 13, title f 18, REED section f 18v; chapter 17, title f 20, REED section f 20v.

E: BL: Harley MS. 3850. Chapter 13, title f 17, REED section f 17v; chapter 17, title f 19, REED section f 20.

F: Bodleian Library: Rawlinson C 565. This manuscript contains post-seventeenth century marginalia that are normally summary titles or section headings. In the section used by REED only one is worthy of note. On p 22, beginning one half-line above the start of the REED section, is the following gloss: 'Durus est hic sermo nostris Diebus.' Chapter 13, title p 21, REED section p 22; chapter 17, title p 24, REED section ff 25–5v.

G: Cambridge, Corpus Christi College: 443. There is some damage or blurring apparent in this manuscript along the gutter between f 27v and 28. Chapter 13, title f 27, REED section ff 27v–8; chapter 17, title f 30v, REED section ff 32–2v.

H: Bodleian Library: Digby 35. Chapter 13, title f 24v, REED section ff 25–5v; chapter 17, title f 27, REED section ff 28–8v.

J: Bodleian Library: Rawlinson C 314. Chapter 13, title f 14, REED section f 14v; chapter 17, title f 16, REED section ff 16v 17.

K: Bodleian Library: Rawlinson C 323. There is a marginal 'Nota bene' next to the first line of the REED text in chapter 17. Chapter 13, title f 19v, REED section f 20; chapter 17, title f 22, REED section ff 22v–3.

L: National Library of Wales: Peniarth 162 part 1. Chapter 13, title f 25, REED section, f 25v; chapter 17, title f 29, REED section ff 31–1v.

N: BL: Additional MS. 24057. This manuscript has been corrected by the scribe or another contemporary hand (*N²*). Chapter 13, title and REED section on f 72 col 2; chapter 17, title f 73v col 1, REED section f 73v col 2.

P: Exeter Cathedral Library: D & C MS 3549A. Chapter 13, title f 31, REED section f 31v; chapter 17, title f 35, REED section ff 36–6v.

According to Barlow (p 983), there are three families: *AC, BDEHKLN,* and *FG.* He assigns *J* to no family. *P* belongs to the same family as *AC.*

468   CRO: P/7/5/1   p 12
This entry appears early in the account before another entry referring to 'men & ther horsys rydyng west.' If this contingent was heading west to Helston to suppress the rebellion that occurred there from 5–7 April 1548 (see pp 380–1), then the Millbrook play may have occurred around Easter, 1 April 1548.

468   CRO: P/7/5/1   p 18
This entry is the penultimate in the account and immediately follows receipts from the Whitsun wardens suggesting that as early as 1553–4 the February/March account year had been changed to an August to August term as in subsequent accounts.

468   CRO: P/7/5/1   p 20
The receipt from 'Robyn Hode' and the 'Maydens' for 41s is entered twice in the 1554–5 accounts. That sum for the play first appears following the accounts of the 'Wytsonday Store Wardens' and is included again on the same page in the accounts of the collectors for the year. These accounts list totals collected from various other church officials and also record again the 'Wytson Store' receipts.

469   CRO: P/7/5/1   p 28
Robert Gache and William Charke (l.14) were the newly elected collectors for the coming year (1558–9). It would appear, on the basis of a note on the preceding page of the document, that the collectors for 1557–8 did not make their account until 13 August 1558, almost a month after Gache and Charke had begun to collect payments. The 40s delivered to them here is entered accordingly into the 1558–9 account.

470   CRO: B/Bod/314/2/15   single mb
The precise date of this document is unknown as the account heading has been lost. It does name, however, Thomas 'Greynfylde,' a knight. A Thomas Grenville or Grenfield was sheriff in Cornwall in 1480

and 1485, and held several commissions in Cornwall and Devon. He was knighted in 1501 and died *c* 1513. The document also lists payment for work to a Robert John. This same name appears in the General Receivers' Accounts for Bodmin in the period 1511–14. Thus the date range of this membrane is presumed to be *c* 1501–13.

471   CRO: B/Bod/314/1/6   mbs [1, 2]
The Berry Tower was built between 1501 and 1514 and was part of the chantry church of the Holy Rood that was 'used by the New, Holy Rood and St. Christopher guilds up to the Reformation' (Munn, *Introducing Bodmin*, p 5).

472   CRO: B/Bod/314/3/31   single mb
The account heading on the MS has been lost but the membrane is dated in a later hand. An antiquarian scholar appears to have wavered between assigning the MS to the reign of Henry VII and Henry VIII. '5 to 6 H.7' and '1489/90' are both written on the membrane but the year date has been crossed out and the '7' of 'H.7' converted to an '8,' thus 1513–14. Also the king's bearward was known to have visited Plymouth in Devon in 1513–14 (see Wasson (ed), *Devon*, p 217).

472   CRO: B/Bod/314/2/12   single mb
The precise date of this document is not known as the account heading has been lost. It is certainly later than 1513 as it refers elsewhere to John Arundell as knight (Arundell was knighted in 1513). It also mentions the prior of Bodmin and therefore presumably predates the dissolution of the priory in 1539.

473   Wallis: *The Bodmin Register*   pp 41–2
John Tregonwell (l.23) (by 1498–1565) in the early years of his law career became a judge in the Admiralty Court and a master in chancery. He was known for playing a part in cases against Sir Thomas More, Anne Boleyn, and the rebels of 1536. His place in the dissolution of the monasteries as one of the three commissioners of Henry VIII (Thomas Cromwell being another) made him one of the most prominent men of the Tudor period. His fair-mindedness toward religious establishments during the Dissolution did not inhibit his interest in the spoils of the Dissolution; Milton Abbas in Dorset was his major acquisition (S.T. Bindoff (ed), *The House of Commons, 1509–1558*, vol 3 (London, 1982), 476–7). Tregonwell was the commissioner to whom the three largest Cornish monasteries, all survivors of the 1536 act of parliament, surrendered in 1539. Bodmin, Launceston, and St Germans priories each gave up its house to the king (Halliday, *History of Cornwall*, p 170). The entry, 'It*em* a sewte of vestyments of cremsyn velvett ... I of the gyft of docter Tregonwell,' may illustrate Tregonwell's willingness to allow a useful item to remain at St Petroc's Church. In *Tudor Cornwall* (p 261), Rowse explains that the Act of Uniformity that initiated use of the Book of Common Prayer made unnecessary much of the extravagant trappings of the Roman church and 'commissions were appointed in every county ... to make a survey of the goods of parish churches, and to see that they were not alienated, except to some good use with the common assent of the parish.' The two Jesus coats and four tormentors' coats, Rowse believes, were used on Good Friday, 'evidently the garments in which they enacted the scenes of the Passion in Holy Week.' Certainly the garments could have been used on Good Friday but they may just as well have been used for dramatic performance of the Passion held at other times.

John Vyvyan (l.24) was the receiver of the manor of Bodmin and a relative of the well-known Thomas Vyvyan, prior of Bodmin and titular bishop of Megara. He was the most important church leader in Cornwall up to the Reformation (Rowse, *Tudor Cornwall*, p 147).

473   CRO: B/Bod/233   single sheet
The manuscript is so faded and torn as to be practically illegible. Maclean's nineteenth-century transcription is found in his *Parochial and Family History of Bodmin*, p 241, reprinted in his later *Parochial and Family History of Trigg Minor*, vol 1, p 341.

475   CRO: PD/322/1   f 7
Thomas John Harvey (l.32) was one of the wardens of the store and light of St Meriadoc and St Martin in 1539–41 (CRO: PD/322/1 ff 8v, 9v, 16).

475   CRO: PD/322/1   f 14
Richard Crane (l.41) was a churchwarden and warden of the Mid-Lent guild *c* 1541 (CRO: PD/322/1 ff 10v, 12v). In 1547 Crane was ale maker with Margery Bray for Our Lady the Purification guild (CRO: PD/322/1 f 25v).

476   CRO: PD/322/2   f 129
The accounts in which these entries are located lack a heading and so the accounting term and type of account are unknown. They follow what appears to be a complete set of records for 1593 but are in a different hand. Folios 129, 129v, 130, and 130v list payments. There is a mix of payments and receipts on f 131 in the same hand. Folio 131v then has accounts for 1596, following which are accounts for 1598. Further evidence for the year 1595–6 is a payment in this set of records for a grave for 'william flecher'; the parish register of burials (CRO: P/27/1/1) notes that William Fleccher was buried 13 July 1595. As surrounding accounts appear to follow a March to March term, the reference to a July 1595 burial confirms a 1595–6 dating.

477–81   PRO: STAC 8/249/4   mb 4
John Rashleigh (1554–1624) from Menabilly was the head of one of the wealthiest and most important families in the Fowey area, a family whose extensive shipping interests developed Fowey as a major Cornish port. Rashleigh was also involved in privateering and his shipping adventures often put him at odds with the law. In 1588 he was arrested for illegal trading in the Baltic. Rashleigh was portreeve of Fowey in 1584, a member of parliament in 1589 and 1597, and sheriff of Cornwall in 1608–9 (P.W. Hasler (ed), *The House of Commons, 1558–1603*, vol 3 (London, 1981), 277–8). In November of 1615 Rashleigh was a defendant in a Star Chamber case in which he was accused of having publicly uttered threats and defamatory remarks against Charles Baret of Golant in October 1614 (PRO: STAC 8/64/17).
    Defendant Sir Anthony Rowse (before 1560–1620) from Halton St Dominick was a member of parliament in 1584 and 1604. Rowse, between the years 1583 and 1603, actively worked as a member of the commission of the peace for Cornwall and, being concerned with privateering in particular, he probably knew John Rashleigh well. Rowse was also a friend of Sir Francis Drake. Rowse was sheriff of Cornwall in 1587–8 and 1602–3. During his second term as sheriff, the protestant Rowse was active against Cornish recusants. He also served as deputy warden of the stannaries and was a recorder for Launceston (Hasler (ed), *House of Commons, 1558–1603*, vol 3, pp 305–6). Another of the defendants, Edward Herle (p 477, l.34) was probably the second son of Thomas Herle (1537–1602) from Trenowth, who was escheator for Devon and Cornwall from February to November 1581 (Bindoff (ed), *House of Commons, 1509–1558*, vol 2, pp 347–8).
    The omitted portion of the bill describes what means the confederates allegedly employed to induce as many 'of the Common people, as they coulde to belieue the saide false and scandalous libell to be

true,' such as by publicly repeating the aspersions against the complainant at the assize and sessions of the peace in Cornwall, by directing petitions to officers of the court demanding the punishment of the complainant, by pointing out individuals in the streets of Fowey and loudly naming them 'Mr Rashleighes Bawdes' or whores, and by bribing, tricking, or coercing women to falsely accuse the complainant.

In his answer (mb 1) to the bill of complaint, defendant Edward Herle simply denied all charges. Defendant Charles Baret responded (mb 2) that he had entered into a bond or recognizance in the amount of 100 marks payable to the king for costs in a case brought against John Rashleigh by a Nicholas Chawner of Devon but that he was not guilty of any of the charges in this case. The bill charged specifically that defendant Thomas Kendall had contrived to bring one Sarah Lillicrapp to his house where, posing as a justice of the peace, he detained her for a day, threatened and bribed her into agreeing to testify to having committed adultery with the complainant, and then sent her home at night with his horse, saddle, and some money in reward. To this Kendall answered (mb 3) that a Margaret Pierce brought Sarah Lillicrapp to his house when he was out of it and that Sarah there complained against Rashleigh and again did so when Kendall returned to his house; this was under no 'examinacion' but done of her own accord, and furthermore Sarah Lillicrapp had previously voiced the same grievances against the complainant Rashleigh. Kendall's wife gave Sarah some needlework to do, for which Kendall gave Sarah a small amount of money, and because Kendall did not want Sarah in his house since she looked sick and lame, he provided her with a horse and saddle so she could return home. Kendall also denied guilt in any other of the matters with which he was charged.

This bill is somewhat unusual in that it has been signed by the attorney-general, Sir Francis Bacon, as well as by two attorneys, Sir Thomas Richardson (later chief justice of the court of King's Bench) and Thomas Hughes. Thomas Hughes was from Lyme Regis and pursued a legal career at Gray's Inn. He served in parliament in 1586 and later in life was a justice in Somerset. He also wrote a blank verse tragedy, *The Misfortunes of Arthur*, performed for the queen in 1588. He was knighted in 1619 and died in 1626 (Hasler, (ed), *House of Commons, 1558–1603*, vol 2, p 352). Normally a bill of complaint was signed by only one attorney, acting for the complainant, and the attorney-general signed only bills of information, which were initiated in his office. These signatures may reflect the seriousness of the charges made as well as the status of the parties involved.

481–5 PRO: STAC 8/27/10 mb 2
This bill of information is presented in the name of the attorney-general, Henry Yelverton (1566–1629), who has signed at the end (p 485, l.36). John Giles and Higgons, the other signers, cannot be identified but were probably a Star Chamber attorney and clerk, respectively. Yelverton succeeded Sir Francis Bacon as solicitor-general in 1613, the same year he was knighted, and as attorney-general in 1617. Eventually Yelverton suffered a reversal of favour; Bacon and others recommended that he be tried before the Star Chamber for his political manoeuvering, even though he had admitted being in error. He was removed as attorney-general in 1620 and imprisoned in the Tower. In 1625 he again resumed public service, becoming a judge in the Court of Common Pleas.

One response (mb 1) is extant; in it defendant Margaret Fetherstone answered that she was not guilty of any of the charges.

486–9 PRO: STAC 8/236/29 mb 2
In his answer (mb 1) John Yeo counter-charged that the complaint was for the purpose of putting himself and the other defendants to trouble (including a long journey of nearly 200 miles to London and various expenses), that the bill was altogether insufficient to be answered in court, and furthermore

that the matters in the complaint, even if true, were 'frivolous idle and for the most parte insensible' and not worthy of presentation in court. For a brief biography of the attorney who signed this bill, Thomas Hughes, see pp 596–7, endnote to PRO: STAC 8/249/4 mb 4.

489–90   CRO: B/Laus/135   mbs [2–2d]
Although this record concerns travel to Plymouth via Tavistock and actually pertains to performance activity in Devon as opposed to Cornwall, it was discovered in the Launceston Borough Accounts (one of several strips of membrane all in the same hand) and is therefore included here. The travel was apparently in connection with a lawsuit since 2d is paid for a copy of the proceedings (p 489, l.34) and 5d is paid for wine for 'Robert Heye by the mayor for his being a good friend in the court of Trematon' (p 490, ll.25–6). It is tempting to suggest that because of difficult travel (one of their horses had to be reshod) the assizes were held in Devon, forcing Launceston people to travel there for matters of suit. The increase in expenditures seems to suggest a larger group on the second trip.

490   CRO: B/Laus/137   single mb
On the basis of a deed of 5 February 1430/1, Peter and Peter, *Histories of Launceston and Dunheved*, p 123, identify William Crese (l.40) as mayor of Launceston in 1430–1.
    The phrase 'pone' le beris' (l.41) is unusual and as the meaning of the abbreviated 'pone'' is not clear in this context, it has not been expanded. The word 'beris' might mean 'beds' or 'litters' (from the same root as 'bier') or 'the bearers.' As it could possibly mean 'bears,' this excerpt, however cryptic, has been included here.

491   CRO: B/Laus/138   f [7]
Peter and Peter believe that this was a draft account, and indeed some sections are crossed out (*Histories of Launceston and Dunheved*, p 128). Walter Colle (l.16) can be identified as a chaplain on the basis of his appearance in other documents. A 1520–1 account (CRO: B/Laus/170 mb [2]), for instance, includes a payment of 4d for priests to pray annually for the soul of Walter Colle, cleric.
    The interlinear 'horn' (ll.16, 18) in proximity to the sums is in reference to a 'Rob*ert* Horn' who is named elsewhere in the manuscript (CRO: B/Laus/138 f [1]). Robert Horn is mentioned in the 1431–2 account (CRO: B/Laus/137) as a provost. Other surnames are inserted interlinearly in this account and presumably are intended to identify the individual responsible for the particular item.

491   CRO: B/Laus/139   f [5]
This may have been a draft since the entire page has an 'X' over it.

491   CRO: B/Laus/141   single mb
The account heading for this account is in very poor and incomplete condition. The endorsement in a later hand dates the account to 29 Henry VI, which is 1450–1. Two members of parliament for Cornwall – 'Borlace' and 'Will*iam* me*n*wynnk' – are named in the account.

492   CRO: B/Laus/153   single mb
This account is in very poor condition and cannot be dated from the heading. Both the CRO catalogue and the antiquarian Seneschals' Accounts (CRO: LR/140) of these documents date them 1465–6. A note, probably by an archivist, dates them *c* 1464–6 (4 or 5 Edward IV). Another hand has cancelled the notation '4° vel 5°' and added the number '6' but the year 1466–7 is already accounted for by CRO: B/Laus/158, which is clearly dated.

492   CRO: B/Laus/160   mb [2]
This manuscript has lost its original account heading but is endorsed '1469 or 1470.' The CRO catalogue and antiquarian Seneschals' Accounts (CRO: LR/140) also date this document 1469 or 1470. The 1470–1 account is extant as CRO: B/Laus/147.

   The left half of the manuscript is totally missing; therefore there are no account section headings either. The word 'Ministrall'' (l.30) is the last word in its line in the MS; the words 'regis ij s.' are visible at the beginning of the line below on the torn left edge but as half of the MS and thus the intervening text is missing it would only be supposition to assume the reward was given to the king's minstrel/s.

492–3   CRO: B/Laus/147   mbs [1, 2]
In the opening formula of this account the scribe has left a blank for the number of the regnal year of Edward IV. Two separate antiquarian notes on the manuscript give the regnal year as either 1 Edward IV (ie, 1461–2) or 11 Edward IV (ie, 1471–2). The correct date, 1470–1, can de deduced from references within the manuscript itself. First, the account makes reference to the forty-ninth regnal year of Henry VI (September–October 1470–11 April 1471), indicating that the account touches upon that period. Second, Richard Neville, sixteenth earl of Warwick (p 492, l.40), and George Plantagenet, duke of Clarence (p 493, l.3), are identified separately. Neville died on 14 April 1471 and the earldom subsequently passed to George Plantagenet, then duke of Clarence. Thus the visit of their respective performers must have occurred before April 1471. The scribe has, however, named Edward IV as reigning sovereign which indicates that, although the accounting year may have begun in November 1470 during Henry VI's short-lived restoration, the account was rendered in November 1471 (that is within 11 Edward IV). At the time, even though Edward had resumed his reign, the scribe may have been uncertain as to how the regnal year was to be reckoned. Beginning this block of external expenses are payments to servants of Hugh Courtenay, who was evidently riding with Warwick and Clarence on their way to Okehampton, Devon.

493   CRO: B/Laus/170   mb [1]
The accounting year for these accounts had changed by 1520–1 from a St Katherine's to St Katherine's period to a Michaelmas to Michaelmas year.

494   CRO: B/Laus/171   mb [2]
The account header of this manuscript has been lost but an antiquarian endorsement 'Hen: 8 | 23 | 1531' is visible on the membrane. As the antiquarian notations on other dated Launceston accounts of this kind consistently give the year in which the account is rendered, 1530–1 is taken to be correct.

   'Greynfild Vicecomit*is*' (l.28) is Richard Grenville (by 1495–1550) of Stowe in Kilkhampton. The Grenvilles of Stowe in northeast Cornwall were a prominent family, related by blood and by marriage to the Arundells of Lanherne and Trerice, the Chamonds, the Roscarrocks, and the St Aubyns. Grenville was appointed to the privy chamber by 1523 and served as sheriff of Cornwall in 1523, 1526–7, and 1544–5 and as member of parliament in 1529. His uncle, Viscount Lisle, deputy of Calais, recommended Grenville for the position of marshal of Calais in 1535 (Bindoff (ed), *House of Commons, 1509–1558*, vol 2, pp 247–8).

495   CRO: B/Laus/173–78   f [12]
The word 'venesicians' (l.16) may refer to actors or dancers. Records of 1548–9 for Plymouth, Devon,

note that people also called 'venycyans' were paid with wine on May Day (Wasson (ed), *Devon*, p 233). See also p 608, endnote to BL: Additional MS. 32243 f 12, for a discussion of a comparable term, 'Egyptians.'

496   CRO: B/Laus/173–78   ff [24v, 26v]
The rings and stones (ll.23–5) were for bullbaiting. William Seymour (l.37) is listed as a Dunheved burgess in 1571–2, 1572–3, 1573–4, and 1575–6 (ff [2, 18, 31]).

497   CRO: B/Laus/179/2/1   single sheets
Each of these sheets is no more than a scrap. Written at the head of the entries from the first of these sheets is the phrase 'Ianuarie the second' and a marginal note (perhaps in a later hand) reads 'X:3°:1643.' The sheet is signed, however, by William Kever who was mayor in 1640–1 (CRO: B/Laus/346). Thus the sheet is dated to 1640/1; the significance of the marginal date is not known.

The 23 January sheet is also signed by Kever, mayor. Although the currency denominations do not appear on the fragment either in column headers or with the sums, these amounts are presumably of shillings and pence as on the preceding scrap from the same year.

498   CRO: B/Lis/284   mb [2]
There is a large stain after 'in anno' in the account heading which nearly obscures the date but the regnal year, 7–8 Charles I, can still be seen. The antiquarian endorsement originally read 5–6 Charles I but has been corrected by the same hand to read 7–8 Charles I (1631–2).

499   CRO: B/Lis/288   mb [2]
Sir William Wrey (l.5) served as sheriff of Cornwall in 1599–1600, when a squire, and later, in 1612–13, after being knighted on 23 July 1603 in the Royal Garden at Whitehall before the king's coronation, along with Sir Anthony Rowse (*List of Sheriffs for England and Wales from the Earliest Times to A.D. 1831*, PRO, Lists and Indexes, no 9 (London, 1898), C3; William Shaw, *Knights of England*, vol 2 (London, 1906), 125). For a brief biography of Rowse, see p 596, endnote to PRO: STAC 8/249/4 mb 4. In 1624–5 Wrey was a member of parliament from Liskeard (Allen, *History of Liskeard*, p 238).

499–500   PRO: E 315/122   ff 19v, 20v, 21, 22
'Nicholas the britton' (p 500, l.7) was probably one of the many Bretons who lived and worked in Cornwall. The Bretons comprised the largest group of non-Cornish people there. County taxation records from 1522–4 indicate their numbers: 'In Trigg and West hundreds, 79 were registered, some 3.5 per cent of all the men listed there. Over much of the county the proportion was similar, but in Penwith in the far west it reached nearly 10 per cent, 112 out of a total of 1,160 persons' (Julian Cornwall, *Revolt of the Peasantry 1549* (London, 1977), 42). Rowse points out that they probably should not be considered 'foreigners' since they spoke the same language as the Cornish people. 'It is clear,' Rowse says, that 'up to the Reformation, they were still coming over in considerable numbers to serve for higher wages in subordinate capacities, as labourers, artisans, curates.' Eventually the surname 'Briton' became common in Cornwall (*Tudor Cornwall*, pp 95–6, 248). Charles Henderson suggested that 'Cornish towns owed their origins to Breton settlers since the natives refused to give up living in hamlets' (as cited by Cornwall, *Revolt of the Peasantry 1549*, p 42).

501–3   PRO: STAC 8/304/38   single mb
No responses from defendants are available; only the bill of complaint is extant.

503–5   Devon Record Office: Chanter 3   ff ccviii verso–ccix verso
The bishop's order was sent to the cathedral chapter at Exeter and three other collegiate churches in the diocese, Holy Cross at Crediton and St Mary's in Ottery St Mary, both in Devon, and St Thomas the Martyr at Glasney in Penryn, Cornwall. All four chapters were ordered to reply in letters which repeated verbatim the text of the original order but in the register only the reply from St Mary's, Ottery, was copied in full, while the replies from the other three were given without repeating the text of the quoted episcopal order. The response from Glasney is given here as fully as it appears in the register but the text of the original order is necessarily given in the form sent to St Mary's, Ottery, whose entire response is printed in Wasson (ed), *Devon*, pp 12–14.

Since the letter was clearly directed against excesses in the seasonal misrule, such as boy bishop celebrations practised by the minor clergy during the Christmas season, it may be inferred that these four churches were the only ones in the diocese whose ministers included a large enough body of boys and youths in minor orders to engage in such behaviour. As Martin R. Dudley has noted, Grandisson was not opposed to all forms of boy bishop observances, for his ordinale for Exeter Cathedral includes liturgical instructions for the boy bishop's participation in the services for the feast of the Holy Innocents ('*Natalis Innocentum*: The Holy Innocents in Liturgy and Drama,' *The Church and Childhood*, Diana Wood (ed), Studies in Church History 31 (Oxford, 1994), 233–42).

505   *STC*: 13309   sig G2
The phrase 'of the same quality' (l.11) refers to the earl of Sussex's players, who feature in the anecdote preceding this one. Also an example of a 'strange accident happening at a play,' it describes a performance in Lynn, Norfolk, during which one of Sussex's players acted the part of a murdered man's ghost. In the audience was a woman who had secretly and fatally poisoned her husband years before. Upon viewing the ghost character she was moved to spontaneously confess her crime.

Believing the strange incident at Penryn refers to a Samson play performed at a barn in Penryn in 1587, William Sandys, 'On the Cornish Drama,' *JRIC* 3 (1865), 18, conjectures that the Spaniards arrived in town when Samson attacked the Philistines; however, there is no evidence that the event Heywood was describing was a Samson play in particular. The source of this account has sometimes mistakenly been identified as Gosson's *School of Abuse*.

505   CRO: P/192/5/1   p 89
The accounting year of this account – that of the 'six men' of the parish – is not specified. Later dated accounts of the 'four men' of the parish (1555–6, p 106) and again of the 'six men' (1577–8 and 1582–3, pp 115, 128) suggest that the accounts of this parish at this time normally began and ended in early to mid-February.

505–6   CRO: P/19/5/1   f 6v
Folios 6 and 6v are comprised of several entries of different dates between 1540 and 1562 and given in roughly chronological order. Dating of these receipts is based on their relative position on the folio. Folio 6 concludes with a payment by the parish for making and setting up of a new rood loft in 1557–8, and the entries following those transcribed here are constables' accounts for the reign of Mary, thus 1553–8. The accounting period at this time cannot be definitely determined although f 8v of these accounts indicates that the churchwardens were to render their accounts on St Andrew's Day in 1556. By 1566 the moveable feast of the Ascension was the start and end date for the accounting year.

506   CRO: P/19/5/1   f 28
The 'west partyes' may simply be in reference to the western area of Cornwall.

506   CRO: P/19/5/1   f 32
The second receipt appears to be for wood. See p 522, ll.18–19 for a reference to the wood of Robin Hood's house.

507   CRO: P/19/5/1   f 51
The Robin Hood players from St Columb Minor also performed in St Ives in 1587–8 (see p 517, l.11).

507   CRO: P/36/8/1   f [10]
The manuscript foliation is partial and inconsistent; this leaf is foliated as '2' but is the tenth leaf after two flyleaves. It may have been the second folio of the original book. Serjeantson, 'Church and Parish Goods of St. Columb Major,' p 345, notes that these imitation velvet and coarse linen streamers were probably not used in church processions because of their lesser quality. The clerk has, unusually, used the Latin conventional sign for the initial syllable 'con' (**9**) to stand for the word 'ut' in his Latin tag, 'ut supra' (l.29).

507–8   CRO: P/36/8/1   f [14]
David Wiles, *The Early Plays of Robin Hood* (Cambridge, 1981), 25, observes, 'Since the bells make up six sets for arms and legs, we infer that the friar is the sixth dancer.'

508–9   CRO: P/36/8/1   f [24v]
The inventory of parish goods for the account year after this (CRO: P/36/8/1 f [25]) reads: 'Adde unto the Churche goods founde the laste yeere one fonte clothe vt supra …' which suggests that, while not mentioned specifically, the dancing costumes were still in the church in 1591–2.

509   CRO: P/36/8/1   f [30v]
In the next year, 1598, there is no reference to morris coats, nor thereafter.

510–12   PRO: STAC 8/202/30   mb 3
John Glanville (1586–1661), the attorney who signed this bill and that in Robins v. Vosse below (PRO: STAC 8/246/13 mb 3), was a member of parliament from Plymouth in 1614, 1620, 1623, 1625, 1626, and 1628. He opposed the Crown in parliament, spoke out against the Crown's extravagant expenditures, and was active in protesting the dissolution of parliament in 1625. Glanville was one of England's most prominent lawyers and a well-known public servant, representing clients in Star Chamber suits and acting at the lord keeper's appointment as a referee in a dispute in Chancery. Glanville was knighted in 1641. He subsequently fell into disfavour in parliament and was imprisoned in the Tower in 1645 for three years, only to return to prominence as a member of parliament during the Commonwealth. During the Restoration he was king's serjeant.

Nothing is known about the complainant or defendants in this suit. A John Strangman (p 510, l.27) appears in the St Columb Churchwardens' Accounts for 1603–4, when Strangman paid 14s 7d to discharge all of his debts (CRO: P/36/8/1 f 37).

In defending himself (mb 1) John Dier denied all charges, specifying that he never spoke or sang any of the libels, nor caused anyone else to do so. Benjamin Strangman said in his answer (mb 2) that his ten-year-old brother found the paper and gave it to him, but as neither of them was literate, Benjamin had a John Coppithorne read it to him; Coppithorne subsequently told one John Carter, who requested the document from Benjamin and kept it for a week before returning it. Benjamin also said that, in an attempt to identify the handwriting, he showed the document to others including his former schoolmaster, who then gave a copy to the complainants. Beyond this acquaintance with the libellous paper, Benjamin Strangman denied the charges.

513–14   St Ives Guildhall   ff 3, 3v, 4, 4v
Due to the condition of this document, the dating of the individual accounts has often proved very difficult. In cases where the accounts themselves do not afford dating information, it has been necessary to resort to the efforts of two antiquarian sources, Matthews, *History of Saint Ives,* and R. Morton Nance, who annotated a copy of Matthews. Nance's RIC copy provides a useful commentary and evaluation of Matthews. Matthews assigned the accounts a single year date only and may not have consistently treated the year in the account heading as the terminus ad quem of the account. In those cases where the account date could not be determined using the manuscript itself, Nance's dating choice has been preferred over that of Matthews. Although Nance may not be infallible, his superior paleographic skills make him the more reliable.

The heading of this particular account is partially torn away and shows only 'The Accompte of Iohn ⟨...⟩ the year of our lorde 157⟨. ...⟩.' Matthews, *History of Saint Ives,* p 147, dates these accounts 1575? but as Nance observes, in 1575 the headwarden was not named John but rather Martin Trewinnard; Nance suggests 1572 or 1574 (the 1573–4 account, however, with a John 'Penheleg' as the headwarden clearly begins on f 7v). In further support of the date 1571–2, this is the second set of accounts in the book and the next account in sequence is for 1572–3 (the account that intervenes on f 5 is assigned to 1594-5 on the basis of an internal reference).

Badcock, *Historical Sketch of St. Ives,* p 19, asserts that the king and queen of the summer games and maypole dances were obliged to turn over all the money they collected to aid the poor but some of their gains may have gone to other uses as well, as these records seem to suggest. The entries here indicate that monies received were used for drink, tithe butter, for wood for the 'playing place,' and for work on the maypole (see Matthews, *History of Saint Ives,* pp 144–92 for other examples).

Several wardens' receipts (p 513, ll.31–7) were given to support entertainments during this year, apparently a banner year for St Ives festivities. Contributors included Thomas James and Pearse Nole (churchwardens); William Teage and Martin Goodall (wardens of the Market House); John Goman and George Goodall (wardens of the quay); and Pearse Goorge and William Mobe (wardens of the aisle), all of whom are listed on f 3v at the opening of the account.

Matthews, *History of Saint Ives,* provides a list of public officers for the borough and parish of St Ives which identifies several individuals named in these accounts. His list of officials is, however, keyed to a single year date only, seemingly without always differentiating between the year in which an individual was elected and the year in which the account was rendered. Occasionally Matthews' list contradicts his own conjectured dating of the accounts themselves. Compounding the difficulty of using Matthews' list of officials for the purpose of identification is the fact that the manuscripts have suffered considerable decay and damage. As a result account headings, which in 1892 may have yielded dates and names to Matthews, are no longer verifiable. Nevertheless, while Matthews' dating may not always be accurate, the fact that the individuals held the said offices in or around the year given is not in dispute and goes to the general picture of their public profile.

'Iames huchin' (p 513, l.15) is probably from the Hichens family of the St Ives area. Matthews provides a history of the family, including the various spellings of the surname: Hechins, Hichings, Huchins, Huchyns, Hutchings, etc (*History of Saint Ives,* pp 428–31, 526). In 1578 a James 'hychen' of St Ives contributed 2d to a local rate and is listed as warden of the quay in 1584. 'william trinwith' (p 513, l.28) is probably William Trenwith from a family of some importance in Lelant, near St Ives. This branch of the family is first mentioned in a *c* 1520 subsidy roll and perhaps even earlier (Matthews, *History of Saint Ives*, p 474). In 1603 William Trenwith served as one of the twelve burgesses; in 1607 the same gentleman was fined for not accepting the office of portreeve. A William Trenwith was head-warden or portreeve in 1573 and another (not necessarily the same man) was headwarden (or portreeve) in 1619 (Matthews, *History of Saint Ives*, pp 476, 517). 'mr Coswarthe' (p 513, l.32) may be a member of the Cosworth family of Cosworth, near St Columb. A John Cosworth was a receiver-general for the duchy and was active in duchy affairs until his death in 1575; he perhaps was in the St Ives area in 1571 or 1572 (Bindoff (ed), *House of Commons, 1509–1558*, vol 1, pp 709–10; Hasler (ed), *House of Commons, 1558–1603*, vol 1, pp 661–2). Mr 'laynyane' (p 514, l.3) may be John Lanyon, listed in the 1573 records as one of the twenty-four councilmen chosen for the coming year. Matthews includes a bracket following this name in the 1575? records, identifying 'laynyane' as Lanyon (Matthews, *History of Saint Ives*, p 147). A William Barratt (p 514, l.5) was headwarden or portreeve in 1587 and constable in 1575 and 1590. Around 1580 he is recorded as one of the twenty-four councilmen. Barratt appears in other accounts as well, one being the 1591 records, where he received payment for timber for build-ing a poor woman's house (Matthews, *History of Saint Ives*, pp 517, 528, 153, 165). A John Goman (p 514, l.6) was warden of the Market House in 1574 and warden of the quay in 1573, 1575, and 1606 (Matthews, *History of Saint Ives*, pp 525–6). John 'carveddris' (p 514, l.14) is listed as one of the 'twelve men' of council in 1578 and again in 1583, and was headwarden in 1579 (Matthews, *History of Saint Ives*, pp 153, 154, 476, 517).

Thomas Hicks (p 514, l.15) was, according to Matthews' reckoning, headwarden in 1572 and 1595 and a capital burgess in 1573, 1580, and 1592 (*History of Saint Ives*, p 433, 517). Names of members of the Hicks family appear in the St Ives records from the earliest times of the town. Matthews gives a brief account of a lost manuscript of the town's history written in 1722 by a Mr Hicks, the town coroner, and discusses the appearance of the names of various Hicks family members down to the nineteenth century (*History of Saint Ives*, pp 431–5). 'Tregerthar' (p 514, l.19) may be Henry Tregerthen, who was warden of the quay in 1601 (*History of Saint Ives*, p 526). A Martin Goodall (p 514, l.22) served with William Teage as warden of the Market House in 1575 according to Matthews, *History of Saint Ives*, p 525.

Although Matthews remarks that the 'white lambes skyns' (p 514, l.18) were for making parchment, Nance disagrees, suggesting they were 'For dressing Adam and Eve; parchment would be bought, not made locally' (RIC copy of Matthews, *History of Saint Ives*, p 148).

514–15   St Ives Guildhall   ff 6, 6v, 7

Matthews speculated that this sum 'for ye enterlude' (p 515, l.5) was 'paid for a manuscript copy of the miracle-play which was to be performed that year' but Nance writes in his annotated copy of Matthews that 'It may also be taken to mean that the sum was contributed for expences of the play' (RIC copy of Matthews, *History of Saint Ives*, p 144).

'Harrie sterrie' (p 514, l.32), king of the summer games, may have been Henry Sterry, who is listed as headwarden or portreeve in 1582. William Trenwith (p 515, l.6) was headwarden or portreeve in 1573 (Matthews, *History of Saint Ives*, p 517). For William Trenwith, see pp 603–4 above, endnote to St Ives Guildhall ff 3, 3v, 4, 4v. 'Iohn *william*' (p 515, l.15) is part of the Williams family, one of the town's first families. A John Williams is listed in a *c* 1520 subsidy roll, having £8 yearly value of goods at both Lelant and Zennor, which Matthews believes to be an 'above average' value. John Williams was a capital burgess in 1573 (Matthews, *History of Saint Ives*, pp 482–3). Thomas Trenwith (p 515, l.17) was headwarden or portreeve in 1625 (Matthews, *History of Saint Ives*, p 517).

See pp 603–4, endnote to St Ives Guildhall ff 3, 3v, 4, 4v, for comment on Matthews' dating of these individuals' terms in office.

515–16　St Ives Guildhall　ff 10, 11
Matthews does not date these accounts at all but Nance suggests 1579, presumably because Matthews gives John Carvoddres, whose name appears in the account heading, as headwarden for the year 1579. Matthews also suggests that Cadwellye (p 516, l.3) 'may be some garment made of Welsh cloth, from Kidwelly'; Nance suggests Cornish 'keas-gwely,' for a bedspread of rough cloth (RIC copy of Matthews, *History of Saint Ives*, p 155).

516　St Ives Guildhall　f 13v
The account is for 1584 according to Matthews and annotated by Nance as 1583–4. Matthews, *History of Saint Ives*, p 155, identifies 'the Roben houde' (l.17) as a group of 'Twelfth Night mummers.' For 'harry stery' (l.18), see p 604–5, endnote to St Ives Guildhall ff 6, 6v, 7.

516　St Ives Guildhall　f 56
'harrye heckes' (l.24), king of the summer games, is probably Henry Hicks, listed as headwarden or portreeve in 1594 and as Henry Hicks, senior, in 1614, 1620, 1631, and 1641. He is listed as warden of the quay in 1590 (Matthews, *History of Saint Ives*, pp 159, 517–18, 526). See pp 603–4, endnote to St Ives Guildhall ff 3, 3v, 4, 4v, for comment on Matthews' dating of the various individuals' terms in office.

'Elyzabeth cockyn' (l.25), queen of the summer games, is probably from the Cocking family that Matthews identifies as one of the town's first families, a typical family of the yeomanry. Elizabeth, like others, is mentioned only in the context of the summer games. Several locations are named after the family, the harbour of St Ives being called 'Porthcocking' from 'ancient times' (Matthews, *History of Saint Ives*, pp 423–4).

516　St Ives Guildhall　f 16
These accounts are undated but Nance dates the account 1587 and notes that Thomas Candrow was the headwarden in the previous year (RIC copy of Matthews, *History of Saint Ives*, pp 155–6, 517). These accounts are followed in order by the accounts for 1587–8.

517　St Ives Guildhall　f 17v
Nance's own transcription of these difficult records inserted into his annotated copy of Matthews, *History of Saint Ives*, p 157, was very helpful to us in deciphering them.

It is likely that the king and queen of the summer games were the sons and daughters of parents who made donations to the games in their childrens' names. 'yonge candrowe' was the son of Thomas Candrow, one of the twenty-four men in 1580, and headwarden or portreeve in 1586 (Matthews, *History of Saint Ives*, pp 153, 517). Matthews identifies 'mr tregera' (l.12) as a member of the Tregenna 'gentle-family' of the Tregenna estate in St Ives. Matthews suggests that this 'master' is John Tregenna, a capital burgess in 1573, 1578, 1583, and 1596 and headwarden in 1597, and adds that his notes say that John Tregenna was bailiff of Penwith in 1581. When John Tregenna died *c* 1607, the male line of the older

Tregenna family ended (Matthews, *History of Saint Ives*, pp 467–9, 517). See pp 603–4, endnote to St Ives Guildhall ff 3, 3v, 4, 4v, for comment on Matthews' dating of these individuals' terms in office.

517   St Ives Guildhall   f 22
Thomas James (l.19) was headwarden or portreeve in 1580 and a churchwarden with Pearse Nole in 1575 according to Matthews; in this case Nance has annotated his copy of Matthews to give the correct date 1571–2 (see pp 603–4, endnote to St Ives Guildhall ff 3, 3v, 4, 4v). In 1578 he was a capital burgess, and one of the twenty-four men in 1602 and 1603 (Matthews, *History of Saint Ives*, pp 517, 522, 169). See pp 603–4, endnote to St Ives Guildhall ff 3, 3v, 4, 4v, for comment on Matthews' dating of these individuals' terms in office.

517   Saint Ives Guildhall   f 24v
'Ioell hicks' (l.29) is probably the same Joel Hicks, warden of the quay in 1596, one of the twenty-four men of council in 1603, and a capital burgess in 1612 (Matthews, *History of Saint Ives*, p 433). See pp 603–4, endnote to St Ives Guildhall ff 3, 3v, 4, 4v, for comment on Matthews' dating of an individual's terms in office.

517   St Ives Guildhall   f 5
No date appears on this set of records, which intervenes between the accounts identified as those for 1571–2 and those of 1572–3. Although Matthews dates this account 1576?, Nance redates it to 1595 (RIC copy of Matthews, *History of Saint Ives*, pp 148–9), the year the Spaniards were in Mounts Bay; in fact, the first entry in the list of payments on this folio is 'for led to make bollat*es* when the Spanyerd*es* were in Mount*es* Bay*e*.' The towns of Paul, Mousehole, and Newlyn were all burned by the Spaniards in 1595. The handwriting appears to be similar to that of the 1596–7 account.

518   St Ives Guildhall   f 19
Nance gives the date 1596 for this account (RIC copy of Matthews, *History of Saint Ives*, p 163). 'Nyclys Hickes' (l.5) is part of the Hicks family discussed in Matthews, *History of Saint Ives*, pp 431–5. See pp 603–4, endnote to St Ives Guildhall ff 3, 3v, 4, 4v, for comment on Matthews' dating of individuals' terms in office.

518   St Ives Guildhall   f 51
This account has only a partial heading but can be dated on the basis of an internal reference to Christmas 1596. A Stephen Barbar (l.13) was headwarden or portreeve in 1634 and served with Thomas Goode as churchwarden in 1636. A Stephen Barbar is also listed as one of the twelve men in 1627, 1630, and 1636. Earlier in this period, a Stephen Barbar (Barboure) was one of the wardens of the quay in 1573 and a warden of the aisle in 1574. (Matthews, *History of Saint Ives*, pp 517, 523, 526, 529, 186, 189, 192). See pp 603–4, endnote St Ives Guildhall ff 3, 3v, 4, 4v, for comment on Matthews' dating of these individuals' terms in office.

518   St Ives Guildhall   f 61
When Matthews saw the records, the word 'maye,' now 'm⟨..⟩' (l.22) was still visible (*History of Saint Ives*, p 177). 'Iames Stearye' (l.21) is James Sterry, headwarden or portreeve in 1615. He also signed documents in 1622 and 1629 as one of the twelve men (Matthews, *History of Saint Ives*, pp 517, 182, 188). See pp 603–4, endnote to St Ives Guildhall ff 3, 3v, 4, 4v, for comment on Matthews' dating of these individuals' terms in office.

518   St Ives Guildhall   f 79

Henry Stephens (l.31), the father of John, king of the summer games this year, was a member of a family begun by a poor Irish immigrant who, according to legend, shipwrecked in Zennor, near St Ives. This Irish ancestor is known as one of the men who introduced seine fishing to St Ives and the nets are called 'Dungarven' after the town in Ireland he came from. The family developed into several branches, the Stevens or Stephens of Tregarthen, who descended from the original immigrant, remaining the main branch. In 1633 Henry Stephens was an overseer of the poor, in 1634, warden of the aisle, and in 1639, warden of the quay (Matthews, *History of Saint Ives*, pp 527–8, 530; Matthews sketches the family biography to 1642 on pp 451–4).

Edward Hammand (l.32), father of Margery, queen of this year's summer games, was one of the twelve men in 1627, warden of the quay in 1632 and 1634, churchwarden in 1634, headwarden or portreeve in 1635, warden of the Market House in 1638, and mayor in 1644 (Matthews, *History of Saint Ives*, pp 186, 517–18, 523, 525, 527). See pp 603–4, endnote to St Ives Guildhall ff 3, 3v, 4, 4v, for comment on Matthews' dating of these individuals' terms in office.

519   St Ives Guildhall   f 3v

The 'Maister' (l.7) on whose behalf Robert Arundell presented the cup to the town was Sir Francis Basset of Tehidy, whose name is engraved on the cup along with the date and the following verse:

     Iff any discord twixt my frends arise
     Within the Burrough of Beloved St. Ives
     Itt is desyred that this my Cupp of Loue
     To eurie one a Peace maker may Proue
     Then am I Blest to have giuen a Legacie
     So like my hartt unto Posteritie.

Matthews relates that on solemn occasions the cup 'was handed round, and its contents sipped by mayor and aldermen, or a draught of mulled wine was presented in it to any distinguished guest' (*History of Saint Ives*, p 211). The St Ives loving cup, given to the town in 1639–40 and dated from around 1620, is housed in the St Ives Guildhall. A description of the cup and its history can be found in Noall, 'The St. Ives Borough Regalia.' St Ives is a good example of a town where civic regalia dating from the Middle Ages continues to instill civic pride.

Robert Arundell (l.6) was the son of Sir John Arundell of Trerice, near Newquay, which is about twenty-five miles from St Ives. Carew, in his *Survey of Cornwall*, remarks that he 'well knew' Robert Arundell, a Cornishman with enviable skill at archery: he could 'shoot 12. score, with his right hand, with his left, and from behinde his head' (sig V). 'mr Hammand*es*' (l.8) is probably Edward Hammand. See above, endnote to St Ives Guildhall f 79.

519   St Ives Guildhall   f 4

After this time the records contain no reference to the lord and lady or king and queen.

519–20   CRO: X/50/5   pp 26–7

If Veal (p 520, l.1) was seventy-eight years old at the time he would have been born in 1490. If he were a boy able to remember at the time of the murder, perhaps between the ages of eight and fifteen years, the murder – and the play in the 'place' at Sancreed – may have occurred between 1498 and 1505. Pool also suggests a date of *c* 1500 for the play at Sancreed ('The Penheleg Manuscript,' p 200 n 160), considering John Veal to be ten years old at the time of the play. A Sir John Treffry (p 520, l.7), knighted in 1485 for his support of the Tudor dynasty, was sheriff in 1489–90 and 1499–1500.

521   BL: Additional MS. 32243   f 12
Customarily REED volumes do not include entries concerning Egyptians, since there is no necessary
connection between them and performance in our period. They were often part of the larger category
of vagabonds and 'rogues,' who were included in acts and proclamations levelled against itinerants.
These entries from Cornwall are noteworthy in that the 'Egyppcions' (l.7) are here (and in 1559–60,
1560–1, and 1561–2) renting the Stratton church house, which, as evidenced by other Stratton records,
was rented to troupes of travelling performers (bearwards in 1526–7; players in 1538–9 and 1539–40).
In the early seventeeth century, Egyptians were included in *Rid's Art of Jugling* (1612), where they are
described as 'being excellent in quaint tricks and devises, not known heere at that time among us, [and]
were esteemed and had in great admiration' (see W. Carew Hazlitt, *Faiths and Folklore of the British Isles*,
vol 1 (London, 1905; rpt New York, 1965), 291). It is possible that the Egyptians or gypsies that visited Stratton were also performers like the 'egypcians' that danced before Sir John Arundell in 1504–5
(see p 530, CRO: AR/26/2 f 19) or even the 'venesicians' that played in Launceston in 1572–3 (see
p 495, CRO: B/Laus/173–78 f [12]).

521   BL: Additional MS. 32244   f 4
Mattingly, 'Medieval Parish Guilds,' p 305, suggests that fund-raising by Robin Hood and his men
coincides with the dates for repairs to the church rood loft and building of the new chancel. The performers may have been members of the parish guild, entertaining to raise money for the church.

522   BL: Additional MS. 32243   f 62
The word 'Iewes' (l.26) is not erased but 'Ieptyons' is written above it in another, but contemporary hand.
As Jews were exiled from England at this time, the use of the word 'Iewes' to describe the visiting group is
very likely an error of association on the part of the Stratton scribe (see Peacock, 'On the Churchwardens'
Accounts of Stratton,' pp 198–9, 225). The corrected reading that identifies these visitors as Egyptians
or gypsies is consistent with other references to them (see above, endnote to BL: Additional MS. 32243
f 12).

522   BL: Additional MS. 32243   f 63v
For a discussion of the significance of these 'Iepsyons' (l.33), see above, endnote to BL: Additional MS.
32243 f 12.

522   BL: Additional MS. 32243   f 65
For a discussion of the significance of these 'Iepcyons' (l.40), see above, endnote to BL: Additional MS.
32243 f 12.

523   CRO: B/WLooe/12/1   p [1]
In B/WLooe/58/3, an antiquarian copy of CRO: B/WLooe/12/1, there is a note that connects the 'showes'
(l.33) to a tale about the queen's ape printed in an appendix in Thomas Bond's *Topographical and Historical Sketches of the Boroughs of East and West Looe*. See Appendix 6 (pp 574–6).

523–6   PRO: STAC 8/246/13   mb [3]
In their joint answer (mb [1]) Vosse and Congdon, after complaining that their names were included
in the complaint out of malice and a desire to cause them vexation, answer that they are not guilty of
the charges. Defendants Thomas Rowe and John Cullacott jointly answer (mb [2]) and also charge

the complainants with malice and deny any guilt in the matter. For the identity of the attorney Glanville, see pp 602–3, endnote to PRO: STAC 8/202/30 mb 3.

The prevailing spelling 'Whitson' or 'Whitsone' is presumably in error for Whitstone, Cornwall.

527–8 Devon Record Office: Chanter 4 f ccxiii verso
The monastery at Tywardreath began as a daughter house of the Benedictine monastery of St Serge in Angers but ceased to be an alien priory around 1400; as this licence shows, its quasi-foreign status before 1400 exposed it to hostility. Not only was it subject, like other coastal communities, to pirate raids but the local population considered its monks to be somehow complicitous in the attacks. In his licence, Grandisson tried to balance a genuine concern for the safety of this small and exposed community, which numbered only six monks in 1333, against his apparent fear that a move to a less remote location would involve more sophisticated temptations to neglect the divine office, such as the worldly and dissolute shows he warns them to eschew ('mundanis spectaculis & lasciuiis,' p 527, l.23).

529–30 RIC, Courtney Library: HK/17/1 ff [3v, 4]
Douch, 'Household Accounts at Lanherne,' p 28 n 25, explains that Betty (p 529, l.7) 'was obviously a general dealer.' The entry for bells 'for the Moruske' (p 529, l.16) most likely refers to morris dancing. Michael Heaney and John Forrest assert that these accounts include a lady's costume but that is not certain; the goods were evidently delivered to Lady Arundell but they could have been used for a variety of costumes or in other ways. See Heaney and Forrest, *Annals of Early Morris* (Sheffield, 1991), 14–15.

530 CRO: AR/26/2 f 19
The accounting period for this account is not given. The date 1504–5 is that suggested for folios 12–23 in the CRO catalogue and is probable on the basis of handwriting. The term 'egypcians' (l.12) is discussed on p 608, endnote to BL: Additional MS. 32243 f 12.

530 CRO: AR/21/22 p [1]
The 'forsaid trouncke' (l.34) is a black trunk valued at 2s which is listed earlier on the page as among the articles in the west chamber of Trebelzue, an Arundell property in St Columb Minor. The sums added interlinearly in the MS presumably represent the appraisal values of the items. Edward Arundell's inventory also includes 'books in several languages, clearly the library of a scholarly and well-educated man' (North, 'The Arundell Archive,' p 54).

531 PRO: SP 46/16 f [9]
Pounds, 'William Carnsew of Bokelly,' p 22, explains Carnsew's use of the dominical letter next to each date (l.7m), with 'January 1 ... denoted by A and the following six days by the letters B to G, before returning to A for January 8.... There is no entry for March 31, and the G which prefixed this date was repeated for April 1, thus throwing out his dominical letters for the rest of the year. Nonetheless he continued the practice until the middle of January, 1577. In the meanwhile he had begun to indicate Sundays by a small, flower-like motif in the left margin.'

The repetition of 'to' (l.7) appears not to be dittography but rather to mean a letter had been written to him suggesting that he meet Mr Mohan. Mr Mohan (l.7) is perhaps William Mohun, sheriff of Cornwall in 1571 and 1577 (*List of Sheriffs for England and Wales*, sig C4).

The 'bodman playes' (l.7) may refer to the Halgavor celebration at Bodmin noted by Carew in his *Survey of Cornwall* (see p 474).

531–3   St Mary's College Library, Oscott: MS 545   pp 89–94
All that is known of Twigges (p 531, l.21), the interlude performer, comes from the trial of Francis Tregian. During Tregian's first trial at the assizes in Launceston in 1578 the main witness for the prosecution was the man Twigges, who entertained at Golden during the Christmas holidays in 1575. As the Oscott MS indicates, Twigges claimed to have seen and lodged with Cuthbert Mayne at Golden, where he claims Mayne admitted that he was a priest and had brought the *Agnus Dei* to Golden; Twigges claims that he very likely celebrated mass there. Twigges was not a credible witness because of his demeanour and because Francis Tregian was able to argue reasonably that Mayne would not have divulged such information to a stranger. Twigges, furthermore, could not provide details of the room he shared with Mayne; in fact, Mayne was actually in Douai in Flanders during that holiday. Joanna Mattingly, in 'Twigges the Informer?' notes that a Twigges appears in the diary of William Carnsew of Bokelly, where Twigges is identified as 'Mr Arundellis man' (the protestant Arundells of Trerice), and raises the question of whether or not the protestant Arundell might have engaged Twigges, if it is the same man, to inform on the Tregians of Golden, specifically Francis Tregian (*Associates Newsletter,* Institute of Cornish Studies, 2nd ser, no 2 (April, 1993), 11). The entry from Carnsew's diary is printed in Pounds, 'William Carnsew of Bokelly,' p 55.

534–8   STC: 4615   sigs S4–T4
F.E. Halliday, who edited Carew's *Survey of Cornwall* in 1953, notes on p 55 that it is surely Carew's own defence of church ales and saints' feasts that is reflected in the passage on those topics here.

William L. Tribby discusses the figure of the on-stage prompter (p 537, l.25) and challenges Carew's account, arguing that Carew's description of the prompter's presence on stage may be unreliable and based on only one medieval performance recalled years later. Carew's singular written account of the prompter's obvious presence on stage, Tribby argues, erroneously feeds the picture of medieval drama as 'naive and highly primitive' ('The Medieval Prompter: A Reinterpretation,' *Theatre Survey* 5.1 (1964), 71–8).

'Sissitia' (p 537, l.11) is a Latin form of the Greek συσσίτια, used by the biographer Plutarch in his life of Lycurgus for the quasi-military common mess founded by Lycurgus at which all Spartan men were expected to take their meals.

PATRONS AND TRAVELLING COMPANIES, GLOSSARIES, AND INDEX

Patrons and
Travelling Companies

ARLEANE RALPH

The following list has two sections. The first section lists companies alphabetically by patron, according to the principal title under which the playing companies and entertainers appear. Cross-references to titles other than the principal, if they are also so named in the Records, are also given. The second section lists companies which have been identified by place of origin.

The biographical information supplied here has come entirely from printed sources, the chief of which are the following: *Acts of the Privy Council*; S.T. Bindoff (ed), *The History of Parliament: The House of Commons, 1509–1558*, 3 vols (London, 1982); *Calendar of Close Rolls* and *Calendar of Patent Rolls* (edited through 1582); *Calendar of State Papers*; C.R. Cheney (ed), *Handbook of Dates for Students of English History*; G.E.C., *The Complete Peerage...*; *The Dictionary of National Biography*; James E. Doyle, *The Official Baronage of England Showing the Succession, Dignities, and Offices of Every Peer from 1066 to 1885*, 3 vols (London, 1886); P.W. Hasler (ed), *The History of Parliament: The House of Commons, 1558–1603*, 3 vols (London, 1981); *Letters and Papers, Foreign and Domestic, Henry VIII*, 21 vols and Addenda (London, 1864–1932); E.B. Fryde, D.E. Greenway, S. Porter, and I. Roy (eds), *Handbook of British Chronology*, 3rd ed (Cambridge, 1986; rpt 1996); J.S. Roskell, Linda Clark, and Carole Rawcliffe (eds), *The History of Parliament: The House of Commons, 1386–1421*, 4 vols (Stroud, 1992); Josiah C. Wedgwood and Anne D. Holt, *History of Parliament: Biographies of the Members of the Commons House, 1439–1509* (London, 1936); and Josiah C. Wedgwood, *History of Parliament: Register of Ministers and of the Members of Both Houses, 1439–1509* (London, 1938).

All dates are given in accordance with the style of the sources used. The authorities sometimes disagree over the dates of birth, death, creation, succession, and office tenure. Where this evidence conflicts, the *Calendar of State Papers*, *Calendar of Patent Rolls*, and similar collections, such as the following, are preferred: J.H. Gleason, *The Justices of the Peace in England: 1558 to 1640* (Oxford, 1969); *List of Sheriffs for England and Wales from the Earliest Times to A.D. 1831*, Public Record Office, Lists and Indexes, no 9 (London, 1898); and J.C. Sainty, 'Lieutenants of Counties, 1585–1642,' *Bulletin of the Institute of Historical Research*, Special Supplement no 8 (May, 1970).

Normally each patron entry is divided into four sections. The first lists relevant personal data and titles of nobility with dates. Succession numbers are given for the most important titles held by a person, as well as for those titles by which he or she is named in the Records.

These numbers follow the absolute sequence given in *The Complete Peerage* rather than the relative ones that begin afresh with each new creation. Knighthood dates are included only for minor gentry not possessing higher titles.

The second section lists, in chronological order, appointments showing local connections and includes those known to have been used within titles of playing companies. Purely expeditionary military titles have been largely omitted, along with most minor Scottish and Irish landed titles. For patrons holding peerage titles, minor civil commissions have been omitted, except for those concerning Cornwall and Dorset, and the geographically proximate counties of Devon, Hampshire, Somerset, and Wiltshire.

Where possible, the date of an appointment is taken from the date of a document assigning that position. If the appointment is stated in the document to be 'for life,' then these words follow the job title. If the original document has not been edited and a secondary source is used that states 'until death,' then this form appears. Otherwise dates of appointment and termination are given, if available. If the length of time an office was held is not known, then only the date of appointment is given. Alternatively, if the only evidence comes from a source dated some time during the period of tenure, then the word 'by' and a date appears. If only the date of termination is known, 'until' is used. For all minor commissions such as commissions of gaol delivery, commissions of array and muster, and commissions of the peace (JP), years only are given. If the dates of these commissions cover several years in sequence, then the earliest and latest years of the sequence are separated by a dash.

The third section, for which information is often incomplete or unavailable, contains the names and locations of the patron's principal seats, and of counties where he or she held lands. Extensive property lists have been condensed by limiting them to Cornwall and Dorset and the surrounding counties.

The fourth section is an annotated index by date of the appearances of each patron's company or companies in the Cornwall and Dorset Records. Following the dates are the page numbers in parentheses where the citations occur. If a patron's company appears under a title other than the usual or principal one, this other title is in parentheses next to the designation of the company. Companies named according to a patron's civil appointment are indexed under the name of that post as it appears in the Records: for example, 'Lord Admiral.' If the patron sponsored more than one type of performer, all entries for a given type (whether singular or plural in number) are grouped together in chronological order. The performer type is only repeated within that grouping to indicate a change in the patron title by which the company is named (see, for example, Edward Tudor under 'King'). Each group of entries is then listed according to the earliest year in which that company appears in the Records. If two or more companies first appear in the same year, alphabetical order is followed. In this section, the annotations 'Possibly' or 'Probably' indicate that the attribution of the performance itinerary item to the particular patron is not definite.

The reader may also wish to refer to the Index for additional references to some of the patrons and to various unnamed companies and their players.

Abbreviations:

acc	acceded	gov	governor
adm	admiral	JP	justice of the peace
bef	before	jt	joint (three or more)
bet	between	KB	Knight of the Bath
br	brother	kt	knighted
capt	captain	lieut	lieutenant
comm	commissioner	m.	married
cr	created	MP	member of parliament
custos rot	custos rotulorum	nd	no date
d.	died	parl	parliament
da	daughter	PC	privy councillor
eccles	ecclesiastical	pres	president
gen	general	succ	succeeded

Companies Named By Patron

Arundel

Thomas Fitz Alan (or Mautravers) (1450–25 Oct 1524), styled Lord Mautravers; succ as 22nd earl of Arundel 1487. Comm of array Southampton, Hants, 1469, 1472, 1475, 1484, Wilts 1469–70, and Dors 1470; JP Southampton, Hants, 1470, 1474–9, 1481, 1483–8, 1493–4, 1498, 1500–2, 1504, Dors 1475, 1483, Wilts 1475, and Hants 1510, 1512–15, 1518, 1523; comm of musters Southampton, Hants, 1472; keeper Alice Holt and Woolmer Forests and park of Worldham, all in Hants, sole 18 Jul 1486 and jt 16 Mar 1510; warden New Forest, Hants, 1489; comm oyer and terminer Southampton, Hants, 1491, 1502, and Wilts 1502; keeper forests of Clarendon, Wilts, and of Buckholt and Melchet, both in Hants, sole 23 Mar 1495 and jt 16 Mar 1510; jt keeper Grovely Wood, Wilts, 16 Mar 1510. Seat at Arundel Castle, Suss; lands in Hants and Somers.

minstrels	Dors	Poole	1524–5 (240)

William Fitz Alan (*c* 1476–23 Jan 1543/4), son of Thomas, 22nd earl of Arundel, *qv*; styled Lord Mautravers 1487–1524; succ as 23rd earl of Arundel 25 Oct 1524. JP Dors 1509–14, Somers 1509, 1512–14, Hants 1510, 1512–15, 1518, 1523, 1525, and Wilts 1510–13; jt warden forests of Clarendon and Groveley, Wilts, and of Melchet and Buckholt, Hants, 16 Mar 1509/10–21. Lands in Dors, Hants, and Somers.

players	Dors	Poole	1530–1 (240)

Bedford (earl)

Edward Russell (20 Dec 1572–3 May 1627), succ as Lord Russell and 5th earl of Bedford Jul 1585. Comm custos rot Devon 1603–19; possibly JP Cornw and Dors nd. Seats at Chenies, Bucks, and Moor Park, Herts; lands in Cornw and Devon.

men	Dors	Bridport	1602–3 (153)

Berkeley

Henry Berkeley (26 Nov 1534–26 Nov 1613), succ as 7th Lord Berkeley at birth. Keeper of Filwood Forest, Somers, for life 26 Jun 1559. Principal residences at Yate Court and Berkeley Castle, Glouc, and Caludon Castle, Warw; lands in Somers.

players	Dors	Lyme Regis	1583–4 (215)
		Dorchester	1608 (177, 183–4, 190–5)

Chandos

Grey Brydges (*c* 1579–10 Aug 1621), succ as 5th Baron Chandos 18 Nov 1602; imprisoned in the Fleet 14 Feb–31 Mar 1601. MP Cricklade, Wilts, 1597; JP Wilts 1603; member Council in the Marches of Wales 1617. Seat at Sudeley Castle, Glouc.

players	Dors	Weymouth– Melcombe-Regis	1603–4 (278)

Clarence

George Plantagenet (21 Oct 1449–18 Feb 1477/8), cr 3rd duke of Clarence 28 Jun 1461 and 17th earl of Warwick and 12th earl of Salisbury 25 Mar 1471/2; attainted and executed 18 Feb 1477/8. Comm oyer and terminer Dors, Somers 1466, Devon 1466, 1468, Southampton, Hants, 1466, 1468, Wilts 1468; JP Cornw 1466–7, 1469–77, Devon 1466, 1468–72, 1474–7, Dors 1466–75, Somers 1466, 1468–70, 1472–6, Wilts 1466, 1470–3, 1475, Southampton, Hants, 1466–8, 1470, 1474–7; chief justice in eyre south of Trent for life 3 Sept 1468; comm of array Cornw, Devon, Dors, Somers, Southampton, Hants, and Wilts 1472; lord chamberlain 20 May 1472. Seats at Warwick Castle, Warw, and Chester, Ches; lands in Devon, Dors, and Wilts.

bearward	Cornw	Launceston	1470–1 (493)

Devon

Edward Courtenay (bef May 1471–28 May 1509), cr 17th earl of Devon 26 Oct 1485. Sheriff Devon 5 Nov 1478; JP Cornw 1483, 1485–8, 1492–8, 1502, 1504, 1506, Somers 1485–8, 1491, 1493–5, 1498–1500, 1502–3, 1505–8, Devon 1487, 1491–2, 1494–6, 1501–2, 1504, 1506; constable Restormel Castle and keeper park of Restormel, Cornw, for life 1 Mar 1486; comm oyer and terminer Cornw 1487, Devon 1487 and 1497; comm of musters Cornw and Devon 1488; comm of array Cornw and Devon 1490; comm of gaol delivery Launceston, Cornw, 1494. Seat at Tiverton Castle, Devon; lands in Cornw, Devon, Dors, Hants, and Somers.

minstrels	Cornw	Bodmin	1505–6 (470)

Dorset

Henry Grey (17 Jan 1517–23 Feb 1554), styled Lord Grey until he succ as 6th marquess of Dorset, 9th Lord Ferrers, 9th Lord Harington, 4th Lord Bonville, and possibly Lord Astley 10 Oct 1530; cr 7th duke of Suffolk 11 Oct 1551; attainted and beheaded 23 Feb 1554. JP Cornw 1539–40, 1544, 1547, Devon 1539–41, 1543–4, 1547, Dors 1539–40, 1547, Somers 1539–40, 1543–4, 1547, Wilts 1539, 1543, 1547; comm oyer and terminer Cornw, Devon, Dors 1540; PC 11 Dec 1549–53; chief justice in eyre south of Trent 2 Feb 1550–3. Seats at Chewton, Somers, and Bradgate and Groby, Leic; lands in Devon and Somers.

players	Dors	Poole	1551–2 (241)

Edgecombe

Peter Edgecombe (1468 or 1469–14 Aug 1539), kt by 1504. Constable Launceston Castle, Cornw, 15 Nov 1489; escheator and feodary duchy of Cornwall 1489 until death; sheriff Devon 5 Nov 1494, 5 Nov 1497, 9 Nov 1517, 7 Nov 1528 and Cornw 1 Dec 1505, 10 Nov 1516, and 14 Nov 1534; JP Cornw 1498, 1502, 1504, 1506, 1509–15, 1520–2, 1524–6, 1530, 1532, 1536–9, Devon 1501–2, 1504, 1506, 1509–15, 1517, 1519, 1522, 1524, 1526, 1530, 1532, 1536, 1538–9; keeper Kerrybullock Park, Cornw, 22 Jun 1509 until death; comm of array Cornw 1511 and 1513; MP Cornw 1515 and 1529; recorder Launceston, Cornw, by 1521 until death; assessor of the stannaries duchy of Cornwall, Cornw and Devon, 11 Jul 1525;

comm of gaol delivery Launceston Castle, Launceston, Cornw, 1532 and 1537; chief steward
Tavistock Abbey, Devon, by 1535; comm oyer and terminer Cornw, Devon, Dors, Hants,
Somers, and Wilts 1538; comm of musters Cornw 1539. Seats at Cotehele and West Stone-
house, Cornw; lands in Cornw and Devon.

minstrels	Cornw	Bodmin	1537–8 (473)

Essex
Robert Devereaux (19 Nov 1566–25 Feb 1600/1), styled Viscount Hereford until he succ as
19th earl of Essex, 6th Lord Ferrers, and 9th Lord Bourchier 22 Sept 1576; beheaded 25 Feb
1600/1. Master of the horse 1587–97; PC 25 Feb 1592/3. Seats at Chartley, Staff, and Lamphey,
Pemb, Wales; residence at Essex House, Midd.

players	Dors	Lyme Regis	1588–9 (216)

King
Henry Tudor (28 Jun 1491–28 Jan 1547), son of Henry VII, and Elizabeth of York; cr prince
of Wales 18 Feb 1503; acc as Henry VIII 22 Apr 1509; crowned 24 Jun 1509.

bearward	Cornw	Bodmin	1513–14 (472)
bearward/s	Cornw	Launceston	1520–1 (494)
juggler	Cornw	Launceston	1520–1 (494)
minstrels	Dors	Poole	1524–5 (240)
	Cornw	Launceston	1530–1 (494)
minstrel/s	Cornw	Launceston	1542–3 (495)
players	Dors	Poole	1524–5 (240)
entertainer	Cornw	Launceston	1530–1 (494)

Edward Tudor (12 Oct 1537–6 Jul 1553), son of Henry VIII, *qv*, and Jane Seymour; acc as
Edward VI 21 Jan 1547; crowned 20 Feb 1547; Edward Seymour, 5th duke of Somerset,
appointed protector, *qv under* **Lord Protector**.

minstrels (prince)	Cornw	Bodmin	1537–8 (473)
minstrels	Dors	Poole	1547–8 (241)
			1552–3 (241)
interlude players	Cornw	Poughill	1550–1 (505)
players	Dors	Lyme Regis	*c* 1552–3 (212)

James Stuart (19 Jun 1566–27 Mar 1625), son of Henry, Lord Darnley, and Mary Stuart, queen
of Scots; acc as James VI of Scotland 24 Jul 1567 and as James I of England 24 Mar 1603;
crowned 25 Jul 1603.

players	Dors	Bridport	1620–1 (167)
			1623–4 (167)
			1624–5 (168)

Charles Stuart (19 Nov 1600–30 Jan 1649), son of James I, *qv*, and Anne of Denmark, *qv*
under **Queen**; cr duke of Albany 23 Dec 1600; duke of York 6 Jan 1605; succ as duke of

Cornwall 6 Nov 1612; cr earl of Chester and prince of Wales 4 Nov 1616; acc as Charles I
27 Mar 1625; crowned 2 Feb 1626; beheaded 30 Jan 1649.

players (prince)	Dors	Dorchester	1615 (198)
children of the revels	Dors	Blandford Forum	1630–1 (137)

Lady Elizabeth

Elizabeth Stuart (mid-Aug 1596–13 Feb 1662), da of James VI (of Scotland) and I (of England),
qv under **King**, and Anne of Denmark, *qv under* **Queen**; m., 14 Feb 1612/13, Frederick V,
elector palatine; crowned queen of Bohemia 7 Nov 1619.

players	Dors	Lyme Regis	1624–5 (223)

Leicester

Robert Dudley (24 Jun 1532 or 1533–4 Sept 1588), cr baron of Denbigh, Denb, Wales,
28 Sept 1564; cr 14th earl of Leicester 29 Sept 1564; imprisoned Jul 1553; attainted 22 Jan
1553/4; pardoned 18 Oct 1554; restored in blood 7 Mar 1557/8. Master of the horse 1559–
87; PC 23 Apr 1559; high steward Andover, Hants, 1574; warden of the New Forest, Lyndhurst
Park, and hundred of Redbridge, all in Hants, 15 Jun 1580; lord steward of the household
1 Nov 1584–8; warden and chief justice in eyre south of Trent 25 Nov 1585 until death.
Seats at Kenilworth, Warw, and Wanstead, Essex; residence at Leicester House, Midd.

players	Dors	Lyme Regis	1569–70 (214)
		Poole	1569–70 (243)
		Lyme Regis	1573–4 (214)
			1577–8 (214)
			1586–7 (216)
players (lord high steward)			1587–8 (216)

Lisle

Arthur Plantagenet (*c* 1480–3 Mar 1541/2), natural son of Edward IV; cr 6th Viscount Lisle
25 Apr 1523; imprisoned in the Tower 19 May 1540; pardoned Feb 1541/2. JP Hants 1512–15,
1518, 1523–6, 1529, 1531–2, 1538; sheriff Hants 9 Nov 1513; warden and keeper forest
and parks of Clarendon, Wilts, and forests of Buckholt and Melchet, Hants, and Grovely,
Wilts, 26 Nov 1524; vice adm 1525; PC 1540. Lands in Devon, Dors, and Wilts.

players	Dors	Poole	1530–1 (240)
minstrel/s	Cornw	Bodmin	1537–8 (473)

Lord Admiral

Thomas Seymour (*c* 1508–20 Mar 1548/9), br of Edward, 5th duke of Somerset, *qv under*
Lord Protector; cr 1st Baron Seymour 16 Feb 1546/7; arrested and imprisoned in the Tower
17 Jan 1548/9; attainted 5 Mar and beheaded 20 Mar 1548/9. Keeper Farleigh Hungerford
Castle and park of Farleigh Hungerford, Somers, 11 Mar 1544; MP Wilts 1545; comm of
musters Wilts 1545/6; eccles comm Wilts 1545/6; PC 23–8 Jan 1547 and 2 Feb 1547–18
Jan 1549; lord high adm 17 Feb 1546/7–18 Jan 1549; JP Devon, Hants, Wilts 1547. Seats at

Sudeley Castle, Glouc, and Bromham, Wilts; London residence at Seymour Place, near Temple Bar, Midd; lands in Hants and Wilts.

| players | Dors | Lyme Regis | 1547–8 (211) |

Charles Howard (c 1536–14 Dec 1624), succ as Baron Howard 11 or 12 Jan 1572/3 and cr 10th earl of Nottingham 22 Oct 1597. Chamberlain of the household 1 Jan 1583/4–Jul 1585; pc by 5 Mar 1583/4 until death; lord high adm 8 Jul 1585–27 Jan 1618/19; chief justice in eyre south of Trent 15 Jun 1597 until death; lord steward of the household 24 Oct 1597–Nov 1615; queen's lieut and capt-gen in the south of England 10 Aug 1599 and 14 Feb 1600/1; JP Somers 1608. Seat at Effingham, Surr.

| players | Dors | Lyme Regis | 1593–4 (217) |

See also John Dudley *under* **Northumberland**

Lord Chancellor
Thomas Rotherham (24 Aug 1423–by 19 Nov 1500). Prebendary Netherhaven, Salisbury Cathedral, Wilts, 1465; archdeacon Canterbury Cathedral, Kent, 1467; keeper privy seal 28 Jul 1467–24 May 1474; provost Beverley College 1468–72; bishop Rochester 1468–71; sole ambassador France 1468, and jt ambassador Burgundy 1471; chancellor Cambridge University 1469, 1473, 1475, 1478, 1483; bishop Lincoln 1471–80 (election 24 Nov 1471; granted 7 Dec 1471; translation c 8 Jan 1472; temporalities restored 10 Mar 1471/2); chancellor England 25 May 1474–27 Apr 1475 and 28 Sept 1475–c 12 May 1483; archbishop York 1480–1500 (translation 7 Jul 1480; temporalities restored 9 Sept 1480). Lands in Somers.

| minstrels | Cornw | Launceston | 1476–7 (493) |

Lord High Steward *See* Robert Dudley *under* **Leicester**.

Lord Protector
Edward Seymour (c 1500–22 Jan 1551/2), br of Thomas, 1st Baron Seymour, *qv under* **Lord Admiral**; cr 1st Viscount Beauchamp 5 Jun 1536; cr 8th earl of Hertford 18 Oct 1537; cr Baron Seymour 15 Feb 1546/7; cr 5th duke of Somerset 16 Feb 1546/7; deprived of all offices and imprisoned in the Tower 14 Oct 1549–6 Feb 1549/50; pardoned 16 Feb 1549/50; imprisoned in the Tower 16 Oct 1551; beheaded 22 Jan 1551/2. JP Wilts 1525–6, 1529, 1532, 1538–9, 1543, 1547, Somers 1538–41, 1543–4, 1547, Cornw, Devon, Dors, Hants, 1547; steward manors of Charlton and Henstridge, Somers, 5 Mar 1528/9; PC 1537 and 10 Apr 1550; lord high adm 28 Dec 1542–Jan 1542/3; lord great chamberlain 16 Feb 1542/3–17 Feb 1546/7; lieut and capt-gen in the North 12 Feb–Jun 1544 and 2 May 1545; councillor of regency and lieut of the realm 9 Jul 1544; protector of the realm 12 Mar 1546/7; lord treasurer of the exchequer 10 Feb 1546/7; earl marshal 17 Feb 1547. Seats at Hatch, Somers, and Wolf Hall, Wilts; residence at Somerset House, Strand, Midd; lands in Cornw, Devon, Dors, Hants, Somers, and Wilts.

| players | Dors | Lyme Regis | 1548–9 (211) |

Monteagle
William Parker (*c* 1575–1 Jul 1622), succ as 5th Lord Monteagle 12 Jun 1585; imprisoned in the Tower Jan 1600/1–Aug 1601; succ as 13th Lord Morley 1 Apr 1618. Seat at Hornby Castle, Lanc; houses at Shingle Hall, Epping, and Great Hallingbury, both in Essex and in Martok, Somers after 1605.

players	Dors	Lyme Regis	1592–3 (217)
man	Dors	Blandford Forum	1594–5 (127)

Mountjoy
James Blount (*c* 1533–20 Oct 1581), succ as 6th Lord Mountjoy 10 Oct 1544. Lord lieut Dors 26 May 1559; JP Dors and Wilts 1562, 1564; comm oyer and terminer Cornw, Devon, Dors, Hants, Somers, and Wilts 1564; shareholder in the company of Mines Royal Cornw and Devon 28 May 1568. Seat at Apethorpe, Northants; house in London.

players	Dors	Poole	1558–9 (242)
			1559–60 (242)
		Lyme Regis	1568–9 (213)
		Poole	1569–70 (243)
		Lyme Regis	1572–3 (214)
			1573–4 (214)
			1577–8 (214)

Neville
Either
Thomas Neville (1501–1569 or 1571), kt Feb 1546/7. Seat at Holt, Leic.

or

Thomas Neville (bet 1525 and 1549, and d. by 10 Dec 1568), 2nd son of Ralph Neville, Lord Neville and 4th earl of Westmorland; kt 3 Oct 1547.

players	Dors	Lyme Regis	1567–8 (213)

Northumberland
John Dudley (*c* 1504–22 Aug 1553), restored in blood 1512; succ as 7th Baron Lisle *c* 1530; cr 7th Viscount Lisle 12 Mar 1541/2, 19th earl of Warwick 16 Feb 1546/7, and 1st duke of Northumberland 11 Oct 1551; imprisoned in the Tower 25 Jul 1553; beheaded 22 Aug 1553. Vice adm Feb 1537–Jan 1543; lord high adm 26 Jan 1543–17 Feb 1547 and 28 Oct 1549–14 May 1550; PC 23 Apr 1543–Jul 1553; lord chamberlain of the household 17 Feb 1547–1 Feb 1550; lieut of the North 17 Jul 1547; lord pres Council in the Marches of Wales 1549–50; lord steward of the household 20 Feb 1550–3; lord pres of the privy council Feb 1550–Jul 1553; earl marshal 20 Apr 1551. Seats at Halden, Kent, Chelsea and Syon, Midd, and Dudley Castle, Staff; residence at Durham House, the Strand, Midd.

players (lord admiral)	Dors	Lyme Regis	*c* 1544–5 (211)
players		Poole	1552–3 (241)

Ogle
Cuthbert Ogle (*c* 1540–20 Nov 1597), succ as 7th Lord Ogle 1 Aug 1562. Member Council of the North Oct 1572–97. Seat at Bothal, Northumb.

players	Dors	Lyme Regis	1594–5 (218)

Oxford
John de Vere (*c* 1516–3 Aug 1562), styled Lord Bolebec 1526 until he succ as 16th earl of Oxford 21 Mar 1539/40. PC 3 Sept 1553. Seat at Hedingham Castle, Essex; manor at Earls Colne, Essex; lands in Devon, Dors, Somers, and Wilts.

players	Dors	Lyme Regis	1559–60 (212)

Edward de Vere (12 Apr 1550–24 Jun 1604), son of John, 16th earl of Oxford, *qv*; styled Lord Bolebec until he succ as 17th earl of Oxford 3 Aug 1562; imprisoned in the Tower *c* Mar–8 Jun 1581. Lord great chamberlain 3 Aug 1562. Seats at Hedingham Castle, Essex, and Hackney, Midd.

men	Dors	Lyme Regis	1583–4 (215)
			1584–5 (215)

Prince
Edward Plantagenet (2 Nov 1470–*c* Aug 1483), son of Edward IV and Elizabeth Wydevill; cr prince of Wales 26 Jun 1471; acc as Edward V 9 Apr 1483; protector, Richard, 3rd duke of Gloucester, appointed 30 Apr–25 Jun 1483; deposed 25 Jun 1483.

bearward	Cornw	Launceston	1476–7 (493)

See also Edward Tudor *and* Charles Stuart *under* **King**

Queen
Elizabeth Tudor (7 Sept 1533–24 Mar 1603), da of Henry VIII, *qv under* **King**, and Anne Boleyn; acc as Elizabeth I 17 Nov 1558; crowned 15 Jan 1559.

players	Dors	Lyme Regis	1558–9 (212)
		Poole	1562–3 (242)
		Lyme Regis	1568–9 (213)
		Sherborne	1571–2 (266)
		Lyme Regis	1573–4 (214)
			1587–8 (216)
			1588–9 (216)
		Poole	1590–1 (246)
		Weymouth–Melcombe-Regis	1590–1 (277)
		Lyme Regis	1592–3 (217)
			1594–5 (217)
		Weymouth–Melcombe-Regis	1596–7 (277)

		Sherborne	1597–8 (272)
			1598–9 (272)
		Poole	1601–2 (246)
jester	Dors	Lyme Regis	1573–4 (214)
tumblers	Dors	Lyme Regis	1588–9 (216)
children of the chapel	Dors	Poole	1590–1 (246)

Anne of Denmark (12 Dec 1574–2 Mar 1619), da of Frederick II of Denmark and Norway and Sophia of Mecklenburg; m., 20 Aug 1589, James VI of Scotland (later James I of England), *qv under* **King**; crowned queen of England 25 Jul 1603.

| players | Dors | Weymouth–Melcombe-Regis | 1605–6 (278) |
| | | | 1615–16 (279) |

Sheffield

Edmund Sheffield (7 Dec 1565–Oct 1646), succ as 3rd Baron Sheffield (of Butterwick, in the Isle of Axholme, Linc) 10 Dec 1568; cr earl of Mulgrave 5 Feb 1625/6. Lord pres Council of the North by 22 Jul 1603–by 11 Feb 1618/19; member Council of the North 21 May 1625. Seat at King's Manor, Yorks.

| players | Dors | Lyme Regis | 1577–8 (215) |

Stafford

Edward Stafford (17 Jan 1535/6–18 Oct 1603), succ as 12th Baron Stafford 1 Jan 1565/6. Member Council in the Marches of Wales Aug 1601. Seat at Stafford Castle, Staff.

interlude players	Cornw	Launceston	1575–6 (497)
man	Dors	Blandford Forum	1594–5 (127)
players	Dors	Lyme Regis	1595–6 (218)

Suffolk (duke)

Charles Brandon (c 1484–22 Aug 1545), cr 5th Viscount Lisle 15 May 1513 and 4th duke of Suffolk 1 Feb 1513/14; surrendered viscountcy 20 Apr 1523. PC bef 15 May 1513 until death; earl marshal 21 May 1524–20 May 1533; pres privy council Feb 1529/30 until death; JP Cornw 1530, 1532, 1536–40, 1544, Devon 1530, 1536, 1538–41, 1543–4, Dors 1530, 1536–40, Hants 1531, 1538, 1540, 1542, Somers 1531, 1538–41, 1543–4, Wilts 1531–2, 1537–9, 1543; chief justice in eyre south of Trent 27 Nov 1534 until death; lord steward of the household bef 13 Apr 1540 until death; comm oyer and terminer Cornw, Devon, Dors, Hants, and Somers 1540; lieut and capt-gen Southampton, Hants, 14 Jun 1545; comm of array Hants, Wilts 1545. Seat at Tattershall Castle, Linc; lands in Wilts.

| bearward/s | Cornw | Launceston | 1520–1 (494) |

Suffolk (duchess)

Katherine Willoughby (22 Mar 1518/19–19 Sept 1580), *de jure suo jure* 12th Baroness Willoughby de Eresby (of Eresby, Linc); m. 1stly, c 7 Sept 1533, Charles Brandon, 4th duke of Suffolk (d. 22 Aug 1545), *qv*, m. 2ndly, probably early 1553, Richard Bertie; fled England 5 Feb 1554/5; returned summer 1559. Residence at Westhorpe, Suff, from *c* 1528; principal seats at Grimsthorpe and Tattershall Castle, Linc, from *c* 1536.

| players | Dors | Lyme Regis | 1560–1 (212) |

Sussex

Henry Radcliffe (by 1533–14 Dec 1593), succ as 9th earl of Sussex, 4th Viscount, and 10th Lord FitzWalter 9 Jun 1583. PC Ireland by 25 Feb 1556/7; constable Porchester Castle and lieut Southbere Forest, Southampton, both in Hants, for life 14 Jun 1560; MP Hants 1571, and Portsmouth, Hants, 1572; warden and capt 4 May 1571 and high steward 9 Sept 1590, Portsmouth, Hants, both until death; JP Hants, 1573/4; comm of musters Hants, sole by 1576 and jt 16 Mar 1579/80; jt lord lieut Hants, and Winchester and Southampton, both in Hants, 3 Jul 1585 until death. Seat at New Hall, Boreham, Essex.

| players | Dors | Lyme Regis | 1584–5 (215) |

Warwick

Richard Neville (22 Nov 1428–14 Apr 1471), in right of marriage styled Lord Bergavenny; confirmed in the earldom of Warwick 23 Jul 1449 and cr 16th earl of Warwick 2 Mar 1449/50; attainted 20 Nov 1459; attainder reversed Oct 1460; succ as 11th earl of Salisbury 30 or 31 Dec 1460. Chamberlain of the exchequer 6 Dec 1450; PC by 6 Dec 1453; JP Cornw 1460, 1462, 1465–7, 1469–71, Devon 1461–6, 1468–71, Dors 1461, 1463, 1465–70, Somers 1461–3, 1466, 1468–70, Wilts 1461, 1463, 1466, 1470, Southampton, Hants, 1461, 1463–8, 1470, Berks 1464, 1467, 1470; lord chamberlain 22 Jan 1460/1 and 7 May 1461; lord high adm 13 Feb–Jul 1462 and 2 Jan 1470/1; chief justice in eyre north of Trent 21 Nov 1466. Seats at Middleham and Sheriff Hutton, Yorks NR.

| bearward | Cornw | Launceston | 1470–1 (492, 493) |
| fool | Cornw | Launceston | 1470–1 (492, 493) |

Probably

Windsor

William Windsor (1498–20 Aug 1558), succ as 2nd Lord Windsor 30 March 1543. Seat at Bradenham, Bucks; lands in Hants and Wilts.

| players (earl of | Dors | Lyme Regis | *c* 1552–3 (212) |
| wynsword) | | | |

Worcester

William Somerset (*c* 1527–21 Feb 1588/9), styled Lord Herbert until succ as 8th earl of Worcester 26 Nov 1549. Member Council in the Marches of Wales Nov 1553 and from 1576. Seat at Raglan, Monm, Wales; residence at Hackney, Midd.

| players | Dors | Lyme Regis | 1567–8 (213) |
| | | Poole | 1570–1 (243) |

Edward Somerset (*c* 1550–3 Mar 1627/8), son of William, 8th earl of Worcester, *qv*; styled

Lord Herbert until succ as 9th earl of Worcester and Baron Herbert 21 Feb 1588/9. Member Council in the Marches of Wales 16 Dec 1590; PC 29 Jun 1601; JP Somers 1626; lord keeper of the privy seal 2 Jan 1615/16 until death. Seat at Raglan, Monm, Wales; residence at Hackney, Midd.

players	Dors	Lyme Regis	1592–3 (217)

Companies Named by Location

Boscastle, Cornw

dancers	Cornw	Bodmin	1505–6 (471)

Bristol, Glouc

players	Dors	Poole	1568–9 (242)

Exeter, Devon

minstrel/s	Cornw	Bodmin	*c* 1501–13 (470)

Germoe, Cornw

players	Cornw	St Ives	1586–7 (516)

Grampound, Cornw

dancers	Cornw	St Breock	1567–8 (506)

Gunwalloe, Cornw

morris dancers	Cornw	Camborne	1595–6 (476)

Possibly
Lanhydrock, Cornw

dancers	Cornw	Bodmin	*c* 1514–39 (472)

Probably
Lanivet, Cornw

dancers	Cornw	Bodmin	*c* 1514–39 (472)

Ludgvan, Cornw

dancers	Cornw	St Breock	1565–6 (506)

Mawgan, Cornw

Robin Hood players	Cornw	St Breock	1591–2 (507)

Millbrook, Cornw

players	Cornw	Antony	1548–9 (468)

Probably
Milton Abbot, Devon
  players   Cornw   Launceston   1573–4 (495)

Minster, Cornw
  dancers   Cornw   Bodmin   1505–6 (471)

Phillack, Cornw
  dancers   Cornw   St Breock   1574–5 (507)

Plymouth, Devon
  players   Cornw   Launceston   1520–1 (494)

St Columb Minor, Cornw
  Robin Hood players   Cornw   St Ives   1587–8 (517)
                                St Breock   1590–1 (507)

St Dennis, Cornw
  interlude players   Cornw   St Breock   1566–7 (506)

St Erme, Cornw
  dancers   Cornw   Bodmin   1505–6 (471)

St Eval, Cornw
  dancers   Cornw   St Breock   1574–5 (507)

St Levan, Cornw
  morris dancers   Cornw   Camborne   1595–6 (476)

St Mabyn, Cornw
  dancers   Cornw   Bodmin   c 1514–39 (472)

Sherborne, Dors
  players   Dors   Lyme Regis   1567–8 (213)

South Tawton, Devon
  singing man   Cornw   Launceston   1573–4 (495)

Possibly
Tywardreath, Cornw
  players   Cornw   Bodmin   c 1514–39 (472)

Glossaries: Introduction

The purpose of the glossaries is to assist the reader in working through the text. The criteria for the selection of glossary entries are discussed below, under the headings Latin Glossary and English Glossary. The glossaries include words found in records printed or quoted in the Records, Introduction, Appendixes, and Endnotes. Definitions are given only for those senses of a particular word which are used in the records printed in these two collections. Within references, page and line numbers are separated by an oblique stroke. Words occurring within marginalia are indicated by a lower-case 'm' following the page and line reference. If the glossed word occurs twice in a single line, superscript numerals are used after the line number to distinguish the occurrences. Manuscript capitalization has not been preserved; however, if proper names are glossed, they are capitalized in accordance with modern usage.

Latin Glossary

Words are included in the Latin Glossary if they are not to be found in the *Oxford Latin Dictionary* (OLD), now the standard reference work for classical Latin. Words listed in the OLD whose meaning has changed or become restricted in medieval or Renaissance usage are also glossed. If a word is found in the OLD but appears in the text in an obscure spelling or anomalous inflectional form for which the OLD provides no cross-reference, that word has been included and its standard lexical entry form indicated, without giving a definition. If the spelling variants or anomalous inflectional forms have been treated as scribal errors and more correct forms given in textual notes, the forms thus noted are not repeated in the glossary.

Most of the Latin words used in the records are common classical words whose spelling has changed, if at all, according to common medieval variations. The results of these common variations are not treated here as new words, nor are forms of glossed words resulting from such variations cross-referenced. These variations are:

ML *c* for CL *t* before *i*
ML *cc* for CL *ct* before *i*
ML *d* for CL *t* in a final position
ML *e* for CL *ae* or *oe*
ML *ff* for CL *f*, common in an initial position
ML addition of *h*
ML omission of CL *h*
ML variation between *i* and *e* before another vowel

ML *n* for CL *m* before another nasal
Intrusion of ML *p* in CL consonant clusters *mm*, *mn,. ms*, or *mt*
ML doubling of CL single consonants
ML singling of CL double consonants

No attempt has been made to correct these spellings to classical norms; rather, scribal practice has been followed in such cases. Where the same word occurs in spellings which differ according to the list above, the most common spelling (or the earliest, when numbers of occurrences are roughly equal) is treated as standard and used for the headword. However, the practice of the *OLD* has been used as regards 'i/j' and 'u/v' variation: in this glossary only the letter forms 'i' and 'u' are used. The genitive singular of first declension nouns appears only as the ML '-e.' All listed variant spellings will be found under the headword, at the end of the definition, set apart in boldface type. Where the variant spelling would not closely follow the headword alphabetically, it is also listed separately and cross-referenced to the main entry.

It is difficult to know in some cases whether certain words are being used in a CL sense or in one of the modified senses acquired in Anglo-Latin usage during the Middle Ages. In these circumstances, the range of possibilities has been fully indicated under the appropriate lexical entry. Unclear, technical, or archaic terms, especially those pertaining to canon or common law, performance, and music, are usually given a stock translation equivalent but receive a fuller treatment in the glossary. In defining the terms excerpted from the Cornish 'Vocabularium' (found in Appendix 1 of the Cornwall collection), it has also been necessary to take into account the vernacular words with which they have been defined there and in the original Old English word-list upon which the 'Vocabularium' is based.

As a rule, only one occurrence of each word, or each sense or form of each word, will be listed for each collection; 'etc' following a reference means that there is at least one more occurrence of that word, sense, or form in that collection. The one occurrence listed is either the sole occurrence or the first chronologically. Since this volume includes two counties and is arranged by locality, the examples cited are not necessarily the first to occur in the page order of the Records; the other occurrence(s) indicated by 'etc' may in fact precede the first occurrence in page order. Page order has only been used if there are two earliest occurrences in different documents assigned to the same year. In such cases, the chronologically first occurrence which also appears earliest in page order is given. Multiple occurrences of each sense may be listed for words defined in more than one sense. Page and line references to different collections are separated by a semicolon.

All headwords are given in a standard dictionary form: nouns are listed by nominative, genitive, and gender; adjectives by the terminations of the nominative singular or, in the case of adjectives of one termination, by the nominative and genitive; verbs by their principal parts.

English Glossary

The English Glossary is not meant to be exhaustive but only to explain words, senses, or spellings apt to puzzle users not familiar with markedly provincial Late Middle and Early Modern English. Accordingly words and senses given in *The New Shorter Oxford English Dictionary* (*NSOED*) have nearly always been passed over and so have their obvious derivatives. Abbreviations have also been omitted if they are still current or widely known, as have forms whose only difficulty is a false word division, errors corrected in the footnotes, and matter corrected and replaced by the original scribe. No attempt is made to gloss words left incomplete by damage to the source texts. Readers are also expected to recognize such spelling variations as 'au/a,' 'c/s,' 'ea/e,' 'ie/e(e),' 'i/j,' 'i/y,' 'o/oo,' 'o/ou,' 'o/u,' 's/z,' 'sch/sh,' 'u/v,' and the presence or absence of final 'e' in the contexts where they commonly occur in older literature. They are presumed to have read enough old-spelling texts to know the values of 'þ,' '3,' and 'y' used for 'þ' and to recognize commonly occurring forms that are nearer to their Old English or Old French originals than the modern standard spelling, such as 'gretter,' 'hider,' 'raunson,' and 'vawtyng.'

A fuller treatment has, however, been given to certain words and phrases likely to hold special interest for users of a REED volume. These are chiefly names of musical instruments (eg, 'bandore') and the specialized vocabularies of civic government (eg, 'baylie,' 'stwerde'), popular custom and pastime (eg, 'ale,' 'Iackalent'), and the performing arts (eg, 'morris dancers,' 'mynstrell').

Normal headword forms are the uninflected singular for nouns, the positive for adjectives, and the infinitive for verbs but nouns occurring only in the plural or possessive, adjectives occurring only in comparative or superlative forms, and verbs occurring only in one participial or finite form are entered under the form that actually occurs in the records. A verbal noun is subsumed under the infinitive when other parts of the same verb are also entered (eg, 'plaing' under 'play').

The capitalization of headwords conforms to modern usage. A word appearing in several noteworthy spellings is normally entered under the one most often found in the text or else – when two noticed spellings are equally or nearly equally common – under the one nearer modern usage. Other noticed spellings are mostly entered in their alphabetical places and cross-referenced to the main entry. As a rule only the earliest occurrence is cited for each inflectional form entered and further occurrences are represented by 'etc,' unless the reader needs to be alerted that the sense in question applies in particular later passages; however, since this volume covers two counties, the earliest occurrence in each is given when the word or form occurs in both sets of records. Two citations given without 'etc' mean that the form or sense in question occurs only twice.

Where the definition repeats the headword in a different spelling, the latter is normally the entry spelling in *The Oxford English Dictionary* and *The New Shorter Oxford English Dictionary* and further information can be found there. When that form is itself an archaism or ambiguous, a further brief definition usually follows. Any further citation of an authority or other succinct account of the glossarian's reasoning appears within square brackets at the end of the entry.

Cornish Texts

There is no glossary for the Cornish texts found in Appendixes 1 and 2. Instead readers should consult R. Morton Nance (ed), *A New Cornish-English Dictionary* (St Ives, 1938; rpt Redruth, 1990).

Works Consulted

Black's Law Dictionary. 5th ed (St Paul, 1979). [*Black's*]
Cheney, C.R. (ed). *Handbook of Dates for Students of English History*. Corrected ed (London, 1978). [Cheney]
Dictionary of Medieval Latin from British Sources. R.E. Latham and D.R. Howlett (eds). Volume 1: A–L (London, 1975–97). [*DML*]
The English Dialect Dictionary. Joseph Wright (ed). 6 vols (London, 1898–1905). [*EDD*]
Graves, Eugene Van Tassel. 'The Old Cornish Vocabulary,' PhD dissertation (Columbia University, 1962).
Latham, R.E. (ed). *Revised Medieval Latin Word-List from British and Irish Sources* (London, 1965). [Latham]

Micklethwaite, J.T. *The Ornaments of the Rubric.* Alcuin Club Tract 1 (London, 1897).

Middle English Dictionary. Hans Kurath and Sherman H. Kuhn, et al (eds). Fascicules A.1–T.10 (Ann Arbor, 1952–97). [*MED*]

Munrow, David. *[Musical] Instruments of the Middle Ages and Renaissance* (London, 1976).

The New Shorter Oxford English Dictionary. Lesley Brown (ed). 2 vols (Oxford, 1993). [*NSOED*]

The Oxford Dictionary of the Christian Church. F.L. Cross and E.A. Livingstone (eds). 2nd ed with corrections (Oxford, 1978) [*ODCC*]

The Oxford English Dictionary. Compact ed. 2 vols (New York, 1971). [*OED*]

Oxford Latin Dictionary. P.G.W. Glare (ed) (Oxford, 1982). [*OLD*]

Page, Christopher. *Voices and Instruments of the Middle Ages.* Appendix 1 (London, 1987).

Young, Abigail Ann. 'Minstrels and Minstrelsy: Household Retainers or Instrumentalists?' *REEDN* 20, no 1 (1995), 11–17.

– . 'Plays and Players: The Latin Terms for Performance.' *REEDN* 9, no 2 (1984), 56–62 and 10, no 1 (1985), 9–16.

Abbreviations

abbrev	abbreviation	m	masculine
abl	ablative	ME	Middle English
acc	accusative	Mk	Mark
adj	adjective	Mt	Matthew
adv	adverb	n	noun
AL	Anglo-Latin	nt	neuter
art	article	pa	past tense
attr	attributive	pass	passive voice
CL	Classical Latin	phr	phrase
coll	collective	pl	plural
comm	common gender	poss	possessive
comp	compound	pp	past participle
compar	comparative	ppl	participial
conj	conjunction	pr	present tense
cp	compare	prep	preposition
decl	declension	pron	pronoun
E	English	prp	present participle
f	feminine	sbst	substantive
gen	genitive	sg	singular
intr	intransitive	tr	transitive
L	Latin	v	verb
LG	Latin Glossary	vb	verbal
LL	Late Latin		

Latin Glossary

ABIGAIL ANN YOUNG

abusio, -onis *n f* misuse, abuse, used of a custom or practice 504/3

actor, -oris *n m literally* one who performs or does (something), *hence* participant, here used of participants in a school play 172/1

actum, -i *n nt* legal proceedings, action, here used of the record of such proceedings 222/41 (*in form* act⟨.⟩)

adinuentus, -a, -um *pp* devised, invented 503/39

Æsopicus, -a, -um *adj* of or pertaining to Aesop, an ancient fabulist; here, with 'opus' understood, referring to his writings as a body 172/7

ager, agri *n m* field; *see* **Dorsettensis**

albus, -a, -um *adj* white; *see* **uinum**

alea, -e *n f* a game of chance played with dice on a board, **ludere ad aleas**, to play at 'alea,' *hence* to gamble 465/6

alias *adv* 1. elsewhere 275/12; 2. otherwise, in other ways 527/12; 3. with alternate names, alias 275/28

amercio, -ere, -i, -itum *v tr* to amerce, assess for a fine 169/7

amicus, -i *n m* friend; *see* **curia**

ammodo *adv* from now on, hereafter 504/38

Anglia, -e *n f* England 296/1

Anglice *adv* in the English language 282/29, etc

animal, -alis *n nt literally* animal, beast: here referring to domesticated animals put to graze, albeit inappropriately 247/18

annus, -i *n m* year 252/11, etc; 493/23, etc; *in various idioms.* **duodecimo aetatis anno inchoato** *literally*, when the twelfth year of (my) age had begun, that is (because of the inclusive counting methods used by CL writers), when I was eleven years old 170/31; **annorum inscius** *literally* unaware of years, *hence,* showing youthful inexperience 172/5; **annus domini** year of the Lord, AD 248/9, etc; 528/5, etc. *See also* **per**

antedictus, -a, -um *adj* said or stated before 504/37

apostolus, -i *n m* apostle, one of the first followers of Jesus; *see* **sollem(p)nis**

apropriatus, -a, -um *pp* (used of churches) appropriated, annexed or attached to a monastery as a benefice owing tithes, etc, to it 527/9, etc

archidiaconatus, -us *n m* archdeaconry, district under the authority of an archdeacon 248/3

archidiaconus, -i *n m* archdeacon, cleric appointed by a bishop to assist him principally in administering justice and in supervising parochial clergy 464/4

articulum, -i *n m* 1. article, a charge or list of charges laid against a person in court 137/34; 2. article, part of a series of charges or allegations upon which witnesses are examined 123/1, etc

assisa, -e *n f* assizes, court sessions held regularly before a panel of judges sent under commission from the central courts in Westminster to each county of England to hear serious charges under common law 288/38, etc; **assizis** (*3rd decl*) 211/7 [*Black's*]

atrium, -ii *n nt* in a Roman house the first main room or entrance hall, traditionally open to the sky, *by extension* the court or yard of a church, churchyard 247/7, etc

attornatus, -i *n m* attorney, counsel, *here in idiom*
attornatus regis the attorney-general 424/34

aula, -e *n f* hall, *here in idiom* **gilda aula** guildhall,
centre of town government 494/11. *See also*
guilhalda

Bailiolensis, -e *adj* of or pertaining to John de
Baliol (d. 1269); *see* **collegium**

balliuus, -i *n m* bailiff, a manorial officer 296/4

beatus, -a, -um *adj* as the title of a saint, blessed
464/12, etc. *See also* **uigilia**

Belgia, -e *n f* Belgium, one of the Low Countries
170/30

benediccio, -onis *n f* blessing 247/10; 527/11

blasphemia, -e *n f* contemptuous words or actions
directed against God directly (or indirectly as
against the saints, the sacraments, etc) and
treated as an offence under canon law 504/1
[*ODCC*]

bonus, -a, -um *adj* good; *see* **curia, gestus**

borialis, -e *adj* north; *see* **uicus**

Brito, -onis *n m originally* an inhabitant of Britain,
Briton, *later by extension* Breton 554/13

burgus, -i *n m* borough, an incorporated town
200/24, etc

campana, -orum *n nt pl* fields, that is, land under,
or prepared for, cultivation 493/9

cancellarius, -ii *n m* 1. chancellor, another name
for a vicar general, deputy of a bishop with
primarily administrative and judicial
responsibility, *here* the chancellor of the diocese
of Bristol 171/14; 2. chancellor, one of the
officers of a cathedral with particular oversight
for the cathedral school 504/26

canon, -onis *n m literally* a model or standard,
hence canon, a provision of church law: **sacri
canones** sacred canons, the authoritative
precepts of ecclesiastical law, *used collectively*,
canon law 464/1

canonice *adv* canonically, in accordance with a
specific canon or with canon law in general
464/5

canonicum, -i *sbst nt* canon, a provision of church
law 248/5

canonicus, -i *sbst m* canon, an ordained member
of a secular chapter 493/14

cantaris, -is *n m* singer, chorister 493/15

cantor, -oris *n m* 1. *literally* a man or boy who
sings, usually a chorister 540/6; 2. *by extension*
chanter, leader of liturgical music in a collegiate
choir, who also acted as an administrative
officer in the chapter 504/26

cantrix, -icis *n f literally* a woman or girl who
sings, *hence either* a female chorister *or* a
female chanter; most likely referring to a
member of a convent or other house for
female religious 540/6

capella, -e *n f* chapel, *specifically* the place of
worship in a chapelry, a subdivision of a parish
527/8, etc

capellanus, -i *n m* chaplain, a priest having charge
of a chapel 491/16

capitulum, -i *n nt* chapter, an organized and
partially self-governing body of secular clerics
serving a cathedral or collegiate church 503/20,
etc

capo, -onis *n m* capon 490/1, etc

caput, -itis *n nt literally* head, *here by extension* a
name used as a heading in a list 283/4

caritas, -atis *n f* love, lovingkindness, *by extension*
charity 491/9

caro, carnis *n f* flesh, meat, *hence* **caro
vitulorum** veal 490/6

castrum, -i *n nt* castle 170/21

cathedralis, -e *adj* of or pertaining to the see of a
bishop or his church; *see* **ecclesia**

catholicus, -a, -um *adj literally* universal, *by
extension* Catholic, of or pertaining to the then
universal church in the Latin West 503/35

cena, -e *n f* supper, the latest of the three main
meals of the day, usually less elaborate than
dinner 489/23, etc

censura, -e *n f* censure, rebuke, punishment
247/13

certifico, -are, -aui, -atum *v tr legal idiom* to
certify formally, eg, the truth of a statement,
compliance with an order, or the performance
of an obligation 248/7, etc; 504/18, etc

ceruisia, -e *n f* 1. beer, ale 489/24; **seruicia**

494/10, etc; 2. ale, a parish fund-raising event at which ale was sold, here called a 'king ale' 252/10, etc

chorus, -i *n m literally* chorus, those who performed the choral passages in classical drama [*OLD*], *by extension in later Latin* a choir, those who performed sacred music in a church or chapel, *here used figuratively in a play on both senses* 171/39

cimiterium, -ii *n nt* churchyard 247/17, etc; 463/5, etc

circa *prep* 1. *with acc* in connection with 247/12; 2. *with abl* about, concerning, with respect to 492/13, etc

circumcisio, -onis *n f* circumcision; *see* **festum**

cithara, -e *n f literally* lyre, *hence by extension* harp 540/10

citharista, -e *n m literally* one who plays on a lyre, *hence by extension* harper; possibly a generic term applied to players of stringed instruments 540/10

cito, -are, -aui, -atum *v tr* cite, issue a citation (to appear before an ecclesiastical court) 247/39; 504/14, etc

Clarencia, -e *n f* Clarence, name of a duchy 493/3

claustralis, -e *adj* suitable for or belonging to a cloister 528/1

clausura, -e *n f* act of enclosing, fencing-in 247/17

clericalis, -e *adj* pertaining to or suitable for a cleric, clerical 503/21, etc

clericus, -i *n m* cleric, one in holy orders 464/10, etc

cognosco, -oscere, -oui, -itum *v tr* to acknowledge, accept (an obligation), here used in bonds 200/23, etc

collectarium, -ii *n nt* collectar, book of collects for liturgical use 504/40

collegiatus, -a, -um *adj* (of churches) collegiate, served by a collegiate chapter; *see* **ecclesia**

collegium, -ii *n nt* college: used of an academic college as a corporate body composed of a head, fellows, and scholars: **collegium Bailiolensis** Balliol College, founded by John de Baliol 170/32-3

comes, -itis *n m* earl, a peer ranking above a viscount but below a marquess 170/35; 492/39, etc

comitatus, -us *n m* county 211/3, etc

commissarius, -ii *n m* commissioner, a royal officer (*possibly* a household officer) delegated to carry out specific responsibilities 493/13

commissio, -onis *n f* commission, a grant of authority: **commissio taxacionis** commission for taxation 494/29 (*in form* **taxa⟨…⟩** *due to manuscript damage*)

commissionarius, -i *n m* commissioner, one empowered by a royal commission to undertake specified responsibilities, here to take statements and conduct examinations 191/35

communis, -e *adj* 1. common, communal, of or pertaining to a community 504/19; 2. common, general 172/31

communitas, -atis *n f* community, commonalty, commons (of a town or city) 493/31

comparencia, -e *n f* appearance before a judge 288/38, etc; **comparancia** 276/5, etc

compareo, -ere, -ui *v intr* to appear before a judge, here in church courts 248/1, etc; 504/14

confessus, -a, -um *pp* having made (sacramental) confession 491/6

confratria, -e *n f* confraternity, brotherhood, guild 491/7

consecracio, -onis *n f literally*, the act of making holy, *here* consecration, the act of ordaining a bishop 248/9; 504/21

conseruator, -oris *n m literally* one who keeps or preserves, *here* keeper of a beast or beasts, either trained or simply captive, for exhibition or baiting: *in idioms* **conseruator ursorum** bearward 494/17 *and* **conseruator unius bestie vocate a camele** camelward 494/18–19

consistorium, -ii *n nt* consistory, originally a council chamber in a bishop's residence which became the site of a court meeting under the bishop or his deputy, *hence* a consistory-court session 248/2

contiguatus, -a, -um *adj* adjoining, contiguous 247/24

contrauenio, -ire, -i, -tum *v tr* to violate or contravene (eg, an order or decree) 247/38

conuenticula, -e *n f* unlawful gathering or assembly 247/14

conuentualis, -e *adj* conventual, belonging to a religious community; *see* **ecclesia**

conuentus, -us *n m* convent, a religious house or the community living therein 527/10

cooperans, -antis *prp* working together with, cooperating 528/4

copia, -e *n f* copy (especially used of a copy of a legal instrument) 489/34, etc

Corderianus, -a, -um *adj* of or pertaining to Mathurin Cordier, a 15th-century French schoolmaster and educational writer, the teacher of John Calvin; here, with 'opus' understood, referring to his writings as a body 172/7

corea, -e *n f* dance, originally a round dance; apparently used to describe a country dance held out of doors 247/15, etc; 463/10

cornicen, -inis *n m* horn player 540/12

cornu, -us *n nt* horn, in CL a horn or trumpet, originally made from animal horn, used for military signals, *here apparently indicating* an instrument used for entertainment or ceremonial purposes 540/12

Cornubia, -e *n f* Cornwall, name of a county and duchy 554/15

corporalis, -e *adj* bodily, physical; *see* **iuramentum**

corpus, -oris *n nt* 1. *literally* the human body, one's physical being 527/17, etc; 2. a dead body, corpse 247/18; 463/7; 3. *in idiom* **corpus Christi** the eucharistic body of Christ: *see* **festum**

crastinum, -i *n f* the morrow, *here* the day after a feast day 492/5; **crastinum Epiphanie Domini** the morrow of the Lord's Epiphany, 2 January 505/4

crux, -cis *n f* cross, symbol of Christ's death or of the Christian faith: here the name of a church **ecclesia ... sancte Crucis** Holy Cross Church 504/26–7

cultus, -us *n m* religious practice, observance, worship 247/28; **cultus diuinus** divine service, used collectively for the regular liturgical observance required in a Christian church 503/37

curia, -e *n f* law court: of a borough 282/40, etc; **curia manerii** manorial court 295/41, *see also*

rotulus; *also in idiom* **bonus amicus in curia** a good friend in court, that is, someone who acts or intervenes on one's behalf in legal proceedings 490/25–6

custos, -odis *n m* 1. warden, head of a collegiate chapter (*see* **capitulum**) 503/20, etc; 2. keeper of a beast or beasts, either trained or simply captive, for exhibition or baiting: **custos ursorum** bearward 494/15

dampnum, -i *n nt* 1. loss, detriment; 2. condemnation, damnation. The occurrence on 503/33 is a play on the two senses.

de *prep with abl* 1. about, concerning 248/3, etc; 464/10, etc; 2. in partitive sense, of, from 491/7; 3. expressing source or origin, from, of 252/10², etc; 470/9, etc; 4. with place names or the equivalent, expressing place of residence, of 137/32, etc; 527/10, etc; 5. substituting for CL genitive, usually (but not exclusively) with vernacular expressions, of 253/18, etc; 493/9, etc; 6. representing E 'of' in expressions in which CL would use an appositive 504/19

decanus, -i *n m* 1. dean, administrative head of a cathedral chapter 504/25; 2. a rural dean, a priest supervising a deanery, an administrative division of a diocese which also functioned as a court division for the diocesan courts 247/7, etc

decetero *adv* hereafter, henceforward 504/5

declino, -are, -aui, -atum *v intr* to resort to, travel to (*with* 'ad' + *acc to express destination*) 527/22

dedimus potestatem *vb phr* name of a writ issued to empower commissioners to take statements on oath from persons involved in a suit before Star Chamber; apparently the name of this writ and a style of cause were normally written on the dorse of interrogatories used, or answers taken, by commissioners in a given suit 61/28

defendens, -entis *sbst comm* defendant (in a lawsuit) 191/31, etc

deliberacio, -onis *n f* clearance, *here in idiom* **generalis gaole deliberacio** general gaol delivery, the clearing out of prisoners from gaols by trying them, generally held concommitantly with the assize sessions 211/7–8; *also with* 'gaole' *understood* **generalis deliberaceo** 246/37

demeritum, -i *n nt* fault, offence 464/4

denunciacio, -onis *n f* denunciation, a public proclamation or announcement of a canonical offence 464/2

denuncio, -are, -aui, -atum *v tr* 1. to announce, proclaim 463/9; 2. to denounce or report (someone, eg, for a crime) 464/4

depono, -onere, -osui, -ositum *v intr* to depose, make a formal statement or give evidence before a court 123/1, etc

deposicio, -onis *n f* deposition, formal statement made in a court 123/28, etc

deputatus, -i *n m* a deputy 296/3

deuocio, -onis *n f* piety, devotion 527/17, etc

deuote *adv* piously, devoutly 527/25; **deuocius** *compar* 503/26, etc

deuotus, -a, -um *adj* pious, devout, characterized by devotion (used of persons and of things) 247/29, etc; 504/31

dies, diei *n m or f* 1. day 248/7, etc; 528/4, etc; 2. day of the week: **dies dominicus** 247/36, *see also* **Iuppiter**, **Luna**, **Mercurius**; 3. day, daytime (as opposed to night) 492/5?; 4. day as a measurement of time 491/9; 5. day set aside for a special purpose: **dies iuridicus** court day, day upon which legal business could be conducted 504/14–15; 6. a saint's day: **dies Marie Magdalene** 491/16, **Marie Magdalene dies** 492/5?, St Mary Magdalene's Day, 22 July; 7. feast day, festival, celebration: **dies Penticostis** Pentecost, festival 50 days after Easter 498/29; **dies … sollempnis** holy day, festival 247/36; 8. *other idioms:* **hiis diebus** in these days, at present 527/13; **nostris diebus** in our times, nowadays 593/32, *see also* **per**

diocesis, -is *n f* diocese, administrative district under the authority of a bishop 527/10, etc

directus, -a, -um *pp* (of a letter or similar document) directed, addressed (to someone) 247/7

displicencia, -e *n f* displeasure, dissatisfaction 503/22

dissolucio, -onis *n f* 1. easing, slackening (eg, of a rule or order); or 2. dissolute behaviour, immorality. The occurrence at 465/4 may represent a play on both senses although the latter is probably primary there.

diuinus, -a, -um *adj* 1. divine, pertaining to or suitable for God 247/9, etc; 503/19, etc; 2. *with* **officium** divine office, the set of daily prayers and scriptural readings to be said by religious at the canonical hours 527/24, etc, *see also* **cultus**

doctor, -oris *n m* 1. *literally* a learned person, here likely referring to members of the Sanhedrin appearing as characters in a Passion play 550/8, etc; 2. *hence* doctor, one holding the highest academic degree in one of the superior faculties (eg, theology or law), used as a title with names 170/32

dominicus, -a, -um *adj* of or pertaining to the Lord; *see* **dies, natiuitas**

dominus, -i *n m* 1. the Lord, title of God or Christ 247/27, etc; 528/5, etc, *see also* **annus, crastinum, festum, uigilia**; 2. lord, honorific for royalty 211/3, etc; 493/13, etc; bishops 137/32; 504/30, etc; royal officials 493/23; and judges 137/33, etc, *see also* **officium**; 3. Sir: title of a knight 170/20; or a priest 548/26; 4. **dominus domus** master of a house, householder 464/16

domorsum *adv* homewards, on the way home 489/36

Dorcestria, -e *n f* Dorchester, name of a town 171/28

Dorseta, -e *n f* Dorset, name of an archdeaconry in the diocese of Salisbury 248/3

Dorsettensis, -e *adj* of or pertaining to the county of Dorset: **ager Dorsettensis** the territory of Dorset 170/22

dux, -cis *n m* duke, highest rank of the hereditary peerage 493/3, etc

ecclesia, -e *n f* specific church or church building 247/23, etc; 463/5, etc; **conuentualis ecclesia** conventual church, church of a religious house 247/8, etc; **ecclesia cathedralis** cathedral, a bishop's seat 504/26; **ecclesia collegiata**

collegiate church, one served by a chapter of priests and other clerics 503/20, etc

ecclesiasticus, -a, -um *adj* ecclesiastical, of or pertaining to the church: **officium ecclesiasticum** another name for the divine office, the set of daily prayers and scriptural readings to be said by religious at the canonical hours 503/26 *See also* **immunitas**

emano, -are, -aui, -atum *v intr* to be promulgated or sent forth, used of an episcopal mandate 504/25

emendacio, -onis *n f* repair, act of mending 252/30, etc

epiphania, -e *n f* epiphany, revelation, here used of the liturgical festival commemorating the revealing of Christ to the gentiles (Mt 2.1–12); *see* **crastinum**

episcopus, -i *n m* bishop, member of the highest of the major orders of clergy 247/9; 503/19, etc

euangelista, -e *n m* evangelist, one of the traditional authors of the four canonical gospels; *see* **sollem(p)nis**

euidencia, -e *n f* (legal) evidence 289/8

examinatus, -a, -um *pp* examined judicially 137/34

excerceo, -ere, -ui, -itum *see* **exerceo**

excercicio, -onis *n f for* exercitio [OLD]

excommunicacio, -onis *n f* excommunication, ecclesiastical penalty under which the guilty party was punished by exclusion from the sacraments and especially the reception of communion 504/4; at various times, further disabilities were imposed as well, such as exclusion from all social intercourse with other church members; this more severe form is also called **excommunicacio maior** greater excommunication 247/38

exerceo, -ere, -ui, -itum *v tr* 1. to carry out, perform (an action or activity) 247/7; 463/10, etc; 2. to spend time at, frequent 465/1 (*in form* **excerceant**)

exnunc *adv* from now on 504/6, etc

Exonia, -e *n f* Exeter, name of a city 470/9

Exoniensis, -is *sbst f* Exeter, name of a city and diocese 503/19, etc

expensus, -a, -um *pp* spent (of sums of money) 490/40, etc; consumed, used (of commodities) 491/17, etc

exulator, -oris *n m* outlaw 554/15 [DML]

faelix, -icis *adj over-correction of* felix [OLD]

fena, -e *n f for* faenum [OLD]

feria, -e *n f* holiday, festival, *in idiom* **ferie natalitie Redemptoris nostri** the Christmas season, the period from Christmas to Epiphany 170/27

ferrum, -i *n nt literally* iron; *by extension* **ferrum equorum** a horseshoe 489/26

festiuitas, -atis *n f* feast day 504/15

festum, -i *n nt* 1. festival, feast 463/11; 2. a specific feast day or festival (secular or religious): **festum Circumcisionis Domini** feast of the Lord's Circumcision, 1 January 504/17–18; **festum Corporis Christi**, feast of Corpus Christi, Thursday after Trinity Sunday 252/16, etc; **ffestum Marie Magdalene** feast of (St) Mary Magdalene, 22 July 493/15, etc; **festum Natalis Domini** Christmas, 25 December 504/10; **ffestum Omnium Sanctorum** feast of All Saints, 1 November 282/32

fiala, -e *n f* fiddle, *possibly by extension* any stringed instrument played with a bow 540/12 [*ultimately from* OLD fides²; *see also* DML fiola]

fidedignus, -a, -um *adj* trustworthy, reliable 247/12

fidelis, -is *comm sbst* faithful believer, *in pl* the faithful 247/18; 503/25, etc

fideliter *adv* 1. faithfully, in a trustworthy manner 137/34; 2. faithfully, exactly 504/12

fidicen, -inis *n m* in CL one who plays upon a stringed instrument, such as a lyre or harp; *here probably by extension* (male) fiddler 540/11

fidicina, -e *n f (feminine of* **fidicen**) in CL one who plays upon a stringed instrument, such as a lyre or harp; *here probably by extension* (female) fiddler 540/11

fidis, -is *n f literally* string for a lyre or harp [OLD fides²] *here by extension probably* fiddle-string 540/10

filius, -ii *n m* son 247/21; *by extension* of a

symbolic or spiritual relationship between a bishop and the clergy of his diocese, especially his administrative subordinates 247/9; 527/10, etc

fistula, -e *n f* pipe, *literally* reed-pipe [*OLD*], possibly a generic term for any wind instrument 540/12

forisfacio, -ere, -feci, -factum *v tr* to forfeit (a sum of money) 282/33

frunitor, -oris *n m* tanner 252/39

fundacio, -onis *n f* act of founding, foundation 503/21

gaola, -e *n f* gaol; *see* **deliberacio**

generalis, -e *adj* general, common; *see* **deliberacio**

generosus, -i *n m* gentleman 211/4, etc

gestus, -us *n m* behaviour, manner, *hence* **bonus gestus** good behaviour (eg, as condition of appearance bond) 276/6, etc

gilda, -e *n f literally*, guild, an association having some common purpose and brought together for mutual benefit and the pursuit of that purpose, *especially* guild merchant, a body made up of the merchants of a town and often acting (under a royal charter) as the town government; *see* **aula**

gracia, -e *n f* 1. grace, a divine gift operating in human beings to sanctify, regenerate, and strengthen (often used in conventional salutation at opening of a letter) 247/10; 527/11; 2. grace, divine favour 504/30; 3. favour, goodwill 50/37; 4. *in abl + genitive of gerund, expressing purpose* for the sake of, so as (to do something) 465/8

gratus, -a, -um *adj* 1. welcome, agreeable, pleasant 247/29; 2. unforced, willing, free 491/8

guilhalda, -e *n f* guildhall, centre of town government 498/29. *See also* **aula, gilda**

gulosus, -i *sbst m* one who enjoys fine food, gourmand, *hence by extension* one who over-indulges in food and drink 464/12

histrio, -onis *n m* 1. actor, as in CL usage 171/29; the pejorative usage in Quinel's Statutes (464/14, 465/6) is more influenced by the patristic sense of 'histrio' for a performer in obscene farces or ritual drama; 2. with a named patron, an entertainer, probably a musician, under his or her patronage **histrio domini regis** 494/29 [*OLD, DML*, and REED *Devon* LG histrio]

hora, -e *n f literally* hour, *here for* **hora canonica**, a canonical hour, one of the set times for worship according to monastic or other community rules, or the form of service, part of the divine office, to be said at one of those set times 503/27

Idus, -uum *n f* the ides, the thirteenth, or (in March, May, July, and October) the fifteenth, day of a month: in the Roman dating system, all other days of a month were designated by counting backwards from three fixed points, its nones (the fifth or seventh day), its ides, and the calends, or first day, of the following month 248/9 [Cheney, pp 75–81]

immunitas, -atis *n f* immunity, exemption, *here in idiom* **ecclesiastica immunitas** ecclesiastical immunity, the church's freedom from secular jurisdiction over the clergy and consecrated buildings or other spaces 247/20

incontinentia, -e *n f* (sexual) incontinence 275/11

indentura, -e *n f* indenture, a legal document drawn up in duplicate on a single sheet and then separated by cutting along a zigzag line; one half was given to each party affected by the document and the matching indentations authenticate the halves 296/2

indulgencia, -e *n f* indulgence: in medieval canon law and theology, a grant of remission for temporal penalties of sin 491/5m, 491/9 [*ODCC*]

infra *prep* within 1. used of extent of space 503/30; 2. *by extension* used of the boundaries of civil authority 283/2

ingressus, -us *n m literally*, an entering, a coming in, *hence* the physical means of entry into an enclosed space 247/19 *and* the action of entering a building 247/29

inhibicio, -onis *n f* prohibition, order forbidding some activity 247/20; 503/19m

Innocentes, -ium *sbst m* the (holy) Innocents,

the children of Bethlehem killed by Herod in an attempt to kill the infant Jesus (Mt 2.16–18); *see* **sollem(p)nis**

instans, -ntis *prp* (of dates) present, instant 504/10

insula, -e *n f literally* island, *here by extension* **insula Purbeck** the Isle of Purbeck, a peninsula bounded by the English Channel, Poole Harbour, and the River Frome 170/21–2

insultus, -us *n m* attack 527/20 [*from* OLD insulto, to leap upon]

interdictum, -i *n nt* interdict, a canonical penalty which included a ban on the administration of the sacraments and restricted the celebration of solemn services; an interdict could be applied to a single church, a group of churches, or a whole diocese or group of dioceses 247/26 [ODCC]

interdictus, -a, -um *adj* forbidden 465/9

interrogatorium, -ii *n nt* interrogatory, article drawn up for the questioning of witnesses 123/16, etc

ioculator, -oris *n m* entertainer, juggler 465/6, etc

iocus, -i *n m, nt in pl* in CL jest, joke (usually verbal); however, in AL senses of entertainment or recreation seem to predominate and verbal humour is not necessarily meant, making the occurrence on 171/15 ambiguous

irrotulo, -are, -aui, -atum *v tr* to enroll (a legal document or record) formally in a record copy 296/2

Iuppiter, Iouis *n m* Jupiter, Jove, chief deity of the Roman pantheon whose name was also given to the fifth planet: *with* 'dies' *understood* **Iouis** Thursday 70/35; 424/26, etc

iuramentum, -i *n nt* oath 137/33; **iuramentum ... corporale** corporal oath, one involving physical contact with a gospel book or relic on the part of the oath-taker 275/12. *See also* **presto**

iurator, -oris *n m* juror: a member of the jury of a court leet 282/28

iuridicus, -a, -um *adj* of or pertaining to a court; *see* **dies**

iuxta *prep* according to 527/27

la, le forms of the Romance definite art usually used to signal the beginning of an English word or phr in an otherwise Latin passage, eg, **la shryne** 252/16, etc; **le May** 490/40; sometimes found as a name element **Thomas le Stulstus** 493/11

laciuius, -a, -um *see* **lasciuius**

lagena, -e *n f* gallon 491/16, etc [OLD lagona, DML lagena]

laicus, -i *n m* layman, one who is not in orders of any kind 465/10

lapsus, -us *n m literally* lapse (of time), *here by extension* the end of a period of time, conclusion 504/15

lasciuius, -a, -um *adj* dissolute, immoral, sexually lax 527/23; **laciuius** 247/15

libellus, -i *n m* libel, a formal listing of charges made by a plaintiff in a suit in an ecclesiastical court 123/1, etc

libertas, -atis *n f* liberty, freedom *here* used of the freedom of the church from secular intervention 247/20

licencia, -e *n f* formal permission, licence 527/8, etc

linthuus, -i *n m* in CL a trumpet, curved at one end, used for military signals, here apparently indicating an instrument used for entertainment or ceremonial purposes 540/13 [*var of* OLD lituus]

literarius, -a, -um *adj* of or pertaining to letters or writing; *see* **ludus**

liticen, -inis *n m literally* one who plays upon the 'lituus,' *hence* trumpeter; it is not clear how it would be distinguished in use from **cornicen** and **tubicen** 540/13

littera, -e *n f literally* a letter of the alphabet, *hence*: 1. (*sg and coll pl*) letter, epistle 247/7, etc; 504/9, etc; **littere ... patentes** letters patent, a type of formal communication sent in the form of a letter not closed by a seal 248/8; **patentes littere** 504/18; 2. literary pursuits or study, education 170/33, etc

ludibrium, -ii *n nt* playful or frivolous behaviour, usually derisive or insulting 463/12 (apparently some scurrilous or otherwise improper performance); 503/30 (describing the seasonal misrule of the minor clergy at cathedrals or collegiate churches)

ludicer, -cra, -crum *adj* of or pertaining to entertainment; pleasant, entertaining (*with* 'res' *understood*) 171/19?; *nt as sbst* 1. pleasantry, entertaining remark 171/20; 2. public entertainment, show, play 171/19?

ludo, -dere, -si, -sum *v tr* to play, with various significances 1. to play a sport or game 170/25; 2. to play a play or interlude 121/8; 3. to play games of chance, gamble 465/6; *prp as sbst* player, gambler 465/7; 4. used without specification, sense unclear 493/30, 498/29

ludus, -i *n m* 1. game, sport, play, pastime; with various significances: a. sport, (folk) game, popular pastime 464/2, 472/25; **ludi inhonesti** 463/10; **ludi teatrales** 463/11–12 (all occurrences of 'ludus' in Quinel's Statutes apparently refer to outdoor activities and are linked with wrestling and dance); b. used to describe the seasonal misrule of the minor clergy: **ludi inepti & noxii** 503/28–9; **ludi inhonesti** 503/20m; c. used of pastimes linked with dance **ludi noxii** 247/7, 247/25; d. entertainment, play (often of an unspecified kind, sense unclear) 489/23, 490/9; 2. play on a classical model, used of school drama 172/13, 172/35; 3. school: **ludus literarius** grammar school 170/23

Luna, -e *n f* the Moon: *with* 'dies' *understood* **Lune** Monday 424/37, etc

lusor, -oris *n m* player, participant in a play, interlude, pastime, or entertainment (apparently used of town players) 494/20

magister, -tri *n m* 1. one who has authority or rank, master, also used as a title of respect with names, Mr 138/2; 2. schoolmaster, teacher 170/29

maior, -oris *n m* mayor 489/40, etc

maior, -ius *compar adj* greater (in size, dignity, or worth) 248/2, etc; *nt pl as sbst* greater or more important matters 172/33; *see* **excommunicacio**

manerium, -ii *n nt* 1. manor, a tract of land held of the Crown, over which the lord exercises jurisdiction through a manorial court, or court baron, in which he or his bailiff sits as judge

and judgments are rendered according to customary usage 296/2, etc, *see also* **curia**; 2. manor house, the place of residence of such a lord within his manor 504/19

manucaptor, -oris *n m* one who acts as a pledge for another's performance of a bond or other obligation, guarantor 246/35m

martiligium, -i *n nt properly* martyrology, a register of martyrs and other saints, giving the dates of their commemoration and other information about them, from which daily readings were customary in religious communities *but sometimes apparently used by extension for* necrology, a register of benefactors and others remembered in prayer in religious communities on the anniversary of their deaths, *here context is insufficient to distinguish* 504/40 [Latham 'martyr'; *ODCC* martyrology; *OED* martyrology, necrology]

martyr, -tiris *n m* martyr, one who dies out of adherence to religious principles, here in the name of a church **ecclesia ... sancti Thome martyris** church of St Thomas the Martyr, that is, St Thomas Becket 504/27–8, etc

matutina, -e *sbst f* matins, one of the canonical hours making up the divine office of clerics; despite its name, matins is the night office, being said at midnight or 2 AM under strict Benedictine observance 503/27

mercatum, -i *n nt* fair, market 463/5

Mercurius, -ii *n m* Mercury, a deity of the Roman pantheon whose name was also given to the first planet: *with* 'dies' *understood* **Mercurij** Wednesday 424/34

mimus, -i *n m* performer, mime, especially in the often obscene farces and pantomimes of the later Roman stage 171/33; 540/13 (where it is glossed by **scurra**) [*OLD*]

minister, -tri *n m literally* servant, *here by extension with reference to Mk 10.43–5*, minister, cleric, used of members of collegiate chapters 503/27, etc

ministrallus, -i *n m literally* a servant (ultimately from LL 'ministerialis'); minstrel, performer, musician, often used either of a musician who

is a member of a household or of a town wait:
1. used without specification 492/30, 493/38;
minnstrellus 494/37; **mynstrallus** 491/25,
493/12; **mynstrellus** 492/13, 492/15 (all
possibly occurrences of sense 3); as members
of a local confraternity 491/7; 2. a minstrel, probably a musician, under named royal,
noble, or other patronage 494/27, 495/9;
mynstrallus 493/23; 3. a minstrel in the
employ of a town, probably a town wait
minstrallus 470/9

miseracio, -onis *n f* mercy 503/19

misericordia, -e *n f literally* mercy; *in idiom* **in
misericordia** (to be) in mercy, that is, subject
to a fine, called an amercement, levied at the
mercy, ie, the discretion, of the judge rather
than at a fixed rate 283/3

missa, -e *n f* mass, liturgical celebration of the
eucharist 503/28

missale, -is *sbst nt* missal, a service book containing
the commons and propers of the mass for
Sundays and festivals throughout the year
504/39

moderator, -oris *n m* head, headmaster (of a
school) 170/23

monasterium, -ii *n nt* monastery, religious house
for a community of monks 527/9, etc

mora, -e *n f* elapse of time, usually with negative
connotation, delay *but in idiom* **moram
trahere** used of a place of residence to stay,
remain, live 527/8, etc

mundanus, -a, -um *adj* worldly, secular 527/23

mundus, -i *n m* the world, the earth; *see* **origo**

musa, -e *n f* pipe, apparently a form of bagpipe
540/11 [*possibly a back-formation from OLD
musicus or an extension of OLD Musa; see OED
Muse, sb.³*]

mynstrallus, mynstrellus *see* **ministrallus**

natalis, -e *adj* of or pertaining to birth, *by extension*
of or pertaining to Christmas; *hence nt sg as
sbst* (with **domini**) Christmas, the Christmas
season; *see* **festum, uigilia**

natalitius, -a, -um *adj* of or pertaining to Christmas; *see* **feria**

natiuitas, -atis *n f literally* birth: *in idiom* **dominica
natiuitas** Christmas; *see* **sollem(p)nis**

nephandus, -a, -um *adj for* nefandus [*OLD*]

nox,-ctis *n f* 1. *literally* night, night-time 489/22;
2. the eve of a feast day, so called from the
liturgical convention of beginning the observance
of a holy day at sunset on the previous day:
nox Marie Magdalene (St) Mary Magdalene's
Eve 491/18, etc

obediencia, -e *n f* obedience, here used with
special reference to the obedience owed by a
cleric to the bishop of the diocese in which he
has a benefice 247/34; 504/32

oblacio, -onis *n f* alms, offerings, gift 489/29, etc

obsequium, -ii *n nt* (religious) service 247/22

officialis, -is *n m* officer, official: 1. official,
specifically an archdeacon's official, a subordinate
officer who supervised legal business in the
archdeaconry courts and often acted as judge
in the archdeacon's place 464/4; 2. official,
here specifically a bishop's official, *probably* the
official principal, another name for the bishop's
vicar general or chancellor, a deputy with
primarily administrative and judicial
responsibility 248/2, etc

officium, -ii *n nt* 1. office, position of responsibility,
specifically a bishop's judicial office or function,
normally exercised by subordinate judges, and
hence a name for a diocesan court: **officium
domini** 137/32, etc; *in idiom* **ex officio**
officially, by virtue of the judicial office 248/3−4;
2. divine office, the set of daily prayers and
scriptural readings to be said by religious at
the canonical hours 503/38, *see also* **diuinus,
ecclesiasticus**

onero, -are, -aui, -atum *v tr* to bind someone by
an oath, swear someone to an oath (*used with
acc of person and simple abl*) 137/33

oracio, -onis *n f* prayer 247/31

ordo, -inis *n m* judicial order 326/26, etc

organista, -e *n m* organist 494/28

originalis, -e *adj* original, *hence* authoritative,
official 504/40

origo, -onis *n f* origin, beginning, *here in phr*

origo mundi the beginning of the world, used as a play title 542/11–12, etc

pacificus, -a, -um *adj* peaceful, peaceable 247/28; 528/4

parochialis, -e *adj* of or pertaining to a parish; *see* **sacerdos**

passio, -onis *n f literally* suffering, endurance, *here in phr* **passio Christi** the Passion, that is, suffering and death, of Christ, used as a play title 542/14, etc

patens, -ntis *adj* open; *see* **littera**

pater, -tris *n m* father: 1. *literally* 170/20; 554/14; 2. *by extension* describing the relationship between the bishop of a diocese and his clergy 504/30, etc

patronatus, -us *n m* patronage, here used of a bishop's fatherly care toward an institution which he founded 503/21

penitencia, -e *n f* penance, act of contrition or restitution imposed by ecclesiastical author-ities upon persons guilty of canonical offences; in case of moral offences such as sabbath breaking, penance often took the form of public confession on a set day or series of days 504/16

peniteo, -ere, -ui *v intr* to repent, be penitent 491/6

per *prep with acc* 1. through, by means of (a person or thing) 248/8, etc; 463/12, etc; 2. through, across (a region or district) 247/10, (a barrier or boundary) 171/41; 3. during, on, at (a period of time) 247/36; 4. *in idioms* **per annum** by the year, annually 493/38; **per consequens** as a consequence, consequently 247/26; **per dies singulos** *literally* each day by day, *hence,* daily 247/26

peregrinacio, -onis *n f* pilgrimage 465/1

peremptorie *adv* in a peremptory manner 222/41; 504/14

perperam *adv* perversely, basely 503/38

personaliter *adv* in person, personally 527/20, etc

pertranseo, -ire *v intr literally* to travel through, cross, *hence by extension* to go on, continue 504/3

placitum, -i *n nt* judicial plea or suit; *by extension,* a court or session at which pleas were heard 463/5

poeta, -e *n m* poet; in this context, one who recites verse is meant, as well as one who composes it 540/13

pompo, -are, -aui, -atum *v intr* (*from Greek* πομπή) to walk in procession, *hence* to march about or parade, often ostentatiously 550/32, etc [*see* OLD **pompa**]

potellum, -i *n nt* pottle, liquid measure of about two quarts 492/6, etc

praesul, -lis *n m* bishop 171/14, etc

prandium, -ii *n nt* dinner, the second and most elaborate of the three main meals of the day 464/17, etc

precentor, -oris *n m* precentor, member of a cathedral chapter responsible for directing the singing of choir services; adminstratively, the precentor is second to the dean 504/25

predepono, -ere, -sui, -situm *v tr* to formally state or depose before 124/24

predictus, -a, -um *adj* aforesaid 247/14, etc; 464/3, etc

premitto, -ittere, -isi, -issum *v tr* to mention before 247/24; *pp in nt as sbst* the afore-mentioned 248/6

prenotatus, -a, -um *adj* noted before, before-mentioned 247/25, etc

prepositus, -i *n m* warden, administrative officer in a collegiate chapter 504/27, etc

presentes, -cium *sbst comm pl* the present docu-ment or letter 527/21, etc

presento, -are, -aui, -atum *v tr* to present findings, used of an officer or jury of a borough court 282/28, etc

presto, -are, -iti, -atum *v tr* to furnish, provide, *in idiom* **iuramentum ... prestare** to swear or take an oath 275/12–13

presumo, -ere, -psi, -ptum *v tr* to take upon oneself (to do something), used of violators of rules or orders 463/11, etc

presumpcio, -onis *n f* presumption, daring, boldness (with strongly negative connotations) 247/39; 504/15

princeps, -ipis *adj* foremost, principal 170/28

princeps, -ipis *n m* 1. prince, son or son-in-law of the king 493/22; 2. head, person in the first rank or position 170/24; 550/9

prior, -oris *n m* prior, head of a priory 527/10

probenda, -e *n f* fodder, provender (for horses) 489/25

processus, -us *n m* (legal) process, proceedings 489/34

professio, -onis *n f* (religious) profession 464/14

promotio, -onis *n f* prompting 247/12

promotus, -a, -um *pp* promoted, used of a proceeding against a person in a church court moved or initiated by someone other than the court itself or a person authorized to make presentment 275/10

prophanus, -a, -um *adj for* profanus [OLD]

puer, -eri *n m* boy: 1. choir-boy 503/27; 2. school-boy 172/2

quarteria -ie *n f* quart, a measurement of volume 491/17, etc

rector, -oris *n m* 1. director, leader 171/39; 2. rector, priest having responsibility for and authority over a parish and entitled to enjoy its tithes 247/35, etc

redditus, -us *n m* rent 493/38

redemptio, -onis *n f literally*, a buying back, *hence*, ransom, redemption, fine 170/26

Redemptor, -oris *n m* Redeemer (as a title of Christ); *see* **feria**

regardum, -i *n nt* reward, gratuity, customary payment 494/15, etc; **rewardum** 493/22, etc

regina, -e *n f* queen, the reigning monarch 79/22, etc

regnum, -i *n nt* reign 79/22, etc

regularis, -e *adj* regular, in accordance with a rule, here of a monastery, with reference to the Benedictine Rule 527/27 [ODCC]

religio, -onis *n f* religion, here Christian religious practice or devotion 465/10

respondeo, -dere, -si, -sum *v intr* 1. (legal term) to answer, reply to (eg, charges or questions) 248/4, etc; 2. to answer for (one's actions or behaviour) 504/16

resurrexio, -onis *n f literally* arising, *here in phr* **resurrexio Christi** Christ's Resurrection from the dead, used as a play title 542/16–17, etc

rewardum, -i *see* **regardum**

rex, -gis *n m* king: 1. a reigning monarch 211/4, etc; 493/13, etc; 2. as a place-name element, **Bere Regis** 123/2, etc; 3. as a divine title 528/4

rotulus, -i *n m* roll (of parchment or paper): **curie rotulus** court roll, the official record of a manorial court 296/2

rubius, -a, -um *adj* red; *see* **uinum**

sacerdos, -otis *n m* priest, a member of the second of the three major orders of clergy 464/3, etc; **sacerdos parochialis** parish priest, priest charged with the cure of souls and other duties within a parish 463/8–9

sacramentum, -i *n nt* oath, especially the oath sworn by jurors to give true findings to the best of their ability 282/28, etc

sacrista, -e *n m* sacrist, one responsible for the communion vessels, plate, and other sacred or valuable objects belonging to a church or other religious institution 252/32

saltator, -oris *n m* (male) dancer 540/14

saltatrix, -icis *n f* (female) dancer 540/14

saluandus, -i *sbst comm* one who ought to be, or should be, saved 463/7

salueto *pl form of* salue[1] [OLD]

salus, -utis *n f* in CL, health, often used in conventional good wishes in epistolary salutations; in Christian usage, salvation; here used in salutations in a play upon both senses 247/10; 527/11, etc

sanctus, -a, -um *adj* holy or blessed, used of things 504/27 or qualities 247/34; *with names as a title* Saint 503/20, etc; *m pl as sbst* holy ones, saints 463/7, etc; *nt sg as sbst* that which is holy, the holy 465/2. *See also* **crux, festum, martyr, sollem(p)nis, Trinitas, uigilia**

Sarisburia, -e *n f* Salisbury 170/30; *also in indecl form* **Sarum** 247/9, etc

scandalum, -i *n nt* scandal, discredit 527/27

scenescallus, -i *n m* steward, a manorial officer 296/3

scenulentum, -i *n nt* bit of mud 503/33 [*diminutive from* OLD caenum]

Scheftonia, -e *n f* Shaftesbury, name of a town and a deanery in the diocese of Salisbury 247/7, etc

schola, -e *n f* school 170/24, etc; **schola publica** public school 170/32

scurilis, -e *adj* scurrilous, offensive (*from* **scurra**) 503/34

scurilitas, -atis *n f* offensive or scurrilous behaviour (*from* **scurra**) 247/33

scurra, -e *n m originally and historically* a Roman raconteur and wit but one distinguished by offensive humour, *by the early Principate*, an entertainer characterized by such humour, *and hence by extension* a buffoon; here a gloss for **mimus** 540/14 [OLD]

secularis, -e *adj* 1. secular, as opposed to sacred, *hence* ordinary or common 463/6; 2. *as legal term* civil, ie, not ecclesiastical 463/5

senatus, -us *n m literally* the Roman Senate, *here by extension* **sacer senatus** sacred assembly, possibly the Houses of Convocation 171/13

series, -ei *n f literally* a series or progression (of objects, people, or events), *hence* the ordered presentation of ideas in a written work, *and thus by extension* a copy of its text 248/8; 504/18

seruicia, -e *see* **ceruisia**

seruiens, -ntis *sbst m* servant 493/3, etc

sessio, -onis *n f* session, sitting (of a court): **sessio pro Burgo** session of the borough court 203/19; **sessiones pro burgo** sessions of the borough court 200/24; **sessiones ad curiam manerii** sessions of the manorial court 295/41; **sessiones** sittings of the court of quarter sessions 275/36, etc

sigillum, -i *n nt* seal (of a community) 504/19

signum, -i *n nt* sign, symbol: 1. personal sign used by an illiterate person instead of a signature; in some cases these signs may be initials 191/29; 2. *by extension*, insigne, a device or object bearing a device, *hence* sign, placard **ad signum le George** at the sign of the George (Inn) 191/33

situatus, -a, -um *adj* located, situated 527/14

sollem(p)nis, -e *adj* 1. ceremonious, pertaining to or suitable to a celebration 170/35; 2. solemn, ceremonious, partaking of religious rites: **dies ... sollempnes** holy days 247/36; 3. *nt pl as sbst* solemn religious observances, high holidays **dominice Natiuitatis ac sanctorum Stephani Iohannis apostoli & euangeliste ac Innocencium sollempnia** the solemnities of Christmas, St Stephen, St John the Apostle and Evangelist, and the (Holy) Innocents, that is, 25–8 December 503/23–5; 4. *n pl as sbst* solemn religious services, often specifically high masses 247/30; 503/28

sparsio, -onis *n f* spattering, sprinkling 503/34

spectaculum, -i *n nt* spectacle, show, usually unspecified but possibly dramatic 170/35; 463/12, 465/7, 527/23; the hostility shown to 'spectacula' in canonical sources probably arises from the term's associations with gladiatorial shows and the like [OLD]

statutum, -i *n nt* statute, regulation, law: **liber statutorum** statute book 504/40–505/1

sto, stare, steti, statum *v intr* 1. to remain, stay, continue in force; 2. to be stayed (of judicial proceedings). It is not clear in which of these senses the occurrence on 169/5m is being used.

stultus, -i *n m* fool, buffoon, here apparently a household entertainer 492/40; **le stulstus** 493/11. *See also* **le**

stupor, -oris *n m* astonishment, surprise, consternation 503/22

subiectio, -onis *n f* subjection (to a legitimate authority), obedience 504/33

subsidium, -ii *n nt* help, aid, *here in idiom* **caritatis subsidia** alms, charitable gifts 491/9

super¹ *adv* above, besides, more 172/41

super² *prep with acc or abl* 1. *literally* above 283/4; 2. above, beyond (used figuratively) 172/30; 3. about, concerning 248/4, etc; 504/15; 4. upon, by virtue of (an oath, a request, an account) 282/28, etc

supradictus, -a, -um *pp* said earlier, stated above 191/31; 528/5, etc

suspensio, -onis *n f* suspension of a cleric from his office and revenues for a limited time 504/4

taberna, -e *n f literally* a shop, but usually in AL a tavern, alehouse, inn 465/1

taxacio, -onis *n f* taxation, assessment; *see* **commissio**

taxillus, -i *n m (formed from* talus + *diminutive suffix)* a small die or playing piece in the shape of a die; **ad ... taxillos ... ludere** to play at 'taxilli,' *hence* to game or gamble with dice or similar objects 465/6

teatralis, -e *adj* of or pertaining to the stage, dramatic, theatrical; *see* **ludus**

tenementum, -i *n nt* tenement, holding; *often specifically* a building 493/38, etc

teneo, -ere, -ui, -tum *v tr literally* to hold, hold on to, *hence*: 1. to take, have (a name) 171/40; 2. to hold a meeting, court session, or other event 211/8, etc; 463/5; 3. to hold (an office or position) 248/7; 4. to have an obligation (to do something), have (to do something) 527/26, etc; 5. *with predicative modifier, here missing,* to hold or regard (someone) as (something) 172/32; 6. *in pass idiom in bonds and the like* to be bound, held accountable (for a sum of money) 246/34, etc

tenor, -oris *n m* tenor, tone, slant (of meaning, eg, in a document) 527/21

Terentianus, -a, -um *adj* of or pertaining to Terence (Publius Terentius Afer, 195 or 185–159 BC), one of the two great extant Roman comedy writers; here, with 'opus' understood, referring to his writings as a body 172/8

tibicen, -inis *n m literally* one who plays a reed pipe (*OLD* tibia), piper; but possibly a generic term for one playing a wind instrument rather than specifically one playing an instrument with a reed mouthpiece 540/11

totalis, -e *adj* total, complete, entire 490/23, etc

totaliter *adv* totally, completely 504/5

tragaedia, -ae *n f* tragedy, a serious drama having an unhappy outcome, here probably either an ancient tragedy or a modern work imitating ancient tragedy at least in form 171/25

tragedio, -onis *n m literally* tragedian, a performer in a tragedy, *here by extension* player 121/8

traho, -here, -xi, -ctum *v tr see* **mora**

Trinitas, -atis *n f* Trinity [*ODCC*], here in the name of a church **ecclesia sancte Trinitatis** church of the Holy Trinity 247/23

tripudium, -ii *n nt originally* ancient Roman ritual dance, in AL apparently a dance containing formal or set elements 472/25 (*in form* ⟨...⟩**pudium** *due to manuscript damage*), etc

tuba, -e *n f* in CL, a trumpet with a straight tube used for military signals, as well as in various civilian processions; here probably any straight wind instrument not having a reed mouthpiece 540/11

tubicen, -inis *n m* trumpeter, one who plays the 'tuba' 540/10

tumulo, -are, -aui, -atum *v tr* to bury, inter 463/8

uersus *prep* to, toward (often with hostile sense): *hence* of evidence, against 289/8

uespera, -e *n f* vespers, one of the canonical hours making up the divine office of clerics; despite its name, also the L word for evening, vespers was usually said before dark, in the late afternoon or early evening 503/27

uestimentum, -i *n nt* (liturgical) vestment 503/32

uicarius, -ii *n m* vicar, one who acts as a deputy for a rector who cannot discharge his duties in a parish 247/35

vicecamerarius, -ii *n m* vice-chamberlain, officer of the royal household serving under the lord chamberlain 170/21

uicecomes, -itis *n m* sheriff, an officer of the Crown within a given county, having particular responsibilities for the county court and other aspects of the administration of justice 494/28

uicis *(gen) n f (nom sg lacking)* occasion, time: **secunda uice** on a second occasion, the second time 490/5; **tertia uice** the third time 490/31

uicus, -i *n m* street 282/31; **borialis uicus** North Street 493/38

uigilacio, -onis *n f* watchkeeping 253/18

uigilia, -e *n f* vigil, eve of a liturgical festival **uigilie ... sanctorum** eves of the saints, that is, of saints' days 463/11; **uigilia beate Marie Magdalane** eve of the feast of St Mary Magdalene, 21 July 492/13–14, etc (*or* **beate**

Marie Magdalene 494/6, etc, *or* **sancte
Marie Magdalane** 492/21–2, etc, *or* **sancte
Marie Magdalene** 493/12 *or* **Marie Magdalene**
492/5, etc); **uigilia Natalis Domini**
Christmas Eve, 24 December 504/34
uilla, -e *n f* town 247/36, etc
uinum, -i *n nt* wine 489/24, etc; *in various idioms*
uinum album white wine 492/23, etc; **uinum
rubium** red wine 492/22

uitulus, -i *n m* calf; *see* **caro**
uoluptuositas, -atis *n f* over-indulgence, love of
pleasure 465/4
ursus, -i *n m* bear; *see* **conseruator, custos**

Warwicum, -i *n nt* Warwick: name of an earldom
492/39, etc

English Glossary

WILLIAM COOKE

abed *v pa 3 pl* abode, ie, endured 487/16 [*OED* Abide *v* 17]

abowght *prep* about 250/5

adowble shamble *n phr* a double shamble, a double stand or pair of stands 127/19–20

a gayne *adv* again 260/4

agreyyd *pp* agreed 239/12

albehit *conj* albeit, although 174/21

ale *n* a convivial public drinking, usually held to raise money for some charitable or civic purpose 138/17, 535/39, etc; **alle** 262/25, 284/29; **ales** *pl* 119/17, etc; **eyle** 513/37; *in comp and phr* **church ale** an ale held under the auspices of a parish church and for its benefit 230/31, 534/17, etc; **charche alle** 257/16; **cherche alle** 255/33, etc; **church ayle** 126/5; **churche ale** 254/34, etc; **churche alle** 260/36, etc; **chyrche ale** 258/26; **church ales** *pl* 117/18–19, 534/8, etc; **clerkes ales** *pl* ales held to benefit parish clerks 120/1; **Cob ale** an ale held to raise money for the Lyme Regis Cobb (*see* p 297) 299/6, etc; **Cobb ale** 302/31, etc; **Cobbe aell** 308/20; **Cobbe alle** 302/17, 303/19; **Cobb ealle** 305/23; **Cobe alle** 298/8, etc; **Cobe ayll** 299/37; **Coobb ealle** 305/13; **kyng alle** an ale at which a parish king presided 257/9; **kynge ale** 254/5, 254/20; **kynges ale** 252/11, etc; **kyngese ale** 252/40; **Robynhode ale** an ale at which a Robin Hood presided 138/15; **Whitsonales** *pl* ales held on or near Whitsunday 203/26, 203/34

amont *n* amount 242/2; **amonte** 242/37

a noder *pron* another 473/24

aparlet *pp* apparelled 399/20

a pone *prep* upon 212/27

apyerith *v pr 3 sg* appeareth 244/23

auter *n* altar 484/4

auysse *n* advice 239/17

avysid *pp* advised, ie, notified 529/18

ayen *adv* again 258/18

ayle, ayll *see* **ale**

az *v pr 3 sg* has 244/22

backer *adj compar* rear 269/38

badye *adj* bawdy 227/27

baighted *see* **bayte**

bailife, bailiff(e) *see* **bayliffe**

baldery *n* baldric(?) *but with puns on the sense* bawdry, unchaste conduct *and on a nonce-sense* making bald, ie, stripping (a victim) of wealth 220/6

bandore *n* bandora, a musical instrument resembling a bass guitar, with wire strings and a fixed bridge 152/6

barkehowse *n comp* a building where bark is used, or stored, for tanning 229/27

batmentes *n pl* abatements, reductions (of sums owing) 245/4

bauners *n pl* fortified enclosures or outworks 245/14 [*OED* Bawn 1]

baylie *n* 1. bailie, the chief officer of a borough, or one of two officers assisting the mayor 140/2, etc; **bayle** 242/1, etc; **baylys** *poss* 245/3; 2. bailie, an officer of the sovereign or another lord, overseeing a manor **bayle** 250/9

bayliewike *n* bailiwick, office or term of office of a bailie 139/15

bayliffe *n* 1. bailiff, the chief officer of a borough, or one of two officers assisting the mayor 134/10, etc; **bailife** 128/12, 136/11; **bailiff** 129/7, etc; **bailiffe** 135/17, etc; **baylief** 147/36; **baylieffe** 134/30, 135/24; **baylif** 186/22; **baylife** 133/36; **bayliff** 186/11, etc; **baylive** 281/20; **bayliefes** *poss* 148/2; **bailiffes** *pl* 154/5, 156/33; **bailives** 191/10; **bayliffes** 184/1, etc; **bayliffs** 184/4, 184/5; 2. bailiff, an officer of the sovereign or another lord, overseeing a manor 248/23, etc; **bailiffe** 294/31; **bayliffes** *pl* 118/22

bayte *v* bait, set dogs to bite and torment (an animal) for sport 283/3; **baytid** *pa 3 sg* 206/37; **baighted** *pp* 249/28; **bayting** *vb n* 288/33; **beatinge** 169/6

bearebeatings *vb n comp pl* bearbaitings (*see* **bayte**) 117/11

bede men *n comp pl* beadsmen, unemployed men maintained in almshouses 256/36

beere hearde *see* **bere hurde**

be ffor wretyne *pp phr* before written, written above 239/12

beof *n* beef 151/15, etc; **beofe** 249/12, etc

bere hurde *n comp* bearherd, one who leads a bear about 492/39, etc; **beere hearde** 496/3; **berehurdes** *pl* 521/14

bereward *n comp* bearward, one who leads a bear about 472/5; **berewarde** 470/26

beyynge *prp* being 239/13

bhare *n* bear 521/19

bocrom *n* buckram 473/35; **bockerom** 261/38; **bocoram** 254/10; **bokeram** 529/21

bodies *see* **French bodies**

bond ffyres *n comp pl* bonfires 224/13

booren *pp* borne 524/17

boote *n* hollow part of a coach, used to hold luggage or extra passengers 312/10 [*OED* Boot *sb*³ 4]

bowchers *n poss* butcher's 186/5

bowgt *pp* bought 358/28

bowth *n* booth 138/18

box *n in phr* **playing the box with** placing in a predicament for sport(?) 474/6 [*OED* Box *sb*² 21]

brand *n* brawn, boar's flesh 130/9

brasell *n* brazil, red dye from Brazil wood 269/23

broking *vb n* acting as a broker or go-between 219/39

brouȝht *v pa 3 sg* brought 258/11

Bryddes *see* **satyn of Bryddes**

bulbayting *vb n comp* bullbaiting (*see* **bayte**) 208/33; **bulbaytinge** 231/8; **bulbeatings** *pl* 117/11; **bulbeatynges** 118/9

bul kepers *n comp poss* bullkeeper's 208/33

bullring *n comp* arena where bulls were publicly baited 163/32, 496/8, etc; **bull ryng** 523/13; **bulrenge** 139/5; **bulring** 153/40; **bulringe** 168/41

burche *n* birch, *presumably* wood for fuel or light 307/27

burgesse *n* 1. burgess, citizen of a borough possessing full municipal rights; **burgesses** *pl* 301/19, 474/32, etc; **burgessis** 475/3; **burgessors** 302/1; 2. burgess, borough's chosen representative in parliament 536/35

busel *n* bushel 307/10; **buselz** *pl* 307/14¹, 307/14²

by causse *conj* because 241/25

bysshopes *n poss* boy bishop's 259/26, etc; **bysshoppes** 259/5, etc; **bysshops** 262/5

cadwellye *n* a kind of cloth 516/3; *see* p 605 (endnote to St Ives Guildhall ff 10,11)

cafehenges *n pl* calves' offal 307/22 [*OED* Henge]

carosing *prp* carousing 222/36

carroure *n* carrier 267/39

charche alle *see* **ale**

Charlamens Weane *n phr* Charlemagne's Wain, a name for the constellation Ursa Major 487/17

chart *n* cart 287/7 [*OED* Charet]

cheldes *n poss* child's, ie, boy bishop's 258/38

chen *n* chain 497/25; **chene** 497/24; **chine** 497/22

cherche alle *see* **ale**

cherimps *n pl* shrimps 307/19

chesable *n* chasuble 262/31

chikiyns *n pl* chickens 307/19

chine *see* **chen**

church(e) ale, churche alle, chyrche ale *see* **ale**

clerkes ales *see* **ale**

Cob(b) ale, Cobbe aell, Cobbe alle, Cobb ealle *see* **ale**

Cobb hall *n comp* hall used for the Lyme Regis

Cobb ale (*see* p 297) 301/25; **Cobb howes** Cobb house *in same sense* 223/1; **Cobb howsse** 304/10, etc

Cobbe kytchyn *n comp* Cobb kitchen, kitchen used to bake and cook food for the Lyme Regis Cobb ale (*see* p 297) 301/23, 301/26

Cobb howsse *see* **Cobb hall**

Cobb warden *n comp* one of the wardens of the Lyme Regis Cobb (*see* p 297); **Cobwardens** *poss* 302/27; **Cob wardinges** *pl* 222/35; **Kob wardens** 223/1–2

Cobe alle, Cobe ayll *see* **ale**

Cob howes *see* **Cobb hall**

cockfistinge *n comp* cockfighting 499/6 ['s' represents ME '3']

cometimber *n comp* potent man(?) 487/13

comitie *n* county 487/37; **comitye** 301/17

cony geere *n* conyger, rabbit warren 275/15

Coobb ealle *see* **ale**

coupes *n* cups 307/34

cremsyn *adj* crimson 473/23

crockes *n pl* crooks, hooks 500/10

crowting house *n comp* a building where bark is used, or stored, for tanning 229/27 [cp *OED* Crut²]

cushinge cloth *n comp* cushion cloth 131/9–10

cutt match candles *n phr pl* candles made from cut lengths of the wick used for igniting firearms 130/33

cytels *n pl* skittles 222/35

d *abbrev for* L dimidium, *used in* E *context for* a half 131/36

dawnce *n* dancer or troop of dancers 506/30, etc; **daunce** 471/4, 506/23; *see also* **morys daunce**

demeasners *n pl* demeanours 162/4

dener *n* dinner 239/6, 505/33, etc; **denors** *pl* 250/15

deput *n in phr* **mayr deput** mayor's deputy 241/15

deveyne *adj* divine 286/34

dieper *adj* diaper, linen cloth woven in diamond pattern 133/10

downe *pp* done 481/13

dowre *n* door 268/29

dowsen *n* dozen 499/34

dreppinge *n* dripping 130/12

ealle *see* **ale**

eaylme *n* elm 268/10; **ieaylmes** *pl* 267/21

Efe *see* **Twelth Efe**

Egypcians *prop n pl* gypsies (often applied to other vagabonds travelling in troupes) 530/12; **Egyppcions** 521/7; **Iepcyons** 522/40; **Iepsyons** 522/33; **Ieptyons** 522/26

endewer *v* endure 158/22; **endwer** 118/38

ensewith *v pr 3 sg* ensueth, follows 508/23

enterlude *n* dramatic performance 218/18, 515/5, etc; **enterclude** 531/25, 532/19; **enterluyd** 505/33; **enterlwd** 506/16; **enterlyde** 497/36; **interclude** 532/40; **interlude** 476/19, etc; **enterludes** *pl* 205/4n, 265/26

epethapthes *n pl* epitaphs, *but here misused for* epigraphs 236/16

ere *n in phr* **thes ere** this year 257/29

erell *n* earl 243/31

escrowes *n pl* scrolls 477/11, etc; **escrolles** 478/24

evninge prear *n phr* evening prayer, the evening service of the Church of England 285/30–1

eyle *see* **ale**

fastneng *vb n* fastening 500/7

feates of actiuity *n phr pl* displays of athletic ability 223/20–1

ferking *ppl adj* apt to strike and hurt(?) 487/15 [*OED* Firk *v* 4]

ffotte men *n comp pl* footmen 239/15–16

firret *n* ferret 220/9, etc; **firrett** 220/4, 220/12

firreted *v pa 3 sg* hunted with a ferret 220/7

fittered *pp* torn or worn to pieces 187/42

foynge *vb n* cleansing 131/28 [*OED* Fow *v*]

French bodies *n phr* French bodices, women's upper garments stiffened with stays of whalebone 180/34

frethinge *vb n* weaving (a structure) out of withies or wattles 153/18 [*OED* Frith *v*²]

Ganmonday *n comp* Gang Monday, ie, Rogation Monday, the traditional day for parishioners to walk round their parish bounds in procession 572/9; **Ganmondaye** 573/5 [*EDD* Gan *v*¹ and *sb*³]

garnement *n* garment 469/38; **garnementes** *pl* 471/31

gayle *n* gaol 500/25; **gaylle** 158/16; **goal** 520/24, 520/26

geat *v pa 3 pl* got 136/34

geather *v* gather 226/36; **geatherd** *pp* 135/1; **geathred** 126/25, etc; **gethryd** 244/2

geere *see* **cony geere**

geeres *v pr 3 sg* jeers 288/22

gerking *vb n* jerking, pulling (posts or boards) loose by moving them to and fro 487/16

gethryd *see* **geather**

giver *vb phr* give her 487/25

goal *see* **gayle**

grone *pp* grown 158/24

gryning *vb n* grinding 307/5

guardes *n pl* ornamental borders or trimmings on garments 114/35

gurswebbe *n comp* girth-web, a strong woven tape used by upholsterers and others 266/36

gyuftes *n pl* gifts 149/3

hall *n* chamber, ie, vagina(?) 511/35

halland *see* **holond**

Hallemasse *n comp* Hallowmass, All Saints' Day 40/23

head *n* foam or froth from the top of beer(?); *or* cream formed on milk(?) 131/37 [*OED* Head *sb* 10]

healpt *v* help 307/13

heir *n* hire 149/22, etc

heiring *vb n* hiring 308/2

hem *pron* them 201/32

hevin *n* heaven 514/25

highe boorde *n phr* high board, *perhaps* a wooden panel filling a gable 266/21

hit *pron* it 248/16, etc

Hock Monday *n phr* the second Monday after Easter 135/2; **Hock Mondaye** 129/17, 135/30; **Hock Munday** 135/17, 136/34; **Hoppe Monday** 126/25

hock monye *n phr* money gathered at Hocktide 128/12, etc; **hock mony** 137/5; **ock monye** 128/14

Hocktyde *n comp* Hocktide, the second Monday

and Tuesday after Easter, when money was often gathered for pious uses, sometimes with a traditional game or other pastime 243/40, etc; **Hocktide** 126/34; **Hoctyd** 169/26

hodgshedd *n comp* hogshead 151/1; **hoset** 304/25, 306/33; **hodgsheddes** *pl* 150/27, 151/1; **hosetz** *pl* 305/1

hole *see* **screame**

holond *n* holland, a kind of linen originally made in Holland 529/15, 529/18; **halland** 133/17

Hoppe Monday *see* **Hock Monday**

horlegoggez *see* **whurlegog**

hoset *see* **hodgshedd**

Iackalent *n phr* Jack o' Lent, an effigy made to represent winter or Lent and carried or driven out of town in a mock ceremony 138/35, 153/26

ieaylmes *see* **eaylme**

Iepcyons, Iepsyons, Ieptyons *see* **Egypcians**

iester *n* jester, professional buffoon or fool 214/25

iis *see* **ys** *pron poss*

ilde halle *see* **yeld hall**

incell *n* sealing material(?); *or* error for 'tinsel'(?) 250/7 [cp *OED* Enseal *v* 2]

indle *prep* within(?) 487/18 [*OED* Inly *adv used as a preposition*?]

interclude, interlude *see* **enterlude**

iogeler *n* juggler, entertainer using feats of balance, conjuring, and sleight of hand 494/3, 494/16

ioyne stoole *n comp* joint-stool, a stool made of joined pieces of wood 133/14

is *see* **ys** *poss suffix*

kay *n* key 252/3; **keay** 268/29

keells *n pl* kayles, bowling pins 308/21

knot *n* coterie 229/35; **knott** 227/27 [*OED* Knot *sb*[1] 18]

Kob wardens *see* **Cobb warden**

kyng *n* a mock king who presided over a parish revel 250/24, etc; **kynge** 255/32; **kyngges** *poss* 255/39; *in phr* **kynges postes** king's posts, alestakes put out to announce a king ale 254/12; *see also* **ale, revell, sommer kinge**

kypinge *vb n* keeping 285/21

kyuerid *pp* covered 20/39

la *see* **le**

lacke pasty *n comp* one who has not so much as a pasty to eat 179/38

laubor *n* labour 267/26¹, 267/26²

laudder *n* ladder 268/16; **lauder** 268/8; **lathers** *pl* 258/3

le *definite art m (French) used to mark the presence of a vernacular noun or phrase in a passage of Latin* 191/33, 490/40, etc; **la** *f* 252/16, etc

leder *n* leather 472/17

Lent clothes *n phr pl* Lent cloths, ie, Lenten hangings; *here* for an altar 473/33

lijnge *vb n* lying 180/26

locrum *n* a kind of coarse linen 508/15, etc; **loccrum** 509/2; **locram** 507/31, 508/1

loffe *n* loaf 248/23

lont *n* loan 508/9

loppyng *prp* ambling or idling about in a slouching way 483/40 [*OED* Lop *v²* 2]

lords of misrule *n phr pl* men chosen to preside over revels, which commonly involved practical jokes and inversion of the usual social hierarchy 113/8 etc; **lordes of misrule** 114/11; **lordes of mysrule** 465/17–18; *see also* **sommer lords or ladyes**

lydes *n pl* leads, strips or sheets of lead used as roofing 267/16

lynclothe *n comp* linen cloth 256/1; **lyneclothe** 515/18

lypping *prp* leaping, *with pun on sense* kissing 483/39

marces *n pl* marks, ie, boundary markers; *or error for* marches 'marches' *in same sense* 220/30 [*OED* Mark *sb¹* 4 and March *sb³* 1c]

marchauntice *n* merchandise, ie, buying and selling commodities for profit 19/3

markes *n* marquess 241/13

marynors *n pl* mariners 147/15

mastarys *see* **maysther**

masty *n* mastiff 219/42

matcheuill *adj* Machiavellian, insidious 221/8; **matchiuell** 219/39

maye *v* take part in the rites of May Day 200/29

maysterys *n* mistress, as title for mayor's wife 241/32

maysther *n* 1. master, as title for a mayor 241/23, 241/31; 2. master, member of the town council **mastarys** *pl* 240/27

mead *n* maid 487/18

meare *n* mayor 305/16, etc; **mear** 240/16; **mere** 241/23, 241/31; **meyrys** *poss* 239/19

meeching *prp* pilfering *or* skulking 219/36, 220/5 [*OED* Miching *ppl a*]

meheamed *pp* maimed 475/13

menstrell *see* **mynstrell**

mere *see* **meare**

merere *n* mayory, mayor's residence 212/11

merys *n* mayoress, mayor's wife 241/32

meyrys *see* **meare**

mich(e) *see* **mych**

ministrelles *see* **mynstrell**

minstrelcye, minstrelsie *see* **mynstrelsey**

minstrele, minstrell, minstrels *see* **mynstrell**

miracle play *n comp* play depicting a miracle or miracles 537/18; **mirable play** 520/12; **miracle** *n in same sense* 537/18m, 537/18; **miracles** *pl* 537/15 [the form 'mirable' has been influenced by L mirabile 'wonderful (thing)']

moccado *n* mockado, an inferior kind of woollen cloth or cloth made of wool and silk 507/31, etc

mont *n* amount 244/4 [*OED* Mount *sb²* 1]

morice dancers *see* **morris dancers**

morishe cootes, morishe cotes, morishe cottes *see* **moryshe coate**

morishe daunce, morishdances *see* **morys daunce**

morris dancers *n comp pl* performers in a morris dance 115/23; **morice dancers** 465/19; **morrisse dauncers** 287/27

morrishe coates *see* **moryshe coate**

moruske *n* morris dance 529/16, etc [*OED* Morisk *a* and *sb* B2]

morys daunce *n comp* 1. morris dance, a kind of traditional dance, performed by a troupe, usually in costume 250/26, etc; **morishdances** *pl* 113/9; 2. a troupe of morris dancers **morishe daunce** 476/33, 476/35

moryshe coate *n comp* coat for a morris dancer

509/23; **morishe cootes** *pl* 509/1; **morishe
cotes** 509/31; **morishe cottes** 509/39; **morrishe
coates** 508/23–4; **morrisshe coates** 508/32;
moryshe cotes 509/22
mowheis *n comp poss* stack-yards, enclosures where
reaped grain or mown hay was laid 487/10,
487/15 [*EDD* Mowhay]
mych *adj* much 244/2, etc; **mich** 242/10, 242/20;
miche 243/39
mynstrell *n* 1. entertainer using music, storytelling,
juggling, etc 529/14, etc; **menstrell** 286/33;
minstrele 285/35; **minstrell** 123/16, 498/5,
etc; **menstrellys** *pl* 240/5; **ministrelles**
470/33; **minstrells** 125/38; **minstrels** 114/12;
mynsterellsse 241/34; **mynsterilles** 285/29;
mynstralls 248/20; **mynstrelles** 238/36,
473/13, etc; **mynstrells** 120/16; **mynstrellys**
239/6, 239/15; **mynstrels** 138/40; **mynstrylles**
241/6; 2. musician retained by a civic or other
corporation 239/27
mynstrelsey *n* entertainment using music, storytelling, juggling, etc, 120/17; **minstrelcye**
118/36; **minstrelsie** 535/41

neales *n pl* nails 266/37
netherkaysse *n phr* nether case, ie, undercasing or
undercovering; *here, probably* a cloth covering
the supports on which the shrine was carried
in the Corpus Christi procession 256/2
noder *see* **a noder**
noen *pron* none 308/22
norcery *n* nursery 530/19
nyw *adj* new 299/22
ny3th *n* night 522/33

ob *abbrev for L* obolus, *used in E context for* half-
penny 251/3, 495/22, etc
obraidinge *prp* upbraiding, reproachful 281/25
ock monye *see* **hock monye**
oder *pron pl* other things 469/38
op *adv* up 258/32; **owppe** 257/35
orsedy *n* arsedine, a gold-coloured alloy of copper
and zinc 529/8 [*OED* Orsidue]
ovis *n pl* eaves? 250/39 [*EDD* Oaves *sb pl*¹]
owppe *see* **op**

owthe *adv* out 241/32

pals *n pl* pales, stakes or upright boards forming a
fence 487/11, etc
par *n* pair 308/21; **pare** 530/38; **payor** 250/9
pasment *n* parchment 267/34
peayd *pp* paid 476/33, 476/35
penes *n pl* pins 250/8
pers *n* purse 246/14
plaers *see* **players**
plaid(e), plaie *see* **play**
plaieares, plaieres, plaiers *see* **players**
plaing *see* **play**
play *n* 1. dramatic performance 261/14, 520/12,
etc; **plaie** 312/4; **playe** 260/12, 476/5, etc;
pley 261/20, 475/33; **plaies** *pl* 127/42, etc;
playes 266/33, 531/7, etc; 2. gambling or
other pastime 285/21; **playes** *pl* 231/23(?);
3. bodily exercise 181/9; **playes** *pl* 231/23(?);
4. playing of a sport or game 567/5, etc
play *v* 1. act a dramatic performance 137/36;
plaie 191/1, etc; **playe** 265/26, 465/21, etc;
pley 241/25; **played** *pa 3 sg* 532/40, 532/41;
plaid *pa 3 pl* 259/36, 495/16; **plaide** 513/5;
playd 241/14, 521/34, etc; **played** 240/35, etc;
playede 246/10; **playing** *prp* 505/12; **played** *pp*
466/7; **plaing** *vb n* 279/11; **playeing** 213/22(?);
playenge 194/39; **playing** 223/37, 523/24(?),
515/7; **playinge** 272/26; **playnge** 286/15; 2.
perform on a musical instrument 124/33, etc;
playe 123/20, 267/36, 523/5; **played** *pa 3 pl*
285/11(?), 288/1; **playing** *prp* 123/17; **playinge**
123/39, etc; **playng** 285/30; **pleyinge** 118/36;
playeing *vb n* 213/22(?), 250/14; **playeynge**
286/33; **playing** 123/18, 496/15, etc; 3. play
a particular game or sport **played** *pp* 568/17;
playeinge *vb n* 231/22; **playing** 222/35;
4. disport or amuse oneself **played** *pa 3 pl*
285/11(?); **playing** *vb n* 523/24(?); *see also*
box *and* **poppett playinge**
players *n pl* 1. entertainers; usually actors, but
early examples may refer to musicians 239/16,
469/30, etc; **plaers** 505/33; **plaieares** 168/22;
plaieres 191/6, 212/37; **plaiers** 266/27, etc;
playeres 259/36, etc; **playors** 211/41; **playres**

242/29; **playrs** 214/10; **plears** 212/5, etc;
plearys 240/21; **pleayers** 126/14, 278/33;
pleers 211/18; **pleersse** 241/24; **pleeyeres**
215/35; **pleyeres** 259/15; **pleyers** 214/22, etc;
plleares 277/9; **plyyeres** 212/26; **playeres** *pl*
poss 263/10, 263/38; **players** 263/5, 264/6;
pleyers 262/18; 2. players of games 114/33,
see also **poppet players**

pley *see* **play**

polling *vb n literally* cutting off heads (of prey)
but with pun on senses plying one's pole (ie,
erection) *and* pillaging with excessive taxation
220/6

poppet players *n comp pl* puppet players (*probably*
marionette players) 496/32; **poppett players**
121/20–1m; **poppit players** 213/40; **puppet**
players 200/10

poppett playinge *vb n comp* puppet playing
(*probably* playing with marionettes) 121/22–3,
121/27

portrive *n comp* portreeve, chief officer of a town
199/24

praijnge *prp* praying 181/42

praty *adj* pretty 29/3

prear *see* **evninge prear**

prese *n* valuation 293/8

presitions *n pl* precisians, over-precise people,
particularly in religion and morals 181/23

prewance *n pl* prunes(?) 152/21

procession dor *n comp* procession door, door in
the wall or rood-screen of a church by which a
procession went in or out 252/3

pugg *n probably* half-yearling lamb 131/19 [*EDD*
Pug *sb*[1] 2]

puppet players *see* **poppet players**

pyces *n pl* pieces 263/28

quare *n* quarry 256/19, 256/21

quauemires *n comp pl* quagmires 474/8

quayers *n* quires 529/17, 530/5; **quayeres** 529/9

quyenes *n poss* queen's 216/34, 217/39; **quynes**
216/29; **quyns** 214/25

rasse *v pr 1 sg* range, place in a row(?) 535/26
[*EDD* Race *sb*[1] & *v*[1]]

reasons *n pl* raisins 572/8, 573/8

reband *n* ribbon 250/7

regoules *n pl for coll* regals, a portative organ
267/35

relive *v* bring to life again 156/3 [*OED* Relive *v*]

ressaywed *pp* received 257/29

restype *v pr 3 sg* resteth, remains 238/12

reuelyng day *n comp* revelling day, the day of a
parish revel 117/9m; **reuelying day** 117/11

revell *n* 1. merrymaking, revelry **rule** 534/15;
reuels *pl* 537/3; 2. *particularly* a parish festival
with feasting, drinking, and entertainment
288/15; **reuells** *pl* 119/16; **revells** 119/38m,
etc; *in comp* **kyng revyll** a revel where a parish
king presided 251/19

reversy *n* revers, material used to line a garment
and turned back over the edge to form a trim
472/14

risshis *n pl* rushes 20/39

robull *n* rubble 256/36

Robynhode ale *see* **ale**

roume *n* room, ie, space 267/10; **rowme** 257/9

rowells *n pl* rolls 480/8

saddele treese *n comp pl* saddle trees, frameworks
of saddles 158/24

sarcenett *n* sarsenet, a kind of superfine silk, usually
scarlet 473/22

satyn of Bryddes *n phr* satin from Bruges in the
Spanish Netherlands 473/36

saudyers *n pl poss* soldiers' 473/37

sayes *n pl* fine cloths of mixed silk and wool 131/18

schafytt *pp* shaved, ie, planed(?) 251/4

scherne, scrynne *see* **shrene**

screame *n* something that causes someone to
scream, whether with pain or with laughter;
here, in phr **the hole screame** complete sexual
congress *with pun on* hole *meaning* pudendum
487/26

seme *n* cart-load 255/38 [*OED* Seam *sb*[2] 2]

sepulker cloth *n comp* sepulchre cloth, a cloth
used in the ceremonies of the Easter sepulchre,
perhaps to wrap the crucifix 265/2

sergenttys *n poss* serjeant's 239/5, 239/14

settin *vb n* setting 497/15; **setteaynge** 268/2

sewt of vestyments *n phr* suit of vestments: a priest's chasuble, deacon's dalmatic, and sub-deacon's tunicle, with accessories, all made to match 473/26; **sewte of vestyments** 473/23

sheerehall *n comp* shire hall, seat of county government 199/14

sheerve *n* sheriff 158/6

shewer *adj* sure 158/10, 158/21

shrene *n* shrine 251/24, 251/26; **scherne** 251/3; **scrynne** 257/36, 257/37

Shroft Tuisdaie *n phr* Shrove Tuesday, the last day before Lent, often kept with feasting, revelling, and entertainments 137/35

sises *n pl* sisters 391/23

skonces *n pl* small forts erected as outlying defences for larger ones 245/14 [*OED* Sconce *sb*³ 1]

skowgens *n pl* scutcheons, shields 500/2

snas *n pl* snares 278/16

sommer game *n comp* summer game, a traditional rite marking the coming of summer, often involving the choosing of a mock king and/or queen 515/26; **somer game** 515/34; **somer games** *pl* 513/36, etc; **sommer games** 518/14

sommer kinge *n comp* a mock king chosen to preside over a summer game 517/19

sommer lords or ladyes *n phr pl* men or women chosen to preside over summer revels 115/22; **summer lordes or ladyes** 465/18; **summer-lords or ladies** 113/8; *see also* **lords of misrule**

sommer pole *n comp* maypole 287/7

souch *adj* such 207/10

soultwyche *n* a kind of canvas or other coarse material made at Saltash in Cornwall(?) 269/16

Soundhey *n* Sunday 248/17

spend *pp* spent 212/27

spleetes *n pl* small strips of split wood 124/9, 124/40; **splites** 123/7

spline *n* spleen, resentment 281/27; **splyne** 197/30

spong *n* sponge 307/33

squalls *n pl* pert, flirtatious girls 236/6 [*OED* Squall *sb*¹ 2]

stapes *n pl* steps(?) 256/18

stere *n* stair 255/39, 256/21

stonninge *vb n* standing room 267/16

stwerde *n* steward, civic officer in charge of finance 129/8; **stweredes** *pl* 129/7

stye *v* climb up, mount 226/32

stypelle *n* steeple 471/12

subordened *pp properly* subordained, ie, deputed; *but here used by confusion for* suborned 531/20

summer lord(e)s or ladyes *see* **sommer lords or ladyes**

surcesse *v* surcease, leave off 281/7

sut *v* suit 201/32

talle *n* tale 179/16; **talls** *pl* 487/10; **tals** 487/14

tapps *n pl* tapes 131/5

teaynt *n* tent 268/11; *see* pp 360–1 (endnote to DRO: PE/SH: CW 1/43 mbs [3, 4])

tethinge *n* tithing, rural division originally reckoned as one tenth of a hundred 248/16

tewluethe *adj* twelfth 235/4

the *pron pl* they 241/25

Thurdsday *n* Thursday 130/4; **Thardsday** 129/32; **Tirsday** 304/13

thynnge *v pr 3 pl* think 239/18

tiche *v* touch 487/24

Tirsday *see* **Thursday**

tomlers *n pl* tumblers, acrobats 216/29

tow *adj* two 149/34, 523/33, etc

trenchers *n pl* wooden platters 572/7; **trenchardes** 152/2

trousse *n* truce, respite from something tedious 537/39

Tudaye *n* Tuesday 304/17; **Twusdaye** 304/10

tuff *n* a piece of light, porous rock 220/5

Twelth Efe *n phr* Twelfth Eve, the eve of the Epiphany 516/18

Twusdaye *see* **Tuday**

unseeme *n?* unseemly conduct 281/17

vant clothes *n comp pl* font cloths, cloths used in connection with the baptismal font 473/34

veaysordes *n pl* vizards, masks 268/32

vellet *n* velvet 530/35

Venesicians *proper n pl* Venetians 495/16

vennigeare *n* vinegar 132/8

Venys *proper n attr* Venice 307/32

vermelon *n* vermilion, cinnabar 529/7

vestyments *see* **sewt of vestyments**

vether *n* feather 226/37

vilme *n* film, membrane; *here*, hymen 511/15

virginall *n coll* virginals; a musical instrument, usually having the strings laid parallel to the keyboard, commonly termed a pair on the analogy of an organ 207/17; **virgynalles** *pl* 530/21

vitelle *n* victual, food 573/10; **vyctelle** 572/12; **vitels** *pl* 307/40, etc; **vittuels** 152/3; **vituels** 153/1

vnly *adv* only 480/34

vyse coote *n phr* vice's coat, ie, coat for a buffoon in a play or skit 270/19

waintres *n pl* bundles of faggots(?) 307/28 [*OED* Wantel]

Wansdaye *n* Wednesday 304/12, 306/26

warde *n* reward 241/25

wate *v pr 3 sg in phr* **God wate** God wot, God knows 156/8

waytes *n pl* waits, musicians retained by a civic or other corporation 470/16, 472/34

weamen *see* **weomen**

Weane *see* **Charlamens Weane**

weathe *n* wheat 307/10

w[ea]youre *n* wire 267/39

weomen *pl* women 135/9, 479/12, etc ; **weamen** 126/25, etc; **wemminge** 135/17; **whomen** 244/3; **woemen** 136/6, 136/19

whas *v pa 3 sg* was 215/35; **whasse** 212/27

Whitsonales *see* **ale**

Whiȝtsontid *n comp* Whitsuntide, Whitsunday and the week following 254/34

whomen *see* **weomen**

whomewarde *adv* homeward 147/28

whurlegog *n* whirligig 250/33; **horlegoggez** *pl* 356/35; *see* p 356 (endnote to DRO: PE/SH: CW 1/2 ff [1, 1v])

whyllys *conj* whilst 241/33

wike *n* week 149/26; **wikes** *poss* 150/23

without that that *conj phr* not admitting that; a technical legal phrase used when denying some matter of fact without admitting some more general allegation with which it is bound up 187/20–1, etc; **withowt that that** 191/8 [*OED* Without 15d]

woemen *see* **weomen**

won *adj and pron* one 268/9

wosterd *n* worsted 473/35

woud *n* wood 307/28

wretyne *see* **be ffor wretyne**

yarncleyers *n comp pl* ironclayers, ie, workers in iron and clay(?); *or* workers of clay ironstone, a clayey iron ore(?) 497/15

yearell *n* earl 153/31; **yeryells** *poss* 212/26

yeld hall *n comp* guildhall, civic hall 127/5, etc; **ilde halle** 470/24; **yeeld hall** 137/12; **yelde hall** 128/1

yeuenyng *n* evening 239/36; **yevenynges** *pl* 239/28

yevyn *pp* given 470/23, etc

yolo *adj* yellow 473/36

y payd *pp* y-paid, ie, paid 256/2, etc

ys *poss suffix* 's, often written and construed in the 15th–17th centuries as a separate word 34/5, 529/14, etc; **is** 475/40, 522/19

ys *pron poss* his 239/35; **iis** 469/30

Index

ARLEANE RALPH

The Index combines subjects with names, places, and book or play titles in a single listing. When identical headwords occur in more than one category, the order is as follows: names of individuals, titles of nobility, names of places, subjects, and titles of books or plays. Often items are grouped under broad topics such as 'animals,' 'musical instruments,' and 'guilds and occupations' to aid research. The pertinent members of these classes are then either given as subentries or referred to by cross-reference.

Place names and surnames appear in modern form where that could be ascertained, and titles and family names of nobility and other public figures appear in forms commonly used by historians. Other surnames are usually cited in the most common form occurring in the Records text except that capitalization and the use of 'i/j' and 'u/v' have been assimilated to modern usage. Names are regularly followed in parentheses by any variant spellings, but these are given for titles only where clarity requires them. Nobles are entered under their family name with cross-references from any titles which occur in the text or apparatus, and royalty under their regnal or given names. Saints' names are indexed under the abbreviation 'St' alphabetized as if spelled out. In many cases (eg, 'Barnes,') it has been necessary to assign numbers to different individuals of the same name to distinguish them; those numbers are in parentheses following the names. Ellipsis dots are used in cases where a person's given name is not known. Occupations or titles of office are given only when considered relevant or to assist in distinguishing individuals of the same name.

The standard source used for determining most place name spellings was Eilert Ekwall (ed), *The Concise Oxford Dictionary of English Place-Names,* 4th ed (Oxford 1960; rpt 1980). The chief sources used for ascertaining the modern spellings of names of individuals were the *DNB*; J.H. Gleason, *The Justices of the Peace in England: 1558 to 1640* (Oxford, 1969); *List of Sheriffs for England and Wales from the Earliest Times to A.D. 1831,* Public Record Office, Lists and Indexes, no 9 (London, 1898); and E.G. Withycombe (ed), *The Oxford Dictionary of English Christian Names,* 3rd ed (Oxford, 1977; rpt 1979). Sources specific to Dorset and Cornwall were the lists of civic officers found in Hutchins, *History and Antiquities*; Matthews, *History of St Ives*; Peter and Peter, *Histories of Launceston and Dunheved*; Roberts, *History of Lyme Regis*; and Sydenham, *History of the Town and County of Poole*. Additional sources for the identification of royalty and nobility are specified in the headnote to 'Patrons and Travelling Companies' to which the Index refers throughout.

RECORDS OF EARLY ENGLISH DRAMA

York edited by Alexandra F. Johnston and Margaret Rogerson. 2 volumes. 1979.

Chester edited by Lawrence M. Clopper. 1979.

Coventry edited by R.W. Ingram. 1981.

Newcastle upon Tyne edited by J.J. Anderson. 1982.

Norwich 1540–1642 edited by David Galloway. 1984.

Cumberland/Westmorland/Gloucestershire
   edited by Audrey Douglas and Peter Greenfield. 1986.

Devon edited by John Wasson. 1986.

Cambridge edited by Alan H. Nelson. 2 volumes. 1988.

Herefordshire/Worcestershire edited by David N. Klausner. 1990.

Lancashire edited by David George. 1991.

Shropshire edited by J. Alan B. Somerset. 2 volumes. 1994.

Somserset including Bath edited by James Stokes,
   with Robert J. Alexander. 2 volumes. 1996.

Bristol edited by Mark C. Pilkinton. 1997.

Dorset/Cornwall edited by Rosalind Conklin Hays and C.E. McGee/
   Sally L. Joyce and Evelyn S. Newlyn. 1999.